SAMUEL M. GREEN, Ph.D., Harvard University, is Chairman, Department of Art, and Director, Davison Art Center, Wesleyan University. He previously taught at Wellesley College, Harvard University, Bowdoin College, and Colby College where he also served as Curator of that institution's art collection. Professor Green has contributed numerous articles and reviews to leading journals of art and architecture.

AMERICAN ART

A Historical Survey

SAMUEL M. GREEN

Wesleyan University

THE RONALD PRESS COMPANY · NEW YORK

Library of Congress Catalog Card Number: 66–16844

PREFACE

This book, an introductory history of American art and architecture from the first European settlement to the present, is designed for courses offered in college departments of art and in schools of fine arts.

Because of the increased importance of American art on the world scene and because many Americans are either unaware of their artistic heritage or indifferent to it, certain persisting aspects of style and tradition have been isolated from the great variety of expression in the arts—ranging from the precise and geometric, seen in so much of our art and architecture, to the amorphous and organic expressed in the paintings of Ryder and the abstract expressionists and in the architecture of Wright. For example, a quick glance at a chronological sequence of illustrations chosen for the rigid and static rectilinearity they have in common should suggest the existence of at least one distinctive aspect of an American tradition, one that gives the art of the United States as specific an identity as that of any other culture.

The art and architecture of the past have been re-examined and assessed from the perspective of the mid-twentieth century, permitting a broader basis of appreciation than did earlier, more academic taste. Thus, folk art is given more importance than before, and artists relatively unnoticed in their own time have been given their rightful place among their formerly more famous contemporaries. Emphasis throughout is on the relative *quality* of a work of art and on its place in the context of artistic style and traditions as seen within the framework of social and historical background.

Although indigenous and intrinsically important, the decorative and minor arts, and the art of the American Indian do not belong to the mainstream of Western or American art. For this reason these areas of art, which are certainly subjects for study in themselves, do not justify coverage in a survey of this nature, and are, therefore, not included.

Throughout, this book is illustrated with hundreds of reproductions covering the full range of American art—painting, sculpture, architecture, graphic arts, photography, and folk or popular art—from the seventeenth century to the present.

In the comprehensive index: (1) the student will find the full name, and dates of birth and death, for the artists and architects mentioned in the book; (2) artists' names are indicated immediately following the titles of their works.

Works of art or buildings referred to in the text are illustrated either in the book itself or in the generally available set of slides distributed jointly by the

College Art Association and the Carnegie Corporation. Throughout the book the slides referred to are numbered in parentheses. This information is for the instructor who wishes to supplement his lectures. Adopters of this textbook may secure from the publisher an *Instructor's Supplement to accompany AMERICAN ART—A Historical Survey: Index to Slides.*

SAMUEL M. GREEN

Middletown, Connecticut
March, 1966

ACKNOWLEDGMENTS

Thanks are given especially to Charles Parkhurst, Director of the Baltimore Museum; Benjamin Rowland, Jr., Professor of Fine Arts, Harvard University; Beaumont Newhall, Director of the George Eastman House, Rochester, New York; Louisa Dresser, Curator of the Worcester Museum; and William H. Jordy, Professor of Art, Brown University, who have read sections of this book in preparation. For their assistance and suggestions I am profoundly in their debt.

For suggestions and information I am also grateful to Professor Henry-Russell Hitchcock, Smith College; Professor Carroll Meeks, Yale University; Professor William H. Pierson, Williams College; Miss Josephine Setze, Yale University Gallery; Professor Nathan Shapira, University of California (Los Angeles); Mrs. Nina Fletcher Little, Mr. Frederick Alan Sharf, Mr. Abbott Lowell Cummings, Society for the Preservation of New England Antiquities; Dr. Heinrich Schwarz and Professor John Frazer, both of Wesleyan University; and to many others, including my students at Colby College, Wesleyan University, and to those in my three seminars in American Art at the Salzburg (Austria) Seminar in American Studies.

I would also like to express my appreciation to the following persons who permitted me to consult their master's or doctoral theses at Yale University: Louise Hunt Averill, Richard G. Carrott, Marion Card Donnelly, Robert W. Duemling, Samuel Huiet Greybill, David Huntington, John M. Jacobus, Robert Koch, Gene E. McCormick, Richard K. Newman, John L. Ward; and to their tutors, especially Carroll Meeks and George Heard Hamilton. I also appreciate the opportunity to consult Gibson Dane's work in progress on William Morris Hunt, as well as the Harvard Ph.D. dissertations of George Downing and Margaret Banton, on American etching and the early Saint-Gaudens, respectively, the Wesleyan University M.A. thesis by Eileen Marie Hayes on abstract expressionism, and the Wesleyan University Distinction thesis by Alan Shestack on contemporary graphic art.

I wish to thank Mr. Whitfield Vye for his adaptations of plans and drawings.

Thanks also are due to the private collectors and museums who have generously permitted their paintings and sculptures to be reproduced.

Finally, I wish to express my gratitude to Wesleyan University for the Faculty Research Grants which have helped defray the costs of typing and illustration.

CONTENTS

> The numbers in parentheses throughout the book refer to slides that are available to instructors for classroom use. See the Preface to this book.

AMERICAN ART

A Historical Survey

PART ONE

THE SEVENTEENTH CENTURY

The architecture and painting of the first century of settlement in what is now the United States are European with as yet very little native flavor. The great decision to leave the old world and to slough off its political and social ways was not accompanied by an equally bold artistic movement. Further, since the Indian of the northeastern coast was a primitive forest dweller with no artistic or architectural achievement to speak of, the rich amalgamation of indigenous and European styles which occurred in Mexico and in the Southwest of the present United States was not repeated in the region of the first European settlements in the Northeast.

Yet, in spite of the lack of originality, there appeared even in this early period a tendency to emphasize certain aspects of the imported styles. Two outstanding instances can be cited. The first is the development of the Protestant meetinghouse, characterized by its revealed structure and general simplicity of design. The second is the prevalence of a provincial style of portraiture, derived from sixteenth-century Tudor models, with its flat pattern and its emphasis upon line and closely detailed observation. The austere meetinghouse and the precise, patterned colonial portrait are the first conspicuous evidences of a stylistic character which gives American art and architecture, isolated in the new world from English prototypes, much of their identity and flavor.

But before discussing these and other examples of early American art and architecture, it would be well to survey briefly where the colonists lived and to touch on the traditions they brought with them.

The settlers built their first shelters on narrow strips of coast in Massachusetts and Virginia, with their backs against a country that was, in the fine Elizabethan words of one of their number in New England, "dauntingly terrible, full of rocky hills and clothed with infinite thick woods. . . . A tract of land God knows how many miles full of delfs and dingles and dangerous precipices, Rocks and inextricable difficulties."[1] By the middle of the century the English settlements, though they had spread inland several miles, were still confined to the shores of Chesapeake Bay and New England, clinging to the tidewater for reasons of accessibility to transportation and trade. In the South the settlements followed the Potomac, the Rappahannock, the York, and the James up from the bay, while in the North the colonies were planted principally on Massachusetts, Plymouth, and Narragansett bays and along Long Island Sound

3

and the tidal portion of the Connecticut River. By 1670 the New Netherlands and the Swedish settlements on the Delaware, recently taken by the Dutch, had been absorbed, and William Penn was about to begin his "noble experiment" at Philadelphia. South of Virginia, settlements had been made in the Carolinas at Albemarle Sound and Charleston harbor. Finally, in territory later to become part of the United States, the French were establishing their wilderness outposts. The Spanish in the South and West had begun a century before to impose their civilization on the Indians.

The gradual progression of the frontier garrison houses from the tidal regions into the Piedmont reflected this expansion of colonial settlement and its struggle with the savages. Later, the "mean howses" of isolated villages were succeeded by the "fayre" ones of thriving seaports, and the wilderness cottages by the sturdy dwellings of the Yankee householders and the manor houses of the Southern planters.

The buildings of the seventeenth century (except at its very end) were in the main late Gothic both in style and in building tradition—even in Pennsylvania, settled so late in the 1600's. There were parts of Ipswich, Massachusetts, in which an Englishman from the eastern shires would have felt perfectly at home, for he would have been surrounded by essentially medieval buildings, like those in his own towns. In Virginia, Bacon's Castle on the James and St. Luke's Church nearby are, respectively, a Tudor manor house and a late Gothic rural church simply transplanted from Essex.

Painting was equally medieval. The portraits displayed today in Pilgrim Hall in Plymouth are essentially the same as their contemporary counterparts in Suffolk guildhalls and reflect the imported provincialism observed in the architecture. They were painted in a late Tudor, or pre-Stuart, style preferred by the Puritan gentry because it was in direct contrast to the imported grandeur and realistic competence of the post-Renaissance tradition favored by Charles I and epitomized by Sir Anthony Van Dyck's Cavalier portraits. Though in England the Renaissance had penetrated in the late sixteenth century to court and metropolitan circles and even to the more sophisticated landed gentry, by the time of the reign of the first James, the older Gothic traditions had not been displaced among the conservative yeomen, husbandmen, and artisans who made up the bulk of the century's "great migration" to America. Nor had the new style influenced the taste of the ministers and lesser gentry who were their leaders.

Architecture in the English Colonies

Since the English settlers were the most numerous in the seventeenth century, their architecture remains the most conspicuous today. The French constructed no significant buildings in this early period, and though the Spanish in combination with the Indians created a new and important style, their buildings are so different from those of the colonists of the eastern seaboard, and belong to so different an architectural tradition, that it is more appropriate to discuss them at a later time. The contribution of the Germans is not significant until the next period, and though the Swedes left some buildings, only the architecture of the Dutch colonists is sufficiently important to be compared with that of the English in this early period.

Domestic Architecture

Since dwellings comprise the largest category of architecture, many more houses have survived than public buildings. While only two important examples of the latter remain, a sufficient number of the former still exist in both the North and the South to give us a fairly lively picture of seventeenth-century domestic architecture.

Types of houses in the colonies were as diversified as the classes of society. In both New England and the South the colonists represented a cross section of English society from indentured servant to landed gentry, and the houses they lived in reflected this hierarchy in a sequence beginning with the "cot" (containing a simple room or "hall" and a loft above), progressing through the one-and-a-half-story house of the husbandman and the two-story house of the yeoman to the manor house of the large proprietor or planter.

Naturally, the first shelters of the earliest settlers were built with the intention of their being only temporary. Some "burrowed themselves in the earth under a hillside, casting the earth aloft upon timber"; [2] others were forced to use the butts of old trees left after the first clearing, covered with bark and thatch, while the more

enterprising built "English wigwams" of sticks "pric't into the ground, binded and fastened at the tops and on the sides . . . matted with boughs and covered with sedge and old mats." [3] At Pioneer Village in Salem, Massachusetts (AA 1, *AA 2), these wigwams, together with the more permanent framed dwellings which soon followed, can now be seen in a careful reconstruction of the probable appearance of this settlement of the 1630's. The clapboarded framed houses are essentially of the medieval type the settlers knew in England and reproduced in the new world until the end of the century, when the new Renaissance style succeeded the earlier one.

The Parson Capen House at Topsfield, Massachusetts, 1683 (AA 30, AA 31, AA 33; Illustration 1–1), and the Scotch-Boardman House at Saugus, Massachusetts, 1686 (AA 28), can be

1–1. Parson Capen House, Topsfield, Massachusetts, 1683.

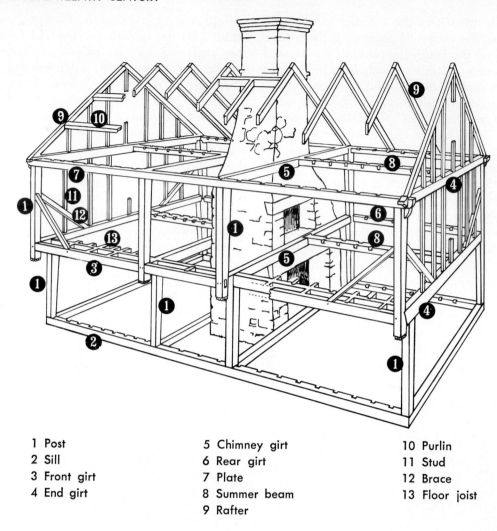

1 Post
2 Sill
3 Front girt
4 End girt
5 Chimney girt
6 Rear girt
7 Plate
8 Summer beam
9 Rafter
10 Purlin
11 Stud
12 Brace
13 Floor joist

1–2. Frame of the Gleason House, Farmington, Connecticut. (Adapted from Norman M. Isham, *Glossary of Colonial Architectural Terms*; Boston: 1939.)

considered as typical of the kind of house that was most numerous and most significant during the first century of settlement. The Capen House is the best preserved and restored, but is not so typical in plan as the Scotch-Boardman House, which has a "lean-to," or addition at the rear, lacking in the other. The appearance, structure, and arrangement of the ideal, fully developed New England frame house of the seventeenth century can be summed up from these two buildings and from the structural diagram in Illustration 1–2.

The principal characteristics, on the exterior, are the prominent central chimney, the high-pitched roof, and the overhang; and, in the interior, the exposed or uncovered framing, the walls of either battened boards or of plaster over split lath, and the fireplace of stone or brick, covered usually by a huge oak lintel or "mantle tree." The variety of flared or "shouldered" posts, the decorative grooves of the boarding, the champfering of the beams, and the ornamentation of the stair balusters comprise the decorative elements of the interior. The relatively austere exterior is relieved by the diamond-paned casement windows, the Tudor profile and ornament of the chimney, the occasional droplets from the overhang, and the nail-studded surface of the door. The Puritan builder was not so unaware of beauty as he is often thought to have been. The decoration of the dwelling itself denies austerity, as do the furnishings (AA 29A, AA 29; Illustration 1–3). Space on shipboard was often taken up with elaborately carved furniture brought from home: high-backed chairs, sometimes upholstered or covered in leather, or turned chests of drawers, decorated with the beginnings of Renaissance detail. After the settlers' arrival, time was soon wrested from more pressing duties to make furniture: benches (DA 3) and trestle tables (DA 68), high settles

to be placed before the fire, dower chests (DA 84), and spindle-decorated chairs (DA 156). Many of these, as well as parts of the framing of the house itself, were highly decorated with color. In the simpler homes, the wood of the framing, walls, and furniture, and even of the tableware and implements, was richly warm in the comfortable glow of the great fireplace in the "hall" or kitchen, with its confusion of pots, spits, and other instruments for cooking and heating. In more elaborate homes, "Turkey carpets" graced the tables, and silverware found enough buyers to employ quite a number of colonial silversmiths in the seventeenth century. The interior of the Hart House (Illustration 1–3) is typical. Even the most down-to-earth of the settlers must have taken at least some

1–3. Parlor from the Thomas Hart House, Ipswich, Massachusetts, c. 1640. Now in the Metropolitan Museum of Art, New York.

esthetic satisfaction in the proper raising, framing, and joining of one of these houses. Governor Bradford, referring to another kind of building, a fort, takes time in his succinct and economical account of the founding of Plymouth to mention that the fort was not only strong but "comly." [4] But, aside from what the builders may or may not have thought of their houses, our contemporary taste for abstract design in form and texture is satisfied by the niceties of their asymmetrical proportions and the alternation of cool white plaster and warm-colored wood. At the same time, the simple, articulated framing of these houses is consistent with our contemporary admiration of revealed structure as seen in modern architecture.

There existed many variations on the pattern of the Capen and Scotch-Boardman houses, the most common being the "Cape Codder" or "saltbox," which eliminated the second story. Descendants of this type in the eighteenth century, and even later, can be seen throughout New England, for it was built wherever the frontier advanced. The only authentic survivor of the saltbox from the seventeenth century, however, is the Jethro Coffin House in Nantucket, 1686 (AA 43). This tall dwelling, with its acutely pitched roof, does not have the more familiar horizontality of the typical Cape Codder of the succeeding century. Perhaps the next most frequent variation of the two-story central-chimney dwelling was the house with end chimney, which eliminated that part of the building on the left or right of the central chimney in the more conventional house. The Paul Revere House in Boston, built about 1676 (AA 35), is typical of the survivors of this kind of building. In Rhode Island the type was developed more fully than elsewhere by the creation of a huge chimney encompassing the entire side of the building and incorporating the fireplaces of both the "hall" and the "lean-to," as in the Eleazer Arnold House at Lincoln, 1687 (AA 41, AA 42).

Another variation, rare in surviving examples but once much more frequent, was the placing of gables on the longitudinal axis as well as on the ends. This can still be seen in the Whipple

1–4. John Ward House, Salem, Massachusetts, 1684.

House, Ipswich, Massachusetts, 1639 (AA 27, AA 27A), and in the John Ward House, Salem, Massachusetts, 1684 (AA 36; Illustration 1–4). The many gabled additions to the Captain John Turner (Seven Gables) House, also in Salem, c. 1668 (AA 39, AA 40), have produced a building of unusual medieval flavor. Only the Fairbanks House in Dedham, Massachusetts, 1637 (AA 19, AA 20), compares in complexity. The original structure of the Fairbanks House can be easily discovered, hemmed in though it is by later accretions. This picturesque building, surrounded by its ancient trees and settled into the ground as though it had grown there, evokes better than any other the seventeenth-century past. The Capen House is also situated in an area that has changed very little since the parson received the house, newly built, from his parishioners in 1683. There are many others nearly equal to the Capen House in charm, the Stanley-Whitman House in Farmington, Connecticut, c. 1660 (AA 29A, AA 29), being among the most interesting in its appearance and situation, and in the correctness of its restoration.[5]

At first it might seem that the cumbersome method of erecting a frame of enormous oak timbers (a method that lasted until the introduction of mass-produced nails in the 1830's, which made possible the lighter balloon frame) must be a very ancient manner of building. But in the seventeenth century the post and truss system had only recently succeeded the cruck (bent-tree) construction of Tudor times. Further, houses of this construction, especially the fully developed type we have been considering, were a fairly recent development in rural England as well, where the husbandmen and yeomen had lived only a few years before in the closely huddled cottages of the manorial village.

The general uniformity of design and the good workmanship of the colonial housewright imply a long tradition of craftsmanship. But craftsmanship was all it was, for the anonymous carpenter was not to be succeeded by the architect for many years to come. The New England builders still lived in a world where a plan could not even be read, let alone drawn; where an inch was determined from the length of three barleycorns in a row; where proportions were based on a framed bay of roughly sixteen feet, derived from the area needed to house two span of oxen. Such casualness explains the lack of exact symmetry and the other little irregularities which add so much to the charm of these houses.

In nearly every respect the early American dwellings reproduced their English counterparts. Southeastern England is filled with framed and weather-boarded barns and outbuildings. Many of the small houses of Essex, Norfolk, and Suffolk are of the same basic construction, and in Surrey, Hertford, and Middlesex fewer brick or stone houses appear than would be expected. It was from these counties, from places like Boston, Ipswich, Dedham, Toppesfield, and Weathersfield, that the settlers came, and it was only natural that they should put up structures similar to those they had known at home.

It was once thought that the New England house evolved gradually, from the simple cottage to the fully developed larger house that was most typical at the end of the century, by a process of accretion. Recent opinion, however, appears to be more reasonable in suggesting that houses of all sizes were built from the beginning of the colonization period: economic status and social position determined whether a dwelling would be a fully developed house or a one-room cot. The end-chimney plan was more prevalent in New England earlier in the century than it was later. Also, a survey of English prototypes shows the central chimney to be much rarer than in New England. Taken together, these facts seem to make the central-chimney plan almost a New England phenomenon. It would be better to say that the late Gothic framed house of the southeastern English counties reached its most consistent and final formulation in the central-chimney house in Massachusetts and Connecticut, not in England.

The great predominance of this kind of house, in contrast to the simple cot and the larger mansion, in New England during the later decades of the century reflects the basically middle-class democracy which developed from the agrarian theocracy of the first decades. Its equivalent in the South—the smaller house of either wood or brick—was less prevalent because of the differences in the historical and economic development of that area. Though both regions drew from the same social and economic strata and both were at first equally agrarian, New England developed a more diversified economy by exploiting the abundant resources of the coastal fishing banks and the opportunities for trade with the West Indies and the mother country. The results were a greater distribution of prosperity, an increased need for a number of tradesmen and skilled craftsmen, and a larger concentration of population in towns. Further, the farmer remained self-sufficient and independent more successfully in the North than in the South, where the small or middling planter found it difficult to hold his own against the rise of the great plantations. It was only natural that the variety of activities in a New England port and the hundred-and-one chores of a Yankee homestead should result in the development of a stronger and more numerous middle class, drawn from a population with diversified occupations and opportunities for advancement which were closed to the slave or indentured servant in the South.

Thus the New England house, perfected for the Yankee farmer or townsman, reflected an essentially middle-class society; as such, it became appropriately the ultimate prototype of the single, isolated dwelling, which has remained an American ideal both in the popular imagination and in the minds of our greatest architectural theorists and practitioners from Andrew Jackson Downing to Frank Lloyd Wright.

A relatively small number of seventeenth-century middle-class houses remain in the South, in contrast to their greater prevalence in New England. This can be partially explained by the difference in economic development between the two regions. There were, of course, other reasons, one being that the wooden houses of the southern colonies rapidly disappeared due to deterioration from humidity and later use as slave quarters. [The appearance of the southern seventeenth-century framed house is probably reflected in the restored kitchen of the Ludwell-Paradise House in Williamsburg, Virginia, 1717 (AA 84).] The typical surviving small dwellings of the southern colonies are brick houses, usually of the story-and-a-half type. The plans of these buildings are of several kinds: the first consists of one room with a large fireplace; the second, of two rooms with a stair hall between them to the loft or attic (or less frequently, two adjacent rooms with stairs in one of them to the attic). In the third plan a porch or vestibule is added; in the fourth the stairway is placed in a projecting addition behind the stair hall, which, in addition to the vestibule at the front, creates the cross plan.

In Princess Anne County, near Norfolk, is the Adam Thoroughgood House, built between 1636 and 1640 (AA 90, AA 91; Illustration 1–5), and challenging the Balch and Fairbanks houses for the position of the oldest dwelling still standing in the former English colonies. Built by a planter who was originally an indentured servant,

1–5. Adam Thoroughgood House, Princess Anne County, Virginia, 1636–1640.

its plan is of the second type. The house is of good, substantial construction, with a great chimney and a steep, sloping roof. It is therefore an impressive example of medieval architecture, sharing in its bold simplicity some of the qualities of the better known New England wooden houses. A similar house is Pinewood, the Warburton House in James City County, Virginia, built in 1680, and representing a similar plan. Crisscross or Christcross in New Kent County, Virginia, and Kiskiskiack in York County, Virginia, both built around 1690, also represent the cross plan and retain some medieval decorative features.

Maryland houses [some of them even more curiously named than those in Virginia: Make Peace, 1663 (AA 101), Parrot's Cage, Want Water, Batchelor's Hope, and Alas the Cow Pasture] are similar in material, plan, and appearance to the Virginia dwellings, although, as in Resurrection Manor, St. Mary's County, c. 1653 (*AA 106), there is a tendency toward considerable decorative pattern with glazed brick in the end walls.

Though the Charleston region in South Carolina was beginning to be settled in 1670, little of architectural significance escaped future rebuilding or alteration. But the Piedmont region of Virginia and North Carolina is particularly rich in examples of the log cabin, which became the favorite type of frontier building after it was introduced by the Swedes and Germans into Delaware and Pennsylvania. The house of square-hewn logs with self-draining dovetailed joints was more common than the type constructed of notched round logs which it soon

succeeded. Several of these houses still exist, carrying on a seventeenth-century tradition though dating actually from the mid-eighteenth century.

The discovery, in the process of remodeling, of medieval features in a house built in 1704 by William Brinton (the younger), in Dilworthtown, Pennsylvania (Illustration 1–6), has recently made it necessary to revise the history of the early architecture of the Philadelphia region. It had been thought that the medieval character of the New England and southern dwellings was not matched elsewhere among the English settlements in the North American colonies, least of all in Pennsylvania, colonized after the Renaissance style had almost entirely super-

1–6. Brinton ("1704") House, Dilworthtown, Pennsylvania.

seded the Gothic in England. The "1704" House, as this masonry house is often called, is not exactly like the medieval dwellings of New England or the South, but it shares with them many features: a steeply pitched roof, large fireplaces, and exposed interior framing. The end-chimney plan is unusual; it consists of two rooms on the main floor with the entrance and stairway both in the larger room rather than in a hallway—an arrangement common in the smaller houses of Virginia and Maryland, which, however, are without the fully developed second story found in the "1704" House. The huge fireplace in the south end covers so much of the wall that there is room only for two very small windows, on either side. The most interesting aspect of the house is the use of the "skirt" or pent roof between the first and second floors of the front elevation and below the gable at the end. This feature had been thought to be of German origin, for though it exists in England, its appearance in the new world only in Pennsylvania, where so many Germans settled, had been in this way explained. But its employment so early in a house which in other ways is so completely English suggests the English origin of this typically Pennsylvanian feature.

The use of the pent roof and the character of the plan (thought by some to have been brought to the Delaware valley by the Swedes) establishes the "1704" House as a prototype for the characteristic architecture of southeastern Pennsylvania (especially the farmhouse, though the plan influenced town houses as well), albeit with Renaissance detail added. The principal importance of the house lies in the fact that its existence corroborates what was formerly very slight evidence of the more widespread presence of equally medieval buildings in Pennsylvania. (The only other evidence consists of, first, a nineteenth-century description of row houses with medieval framing in Philadelphia; and, second, the recent uncovering of half-timber construction in a Philadelphia back building.)

One kind of dwelling—the row house—unique in the early years of settlement, has completely disappeared. Though it is known only through contemporary description and through research, the type is of sufficient interest to be at least mentioned here. Groups of these attached houses existed within the fortifications of Jamestown as early as 1611 and at Henrico, a settlement farther up the James, a few years later. Row houses were specified by the London Company for the plantations on Long Island Sound in Connecticut, and old descriptions and prints of Boston indicate that they were probably in existence there as well. They were certainly prevalent in New Amsterdam. In such busy and fast growing ports, the persistence of a familiar European urban, medieval type is to be expected, while the existence of the form at Jamestown and in Connecticut is explained by the fact that this arrangement of dwellings afforded greater protection in a hostile region. (This plan was earlier specified in the Ulster plantations in Ireland, financed by the same London Company which invested in the Connecticut settlement.) Apparently row houses were built in Jamestown as late as 1685, and four Virginia State Houses were comprised of a successive combination of three row houses each.

In both the North and the South the isolated dwellings of the middle class constitute the most numerous group of structures surviving from the seventeenth century. A few examples of larger houses still remain, but the great majority have disappeared. Soon after the very first settlement in the Massachusetts Bay Colony, its leader, John Winthrop, built his "fayre" house, a procedure which was followed not much later by the other proprietors of the colony. Thus, as early as 1630, even larger houses than the fully developed yeoman's house were in existence. It is interesting to notice that, as soon as they could manage to do so, the important figures of the New England migration continued to live in the new world among surroundings to which they were formerly accustomed. The famous Puritan preacher Thomas Hooker, once of Trinity College, Cambridge, and founder of Hartford, built a mansion which was similar to the less pretentious English manor houses, with a projecting vestibule surmounted by a chamber. The great merchant Theophilus Eaton, after he turned his attention from the Baltic trade to the commercial possibilities of the New England plantations, built in New Haven, soon after its founding, a two-story house of ten rooms with a U-shaped plan. These dwellings and many like them—all probably built of wood—have disappeared.

The foundations of the first really great house of the southern colonies, built about 1646 by the infamous royal governor Sir William Berkeley, still exist in James City County, Virginia. From them, it can be seen that the mansion was a long building with a succession of several large rooms (where Sir William used to entertain escaped Royalists during the Commonwealth).

There is also evidence that Berkeley's house had a curvilinear gable similar to those at Bacon's Castle (AA 93, AA 94; Illustration 1–7), which still stands intact in Surry County. Built

1–7. Bacon's Castle, Surry County, Virginia, c. 1655.

between 1650 and 1660, the Castle, like the nearby church at Smithfield, is an important Gothic survival. The two-story brick structure is of the cross plan, with two large halls, an entrance porch, and a stair hall. This, the earliest such plan in the colonies, was the prototype for many smaller houses in the South. But the decorative design of the Castle is even more noteworthy. The cross-mullioned windows (since replaced by sash) and the belt course (a projecting row of bricks indicating the floor division), are common enough. But the clustered and diagonally set chimneys are a comparatively rare Gothic survival in the colonies, as are the end gables which are both stepped and curved (technically, cusped).

Bacon's Castle and a few other surviving large houses reflect the burgeoning plantation economy of the South and are the forerunners of the great mansions of the Georgian period. But in the North, after the first generation of landed proprietors and ministers had passed, the great houses ceased to be built because of the equalization of wealth and the high price of labor in the expanding and diversified economy of mid-seventeenth-century New England. It was not until the end of the period that the houses of the new merchant class, made rich by the growth of manufacturing and trade, began to be built. In Boston alone there were thirty merchants in 1676 "of considerable estates and very great trade" [6] with fortunes of between ten and twenty thousand pounds. Yet only one of the residences of this group has survived, the Usher House at Medford, Massachusetts, built of brick in 1677 but so remodeled in the eighteenth century by Isaac Royall that it is hardly recognizable as a house of this period. The more noteworthy Foster-Hutchinson House, built about 1683, and the Peter Sergeant House, built between 1676 and 1679, both also constructed of brick, have disappeared, though enough evidence of the latter (the remodeled Province House of historical and literary fame) remains to indicate that the house was similar in its decorative details to Bacon's Castle. Another fairly large brick building, the Tufts House in Medford, built in 1674,

1—8. Pierce-Little House, Newbury, Massachusetts, 1667 (?).

is almost Georgian in its simplicity, plan, and proportion. Its gambrel roof, which it shares only with Harvard Hall during the seventeenth century, is very advanced. Another large house in the North is worth consideration—the Pierce-Little House in old Newbury, Massachusetts, probably erected in 1667 (Illustration 1–8). Even today, surrounded by its outbuildings and approached by a long avenue of shade trees, it looks out across the salt marshes to the ocean like an English manor house on the North Sea. Remarkable for its construction in stone, very rare in New England, and for the Gothic details of its projecting two-story vestibule, including an arched niche, the existence of the Pierce-Little House suggests the possibility that there were more of its kind in New England than has been commonly thought to be the case.

The first permanent buildings were fortifications. Soon after the arrival of the Pilgrims at Plymouth, Governor Bradford wrote that "they built a fort with good timber." [7] This structure was described by a Dutch traveler in 1627 as a "large square house made of thick sawn planks staid with oak beams" [8]—a succinct description, incidentally, of the traditional building methods of East Anglia. Though no forts dating from the seventeenth century still exist, the eighteenth-century block houses of split logs with an overhanging second story at Kittery Point, Edgecomb, Winslow, and Augusta, all in Maine, and such sites as Old Fort Harrod at Harrodburg, Kentucky, 1775, preserve what must have been common earlier forms on the advancing frontier. But more numerous than the fort was the garrison house, a strong building used as a one-family residence in peaceful times but as a place for protection and retreat for the community in times of danger. Most of these buildings were of wood—not framed like the ordinary dwelling, but constructed of squared, dovetailed logs for greater protection against attack. One of the most interesting is the McIntire Garrison House, c. 1645 (*AA 5), still standing in the Scotland section of York, Maine, a survivor of a succession of plunderings, burnings, and murders which wiped out all but two of the settlements on the coasts of that province. Though garrison houses of masonry were more effective than those of wood, scarcity of lime for mortar made their appearance rarer. Two brick "strong houses" built during the late seventeenth century in Haverhill, Massachusetts, and its vicinity still exist, but later remodeling has made them much less typical and impressive than the one remaining "strong house," the Whitfield House at Guilford, Connecticut, 1639 (AA 44, AA 45; Illustration 1–9), which is apparently similar to those put up a few years before in the English-Scotch planta-

tions in Ulster for protection against the recently conquered Irish. Though the building may suffer from a too romantic restoration, the great hall, with its huge fireplace, is certainly original and implies a house of considerable strength and size. The massive solidity of the chimney, the steep pitch of the roof, and the narrow, fortress-like windows give an air of medieval strength to this one surviving "castle" in the English new world.

Non-domestic Architecture

In the theocentric seventeenth century the most important buildings were the places of worship; in the colonies, therefore, meeting-houses and church buildings were the most conspicuous structures. Both were symbols of authority, the former of the Puritan theocracy, the latter of either the Anglican Establishment or, in Maryland, the Catholic Church. Outstanding examples of each type still exist: the Newport Parish Church, now St. Luke's, in the vicinity of Smithfield, Isle of Wight County, Virginia, 1632–1680's (AA 98, AA 99, AA 100; Illustration 1–10), and the Old Ship Meetinghouse at Hingham, Massachusetts, 1681, with later additions (AA 9, AA 11; Illustration 1–11). Built as early as 1632,[9] St. Luke's, situated in a now remote part of the tidewater, is an authentically Gothic brick building very similar to several parish churches in Essex, England, though erected a hundred or more years after its English prototypes. Though St. Luke's has no such Gothic characteristics as flying buttresses or pinnacles, it does possess wall buttressing, Gothic tracery in the windows, and the "corbie" (or crow) stepped gables of the eastern shires. An odd triangular shape over the entrance, seemingly an awkward attempt at a pediment, and the angle quoining of the tower (added, with the top floor, after 1657) mark the only concessions to the classic style, established by this time in metropolitan England for three-quarters of a century. The plan is that of a simple aisleless nave, like that of similar structures in England. The recently restored building has many interesting interior

1–9. Whitfield House, Guilford, Connecticut, 1639.

1–10. St. Luke's Church, Smithfield, Isle of Wight County, Virginia, 1632–1680's.

the meetinghouse of the late seventeenth century is apparently a phenomenon unique to America; [10] some precedent for its large size, its centrally placed pulpit, and its galleries can be found in Protestant meetinghouses and churches on the Continent, but few examples survive. It might seem strange that there was no marked precedent in England for the New England meetinghouse until it is remembered that the English Puritans, prevented from worshiping in the buildings of the established Church and thus compelled to meet elsewhere (sometimes in taverns), were also generally forbidden to build places of worship of their own. Between 1630 and 1640, thirty-five meetinghouses were erected in New England and the type was more or less established, so that when construction of non-conformist meetinghouses was permitted later in England, their design was influenced by American prototypes.

features, including a rood screen, and an unusual tie-beam-reinforced truss roof (reconstructed upon evidence found in the remodeled building), which is peaked into the gable roof but has an effect similar to a low vault. The early churches at Jamestown and at Williamsburg were of this general plan. All that is known of the first Catholic church in the English colonies, St. Mary's Chapel at Old St. Mary's City, Maryland, is that it was built with a cruciform plan.

These early church buildings were traditionally longitudinal in axis with attention directed toward the altar and its liturgy. The meetinghouse, on the other hand, was oriented toward the pulpit and was wider in dimension, sometimes even square, with galleries added to accommodate more worshipers. These changes, incorporated in a relatively simple structure of exposed framing and unembellished walls, resulted in what might be called a new building type. Furthermore, in its fully developed form,

1–11. Interior, Old Ship Meetinghouse, Hingham, Massachusetts, 1681.

It would be absurd, however, to state that the colonial meetinghouse was not influenced by English architecture. In its earliest form, in both structure and appearance, it was hardly different from a large framed dwelling; later, it resembled the typical town hall in England, with its numerous gables and the addition of what the early records called "lanthornes" or "cupilos." Indeed, the fact that ecclesiastical and civil functions were interrelated to such an extent in New England made it only natural for civil architecture to have influenced the meetinghouse.

The survival of the Old Ship Meetinghouse as a rare example of its building type is perhaps not entirely fortuitous, for it was the largest in New England with the exception of the Third Church's meetinghouse in Boston, and continued to be adequate for Hingham, a town which declined rather than increased in population. Its congregation, instead of pulling it down and replacing it with a more up-to-date building in the eighteenth or early nineteenth century (the fate of others that had survived the seventeenth century), decided instead to remodel it, adding two porches and classical detail to the exterior, and covering up the roof framing by means of a flat ceiling hung from the tie beams. When this was removed in 1930 there was revealed the finest example of exposed framing surviving from the early colonial period, a complex system of tie beams, rafters, and struts supporting the wide roof in a configuration similar to the lofty timber-covered halls of medieval England (and also coincidentally resembling the upturned hull of a ship). Though the exterior has been altered as described, its general proportions, its steep, hipped roof, and the presence of a cupola reflect its former appearance. The Hingham meetinghouse must have been somewhat plainer and less picturesque than earlier examples (which often had gables and more highly pitched roofs, frequently of pyramidal shape—a logical development of the hip roof), as illustrated in an old print of what must have been a more typical example—the West Springfield Meetinghouse, 1702 (Illustration 1–12).

The Old Ship Meetinghouse is important historically and esthetically as the sole survivor of

1–12. West Springfield Meetinghouse (destroyed), West Springfield, Massachusetts, 1702. Wood engraving from John Warner Barber's *Massachusetts Historical Collections* (Worcester: 1839).

a host of similar buildings in New England, and as a respectable addition to the great tradition of the framed Gothic halls in England. This edifice and a few eighteenth-century examples, less complex in structure and with classic ornament added, such as the West Parish Meetinghouse, West Barnstable, Massachusetts, are all that remain of a once typical American architectural type which in its simplicity, plainness, and clearly organized plan represented a fitting setting for the austere service of the Puritan creed, and at the same time was both appropriate and convenient for the conduct of the town's civic business.

Toward the end of the century, the town hall began to replace the meetinghouse as the "house for the town." Though all vestiges of this kind of structure have disappeared, the reputation of at least one, the Town House at Boston, 1656 (*AA 14), which burned in 1771, was such that its probable appearance can be surmised from contemporaneous records. Public rooms, sheathed in broad vertical planks, were on the second story and connected with the street level by an awkwardly placed outside stairway. Below was an open market punctuated with the huge oak supports for the upper floors. The third story was covered by a hip roof and lighted by windows in a row of three gables on each longitudinal side. A more thoroughly medieval building can hardly be imagined.

In the South, public buildings were more prominent than in New England. The Chesapeake Bay colonists brought with them the official church (with the exception, of course, of the Catholic proprietor of Maryland and his coreligionists) and a simulacrum of the English Parliament in the House of Burgesses in Virginia and the Assembly in Maryland. As has been noted, the earliest State Houses in Virginia were composed of row houses, but the Old State House at St. Mary's, built in 1676 and destroyed in 1829, was a different matter, as can be seen in an authoritative restoration completed in 1934 (AA 103, AA 104). The building consists almost entirely of an impressive assembly room, thirty-six by forty-one feet, spanned by massive exposed beams, illuminated by casement windows, floored with brick, and heated by a large fireplace at either end. A stair hall to the small upper rooms and an entrance vestibule, on opposite sides of the hall, created a cruciform plan similar to so many early houses in the South.

Turning now to school and college buildings, we find that most of them were in New England, where education at all levels was a public responsibility. Schools were started there relatively early (Boston Latin School was founded in 1643), but we know nothing of these first institutions except that they were frequently conducted in outgrown meetinghouses. Two colleges had been founded in the colonies by the end of the seventeenth century. As early as 1636 the Massachusetts Bay Colony had been concerned about its future supply of ministers, but the Anglicans of the South were not sufficiently bothered about the lack of parish incumbents to found a college until 1693, when they erected the first building of William and Mary College at Williamsburg. This structure was built in the Georgian style, newly imported to the colonies, and therefore

will be taken up in the succeeding Part. Harvard's first building (*AA 12), begun in 1638, was entirely Gothic, with overhangs and many gables. Its E-shaped plan added further to its medieval appearance, to the extent that it probably surpassed even the Boston Town House in picturesqueness. Poorly constructed, this wooden building was "ruinous" in 1655 and had to be demolished in 1678. The new college building, Harvard Hall, was put up in the years 1674–1677 in the more permanent material of brick. Though not designed with an E-plan, its many gables, surrounding a gambrel roof (perhaps the first in the colonies), its irregular string course between the floors, its segmental arched windows with diamond panes, and its absence of classical detail gave it almost as medieval an appearance as that of the first building. Stoughton Hall at Harvard, built in the last few years of the century, was Georgian. These two buildings, together with Massachusetts Hall (the only one of the three which remains today), can be seen in the 1726 print by William Burgis, *A Prospect of the Colleges in Cambridge in New England* (*GB 35; Illustration 2–52, on page 103).

There were, of course, other kinds of buildings than those included under the categories of domestic and public architecture: business and commercial buildings and similar practical structures. The former were often row houses or individual buildings resembling dwellings, as was the case in England. One of these, the Aptucxet Trading Post at Bourne, Massachusetts, built in 1627 and restored in 1930 (AA 15), is essentially a story-and-a-half house with an end chimney, a gabled wing, and a pitched roof that provided a storage area (even higher and steeper than that of the Jethro Coffin House at Nantucket). The Old Wind Mill at Nantucket, 1746 (AA 16), though of the eighteenth century, is a survival of a type of timber structure brought from East Anglia (where many of them exist today), impressive for the complexity of the interior framing constructed as bracing against the wind.

Though Hugh Morrison, author of the most inclusive history of our early architecture, says that there was no new construction technique and no essentially new architectural form invented in colonial American building, nevertheless the quality which these remaining structures lend to the American scene in their contribution to its present beauty, their evocation of another age, and their appeal to our modern critical sympathies, makes them no less important intrinsically in spite of their relative lack of originality. The New England meetinghouse and framed dwelling were the last representatives, no matter how insignificant, of that great Gothic style which has so much in common with modern architecture in its emphasis on the organic beauty derived from the exploitation of revealed structure. To the still classically oriented taste of the early nineteenth century, the old New England houses were "wooden enormities." [11] Today the pendulum has swung in the opposite direction. These basically functional houses with their clearly revealed structure are nearer to

contemporary building than any that have intervened except the immediate ancestors of the modern movement. To look at them only to enjoy their quaintness or romantic association with the past is hardly to do them justice. It is even worse to copy them. When a seventeenth-century design is reproduced in the twentieth century because the analogies of its structure to that of contemporary building are considered appropriate for our time, there is no true understanding or appreciation of the original, but only a historically naïve sentimentality. The seventeenth-century house is only analogous to the good contemporary house, not the same. Functional as this old house was, it was not self-consciously so on the part of the builder, who constructed naturally out of the materials and traditions of his seventeenth-century environment—a very primitive one in comparison with our own highly developed technology of new methods and materials.

Painting and Sculpture

Painting

The craft of the "paynter-stayner" was needed as much in the new world as in the old; fences had to be painted, floors and walls "layd in oil," and parts of the interiors of houses trimmed in Indian red. There was also a need for guild and trade signs and for heraldic devices, including hatchments (family arms on a black ground) for funerals. In England the artisans who executed such work were usually guild members who had first served an apprenticeship. But in the new world there were other painters as well, more properly called amateurs, who flourished in a pioneering country where any skill was at a premium. There are records of both kinds of painter-craftsmen in the colonies, the artisan and amateur, but since most of the work they did was ephemeral, not enough is left to give us any significant notion of its kind or quality. But the fact that they existed and the survival of a few remnants of their work in historical collections justify these few words about them.

The only paintings which have survived in any number from this early period are portraits, a few obviously brought from the old world, but most of them painted here. The best of the native products are of considerable interest, since they are painted in a provincial English style at variance with the fashionable mode abroad, thereby establishing a tendency which, as we shall see, influenced the development of a native school.

From the evidence of the lack of skill displayed in many of these early painted visages it might be surmised that they were executed either by amateurs or by the artisan jacks-of-all-trades, the "paynter-stayners." The professional portrait limners, already set aside from their artisan contemporaries in England, were naturally an exception in the newly settled colonies. Perhaps only the anonymous painter of the Freake and Gibbs portraits, which are so much better than the majority, could have been a trained professional.

It is interesting to note that most of the pictures to be discussed were painted in the New Netherlands and in New England, not in the southern colonies. Economic and cultural dependence on the mother country was much greater in the South than in the semiautonomous northern colonies. Pictures were brought to Virginia and Maryland from London and Bristol with other items of luxury, and it was not until the late eighteenth century that the region produced in Charles Willson Peale a native artist of prominence.

The Dutch settlers in the New Netherlands, due to the vigorous artistic life of seventeenth-century Holland, were much more familiar with painting than were any of their English contemporaries in America. It is therefore not astonishing that by the beginning of the eighteenth century a strong local school had developed in New York. But it was to be far excelled later in Boston. By 1670 in the Massachusetts Bay Colony there were portraits of some distinction, even if in an old-fashioned style. By the mid-eighteenth century this antique manner, combined with later European influence, coalesced into a distinctive regional style, culminating in one of the greatest artists of the eighteenth-century British world, John Singleton Copley of Boston.

There were several causes for this development in Massachusetts. Here was the greatest concentration of population in the colonies by the middle of the century, and Boston was the largest town. Economic and political ties with England were less binding than elsewhere. The mother country needed the products of the southern plantations but could do without those of New England. As a result there was less traffic in English goods and consequently in the newer English tastes. A largely homogeneous population—middle-class, generally of one religion, originally from one part of England, and isolated from the mother country largely by choice—would naturally produce different social and political forms. New England, in desiring to be free of English legal and religious restraints, developed early an independence of attitude which in the field of politics led eventually to

1–13. Sir Peter Lely, *Elizabeth, Countess of Kildare,* 1679. Oil on canvas. 49½ x 40¼ inches. (Reproduced by courtesy of the Trustees of the Tate Gallery, London.)

the Revolution. In artistic matters this independence resulted in an isolation from the main currents of artistic development, thus prolonging the older conservative style brought to the colony and influencing the creation of a local school.

When a typical portrait is seen for the first time, its old-fashioned look is surprising (see Illustration 1–14). The figures are stiff, wooden, even incorrect in their anatomy and articulation, and, above all, flat. They seem to be silhouettes in an unreal space, like paper dolls pasted to a cardboard background. An effect of three-dimensionality has been attempted by both modeling and perspective, but very tentatively and inaccurately; what modeling there is is definitely subordinated to line. All of these characteristics are certainly strictures from the point of view of the realism that has prevailed since the Renaissance and still somewhat influences our judgment of pictures.

As an example of this kind of realism, Sir Peter Lely's portrait of *Elizabeth, Countess of Kildare,* 1679 (Illustration 1–13), can be taken as typical. At the same time it serves as an example of the best and most characteristic European portrait style, a style brought to England by Van Dyck during the reign of Charles I, and continued by his followers during the Restoration later in the century. Pictures like it, then, were contemporaneous with the New England painters. But how different the Lely is from a Boston picture! It is correct in anatomy and perspective and convincing in modeling, while a pleasing blend of line and tone gives an illusion of surrounding space. It is in these character-

1–14. Anonymous (the Freake limner), *Mrs. Freake and Baby Mary (?),* 1674 (?). Oil on canvas. 42½ x 36¾ inches. (Worcester Art Museum, Worcester, Massachusetts.)

istics that the picture's realism lies. But in addition to this simulation of natural appearance the painting has rich and subtle color, liveliness of execution, and a fashionable and refined interpretation of the subject. These characteristics give it the brilliance and elegance of the great portrait tradition that culminated in Van Dyck himself and which stylistically belongs to the post-Renaissance period called baroque. In contrast, the seemingly primitive colonial effigies do not belong at all to this school; though they were painted fifty years after Van Dyck died in England, they belong to another tradition, an earlier one. Like the houses the New England colonists were still building in the 1690's, these paintings are medieval. If we examine them not as the contemporaries of those by Van Dyck's followers after the Restoration (such as Sir Peter Lely and Sir Godfrey Kneller), but as later examples of a surviving Gothic tradition, we can better countenance their unnaturalness and concentrate on their virtues—design, pattern, and sensitive linearism.

Today pictures of this type are hung in museums of art as well as on the walls of historical and genealogical societies because their abstract qualities recommend them to modern taste, which is no longer satisfied with mere imitation.

But why are these pictures so different from contemporaneous portraits of the Van Dyck school? Most observers would probably answer in one of two ways: they would consider the American pictures as products of a provincial and backward English school, or, on the other hand, as first examples of an indigenous American one. Both opinions would be to a certain degree correct. These portraits are indeed backward and provincial English, but the colonists brought this school, not the fashionable Cavalier manner, with them. Thus the direction given to the development of painting in this country was quite different from that in England, where the baroque Van Dyck tradition was to prevail.

It is worthwhile to consider the significance and origin of this provincial English school and its relationship with its colonial offshoot in New England.[12] It is not too generally recognized that this relationship exists. As a matter of fact, even histories of English art largely ignore the persistence of this retardataire school in Britain itself, and concentrate instead on the better known paintings of the Stuart court and the Cavalier gentry. But there was another group of patrons in England who had their own, very different tastes and who consequently employed different artists. This school is a continuation of the older and indigenous Tudor school of late medieval times, which preceded the influence of Van Dyck and his immediate predecessors in England. Even a cursory examination of some English provincial portraiture during the reigns of Charles I, of the Protector, and even of Charles II, shows how similar this little known facet of English art is to the painting done in New England at the same time. This is generally true of most English ecclesiastical and academic portraiture, at least until the mid-seventeenth century (as can be seen at Lambeth Palace and at Oxford and Cambridge). It is certainly true of Norfolk and Suffolk, the heart of East Anglia, the origin of most of the New England colonists (where, incidentally, a preference for the patterned and linear continued well into the eighteenth century). It is understandable how such a tradition would be long in resisting new styles. It had existed before the reign of Henry VII, and had even influenced the great Hans Holbein the Younger to change his rounded three-dimensional Renaissance style to the flat patterns seen in the portraits of Henry VIII's unfortunate wives, who look like medieval queens on playing cards. The tradition continued in the reign of Elizabeth, whose artistic preferences were still somewhat medieval (or at any rate, patriotically English), and lingered on into the reign of her conservative successor, James I. It required the forceful artistic personality of Prince Charles (later Charles I, one of the greatest and most perspicacious collectors in history) to end this "Jacobethan" taste by introducing Flemish and Dutch artists who painted in a more up-to-date continental manner. The new style gained favor at the court and among the Cavalier gentry, but elsewhere the old tradition did not succumb to the sensuous wiles of Van

Dyck's followers until the beginning of the eighteenth century.

It would be an oversimplification to say that the Cavaliers were painted exclusively by Van Dyck and his followers, and that the Roundheads and Puritans sat only for artists of the conservative school out of protest against the fripperies of Royalist taste. But though it cannot be categorically stated that the provincial school in Puritan East Anglia and the provincial school in Puritan New England are the same, it can at least be said that the New England portraits of the seventeenth century are thoroughly English, that the largest body of English work they resemble can be found in East Anglia, and that this style persisted there longer than elsewhere in England.

Before discussing the actual pictures, an explanation should be given for the fact that they are all portraits. After the iconoclastic fervor of the Reformation had made religious art a thing of the past, portraiture was nearly the only form of art, since landscape and genre were not prevalent in England until the eighteenth century. Only after Charles I brought Rubens to decorate the ceiling of Whitehall Palace in London did mythological and historical subjects gain any prominence. But mere decoration and pompous allegory were offensive to Puritan taste, as they were to middle-class taste in general (witness the art of seventeenth-century Holland, that epitome of bourgeois culture). Thus the staid portraiture of East Anglia and the colonies (and, in fact, of the non-Cavalier British community in general) represented a middle-class resistance against royal and aristocratic affectation, especially hateful to the Puritan who was not only one of the most typical manifestations of the rising middle class, but whose forebears had been the most active iconoclasts against what they considered to be the papist idolatry of medieval religious art.

And now let us turn to these few but fascinating pictures, among the last representatives of the dying medieval style—long since dead on the Continent except in remoter parts such as the Scandinavian countries and the Alpine regions.

The best pictures of the New England school are undoubtedly those by the anonymous artist who has been called the Freake limner. His portraits, *John Freake* and *Mrs. Freake and Baby Mary (?)* (Illustration 1–14), painted in 1674,[13] at first glance have all the unsophisticated charm of folk art. But when compared with less expert examples of their own kind, they are far from naïve. Interest in line, flat color, and pattern are typical of popular art at all periods, but these are also qualities of medieval art in general. The two portraits are too sophisticated and refined in their careful drawing, exquisite patterning, and keen observation of particulars of costume and face to be anything but the consequence of a long and expert tradition. Further, the prominence of Mr. Freake, merchant and attorney, and of his wife, the daughter of Thomas Clarke, one of Boston's wealthiest merchants, would not be consistent with the employment of a mere artisan or amateur. The Freake painter is too close in quality to the best of early sixteenth-century English provincial painters to be anything but a professional.

Besides the Freake portraits, the same limner probably painted the three separate portraits of the Gibbs children, Robert (*PA 16B), and Henry and Margaret (both in the collection of Mrs. David M. Giltinan, Charleston, West Virginia)—all done in 1670. The decorative effect of the design, the detail of certain areas, and the expert surety of line indicate the same hand in all five pictures. The care in the rendering of the children's dresses and the sympathetic recording of the subjects' childishness create an impression very different from the stereotyped one of the Puritan child. These were certainly not among the "wretched" children so difficult for the tithing man to control at Sunday meeting. The little subjects are as gaily dressed as their counterparts in Elizabethan and Jacobean portraits in England (and in miniature adult fashion, as was the seventeenth-century custom), and they look as though their childish learning went beyond the dour *New England Primer* and Michael Wigglesworth's *Day of Doom,* which were prescribed reading for Puritan children. Robert, Henry, and Margaret Gibbs seem to be the off-

spring more of Irresistible Grace than of Total Depravity, those twin doctrines of the Calvinist creed.

Another artist, close in style to the Freake limner and, like him, anonymous, is the painter of the Mason children: *David, Joanna and Abigail Mason* (*PA 13) in a group portrait, and *Alice* alone (Adams Memorial Society, Quincy, Massachusetts). Although executed in 1670 also, their quality is not quite that of the painter of the Freake and Gibbs portraits. The compositions are not so expert and the detail and line are less sure.

The pictures by the Freake and Mason limners are outstanding in the group of similar paintings done in the Bay Colony. While they represent a breakdown of the austere Puritan ideal and a reversion to late Elizabethan gaiety, they continue the older style rejected by the Cavalier group but favored by middle-class Puritanism on both sides of the Atlantic.

The portrait believed to be that of *Elizabeth Eggington,* 1664 (PA 152), and one possibly representing *Thomas Thacher,* c. 1670–1678, though perhaps considerably later (PA 6), can be taken as typical examples of less expert work. A first glance at the *Elizabeth Eggington* reveals the flat pattern of the seventeenth-century style, but a further examination shows that there is far less refinement and surety of line than in the work of the Freake limner. The *Thomas Thacher* has a certain boldness of design but lacks precision in delineation and detail, and therefore seems more amateur than professional. This picture is typical of a whole group of New England portraits, among them some tentatively attributed (on very little evidence) to John Foster, who, it is known, executed the first American example of the graphic arts, a woodcut *Portrait of Richard Mather,* c. 1670 (GB 81). Its stark crudity has a certain effectiveness, but if Foster is the author of such a portrait as that of *John Davenport,* 1670 (PA 9), it is evident that the subtler demands of the medium of paint were beyond his abilities. Here there is pattern, but little else, including character, which the bolder *Thomas Thacher* does have. The fact that Foster, a graduate of Harvard, sometime teacher of Latin and Greek, printer, publisher, and amateur painter should have been compared to the famous ancient Greek painter Apelles is a sad commentary on art in the Massachusetts Bay Colony, the most flourishing artistic region in the colonies.

But this early school was soon to die out. The costumes of the Freakes and of the Mason children already presaged the loosening of the old order. The same forces that confounded Puritanism in England and caused the multitude to run to Dover to welcome Charles II were working in the Massachusetts Zion; after the last upheaval of the witchcraft trials, even the Puritan church itself seemed discredited. Indeed, not only the wealthy merchants but the descendants of the old Puritan aristocracy were forming the fashionable Anglican congregation of King's Chapel. The writer of 1652 who describes Boston even then as a "City-like Towne . . . wharfed out with great industry and cost, the buildings beautiful and large . . . and orderly places with comely streets," predicts correctly a "sumptuous city." [14] Merchant Hutchinson's house, built in 1685–1692 for John and Abigail Foster, was already a fully Renaissance three-story building of brick with giant pilasters. And this would hardly be the only mansion in this style in so large a city, soon to be exceeded in population in the British world only by London, Bristol, and Norwich. In such an environment the new style of the Stuart court was not to be long in coming. It arrived in the person of an amateur, one Thomas Smith, apparently a sea captain who came to Boston around 1650 and about whom nothing is known except that it was probably he who was paid four guineas by Harvard College for a portrait of Dr. Ames, now lost.

In the two pictures definitely attributed to him, a *Self-Portrait*, c. 1690 (PA 16), and one of his daughter, *Maria Catherine Smith*, c. 1680 (Illustration 1–15), we see the work of a man who had rejected the late medieval style, with its line, pattern, and precise observation of decorative detail. He substituted in their stead modeling and other form-realizing techniques of the baroque style evidenced by his contem-

1–15. (Captain) Thomas Smith, *Maria Catherine Smith*, c. 1680. Oil on canvas. 26⅞ x 25¼ inches. (Collection American Antiquarian Society, Worcester, Massachusetts.)

poraries, the followers of Van Dyck. The captain was also aware of the fashionable manner of these artists, for Maria Catherine has the elegant dress, the elaborate coiffure, and the lush and well-realized charms of the ladies of the court of Charles II as painted by Sir Peter Lely (Illustration 1–13). But his grasp of the professional refinements of such artists was slight; Captain Smith was veritably an amateur, even if he attempted a more advanced manner than his fellow colonials. Convincing anatomy and articulation are lacking in these pictures, not as the result of ignoring these qualities (as was the case in the late medieval style), but because of lack of skill. Even the realization of form by modeling and the painterly blending of objects with each other and with their background are crudely done in Maria Catherine's portrait. The captain's *Self-Portrait* is not without its naïve charm, however, in spite of its pretentions. The subject looks a little dolefully out of the canvas, his hand resting on a skull placed over a poem presumably of his own composition in which he bids farewell to the evil world—a Puritan attitude somewhat at variance with the worldly mood expressed in his daughter's portrait. The poem's lugubrious sentiment, "Farwell World, / Farwell thy Jarres / thy Joies, thy Toies, thy Wiles, thy Warrs," is somewhat lessened by the representation of a lively encounter of ships engaged in a naval battle.

Several other portraits, such as that of a *Major Thomas Savage*, c. 1679 (PA 14), may be by the hand of Captain Smith, or by painters with similar background and training—or lack of them. But no matter how up-to-date these rounded bodies by some pedestrian amateur may be, the added reality is plodding and dull when com-

1–16. Anonymous (the Pierpont limner), *Reverend James Pierpont*, 1711. Oil on canvas. 31½ x 25 inches. (Courtesy of Yale University Art Gallery, New Haven, Connecticut. Loaned by Allen Evarts Foster.)

pared with the linear grace and delicacy of the backward but still professional painting of Mrs. Freake and her daughter.

A much more interesting portrait is that of *Elisabeth Paddy (Mrs. John Wensley)*, 1670–1680 (PA 8), a resident of the Plymouth Colony, a more provincial place than Boston in the Bay Colony. Though her face and some of her outlandishly elaborate costume are rendered with some knowledge of three-dimensionality, this is inconsistent with the remainder of the picture and was obviously learned only secondhand from a Captain Smith or a Dutchman from New Amsterdam. But the charm of the detail, the close observation of it and of the rather sensitively realized face, show the persistence of the older tradition.

One other painter, though he worked in the early eighteenth century, could still be considered among the New England group, since he was also untutored and not yet fully aware of the new fashions. This is the painter of the New Haven divine, *Reverend James Pierpont* (PA 17; Illustration 1–16) and of his wife (PA 18), both done in 1711. In his portrait of Mrs. Pierpont the artist struggled as hard as did Captain Smith, in his portrait of his daughter, to make his subject fashionable; indeed, Mrs. Pierpont does have a certain dark-eyed grace, like Lely's creatures, but more dignity. The *Reverend Pierpont*, gazing unseeingly out of the otherwise almost blank area of the picture, is the most arresting American portrait before Copley, not for its professional competence but for its insight into the sitter's personality. One sees in this face not the aggressive assurance of early Puritans like John Cotton or Increase Mather nor the hysterically stimulated faith of a Cotton Mather, but the melancholy of a man who begins to doubt the validity of Limited Atonement, Predestination, and Total Depravity. This extraordinary visage compensates for the lack of anatomical knowledge shown in the rest of the figure (hands and arms are studiously avoided in this and other paintings attributed to the Pierpont limner), and for the uninteresting composition (the elements represented are so few as to require little skill in composing them). In view of all this, it would be a pity if the face of the Reverend were only a happy accident.

What of the other artisans and amateurs like John Foster? There must have been many, but nothing can be definitely attributed to them, even when their names are mentioned in the old records. The "paynter-stayner" Tom Childs, for instance, who died in Boston in 1706, must have done many of the other tasks his kind were supposed to do. (Henry VIII's "sergeant paynter," for example, painted barges, coaches, chariots, litters and wagons, tents and pavilions, heralds' coats, trumpet banners, "and funerals to be solomnized." [15]) We know that John Foster executed tombstones and mortuary painting, which was apparently a very important branch of art, elaborate and rich in symbolism. These were probably as embellished with old-fashioned folk motifs as were the splendid chests and other furniture made throughout New England by various craftsmen. One of the best of these was Thomas Dennis of Ipswich, who covered his furniture with complex patterns of rosettes, arabesques, and foliations in a still-Tudor exuberance of wood carving (DA 84).

In the New Netherlands, it was also the artisan-craftsman who was most likely to paint portraits. Evert Duyckinck came to New Amsterdam in the 1630's to make, engrave, stain, and paint glass. He also executed the city's coats of arms that were painted on the fire buckets. But of his pictures we know nothing definite. His son Gerret was also a glazier (the Duyckinck dynasty continued well into the eighteenth century), and in his case scholars are on surer ground, attributing to him a portrait of himself and one of his wife. Several other artisan-craftsmen are mentioned in New Amsterdam and in early New York, after the city was taken by the English. These include a painter called the Stuyvesant limner because he painted portraits of the crusty old Dutch governor and his son Nicolas. The Dutch settlers brought with them from their art-loving homeland an almost unbelievable number of paintings, according to New Netherlands inventories. It is not surprising, therefore, that the Stuyvesant limner should be competent

in modeling and in the representation of landscape, as seen in his *Nicolas William Stuyvesant, 1666* (PA 19). Even the anatomy of the horse upon which the young man sits is not unconvincing, though its small size in relation to its rider would have been unthinkable in the Netherlands. Gerret Duyckinck is also convincing as far as modeling is concerned, and therefore shows some knowledge of professional standards, though his figures appear more pneumatic than three-dimensional, as can be seen in his *Self-Portrait* and in the portrait of his wife (PA 20, PA 21). His work also possesses some of the realistic approach to a subject that characterizes seventeenth-century Dutch art. (His pudgy self and his pug-nosed wife were not made to appear more attractive than they were.) This realism and a certain boldness of design typical of naïve painters continued into the next century, giving a certain individuality to the otherwise generally fashionable eighteenth-century portraiture throughout the colonies, including the former New Netherlands.

Some writers have seen the tradition of realism associated with certain aspects of American art (and appropriate to that pragmatism so characteristic of America) as beginning with the Dutch school in New Amsterdam. Although there may be a certain justice to this observation, more credible would be the following suggestion: that out of the flat, patterned, linear work of the early New England school came a certain dry, planometric style which can be observed from the time of Robert Feke in New England, culminating in Copley and continuing in the Connecticut school surrounding Ralph Earl after the Revolution—if not longer. At any rate, the presence of these seventeenth-century medieval pictures on New England walls, combined with the austerity of the meetinghouse and the conservative simplicity of the seventeenth-century dwelling, must have had some part in forming a taste, even if entirely unconsciously. Perhaps this taste contributed something to what may be called an American style which can still be discovered in some of our painting today.

Sculpture

If there was any other sculpture or carving besides painted trade signs and tombstones during the seventeenth century, it has been lost. In any event, aside from portraits, the most impressive remnants of the figurative arts of the seventeenth century are tombstones, by far the best of which are in New England, and more especially in Massachusetts.

These monuments probably reflect the funeral art of the Puritans, by its nature ephemeral but nonetheless important, considering how concerned these people were with mortality. The earlier stones [16] derive from the baroque tradition of the naturalistic rendition of figures and of foliate and other decorations in an illusionistic style, and often incorporated iconography taken from seventeenth-century English emblem books.

1–17. The "Stonecarver of Boston," gravestone of Joseph Tapping, King's Chapel Burying Ground, Boston, Massachusetts, 1678.

Some of these stones are quite elaborate. John Foster's stone, 1681, in the Dorchester graveyard, and that of Joseph Tapping, 1678, in King's Chapel Burying Ground, Boston (Illustration 1–17), were evidently too complex in conception to be successfully executed by the provincial carver (the "Stonecarver of Boston"), who was not too skilled in the representation of such subtleties as a lighted candle, a terrestrial globe, winged Father Time, and horrid Death himself, which appear in both stones. More successful are the less pretentious *momenti mori,* where conventional baroque ornament is combined with heraldry and some reminiscence of late medieval decorative formulas, as in the elaborately cut tulip, symbol of immortality. The best examples of this kind are signed "J. N." Typical is the stone of Thaddeus MacCarty in the Granary Burying Ground in Boston, 1705 (SB 2), which represents the refined competence seen in all "J. N."'s work. Many stones were more complex than those by "J. N.," however, though not as elaborate as those by the "Stonecarver of Boston." In them much use is made of the conventional skulls, skeletons, winged angel heads, and other stock symbols of death: shovels, coffins, and the like. These motifs are usually framed in an elaborate vocabulary of foliate motifs, more conventionalized and less naturalistic than the work of the two carvers already mentioned. The most productive carver of this kind of stone was Joseph Lamson, whose gravestone of William Dickson, 1692 (Illustration 1–18), in the First Parish Burying Ground, Cambridge, Massachusetts, is one of the most original and forceful in the colonies. Here grotesque imps of death and benign little angels cheerfully busying themselves with coffins are incorporated in a design of unusually sophisticated lettering and bold floriate pattern, expressive and decorative at the same time. Another of Lamson's stones, that of Rebekah Row, 1680 (SB 1), in the Phipps Street Burying Ground, Charlestown, Massachusetts, is less elaborate, but perhaps can be considered more typical of his work, especially in its sure mastery of well-defined design.

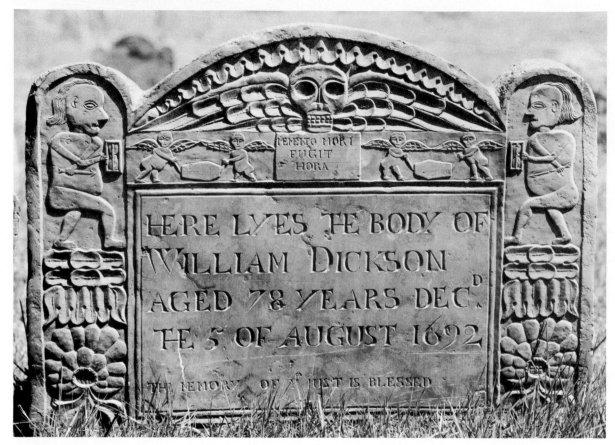

1–18. (Attributed to) Joseph Lamson, gravestone of William Dickson, First Parish Burying Ground, Cambridge, Massachusetts, 1692.

Lamson's stones indicate the qualities that were later developed in the more conventional gravestone carving of the seaboard region and in the original and indigenous styles of the rural areas when an even surer mastery of design was developed. These early stones and their successors of the eighteenth and early nineteenth centuries are coming to be more appreciated with the increase in contemporary admiration for the abstract and expressive.

PART TWO

THE EIGHTEENTH CENTURY

During the eighteenth century the colonists became metropolitan and were no longer exiles on the periphery of the European world.

By 1760 the thirteen colonies stretched uninterruptedly from the Spanish border in Georgia to the regions in the Province of Maine disputed by the English and French. At the time of the Revolution the Piedmont had been settled up to the Appalachians and in a few places beyond, though the bulk of the population dwelt in the tidewater. Into this country had poured settlers not only of English but of other British stock, particularly Scotch-Irish, and many Germans, mostly from the Palatinate. Throughout the territories united by the British crown, the population grew from about a half-million at the beginning of the century to nearly four million at the outbreak of the Revolution. The number of inhabitants of Philadelphia, less than a hundred years after its founding, was second only to London in the British Empire.

In this vast region, with its large and heterogeneous population, the old divisions among the Puritans of New England, the English of the South, and the Dutch of the Hudson valley were no longer possible. Philadelphia and New York were cities of mixed population and religious beliefs. New England was no longer an exclusively Puritan stronghold, for Newport and Portsmouth, the second and third largest cities in the region, were strongly Anglican and Royalist.

Even Connecticut was dotted with the churches of the Anglican Establishment.

Society was extremely varied, ranging from slaves and indentured servants to the proprietors of princely domains and of great merchant fleets. Slavery had greatly increased as the tobacco plantations spread throughout the South and the similar one-crop economies of rice, cotton, and indigo took hold in the Carolinas and Georgia, creating numerous and rich large-scale planters. The more diversified economy of New England and the Middle Colonies became increasingly prosperous, creating more business and wealth. This was naturally accompanied by further class stratification, from the "rabble" of free labor to the merchant, already in the seventeenth century called "damnably rich."

Though the middle class (even in a colony of plantations like Virginia) was the most numerous and assumed much of the leadership in the Revolution (with the assistance of the merchants and planters, chafing under British restrictions which interfered with the increase of their income), it was the members of the upper classes who built the important buildings and set the standards of taste. Especially in Virginia, the southern planters, always requiring more land for a crop that exhausted the soil, were the owners of huge domains. Baronial grants of land in the proprietorships, the legalization by the British of the Dutch patroon system, and the exploitation of private privilege on the part of officials who sold or granted land—increasing their own holdings with each transfer—created other sizable estates. In New England, large grants were made to the proprietors of the South Counties in Rhode Island; land speculation, plus the exploitation of official favor, resulted in vast tracts coming under single ownership in Connecticut; and both of these devices, together with a canny marriage, created in Maine one of the largest of private domains.

The landed gentry, together with the merchant class, were in constant contact with England and its tastes. Further, the presence of the royal governor and his entourage in most of the colonial capitals, of the officers of the British army in some cities, and of His Majesty's Custom, Post, and other offices everywhere, gave a London polish and glamour to the upper levels of colonial society. The commercial cities of Portsmouth, Boston, Newport, New York, and Philadelphia; the political and social capitals of Williamsburg and Annapolis; the plantation port of Charleston; and the great Maryland and Virginia plantations (with their own wharves in direct contact with London and their own ships bringing back ballast of English bricks and mantelpieces), were the most closely related to England by commercial contact, and the most motivated to emulate the ways of metropolitan Britain. For instance, the commerce that trans-formed Boston from a stubborn provincial enclave of a sect dying out in England into a great metropolitan port also accounted for a sweeping change in taste: originally a medieval market town, it became a classic Georgian city, and its backward and provincial school of painting eventually produced one of the greatest painters of the eighteenth century, John Singleton Copley. The presence in Newport of an important Tory population accounts for the existence there of the most sophisticated Georgian buildings in the colonies, by the first American architect, Peter Harrison.

It must not be forgotten, however, that the changes in colonial society finally culminated in the rejection of British rule and the expulsion of the Tories. The American Revolution was not only economic and political, but social as well, for in the British colonies, especially in the North, the concept of an American egalitarianism had already developed from various causes. This was reflected in the arts by the growth of an American portrait school, wherein the subjects were represented as unassuming individuals and not as symbols of a ruling class, and in provincial building, where a pragmatic adherence to older forms and to native and easily available materials gave a character that was lacking in the more conspicuous architecture of this era, which aspired to a more urbane taste.

Architecture in the English Colonies

At the end of the seventeenth century only the successful planters and merchants had sufficient leisure and wealth to surround themselves with "all accommodations for a comfortable and gentle living." By the time of the Revolution even the lower middle class, comprised of small planters, artisans, and shopkeepers, had larger and better constructed dwellings than the huts and cots of the first years of settlement, while the wealthy lived in houses of which "the splendor of the rooms [does] not suffer in comparison with Europe," in the words of the Duke de la Rochefoucault-Liancourt.[1]

All of these buildings shared a common English post-Renaissance style, generally called Georgian, even though local idiosyncrasies gave flavor to them, as in New England where the conservative simplicity of the seventeenth-century dwelling and meetinghouse had some effect on the more elegant later style.

Though there is little that is original in American architecture of the eighteenth century, the greater part of it being a postscript to English

Georgian, it does thereby belong to the great tradition of the Renaissance in its last phase. As such, its dignity and monumentality, its beauty of proportion and refinement of detail have an intrinsic merit which also can serve as general norms of measure and restraint, provided they do not seduce us into the literal copying so prevalent in our recent past. Furthermore, the architecture of this period is an eloquent commentary on the history of colonial society, and like that of the seventeenth century it contributes to the character of the older sections of the nation.

The Georgian Style: Origins, Designers, and Builders

Georgian architecture descends from the Renaissance style, which began in the fifteenth century in Italy as a reaction against the Gothic style and a revival of classical antiquity, and which received its final academic formulation during the sixteenth century in the work of Palladio and his contemporaries. In contrast to the medieval, much of whose beauty is that of revealed structure, the Renaissance is not an organic architecture but one in which principles of abstract form are more important. The picturesque arrangement of plan or elevation which was possible in the accidental and casual functionalism of medieval architecture was not permitted in the Renaissance; arbitrary rules of symmetry and order required deliberate compositions of space, mass, and surface. These are the general or fundamental principles of the Renaissance. A surface aspect of the style is its emulation of the detail of the architecture of Greece and Rome, that is, of the classical orders—Doric, Ionic, Corinthian, Tuscan, and Composite—which were systematized and adapted in a series of publications with engraved illustrations that date from before the time of Palladio through the mid-nineteenth century, or as long as classical taste lasted. The superficial element of the style—its classic detail—was first brought to England and applied to basically medieval buildings, creating the interesting yet stylistically confused buildings of Elizabethan England and much of Jacobean. But during the reign of

James I, Inigo Jones brought a correct classicism, derived largely from Palladio, to England, where his followers so established it that the later baroque phase of the Renaissance hardly penetrated the country or, consequently, its colonies. (The baroque—one of the great architectural styles, characterized for its casualness in the treatment of the orders, its introduction of curvilinear, even undulating, space and volume, and its enthusiastic ornamentation—left little mark on English architecture except in large-scale planning and the use of some decorative elements such as the broken and curved pediment.)

The influence of Jones's Palladianism was strengthened in the early eighteenth century by a group of architects led by Lord Burlington, so that much English Georgian is largely Palladian and therefore more restrained than the baroque.

In America, only the work of Peter Harrison and the early Thomas Jefferson clearly reflect this aspect of the Georgian style very specifically. A more prevalent English influence on the architecture of the colonies was the less pretentious domestic work of Sir Christopher Wren's followers during the reign of Queen Anne and the first two Georges. These houses comprise one of the most agreeable varieties of domestic architecture, combining a warm and comfortable adaptability with enough classical simplicity, balance, and detail to give them restful proportions and some grace. Dwellings of this kind (in contradistinction to the halls and castles of the great nobles) were familiar in provincial areas, whether they were in Great Britain itself or across the Atlantic in America.

The principal means by which the Georgian mode was distributed both in America and in provincial England were the English carpenter handbooks, meant for the great majority of builders who had no training in professional architecture, be they gentleman-amateurs like George Washington, who designed his own plantation house, Mount Vernon, or "housewrights" like the mulatto Hopestill Caswell (possibly an ex-slave) who built many of the great houses in and around Portsmouth, New Hampshire. In this connection the full title of one of the most popular of these books (by one Batty Langley) is suggestive: *The City and Country Builder's and Workman's Treasury of Designs* (London, 1740). Other frequently used books were Abraham Swan's *British Architect* (London, 1745; an edition was published in Philadelphia in 1775), and Halfpenny's *Modern Builder's Assistant* (London, 1742). Carpenter handbooks were supplemented by other volumes devoted to theory and composition and to the works of great architects, all lavishly illustrated with fine engravings, as were the carpenter handbooks. The most influential of these was *A Book of Architecture* (London, 1728) by James Gibbs, a follower of Wren who carried on the sturdier, less academic aspect of post-Renaissance English architecture. The stricter classicism was represented chiefly by the publication, under the aegis of Lord Burlington, of the Leoni edition of Palladio (1715), of Inigo Jones's buildings (1727), and of works by architects in the Burlington circle [the most popular of these in America were William Adams' *Vitruvius Scotticus* (Edinburgh, 1750) and *Palladio Londonensis* (London, 1734), though Robert Morris' *Select Architecture* (London, 1757) was used almost as much].

The importance of carpenter handbooks and design or pattern books in the transmission of the Georgian style to America can be indicated by citing only a few examples. George Washington used Batty Langley for the design of the library fireplace, the main entrance (AA 220), and the large Palladian window on the north end (AA 221) at Mount Vernon, and Swan for much of the other detail, especially in the mantelpieces, as in the dining room (AA 222). Swan's book was also used by the designers of the Lee Mansion, Marblehead, Massachusetts (AA 296), the Miles Brewton House, Charleston, South Carolina (AA 250), and many less pretentious houses; and *Halfpenny's* is the source of the fine portico at Whitehall, near Annapolis (AA 232; Illustration 2–13). Gibbs was the chief influence in the design of a number of plantation houses, and one of his alternate projects for the steeple of St. Martin's-in-the-Fields, London (Illustration 2–15) was the direct inspiration for a number of church towers in the colonies, perhaps the most faithful copy being the First Baptist Meetinghouse in Providence (AA 257; Illustration 2–23), and indirectly was responsible for nearly all the so-called Wren steeples in the colonial period and during the early republic. The two facades of one of the great houses of Virginia, Mount Airy, were taken from Gibbs (Illustration 2–11) and from the *Vitruvius Scotticus*, while the young Jefferson leaned heavily on Gibbs, Palladio, and Robert Morris.

Designers (there were really no professional architects as we know them today), as opposed to carpenter-builders, derived their knowledge of architecture from such books, and their example filtered down to the housewrights and builders, who were further aided by the carpenter handbooks. An indication of the need for such exemplars is illustrated by the completely unprofessional character of one of the few architectural drawings which has come down to us from the colonial period, a plan for a house, hardly more than a scrawl. Yet it is by Richard Munday, a master builder who was responsible for some of the most important structures in the colonies.

Gentleman-amateurs like Jefferson and Colonel Alexander Spotswood, an early governor of Virginia, were more sophisticated, using mathematics in devising the proportions of their buildings, but even they would have been at a loss without architectural source books. At the same time, the builders would have been equally lost without the details of framing and other construction found in the carpenter handbooks.

Georgian architecture, then, has stylistic unity not because it was designed by a single group of architects or followed the lead of one guiding genius, but because of two factors: first, the existence of a common body of knowledge among designers who were sometimes gentleman-amateurs and sometimes master builders; and second, traditional practices among carpenters and housewrights, who had absorbed them from the time they were apprentices. A pleasingly high level of taste can be expected of architecture under these circumstances, but no great variation of type or originality of conception.

Architects, in the strict sense of the word, did not design buildings in the colonies. The only known exception is John Hawks, who was brought from England by Governor Tryon to build an official residence at New Bern, North Carolina (AA 253), though a good, but far from conclusive, case has been made for attributing two buildings at Williamsburg to Sir Christopher Wren. The gentleman-amateur, typified best by Thomas Jefferson, was a man who was expected to be as familiar with his classical orders as he was with Greek and Latin, and though each varied in the degree of talent he showed in the arrangement of motifs derived from his various sources, most of the results are tasteful, if not always outstanding. Among the most talented amateurs besides Jefferson and Spotswood (Washington was less skillful, as will be seen) were two colonial officials, Richard Taliaferro (pronounced *Toliver*, and sometimes spelled that way) of Virginia, and Peter Harrison of Newport, who designed some of the most distinguished buildings in the colonies in Newport and greater Boston. Other amateurs whose names are known were Dr. John Kearsley, the English physician who designed Christ Church, Philadelphia; Andrew Hamilton, the distinguished lawyer who had a part in the plans for Independence Hall; Thomas McBean, the Scotsman who built St. Paul's Chapel, New York; and Joseph Brown of Providence, who was responsible for the Baptist Church there, the old college building at Brown University, and some private houses. Among professional builders Henry Cary of Williamsburg and another prominent Virginian, John Ariss, are notable, as are two wood carvers turned master builders, William Buckland, who worked in Annapolis, and Ezra Waite, who was probably responsible for the all-over design of the Miles Brewton House as well as for its carving. Less sophisticated were such carpenter-builders as Munday and Caswell, who, however, represent the great majority of designers, most of whom are still unknown.

Thus, much colonial architecture was designed by essentially untrained men, either cultivated amateurs or master builders. The great majority of it, however, is anonymous, and represents a tradition of craftsmanship wherein excellence was not always deliberately and consciously taught and learned but was absorbed through apprenticeship, example, and practice. Perhaps these anonymous designers benefited from not having been constrained by academic training, for they could devise their own solutions to problems not in the books and consequently often introduced in their buildings an original and pleasing aspect lacking in more "correct" ones. This was especially true in provincial places (the Connecticut valley in Massachusetts, for example, noted for charming late medieval carving), and in non-classical irregularities of plan and elevation seen in all but the most pretentious structures.

Analysis of the Georgian Style in America

The Georgian style, like all classical architecture, is formal, symmetrical, and ordered. A balanced mass and facade are the rule, and the hit-or-miss asymmetry of a House of Seven Gables is unthinkable. The plans are as rational as the design, at least from the point of view of geometry, if not of common sense.

Plan. The typically developed eighteenth-century plan consisted of a double file of rooms separated by a central hall which ran the entire width of the house and which contained the stairway. The larger houses usually had two sets of formal rooms on either side of the hall, with chimneys on the end walls or between the two rooms with fireplaces back to back. The smaller dwellings, however, often retained a central-chimney arrangement, as in the small Cape Cod and two-story houses in the more provincial sections. This was especially true in conservative Connecticut, which clung generally to the seventeenth-century tradition until the Revolution. In New England, the kitchen and service areas were usually placed in an ell; in the large southern houses they were situated in outbuildings, often connected by an arcade or passageway to the principal structure (Illustration 2–1).

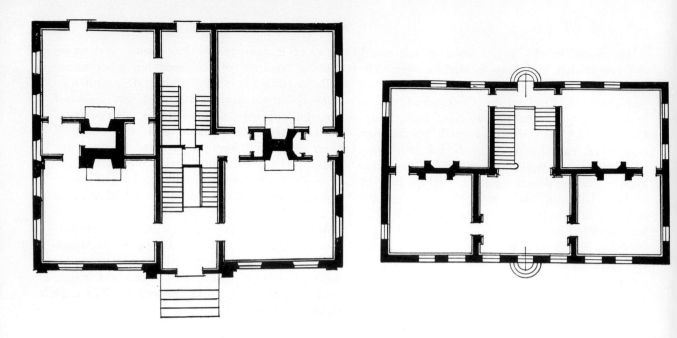

2–1. Plans of eighteenth-century houses. *Above, left:* Vassall-Longfellow House, Cambridge, Massachusetts, 1759. *Above, right:* Carter's Grove, James City County, Virginia, 1751. *Below:* Mount Airy, near Warsaw, Virginia, 1758–1762. (Adapted from Fiske Kimball's *Domestic Architecture of the American Colonies and of the Early Republic;* New York: 1922.)

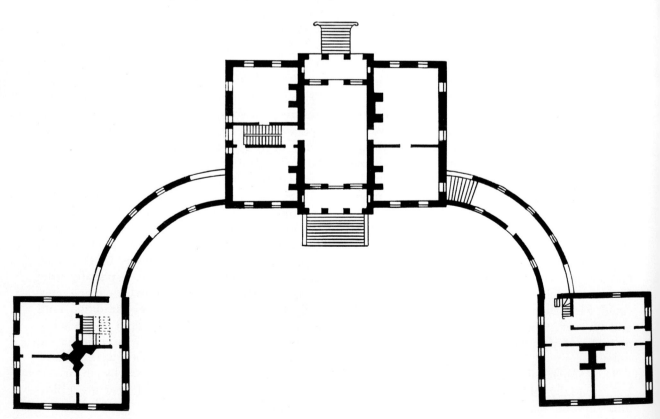

2–2. *Left:* Broken and curved pediment; *right:* curved or segmental pediment. Both from Abraham Swan, *British Architect* (London: 1745).

Ornament. At the beginning of the period there was little exterior detail in houses of classical taste except parts of cornices and moldings, from which eaves and window and door frames were largely composed. Later, more decorative elements were added, and doorways became the principal feature of the design. They were essentially of several types, all flanked with pilasters. Some were terminated simply by a cornice or an entire entablature (Illustration 2–19), while the cornices of the other types were crowned by three kinds of pediments: the angular (Illustration 2–21); the broken, either angular or curved (Illustration 2–2); or the curved (Illustration 2–2). Windows were sometimes similarly terminated with angular or segmental pediments or with an alternating sequence of the two (Illustration 2–26). If

there was a more prominent window, it was often of the Palladian type (Illustration 2–3; see also Illustration 2–29).

Treatments of the Wall. Walls, whether composed of brick, masonry, or wood, were usually varied in some way. Angle quoins (alternating blocks of different widths) were often used to give an expression of structural strength to the corners (Illustration 2–10). In brick construction, a water table of molded bricks customarily set back the main body of the house a few inches from the basement, thus making the latter appear more like the base of the building (Illustration 2–6), and belt courses in brick (or stone) expressed the floor levels (Illustration 2–8). The two boldest elements used in the design of the facade were the projecting central pavilion

Venetian Windows *of the* Tuscan   Order *whose* Members *are described at large in Plates* I. II.   Plate LI.

Batty Langley Invent and Delin. 1750.   Tho.' Langley Sculp.

2–3. Palladian window from Batty Langley's *The City and Country Builder's and Workman's Treasury of Designs* (London: 1740).

topped by a pediment-like gable (Illustration 2–29) and the giant pilaster which was placed at the corners of the main blocks of the house or of the pavilion (Illustration 2–19). The wall was terminated by the entire entablature, or most of it, though often only the cornice was used (except over the pilaster itself) in order for the windows to be of greater height (Illustration 2–19). Sometimes when the pavilion was omitted, a gable was placed over the central portion even though it did not project (Illustration 2–25).

Roofs. Roofs were of three basic types: hip, gambrel, and gable (Illustration 2–4).

Material. Brick was the commonest material for the larger houses, except in New England where the use of wood persisted. The brick courses were often varied for textural effect by the alternation of headers, sometimes glazed to enhance their pattern—a practice used in the

New Jersey and Maryland houses of the seventeenth century. Stone construction was usually of smooth-faced ashlar (Illustration 2–10), but in parts of Pennsylvania and the Middle Colonies in general, the earlier tradition of rough field-stone survived (*AA 306). Occasionally brick or stone was plastered over, especially in Philadelphia (Illustration 2–29) and in places influenced by that metropolis—Newcastle, Delaware, and Alexandria, Virginia—and in Charleston, South Carolina. In frame buildings, sheathing (Illustration 2–19) was sometimes substituted for clapboard to give an illusion of masonry or plaster, or wood was sanded and incised to resemble smooth-faced ashlar.

Interiors. Interiors were in general more elaborate than exteriors. The decorative motifs employed were classical in derivation, but occasionally motifs which were ultimately baroque were used in interior as well as exterior design. This was especially true of chimney pieces where curved and broken pediments frequently appeared (Illustration 2–28). Curvilinear rococo elements (such as Chippendale employed) were also used in these areas and on ceilings.

Doors were paneled, and some frames were pedimented and others were even arched. Windows usually were not as elaborately enframed as doors, but some had cornices and, in several instances, flanking pilasters. The mantelpiece or chimneypiece was the most complex and elaborate element of the interior design, after the huge hearth of the seventeenth century (used as much for the preparation of food as for warmth) had given way—except in the kitchen—to the small fireplace whose function was heating alone. During the early part of the century, the fireplace was simply framed by a molding, sometimes quite thick and heavy, and had no mantel (Illustration 2–5). The later Georgian fireplace was more ornate, employing as a frame around the opening a mantel shelf supported by consoles (Illustration 2–28) or placed above elaborate carvings. The overmantel was distinguished in some way from the surrounding wall treatment—often by pediments, broken or otherwise (Illustration 2–28). Wall surfaces were paneled or papered. Paneling from floor

2–4. Roofs. *Left to right:* Gable; gambrel; hip.

to ceiling was commoner in the early eighteenth century than later, and was most usually on the fireplace wall (Illustration 2–5). This treatment persisted into the latter part of the century in the more elaborate houses, but wainscoting (waist-high paneling) sufficed for most later rooms, except for the area immediately above the fireplace (Illustration 2–28). Some walls were pilastered and, in the finer houses of the earlier period, even painted to imitate marble. Occasionally, figurative or landscape painting was executed in panels, though such treatment was more usually reserved for the overmantel. Figured "wall papers," some of them imported, were frequently used, especially later in the century.

Ceilings were ordinarily plain above the sometimes elaborate cornice, but toward the middle of the century a few were highly ornamented (*AA 204, AA 205).

Stairways were usually broad and open (Illustration 2–9) and thus very different from the cramped seventeenth-century stairway, and were often broken by a landing and one or two runs to left and right, with lathe-turned balusters, and carved newel posts that were masterpieces of the carpenter's art (AA 284).

Thomas Jefferson, in his *Notes on the State of Virginia*, refers to the public buildings of the early Georgian period as "rude misshapen piles which but that they have roofs would be taken for brick-kilns." [2] To the present-day enthusiast of Georgian architecture, the subtleties of Jefferson's taste might seem too refined. Yet

certain characteristics do distinguish an earlier from a later colonial building. During the first quarter of the century, in general, the sturdy and simple structure of brick or wood was the norm, scarcely ornamented except at the cornice and sometimes at the doors, and with a simple hip or gable roof (Illustration 2–6). The earlier houses were steep-roofed (Illustration 2–8) while the later ones adjusted the pitch to comply with the less acute angle of the classical gable or pediment (Illustration 2–16). The earlier wooden house usually remained clapboarded, smooth sheathing being a later development. As the century advanced, a variety of formal elements made their appearance as the carpentry and other architectural books became more known. Giant pilasters began to take the place of angle quoins; windows, both wall and dormer, began to be crowned with pediments; and Palladian windows appeared in stair halls and over front entrances. Projecting central pavilions (usually crowned with a pediment) replaced the flush walls, giving a more monumental accent to the facade (Illustrations 2–19 and 2–29). Porticos were added to doors (Illustration 2–20) and even two-story porches to the facade (Illustration 2–12); in a very few instances, the giant portico was employed (Illustration 2–13), but this became commoner after the Revolution.

Transitional Building

Though the Georgian style entered the colonies during the late seventeenth century in a few important buildings of advanced Renaissance style, classical detail (let alone classical planning) was generally slow in gaining ground.

The central chimney often persisted, and with it a somewhat casual and functional plan evidenced in asymmetries of design; but framing and battened boarding of interiors gave way to smooth walls of lath and plaster or to paneling with classical molding and other detail, though these were usually combined in a naïve way with surviving medieval detail, as in the room from Newington, Connecticut, c. 1725–1750 (Illustration 2–5). The story-and-a-half house also persisted and, though retaining the essential shape of the Jethro Coffin House in Nantucket,

it had less acute gables and its eaves and openings were trimmed with classical moldings. Though basically seventeenth-century, this kind of house persisted along the frontier and as a simple type of rural, and even urban, dwelling well into the nineteenth century, and thus is a peculiarly American type hardly matched in the mother country.

In the South the basic seventeenth-century form of the simple story-and-a-half, steep-roofed, end-chimney house in brick or in wood was likewise given a few classical embellishments early in the next century, as in a number of buildings in Williamsburg, Virginia [such as the Repiton

2–5. Room from Newington, Connecticut, c. 1725–1750. Now in the Metropolitan Museum of Art, New York.

Brick Office (AA 85)], whose unpretentious charm was quite lost on Jefferson, who felt that it was "impossible to devise things more ugly and uncomfortable."[2]

The South

The most impressive buildings in the new Georgian style (literally "Georgian" is incorrect, for in the early eighteenth century William and Mary ruled England) were built in Williamsburg, the colonial capital of Virginia, and though the two most important structures, the Capitol and the Governor's Palace, are not original, they have been restored according to the best authority (1928–1932).

The design for the "Wren Building" at the College of William and Mary, erected first from 1698 to 1702 and rebuilt after a fire in 1716 (AA 185), and the Capitol, 1701–1705 (AA 188, AA 190), are stylistically close to the work of Wren in certain details, such as the narrow pavilion crowned by an acute-angled pediment on the college building, and in the overall exterior simplicity of both, which expresses the functions of the interiors. As Chief of the Office of Works, Wren might well have overseen these two structures in his official capacity, but evidence points to the probability that Governor Spotswood designed the college building, and that the Capitol was also locally designed, since it is composed basically of two buildings joined together, a precedent which existed only in the old Jamestown Capitol buildings. Henry Cary was the overseer in charge of work on the Capitol, as he was at the Governor's Palace, 1706–1720 (AA 191). This building, somewhat Wren-like in its high-pitched roof and not over-elaborate ornament, is a dignified structure of considerable size, the first of the Virginia mansions to be two rooms deep. The Palace served as a model for at least one of the great Virginia plantations, Westover. Brafferton Hall (or The Brafferton), 1723 (AA 198; Illustration 2–6), and the very similar President's House, both at the College of William and Mary and probably built by Cary if not designed by him, are Governor's Palaces on a smaller scale. Spotswood, a soldier and amateur architect, is certainly the

2–6. Brafferton Hall, College of William and Mary, Williamsburg, Virginia, 1723.

author of Bruton Parish Church in Williamsburg, 1711–1715 (the tower spire is later: 1769) (AA 196, AA 197). The beauty of this church lies in its proportions, for the classical detail is very restrained and inconspicuous. It is known that the governor used geometry very deliberately in its composition, as was done at the "Wren Building," where the golden section ratio was used. Since the proportions of the Palace are also mathematically worked out, in this case in integers of six, weight is lent to the possibility that Spotswood was the designer and Cary used his plans. Yet, the presence in Williamsburg and elsewhere in Virginia of later dwellings as carefully composed mathematically as those of Spotswood (for instance, it was usual for the height of a chimney above the roof line to be based on the height of an equilateral triangle whose sides equaled the height of the walls of the house) somewhat undermines the case for Spotswood's authorship of the Palace.

But whoever their designers may be, these structures combine the solid dignity of public buildings with an informal warmth associated more with domestic architecture and with the less pretentious English buildings of the time by

2–7. Views of Williamsburg from the "Bodleian Print," Bodleian Library, Oxford.

Wren and others. (Similar characteristics were common in contemporaneous Dutch architecture, which was influential in England but especially so during the reign of William III, who was also ruler of the Netherlands.)

The Capitol and the Governor's Palace now at Colonial Williamsburg are complete reconstructions but their present appearance must be a simulacrum of their former state since the exterior restorations were based largely on the evidence of an engraving in the Bodleian Library at Oxford (Illustration 2–7), supplemented by excavation which revealed the plans and some ornamental detail. The interiors, however, except for the evidence of a tiled floor and parts of two mantels found in the debris, are hypothetical and comprise a summary of the best eighteenth-century detail in the southern colonies, various motifs having been taken from such famous houses as Carter's Grove in Virginia, Whitehall in Maryland, and the Miles Brewton House in South Carolina.

The repair, restoration, and reproduction of these buildings and many others of all types at Williamsburg (and the careful weeding out of inappropriate later buildings), together with the restoration of gardens and of the original town plan, constitute a scrupulous re-creation of the eighteenth-century colonial capital. Though it may suffer a little from artificiality, Colonial Williamsburg is nevertheless an impressive record of a significant aspect of America's past.

But this town was not a metropolitan center like Charleston or Philadelphia, for it flourished only at the time of legislative sessions. The architecture of Virginia, the largest, wealthiest, and most populous of the colonies, is therefore more characteristically reflected in the plantation buildings. The mansions of Virginia constitute the finest group of Georgian architecture in America. On the typical great plantation, the main house was the center of a kind of community which incorporated, as in the case of "King" Carter's, three hundred thousand acres and a thousand slaves, and employed not only field hands, but those who contributed to the self-supporting whole—coopers, sawyers, blacksmiths, tanners, shoemakers, spinners, weavers, and even distillers. Among Washington's dependencies at Mount Vernon, besides conspicuous offices, stables, "necessaries," and houses for butler and chief gardener, there were also smokehouses, wash houses, a carpenter's shop, spinning houses, dairy and seed houses, and a school, as well as the quarters for the field hands and for the domestic slaves. Aside from the income-producing fields, there were five hundred acres laid out in gardens and parks. Mount Vernon (one of five houses in Washington's total property), with its gardens and dependencies, is a typical Virginia plantation and demonstrates for its type what Williamsburg does for a town.

Of the several large plantations of the early eighteenth century, the Lee Mansion, Stratford, on the Potomac near Montross in Westmoreland County, c. 1725–1730 (AA 199, AA 200), is the most prominent that survives. It was unique in the colonies—except for the Williamsburg Capitol—in having an H-plan consisting of two blocks, each surmounted by a cluster of four chimneys joined by arches, and connected by a central area entered by an unelaborated door. The basically simple design is enhanced by the nicely spaced windows and by the quality of the brick work, while the greater elaboration of the interior is the more effective because of its contrast with the bold masses and unornamented simplicity of the exterior.

A far more characteristic house than Stratford, and in its setting perhaps the most beautiful of all the plantation mansions, is Westover, on the James in Charles City County, c. 1730–1734 (AA 202, *AA 203; Illustration 2–8). Its builder, William Byrd II, president of the Governor's Council, had been educated in England and was later the colony's representative there; he increased the 27,000 acres inherited from his father to 218 square miles, and gave great attention to his house. Westover, with its relatively plain facade, is basically an English country house in the Queen Anne style of Wren's followers, but the pitch of its roof, the narrow rhythm of its dormers, and the conspicuous height of its chimneys bear a marked resemblance to the Governor's Palace in nearby Williamsburg. These characteristics and the restriction

2–8. Westover, Charles City County, Virginia, c. 1730–1734, by Richard Taliaferro (?).

of external decoration to the main cornice, a belt course, and the two doorways are typical of the early period. Subtleties of proportion, as at Stratford, compensate for the lack of the pilastered and pavilioned monumentality of later houses. Among these refinements are the diminution of the size of the windowpanes from bottom to top and the graduation of the spacing of the slates of the roof—devices which add to the height of the building, already picturesque with its exaggeratedly tall chimneys. The interiors are quite elaborate, especially the drawing room and stair hall, which have rococo ceilings (*AA 204, AA 205). Westover is the grandest of the Virginia mansions and the partial prototype of several others. Carter's Grove, 1750–1753 (AA 206, *AA 207), in James City County six miles south of Williamsburg, was built by "King" Carter's grandson, Carter Burwell, in 1750, and represents the culmination of the early Georgian. (As at Westover, the main block of Carter's Grove is situated at the center of two simple dependencies not originally attached to the main house.) Carter's Grove is a quieter, more reposeful building than Westover, not quite so grand; its hipped roof (originally with-

2–9. Hallway at Carter's Grove, James City County, Virginia, 1750–1753, by Richard Taliaferro (?).

out dormers) is not so steep, nor its chimneys so tall, and a simple brick pedimented doorway is substituted for the elaborate ones at Westover. But the interior paneling, especially in the great entrance hall and adjacent stair hall (AA 209, *AA 210; Illustration 2–9), is more magnificent even than in the living room at William Byrd's mansion. Carved by an Englishman, Richard Bayliss, who was brought to Virginia for this purpose, it is perhaps the most elegant and correct room in all of the colonies, with its fine Ionic pilasters supporting a complete entablature.

These two houses in their effective, simple boldness and their relative rejection of academic detail are the best of a whole group which may well be from the same hand. It has been established that Richard Taliaferro, a prominent landowner and sometime official in the colony, built for himself in 1755 a dwelling in Williamsburg known by the name of his son-in-law, the George Wythe House. The exterior of this building is a smaller version of the main block at Carter's Grove, though plainer, without even a brick pediment over the door. But the nicety of its proportion (based on a mathematical module), combined with its simplicity, make it easy to include it with other larger mansions, especially Westover. These characteristics and the presence of certain other details (especially the frequent use of motifs derived from *Palladio Londonensis*) have led to the acceptance of the probability that Westover and Carter's Grove and others may indeed be by Taliaferro.

If Taliaferro is perhaps a somewhat unsure figure, the designer and builder of the most distinguished Virginia mansions of the decades following the turn of the mid-century is known. He is John Ariss, who was responsible for a number of houses erected between 1750 and 1775. Several have been destroyed, some are ruinous or have disfiguring dependencies, but Mount Airy, 1758–1762, in Richmond County, near Warsaw, is still well preserved (Illustration 2–10; see also Illustration 2–1). Another important building which in its present state may have been at least partially designed by Ariss (working together with Washington himself) is Mount Vernon, in Fairfax County, 1751–1789 (AA 220, AA 221, AA 222). Ariss was known to possess several design books; the most important of which he made use were Gibbs and *Vitruvius Scotticus*. Also, he had traveled in England, as an advertisement in the *Maryland Gazette* in 1751 attests. Unfortunately the original interiors of Mount Airy were burned out in 1844, but the exterior remains intact. Like Ariss' Carlyle House (as it was originally designed) in Alexandria, Virginia, and like Mount Vernon and others attributed to him, the plan of Mount Airy is characterized by the joining of the dependencies to the main house by an arcade. The facades, each with recessed vestibules, are clearly derived from Ariss' favorite sources, the one on the north adapted from a plate in *Vitruvius Scotticus* for Haddo House, Aberdeenshire, and that on the south copied in detail from plate LVIII in Gibbs's *A Book of Architecture* (Illustration 2–11). A magnificent building of random ashlar trimmed in light-colored limestone, with its formal composition enhanced by an entrance stairway with paths flanked by urns, Mount Airy is one of the most impressive in the country. It may not have the intimate charm of the earlier houses, but its projecting pedimented pavilions, its quoined corners (all except the quoins being characteristic of the later, more classical Georgian), coupled with the strength and boldness of Gibbs's heavily rusticated stonework, comprise a most effective design.

Mount Vernon, as it presently appears, with the exception of the porch added after 1784, consists principally of work done from 1757 to 1771. But the enlargement of the house in two successive waves during this time necessitated a number of unfortunate compromises between convenience and formality, as an examination of the entrance facade will make only too clear (AA 220). The conspicuous detail of the central doorway does not hide the fact that it is not in the center of the flanking windows; the ends of the pediment gable over the center fall in one place over the wall and in another over the windows. The banquet hall has no second story but, for the sake of symmetry, two stories of false windows are placed in the walls, though the large Palladian window on the side makes it clear that the room is not divided in two horizontally. Such attempted deceptions in the design, taken together with Washington's specific order for simulated stone in the form of champfered and sanded wood, might indicate that the owner had far more hand in the design than did Ariss. But the latter's association with the Washington family by blood relationship and the appearance of so many details from books which Arris used in his other buildings would indicate that he must have at least been of considerable assistance to Washington. The interiors of Mount Vernon have not the grandeur of Westover, Carter's Grove, or the great houses of Charleston or Annapolis, but they are typical, especially in their fine mantelpieces (AA 222). Only the ornamented ceilings are rather unusual (AA 222), rivaling the finest ones in the colonies at Washington's sister's house, Kenmore, built about 1753 in Fredericksburg.

When Latrobe, the English-born architect of the early republic, visited Mount Vernon, he remarked that parts of the building were "in very indifferent taste,"[3] a comment which he probably would not have made of Jefferson's work, for it was Jefferson who was largely responsible for the introduction into the colonies of a stricter Palladian classicism seen especially in the "strung-out" house plan (based on Palladio's Roman country house style), and of the motif of the two-story portico. Another source

2—13. Whitehall, near Annapolis, Anne Arundel County, Maryland, 1764—1768.

near Charleston, and the second is the Miles Brewton House, 1765–1769 (AA 250), in Charleston itself. At any rate, both derive more or less from Palladio, Book II, plate 16 in the Leoni Edition, but the portico of Jefferson's own house, Monticello, before he later rebuilt it, was more strictly Palladian than the others, as Jefferson's drawing of the original building shows.

As early as 1772, Jefferson was also interested in the giant temple portico, using it in his proposals for the remodeling of the Governor's Palace in Williamsburg. This desire to surround the old building with a temple colonnade prophesied his turning to that form in the new Capitol he designed for Richmond during the next decade and his whole change of attitude from late Georgian Palladianism to neo-classicism after the Revolution.

A house with both the elongated country house plan and the giant portico, and one of the most important examples of domestic architecture in the colonies, is Whitehall, 1764–1768 (AA 232, AA 233; Illustration 2–13), in Anne Arundel County, Maryland, across the Severn from Annapolis. The free-standing temple portico is the first instance of this form in domestic architecture in the colonies. (Peter Harrison's Redwood Library in Newport, 1748–1750, a public building, is the only one that precedes it.) The plan and the portico of Whitehall suggest the possibility of the young Jefferson as designer, but the house was built when he was only twenty, six years before he acquired his copy of Palladio.

In view of the advanced design of Whitehall and its magnificent interior carving, more elaborate than anywhere else in the colonies, the probability is that this charming building (the only example of the "pleasure dome" to be erected in the colonies) was the work of a designer in the entourage of Governor Sharpe. The combination of the extraordinary skill and refinement of carving with the use of certain recurring motifs suggests that the ornament at Whitehall was executed by the same craftsman who is known to have done other work in Virginia and Maryland, William Buckland, an Englishman trained as a master joiner, and the only one in that part of the country so competent and well known in the profession. Indentured to James Mason to decorate his newly built Gunston Hall, 1755–1758 (°AA 213, °AA 214, AA 215; Illustration 2–14), in Fairfax County, Virginia, Buckland worked on its lavish interior (and probably its two porticos), overwhelming this otherwise simple, one-and-a-half-story house of the basic seventeenth-century plan and elevation with rich Palladian decoration.

2–14. Dining room, Gunston Hall, Fairfax County, Virginia, 1755–1758. (The Board of Regents, Gunston Hall.)

Buckland's reputation was carried to the colonial capital of Maryland, Annapolis, where his work contributed in large measure to the distinction of that port city, the residence of a wealthy merchant and shipping class as well as the urban center for the neighboring planters— a place as notable as Williamsburg for its gaiety and taste. Buckland worked first on the interiors of the Brice House, which had been built in 1740 (AA 237), embellishing the rooms of this dignified and beautifully proportioned house (almost austere in its lack of exterior decora-

tion) with elaborate and sophisticated carving. He not only executed the joinery and ornament of the Hammond-Harwood House, 1773–1774 (AA 237, AA 238, AA 239), but the building itself was designed by him, as is attested in a portrait by Charles Willson Peale of Buckland holding a plan of the house. The design is of a central type with unusual polygonal dependencies, the central block graced by a pedimented pavilion with perhaps the finest carved door in the colonies. The outstanding interiors are in the drawing room and the ballroom above it, where Buckland's rich carving is more concentrated and in scale with the larger proportions of the room than is the case in the perhaps over-elaborate interiors at Gunston Hall. In the Annapolis house, Buckland proved himself not only a great joiner, but a very competent architect as well.

It has been suggested that Buckland executed the interiors of several other houses at Annapolis, and that he even designed some of the buildings themselves. The only one that possesses interiors equal in quality and elaboration to those of Gunston Hall, and of the Brice and Hammond-Harwood houses, is the Chase-Lloyd House, 1769–1771 (AA 235), the most impressive of the mansions of Annapolis, a city famous for its great houses, where it is quite certain that Buckland executed the carving. Also connected with Buckland's name are the Paca and Rideout houses (similar to the Brice House in the unacademic boldness of their exteriors), and the Scott House, which resembles the Hammond-Harwood. In any event, Buckland contributed a great deal to the opulence of eighteenth-century Annapolis, much of which remains due to the growth of neighboring Baltimore.

Except for Annapolis and Williamsburg, and of course Charleston, the only other town where there is much colonial architecture preserved in the South is Alexandria. It is not a typical southern town, however. Aside from Ariss' Carlyle House, there is little that is reminiscent of the great Virginia plantations or the town houses of nearby Annapolis. A port settled largely by Scotch merchants, its houses resemble those of Philadelphia, often in rows, distinguished only by pedimented doorways and mid-century Georgian interior paneling. The Fairfax House is typical of the row houses, as is the famous Gadsby's Tavern. The best interiors, as those of the Delaunay House, are often just post-Revolution in date, but carry on a conventional mid-century taste. These unpretentious, clear-cut houses give distinction to a town that has recently been zoned to preserve its quality.

Few Maryland plantations survive from the pre-Revolution period. Two may be mentioned: Montpelier, near Laurel, in Prince George

County, in the northern part of the state, built in two periods, 1751 and c. 1770 (*AA 229); and Tulip Hall, near Annapolis, in Anne Arundel County, c. 1756 (*AA 230), with later carving by Buckland. The former has a high-pitched roof, similar to the Governor's Palace at Williamsburg and to Westover, but its pedimented pavilion and its elaborate doorway with fanlight in a broken pediment indicate a later taste. The attached wings with polygonal ends (added c. 1770) recall Buckland's Hammond-Harwood House. This factor and the quality of the interior reflect this designer's work and it has been suggested that he may have remodeled it entirely in 1771.

Elsewhere in the South, the architecture of Charleston is the most important, but there are certain plantations and other buildings in the Carolinas which are also of interest. There is, for instance, an early eighteenth-century plantation near Charleston which is almost unique: The Mulberry, Moncks Corner, 1714 (AA 113, AA 114), a rectangle with four little square pavilions at the corners. This is a common enough form in France, but the origins of the house are confused by the appearance of Dutch roofs on the corner sections.

The legend of numerous great plantation houses in the Carolinas destroyed by war and a declining economy is largely unfounded. The ruins of Middleton Place (still surrounded by its magnificent gardens) on the Ashley, and Fairlawn, in Botany, near Moncks Corner, and the magnificent Drayton Hall, 1738–1742 (*AA 240, *AA 240A) on the Ashley ten miles from Charleston, are exceptions. The latter is perhaps the greatest of the southern mansions surviving in their original form. Surpassing even Westover and Mount Airy, it possesses a two-story frontispiece projecting from a central pavilion of Palladian design, and a magnificent hall with a double flight of stairs. The detail of the paneling and carving throughout represents the taste illustrated in William Kent's *Inigo Jones*. Such magnificence implies possibly a British architect, perhaps brought over by the Honorable John Drayton when he came from Barbados, a supposition supported by the early use of a double portico, common already in the West Indies. This first open porch in the mainland colonies was a feature which was to become, after the Revolution, ubiquitous in Charleston and frequent elsewhere in the hot and humid South. Hampton, 1735, 1757 (portico, 1791) (AA 242), on Wambaw Creek near the Santee, is another moderately large house (though of frame) of considerable interest, including the largest paneled room in the colonies and another room with a coved ceiling. Most of the other houses in South Carolina were relatively small, because the great planters lived in the low country only part of the year, spending the "sickly season" of fever in Charleston.

There were a few important plantation houses in North Carolina; the greatest mansion in all the colonies was Tryon's Palace (completely restored) at New Bern, 1767–1770 (AA 253), built for Governor Tryon by a British architect, John Hawks. Though the building was burned in 1798, the drawings by Hawks were so professional and detailed that they could be used for the present restoration of the building. A combination of state house and mansion, the Palace resembles in general the pedimented, pavilioned, dependencied buildings of the period and, in particular, a plate in Morris' *Select Architecture*.

Charleston was the only genuinely urban town in the South. The Carolina planters who lived here most of the year were their own merchants and did not depend on the English factor and agent. This circumstance made the city not only the center of a great feudal empire, but also a prosperous port. It is no wonder, then, that Charleston, in spite of its relatively small population, in comparison with that of Philadelphia, for example, was the most distinguished colonial city in America, architecturally speaking. It is to the great credit of Charlestonians that, due to a zoning law passed some time ago (the first of its kind), most of its early architecture has been preserved. Since the buildings are still part of an organic city, Charleston offers great contrast in its living reality to the artificially reconstructed Williamsburg.

Josiah Quincy, Jr., the Massachusetts aristocrat, was overwhelmed by the "state, magnifi-

cence and ostentation" of Charleston. He stayed with Miles Brewton, where the "sumptuous dinners, the richness of the fittings and the elegance of the architecture"[4] made a deep impression on him. The Brewton House, 1765–1769 (AA 250), is the handsomest of the city's residences and is among the finest urban dwellings in the colonies. It was probably built by one Ezra Waite, who called himself in an advertisement, "civil architect Housebuilder in general and Carver from London."[5] An impressive stone double portico with a fanlighted door distinguishes the facade, while the great drawing room on the second floor is perhaps the grandest single room in the colonies, with its original Waterford chandeliers still in place, its fine mantel from *Palladio Londonensis*, its broken-pedimented and pilaster-framed doors, its elaborate entablature with fully projecting cornice, the coved ceiling enframing a painting at its center. This house, and several others [outstanding among them is the William Gibbes House, c. 1779 (AA 252)], are conventionally planned with central hall and flanking rooms.

Though Williamsburg has the only distinguished public buildings in the South from the colonial period, and these are restored, there are a few fine churches left. Christ Church in Lancaster County, 1732 (AA 211, AA 212), is the oldest remaining in Virginia. The workmanship in the stone trim, the brick, and the wood is especially refined in its classical correctness, and the extremely simple interior is most effective, wherein the openings in the white walls are the only elements in a severe and elegant geometry. Christ Church, like Bruton Parish Church in Williamsburg, is cruciform in plan, whereas later churches are rectangular. The esthetic effect of these buildings, depending on good proportion or an embellished doorway for their exterior design—though their interiors are more elaborate—is illustrated in Christ Church, Alexandria, 1767 (AA 384), and Pohick Church in Fairfax County, near Mount Vernon, 1771–1772 (AA 224, AA 225), possibly designed by Washington, who was a vestryman in both churches.

No important church remains in Maryland, but South Carolina possesses several, all belonging to the Anglican Establishment, the less permanent buildings of other sects having disappeared. One of the oldest is St. James, at Goose Creek, 1711 (AA 243), where the rectangular form covered by a gabled roof cut off at the top corner is so simple that it is even without eaves. But the decoration of the doorway, the little cherub heads at the keystones of the architraves over the windows, and the elaborate, really baroque reredos in the interior, with its heavily ornamented broken pediment—none of these very correct—reflect the opulent if somewhat naïve tastes of the rich Barbados planters, recently come to the lusher shores of Carolina. But the unacademic columns, supporting planks cut to resemble arches, belie the magnificence. In contrast, St. Michael's in Charleston, begun in 1752 (AA 245), is in no way naïve, being extremely careful in its classicism. The mass of the building is prefaced by a portico of Doric columns bearing a pediment—the first since Redwood Library of four years before at Newport—and supports a beautifully proportioned tower. Both portico and tower recall Gibbs's St. Martin's-in-the-Fields (Illustration 2–15), though the tower is not as slavish an imitation as are most of those inspired from that source. (This relative originality in the tower and the somewhat heavy but powerful and masterful design of the whole edifice give credence to the suggestion of Peter Harrison's biographer that the Newport architect was its designer, though no documentary proof for this exists.)

The parishes of the plantations naturally emulated this metropolitan church. Though many Anglican churches fell into disuse and ruin after the disestablishment, and though both the Revolution and the Civil War destroyed many others, enough of them remain to comprise one of the most charming groups of small, unpretentious buildings in the country. Pompion Hill Chapel, Pompion Hill, 1763 (AA 247), may be taken as an example. Here the misunderstood baroque detail of the church at Goose Creek has been replaced by a correct entablature and a beautiful little Palladian window, careful in proportion

2–15. Alternate designs for St. Martin's-in-the-Fields, from James Gibbs, *A Book of Architecture* (London: 1728).

and detail, and simple and clear in effect. St. James Church, Santee, 1768 (AA 244A), is even more academic in that it possesses a full portico.

Public buildings in the South were neither so numerous nor remain so well preserved as in the North—with the obvious exception of Colonial Williamsburg. One example, however, the Chowan County Courthouse, 1767 (Illustration 2–16), at Edenton, North Carolina (the center of the tidewater area in that colony, settled largely by Virginians from a few miles to the north), is an unpretentious version of the pavilion type. Its clean edges, nicety of propor-

2–16. Chowan County Courthouse, Edenton, North Carolina, 1767.

from the same source books, they were very much the same in plan and detail, except in the employment of wood as the most important material and in the relative absence of longitudinal plans like that of Brandon, more suitable for the climate of the South.

Two houses, the McPhedris-Warner House, Portsmouth, New Hampshire, 1718–1723 (AA 281), and the Richard Derby House, Salem, Massachusetts, 1762 (*AA 294), show the norm of the less pretentious large house which depends for its effect on the simple dignity of the masses relieved only by openings and by a few details in cornices, rather than by elaborate ornamental devices.

The Thomas Hancock House, 1737–1740 (*AA 256; Illustration 2–17), destroyed in 1865, was the finest residence in early Georgian Boston. Constructed of masonry, it was distin-

tion, and the relation of pedimented door to pediment above, suggest an almost mathematical refinement of design and indicate a master builder of sensibility. Constructed within the framework of the late Georgian but reducing its formulas to quintessential simplicity, it approximated a kind of abstract planometric shape which approaches the feeling of the plain surfaces of the seventeenth-century meetinghouse— for all the difference in formal vocabulary.

New England

In New England a larger number of modest dwellings remain than in the South where the great plantation houses are the most conspicuous survivors of the eighteenth century. They follow in general the transitional type and are often characterized by covered porches and connected outbuildings built against the rigors of the New England winter.

Though the great majority of New England dwellings were of this sort, the wealthy merchants of Boston and other ports built what were the equivalents of the great mansions of the South, a few of which even surpassed their southern counterparts in magnificence. Derived

2–17. Thomas Hancock House (destroyed), Boston, Massachusetts, 1737–1740. From an old photograph.

guished by its elaborate detail, especially its quoining, its balcony supported on consoles, and the great French window, dignified by pilasters and an ornate broken pediment, that opened out onto the balcony. The Royall House, Medford, Massachusetts, east facade, 1733–1737, west facade and chimneys, 1747–1750 (AA 282, AA 283, AA 284, AA 285), represents the style of the first half of the eighteenth century in transition to that of the second. The earlier east facade (AA 282) has angle quoins, a non-pedimented doorway, and clapboarding; the west facade (AA 283) has not only a segmentally pedimented door but cornices over the windows. The quoining on the older facade is replaced here by pilaster strips and the clapboarding gives way to simulated, rusticated stonework in sanded wood.

The interior of The Lindens, formerly at Danvers, Massachusetts, 1754 (AA 287, AA 288, AA 290) (the house was removed to Washington, D. C., except for the drawing room which is in the Museum at Kansas City), is equally refined and perhaps more academic than the earlier Virginia houses, at least in its interiors. But the exterior, for all the pretentiousness of its engaged columns, supports a very awkward equilateral triangle which simulates a pediment; in this detail the hand of the owner, Robert "King" Hooper, as designer is probably seen. But except for this, the house is one of the finer New England mansions and must reflect on the whole the taste of an accomplished master builder rather than that of the supposed designer. The stair hall is worthy of comparison with that at Carter's Grove, incorporating a stairway with a magnificent example of that triumph of carpentry, the double twisted newel post. Another important mansion is the Wentworth-Gardner House at Portsmouth, New Hampshire, 1760 (AA 292, *AA 293; Illustration 2–18), built by a member of the enormously wealthy family of the royal governor. Beautifully elaborate in its interior paneling and other detail (its classicism is almost Burlingtonian) and forceful in its composition, it is dramatically situated at the water's edge, and partially shaded by a magnificent linden brought from England

2–18. Wentworth-Gardner House, Portsmouth, New Hampshire, 1760.

as a sapling by the first Wentworth owner. The exterior is less correctly academic than the interior, incorporating a prominent curved and broken pediment (an exuberant motif not usually permitted in the restrained classicism of the later Georgian), unusually large windows with greatly projecting pediments and sills, and conspicuous quoining at the corners. Even the simulated stone adds to the general boldness of the composition, which is enhanced by a somewhat abruptly oblique hip roof pierced by imposing dormers and several large chimneys. Yet the carefully detailed pediments over the windows of the first floor and the correct, almost Palladian, interior details bespeak a classical sophistication. This paradoxically classical and at the same time picturesquely composed house is one of the most interesting Georgian houses in the colonies, as well as one of the finest.

Two houses quite similar to one another express more consistently the classicism found later in the century: the Vassall-Longfellow House, Cambridge, Massachusetts, 1759 (AA 291), and the Lady Pepperell House, 1760, at Kittery Point, Maine, across the river from Portsmouth (Illustration 2–19). Each house has a central pavilion with pediment, giant pilasters, and a prominent cornice, and each is characterized by great restraint in detail and proportion. The

2–19. Lady Pepperell House, Kittery Point, Maine, 1760.

Lady Pepperell House (built for the widow of the first American baronet, knighted for his financial and military assistance at the siege of Louisburg) partially solved the problem of the homely New England convention of using wood, so inconsistent with the standards of classical monumentality required by advanced Georgian taste: the pavilion is simply sheathed, while the remainder of the facade remains clapboarded. The contrast of texture in this solution, combined with the graceful monumentality of the house and the beauty of its carving, make the Lady Pepperell House one of the most charming examples of architecture in the North. This building and several in neighboring Maine and in Portsmouth (including the Hamilton House at South Berwick, Maine), in the delicacy of their joinery and the refinement of their proportions, suggest a single designer; it is tempting to think he may have been the mulatto Hopestill Caswell.

The Jeremiah Lee House, Marblehead, Massachusetts, 1768 (°AA 296, AA 297, AA 298; Illustration 2–20), pedimented and with an elegant portico, is typical of the greater classicism of the later part of the Georgian period, and its three-story height sets a pattern for the large house of the post-Revolution period.

These were the outstanding houses in New England. There were many others, but relatively few were as impressive. The more common type was the respectable, large house, with many of the features of the high Georgian style but not so ample in scale or so elaborate in exterior or interior ornamentation. Newport,

2–20. Jeremiah Lee House, Marblehead, Massachusetts, 1768.

Rhode Island, and Portsmouth, New Hampshire, are particularly rich in examples, since neither town after the time of the Revolution had the relative population growth that occurred, say, in Boston or New Haven. The Tobias Lear House in Portsmouth, c. 1750 (Illustration 2–21), is a good example of the norm of the mid-century. Its steep hip roof, central hall, pedimented doorway, and narrow cornice are conventional enough; but the "four-square" proportions and the small windows, the angle line of an unusually steep roof, and the emphatic placing of the chimneys reveal a local building taste which in its simplicity and boldness combines the straightforward quality of the seventeenth-century building with the picturesque proportions of the earlier eighteenth century. A comparison with its near neighbor, the Wentworth-Gardner House, with its elaborate doorway, simulated masonry, and more conventional proportions makes the homely virtues of the Lear House all the more notable.

Elaborate entrances, not seen as frequently in the South, were fairly conventional in New England, and resembled a similar early type of local Georgian interior carving. Examples are found in the early eighteenth-century room from

Newington, Connecticut (Illustration 2–5), with its scroll and diagonal panels and its "folk art" rosettes in the entablature above the naïvely proportioned pilasters surrounding the mantel, or in the pilastered and pedimented doorways of the Connecticut valley in western Massachusetts. The latter were derived from more correct prototypes farther east and south (a good example is one from Hatfield, Massachusetts, in the Boston Museum of Fine Arts), in which late Tudor devices of boldly cut leaves and curving vines are substituted with cavalier assurance for correct pilasters, flutings, and capitals, in an altogether delightful and indigenous variation on classical themes.

Local idiosyncrasies, such as those illustrated in the Tobias Lear House, give character to each region and indicate how the sometimes monotonous classicism of the more correct architecture was varied to good effect. This is particularly true of details, where considerable liberties were taken in provincial areas or on the part of unsophisticated builders.

In contrast to the South, New England remains rich in examples of religious and other non-domestic architecture, and in buildings for

2–21. Tobias Lear House, Portsmouth, New Hampshire, c. 1750.

2–22.   Interior, Alna Meetinghouse, Alna, Maine, 1789.

colleges. Both the plan and the simplicity of the seventeenth-century meetinghouse were slow in dying out. The Elder Ballou Meetinghouse in the northeast corner of Rhode Island at Cumberland, built as late as 1747, is more functional and severe even than the Old Ship. St. Paul's, Wickford, Rhode Island, 1707 (*AA 382) (removed from Narragansett to Wickford in the early nineteenth century), shows the beginning of the classical style, but does so only in detail. Otherwise, it is completely seventeenth-century. Even as late as 1785, the Rocky Hill Meetinghouse in Amesbury, Massachusetts (*AA 300), and the Rockingham (Vermont) Meetinghouse, 1787 (AA 380A), still belong to the earlier type, though more classical in detail; their frame structures are still exposed and their exteriors are

notable for their pared-down simplicity and crisp outline. Nearer the frontier, certain Maine meetinghouses of the late eighteenth century are even more interesting in the extent of their stylistic backwardness. The Alna Meetinghouse, 1789 (Illustration 2–22), especially preserves the appearance of a seventeenth-century structure in its framing and in its supports, wherein the classical orders are completely ignored and the result is a form similar to the interiors of wooden ships of the time.

The first important New England church to turn away from this seventeenth-century tradition was Christ Church ("Old North"), Boston, 1723 (AA 273), put up by the second Anglican congregation there and designed by William Price. It is completely Renaissance in its longitudinal axis, its classical supports and vaults, and its tower, as well as in the general arrangement of the interior galleries supported on square pilasters. In these respects, it resembles the Wren London churches and most of all, St. James, Piccadilly. The tower, ancestor of dozens like it, derives principally from Wren's St. Lawrence Jewery in London. (The steeple has been blown down twice, the last time during a 1954 hurricane, but has been reconstructed as accurately as possible each time.) "Old North" was copied for Trinity Church, Newport, in 1725 (AA 269, *AA 270, AA 270A), and for "Old South," Boston, 1729 (AA 277), designed by Robert Twelves. Both adopted the tower and arched windows of the original, but the Newport church, though in wood, is closer in its interior design. The latter was designed by the builder Richard Munday and shows the same boldness of conception that we shall see in his Old Colony House, Newport, where there are similar naïvetés, as in the strange pediments placed over the door of the church.

The church that represents best the taste of the later century is the First Baptist Meetinghouse, Providence, 1774–1775 (AA 257; Illustration 2–23), by Joseph Brown, professor of philosophy at Rhode Island College (later Brown University), who also was responsible for the college building there and for several fine houses. This meetinghouse, the oldest Baptist church in the United States, though a handsome building, is much more academic than Munday's ingenuous Trinity. The general conception of most of the details of both interior and exterior is derived from Gibbs; the tower (Illustration 2–15) is a perfect reproduction of one of the rejected designs for St. Martin's-in-the-Fields. The difficult task of expressing in wood the masonry structure intended by Gibbs was facilitated by painting the building in various colors and textures to imitate stone (now replaced by the more conventional white paint), thereby emphasizing the effect of the imitative character of Brown's church. In contrast, Munday's less slavishly copied church, which makes concessions to its wooden material in its design, has a more pleasing directness.

2–23. First Baptist Meetinghouse, Providence, Rhode Island, 1774–1775, by Joseph Brown.

Most New England meetinghouses of the late eighteenth century, however, were not as academically correct as the Providence meetinghouse, and tended to combine the decorative vocabulary and proportion of classicism with the forthright and picturesque virtues of the earlier period. Two typical examples in Connecticut are the contemporaneous Farmington Meetinghouse, designed by Captain Judah Woodruff (AA 278), and the Brooklin Meetinghouse (Illustration 2–24), built in 1771. These buildings share a sturdy simplicity of shape and a crisp precision of plane surface. The interior at Farmington is original; that at Brooklin is being reconstructed. But the exterior of the latter is more satisfactory since the original doors are in place, and the proportions of the windows are more pleasing.

2–24. Meetinghouse, Brooklin, Connecticut, 1771.

New England is particularly rich in the number of college buildings which have been preserved from the colonial period; Massachusetts Hall at Harvard University, Cambridge, Massachusetts, 1718–1720 (AA 268; see also Illustration 2–52), designed by President J. Leverett and B. Wadsworth, is the oldest surviving. Constructed of brick, solid and massive, with very little detail, and unified by the two great stacks of paired chimneys at the ends, it expresses the logical arrangement of a series of studies and bedrooms in an unpretentious and practical design. Connecticut Hall at Yale University, New Haven, Connecticut, 1750–1752 (AA 286), also of brick, is closely modeled after the Harvard building, but not so effective in its total impact,

lacking the strong accent of the paired chimneys. Later buildings—Hollis Hall at Harvard, 1763 (AA 295), and University Hall, Brown University, Providence, Rhode Island, 1770–1771, by Joseph Brown (AA 259), both of brick, and Dartmouth Hall, the later wooden example of the type at Hanover, New Hampshire, 1784–1791 (AA 299)—share a central pavilion and cupola modeled on the old Nassau Hall at Princeton, New Jersey, by Robert Smith of the Carpenter Company of Philadelphia and William Shippen, 1754–1756 (AA 323). These buildings are practical and lacking in pretention, their somewhat austere beauty depending on their general proportions and the arrangement of openings, as well as upon the quality of their honest workmanship. Only two academic buildings, both at Harvard, differ from this general norm: Holden Chapel, 1742 (AA 276), designed by the painter John Smibert, a quaint little cube elaborated with the enormous arms of England in the pediment, and otherwise distinguished by excellent detail; and Harvard Hall, 1764–1766, with a more monumental pavilioned facade than the other academic buildings, an effect enhanced by a large cupola.

Among public buildings, the Second Town Hall, later the Old State House, Boston, 1712 (rebuilt in 1748) (AA 280), though much altered, is notable chiefly for its size, its fine facade with the pilastered and pedimented door opening from the governor's council chambers to the balcony (from which laws and other pronouncements were made), and its richly ornamented stepped gable adorned with the handsomely carved lion and unicorn of the British arms. Unfortunately restored too early (1881–1882) for subsequently gained architectural knowledge to have been incorporated in it, the structure is not as satisfactory a monument as the better preserved Old Colony House in Newport, 1739–1741 (AA 271, *AA 272; Illustration 2–25), by Richard Munday, which, though somewhat altered, has been restored in general to its pre-Revolution appearance. The principal feature of the facade is a doorway crowned by a balcony window deriving from that of the Hancock House in Boston. Indeed, the whole

2–25. Old Colony House, Newport, Rhode Island, 1739–1741, by Richard Munday.

appearance is more like a large Queen Anne house than an academically monumental building. But this is compensated for by the almost baroque elaboration of the pediment over the balcony window, and by the scroll-topped paneling and the piling up of architraves in the entablatures on the interior. Though Henry James called the building "an edifice ample, majestic and of the finest proportions," [6] to compare it with Harrison's expert work in the same town is to measure it by the standards of classical taste, which are essentially more logical, and thus to reveal its inadequacies: the awkward truncated gable, the three absurd circular elements confined restlessly within it, and the lack of pleasing proportion in the relationship of the gable windows to the main window and of the balcony window to both.

Peter Harrison's Redwood Library, Newport, 1748 (AA 260, *AA 260A), is infinitely more sophisticated but equally less original than the Old Colony House. Harrison, Yorkshire-born, was primarily a successful merchant shipbuilder and military engineer. He was a stubborn Tory, appointed in his last years as Collector of His Majesty's Customs in New Haven. He died there of a stroke after Lexington and Concord. Harrison's British background, his knowledge of the Assembly Hall at York (designed by Lord Burlington himself), and his possible acquaintance with William Kent, a fellow Yorkshireman and the most Palladian of the Burlingtonian architects, all prejudiced him against the kind of homely awkwardness he saw in colonial Newport. In the Redwood Library and other buildings in Newport—the Touro Synagogue, 1759–1763 (AA 266); the Brick Market, 1761–1772 (AA 267; Illustration 2–26); and several houses that have since disappeared—Harrison initiated a new architectural standard not only in Newport but in the whole of the colonies, preceding the classicism of Thomas Jefferson by almost a generation. The Library introduced the temple portico to America, and though small

in scale and ridiculous in its use of wood as a material, it does not lose the dignity of its prototypes, so clearly copied from Palladio. The Brick Market, which gives such miniature dignity to Thames Street, is a kind of toy-like version in brick and white-painted wood of a part of Old Somerset House by Inigo Jones as it appears in an engraving in *Vitruvius Britannicus*. The richly elegant interior of the synagogue, built by the Sephardan Jewish Community and carefully planned with Rabbi Touro, comprises a kind of parade of English examples from Kent to Batty Langley—unoriginal but put together with impeccable taste (the present ark is a later, 1828 edition). The interior of King's Chapel, Boston, 1749–1754 (AA 262), built by Harrison for the wealthiest Anglican congregation in the North, is very strongly

2–26. Brick Market, Newport, Rhode Island, 1761–1772, by Peter Harrison. From an old photograph.

2–27. Interior, Christ Church, Cambridge, Massachusetts, 1759, by Peter Harrison.

reminiscent of Gibbs's Marylebone Chapel in London. It is a masterpiece in scale, proportion, finish, and elegance of design, and is principally notable for its handsome, paired giant order of Corinthian columns, which replace the two-story colonnades that usually supported the balcony. The plan, exterior, and portico (AA 261) derive from a book by Gibbs (a tower or steeple was originally intended), but the character of the masonry has a heavy grandeur recalling the stonework of Yorkshire. Christ Church in Cambridge, 1759 (AA 263, AA 264; Illustration 2–27), is equally elegant, though of wood. The main mass of the exterior derives

from Gibbs; the rest is apparently Harrison's solution for a place of worship for a parsimonious parish which rejected both balcony and steeple. The building is singularly successful in its well-lit spaciousness, its very simple architectural elements, and the substitution of a simple curved ceiling for the usual lath and plaster vault. The omission of a continuous entablature between the columns was particularly happy, giving lightness and even gaiety to the design. In this charming building, Harrison's classical sensibility, trained in good academic examples, freed itself from a too slavish imitation and created an interior of airy spaciousness and grace and a fine, simple exterior of considerable dignity.

Harrison also introduced the pilastered facade to New England in a home for Governor Shirley, Shirley Place, 1747, in Roxbury, Massachusetts, and one near Newport (about 1750) for Charles Dudley, the Newport Customs Collector; both buildings were later destroyed. These houses and the Redwood Library brought the gentility of Burlingtonian classical taste to New England, and initiated the use of wood to imitate stone. (The simulated masonry of the Royall House is of the same year as the library in Newport.) Harrison's work presents the two sides of the coin of classicism: judgment, refinement, and good taste on the one hand, mere appearances on the other. Perhaps the Old Colony House is ample and majestic after all.

The Middle Colonies

The architecture of the three Middle Colonies, like the composition of their population, is less homogeneous than in New England and the South, that of New York being confused with Dutch influence, Pennsylvania with German, and New Jersey being a combination of many influences, including a considerable amount from New England. Yet at the end of the period, Philadelphia had achieved the most impressive architecture in the colonies. In New York, the Dutch influence, particularly in the country regions, was remarkably tenacious, and the Dutch and Flemish style cottages, discussed later, permeated the Hudson valley, Long Island, and much of northern New Jersey.

The prosperity of New York and its subsequent growth have left very little of its early building, so that a full discussion of it would involve more antiquarian and local history than extant architecture. New York City, for instance, has preserved only two important houses and a church from the colonial period, the Van Cortlandt House in Van Cortlandt Park, the Madame Jumel (Morris) Mansion on the Harlem River, and St. Paul's Chapel in downtown Manhattan.

The great manor houses of the patroonships of the Hudson valley were never as impressive as the size of their domains would suggest, and most of them were remodeled later. Johnson Hall, in Johnstown, 1762 (*AA 333), is a fine formal Georgian house, hip-roofed, pedimented, with a great stair hall in correct detail, but hardly the mansion expected of Sir William Johnston, the owner of a great patroonship. Philipse Manor Hall in Yonkers, c. 1720 (*AA 327), was built by Frederick Philipse, who bought out most of a former patroonship extending from Spuyten Duyvil to the Croton after acquiring a great maritime fortune in the late seventeenth century. There is some doubt whether the older portion of the house is as ancient as 1682; if so, it has Georgian features at a very early date. Most of the present house is large, though it is built of undressed stone like a farmhouse; the interior, especially the southeast parlor, is of unusual richness, and constitutes one of the showpieces of the colonies. The exterior of the nearby Van Cortlandt House, 1748–1749, seems a rougher version of Philipse Manor, and its interior is so simple as to be almost pre-Georgian. The Madame Jumel (Morris) Mansion in Manhattan, 1765 (AA 331), is a house of an entirely different character displaying a sophistication of design (especially in its detail) which is as far ahead of its times as that of the Van Cortlandt House is behind. Much of the detail seems too fine-scaled to be anything but very late Georgian. At the same time, both the fact of the giant portico itself and the extreme attenuation of its columns would point to a post-Revolution date, though there is no evidence to prove conclusively that it is not contemporaneous with the rest of the house. (The elliptically arched front entrance is known to be later.)

The most important colonial structure to be built in New York City still stands, St. Paul's Chapel, 1764 (AA 324), by the Scotsman Thomas McBean. The interior is similar to King's Chapel in Boston and St. Michael's in Charleston, closely reflecting Gibbs's St. Martin's-in-the-Fields, as do the portico and tower (both added in 1794). The name of Pierre

Charles L'Enfant, the planner of the city of Washington, has been associated with that of McBean in the design of the chapel, but his connection would have been chiefly as an executant, since the building is so eminently Georgian and not at all French. One of the handsomest early structures in the United States, the beauty of St. Paul's is all the more remarkable in its situation among the skyscrapers of lower Manhattan.

New Jersey reflects the influences of the Flemish type of Dutch colonial in Hackensack and in its environs, but parts of the northern region of the state, at one time politically a part of Connecticut, were settled by Puritan enclaves. The older architecture of Plainfield, Morristown, Elizabeth, Newark, and Woodbridge, therefore, seems little different from that of provincial New England. Buildings in the area near Pennsylvania reflect the architecture of that region, as illustrated in the Trent House in Trenton, an early Georgian mansion with certain local idiosyncrasies of plan, the corner fireplaces and some details deriving from Quaker usage, which may in turn have derived from Swedish or German precedent. These are discussed at greater length in the next section.

Some German influence was undoubtedly present in the architecture of the English settlements of Pennsylvania, especially in the rural areas, but German colonial architecture as such was confined to the Pennsylvania "Dutch" (German) enclaves. Some of the simple character of Pennsylvania architecture—its relative neglect of classical detail (largely confined to openings and to cornices) and the use of rough fieldstone—may be due to the influence of the Pennsylvania "Dutch." At any rate, nearly all the Georgian houses of the Philadelphia region have these characteristics, enduring in the countryside until much later, and giving to the farm and village houses a warm, informal dignity that makes rural Berks, Bucks, and Chester counties so attractive. The amplitude of the barns of this region, usually constructed with a stone basement and ends, but elsewhere vertically planked, recalls the great house-barns of the Black Forest

in Germany, and may ultimately derive from them through the Pennsylvania Germans.

There is little left of the Philadelphia which was described by an eighteenth-century traveler as having been built "after the London Way," that is, the London of row houses built in the post-medieval style after the Great Fire. The only remnant of the continuous rows of early Georgian houses is Elfrith Alley near the Delaware River. But this short street lacks a single example of what were very conspicuous features of the urban scene, the pent roof and the hooded entrance, which are still seen in the suburbs and countryside. A hooded entrance survives in one city dwelling, the Letitia Street House, 1703–1715 (AA 301), preserved in Fairmount Park. This two-story building is probably typical of the smaller town house in other ways as well (though early records speak of three-story houses also), possessing the two corner fireplaces of the Quaker or Swedish plan, and being marked by a relative lack of classical ornament. Charles Bulfinch, after a visit to Philadelphia, probably summed up its general appearance very well when he commented on its "plain Style" and "Quakerish neatness."[7] Even the early larger houses in the vicinity of Philadelphia are certainly plain and simple enough, reflecting the design characteristics of the farmhouses. Typical is the Pastorius House (Green Tree Inn), Germantown, 1748 (AA 310); Moore Hall in Phoenixville, built after 1722 (AA 306); or Waynesborough, Paoli, 1724, 1740 (*AA 307), the home of General Anthony ("Mad Anthony") Wayne. The important houses of this region share in a tradition of simplicity which was common to most of the early large houses throughout the colonies. Stenton, in Germantown, 1728 (*AA 308), for instance, has no exterior ornament except its door and window trim, though the interiors are nicely paneled. One of the best early interiors is at Graeme Park, Horsham, 1721–1722 (AA 304, AA 305), executed in the Georgian manner and quite Palladian in detail for so early in the century. The reason for the presence of these elegant interiors in such an austerely simple stone house remained a mystery until it was discovered recently that Governor Keith built it first as a factory and that the Graemes remodeled it afterward.

It was not until the second half of the century that Quaker wealth and tolerance overcame Quaker plainness, a tendency aided, to be sure, by an increase of Anglicans in the Pennsylvania colony. Then Philadelphia and its environs blossomed with masterpieces of the Georgian style. Though exteriors in the city remained relatively plain, still lacking pilasters, pavilions, and other details and variation in massing, the interiors were magnificent. Typical are those of the Steadman-Powell House, 1768, one room of which is preserved in the Metropolitan Museum (AA 315) and another in the Philadelphia Museum; and of the Stamper-Blackwell House, 1764 (Illustration 2–28), characterized by elaborate

2–28. Room from the Stamper-Blackwell House, Philadelphia, Pennsylvania, 1764. Now in Henry Francis du Pont Winterthur Museum.

carving and concentration of detail in the fireplace area, with an occasional bookcase or arched embrasure appearing in the room as well.

Some suburban houses have elaborate interiors, and nearly all of them have equally imposing exteriors. One of the finest of these, in Fairmount Park, is Mount Pleasant, 1761 (AA 311, *AA 312; Illustration 2–29), which, with its fine doorway and Palladian window, is a masterly example of the best Philadelphia craftsmanship, equal to that of Buckland's at Annapolis. Perhaps the finest Palladian house in the North is Cliveden (the Chew House), Germantown, 1761 (AA 313), constructed of carefully cut ashlar. Restrained and correct, it has a dignity of proportion and scale unmatched in the colonies. Its pedimented Doric portico and its urns (though they may seem a little gratuitous) contribute a good deal to the classicism of the building. The interior is as distinguished as the exterior, being graced with a large entrance hall separated from the stairway by a pair of Doric columns (unlike any other house in the colonies except the Chase-Lloyd House at Annapolis).

These houses are only some of the outstanding ones in the Philadelphia region. Charming little Laurel Hill, 1762, with its fine Palladian facade, or the larger Woodford, 1756, both in Fairmount Park, are other examples. (The latter is the earliest still surviving example of the late Georgian style in the Philadelphia area.) Smaller houses, like the Amstil House in Newcastle, Delaware, and the elegant and not at all provincial Corbitt House in Odessa, Delaware, 1772–1774 (AA 322), with its magnificent interiors, exemplify the influence of Philadelphia down the Delaware valley. The whole town of Newcastle, Delaware, preserves an effect which must reflect well the Philadelphia of two centuries ago.

The Quaker meetinghouses scattered about Philadelphia and its environs were simple from the beginning and remained so. The Radner Meetinghouse of 1713, for instance, is not much different from the Media one of 1814. Eschewing decoration, they depended entirely on good proportion and workmanlike execution for their

2–29. Mount Pleasant, Fairmount Park, Philadelphia, Pennsylvania, 1761.

effect. But Anglican Christ Church, Philadelphia, 1727–1744 (steeple, 1754) (AA 320, AA 321), is a different matter, being one of the most elaborate in the colonies. Its detail derives from the usual architectural books, it bears some resemblance to Wren's St. Andrew's-by-the-Wardrobe in London, and its tower derives in part from Gibbs's St. Martin's-in-the-Fields (as might be expected)—nevertheless, the building has more character than others in the colonies. The huge pedimented chancel walls facing the street and the enormous Palladian window lighting the interior give an importance to this facade which counterbalances the front of the building and the tower, and permits the use of such elegant details as niches and urns. At the same time, the grand scale of the interior affords a more lavish use of various elements from the classical repertoire than is usually permissible. The total effect of the interior, however, when compared with Munday's Trinity Church and Harrison's two masterpieces, King's Chapel and Christ Church, by not being long enough to carry the weight of its elaborate detail, is one of awkward proportions. This may be due to the fact that the building was designed by an amateur, Dr. John Kearsley, a physician from London. Yet, on the whole, the edifice is a very successful example of the work of an amateur designer.

Both Dr. Kearsley and Andrew Hamilton, a prominent lawyer and Speaker of the Pennsylvania Assembly, submitted designs in 1730 for the State House. Hamilton, who won the competition, was an equally successful amateur, for "Independence Hall," 1732–1753 and after (AA 316, AA 317, AA 318, AA 319), as it later came to be known, is a thoroughly satisfactory venture and has the virtue of not being imitative in specific details, but only in general. The south front, with its very nicely graduated tower and cupola (not derived from Gibbs), its fine detail, and its effective use of advanced forms like the Palladian window, shows an acquaintance with architectural style on the part of the designer which was remarkable in 1730, especially for a man whose first and only design this was. The beauty of the building also shows how widespread were architectural interest and taste, though Hamilton was undoubtedly helped by the numerous joiners and other craftsmen necessary for the job, which took many years to finish.

The north facade is perhaps a little monotonous; the central door cries out for more accent. Yet the flat simplicity is rather pleasing in its repetition of forms. The buildings were formerly joined to the main block by an arcade, one side of which was not open. This curtain wall probably added to the flat continuous effect of the design on the north front. After all, this section of the building was to be seen only across a narrow street closed in on the opposite side by buildings. (The present clearing away of a large area north of Independence Hall in order to permit a vista is therefore somewhat at variance with the purpose of the designer.)

The interiors are impressive in their scale, with fine, heavy, early Georgian carving which is always correct, showing nothing of the naïveté of Stuart survival as seen in Munday's Old Colony House in Newport. This building and the others surrounding it comprise certainly a most impressive group and on the whole it is gratifying that the complex is being restored to its early appearance by the removal of incongruous buildings.

Non-English Architecture in the Colonial Era

In most instances the architecture brought to America by colonists other than those from Great Britain has had little influence on American building as a whole, except for the Spanish in the Southwest. Yet some attention should be given to the architecture of these cultural enclaves which gave local flavor to the areas in which they existed.

Swedish and German

The Swedes were the first to settle the Delaware valley region, but their contributions to the history of American architecture were slight. One of them, however, is significant, certainly in American lore: the log cabin, of round logs and later of hewn ones. This form of construction was much used by the Germans who entered Pennsylvania through the former Swedish settlements and they carried it to the frontier where it was picked up by other settlers who took it into the valleys of Virginia, the Piedmont areas of the Carolinas, and over the Alleghenies. Two early examples exist at Darby, Pennsylvania, but the John Morton Birthplace, Prospect Park, near Chester, Pennsylvania, 1654 with later additions (*AA 73), is a more available example. The plan of these houses, consisting of a large room with a corner fireplace, and two small rooms, may have originated with the Swedes. At any rate, it was favored by William Penn and used frequently by the British settlers in the same areas in which the Swedes had settled.

There is something of a Scandinavian look in the steep roofs and details of Holy Trinity Church ("Old Swedes"), Wilmington, Delaware, 1698 (AA 72), and, to a lesser extent, in Gloria Dei Church (also called "Old Swedes"), Philadelphia, built at the same time (AA 74, AA 75), both by Swedish congregations. These buildings are among the first in the colonies to reflect the general principles of Renaissance design though later additions have increased their specifically Georgian character.

Very few actual German structures remain in the colonies, though some influence of the earliest German domestic and agricultural buildings in the Pennsylvania colony may be seen in the architecture of the British settlers in the same region. The tradition of the large house-barns survived in later barns, often elaborated with geometric "hex" signs to ward off evil spells, as at Oley Valley Farms, Pikeville (*AA 78) and other "hex" barns found mostly in Berks County (AA 79).

Among the few remaining German dwellings is the Georg Müller House in Milbach, Pennsylvania, 1752 (AA 76), whose interiors have been removed to the Philadelphia Museum (AA 77).

and windows, and the bold framing, neat cupboards, built-in curtained beds, fine iron work, and cheerful color of the interiors combine to make these Dutch houses, rare as they are, a most interesting instance of what is essentially a foreign architecture in this country. There are very few more of this type left: among them are the Adam Van Allen House near Kinderhook, the Arendt Brandt House in Schenectady, and the Hendrick Bries House in East Greenbush (1723), now almost ruinous.

In Ulster and Dutchess counties, the favored material was fieldstone, though the builders would probably have preferred their traditional brick had the stone not been so easily available. There are two types of story-and-a-half dwellings in this region: one with a gently sloping gable roof, with or without dormers; the other with an acute, tall gable including two garrets. Both the attic and gable were usually covered with clapboards, as was the kitchen wing, a frequent addition. The first group is seen best at Hurley, where a whole street of unspoiled houses exists; there are a few at New Paltz and Kingston as well. The second group is seen also at New Paltz, and in one example at Newburgh. The houses of the first group are more numerous, and can be represented at their most typical in the Freer House, New Paltz, 1720 (AA 55), though the Senate House at Kingston is more picturesque with its very obliquely sloped roof, its narrow, sloping dormers, and its sequence of three rooms with two doors opening on the facade—an extension of the usual basic plan of the Dutch colonial house, one room in width.

The second type of dwelling is more picturesque by reason of its very high and steep gables. The most arresting of the five original "Huguenot" houses in New Paltz is the one built by Abraham Hasbrouck in 1712 (*AA 56) (now Memorial Hall, the headquarters of the Huguenot Patriotic Society).

The so-called Old Stone House at Gowanus, 1699 (*AA 57), a reconstruction (1934) in Prospect Park, Brooklyn, of a building erected in Gowanus in 1699, is another well-known stone dwelling, but not typical, since it comprises two stories and has no high gables, and is therefore more like the houses of the Albany region. It is also atypical for Long Island, where wood was the favored material, a circumstance perhaps influenced by the building tradition of the settlers from New England in the central and eastern part of the island.

It was probably in Dutch Long Island that there occurred the first stages of a development which was to become common in southern New York and northern New Jersey, a style characterized by a flared overhanging roof introduced in the mid-seventeenth century and combined in the eighteenth century with the Dutch gambrel roof (the break comes higher and the angles are more obtuse than in the English gambrel). This "Dutch colonial" roof was actually not Dutch at all, having been originated in Flanders and imported into Holland in the early seventeenth century by Flemings, who also brought with them the "mouse-tooth" gable referred to earlier.

One of the earliest examples is the Jacobus Demarest House (now the Englewood Public Library), River Edge, New Jersey, before 1720 (AA 65), characteristic in that it lacked a porch, a feature which developed later. The Roelof Westervelt House, Tenafly, New Jersey, 1798 (AA 63), is a later example of this type. The Dyckman House on upper Broadway, New York, c. 1783 (AA 66, AA 68; Illustration 2–32), exemplifies the incorporation of a porch under the overhanging roof; the Vreeland House, Leonia Borough, New Jersey, 1818 (AA 69), shows the ultimate development wherein the porch posts acquire classical detail.

No public buildings and few churches in Dutch colonial architecture have survived. The octagonal meetinghouse of Dutch Protestantism was seen occasionally, but was soon overwhelmed by the Georgian-detailed rectangular meetinghouse or church. These later buildings, however, preserved an unpretentious solidity not unlike the simple forms of the Quaker meetinghouse, as can be seen at the Old Tennent Church, Tennent, New Jersey, 1751 (AA 70), and the First Dutch Reformed Church, Fishkill, New York, 1784 (*AA 71), which has some later remodeling.

2–32. Dyckman House, New York, New York, c. 1783.

French

Though the French territory in what is now the United States covered more area than that of any other European nation, the French left relatively little architecture, and none had any influence to speak of except in the Louisiana plantations. Furs and the possibility of precious metals—not the desire for permanent settlement —spurred exploration and what sparse settlement there was. The most important town was New Orleans, founded in 1721 as a strategic trading post. After 1763 the French ceded to England their territory east of the Mississippi, except for New Orleans; that city and the west bank were given to Spain, to be restored to France again for only a few years before Napoleon sold it to the United States in 1803. The years of Spanish occupation had little effect on the population, customs, or architecture, which remained predominantly French, reinforced in New Orleans and the bayou country by French settlers, the

Cajons, formerly situated in Nova Scotia, who were expelled by the British after 1760.

The typical French building in this vast country is well represented by a dwelling later called the Courthouse, in Cahokia, Illinois, c. 1737 (AA 169). The structure is surrounded by a porch; its hip roof, which becomes less acutely pitched over the porch, is supported by upright posts filled with clay pots (the origin of this method is obscure). Houses of this sort still exist in St. Louis and St. Genevieve, Missouri, where there were also a few stone dwellings of the same general design. In river bottom country this type of dwelling (usually of two or more rooms in a row) was supported on brick piers to protect it from floods, as in the house in New Orleans called Madame John's Legacy, c. 1727 (AA 171), and became a popular type called the "raised cottage," even in areas not subject to floods.

The first building of the large three-story Ursuline Convent in New Orleans (1734) exposed its framing in a still medieval way, and was filled in with brick, as the architect's drawings in the National Archives in Paris show. The second convent of 1748 (now the Archbishopric) was of stone with the typically French steep mansard roof and reflected the simplified classicism stripped of orders which was becoming popular in mid-eighteenth-century France. Unfortunately, the original building is difficult to recognize under a series of remodelings.

Another old house in New Orleans, Lafitte's Blacksmith Shop, built between 1772 and 1791, shows under its peeling plaster the post construction filled not with pots as in the Illinois and Missouri country, but with soft bricks as was the custom in New Orleans.

Little of the original French New Orleans remains, due to two fires in 1788 and 1794. But the *Vieux Carré*, the original gridiron-plan city (with the former Place d'Armes, now Jackson Square, as a focal point on the banks of the Mississippi), with its narrow streets and closely packed row houses, has the air of a foreign town. This is partly because it shares with other cities of the South wrought iron decorated porches (*galleries*), balconies, long wings (*garçonières*) and courtyards or yards—the latter very like Charleston; and partly because the French taste, smaller scaled and more delicate than the English, persisted in the rebuilding after 1794. Preserved by law from change of design, this area is one of the most architecturally attractive in the United States, a section enhanced by the nostalgia of the French appearance of its streets, and its still Creole ways.

The plantations in the lower Mississippi valley and along the Louisiana bayous developed out of the raised cottage: the lower floor was covered with brick or stone, the upper one with wood, with a *gallerie* supported on piers over an open porch on one side (sometimes on two or three and frequently four) for cross ventilation. Such a house is Parlange, Pointe Coupée Parish, Mix, Louisiana, 1750 (AA 176, AA 177), and another, Homeplace Plantation, Hahnville, St. Charles Parish, Louisiana, 1801 (AA 179). Here the four-sided *gallerie* and the "bonnet" double-pitched roof reflect the tradition of the pioneer house in

French Missouri and Illinois, while the two stories of porches reflect that of the "raised cottage." These traditions are seen elsewhere in the lower Mississippi, as at Connelly's Tavern, Natchez, Mississippi, built before 1800 (AA 182), though here the porch and *gallerie* cover only one side.

Spanish

The architecture in the former Spanish domains now within the continental boundaries of the United States was conspicuous for its ecclesiastical buildings, consisting of churches and monasteries established for the conversion and teaching of the Indians by the various monastic orders, principally the Franciscans. An occasional fort or governor's palace, ranch house or hacienda, and a few humbler dwellings make up the rest. Much of this architecture is as European as is that of the Dutch or, for that matter, of the English. But in some instances it becomes more original, especially in the combination of the Spanish with the indigenous Indian building traditions in New Mexico, and in the development of the ranch house in California.

Buildings in the region around San Antonio in Texas, Tucson in Arizona, and to a lesser extent the string of missions along the California coast are of the more conventional sort and belong as properly to the history of Mexican architecture as to that of the United States, though their presence in this country has inspired or excused considerable Spanish revivalism in this century.

Florida, once part of the Spanish domain in the new world, has few buildings left from this regime: the "oldest house" in St. Augustine—more probably built in 1763 than in 1564, since all the buildings in the town were supposed to have been destroyed in 1702 by Governor Moore of South Carolina—is a very simple two-story structure of local limestone and wood clapboarding. But the great fort there, the correctly restored Castillo de San Marcos, 1672–1756 (AA 118, AA 119), is a massive and formidable structure indeed (as is the still ruined Fort San Carlos, a few miles south), the best representa-

2–33. Detail of facade, San Xavier del Bac, near Tucson, Arizona, 1783–1797.

tive in the United States of the European fortress with its projecting bastions.

The San Antonio area is much richer in remains of the Spanish regime. The famous Álamo, 1744–1757 (AA 133), the church for the first mission, founded in 1718, is less impressive than its successors, especially San José y San Miguel de Aguayo, 1720–1731 (AA 136, AA 137, AA 138, AA 139, °AA 139A), the most ambitious and sophisticated of the Spanish missions north of what is now the Mexican border. Its nave is covered with three groined vaults, with a dome over the fourth bay, and its facade includes a great tower. But the accomplished fabric of the structure is matched by the elaborate baroque decoration in the style called generally "Chur-

rigueresque" (after a Spanish architect who originated in the seventeenth century an extreme form of elaborate ornamentation), as developed and distinguished in eighteenth-century Mexico as it was in Spain. The main portal and other details were carried out by one Pedro Huizar, and comprise the most notable instance of this baroque form in the United States. Though perhaps too exuberant for Anglo-Saxon taste, it is magnificently effective, isolated as it is against the otherwise undecorated simplicity of the heavy geometric shapes of the structure. The Álamo and the other San Antonio missions, such as Nuestra Señora de la Purísima Concepción de Acuña, 1731 (AA 140), and San Francisco de la Espada, 1731 (AA 141), are less elaborate and more conventional.

Almost as ambitious, but less sophisticated than San José y San Miguel de Aguayo, one of the most distinguished and ambitious examples of Mexican architecture in the United States is the mission church of San Xavier del Bac, 1783–1797 (AA 142; Illustration 2–33), a few miles south of Tucson, Arizona. The only survivor of a series of Arizona missions, it is a fully developed cruciform structure with low dome-like vaults, except at the crossing where there is an impressive dome. A facade flanked by two towers is especially imposing in its width and in the richly decorated central area of brick which contrasts with the plain white stucco of the flanking areas. The towers are particularly bold, displaying large baroque scrolls of powerful design. The brilliant white architectural forms of San Xavier standing out in bold relief under the intense light of the desert sun give an austere geometry to the classically derived shapes which would not be seen in the gentler radiance of the Mediterranean area where the forms originated. After dark, the dramatic simplicity in the blending of the white surface and the black shadows of the desert night act as a foil for the unbelievably complex ornamentation of the central "frontispiece" (as the Spanish call their decorated portals) in molded brick, making it all the more compelling. This decoration and that of the interior, though not as "primitive" or provincial as the work of Indians or Spanish-

Americans in New Mexico, is nevertheless not of the urban sort seen in the great late baroque churches of metropolitan Mexico—or, for that matter, in San Antonio. This ornament belongs to the more naïve combination of European design and Indian workmanship which had been in existence from the time of settlement in the sixteenth century, becoming a continuing tradition through a succession of styles from late Gothic to rococo.

The mission churches of Alta California, some of which are in ruins and others restored, stretch from San Diego to San Francisco Solano in Marin County along the old *Camino Real.* Most of them, founded by the indefatigable Padre Junipero Serra, were extremely successful until the secularization by the Mexican government of the monastic orders in the 1830's. The majority of the present edifices were built in the two decades before and after 1800, and reflect a variety of architectural tastes. None is as large or as competently designed as San Xavier or San José y San Miguel, though San Carlos Borromeo at Carmel, 1793–1797 (AA 152, *AA 152A), has ambitious decoration, obviously copied from Mexican sources by the master stonemason who designed it, Manuel Estevan Ruiz. It has details which it is unlikely that he would have known otherwise, such as the elaborate window over the portal. But with this Spanish baroque form, partly Moorish in derivation, he combined more conventional baroque details in the tower and in a strictly Renaissance portico of very conservative design, showing thereby a somewhat naïve and unsure taste. A restored wooden barrel vault carried on three great stone ribs indicates considerable originality. Innocent of correct design as Ruiz may have been, nevertheless this vault and the fact that the walls and their supports continue the curve of the ribs down to the ground show him to be an accomplished engineer. Ruiz may have worked on the neighboring Capilla Real, Monterey, 1794 (AA 153), whose facade, the most elaborate among the California missions, is derived from several sources, the lower story being fairly classical with a gable derived from Juan de Herrera (the architect of Philip II's

El Escorial outside of Madrid), while the upper is crowned with a design of later baroque origin. The whole facade is covered with a froth of rather timid carving—altogether a design far removed from the sure touch of Pedro Huizar in Texas.

More elaborate in construction is the still unrestored church of San Juan Capistrano, 1797–1806 (AA 154, AA 155, *AA 155B) (most of the missions have been destroyed more than once by earthquakes), which displayed three domical vaults. The conjectural restoration by Rexford Newcomb shows a building with the austere walls and impressive height of the great mission churches in sixteenth-century Mexico. The builder was in fact a Mexican, Isidoro Aguilar.

Only San Luis Rey, 1811–1815 (AA 159), north of San Diego, has a similar scale and as impressive an interior as San Juan Capistrano once had. But its dome is wooden, though supported on an interesting system of pendentives forming an octagon as the support of the drum. By this time (1811–1815), after several earthquakes, the builder, Padre Antonio Peyri, had decided not to tempt fate with masonry domes or vaults.

The mission church at Santa Barbara, 1815–1820 (AA 156), is among the most beautifully restored and kept, and the only one which reflects the neo-classic taste permeating both Europe and America at the date of its erection. A Doric facade of engaged columns, with a Greek fret design in the entablature (taken out of context from an edition of Vitruvius still at the mission), lends an elegant and fragile look to an otherwise heavy building crowned with the bold, simplified baroque forms of the domed towers. This powerful but unconventional design, together with the naïve detailing of the Ionic order, betray the hand of the untutored builder, who was in fact the priest himself, Padre Ripoll.

The mission church at Santa Barbara is unusual in being five-aisled. The great majority of the missions have only an aisleless nave, sometimes with a curved or trapezoidal sanctuary, and are roofed simply with beams, usually carved and resting on corbels projecting from the walls, as at San Diego de Alcalá, San Diego,

1808–1813 (AA 149). Most are constructed of adobe, trimmed with stone or with a mixture of lime and stones forming a kind of crude concrete, and are faced with either white or pastel-tinted stucco. The more ambitious buildings are of stone, easily quarried, of a pleasant light yellow color. Some have patios and arcades and are still used as convent buildings. The latter are especially attractive at Santa Barbara, where the friars have been in uninterrupted possession of the mission since its founding in 1786, at San Juan Capistrano (*AA 155, *AA 155B), at San Juan Batista, and at Santa Inéz at Solvang, 1804 (*AA 163, *AA 164).

Though this long succession of missions was a social phenomenon unique even in Latin America (the San Luis Rey mission, for instance, had a resident population of 2,869 and was the largest in the new world), architecturally they are not equally remarkable. Charming and full of character as they are, serving as touchstones to the past and offering inspiration for modern architects in the adaptation of their forms and materials to their environment, the California missions nevertheless have neither the sophistication of their Mexican prototypes nor the unpretentious originality of their earlier New Mexican counterparts. The priests in California had to educate a particularly backward and unskilled group of Indians, and this fact, combined with their enormous missionary effort, required more important tasks and moneys than the employment of trained carvers or the importation from Mexico of architects beyond the rank of master mason.

The missionaries in New Mexico were no less busy, but they encountered a race of Indians, the Pueblos, who were already proficient in the arts of building, and of whose traditions and techniques they were glad to take advantage. This factor, together with circumstances unfavorable to building on a large and elaborate scale (the remoteness of the mission field and the relative hostility of the natives) caused Indian elements to play a much greater part in the Spanish architecture of New Mexico than was the case elsewhere in the United States, or anywhere else under the crown of Spain.

The Franciscan fathers set out from the centers of New Spain into the northern desert supplied with enough equipment to build a mission: axes, adzes, a saw, a chisel, two augers, a plane, and some 6,000 nails of various sizes. These basic necessities and their memories of the general appearance of the architecture of Spain and New Spain were all they had. But for at least five hundred years the Pueblo Indians had been building groups of terraced dwellings, or "apartment houses" above and around storehouses, safe from attack because they were inaccessible from the ground level except by easily retrievable ladders. The buildings at the Taos Pueblo are perhaps the most impressive, as well as the most familiar, but those at Ácoma Pueblo are as typical, and much older. They are not so like fortresses as at Taos, because the almost inaccessible mesa upon which the village was built in the ninth century was itself inaccessible except by a narrow, steep path which could be easily controlled. It was here that the indomitable Padre Juan Ramírez induced his converts to build perhaps the finest of the New Mexican churches and it was up these steps that the faithful for many years carried the earth to build the great edifice and to fill in the consecrated ground for the cemetery. The simple, massive forms of this mission of San Estevan, 1629–c. 1642 (AA 122, AA 123; Illustration 2–34), seem to be a reflection of the basic shapes, material, and color of the Ácoma Pueblo itself. The large nave and the towers are of course essential to an architecture which is foreign to the Indian tradition, as are the monastery rooms, the patio, and the balconied corner tower. But the material of adobe, and the great timbers (called *vigas*) supporting the planks and adobe of the roof and protruding into the exterior are Indian elements. So are the sculpturesque forms of the walls, buttressed at the corner of the monastery and wider at the base of the church walls in order to bear more easily the weight of adobe and ceiling. The sanctuary of San Estevan, as in most churches in the New Mexico area, was trapezoidal but otherwise the interior was completely rectangular, insofar as adobe (which always appears to have been directly patted into place

2–34.   San Estevan, Ácoma Pueblo, New Mexico, 1629–c. 1642.

by human hands) can be mechanically rectangular. This simplicity is relieved only by the sometimes elaborately carved and painted brackets inserted into the walls, which help support the *vigas,* and by painted and sometimes carved altarpieces. Both of these features are at their best at the San José mission, Old Laguna Pueblo, 1699–1706 (AA 126, AA 127, *AA 128). Occasionally there is also supplementary decoration painted directly on the walls. A narrow transept was occasionally added, but did not become conspicuous until the late eighteenth century in some of the mission churches, as at San Francisco de Asis at Ranchos de Taos, 1772 (AA 131, AA 132). A curious feature, which also explains the unusual orientation of the churches to the east, is the raising of the roof to enough height to accommodate a transverse window (at the crossing of the transept, or when this does not exist, at about the point where it would be) in order that a light be cast dramatically on the sanctuary, in an otherwise almost unlighted interior. This typically baroque "stage prop" must have been

especially effective when the first light of dawn was caught and concentrated on the altar at matins.

The exterior of the churches was graced usually by two towers as at Ácoma and Ranchos de Taos, but occasionally by a residual baroque pinnacle and a scroll facade, as at Laguna. A rare but extremely effective facade is that of San José de Gracia mission, at Trampas, 1760 (AA 129), where a balcony is hung between the two supporting buttresses of the facade. The almost primitive simplicity of the exteriors is in most instances enhanced by great earthen buttresses to prop up the adobe walls in the older buildings, or built into the original fabric during the eighteenth century as at Ranchos de Taos (*AA 132). The stark simplicity of these walls, covered with white gypsum, is the background for very little decoration: doors are sometimes paneled, even carved and occasionally decorated with spindles. The effect of the facade is often further emphasized by an enclosure in front of the church, a reappearance of the atrium of early Christian times, which was revived in the days of the early conversions of the Indians in Mexico, when larger groups than could be accommodated even in the great Dominican and Franciscan monastery churches had to be encompassed. At Trampas and Chimayo this atrium-like area is dignified by a gateway and a fine carved door.

The simple directness of these Spanish-American churches (softened and made irregular by the use of adobe), the organic relationship of their material and form to the environment, and the baroque decoration, translated enthusiastically into native terms, comprise a combination of Spanish and Indian factors which results in one of the most beautiful and certainly the most original accomplishments in the early architecture in the United States.

Of the other Spanish colonial buildings, only the dwellings of the former Mexican areas can equal these churches and monasteries in importance. Some residences, such as the Palace of the Governor at San Antonio, 1749 (AA 134, AA 135), for all its rather stark simplicity and its beamed and boarded ceiling, is not un-Spanish with its carved keystone over the main portal, its grilled windows, and projecting water spouts. Earlier and far more indigenous is the Palace of the Governors at Santa Fe, 1610 1614 (AA 121), where the ends of the *vigas* project, and where the basic forms are tapered and softly rounded in typical adobe fashion, even though the details of the supports of the long covered porch (*portale*) and other decorative details are obviously Spanish in derivation. Though most of the smaller old houses in the territory of which Santa Fe was the capital have disappeared, the adobe type with *vigas* was standard. This kind of structure, designed to keep out heat and fitted so beautifully into the environment, could be enlarged by extending its plan longitudinally or at right angles, and varied by the addition of doorways, patios, and balconies in the Spanish tradition, as seen in a few houses in Taos and Santa Fe. Dwellings like this—simple, flexible, completely related to their environment, and retaining little if anything of the European decorative vocabulary, classical or otherwise—are basically contemporary in their esthetic and are, in fact, the basis for a modern indigenous style which is presently flourishing in the region.

Perhaps more important as a background for contemporary architecture in densely populated California is the early domestic architecture of that region. Though the Franciscan fathers were not too original in their use of established architectural designs, their planning, orientation, and planting of the mission complexes and villages (the latter have almost entirely disappeared), as seen at Santa Inéz, was admirably adapted to circumstances of the environment, and served as an excellent prototype for the country houses (*haciendas*) and the *ranchos*, which were introduced by the Mexican government after the separation from Spain in 1821, to counteract the exclusive hold of the missions on the territory. Not basically different from the New Mexican houses and, like them, usually of adobe, they exploited the principle of corridor-bounded patios with more freedom, being usually larger establishments.

In the more northern area the *ranchos* were usually of two stories, with a balcony which was often carried all around the house, or at least on three sides, as in the old Larkin House, 1834, and the old Pacific House, 1847 (AA 166, AA 167, *AA 161), both at Monterey. But the most interesting example of the *rancho* is the house built by Governor Vellejo near Petaluma, in Sonoma County at the northernmost point of Spanish-Mexican colonization. Here the almost rambling plan of patio and wings, the use of porches, balconies, and wide overhanging eaves, the orientation for air and view, as well as the employment of local material (traditional adobe and wood, with vertical redwood planking), combine to make an extremely successful dwelling for the area. After the arrival of the North Americans, the local tradition represented by this house was augmented by the framing and clapboarding techniques of the East which, added to the adobe and patio plan, formed an equally successful solution. Residences such as these, using the materials of the environment, exploiting the site and view, and providing for the interpenetration of interior and exterior and for a free-flowing plan are the very real prototypes for the exciting and equally indigenous contemporary architecture of California, both in the bay region and farther to the south.

A word should be said about the Cabildo at New Orleans, 1795 (AA 184A), built by the Spanish regime to house government offices. Reflecting in its detail and proportion the anti-baroque neo-classical taste of the end of the eighteenth century in both Spain and Mexico—

the arcaded lower floor repeated in the arched fenestration of the second floor, and the central area of its facade crowned with a clear cut pediment (the mansard roof is a later addition) —it ranks with City Hall in New York as an example of the late eighteenth-century style of the Continent. This building, together with its counterpart on the other side of the New Orleans cathedral, gives to Jackson Square a great deal of that monumental unity later enhanced by the beautiful Greek Revival Pontalba apartments.

Community Planning in the Colonial Era

The subject of town and city planning was more crucial in colonial times than during any other era (except the present) in American history, because the patterns were set for future development and for much of the appearance of the American scene as it exists today.

The most commonly utilized town plan consisted of the simple grid, usually with an open square in the middle, used for marketplace or public buildings, which derived ultimately from Vitruvius' ideal plan for a Roman military camp. The popularity of this plan—incidentally, quite common throughout history for port towns— had been enhanced at the time of the English colonization by its use not only in colonial settlement by the Spanish and Portuguese but also in the English settlements in Northern Ireland.

When the danger from the Indians had passed, the Vitruvian grid pattern of the *bastide* settlement (or garrison town around a fort) continued to be used in the new unfortified towns, and the fort or strong house (called *bawne* in Ireland and in early America) in its center was replaced by the meetinghouse in New England, and by the courthouse in Virginia. Thus, from the beginning of colonization the nucleated manorial village (houses clustered around a manor house, with radiating fields) was a thing of the past not only for the settlers who were already independent yeomen and husbandmen, but also for those who hoped to achieve a similar position in the social scale by migrating.

New Haven, laid out in a gridiron around a central square in 1638, was the most conspicuous and the earliest example of a town which was deliberately planned and did not simply grow out of a fort or *bastide* for defense (*CPA 6; Illustration 2–35). This basic plan was repeated at Charleston in 1704 (*CPA 4), Savannah in 1733 (*CPA 12), and Alexandria in 1749 (*CPA 1), and was varied in the Philadelphia plan of 1682 by the addition of four supplementary squares. [New Orleans had an elaborate gridiron plan in 1721, laid out by its French rulers, of eighty blocks around a large central square, now Jackson Square—still the basic plan of the *Vieux Carré* (*CPA 7).] These plans might be called classical in contrast to those of Annapolis, 1694, and Williamsburg, 1699, which could be termed baroque, since diagonal streets, avenues, and circuses (curved open areas) were superimposed over the grid. These later plans contributed much to the effect of the individual buildings by enhancing their spatial relationship to one another.

Even though such circumstances as the contour of shore and depth of harbor caused some variations in the ideal plan of port towns, only Boston's remained conspicuously like that of the medieval city (that is, essentially accidental, growing up along the lanes which legend claims were originally cowpaths), a local restriction due to the unusually irregular shoreline and the hilly terrain of the site (*CPA 3). The crowded,

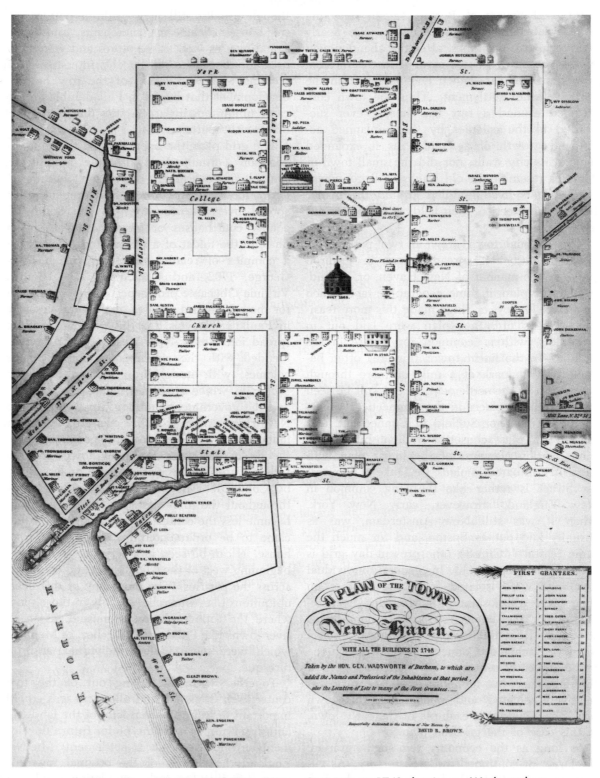

2—35. Manuscript map of New Haven, Connecticut, 1748, by James Wadsworth.

veloped which were different from those of Europe, and which set the pattern for future development, giving a special character to the American scene. The open lot with its single isolated dwelling in a township or in a clearing was the prototype of a continuing ideal of individual property ownership—even if today it can be satisfied only in much restricted dimensions. The tradition of open spaces and trees, expressing a desire for the non-urban, has led to extensive suburban development and inspired the idealism of Frank Lloyd Wright and other city planners. Finally, the rectangular geometry of the grid plan supplemented a tendency toward the planometric and prismatic forms already seen in American building by enhancing them with a similar rectangular enframement.

Painting

Before Copley

American painting came of age during the eighteenth century. In the work of men such as Copley and to a lesser extent his predecessor Feke, we are dealing with artists who can be favorably compared with the accepted English artists of the period.

Fashions in art from abroad were eagerly imitated by colonial painters, but their sources were secondhand or second-rate, consisting of engraved reproductions of English portraits or original work by inferior English artists who immigrated here. It was inevitable that these factors, together with the existence of a body of earlier colonial painting (either in the older English tradition or with a native character), should dilute and transform the imported English taste. From one point of view, the American colonial school even at its best is only a distant reflection of the great portrait tradition of Rubens and Van Dyck, which reached its final phase in the work of such eighteenth-century English portraitists as Gainsborough. Yet, because of this very distance, the American work achieves a certain individual character which at its worst is still distinctive and at its best, even distinguished.

Though there were some other forms of art during the eighteenth century, portraiture continued to be in America, as it was in England, the most important branch of painting. As the upper classes added to their ranks, both the established aristocracy and the representatives of the newer mercantile wealth demanded painted replicas of their faces. The portrait painter in America was undoubtedly the most skilled of the pictorial artisans of his time, but he remained basically an artisan. He still had to paint coats of arms and signs, and he was frequently a house painter as well. His training was usually acquired as an apprentice to one of these trades, and until Smibert arrived with his copies of European masterpieces, the colonial portraitist had no pictures of the European tradition to see and imitate. There was in America certainly no academy like the one Smibert attended in London. Even the greatest of the colonial masters, Copley, was essentially self-taught, though he was more fortunate than most in having been trained in engraving by his stepfather, a professional though inferior English artist. The colonial artist was essentially only a craftsman and his social position reflected this fact. As late as the 1760's, Copley himself wrote that it was "not a little mortifying that the people regarded painting no more than any useful trade, as they sometimes term it, like that of a carpenter and shoemaker." [8] The justness of such a complaint is corroborated by the tenor of certain newspaper advertisements: "Old Madeira and other wines, groceries, most kinds of painting done as usual at reasonable prices" (New York, 1711); "a choice collection of books pictures and pickles [for sale]" (Charleston, 1744). It is because of its basis in the crafts that colonial art has so much of the flavor of

2–36.   Anonymous, *Thomas Van Alstyne,* 1721. Oil on canvas.   39½ x 30 inches.   (Courtesy of The New-York Historical Society, New York City.)

amateur work. Its naïveté about academic essentials and its directness of design, derived from sign painting, contribute a great deal to its special character and its esthetic appeal.

Yet, increasing contact with England after the Restoration and especially after the "Glorious Revolution" brought a desire to emulate its fashions so that at the beginning of the eighteenth century this native school was often disguised by a superficial British manner. Several painters illustrate this tendency at the opening of the period. Though their work is not very important esthetically, a brief description of some of their pictures will offer some knowledge of the early years which were the background for the more significant developments later in the century. A certain J. Cooper (who may never have lived in the colonies) left, especially

in the Boston area, a number of small portraits executed in the second decade of the century, in which he added to the essentially bold design of the sign-painter tradition certain pretentious accessories and a kind of nervous highlight representing the sheen of expensive stuffs. These and the mannered poses of his gentlefolk and allegorical figures were doubtlessly derived from the small, coarsely executed engravings of royalty which were common at the time. A similar technique and approach were used by the anonymous painter of members of the Broadnax and Jaquelin families in Virginia, as seen in *Edward Jaquelin II as a Child,* c. 1722 (PA 26A). Nathaniel Emmons of Boston catered more specifically than did Cooper to the tastes of what a Puritan divine called a "giddy, carnal rising generation"[9] in little portraits which in their size and sheen imitated English engravings. Anglo-Dutch New York, which was rapidly increasing in mercantile wealth, attracted the Scotsman John Watson, who brought with him an authentic (though third-rate) metropolitan style to add to that of the local artisans, as seen in the portrait said to be of *Governor Lewis Morris,* 1726 (*PA 44A).

Typical of the older portrait manner persisting in the former Dutch colony at about the time of Watson's arrival was the work of an interesting limner known as the "Aetatis Sui" painter because of his custom of noting the age of his subject prefixed with this Latin phrase. In his portrait of *Thomas Van Alstyne,* 1721 (PA 22; Illustration 2–36), the force of the characterization approaches the intensity of caricature. In his *Mrs. Van Alstyne,* 1721 (PA 23), however, as in his other feminine portraits, this forcefulness is softened by an attempt at elegance which would be ridiculous were it not for the boldness of the shapes—a characteristic of all the portraits by this still naïve artist.

Under the influence of Watson and others, the bourgeois forthrightness of the earlier Dutch approach to subjects and design was changed to a more aristocratic one, accompanied by greater refinement in anatomy, modeling, and the representation of surrounding atmosphere, and by a more careful technique.

Among the best of these later Hudson River artists is the portraitist of the de Peyster family, who was much influenced by at least the composition of English prints. His most interesting picture, *James A. de Peyster* (?), 1720–1730 (*PA 41), depicts a child clothed in a fashionable dressing gown standing in a park and tentatively making the acquaintance of a fawn. In this picture and in a very similar portrait of *John Van Cortlandt* painted about the same date (PA 42), and in others, a certain boldness of design and oversimplified modeling persist from the more primitive style, in spite of the additions of new technical subtleties and a greater artificiality of pose. Perhaps more pleasing to modern taste for their naïve and flat design are the portraits of the Gansevoort family, such as *Magdelena Gansevoort,* c. 1720 (Illustration 2–37), which bear a striking similarity to the "popular" or "folk" portraits of the nineteenth century.

About 1770, painting in the former New Netherlands came to resemble more and more that of the other English colonies, or English provincial painting in general. A handsome double portrait of *Captain and Mrs. Johannes Schuyler* by an unidentified Hudson Valley artist (though sometimes attributed to Watson), c. 1725 (PA 24), can be used as an example, for Mrs. Schuyler is almost identical in costume and pose to the subject in a portrait by John Smibert done in 1724, before he came to America. This fact suggests that the Hudson Valley painter knew the Smibert, which is most unlikely, or that both artists copied details from the same source, probably an engraving. The use of engravings for pose, dress, and even features was a frequent practice in colonial painting from this time on, and in the former New Netherlands was undoubtedly one of the means by which the local style became less individual in character.

The South had a more impressive immigrant than Watson in the person of the German painter Justus Engelhardt Kuhn, who tried his skill in Maryland. Yet he is not a very distinguished artist when judged in the framework of the great international tradition from which

2–37. Anonymous, *Magdelena Gansevoort,* c. 1720. Oil on canvas. 50¼ x 32¼ inches. (Courtesy, Henry Francis du Pont Winterthur Museum, Winterthur, Delaware.)

he came or with which he was at least acquainted; he probably was not competent enough to have prospered had he remained in Europe. But his ability to paint stuffs and accessories with a certain flourish, to put sufficiently convincing bodies in their midst, and to place them in fantastically elaborate backgrounds involving columns and architectural vistas (surroundings worthy of a German princeling) met the need for pretension on the part of the rising tobacco aristocracy of the tidewater. Kuhn's portraits of *Eleanor Darnall* and of *Henry Darnall III,* c. 1710 (PA 20B, PA 21B), may be taken as typical of his work. The children, about six and ten respectively, dressed and coifed in the style of their elders as was customary, stand before elaborate backdrops, one of them including a formal garden and palace which would have been most improbable in Maryland; the boy is accompanied by a Negro page, and the girl is patting the head of what appears to be a large china dog.

Another immigrant, Henrietta Johnston, who executed pastels in burgeoning Charleston, is a more attractive if more limited figure. Though her talents were circumscribed (she hardly ever attempted anything more than the face itself, and even this is not well constructed), her work has a kind of doll-like insubstantiality which, though singularly inappropriate in her masculine portraits—as in that of *Colonel William Rhett,* c. 1710 (PA 28)—gives charm and grace to her representations of women, as seen in her portrait of *Mrs. Samuel Wragg,* 1708 (PA 27). Mrs. Johnston's talents would hardly have been noticed except in a country and a period where so little of artistic quality or significance was as yet being done.

The first quarter of the eighteenth century is, on the whole, rather unrewarding. New fashions in technique and new attitudes toward the sitter were introduced; and the first really American school developed in New York, characterized by a combination of an earlier seventeenth-century Dutch provincialism with the courtly elegance of early eighteenth-century England.

But the next quarter-century saw the arrival of a British painter, John Smibert, whose talents, though not first-rate, were at least professional. Through him both the public and the fledgling colonial artists were for the first time put in contact with the great baroque tradition, known previously only through engravings of its masterpieces. For Smibert brought with him not only a knowledge of European painting but self-executed copies of some outstanding examples, which were the only actual European pictures in the grand manner in the colonies.

Smibert was trained in one of the first British academies and further self-educated in Italy. He came to America with the philosopher George Berkeley, who settled in Newport, Rhode Island, for two and a half years to await funds for the founding of a university for the Indians in Bermuda until, disappointed, he returned to Ireland and the consolation of a bishopric. Smibert, who was to have been in charge of the artistic aspects of the college, did not return with Berkeley but remained in Boston in spite of the bishop's urging him to take up his profession again as a portrait artist in Cork. For Smibert, who had begun his career as a house painter and plasterer's apprentice in Edinburgh and had achieved only minor recognition in England, was happy enough with the praise and commissions of Boston's best families, into whose ranks he had entered through marriage.

He was not always the portraitist of fashion, unlike his British contemporary, Thomas Hudson, who worked in an elegant formula inherited from Lely and Kneller. In contrast, many of Smibert's figures have a kind of bluff reality which is quite reminiscent of another of his English contemporaries, William Hogarth, and may even derive from a revolt on the part of both artists against aristocratic fashion. One of Smibert's first pictures in America, the portrait of the toothless and jolly *Nathaniel Byfield,* 1730 (PA 36) is very similar indeed to several portraits by Hogarth of *Reverend Hoadley.* Both artists express an uncompromising though sympathetic realism and a very convincing, almost exaggerated, sense of three-dimensionality (perhaps the result of the fact that both were professionally trained). Others of Smibert's early American pictures are equally unpretentious in attitude and voluminously three-dimensional in treatment as, for instance, the group portrait of *Daniel, Peter, and Andrew Oliver,* c. 1730 (PA 35).

At times Smibert can be quite charming as in such portraits as that of *Jane Clark,* 1739 (PA 37B), where he loses some of his emphasis on roundness, indulging in depiction of surface play of light, decorative treatment of landscape, and details of his pretty sitter's dress.

2–38. John Smibert, *Dean George Berkeley and His Family*, 1729–1730. Oil on canvas. 69½ x 93 inches. (Courtesy of Yale University Art Gallery, New Haven, Connecticut. Gift of Isaac Lathrop.)

Both tendencies in Smibert influenced New England painting: his forthright bourgeois attitude and his elegant aristocratic approach. Robert Feke vacillated and finally chose the latter; and even Copley, generally a master of honest observation, often lapses into the mannerisms of courtly attitudes, partially on the basis of Smibert's precedent.

Characteristic of Smibert's less artificial manner is his best and most important—and first—picture in this country, *Dean George Berkeley and His Family*, 1729–1730 (PA 34; Illustration 2–38). The good dean is represented with members of his family, a secretary, a Newport friend, and, at the far left, Smibert himself. The

Idealist philosopher stands at the far right, his hand resting on a volume of Plato. In this picture Smibert shows himself the heir of the great post-Renaissance portrait tradition in his at least rudimentary knowledge of human anatomy and in the baroque technique which creates the illusion of surrounding air as well as of distance in the landscape. Though Smibert is a vastly more competent artist than any in this tradition who preceded him to the colonies, he is hardly an outstanding painter. The anatomy is barely adequate and the modeling is not subtle. The arms are round, but the sleeves might be stuffed with something other than flesh and blood. The brilliant and lively brush strokes in the secretary's velvet jacket only superficially describe its sheen, for the highlights thus created are misplaced for rational articulation, for consistent source of light, and even from the point of view of composition. The poses are awkward and the organization is hardly effectual: Berkeley is almost the least important figure. But the faces are well-painted; there is a certain briskness in the baby, though his mother and her friend seem only partially alive, and the color is gay and rich. Taken together with the best of Smibert's other portraits, this painting at least dimly reflects in the colonies the achievements of the European portrait school. Smibert's technical knowledge and his collection of classical models, ancient and modern, all played an important part in the development of American art. Smibert personally influenced Robert Feke, the first native-born artist in America, and his collections continued to have their effect after his death, not only on Copley but also on Allston and Trumbull, important artists in the next generation.

Very similar to Smibert's Berkeley picture is Robert Feke's *Isaac Royall and Family*, 1741 (PA 67; Illustration 2–39). In this painting the Boston merchant, the builder of the great house in Medford, and later a prominent Tory, is represented as a youth of twenty-two with his wife and child, and some female relatives.

2–39. Robert Feke, *Isaac Royall and Family*, 1741. Oil on canvas. 54⅝ x 77¾ inches. (The Fogg Art Museum, Harvard University, Cambridge, Massachusetts. Harvard University Law School Collection.)

Royall's position in the picture is the same as that of Berkeley in the Smibert painting, and the other figures are arranged around a carpet-covered table as in the earlier picture. But even though Feke was obviously emulating Smibert in composition, modeling, and the poses and attitudes of the figures, nevertheless the result is very different from the Berkeley picture. In Feke's painting the unity of Smibert's composition is broken by the isolation of each figure from the other and by the rejection of curved accents in the design. There is a much greater emphasis on line, and the modeling is inconsistent—Royall's own figure is practically flat, for instance. Where three-dimensionality is attempted it becomes almost block-like and has defined edges, as in the faces with their hard shadows and their almost metallic reflected light. But the most outstanding difference between the two pictures is the greater emphasis on pattern in the Feke. The "Turkey carpet," the linen, and details of costume are relatively unimportant in Smibert's picture. But Feke takes obvious delight in the design of the rug covering his table, in the linen, in the embroidered waist-coat, and above all, in the silhouette of Mr. Royall's hands and well-turned calf.

Another picture, the portrait of *Reverend Thomas Hiscox,* 1745 (PA 68), invites comparison with Smibert's *Nathaniel Byfield.* Again Feke's figure is lacking in three-dimensionality, is sharp, metallic, and basically linear in contrast to the well-rounded Byfield, whose portly image blends easily into the surrounding atmosphere.

Nothing definite is known about Feke's life (although many surmises have been made), except that he was married in Newport and was at one time a "mariner," as is indicated in his marriage license. But it is probable that he grew up on Long Island or somewhere in New England. In either place, the pictures with which he would have been familiar would have been those stemming from the late medieval, provincial portrait tradition; their characteristics of line, flat pattern, and careful observation of detail remain very much a part of his own work, whether he consciously wanted them to be or not. To compare the *Dean Berkeley* and *Isaac Royall* is to contrast an unexciting, competent hack work of early eighteenth-century English portraiture (from one of the dullest periods in the history of English art) with a picture that has individual character and real distinction. The combination of the then current European mode with the earlier colonial stylistic tradition resulted in the creation of a distinctively native style in Robert Feke's work, a style which was taken over and improved upon by Copley. In the Royall picture, the outline of the neck and hand of the woman to the extreme left, the silhouetted hands and cuffs of Royall himself, the pattern of his waistcoat and coat, and the meticulous threads of carpets and lace are all exceptionally sensitive. These qualities combine in an esthetic effect as rewarding as in any colonial painting since the Freake limner. But this is the opinion of modern taste. Feke himself would have been annoyed to have anything provincial discovered in his works, for he assiduously imitated what were to him more sophisticated models than those afforded by the local tradition. The series of portraits painted between 1741 and 1750 (the artist seems to have disappeared after that) are almost all of a piece in their desire to be overwhelmingly aristocratic. In these pictures, Feke supplements the influence of Smibert's later, more conventional style with imitations of the most elegant of English examples, known to him either through engravings or through an actual acquaintance with the originals, perhaps when he was a "mariner." His *Isaac Winslow,* c. 1748 (PA 49B), and *James Bowdoin II,* 1748 (PA 45B), stand in their silken flowered waistcoats and powdered wigs, gesturing emptily, characterless except for the appurtenances that make them gentlemen. His women have features so little distinguished from one another that they appear to be twins, standing or seated at the base of an unlikely column with their flowered satin dresses spread out decoratively over the lower part of the picture, as in the portraits of *Mrs. John Vinal* (?), c. 1748–1750 (PA 69), and *Mrs. James Bowdoin II,* 1748 (PA 46B).

But for all the mincing mannerisms of new world aristocracy in Feke's subjects, his style has certain virtues: hard, linear, exact, and patterned—characteristics indicating the persistence of the artist's colonial heritage in spite of all his efforts to be British.

The large, full-length portrait of the great landowner, *Brigadier-General Samuel Waldo*, 1748–1750 (?) (PA 70; Illustration 2–40), sums up Feke's characteristic single portraits, though it is the most pretentious of the lot. The figure is impersonal and aristocratic, attitudinizing in a landscape cared for like an English park, scarcely the wilds of North America. The hardness of modeling, the metallic highlights, the artificial though subtle color have a distinction which is entirely Feke's and which derives from the peculiar circumstances of his colonial environment. For, though the point of view is that of the English aristocracy, the manner remains American. It is in this piquant contradiction between purpose and effect that much of Feke's charm lies.

Though General Waldo's features have more character than those of most of Feke's sitters, the most interesting face that he painted is his own, which appears in the early *Self-Portrait*, c. 1730 (PA 65). It seems, indeed, an accurate representation of the face described by the Scotch diarist, Alexander Hamilton, who said of Feke, whose studio he visited in Newport, "This man has exactly the phiz of a painter, having a long, pale face, sharp nose, large eyes with which he looked upon you steadfastly, long, curled, black hair, a delicate, white hand and long fingers." [10] Not only is this picture unusual as being the most individualized of the artist's portraits, but it is one of the most charming paintings of the colonial era. This and the Royall picture remain his best work, though all have some distinction even if they do demonstrate a limited repertoire. But this last characteristic is only natural in a man who was said by Hamilton to be self-taught. In Feke, America can be said to have produced its first distinctive painter—and until that time its most distinguished.

While the example of Smibert was inspiring the development of a New England school, a painter of less ability and significance but of moderate competence, Gustavus Hesselius, was working in Philadelphia and Maryland. He ar-

2–40. Robert Feke, *Brigadier-General Samuel Waldo*, 1748–1750 (?). Oil on canvas. 96 x 59¼ inches. (Courtesy of The Bowdoin College Museum of Fine Arts, Brunswick, Maine.)

rived from Sweden in 1712, bringing with him a somewhat below-average norm of baroque portraiture, hardly above the artisan class. In fact, Hesselius advertised himself as a "ship, house and show board" painter, able also to execute "coats of arms for coaches, chaises, etc." [11] Yet his work has not the bold naïveté of the real artisan tradition. Nor is this lack compensated for by a grasp of the realism and "painterliness" of the great tradition which he reflected but dimly. But Hesselius' best portraits, though lacking convincing drawing and brilliant execution, are notably serious and honest in an era when the trappings of position were more important than the worth of the individual. His own *Self-Portrait* and the portrait of *Mrs. Lydia Hesselius*, c. 1740 (PA 53, PA 54), are cases in point; but his masterpieces are the portraits of two Indian chiefs, *Tishcohan* and *Lapowinska* (*PA 52; Illustration 2–41), painted in 1735 at the behest of the proprietor John Penn, who was treating with them for their lands. Both Indians are painted with sympathy, but the troubled face of Lapowinska, puzzled by the negotiations which he did not understand but rightly suspected were not to the advantage of his people, shows particular insight on the part of the artist. Unfortunately, the psychological penetration is not matched by the form, for the drawing lacks surety and the modeling is hazy and hesitant.

Besides portraits, Hesselius painted mythological pieces, apparently the first such pictures in the colonies. Whether they were executed for some patron is not known. If they were, the presence of such an advanced aristocratic taste would be an interesting commentary on the society of the southern colonies, though the fact that they were painted in America at all is not without significance. However, their chief importance lies in their being historical curiosities. Both paintings, a *Bacchanale* (Pennsylvania Academy) and a *Bacchus and Ariadne*, undated (*PA 50), are remotely derived from seventeenth-century classicizing models, but they are so marred by awkwardness of composition and drawing and by inadequacies of anatomical knowledge that they are travesties of the grand style. But in the portraits he painted in Philadelphia and the South, Hesselius left a tradition of moderately competent craftsmanship which was to be carried on by his son John. The latter, however, was less influenced by his father than by the next generation of immigrants.

This group, the successors of Smibert and the elder Hesselius, painted in the rococo style, an extension or corollary of the baroque of Van Dyck and his followers, and characterized by a refinement of baroque qualities. Movement in the composition is still curvilinear, but the curves have been broken down into smaller ones, giving a highly decorative effect. The human figure is more elongated, graceful, and

2–41. Gustavus Hesselius, *Lapowinska*, 1735. Oil on canvas. 33 x 25 inches. (The Historical Society of Pennsylvania, Philadelphia.)

insubstantial; its solidity is broken up by highlights. This glancing play of light comprises a further decorative effect, vivifying the composition and giving greater opportunity for brilliant and scintillating brush strokes than was the case even in the baroque. The rococo style, more adaptable than the earlier one to the representation of refined elegance, sometimes sinks into simpering, overgraceful attitudinizing. Yet the lightness and gaiety of the effect often compensate for this superficiality. For an illustration of the differences (and the similarities) between the two styles at their most typical and on their highest level, a comparison should be made between Sir Peter Lely's *Elizabeth, Countess of Kildare* (Illustration 1–13) and Thomas Gainsborough's *The Honourable Mrs. Graham*, 1767 (Illustration 2–49). In looking back at Smibert and Feke, it will be seen that the division between baroque and rococo in their styles is not too distinct, for both artists are in a sense transitional. Especially in Feke the decorative effects of foliage and highlights reflect some rococo qualities, though the solidity of the figures is more baroque. But these general stylistic divisions of European painting must not be used too categorically in American art, for Copley, the greatest painter of the rococo if this word is a historical as well as a stylistic definition, is stylistically hardly rococo at all.

The second generation of artistic immigrants in the eighteenth century were no more esthetically distinguished than their predecessors. (Had they been better, in all probability they would have been successful at home and not have tried their luck in the remote colonies.) Their significance is therefore largely historical in that they painted certain portraits in certain places and influenced certain better or more interesting artists. Yet, though these painters are intrinsically much less important in the history of art than are the best of their British contemporaries, the rococo inheritors of the Van Dyck tradition, their work has a certain charm. Indeed, most of their portraits are pleasing in a superficial, gracile way, and their mincing and fashionable refinement must certainly have been satisfactory to their owners.

Charles Bridges, whom William Byrd of Westover recommended to his fellow planters as "a man of good family forced to earn his bread," [12] painted in Virginia in the 1740's in an agreeable but unexciting Lely-like manner with some rococo charm, as can be seen in his *Mrs. Maria Taylor Byrd of Westover*, 1724 (?) (PA 37). Most of the portraits attributed to him have a superficial assurance which his inferior local imitators could not quite achieve. John Wollaston arrived in the colonies in 1749 and painted first in New York and later in the South, recording the faces of Carrolls and Calverts in Maryland, of Randolphs and Byrds in the Old Dominion, and settling for a few months in Charleston until he left for India in 1758. His style is easier to identify than that of Bridges because of a mannerism peculiar to him: the employment of almost oriental, almond-shaped eyes.

Less competent than Bridges, his somewhat puffy forms and awkward articulation are hardly compensated for by his only moderate ability to paint such eighteenth-century essentials as lace and ribbons. Typical of his work are his portraits of the Lewis family: *Warner Lewis, Mrs. Warner Lewis*, and *Warner Lewis II and Rebecca*, c. 1756 (PA 60A, PA 61A, *PA 62A). Jeremiah Theus, a Swiss, arrived in Charleston in 1739, not long after the death of Henrietta Johnston, and dominated the Carolinian school until his death at the outbreak of the Revolution. More workmanlike than Wollaston but with a plodding stolidity which somewhat effaced his rococo delicacy, he managed to give some sheen and glamour to the clothes into which his solid figures were thrust, as in his portraits of *Mrs. Peter Manigault (Elizabeth Wragg)*, 1757 (PA 56), and *Elizabeth Rothmaler*, 1757 (PA 55). Charleston, with its fine architecture and urbane graces, deserved better than Wollaston and Theus. But it must be remembered that many of the southerners were painted abroad or ordered their pictures from English studios, since a picture painted from a written description would do provided it was properly aristocratic in attitude and dress.

William Williams, who painted in Philadelphia, is a more rewarding figure. Though a certain naïveté emerges from his somewhat grandiose compositions, replete with gardens, ruins, and statuary, and though his figures in their very shiny silks and satins are not too accurately drawn, his incident-filled canvases with their rococo colors have genuine charm. His *William Hall* (PA 36B) and *Deborah Hall* (PA 48), both painted in 1766, are very pleasing in design and in their gay color. Williams introduced the conversation piece (a group in an informal situation or arrangement) to America. His *John Wiley, His Mother and Sisters*, 1771 (*PA 49), is an interestingly arranged group in a landscape which is not too contrived, while his *Husband and Wife in a Landscape*, 1775 (Illustration 2–42), though somewhat unconvincing in anatomy and mannered in gesture, is nevertheless a valid characterization and, as usual with Williams, delightfully decorative.

2–42. William Williams, *Husband and Wife in a Landscape*, 1775. Oil on canvas. 32¼ x 38 inches. (Courtesy, Henry Francis du Pont Winterthur Museum, Winterthur, Delaware.)

A more important figure than Williams was Joseph Blackburn, who landed in Boston about 1755, shortly after Smibert's death, and stepped into that artist's shoes. Almost as empty and relatively as incompetent as the rest of the group, he does have a lighter and more graceful touch, and gay, charming color, as can be observed in his best-known work, *Isaac Winslow and His Family*, 1755 (PA 57). Though his vivacious, multicurvilinear compositions and his mincing poses are sometimes almost a caricature of the rococo style, as seen in his portrait of the children *Elizabeth and James Bowdoin*, 1760 (PA 39B), his facility in the new taste brought him

many sitters. Occasionally he executed a more solid portrait, as in the *Mrs. Theodore Atkinson (Hannah Wentworth)*, 1760 (PA 59A), and *Lord Geoffrey Amherst*, 1758 (Illustration 2–43), in which the coloristic richness and subtlety of modeling and light reflect the best of the rococo tradition. The influence of Blackburn's easy and superficial skill might have ruined the young Copley if the latter's artistic personality had been less strong. In point of fact, Blackburn himself benefited in some of his later pictures from the strong characterization of the youthful Massachusetts-born artist.

All of these portraitists from abroad display

2–43. Joseph Blackburn, *Lord Geoffrey Amherst*, 1758. Oil on canvas. 31½ x 26⅛ inches. (Collection of Frederic R. Pratt. Photo courtesy of the Metropolitan Museum of Art, New York.)

only the surface refinements of the period and not its solider virtues. Their work could be summed up in very much the same terms that Gilbert Stuart, a much better painter, used to describe the typical, run-of-the-mill British portrait: "How delicately the face is drawn. Did you ever see such rich satin, and the ermine is wonderful in its finish. And, by Jove, the thing has a head!" [13]

Of the native-born colonial artists of the mid-century and shortly thereafter, John Hesselius, John Greenwood, and Joseph Badger are the most outstanding. John, Gustavus Hesselius' son, is the least distinguished of the three, but the only one of importance in the South. His early work is like that of his father and is still somewhat influenced by the pseudo-grandeur of Kuhn's elaborate settings. His portrait of the young and aristocratic *Charles Calvert and Colored Slave*, 1761 (PA 80), recalls Kuhn's

Darnall portraits and improves on the earlier artist's limited ability to paint a convincing figure. But, fascinated by Wollaston's easy rococo glamour, Hesselius later gave up the somewhat pedestrian manner of his father to paint portraits in Philadelphia, Annapolis, and Virginia; these are perhaps a little too pretty and superficially fashionable. *Mrs. Richard Galloway, Jr., of Cedar Park, Maryland*, 1764 (PA 81), for instance, is all sheen and elegance.

Joseph Badger, at first a house painter and glazier, became Boston's most solid portraitist after Feke, until the rise of Copley. He derived his forthright style from a combination of the workmanlike limner tradition with the greater sophistication of Smibert and Feke. Though never giving up the homely virtues of the sign painter, he borrowed his poses from his betters, and infused his sitters with a kind of dogged, wooden dignity that is reminiscent of the preceding century. His *Captain John Larrabee*, c. 1760 (PA 51B), stands in an elegant pose that does not quite ring true because, though it derives from Feke, it is not accompanied by his refinement of manner. Instead, a primitive vigor of drawing and design breaks through. In his portrait of *Mrs. John Edwards*, 1750–1760 (PA 50B), the silhouette-like treatment of the face, arms, and chair seems more accidental than planned —the consequence of a lingering, older way of seeing rather than a deliberate exploitation of the design (such as Feke would have done). Yet Badger's faces and figures have more personality than any of those painted by more stylish artists. His pictures of children are real and charming, and reveal somewhat more the influence of the encroaching rococo than do his representations of adults. The outstanding example is the portrait of his grandson, *James Badger*, c. 1760 (PA 73), more engaging in its still somewhat awkward rigidity than the Bowdoin children by Blackburn, for all their prettiness.

John Greenwood, painting during the last years of Feke's productivity and the early years of Badger's, is perhaps the most interesting of the mid-century artists, excepting Feke. The son of a Boston merchant and shipbuilder,

2–44. John Greenwood, *Sea Captains Carousing at Surinam,* c. 1775. Oil on canvas. 37¾ x 75¼ inches. (Courtesy of the City Art Museum of St. Louis.)

young John, after his father died leaving no estate, apprenticed himself to a typical artisan of the period, who was a house painter, printer, engraver, and gravestone cutter. But he soon started to paint portraits, of which he did a number with great verve and in a variety of manners in Boston during the 1740's and continued until he left for the Caribbean in 1752. This was a year or two before Blackburn personally brought the rococo manner to the Massachusetts metropolis, so that Greenwood's sometimes rococo style must have derived from aspects of Feke and from engravings after such early rococo English portraitists as Thomas Hudson. His most notable picture is a portrait of *The Greenwood-Lee Family Group,* c. 1747 (PA 74), obviously patterned after the Berkeley and Royall pictures, but very different in effect. The artist seems to delight in his new-found facility, enlivening his composition with a spirited and dynamic rococo composition and with lively color and smiling faces.

Greenwood was also the author of *Sea Captains Carousing at Surinam,* c. 1755 (PA 76; Illustration 2–44), a delightful genre picture (perhaps the first of this kind by a colonial artist) of no great esthetic value but of considerable topical interest. This Caribbean scene is lit dramatically by candlelight, exposing some figures and hiding others in darkness, and casting bold and interestingly shaped shadows. All manner of figures are portrayed: drinking, dancing, pantomiming, being sick, sleeping, waiting on tables. Though the composition is as chaotic as the scene being represented, certain areas show a nice sense of pattern, and the whole is very lively.

Sea Captains Carousing was undoubtedly inspired by Hogarth's engravings of tavern life from *The Rake's Progress;* but this influence is so nicely adapted to the local scene, there is so much acute observation, and such flashes of design are evident in certain passages that it is a pity no other of Greenwood's West Indian pictures has turned up. A potentially very interesting artist was lost, for John Greenwood, after painting a few portraits in Surinam (it is said), went to Holland to deal in pictures and ended his days as a wealthy purveyor of old masters in London.

Copley and the Later Eighteenth-Century Portraitists

John Singleton Copley is the one really important artist produced by the American colonies. He was born in Boston in 1738 and started to paint as an adolescent under the tutelage of his stepfather, a mediocre English portraitist and engraver. He also learned much from the example of Smibert and Feke, Greenwood and Badger (the latter his rival during his early years), and Blackburn, who was a passing influence. Copley was, of course, also familiar with the earlier New England school, although he seems to have consciously ignored it. Out of this limited artistic environment Copley took all that he could use and, after a short time of trying out different modes, he settled into his own manner. Copley's style before he went to England is one of the great achievements of American culture. No other figure in the arts can match it, and in other fields only our revolutionary political thinkers can equal his distinction. Yet the moment he found himself in Europe, in the presence of the paintings of the masters of the past and of his own generation, he jettisoned his American style. Like Feke, he recognized in his own artistic environment only its lacks and limitations and was unaware of its advantages. For, the isolation from the great tradition, which Copley regretted, carried with it the necessity to teach himself to work at the solution of artistic problems without the benefit of the methods and formulas handed down by custom and precedent. At the same time, it forced him to depend mostly on colonial work, the best of which already had a local flavor. Therefore, in spite of himself, Copley became an American painter.

The young Copley was fortunate to have Peter Pelham as his stepfather. The technical training he received before the latter's death when the boy was thirteen was probably as exacting and as beneficial as any he could have acquired in this country, because an engraver must be precise and extremely careful, and know his tools. Further, by the magic of genius, Copley turned this limited technique, with its hard, metallic quality and its emphasis on line and black and white, into a definite stylistic advantage. His English critics found his work hard and "liney," but these very qualities are at the basis of his personal style. Pelham's colors in the few portraits he painted are raw, bright, and not blended, as seen in *Reverend Cotton Mather*, 1727 (PA 32). But even this harsh chromatic quality (combined with the definite modeling of the engraver) was used to advantage by Copley; though he toned down his hues and related them sensitively, they remain local and isolated and do not permeate and unify the whole canvas, as in the baroque tradition.

When the young artist was about fifteen he painted the children of Christopher Gore, *The Gore Children*, c. 1753 (PA 84A), in a kind of Feke-like elegance of pose and impersonality of feature, without the awkwardness of Badger but also without the latter's naïve and wooden honesty. Three years later, after several essays in Feke's grander manner, supplemented by the example of English engravings, Copley painted *Ann Tyng (Mrs. Thomas Smelt)*, 1756 (PA 86), showing the influence of Blackburn's insubstantial and frothy figures as well as his coy artificiality of arrangement. Early pictures such as these must have given great satisfaction to the mere boy who was equaling, perhaps even excelling, the best of Boston's older painters. In the next few years Copley improved in subtlety of modeling; his bodies are adequately suggested beneath their clothing, losing that ambiguity as to whether a surface is concave or convex which is so confusing in Greenwood or Blackburn—or even in Badger, for all that artist's solidity. Copley also developed a sense of exact observation which he conveyed with a precise outline as well as by careful modeling. His portraits of the silversmiths *Nathaniel Hurd, Portrait A*, 1765–1770 (PA 98, PA 99), and *Paul Revere*, 1765–1770 (PA 66B, PA 67B), demonstrate these qualities admirably, especially the detail of the hand and teapot in the *Paul Revere*. The artist's attitude toward these sitters is forthright and unassuming. No excuses are made for Paul Revere's trade nor for his shirt-sleeves. Yet Copley could be as class-conscious as any English painter. He did not hesitate to employ

2–45. After Sir Joshua Reynolds, *Lady Caroline Russell.* Mezzotint by MacArdell. 14⅝ x 9⅞ inches. (Courtesy of Prints Division, New York Public Library.)

2–46. John Singleton Copley, *Mrs. Jerathmiel Bowers,* c. 1765. Oil on canvas. 49¾ x 39¾ inches. (The Metropolitan Museum of Art, New York. Rogers Fund, 1915.)

fashionable English models for his own purposes. For instance, he used a print after Sir Joshua Reynolds' *Lady Caroline Russell* (Illustration 2–45) for his portrait of *Mrs. Jerathmiel Bowers,* c. 1765 (PA 89; Illustration 2–46), changing only the face. Even the spaniel in both laps is the same.

Though many of Copley's portraits, especially of women, in the late 1750's and early 1760's are affected and overelaborate, some of them are not so at all, suggesting that it was the taste of the sitters rather than that of the artist which dictated the manner. Copley turned easily from the portrayal of fashionable Anglican and Tory ladies, dressed in their mundane frippery, to the depiction of plain Yankee women, wives of Puritan clergymen, clad in their homespun and kerchiefs.

Perhaps the outstanding picture of Copley's middle period, among a number of distinguished masculine portraits, is that of *Epes Sargent,* c. 1760 (PA 87, PA 87A), a Gloucester merchant and representative to the Great and General Assembly. Convincing and sympathetic in characterization, the figure is realized with a surety of technique which is that of a master. The hard outline and slickness of surface, sometimes oppressive in Copley's more mechanical renderings, is here softened by a feeling for the paint, which he applied thickly and richly.

The culminating period of Copley's work is from 1766 until the painter's departure for his continental tour eight years later. Though he had to execute an occasional commission in the grand manner [such as the two huge full-length pictures of *Mr. Jeremiah Lee* and *Mrs. Jeremiah Lee,* 1769 (PA 72B, PA 73B), painted to hang in the wealthy merchant's mansion], Copley is sufficiently sure of himself and his popularity as the leading portraitist of his time not to feel required to cater too much to his sitters' fancies, should they disagree with his own point of view. One after another the leaders of the community came to sit for him, and all of them were portrayed in Copley's sober and unaffected manner. His subjects all seem to be individuals, important in their own right and not only because of some lucky chance of birth. John Hancock and Sam Adams were among them, as well as the great merchants, Thomas and Nicholas Boylston. Mr. and Mrs. Thomas Mifflin came all the way from Philadelphia to Boston to be painted in 1773 (PA 105) in a picture wherein the rigorous and exacting realism of the artist still permits his subjects to be portrayed in a relaxed and intimate manner.

The portraits of *Isaac Smith* and *Mrs. Isaac Smith,* 1769 (PA 94, PA 95), demonstrate one

2–47. John Singleton Copley, *Dr. Sylvester Gardiner,* c. 1770. Oil on canvas. 50 x 40 inches. (Collection of Robert Hallowell Gardiner, Gardiner, Maine. Photo courtesy of Mr. Gardiner.)

of Copley's greatest accomplishments: his ability to blend the rather stiff poses and patterned compositions of the earlier tradition (probably preferred by some of his sitters) with a firm grasp of structure and depth and extremely careful detail. This meticulousness becomes sometimes almost uncanny, resembling what has sometimes been called "magic realism" today. Such a picture is that of *Mrs. Ezekiel Goldthwait,* 1771 (*PA 103), where the representation of a bowl of fruit and its reflection on a highly polished surface is a triumph of the love of careful detail seen in the portrait of *Paul Revere* and, before Copley, in the paintings of Feke and of the Freake limner. *Ezekiel Goldthwait*'s portrait of the same date (PA 102) is equally convincing, but the *Dr. Sylvester Gardiner,* c. 1770 (Illustration 2–47), a London-educated surgeon and a great Tory landowner, is outstanding among Copley's masculine portraits. The observer feels the accomplished authority in the artist's easy portrayal of the intelligent face and relaxed pose, well-realized in space and monumental in its forthright dignity.

Each of these portraits is a new solution to a new problem. A large part of Copley's genius consisted of perseverance. He worked with a subject for fifteen or sixteen sittings at an average of six hours at a stretch. This conscientiousness exhibits not only determination to bring the visual world to terms but also a love of every facet of that visual reality, for Copley could not have borne working at his subject in this meticulous way without a fondness for what he was doing. The mystery is that each picture, though it is indeed a painstaking reconstruction of reality, does not overwhelm the observer with a feeling of weariness at the amount of effort involved. Instead, the result gives an impression of being natural and unforced.

The portrait of *Mrs. Thomas Boylston,* 1766 (Illustration 2–48), painted at the beginning of the artist's most accomplished and productive period, sums up Copley's best and most characteristic work. Though a column, a tassel, and a great curtain appear in the composition as symbols of her social position, the old lady sits in a chair which obviously needs reupholstering,

2–48. John Singleton Copley, *Mrs. Thomas Boylston,* 1766. Oil on canvas. 49 x 38 inches. (The Fogg Art Museum, Harvard University, Cambridge, Massachusetts.)

personal style of meticulous realism rendered with sharply modeled linearism and some abstract pattern. Copley's pictures are very different from the contemporary British school he was attempting to emulate at least in style if not in manner. English eighteenth-century portraiture in the hands of Reynolds, Gainsborough, or Raeburn was the culmination of the tradition begun by Van Dyck, with its emphasis on the position of the sitter in the class hierarchy. It was the grand style of the baroque brought to its ultimate rococo refinement of coloristic and atmospheric charm.

2–49. Thomas Gainsborough, *The Honourable Mrs. Graham,* 1775. Oil on canvas. 93½ x 60¼ inches. (National Galleries of Scotland, Edinburgh.)

as the little depression in the back indicates. This homely detail is matched in the sitter's face by a conspicuous mole which the artist only partially tries to hide with a shadow. The wife of a saddler and shopkeeper, and the mother of eight children, Mrs. Boylston looks out of the canvas benignly, hoping to please her two sons who have become the wealthiest merchants in Boston and who undoubtedly are paying Mr. Copley for her image. Perhaps the drapery has too metallic a sheen for some tastes, but the figure beneath is well indicated and the texture and quality in the olive-green cloth are well realized. The brown, old skin, the snapping black eyes, and the still-dark hair under the bonnet reflect the kind of vitality which helped Mrs. Boylston survive eight eighteenth-century confinements. The *Mrs. Boylston* shows admirably Copley's insight into character, and demonstrates in a distinguished way his very

A comparison of *Mrs. Thomas Boylston* with Gainsborough's *The Honourable Mrs. Graham*, 1775 (Illustration 2–49), demonstrates the differences in the point of view of painter and sitter and in the manner or style of the artists. Mrs. Boylston is an individual, important in the merchant aristocracy of Boston, but she is made to be no different from what she is, a plain woman of character whose sons have come up in the world. Mrs. Graham is portrayed very successfully as "the honourable." There is no doubt as to her social position, but what kind of a woman she was no one can tell—except that she was probably not ugly. The observer feels that he knows Mrs. Boylston; Mrs. Graham is merely a symbol. He feels that Mrs. Bolyston could go to the kitchen to supervise the preparation of a clam chowder; Mrs. Graham would not know where the kitchen was, let alone how to use it.

On the level of stylistic analysis, the difference between the two pictures is equally marked. Copley's figure has bulk and weight and is isolated from the background by a strong defining line. This line is also important to the design within the figure, being the means by which the parts of the body and the various planes of the drapery are differentiated. The line describes and models at the same time; the latter function is emphatically supported by the modeling in tones, but always controlled by the hard outline. There is a rational consistency of planes in interrelation, building up to an effect of boldly static monumentality. Gainsborough's figure, in contrast, loses its solidity through a brilliant and complex play of ephemeral light and shade which dances and shimmers in a soft maze of bows, ruffles, and feathers. The over-elegant and affected manner and the elongated proportions of the human figure add to the impression of refined disembodiment. Line has disappeared and with it the isolation of the figure from surrounding space. An evanescent interplay of light and shade unite the already unreal figure with its envelope of air. The liveliness of this interplay, with its curvilinear accents against the larger curves of the design as a whole, makes the composition nervously dynamic, in great contrast to the solid and static

clarity of the Copley. The Gainsborough is a species of brilliant decoration achieved by a scintillating, glancing brush and a chromatic variety and subtlety—a rococo refinement of the great coloristic tradition of the baroque.

Though in much British portraiture there was often a greater emphasis on characterization than in this Gainsborough, and though there existed a more solid, classical kind of painting (witness Reynolds), nevertheless, the *Mrs. Graham* reflects the aristocratic bias of British painting, as well as its stylistic character, in not too exaggerated a form. The conclusion to be drawn from this comparison is inevitably that there is a difference between English art and American art. It would be chauvinistic to claim that the latter is better. Indeed, many would prefer the skill and enchantments of the Gainsborough to the more stolid virtues of the Copley. The two are simply different.

The reasons for Copley's differences are not difficult to find. In its attitude toward the sitter, the American picture could be said to be democratic. Though Copley could, on occasion, portray all the airs and graces demanded by some of his Tory sitters, his best and most characteristic portrayals are of more rugged individuals who are convincing in themselves without the need of props. These are men of a generation of whom a royal governor complained that they did not raise their hats in the presence of himself, the representative of the king. The hardy Yankee individualism that sought and won freedom was an American trait, and Copley's portraits of both men and women reflect it.

Copley's style was as much the consequence of his artistic environment as his point of view was the result of his social surroundings. Try as he would, it was not until he made the "grand tour" and finally arrived in England that Copley was able to rid himself of what Benjamin West called the hardness and overmeticulousness of his drawing, his "lineyness." Yet, these are the very qualities that help to distinguish Copley's work. Together with a love of pattern and detail, they also distinguish what we may be given license to call an American tradition, since it culminated in so important an artist as Copley.

The Freake limner and the best of the primitives displayed linearism and a close observation of detail. The self-taught Feke had these qualities together with his own particular block-like and metallic interpretation of Smibert's more painterly three-dimensionality. Copley added to this tradition the technical training of engraving and the study of imported prints, both of which fortified his linearism and his emphatic modeling. Though he de-emphasized the obvious pattern of the earlier painters, he retained enough abstract, formal effect in his defining outline and his contrasts of darks and lights to be closer to these older artists than to his English contemporaries with their broken up, all-over decorative effects. (It is an interesting and curious fact that the fusion of these various influences in Copley created in his work a stylistic character hardly different from that of the Renaissance. The analysis of the style seen in the portrait of *Mrs. Boylston* could be readily applied to the work of Holbein or of any other Renaissance artist in contradistinction to that of painters in the baroque or rococo periods.) From the work of Copley, it seems quite clear that there is no longer a question of whether there is a genuine colonial art in America or merely a second-rate English school.

Copley's career in England began when *Henry Pelham (The Boy With the Squirrel)*, c. 1765 (PA 96, PA 97), was shown at The Royal Academy in London. This typically "liney" picture is a tenderly observed portrait of the artist's half-brother, still a boy, intent on playing with a flying squirrel on a shiny tabletop. The qualities of this picture, though antithetical to the English school, aroused great interest and established Copley's reputation; even Sir Joshua Reynolds urged him to come to England before his manner was "fixed by working in" his "own little way in Boston."[14] Copley left America in 1774, arriving in England the following year after a tour of the Continent.

Married to the daughter of Richard Clarke, a wealthy merchant to whom the tea thrown overboard in the Boston Tea Party had been consigned, Copley had been torn between Tories and Patriots, even acting as a go-between for the British and the Bostonians in attempts to resolve differences before the Revolution. When he finally left for Europe it must have been with mixed feelings as an American. However, he never returned, but established himself and his family so successfully in England that he made it possible for his son John Singleton Copley, Jr. (later Lord Lyndhurst) to become Lord Chief Justice.

Copley's artistic career in London was a distinguished one, but it is not properly part of the history of American art. His style partook of the European breadth and fluidity he had envied, and his portraits, like that of *Mrs. Seymour Fort*, c. 1776 (PA 100), while they retain much of their keen observation and individuality, become enriched with a more painterly and colorful technique. The "English" Copley is principally important in the world history of art for his lively paintings of topical events, such as the exciting *Watson and the Shark*, 1778 (PA 109), recording a near-fatal accident in Havana harbor, and for his large canvases depicting contemporary and earlier events in British history. These pictures, patronized by royalty, attracted such curiosity that they had to be exhibited in tents to accommodate the crowds.

Though the later Copley became celebrated as an English artist, his American work is also much admired today. When the eighteenth-century American artists who preceded him are re-examined in the light of his accomplishments, the extent of their contribution to the formation of the American tradition should have some bearing on our judgment of them. Thus, Feke is more significant by this measure than is Smibert, and even the good and plodding Badger is as interesting as the more various, inconstant Greenwood.

Certain other artists of the late eighteenth century have only recently been identified and become admired. Provincials they were, men subjected to the same artistic environment, with all its limitations, as was Copley; but they lacked his genius and they had more resistance to international fashion—or less ability to reconstruct it from verbal descriptions or from prints. Wil-

2–50. (Attributed to) William Johnston, *Jabez Hamlin*, 1760's. Oil on canvas. 50 x 41 inches. (The Connecticut Historical Society, Hartford; photo courtesy of Frick Art Reference Library.)

liam Johnston is perhaps the most important because of his influence on a group of painters who bridge the colonial period and that of the early republic. It is known that he painted in Connecticut in the 1760's and was probably the author of a group of portraits originating in Hartford, New Haven, and New London. Typical is the *Jabez Hamlin* (Illustration 2–50), a portrait of the mayor of Middletown, Connecticut, which has been attributed to him. Characteristic in this picture are the bold silhouette design, the emphasis on line, the rather abrupt modeling, the attention paid to detail (as seen in the book, table, folded paper, and inkwell), the pose of the figure, and the intense characterization of the face. These qualities were also in Copley's work, to a lesser or greater degree. The design is bolder and more obvious in the

Johnston, more like the earlier painters with their greater emphasis on pattern; the line is less subtle and descriptively less competent than in Copley. The drawing, on the whole, is inferior in its implied knowledge of anatomy, and the modeling is too abrupt, lacking the more sophisticated transitions of Copley. The realism in the pose and the face is exaggerated into what amounts almost to caricature, and the detail is not so expert or painstaking as in Copley. The characteristics of Johnston's work suggest a closer association with Copley than merely the general influence that would be inevitable in the case of such a prominent artist. In any case, the same factors that contributed to the making of Copley are present in an artist like Johnston. (William Johnston may have been the son of Thomas Johnston, the artisan and portrait limner who trained Greenwood; in that case his connection with the Boston school would be explained.)

John Durand better represents the artisan tradition than Johnston, for he remained seemingly quite satisfied with his provincial style. It is known that he painted in New York during the late 1760's and in Connecticut in 1772; afterward he returned to New York, and then worked in Virginia until the end of the Revolution—the typical itinerant limner. His *Rapalje Children*, c. 1769 (PA 127), is wonderfully designed with a strong sign painter's outline, a vigorous sense of pattern, and a delightful laying on of flat color—though the mouths simper a little in unsuccessful emulation of some foreign-born artist like Blackburn.

Among others who could be mentioned in this group of artists characterized by an American style—deliberate or unconscious, as the case may be—is John Mare. His portrait of *John Keteltas*, 1767 (PA 82), has the rigidity characteristic of the somewhat primitive artist, with the hard, exact linearism and modeling and the exquisite attention to detail which are the hallmarks of the group. (Mare's detail is so precise that he even records a fly on the sitter's cuff in the most illusionistic manner.) Samuel King of Newport could also be mentioned in this group, though a typical portrait, that of *Reverend John*

Eliot, 1779 (PA 142), is not as meticulous or "liney." But by far the best of these later contemporaries of Copley, though still less professional than he, was Winthrop Chandler of Woodstock, in provincial northeastern Connecticut. Here, except for a brief sojourn in neighboring Worcester, Massachusetts, he spent his uneventful life, a house-painter by profession but occasionally painting portraits of his friends and relatives. Chandler was influenced by Johnston, as can be seen in the similarity of his poses and the repetition of some of his motifs, and probably through Johnston by Copley, though he may have gone to see the latter's work in Boston. Chandler compensated for his lesser competence in the subtleties of realism by a strong sense of design and an expressiveness of drawing which are extraordinary in their ability to characterize his sitter through physiognomy and pose. His *Reverend Ebenezer Devotion,* 1770 (*PA 95B; Illustration 2–51), is probably his best and one of his most ambitious portraits. The pastor of Scotland, Connecticut, sits in an exaggerated pose, with his legs parted like Jabez Hamlin and his figure silhouetted against a great case of books. (Among the legible titles, besides the *Concordances* and *Sermons,* are works by Locke, Newton's *Optics,* and the *Spectator.*) The boldness of the composition, the expressive drawing of the figure, and the incisiveness of the characterization of the rural divine make this one of the outstanding works of the eighteenth century. The effectiveness of the painting is not due to mere accidents of unsophisticated primitivism; Chandler is far from naïve in this portrait and in others, including that of *Mrs. Ebenezer Devotion,* 1770 (*PA 96B). He knew what he was doing within the limitations of his technique.

Artists of the caliber of Copley and, to a lesser extent, Feke and Chandler, are outstanding in any history of art. Even when we deal with craftsmen like Johnston and Durand, in contrast to more conventionally accomplished painters such as Blackburn, there is a certain significance in the individuality of their style which in its abstract qualities of design appeals to our contemporary taste more than the facility of lesser Europeans or of those who trained them.

2–51. Winthrop Chandler, *Reverend Ebenezer Devotion,* 1770. Oil on canvas. 55 x 43¾ inches. (Brookline Historical Society, Brookline, Massachusetts; photo courtesy of Museum of Fine Arts, Boston.)

Painting Other Than Portraiture

Though portrait painting was by far the most important of the colonial branches of painting, we should not ignore the fact that there were others. An artist of Copley's standing could rely on his portraits for a living, but the limner who was primarily an artisan had to paint more than faces. In addition to house-painting and the execution of the usual signs and heraldic devices, an artisan or amateur tried his hand at landscape, genre, and occasionally even allegorical or decorative wall painting. In eighteenth-century England there was ample precedent for all these branches of art. Landscape painting had come into favor during the seventeenth century, and was thoroughly established by the eighteenth. Genre painting, derived largely from Dutch sources, made frequent appearances, and was seen at its best in Hogarth. Wall decoration was less prevalent than on the Continent, yet a number of palaces and great houses were decorated in the pompous baroque manner of allegory.

In America, all of these kinds of painting were reflected only dimly. Genre rarely appeared; a unique painting in this category is Greenwood's *Sea Captains Carousing at Surinam*. A few others exist, most of them executed as overmantel panels, but they are so rare as to be curiosities. Their depictions are crude, and because they are not primarily decorations but representations of events, the traditional skills of the artisans who probably executed them were not up to coping with such complexities as groups of persons represented convincingly in space.

Because in the colonies there were no palatial wall surfaces requiring decoration, this branch of painting, rare enough in England, was neglected in America. Though John Durand advertised himself as willing to be a "history" painter, there is little evidence of anything of this kind by him or anyone else. Only one example can be cited, and though it has no esthetic quality to speak of, its rarity and the subject matter treated are curious enough to be mentioned. This is a scheme of decoration comprising several scenes and painted by more than one hand in the McPhedris-Warner House in Portsmouth, New Hampshire, c. 1750 (PA 132, PA 133). The earlier group, copied crudely from engravings, represents two Mohawk chiefs who had been taken to London and feted there with royal honors; the others depict Sir William Pepperell and, oddly enough, *Abraham and Isaac*. But these pictures are so crudely executed that they lack even the decorative charm of the sign painter's bold, linear design and his patterned use of color.

The more usual decorative painting consisted of small panels with conventional but charming motifs of flowers and plants, usually comprising some elements of folk tradition, though an unusually elegant decoration in the Vernon House in Newport, consisting of quite competent lacquered panels in the Chinese manner, exhibits a training and competence unusual in the colo-

nies. In discussing decorative painting it must not be forgotten how important non-representational ornamentation was. The skill of housepainting was a very different one from today. The man who painted interiors in "shining colors"—that is, in successive transparent glazes—was no mean craftsman. The graining of wood and other imitative techniques, such as marbleizing, could become very complex. The *tour de force* accomplishments of some of the "paynterstayners" and "grainers" were indeed remarkable, as can be seen in a room from Marmion, Virginia (PA 131), and in many another.

Landscape was the most frequently painted subject after portraits. It appeared fairly early in the century, for Nathaniel Emmons' obituary in the *Boston Newsletter* of May 29, 1740, mentions that "Apelles" as having painted not only "faces" but "rivers, banks, and rural scenes." Gustavus Hesselius, in addition to portrait painting and his artisan activities, is said to have done landscapes, and Theus also published abroad that he could do "landscapes of all sizes." [15] The versatile William Williams, besides executing portraits and conversation pieces as well as "teaching the different branches of drawing and to sound the Hautboy, German and common flutes," [16] did landscapes and "cow pieces." But whatever these artists did in this genre is lost. The topographical view was apparently one of the more prominent aspects of landscape art in the colonies. "Perspective views" of "Gentlemen's County Seats" were advertised, but only one has turned up: on the wall at Mount Holly near Annapolis in Maryland there is a rather inadequate representation of the house and a bird's-eye map. Though Smibert wrote on one occasion that he was "diverting [himself] with some things in a landskip way," [17] and though an advertiser mentions landscapes in gold frames by a "genuine painter," suggesting the possibility of the existence of at least one artist with more than amateur or artisan skill in this department of painting, nothing of professional character has been found. There are some charming odd examples here and there, such as a *Landscape* on a wooden panel probably meant for an overmantel decoration, c. 1775–1800 (PA 130);

or a similar wooden panel in the Pennsylvania Hospital in Philadelphia, *Landscape With Cow,* 1749–1752 (PA 113), a potpourri of castles, windmills, ships riding at anchor, fishermen, and a cow all topsy-turvy in a swatch of foliage —the work of the youthful Benjamin West. Such decorative landscapes appear throughout the colonies, but most frequently in New England, most of them executed with engaging naïveté in a decorative pattern characteristic of the amateur or artisan. Among the best of these is one by Winthrop Chandler, the view of a *Winding River With a Mansion House,* executed between 1772 and 1790 (Collection of Mrs. Nina Fletcher Little, Brookline, Massachusetts), painted for a house in Scotland, Connecticut. These paintings are characterized by delightfully conventional trees (they seem to be patterned after English needlework subjects), precise, conventionalized buildings, and colorful little figures. A few panels which could be called more professional than amateur, though certainly not first-rate, were painted in emulation of the classical landscapes of Claude Lorrain and his imitators, both subject and treat-

ment probably derived from engravings. Perhaps the most competent were painted on the paneled walls of the room from Marmion, Virginia, between 1775 and 1800 (PA 131). They are typical not only for their classical composition but for their decorative rococo quality, quite different in effect from the linear and patterned designs of the amateurs in the more indigenous tradition.

The work of Copley was the outstanding achievement of eighteenth-century colonial painting. Its style, of which he was the best representative, was the result of the American environment; on the eve of the Revolution, American art can be said to have already made its declaration of independence. The predecessors of Copley—above all, Feke and, in their lesser way, Greenwood and Badger—contributed to this native quality, as did the anonymous limners who were also part of Copley's heritage. During and after the Revolution this native style was continued in the work of Chandler and Ralph Earl, who formed the nucleus of a local tradition which was strong enough to withstand even the imported graces of the great Gilbert Stuart.

The Graphic Arts

The graphic arts produced in colonial America are on the whole negligible; even the more amateur examples lack the impressive quality of the primitive or naïve beauty which is present in the sculpture of the same period.

Peter Pelham's mezzotint of *Reverend Cotton Mather,* 1727 (GB 162), generally accepted as the first single print (as opposed to one bound in a book) to be done in America, is a competent representation in the contemporary English manner, one which the young Copley emulated with considerable skill in his *Portrait of Reverend William Welsteed,* 1753 (GB 55). John Greenwood's *Jersey Nanny,* another mezzotint, 1748 (GB 83B), is far less conventional, reflecting the liveliness and humor of this unconventional artist.

Topographical views and depictions of events make up the bulk of print-making in the colonial period. The early professional style in this genre can be exemplified at its best in William Burgis' *A Prospect of the Colleges in Cambridge in New England,* 1726 (*GB 35; Illustration 2–52), a hand-colored copper engraving, typical of views of American cities that were engraved mostly by foreigners who improved on what must have resembled surveyors' drawings. Native engravers were less skillful. Paul Revere's *View of Part of the Town of Boston and British Ships of War Landing Their Troops,* 1770 (*GB 175), for instance, is hardly professional in its poor perspective and awkward composition.

Henry Dawkins in his *Paxton Expedition,* 1764 (*GB 64), incorporates a town view which

2–52. William Burgis, *A Prospect of the Colleges in Cambridge in New England*, 1726. Engraving. 18¼ x 24½ inches. (Photo courtesy of the Harvard College Library, Cambridge, Massachusetts.)

is considerably less competent than the work of Burgis or of other engravers of European origin, though it has a naïve charm. This is not to say that Dawkins and his Connecticut counterpart, Abel Bowen (engraver of charts and maps, as well as printer and publisher), were not respectable decorative artists; they were simply not trained representational ones. Even so, Dawkins' lively little scenes of American life, set in the elaborate rococo borders of his maps, are delightful enough.

Revere is the outstanding engraver of the colonial era, at least from the point of view of quantity. But it must be admitted that the work of this man, rightly famous as a silversmith and patriot, cannot be compared with any of the prints of the reproductive engravers in England or on the Continent—not to mention original works in the medium. Revere copied many sources, but seldom if ever with what could be called professional skill. Even his most famous print, the *Boston Massacre*, 1770 (GB 176), was derived from Peter Pelham's rendering of it, which Revere saw, copied, and successfully published before Pelham had a chance to market his. Pelham's indignant letter to Revere documents very clearly the latter's lack of originality. "When I heard you was cutting a plate of the late murder, I thought it impossible, as I known you was not capable of doing it unless you copied it from me." [18] Pelham's engraving of the subject is not much better, but it does reproduce his own original drawing. Only one print survives (GB 161). Revere's work is sometimes topically interesting, but most of it is not even that and none of it is of real artistic interest. Another notable engraver, Amos Doolittle, is even less competent. His famous engravings after Ralph Earl's far from adequate rendering of the battles of Lexington and Concord, *Engage-ment at the North Bridge in Concord*, 1775 (GB 66), are even cruder and more amateurish than Revere's. But it must be admitted that when Doolittle had a respectable English original to copy, he did it with considerable skill—something Revere was incapable of.

Actually, more interesting graphic work occurs in connection with letter press, particularly in journals and broadsides. This is usually marked by the strong and effective design of the amateur (later called the "folk" artist), nicely adapted to decorative treatment in black and white. But illustration is outside the province of this book.

Sculpture

Sculpture, in its conventional form of academically correct monuments and memorials, hardly existed in the colonies. What sculpture there was of this sort, as far as is known today, was represented by four statues, two of the elder Pitt (one in New York, the other in Charleston), one of Lord Botetourt, Governor of Virginia, still standing before the Wren building at Williamsburg, and an equestrian statue of George III, melted down during the Revolution. Since all were imported from London studios, they were scarcely American, nor did they exert any influence on a native school.

Less pretentious objects such as weather vanes and carved trade signs were more numerous, though few remain; these, together with gravestones, were the only indigenous examples of the three-dimensional art in the colonies. Shem Drowne, the hero of Hawthorne's short story, *The Wooden Image,* fashioned in Boston the lively but brutally primitive image of the Indian, c. 1750 (Illustration 2–53), which topped the old Province House, and the famous grasshopper which is still on the cupola of Faneuil Hall, where it was placed in 1749. Both are extremely effective in design, bold in pattern, and admirably simple in their use of the medium of molded and hammered copper. It is a pity that Drowne's ships' figureheads have been lost, along with all the other eighteenth-century examples of this once prominent art. The wooden figure of the *Little Admiral* now in the Old State House, Boston, made in 1770 for a mathematical instrument maker on Long Wharf in Boston, may reflect the craftsmanship of Drowne or the Skillins, famous carvers in Boston in the generation after Drowne, but it is not very impressive. At least one trade sign remains, that of Thomas Child, advertising his painting shop (SB 218). But since it was carved in England and used for his shop in London, it can hardly be called American.

The colonial gravestones offer much richer material than any other form of carving. The artisans who did the interior finish of rooms and painted heraldic devices were as likely to branch out into the carving of gravestones as into the painting of portraits, especially since the need for the former was constant. Such an artisan was John Holliman, whose stones in Beverly and Salem, Massachusetts, were as famous as the rooms he grained and stained. Another was John Johnston (Greenwood's teacher, and probably the father of William

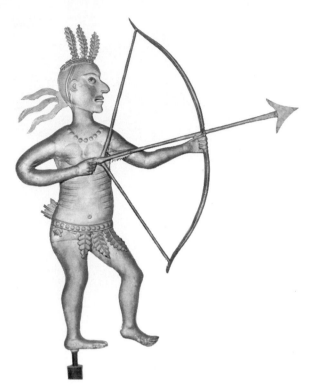

2–53. Shem Drowne, *Indian Weathervane,* c. 1750. Cut copper. Height: 54 inches. (Massachusetts Historical Society, Boston.)

guished by the refinement of their representational carving of portraits, angels, and even clouds. The most conspicuous change in gravestone design in the eighteenth century was the introduction of portrait heads, which were sometimes rendered with considerable representational skill. But even these more complex motifs were usually kept within the bounds of a respect for the sculptural limitations and character of the stone—slate was cut in flat planes, marble in rounded relief, and granite more boldly.

In contrast to the designs of the coastal areas of New England and of regions in the middle and southern states (where the gravestones were either imported, as in parts of Virginia, or carved by New England craftsmen, as in Charleston, South Carolina),[19] the stones from the hinterland of New England are far more interesting. In fact, the variety and the originality of these stones make of them one of the most fascinating and esthetically rewarding groups of objects in the history of American art. There were many quite distinctive schools as well as individual carvers of considerable originality, some of them quite uninfluenced by conventional motifs and styles, which were derived from the emblem books, from more academic carving, or from the other arts. The designs are remarkable for their often startling directness and for their decorative and expressive power. Seemingly archaic or primitive, they are actually the end product of a process of increasingly sophisticated treatment of a motif or group of motifs. Especially notable in this respect are a group of stones cut by numbers of the Worcester family of Groton, Massachusetts, found in various parts of the state stretching from Watertown to west of the Connecticut River. One of the most arresting is the gravestone of Hannah Converse (Illustration 2–54) at the Burying Ground at Brookfield, Massachusetts, which represents the culmination of a tradition originating in Haverhill, Massachusetts, during the late seventeenth century. (The earlier example is all the more crude when compared with this descendant of three quarters of a century later.) The Converse stone is carved with such decorative force and such feeling for the resistant character of the stone that it coin-

Johnston), who was not only an engraver, printer, and portrait painter, but a designer and carver of gravestones as well.

The decorative and symbolic motifs of the seventeenth century persisted into the eighteenth in the conservative regions of the seacoast, as illustrated in the John Holyoke stone, 1775 (SB 4), in the Centre Street Burying Ground, Newton, Massachusetts, possibly by Daniel Hastings, a well-known carver. In general, however, there was an increase in classically derived motifs—such as acanthus leaves and naturalistically rendered flora. Many of these examples are quite equal if not superior in sophisticated craftsmanship to the most important stones in the greater Boston area. This is especially true of Newport, Rhode Island, where three generations of the Stevens family (all named John) and John Bull produced beautifully proportioned and lettered stones further distin-

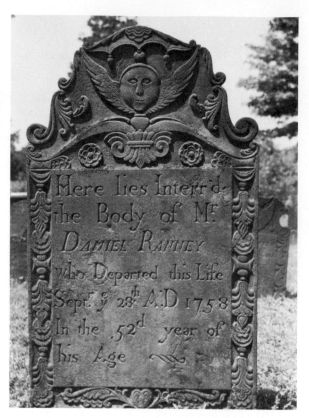

2–54. Member of the Worcester family, gravestone of Hannah Converse, Burying Ground, Brookfield, Massachusetts.

2–55. Thomas Johnson, gravestone of Daniel Ranney, c. 1758, Cromwell Burying Ground, Cromwell, Connecticut.

cidentally resembles some of the best West African masks carved out of hardwood. Another fascinating group of stones is by a carver working in Windham, Connecticut, called the "Celtic Carver" because of the extraordinary coincidence of his decorative motifs with the dynamic abstract design of the carvers of the Gaelic crosses and of the Anglo-Irish manuscript illuminators of the eighth century. These lively designs are among the curiosities of art history, for it seems as unlikely that the "Celtic Carver" originated the designs himself as it does that they are a survival or a revival of an artistic vocabulary which had not been used for centuries.

Less extraordinary from the historical point of view, but almost bizarre in the provincial adaptation of conventional baroque motifs, is the work of the Johnson family, Thomas ("Deacon"), his brother Joseph, and his son Thomas, Jr., who flourished in the Connecticut valley, their work appearing mostly in the Windsors, Hartford, and Middletown. A good example representing the exuberant style of the group is the Daniel Ranney stone, c. 1758 (Illustration 2-55), in the Cromwell Burying Ground, by the elder Thomas Johnson. Somewhat similar, though more ambitious in the recurring use of a motif of paired angels, is the work of Nathaniel Phelps in the Northampton region in western Massachusetts. These are only a few examples of a most unusual and rewarding kind of sculpture, hitherto relatively unknown and largely unappreciated.

PART THREE

THE EARLY REPUBLIC

The political and cultural coming of age of the North American colonies, which had been taking place during the eighteenth century, reached its symbolic climax in the achievement of independence. The removal of restrictions formerly imposed by the British on manufacturing and trade, and the creation of a federal union to replace a loose confederation of states gave great impetus to the economic and geographic growth of the new country. The population was increased by new immigration, and expanded beyond the Alleghenies from the territories of the old Western Reserve down to the Gulf region where the cotton economy of the South was already seeking new lands. With the Louisiana purchase and the explorations of Lewis and Clark other vast territories were opened for settlement. The ever present frontier added a democratic aspect to society which, with the election of Jackson, was soon to play an increasing part in political and social life. Meanwhile, the planter aristocracy in the South and the merchant, manufacturer, and businessman in the Middle States and New England continued to dominate the social scene and with it the taste of the country. What some sociologists call "high culture" remained generally in the hands of this class, in the older sections of the country; at the same time, however, the gradual rise in the standard of living enabled the less wealthy to patronize the arts. Portrait painting and other art forms of a naïve or folk quality increased, not only in the cities and the remote farms and towns of the East, but also in the hinterland where the old-time artisans were not so readily available and where self-taught native craftsmen came to the fore.

The greatest single factor distinguishing this period from the colonial era is the consciousness of independence. The realization of nationality unified the country both politically and culturally. Puritans and Episcopalians, farmers, mechanics, and merchants were first of all Americans, in spite of sectional differences and local idiosyncrasies. The new self-consciousness was naturally reflected in American art, different from that of England even before the Revolution.

This awareness is reflected in the subject matter of painting and in the creation of a distinctive architecture. The events and prominent figures of the Revolution were immortalized on canvas, and an added impetus was given to landscape and genre painting by an interest in the specifically American scene. At the same time the country's pride in its new sense of identity was reflected in the government buildings, designed in the international neo-classical style but given a certain national stamp and grandeur (resulting in a kind of "officialese" architecture very appropriate to the new country, but persisting into our own times with somewhat different effect).

The psychological factor of national unity together with the practical factor of improvement in transportation and communication by land, sea, and inland waterways (the steamboat was invented in 1807, construction of turnpikes began in 1817, and railroad building got under way in 1830) tended to concentrate centers of activity, including artistic ones, in a few populous areas. The consequent formation of groups of like-minded professionals who could pool their experience and taste in schools and discussions was supplemented by the increased immigration of trained artists who were among those fleeing the troubled times of the French Revolution and the Napoleonic wars. Furthermore, the founding of the capital city at Washington brought to the new country European decorators and, especially, trained architects who set professional standards where only gifted amateurs had existed before, and created a monumental architecture on a par with that elsewhere in the world.

Schools, academies, and even architectural studios were established; there was even an academy of drawing in Cincinnati in 1812. The two most significant were the Pennsylvania Academy in Philadelphia and the American Academy of the Fine Arts in New York. The former, founded in 1805, was an outgrowth of Charles Willson Peale's drawing school begun in 1795; the latter, formed in 1802, was not effective until Colonel John Trumbull became president in 1817. (Both institutions exhibited and bought works of art.) In these schools the principal training consisted of drawing from the cast, supervised in a more or less desultory manner. Foreign artists, mostly Frenchmen escaping the Terror, advertised the teaching of drawing and painting, and a whole school of American painters returned to this country after having traveled on the Continent or studied in England, most of them with Benjamin West. Though these artists were not always distinguished, they brought with them a generally high level of technical ability which resulted in a more widespread competence. Schools were soon followed by exhibition galleries, formed contemporaneously with libraries and athenaeums and sometimes incorporated with them, as at Boston. But more frequently, art was exhibited with natural history and curiosities, as in Joseph Steward's museum in Hartford, Connecticut, founded in 1802, and in the most famous of them all, Charles Willson Peale's museum in Philadelphia. This was situated in Independence Hall, where the artist exhibited his gallery of portraits of famous Americans together with his mastodon. Much of this collection went later to the Peale Museum in Baltimore, where it was carried on by Charles's son, Rembrandt. Moreover, a few dealers imported pictures, especially in New York and Philadelphia; and a few collectors, such as the wealthy Baltimore merchant Robert Gilmore, made their appearance.

The greater sophistication of artistic talent and taste resulting from such factors was naturally followed by the increasing separation of the artisan from the artist and by the growth of a folk or popular art whose practitioners became further isolated from the main centers of art than had been the case among the colonial artisans, who belonged to an artistic community that was consistently provincial. Thus, though a greater cultural unity came into existence during this period than during the more diverse colonial era, the persistence of artistic peculiarities due to differences of geography, climate, and social structure must not be overlooked. The balconies of New Orleans and the Carolinas, the fieldstone of Pennsylvania, the smooth and precise wooden joinery of New England continued to give American architecture a regional flavor. While Jefferson's new classicism strongly influenced architecture in Virginia, Maryland, and the national capital, the late Georgian taste of England was followed in many other areas, especially in New England. Fewer distinctions caused by local circumstances appeared in painting and sculpture than in architecture; nevertheless each region could boast not only its professional group (which was like those of other areas) but also its own quasi-primitives who carried on an older, indigenous tradition which was less sophisticated but often more esthetically rewarding than that of the increasingly numerous, more conventionally competent artists. A case in point is the school of portraitists centering around Ralph Earl and his followers, who had a considerable popularity in the face of competition from the brilliant European technique of Stuart and his followers.

In summation it can be said that art and architecture in the United States during its first decades as an independent country became more conspicuously national and at the same time reflected more strikingly the mainstreams of European art.

Architecture

There are two principal currents to be distinguished in the architecture of the early republic. The first is a late Georgian style practiced by a group of architects in England, most notably by the Adam brothers, Robert and James, and represented at its best in the United States by Charles Bulfinch of Boston—a group somewhat influenced by a classicism that emphasized late Roman practice. The second is the neo-classicism (and related romantic classicism) exemplified in the works and taste of Thomas Jefferson, broader in its choice of classical inspiration and centering around the architects whom Jefferson sponsored, notably Benjamin Latrobe.

Both styles or manners share certain characteristics of plan, composition, and detail. The basic plans (Illustration 3–1) are of two kinds (and are used equally in domestic and non-domestic architecture): the rectangle with or without a portico, and the rectangle in which a curved or elliptical projection plays an important part. (The rotunda also appears occasionally, especially in Jefferson's work.) Most plans, no matter how rectilinear their exterior walls may be, include curved forms in the interior arrangement in halls, stairways, or drawing rooms—elements which add variety and grace. Plans are also more convenient, incorporating closets and supplementary corridors, passages, and stairways. (The typical old central stairway was no longer the public exposition place of every intimacy of service.) Jefferson's Monticello exhibits many of these characteristics, as seen in the plan (Illustration 3–12) and in the compact service stairway (°AB 2).

Both in the composition of exteriors and in the design of individual rooms there is a tendency to concentrate upon a central motive, such as the portico or elaborate entrance, and to leave large surfaces deliberately plain in contrast. This last characteristic results in an effect of simple cubical mass with precise edges and plane surfaces. In the Adam style, where the decoration is small-scaled and relatively flat, this tends to give buildings an insubstantial and clean-cut grace, whereas in neo-classicism the simple walls, usually combined with the antique orders, have great monumentality. The difference is well illustrated in a comparison of two pairs of buildings, domestic and public, respectively: Bulfinch's first Harrison Gray Otis House (Illustration 3–4) contrasted with Jefferson's Monticello (Illustration 3–12); and Bulfinch's State House at Boston (Illustration 3–3) contrasted with Latrobe's Baltimore Cathedral (Illustration 3–17). The most significant addition to the architectural design of this period is the use of various forms of domes and vaults. Even in domestic buildings, coved and vaulted ceilings often cover the oval or elliptical rooms; Monticello even has a dome. In public buildings these forms appear with greater frequency. The formal satisfaction derived from the juxtaposition of the curved shapes of the enclosures with the severely simple walls is characteristic of the most interesting buildings of the time, and is seen most clearly in the work of Latrobe.

The third characteristic shared by the two principal styles of the early republic—the use of detail—is more complex, requiring some knowledge of the archaeological classicism of these years as well as of the Renaissance tradition, one of whose last manifestations was the Georgian architecture of the English colonies.

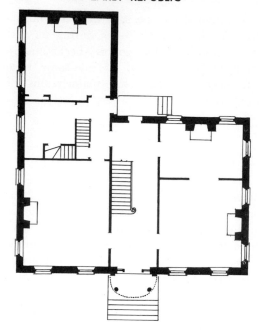

3–1. Plans of buildings of the early republic. *Left:* (First) Harrison Gray Otis House, Boston, Massachusetts, 1795–1796, by Charles Bulfinch. (Adapted from *Great Georgian Houses of America,* Architects' Emergency Committee; New York: 1933.) *Below:* Bank of Pennsylvania (destroyed), Philadelphia, Pennsylvania, 1800, by Benjamin H. Latrobe. (Adapted from Talbot Hamlin, *Benjamin Henry Latrobe;* New York: 1955.)

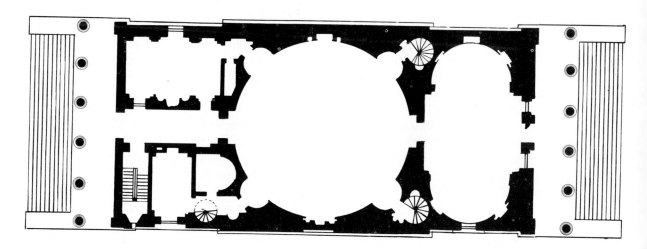

The young Jefferson's admiration for correct classicism, derived from a study of Palladio, was increased when he later saw actual classical buildings. In fact, Jefferson was among the first in America or in Europe to turn to neo-classicism. His State Capitol at Richmond (Illustration 3–9) is the first building of this style in the sense that it is derived from an actual antique building (the Maison Carrée, a Roman temple of the first century A.D., still standing in Nîmes, France) and precedes similar examples in Eu-rope by a few years. It is this phase of neo-classicism, the imitation of actual correct classical examples, which distinguishes it from the less specifically inspired classicism that preceded it. Jefferson's architectural ideals were those of a generation upon whom the discovery of the ruins of Pompeii and Herculaneum had had great effect, a generation indoctrinated by the esthetic of Johann Winckelmann, who urged the imitation of antiquity on the grounds that the Greeks especially had reached perfection in all the arts. A flood of archaeological publications, led by Stuart and Revet's *Antiquities of Athens* (the first volume of which appeared in 1762), added example to enthusiasm. The preference for an "authentic" classical architecture was also aided in France and America by the political ideology of this generation, for republican sentiment found much to inspire it in the city-states of antiquity.

Perhaps it is too much to expect of most readers, however, that they recognize the difference between the correctness of actual Roman and Greek detail as opposed to the less archaeological designs derived from Palladio and his contemporaries. It is perhaps more practical to judge on matters of plan and general design —except in the case of the Adam style whose eccentric decorative vocabulary is fairly easy to isolate from the more conventional classicism of both the Renaissance and neo-classicism. This vocabulary was derived from excavations at the palace of the Emperor Diocletian at Spalato (now Split, Yugoslavia), and more especially at the so-called Golden House of Nero on the Palatine Hill in Rome, where were discovered the orders with attenuated and graceful proportions and the late Roman decorative vocabulary of urns, swags, rosettes, and other similar details. The earlier Georgian concentration on pavilions, pediments, heavy cornices, and monumental doorways was succeeded in the Adam style by a graceful vocabulary of pilasters, engaged columns, blind arcades, and doors with open sidelights, all of which were supplemented by the small-scaled detail just described; these can be seen in the Derby-Crowninshield House, Salem, Massachusetts (Illustration 3–8). This Adam style, exemplified by the work of Bulfinch, popularized by his follower Asher Benjamin, and spread throughout the country by both American and English carpenter handbooks, is much more widespread than the neo-classicism of Jefferson and his circle. In fairness it must be said, however, that for all the surface delicacy and grace of Bulfinch and his group, there is occasionally a certain grandeur of simple forms to be discovered underneath, as in the Massachusetts General Hospital (Illustration 3–6).

But it is in neo-classicism that this last characteristic is more generally found, and it is in this quality rather than in matters of mere detail that more significant distinctions between Georgian architecture and that of the early republic can be seen.

It might be expected that the influence of the new scientific archaeology would lead neo-classical architecture into an excessively academic and expressionless style accompanied by little, if any, creative originality (as was the case in such European buildings as the Madeleine in Paris, its exterior so like the Temple of Jupiter in ancient Rome). But the correctness of the new classicism is actually its least interesting aspect, if also, unfortunately, its most conspicuous. Far more significant than the matter of surface ornament and detail was the effect of the totality of the spatial organization of the buildings. This was partly inspired by archaeology, that is, the discovery of late Roman buildings remarkable for their "unclassical" plan and structure. This aspect of antique inspiration rather than the mere imitation of classical orders stimulated the most creative architects into more original surface compositions and disposition of vistas and volumes, thereby releasing them from the stereotyped rationalism of the post-Renaissance or Burlingtonian theory. In France, this group was led by Claude-Nicolas Ledoux and in England by Sir John Soane, whose imaginative vaults and domes, sense of proportion, and simple geometric decoration caused a revolution in English and consequently (through Latrobe) in American architecture. Thus the unconventional surfaces and volumes of some aspects of English neo-classicism, austere and undecorated (even awesome and Cyclopean in the so-called "plain style," its most individual manifestation), and the ingenious, elegant, and spaciously complex work of Soane and Ledoux cannot possibly be equated with the conventional neo-classicism which the mere imitation of the Parthenon portico implies.

There was, in fact, a revolution in architecture as well as in politics—a revolution as romantic as it was neo-classic, stimulated and popularized by scholarly publications illustrating the scale, scope, and spatial imagination of Roman architecture, and supplemented by the works of such artists as the Italian etcher Giovanni Battista Piranesi, who dramatized in his prints of Roman ruins their shadowed vastness, and played upon the theme of the sublime and enormous in architecture in his series *The Prisons (I Carceri)*. The work of Latrobe, exemplified in the Bank of Pennsylvania, in Philadelphia (Illustrations 3–15 and 3–16), and in the monumental Baltimore Cathedral (Illustrations 3–17 and 3–18), represents this aspect of neo-classicism: that is, romantic classicism, to distinguish it from more archaeological neo-classicism.

The eclecticism represented by neo-classicism is only the first of a series of revivals signaling the end of the consistent organic process of stylistic change from the Renaissance through rococo, and the beginning of that search for a style which seems to represent the history of nineteenth-century architecture until it achieves its goal at the beginning of the twentieth. Yet, on the other hand, in the best of romantic classicism there is more intimation of modern style, at least in surface design and imaginative use of space, than in most of the revivalist architecture which intervenes.

Though Jefferson and some of the early official architects of the republic reflect the stricter aspects of neo-classicism, and though Bulfinch and his followers in the Adam manner prevail in numbers, the work of Latrobe in the spirit of romantic classicism sets the tone for the best architecture of the generation, which was further developed in the next period in the style called the Greek revival.

It is interesting to speculate how neo-classicism became so solidly rooted in America. Beyond the incalculable influence of Jefferson's interest in architecture and his preference for this style, there must also have been a predisposition for it in America. The coincidence of republican forms of government in ancient Greece and Rome undoubtedly had some significance, but probably more important was the persisting influence of a stricter Palladianism in colonial America than in England (where there was

much more resistance offered from the continental baroque and rococo architectural vocabularies); thus America was a more fertile soil for the nourishment of a purer classicism.

As in the Georgian period, the new styles were spread mostly by books, with the exception of the direct example of such men as Bulfinch, Jefferson, and Latrobe. Though these and other professionals entered the architectural scene during this period, they could hardly supply the enormous demand for building in a country so rapidly expanding in population and area as the United States. Consequently the pattern books remained as important as formerly. Some of these books were as conservative as much of the architecture of the period, hardly different from the Georgian of the mid-century (for instance, Biddle's *Young Carpenter's Assistant,* 1805), but the rest were more up-to-date. Many were British in origin; especially popular were the publications of William Paine (notably the *British Palladio*), representing a kind of conservative Adam style which ignored the larger conceptions of the Adam brothers and their contemporaries, concentrating rather on their refined detail. Books published in America began to take the place of imported ones, however, and consequently a kind of American Adam style began to emerge. The subtitle of one of the most influential of these pattern books, Asher Benjamin's *American Builders Companion* (Boston, 1806), even announced on its title page "a new system of architecture, particularly adapted to the present style of building in the United States of America." This system consisted mainly of minor changes in English design which were more readily "turned in wood," yet this often led to further elongation of proportion and greater insubstantiality of effect in the American imitations of a style already overrefined.

These books reflect the continuing importance of the anonymous builder in the rapidly expanding country, but it must be emphasized that whereas in the colonial era only two amateurs, the young Jefferson and Peter Harrison, could be even considered as architects, in the

3–2. General Epaphradatus Champion House, East Haddam, Connecticut, 1790, by William Spratt.

Transitional Building

Before discussing the architecture of the early republic proper, notice should be taken of a few buildings among those which were put up after the Revolution but still belong stylistically to the colonial period. After all, not enough building was executed in the years of recovery following the Revolution for the new taste to make much headway until about 1790.

One very distinguished example of the retardataire style is the Pierce-Nichols House built at Salem, c. 1782 (AB 755), by the young carpenter and wood carver Samuel McIntire, who was to become so prominent a few years later. A three-story mansion with giant pilasters and a fine one-story portico, Palladian in proportion and detail, it repeats and brings to a culmination the characteristics of the Georgian era. Another important building is the General Epaphradatus Champion House, 1790 (Illustration 3–2) in East Haddam, Connecticut, designed by William Spratt, a former captain of the British army who, on his release as a prisoner of war, chose to remain in the former colonies. The elegant proportions and detailing of this house, in spite of its typically New England wooden construction, bring something of the refinement of London to this little Connecticut River town. Though the style of the house is provincial English in that it lags a decade or so behind metropolitan standards, the ornament is in the more delicate scale of Adam and Paine and thus, in this respect, it is one of the first buildings in the United States in the Adamesque style. The situation of the house high on a series of terraces above the river made necessary a certain ingenuity in adapting the formal symmetry of the Georgian elevation and plan to the dramatic site. Spratt also designed a dwelling in Farmington (the Cowles House) and two buildings in Litchfield, Connecticut (the John Deming House and the Sheldon Tavern), which in their refined detail add great charm to two unusually well-preserved colonial and early republican towns.

Another of the most impressive houses of the late eighteenth century, still essentially Georgian

period under consideration the employment of actual professionals, particularly in the capital, created an entirely different situation from that prevailing in the eighteenth century. The buildings of these architects were extensively emulated; Latrobe's professional standards were taught to his apprentices who later established their own practice.

Yet the builders' powers died hard. The Carpenter Company of Philadelphia, for instance, made it as difficult for Latrobe when he came there to erect his epoch-making Pennsylvania Bank as present-day builders' codes, backed by contractors, sometimes made it difficult for Frank Lloyd Wright. To do justice to the period as a whole, hindsight shows us that buildings by anonymous carpenters (and masons), not even as professional as those in the Carpenter Company of Philadelphia, have a quality which their predecessors in colonial times did not have. These amateurs absorbed the general stylistic character of the three phases of current taste— the Adamesque, neo-classical, and romantic classical—and made them into something new and indigenous, transforming the monumental architecture imported from abroad to make it appropriate for local conditions and materials and the talents of local carpenters or masons.

in plan and proportion, is the John Brown House in Providence, Rhode Island, 1786 (AA 366). Like the Lee Mansion in Marblehead, Massachusetts, it is three stories high and has a projecting portico. But it is more massive, being constructed of brick. Only the elaborate and small-scaled detail places the house in the post-Revolution period.

Late Georgian or Adamesque

Though the neo-classicism and romantic classicism of Jefferson and Latrobe are the more significant styles of the early republic, late Georgian or Adamesque was nearly ubiquitous until about 1800, and remained by far the most popular until the end of the period, with the exception of the work of Jefferson and those associated with him in Virginia, Washington, Baltimore, and Philadelphia.

Most of the best buildings in this style were put up in New England and it was through the example of Bulfinch, who began to build in Boston during the early 1790's, and of McIntire, working in Salem about the same time, that the Adamesque influence spread throughout New England from the rich seaboard cities to the Province of Maine and to the wilderness of the Western Reserve, where, as in parts of New York State, the area was settled largely by New Englanders.

Like the rest of the country New England was glad enough to be rid of the mother country's taxation and restrictions on trade. But the rich Federalist merchant class and the new manufacturers who profited from independence were no less aristocratic in their tastes than before, and their predilections remained English; their sympathies could scarcely be Gallic during and after the French Revolution. The Francophile Democrats were more open to architectural ideas from the Continent, ideas which their leader Jefferson called the "modern" style as opposed to the late Georgian.

Charles Bulfinch, New England's foremost architect, was a conservative both in architecture and politics. (He was a selectman of Boston for nearly three decades and Chairman of the Board for nineteen years.) After a grand tour of Europe, Bulfinch wrote in 1786 that he then "passed a season of leisure, pursuing no business but giving gratuitous advice on architecture." [1] His recommendations could hardly have been in the most advanced taste, for on his trip he had not been impressed by those buildings, ancient or modern, which had appealed to Jefferson. He had seen the Maison Carrée at Nîmes, but had not remarked on it, and if he saw anything by Ledoux he did not notice it. While in England Bulfinch commented upon John Nash's London Crescents and he obviously admired the work of William Paine and Sir William Chambers, which reflected a more conservative taste than that represented by Sir John Soane. The books Bulfinch brought back to America reflect a similar conservatism. On his return to the United States then, Bulfinch represented a taste already moribund in England, but he did so with charm and distinction.

Bulfinch's first buildings were not very impressive or original, but two of his early churches (no longer in existence), at Taunton and Pittsfield, both in Massachusetts, had considerable influence through the combination of their designs in an early publication by Asher Benjamin. The Bulfinch–Benjamin variation on the Wren–Gibbs steeple can be seen in the Congregational churches at Old Bennington, 1806 (AB 700), and Middlebury, Vermont, 1806 (both by Colonel Lavius Fillmore), buildings which follow the Benjamin plate closely and are also similar to a church in Windsor, Vermont, where Benjamin himself lived in 1790. They reflect a delicate Adamesque taste which in its translation from stone to wood becomes almost fragile in its attenuation.

The two most important of Bulfinch's early buildings were the State Houses at Hartford and Boston. The first to be built was the one for Connecticut, still standing in downtown Hartford and known as the Old State House, 1793–1796 (AB 744). This first public building of any consequence to be erected in New England after the Revolution seems less impressive in its late Georgian grace than the more classical designs then being presented in Washington for the Capitol and President's House. But it is

3–3. State House, Boston, Massachusetts, 1795–1798, by Charles Bulfinch. From an old photograph taken before the addition of the present wings, appearing in the *American Architect and Building News,* 1903.

Though Bulfinch began in 1787—earlier than the conception of the Hartford building—to design the Massachusetts State House, 1795–1798 (AB 774; Illustration 3–3), it is more impressive in its size and site and in the accent of its dome. It is also more interesting in its interior design. The charm of the finely scaled detail of the late Roman Adamesque type is even more noticeable than at Hartford, and the rooms are more complexly shaped. The segmental dome on pendentives in the House of Representatives (AB 32, AB 775) is especially fine in spite of all its superimposed and fussy detail; Latrobe's far simpler use of coffers permits the sweep of the construction to be its own excuse (compare Illustration 3–16). More typical is the Old Senate Chamber (AB 33) with its delicate, small-scaled ornateness. The exterior of the State House, not unlike that at Hartford, has a colonnade with paired columns at the corners, and an arcade. The latter, however, is far less tall, with the consequence that there is a better relationship between the portico and its support. The dome rests on a pedimental base which enhances the geometry of the total composition and is therefore more "modern" than most of Bulfinch, deriving from a similar motif in Sir William Chambers' Somerset House in London. (The stone wings are later additions.)

While Bulfinch was involved in constructing the State Houses, he was also putting up one of the most interesting buildings of his career, the Franklin Place row houses (long since disappeared), 1793–1794, stretching in a crescent along a small park, and housing the Tontine Buildings and the Boston Library as well as dwellings. These very early row houses were more impressive than those in New York, Philadelphia, and Baltimore because they were part of a complex resembling the large-scale planning of Nash's London Crescents. The design of the group was particularly effective since the detail was restricted largely to the central and end blocks, permitting the simple intervening wall surfaces to act as a foil to the more decorated areas. It is a pity that these buildings were demolished, for they are hardly equaled in Bulfinch's later houses.

a nicely proportioned and consistent edifice graced with a dignified colonnade, although the columns are paired at the corners and raised on an arcade, which tends to minimize their monumentality. Furthermore, the columns, the arcade, and the blind arcade are unusually elongated. The balustrade, with accenting urns, and the cupola (added later, and very similar to the one at City Hall in New York) are even more gracefully fragile than is usual with Bulfinch, and add to the impression of delicacy. The interiors are charming in their detail, but the plan and spatial treatment of the rooms are not particularly noteworthy.

3–4. (First) Harrison Gray Otis House, Boston, Massachusetts, 1795–1796, by Charles Bulfinch.

Most of Bulfinch's work until the War of 1812 was domestic. He built three Boston houses for Harrison Gray Otis. The first, on Cambridge Street, 1795–1796 (AB 741; Illustrations 3–1 and 3–4), beautifully kept as the headquarters of the Society for the Preservation of New England Antiquities, is the most conservative as well as the most typical. Essentially it is no different in plan or elevation from the late colonial three-story houses. But its attenuated proportions and small-scaled, Adam-derived detail make it definitely post-Revolution. The second, on Mount Vernon Street, 1800 (AB 29), is equally conservative in plan, but the elevation, with graceful pilaster strips resting on a blind arcade of segmental arches, affords an elegant framework for exquisite small-scaled detail largely confined to the order itself. The third Otis house, 1806 (AB 30), on Beacon Street facing the Common, is more like those of Latrobe, with low service rooms on the ground floor beneath the formal rooms above, as in Europe. Its very plain facade is relieved only by a beautifully detailed classical portico on the ground floor, and by restrained ornament appearing only in the railing, cornice, and window enframements.

These three houses epitomize the many more that Bulfinch and his followers and contemporaries built throughout New England, but especially in Boston itself. (The older sections of that city are the most British-looking in America. This is especially true of the Beacon Hill area; legislative action has assured its preservation as a monument to this era of our early history and it is unmatched except by Charleston, South Carolina, similarly preserved.)

Bulfinch also built houses in which curved elements were more conspicuous than the more conventional rectilinear ones. The most distinguished of these, the Barrell Mansion (destroyed), in Charlestown, 1792, is reflected in the Knox House, Montpelier, 1793 (Illustration 3–5), in Thomaston, Maine. The design of this house is generally ascribed to Bulfinch, and though not the original building, it was reconstructed on very good authority. The inclusion of oval rooms in a curved bay is the most outstanding element in the plan and gives the house its essential character. The fine facade is enhanced by a splendid site similar to the one on which the house was originally built, looking down the St. George to the sea. A famous mansion in its day, it was the center of a vast domain —originally a royal grant—inherited by General

3–5. Montpelier, Thomaston, Maine, 1793, by Charles Bulfinch. Built by Ebenezer Denton. (A restoration.)

3–6. Massachusetts General Hospital, Boston, Massachusetts, 1818, by Charles Bulfinch.

Knox's wife, and the principal edifice of a complex arranged in two wings with nine buildings in each wing. The general's extravagance (there were at one time three-hundred household servants) brought the estate to ruin, and already in the 1840's Hawthorne described it as "a large, rusty looking edifice of wood . . . a ruinous mansion." [2]

The Larkin–Rice House in Portsmouth, New Hampshire, 1815 (AB 70), generally attributed to Bulfinch, can be taken as typical of Bulfinch's work outside Boston. It is a handsome example of his later style, essentially a simplified brick cube with scarcely any projection or recession except the shallow blind arcades surrounding the openings.

During the first eighteen years of the century, until Bulfinch went to Washington to become architect of the Capitol, his non-domestic buildings show a curious alternation between the conservative, refined Adamesque and a newer, bolder, and simpler style. Since the former are

constructed mostly of brick with wood trim (though sometimes of masonry) and the latter are of granite, this difference in material may be the decisive factor. The first of the granite buildings is the State Prison in Charlestown, 1803, solid and undecorated, where the functional use of masonry can be pointed out in a typical detail: the single granite blocks of the stairways are cantilevered out of the wall itself, an ingenious and expressive structural use.

It is interesting to contrast this granite building with Bulfinch Hall, Phillips Academy, Andover, Massachusetts, 1818 (*AB 76). This building, similar in plan and elevation, is, however, of brick. Apparently Bulfinch felt that this material warranted more graceful treatment, and it is therefore elaborated with his more usual delicate ornamentation.

The finest of Bulfinch's granite structures still standing is the original building of the Massachusetts General Hospital (Illustration 3–6) in Boston, erected in 1818. An elevation from a book in Bulfinch's collection (by William Thomas) has been suggested as a source of the design; but, if so, it has been greatly changed. The engraving features a rotunda and colonnade, as does the actual hospital, but all Thomas' decoration has been removed. The entablature has been reduced to two elements: a large block of granite to serve for both architrave and frieze and another for an undetailed cornice. These elements together with the Ionic capitals of the colonnade are the only decoration, for even doors and windows are simple openings so devoid of decoration that they seem to be cut into the solid granite. The flat surfaces of the walls are relieved otherwise only by the fanlighted arches of the main doors and the semicircular window of the pediment. Even more impressive is the clear arrangement of the basic shapes which consist of a central mass (partially wrapped around with a colonnade and crowned with a low dome) to which the long, block-like wings are attached. The direct expression of plan and structure in terms of a pared-down geometry of form is further enhanced by large chimneys on each corner of the central block, which are frankly part of the design and not in any way minimized. What could be the reason for this masterpiece of the "plain style"? One explanation is that the building is the logical culmination of a development begun in the Charlestown prison. Another might be that Bulfinch felt his Adamesque style was growing old-fashioned. This feeling may have been increased by a visit to Washington (in connection with a trip in 1816 to Philadelphia and Baltimore to study hospitals in preparation for the Boston commission) where he must have been struck with Latrobe's designs for the Capitol, even in its still ruinous state after the War of 1812. (He wrote that he was impressed by the general monumentality of the city.) Probably the first explanation is the most likely, since Bulfinch's own later work in Washington reverts to his earlier manner.

In contrast to these simple and monumental structures, Bulfinch at the same time had done buildings in the typical Adamesque manner represented by Bulfinch Hall at Phillips Acad-

emy. Most of these were not so significant as the others, and since many have been destroyed, it is better to consider only one example as the culmination or masterpiece of Bulfinch in this style, the First Church of Christ, at Lancaster, Massachusetts, 1816–1817 (AB 75; Illustration 3–7). Here the portico and tower, and their relationship to each other and to the building as a whole are all impeccably composed. This is seen especially in the transition from the larger block which acts as the background for the pediment of the portico to the smaller block which serves as the base for the round tower (AB 74). This potentially awkward transition is solved by a very ingenious device—a simple curve with a kind of Adamesque (or late Roman) shell pattern incised on its surface—which replaces the more conventional enlarged console or bracket used by architects of the baroque period; this exuberantly curvilinear form could hardly have been successfully used in the chaste context of Bulfinch's more classical design. The opposition of curved and rectangular elements so aptly related in this detail is typical of the basic rationale of the design as a whole. The circular shape of the tower, crowned with its dome, is nicely contrasted with the two cubical steps of its base, and is picked up again by the arcade which fills in between pilasters in what otherwise would be a portico. This unusual treatment not only adds grace to the lower part of the facade, but the solid area of the brick work (which partly fills in the space ordinarily left open between the columns in a conventional portico) eliminates what is often the too great contrast between an open portico and the mass of the building which it prefaces. At the same time Bulfinch exploits the opportunity afforded by this red brick area to silhouette against it a beautifully detailed pilastered order executed in white painted wood. The rare combination of the consistent, well-designed monumentality with the beautifully detailed ornament of the Lancaster church is perhaps summed up in the graceful tower. Here the Gibbs steeple tradition has no echo, and the spindly openness of Bulfinch's earlier towers is replaced by the arch-interrupted masonry of the tower itself, sur-

3–7. First Church of Christ, Lancaster, Massachusetts, 1816–1817, by Charles Bulfinch.

rounded by a procession of well-designed en-gaged columns. The dome and its swag-draped drum are a more dignified climax than the more conventional steeple would have been and are more suited to the restrained mathematics of circle and square which is the underlying dy-namic of this accomplished design. The con-ventional eighteenth-century interior (AB 75A) is not so spectacular as the exterior, but the de-tailing of pulpit and gallery is refined.

Perhaps this should be the point where the discussion of Bulfinch's architecture should end,

for his work at the Capitol, where he remained from 1818 until 1830, was not his best. The Maine Capitol at Augusta, 1828–1829, however, deserves mention (particularly if its former ap-pearance, before the additions of the wings and the present dome, can be envisaged) as a late example of Bulfinch's simple monumental work in granite, represented at its best by the Massa-chusetts General Hospital.

Though Bulfinch was a respected leader in his community after his return from Washington, he had no offers for professional work. The style he represented had been replaced entirely by that of his contemporaries—Jefferson, Latrobe, and their followers.

Samuel McIntire did for the appearance of Salem what Bulfinch did for Boston. The wealth of a suddenly very prosperous generation which had led the way in the exploitation of the East India trade transformed the medieval and Georgian town into a simulacrum of a provincial English city of the late eighteenth century. Federal, Essex, and especially Chestnut Streets (and part of the Common) still comprise a remarkable architectural monument to the maritime culture of the early republic.

At first McIntire was a carpenter-designer very much in the older tradition, as has already been seen in the Pierce–Nichols House of 1782. But he was ambitious to be an architect, for in 1792 he sent to Washington a design for the Capitol derived partly from Gibbs but appropriately monumental, which, had it been built, would have been perhaps his masterpiece. Yet, in spite of this excursion into the monumental, McIntire persisted in following a conservative norm, building houses rather like Bulfinch's first Harrison Grey Otis House, as seen in such a typical mansion as the Pingree House, Salem, 1804–1805 (AB 44, *AB 45). Only occasionally did McIntire do the unusual, most notably in the Elias Hasket Derby House, the showplace of New England until pulled down by the great shipowner's children. This building, pretentious and grand, was inspired largely by a design of Bulfinch which was in turn inspired by a design by Lord Burlington. McIntire built another elegant house from a design attributed to Bulfinch, the Ezekial Hersey Derby (later Crowninshield)

3–8. (Ezekial Hersey) Derby-Crowninshield House (partially destroyed), Salem, Massachusetts, after 1798, built by Samuel McIntire, after designs by Charles Bulfinch (?). From an old photograph.

3–9. Dining room from Oak Hill, Peabody, Massachusetts, c. 1800, by Samuel McIntire. Now in the Museum of Fine Arts, Boston.

House (Illustration 3–8), built shortly after 1798 and especially rich in late Georgian ornament. These two Derby houses were among the finest of the Adamesque group in the United States. Occasionally McIntire rejected this norm for a more elaborate and less conventional charm, as seen in the Assembly House, Salem, c. 1796 (AB 758), later made into a private residence.

McIntire's interiors comprise his most distinguished and characteristic work. These are epitomes of the delicacy of the Adam style, wherein he seems to play even more gracefully on the theme of urns, beading, rosettes, wreaths, and brackets than his mentor William Paine, and with even more elaboration. Outstanding examples are seen in the remodeled parlor for the Pierce–Nichols House, Salem, 1801 (AB 756), the interior of the Pingree House (AB 41, AB 43, AB 46), and the dining room from Oak Hill, Peabody, Massachusetts, c. 1800 (Illustration 3–9). Though McIntire's Salem church is gone, the steeple of the Unitarian Church at Newburyport owes to him its design (the Gibbs formula with Adamesque delicacy), as must much else in that charmingly preserved town and

3-10. Gore Place, Waltham, Massachusetts, 1806. (Courtesy of Gore Place Associates.)

elsewhere in Essex and Middlesex counties, Massachusetts.

It would be rather rash on the basis of the evidence available to attribute to either Bulfinch or McIntire what is perhaps the most satisfactorily designed and impressive house of the style and period, Gore Place, Waltham, Massachusetts, 1806 (AB 51, *AB 52, *AB 53; Illustration 3–10), built by the Federalist governor, Christopher Gore. One of the largest mansions in the country, flanked by wings leading to pavilion-like ends, the main part of the building consists of a long and narrow central block with great windows opening onto an entrance terrace on one side and, on the other, into a garden with a view to the Charles River. There are semicircular and oval rooms on both floors, and a magnificent but graceful curving staircase. Though the interior (*AB 53) is filled with details from Paine and in general reflects the elaborate surface ornament of the Adam brothers, the exterior is a masterpiece of decorative restraint. The detail of the French windows, the finely scaled cornice, and a roofline lightened by a continuous balustrade comprise the only ornament. This acts as a foil for the concentration of the design on the shapes of the building itself and of its openings: the long doors and windows of the central block, the graceful curve of the garden facade, and the prominent fanlights used as fenestration and over the principal doors. But the most effective elements of the sure and basically simple design are seen best in the wings; their geometry of two-stepped recession somewhat resembles pilasters stripped of their capitals and other detail, and even of their entablature (which is merely hinted at by the cornice-like strip under the triangles of the pediments). This house, an essay in pure architectural form which only suggests but does not actually employ classical detail, comes close to some of the "plain style" Regency houses of England which influenced George Hadfield and Latrobe while at the same time showing certain analogies to the style of Ledoux. Though no documentary evidence exists to indicate a specific designer, the distinction of this mansion implies an architect of importance and therefore seems to point most forcibly to Bulfinch, though nothing in his work up to this time would give any precedent for his authorship except perhaps the treatment of the French window enframements with an entablature supported by a bracket (used also in the second Harrison Gray Otis House), and the more suggestive fact that the design of the elevations bears some resemblance to several in the book by William Thomas which Bulfinch owned. The plan, however, is closer to French precedent than is usual with Bulfinch, exhibiting even more conveniences such as closets, stairways, and passages than Jefferson's Monticello. The plan is in fact so accomplished in this respect and otherwise that it may well be the work of the French architect of the Revolutionary period, Jacques Guillaume Legrand (the contemporary of Ledoux), with whom Mrs. Gore worked very closely in Paris in 1801 and 1802 over the design of Gore Place.[3] The elegant simplicity of both the exterior and interior may also reflect the taste prevalent among Legrand's generation, but may also be the result of Mr. Gore's desire that his house be built "with the greatest economy and absence of ornamentation."[4] In any case, the decorative detail of the interior is English and the materials and construction are certainly not French. McIntire, who did the Lyman House in nearby Waltham, has also been suggested as the possible designer of Gore Place, but largely on the basis of the interior details. Certainly the large plane surfaces of the interiors, acting as foils to the restricted decorated areas, are far more restrained, and deliberately so, than is McIntire's custom. It would be more reasonable to attribute the plan and the basic elements of at least the river facade to Legrand and Mrs. Gore than to McIntire or even to Bulfinch, assuming that the construction and details were executed by New England builders and craftsmen. It is interesting to conjecture how much Gore Place, with its successful combination of several stylistic ingredients, may have influenced the later Bulfinch, since it seems unlikely that he had anything to do with its design in view of the recent publication of Governor Gore's remarks about Legrand.

Asher Benjamin's books popularized the kind of work that McIntire and Bulfinch were doing; specific designs by the latter were published by him. Most were of Benjamin's own design, however, though his first book, *The Country Builders' Assistant* (1797), is dependent to a large degree on designs published by Sir William Chambers in 1759 and on construction diagrams in a carpentry book by Peter Nicholson, also English. Two of Benjamin's buildings are still standing and, though they are of masonry, are quite solid and impressive in comparison with the elevations published in his carpenter handbooks. One, the Center Church, New Haven, 1812–1814 (*AB 26) (long thought to be an early work by Ithiel Town, who became a prominent architect in the next period), is quite Gibbsian in its massiveness and lack of attenuation. Here the architect even employs rustication, so out of keeping with the delicacy of the Adamesque. Perhaps the former West Church in Boston (now a branch of the Boston Public Library) adjacent to the first Harrison Gray Otis House is more typical, being in general more delicate in detail though still impressively solid.

Outside of Boston, the best architecture in New England appeared in the coastal towns, especially in Providence and north of Boston, not only in Salem and Newburyport, but most notably in Portsmouth, New Hampshire, and in the new and flourishing coastal towns in Maine. The Providence houses of the period (on the hill near Brown University and the Rhode Island School of Design), among them the Thomas Poynton Ives House, 1806 (AB 56), and several mansions by John Holden Green, combine with the still somewhat colonial building of Joseph Brown to form one of the most distinguished architectural complexes in the country.

Equally notable, but in a more provincial way, is Wiscasset, Maine, which preserves almost intact the architecture of its brief period of prosperity before Jefferson's embargo, and thus represents today the former appearance of much of maritime New England. Among the most impressive of Wiscasset's larger houses is the Nichols–Sortwell House, 1807–1812 (AB 716), an example of the common three-story type best represented by the first Harrison Gray Otis House. But its proportions, in comparison, reflect a certain provinciality, as can be seen in the awkward relationship between the scale of the blind arcade and the rest of the facade and between the Palladian window on the second floor and the fanlight on the third, although the detail throughout the house is exquisite. Alexander Parris' elegant houses in Portland, Maine, of which the McLellan-Sweat House (now part of the Portland Museum of Art) is the finest remaining, are far more sophisticated, and illustrate the prevalence of good design beyond the larger cities.

Each region (and sometimes individual towns) possessed similar distinction, which it often owed to the work of such a local designer as Lavius Fillmore, whose General Samuel Strong House in Vergennes, Vermont, 1796 (AB 700A), represents the quite typical combination of a Georgian plan and general canon of proportion with Adamesque detail. David Hoadley, a more original designer-builder, contributed a great deal to Connecticut architecture of the period, designing a number of meetinghouses throughout the state, partly under the influence of Bulfinch, with whom he had been associated in the building of the Old State House in Hartford. The best of these, and one of the finest of the period, is the United Church in New Haven, 1814–1815 (AB 36, AB 38), which has the refinement of the Adamesque without its fragility, and an unusually spacious interior spanned by a shallow saucer dome (AB 37, AB 38) suspended from the roof in what must have been a very skillful feat of carpentry.

Beyond New England the Adamesque style also predominated, except in parts of Virginia, in Baltimore and Philadelphia, and of course in the national capital, where the neo-classicism of Jefferson and Latrobe prevailed. New York was not as architecturally prominent as its position as the federal capital for two years might warrant, though its predominantly Dutch and Georgian character was somewhat altered by row houses with Adamesque details by John McComb, Jr., and by several public buildings which have since disappeared. The fine portico and steeple (attenuated versions of the familiar Gibbsian motifs) added to St. Paul's Chapel (1794–1796) by Major Pierre Charles L'Enfant have already been mentioned. Philadelphia had its share of Adamesque buildings, from its row houses with their fanlighted doorways to the Pennsylvania Hospital, designed by David Evans, Jr., 1796 (AB 777), distinguished by its surgical amphitheater and the elegant row of pilasters surmounting a blind arcade on its facade, a motif derived from a more notable building (later destroyed), the old Library Company of Philadelphia by William Thornton (the first architect of the Capitol at Washington). The George Read II House, Newcastle, Delaware, 1797–1801 (AB 778, AB 779, AB 780), is a typical great house of the period in the Philadelphia area, other examples of which have disappeared in the larger city itself. A fanlighted and side-lighted doorway and Palladian window grace the facade, while the interior is beautifully carved with motifs from Paine. One of the most distinguished mansions of the period is Woodlands in West Philadelphia (AB 766), remodeled in the new style in 1788 and incorporating many of its most prominent features: elliptical rooms, an attenuated portico, niches, and much elegant, small-scaled decoration. Baltimore possessed an equally distinguished mansion, Homewood, 1801–1803 (AB 762), possibly designed by Thornton, and built by Charles Carroll. The delicate interplay of white-painted Adamesque detail and trim red brick in this well-proportioned house make it a distinguished example of the transition between the southern colonial mansion and its Greek Revival successors of the next period. Further south, in Charleston, South Carolina, many fine examples of the Adamesque style were built after the city recovered from the Revolution and assumed her preeminence as the largest city in the South. In fact the later phase of the classical revival in the 1820's and 1830's had difficulty in replacing the well-entrenched earlier mode. Among the most elaborate of the Charleston houses of the early republic is the Nathaniel Russell House, possibly designed by the Providence architect Russell Warren, and built shortly before 1809. Here the proportions of the narrow facade (allowing space for a lateral piazza and a garden, a plan common in the hot climate) are exploited as a framework for the attenuated details of the period. The William Drayton House, 1820 (AB 61), is an even more indigenous building, since the elliptical garden facade is covered by a two-storied porch, an early instance of one of several similar devices to mitigate the heat of the South.

The Adamesque style was carried west across the Alleghenies into Tennessee and Kentucky and into western Pennsylvania and Ohio. The Eagle Hotel at Waterford, Pennsylvania, 1826 (AB 329), the Taft House at Cincinnati, and numerous buildings in other Ohio towns built by settlers from Massachusetts and Connecticut (some of Ohio was once part of the State of Connecticut) are evidence of the ubiquity of the style wherever settlement became permanent.

It would be interesting to discuss certain vernacular variations on the Adamesque style— quaint inconsistencies in the use of classical orders where the wood carver's chisel got out of hand, resulting in some delightful abstract patterns—or the persistence of certain medieval structural survivals like that of the Alna Meetinghouse, discussed in Part Two. But these manifestations are curious byways and not as profitable for a general study as are similar instances in the next period, when both design and structure assumed a vernacular character important enough to be a real contribution to an indigenous style.

Jefferson and Neo-Classicism

Thomas Jefferson was the catalyst for the classicism which became the hallmark of most of our architecture before the Civil War, and of our official architecture ever since. The statesman who formulated effectively for the first time some of the political ideas vaguely current in his time into the clear statements of the Declaration of Independence and the Constitution was an equally sensitive barometer to the artistic sensibilities of his era. Jefferson brought back from Europe, where he had served as minister to France, a clear expression of the general yearning for classical style and standards. No one could have been better prepared for this task or more aware of the appropriateness of the new classicism as an architectural symbol of our national dignity. We have seen that Jefferson's skill was already mature and practiced before the Revolution. He had sought

to replace the Georgian vernacular he saw around him; just before the Revolution, he had drawn up a plan to dignify the Governor's Palace at Williamsburg with giant porticos on each side. Already oriented toward the classicism of Palladio, more correct than any other before the actual archaeological neo-classicism with which he came in contact abroad, Jefferson's background was most congenial to the style of Louis XVI and immediately receptive to the impact of his first sight of an actual antique building, the Maison Carrée at Nîmes. Though he admired the elegant architecture of Jacques-Anges Gabriel in the Place de la Concorde, and wrote that he was violently smitten with the Hôtel de Salm (palace of the Legion of Honor), the proto-neo-classicism of these Parisian buildings paled before the impact of a veritable ancient "fabrick." We are not surprised at his hyperbole when he remarks in a letter to one of his female correspondents that he gazed "whole hours at the Maison Quarree [sic] like a lover at his mistress."[5] It is this building that inspired the Virginia Capitol at Richmond, 1785–1789 (AB 753; Illustration 3–11), which Jefferson designed with the help of the French architect Charles-Louis Clérisseau.

3–11.   Capitol, Richmond, Virginia, 1785–1789, by Thomas Jefferson, with Charles-Louis Clérisseau. Detail from an old photograph taken after the fall of Richmond, 1865, by Mathew Brady or one of his assistants. (Library of Congress.)

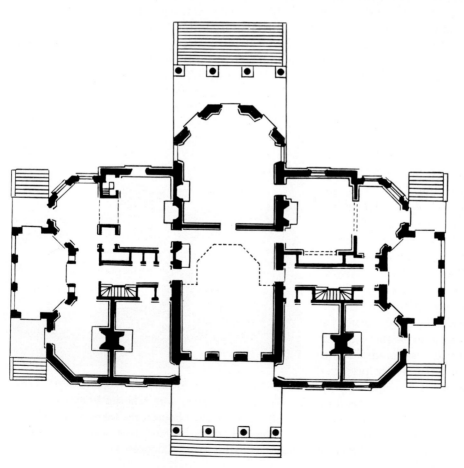

3–12. Monticello, Charlottesville, Virginia, 1793–1809, by Thomas Jefferson. (Floor plan adapted from *Great Georgian Houses of America*, Architects' Emergency Committee; New York: 1933.)

The adaptation of this refined miniature of classical architecture to the dimensions and multifarious uses of the executive and legislative branches of a Commonwealth could hardly be a direct imitation, necessitating as it did a complex interior plan, a need for several floors, and the intrusion of fenestration. But the basic design and the proportions of the original are followed, though the Ionic order has been substituted for the Corinthian. The Maison Carrée has been adapted to a far more complex use than was the case with the Madeleine in Paris, which was to function as a place of worship, like the Temple of Jupiter which inspired it; the Richmond Capitol, designed in 1784, was the first public building to use the full temple form. But more important than this interesting fact is the total effect of the building whose huge scale and magnificent site above the city symbolize the importance and dignity of the Commonwealth. It is an edifice inspired by Roman taste, genius, and magnificence, to use its designer's own words, but it is not slavishly copied.

Jefferson's neo-classicism continued to be his chief inspiration, but it was not unmixed with the Palladianism he had long admired—as witness his design for the President's House, 1792, which is very close indeed to the Italian's Villa Rotunda. But Palladio himself was, in a manner of speaking, a neo-classicist in the seventeenth century. His rendition of the Temple of Vesta in Rome was combined with a Gibbsian prototype and used by Jefferson for the dome of his own remodeled Monticello. This mansion (AB 10A; Illustration 3–12) near Charlottesville, reconstructed from 1793 to 1809, embodies its builder's ideal of a proper country house, not unlike the half-urban, half-rustic villas of his beloved Rome, as described by Cicero, Horace, and the younger Pliny. Dominating its environment, but very much a part of it, Monticello is dignified and convenient, the principal structure of a considerable estate which was almost self-supporting and self-sufficient, and was manned by a large number of household slaves. Jefferson combined the convenience of underground passages derived from the Roman precedent of Hadrian's Villa with a number of further con-

veniences of his own, some of them remarkably inventive examples of typical American gadgetry: a compass combined with a weather vane which could be read indoors; a system of cannon balls whose balanced weights told the day of the week; double doors, triple sashes, dumbwaiters in the dining room mantelpieces, and beds which could be folded up and made to disappear. There were even water closets of a sort, with an ingenious method of disposal, dependent, however, on the ample human labor provided by the slave system. These innovations were combined with instances of the advanced planning of the time—closets, tucked-away stairways, and supplementary passages. Interesting as these practical innovations are, they are less impressive than the formal beauty of the structure whose scale is neither too monumental nor too domestic. The most unusual aspect of Monticello is the prominence of the entablature which serves to unify the design. This is made possible by concealing the low second story behind a parapet, thus permitting the use of the full area of the entablature, part of which was customarily sacrificed in order to accommodate more fenestration. This prominent feature, together with the dome and porticos, comprise the principal ingredients of the building's restrained magnificence. The perfect relationship of part to part makes Monticello a very much more impressive house than even the grandest of the Adamesque, which seem in comparison fragile and overdetailed.

Other houses either designed by Jefferson or whose design he strongly influenced have a similar monumentality. Perhaps the best is Bremo, in Fluvanna County, Virginia, 1815–1819 (AB 15, AB 16), a basically Palladian villa with twin dependencies, each with a portico, joined to a massive central block which is also distinguished by porticos—one projecting and the other *in antis*. The basic composition of this plantation house approaches more closely the simplicity of Latrobe's forms than is usual with Jefferson. Poplar Forest near Lynchburg (where the great man fled occasionally when the mass of his admirers threatened to eat him out of house and home at Monticello) is an attractive octagonal building, concise and neatly effective in design. Farmington (now the Charlottesville Country Club) was remodeled by Jefferson with fine, large-scaled, and correctly detailed rooms and a classical portico. (He added a similar portico to Montpelier, Madison's home.) Other Virginia plantations connected with Jefferson's name are Barboursville, Frascati, Oak Hill, and Edgehill, the last deriving from Kent's *Inigo Jones*, a source earlier than usual for Jefferson, but respectably classical.

Jefferson's most impressive work is the University of Virginia, 1817–1826 (AB 17, AB 21A; Illustrations 3–13 and 3–14), probably the finest complex of buildings in the United States until Southern Florida University, by Frank Lloyd Wright, and Saarinen's General Motors Research Center were built. The proportions of the individual buildings, their relation to each other, and the satisfying incorporation of a great variety of both architectural and landscape elements into an ordered whole are the ingredients which make the University extremely successful. Yet this is accomplished in the face of extreme pedantry. Jefferson wanted the pavilions "as they show themselves above the dormitories" to be "models of taste and correct architecture." [6] The pavilion illustrating the Doric order was inspired by the Baths of Diocletian in Rome; that demonstrating the Ionic, by the Temple of Fortuna Virilis. Other orders came from the Theater of Marcellus and the Albano dome, also in Rome. (Palladio, however, contributed three variations.) Though the idea of the Rotunda (modeled after the Roman Pantheon) as the climax of the design was Latrobe's, it was eagerly taken up by Jefferson, and the conception and detailing are his. A description of the University of Virginia, a knowledge of the influences that went into it, and even the study of adequate photographs do not prepare the observer for the impression the actual buildings make on him. What should be overformal or academic is not. This is very difficult to account for; the explanation probably lies in these two factors: Jefferson's feeling for proportion and basic design, and his intimate concern with every stage of the building. Jefferson had ex-

3–13. Two pavilions, University of Virginia, Charlottesville, Virginia, 1817–1826, by Thomas Jefferson.

traordinary sensitivity to that beauty of form which is the essence of authentic classical architecture, but this was supplemented by his interest in the underlying mathematics of architecture. The nobility, grandeur, and chastity of classical architecture—to use Winckelmann's terms—were expressed for Jefferson not only in correct detail, but in a very real appreciation for basic cubes, spheres, and surface arrangements. The designs for the University of Virginia and especially for the Rotunda, which survive at the Massachusetts Historical Society and at the University itself (AB 18B), are essentially exercises in geometry. Jefferson's theories and statements to the contrary, he was no doctrinaire, for he changed the Roman Pantheon design, which inspired the Rotunda, both in detail and

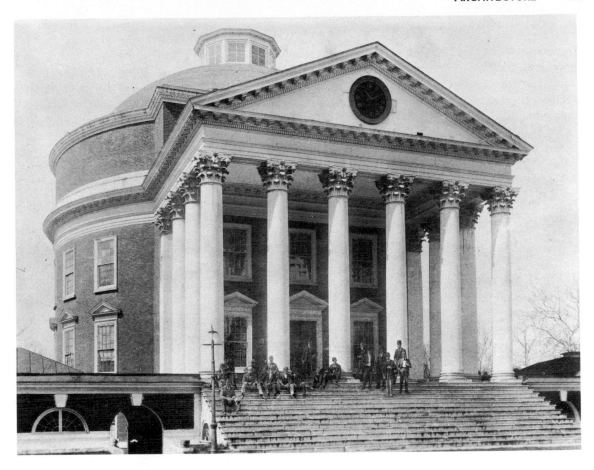

3–14. Rotunda, University of Virginia, Charlottesville, Virginia, by Thomas Jefferson. From an old photograph.

in proportion. For instance, Jefferson has united the Rotunda and the portico (not satisfactorily combined in the Roman original) by joining the two together with an entablature running all around the edifice (AB 20; Illustration 3–14). Though Jefferson lacked much technical knowledge, and though he availed himself of the assistance of a trained professional in his Virginia Capitol, he nevertheless was far more involved in the practical matters of building than was the usual gentleman-amateur. Jefferson once said that putting up and taking down buildings was one of his favorite amusements. In this he is a typical American, if we agree with a German-born modern architect who said that building seemed to be a national passion in the United States. Jefferson's inquisitive and creative mind not only designed astronomical observatories and anatomical laboratories, but was concerned with experiments in mortar and brick-making.

Every aspect of the construction of the University was under Jefferson's close supervision. The use of curved brick walls (AB 21B) to entwine the garden parterres in their serpentine coils is only one of the instances of his ingenuity. Out of such concerns came his feeling for the traditional materials of brick and wood. Undoubtedly it is the bright, cheerful red and the brilliant contrasting white of the materials which gives the buildings much of their sparkle and variety. Seen in any setting—green, russet, white, or brown, depending on the season—they always give a fresh and lively impression.

One critic has described Jefferson as a "creative revivalist"; but more than that, he was a humanist in the best sense of the word and not a doctrinaire classicist, as the finest of his architecture amply demonstrates.

Jefferson's official positions, culminating in the presidency, made him the key figure in the development of neo-classicism in this country. The extent of government patronage of the arts during Jefferson's Administration has not been equaled by any other, except perhaps that of Franklin Delano Roosevelt. Jefferson was the prime mover in initiating the planning and building of the new capital, advising and even contributing designs himself. The effects of Jefferson's interest in a stricter classicism than that which prevailed in either the late English Georgian or the French Louis XVI style, and of his sense for the monumental (particularly as expressive of the new dignity of nationality) were far-reaching. Even at the very beginning of official post-Revolution architecture, these aspects of Jefferson's taste were reflected in the work of Pierre L'Enfant, a French architect and engineer who had been attached to Lafayette's staff, and who had been appointed by President Washington at Jefferson's suggestion. His master plan for the development of the capital city was on a grander scale and more ambitious for potential magnificence than either that of Versailles or of Wren's London, both of which inspired it. A prominent critic feels that not only L'Enfant's Federal Hall (a remodeling of the old New York City Hall) but also the design for the Capitol by another Frenchman, Stephen Hallet, were transformed by the American environment into something quite different from the Louis XVI taste of France, and that a large ingredient of this environment was Jefferson's archaeological predilections. But it was a while before any of the architecture in Washington or elsewhere in the United States was to equal Jefferson's own Capitol at Richmond in correct neo-classicism.

Meanwhile, one interesting official building in the Louis XVI style and several in a conservative Georgian manner were being erected. The first was the City Hall at New York, 1811 (AB 47, AB 48, AB 48A), designed by a Frenchman, Joseph-François Mangin, and partly changed by John McComb. This elegant building, almost overrefined and even somewhat rococo in delicacy of proportion and scale, is a remarkable example of the architectural grace of late eighteenth-century France. It is all the more charming in the midst of the contrasting modernity of downtown New York, an actual example in this country of one of the most engaging styles (though not the grandest) in Europe's architectural history. Only one other building, Maginault's City Hall in Charleston, is comparable in any way, though perhaps the delicacy of Maximilian Godefroy's interior decoration in the Unitarian Church at Baltimore (AB 104) should be mentioned as another instance of the Louis XVI style. These buildings, taken together with Jefferson's importation of the convenient plan and curved forms of that style (plus the possible influence of the imaginative simplicity and monumentality of Ledoux), comprise the French ingredient in the architecture of the early republic. But the outrages of the Terror and the blunderings of Citizen Genêt (the new French republic's minister to this country) served to discourage the continuation of the French influence; the style of the Directoire or of the Empire had little effect. Instead, late Georgian and Adamesque were supplemented by further injection of English influence. William Thornton's commission-winning design for the United States Capitol, in spite of its monumental plan, was still very Georgian in design and detail, as can be seen in the facades of the areas flanking the Rotunda. There, walls give an almost amateurish awkwardness to a building dignified by later, more competently designed additions. Thornton, a physician by profession, was one of the last representatives of the eighteenth-century amateur architects; and a rather casual one at that, if we may judge from his own comments about his design for the

Philadelphia Library: "When I travelled I never thought of architecture, but I got books and worked a few days, then gave a plan in the ancient ionic order which carried the day." [7]

Though Thornton's talents were not quite sufficient for an important building like the Capitol, he was successful in his domestic architecture. Woodlawn, near Mount Vernon, and Tudor Place, 1815, in Georgetown (each built for one of Washington's step-granddaughters) are good examples, the former being a handsome but conventional Georgian building no more advanced than the Philadelphia Library, while the Georgetown house is more classical, with a central block and prominent temple-like portico, showing that Thornton did advance with the years, following the precedent of Jefferson and others. The Octagon House, 1798–1800 (AB 759, AB 761), now the headquarters of the American Institute of Architects in Washington, is perhaps the most effective and original in its nice proportions and in the frank geometry reflected in its name. The detail, however, is finicking in comparison to Latrobe's and Jefferson's.

Though the White House in Washington, 1815 (AB 745, AB 751), is considered one of the early examples of classicist federal architecture, actually only its proportions suggest antiquity. A comparison with the nearby Treasury Building (though the latter is of a later date), for instance, shows how lacking in real monumental feeling it is. Its designer, James Hoban, should not be considered among the group of architects in the style Jefferson called "modern," because the building, for all its effectiveness, is really Georgian, resembling both Leinster House in Dublin (Hoban was Irish) and a house in Gibbs's ubiquitous *A Book of Architecture* of exactly three-quarters of a century before. (The colonnades which give the building much of its character are actually the result of a suggestion by Latrobe.)

Latrobe and Romantic Classicism

Perhaps Jefferson's most far-reaching act in his capacity of stimulating the official architecture of the new country was to encourage Benjamin Latrobe and finally to appoint him in 1803 as Surveyor of the public buildings of the United States. Without the President's interest in architecture, Latrobe would not have succeeded in imposing his authority on relative incompetents like Thornton. Even Jefferson himself, the gifted amateur, bowed out before this professional, whose romantic classicism influenced the character of American architecture for decades to come. Latrobe's improvements on Thornton's Capitol and Hoban's President's House were so accomplished, monumental, and symbolic of the nation's greatness that they could not but recommend him to the country at large, though his two other outstanding buildings, the Philadelphia Bank and the Baltimore Cathedral, had already made him famous in more restricted circles.

After Latrobe had been in the country for three years and had designed a number of Virginia country houses and some town houses in Richmond, he received the first commission worthy of his talents, the Bank of Pennsylvania, 1799–1801 (AB 113; Illustrations 3–1, 3–15, and 3–16). This building, unfortunately demolished, was significant in American architecture for several reasons. It was the first important edifice by a professional architect; it introduced a Greek order; and, most important, it was so beautiful and perfect an edifice that it immediately won favor and consequently set the style of expressive monumentality (in spite of its relatively small scale) which was to distinguish the important early official architecture of the nation. The beauty of the building depended not only on its proportions and the relationship of its parts, as seen in Latrobe's drawing of the exterior (AB 113; Illustration 3–15), but apparently on the design of the interior as well, where the low dome of the central rotunda of the Banking Hall was complemented by the vaults of the stockholders' and directors' rooms on the first and second floors (Illustration 3–16). The segmental shape of the dome, the first example of masonry vaulting in a public building in the country, was relieved only by coffers, not very deep; its supporting walls were ornamented

3–15. Bank of Pennsylvania (destroyed), Philadelphia, Pennsylvania, 1799–1801, by Benjamin H. Latrobe. Watercolor drawing by Latrobe. (Maryland Historical Society, Baltimore.)

only by simple panels above the arches and windows, and by niches. The graceful austerity of this building has the strength of the English "plain style," the grace of the Adam Brothers, and the clear structural statement of Soane. The combination of these factors in a distinctively personal style of accomplished dignity inevitably made a great impression in old-fashioned Georgian Philadelphia. The water pumping station in Central Square, where the Philadelphia City Hall now stands, was a closer reflection of Ledoux and the late work of Soane, and was a masterpiece of romantic classicism in this country, as can be seen in a genre painting in which it is depicted in the background, *Fourth of July in Centre Square,* by J. L. Krimmel (PB 287).

Baltimore Cathedral, 1804–c. 1818 (AB 119, AB 120, AB 121; Illustrations 3–17 and 3–18), the seat of the large and prominent Catholic diocese of Maryland, is a more impressive build-ing in size than the bank, though perhaps not ultimately as successful in its final proportions. The result of seven plans and much negotiation, it is a magnificent structure with which even Frances Trollope, who found so little to praise in America, was impressed. The exterior (except for the onion domes of the towers, added later) is powerful, expressing in uncomplicated forms the basic plan and enclosure. Prefaced by a magnificent Ionic portico, the masses and volumes of the structure are enhanced by the rectangular panels in the walls and by the emphatic continuous entablature. Severity is relieved by the arches of the windows and the openings of the belfries, whose curved forms are recapitulations of those of the dome. The dome itself, accompanied by a succession of half-domes and barrel vaults, creates a spatial effect that makes the interior as impressive as it is unique; it was the largest enclosure constructed up to this time in the United States. The varying geometry of

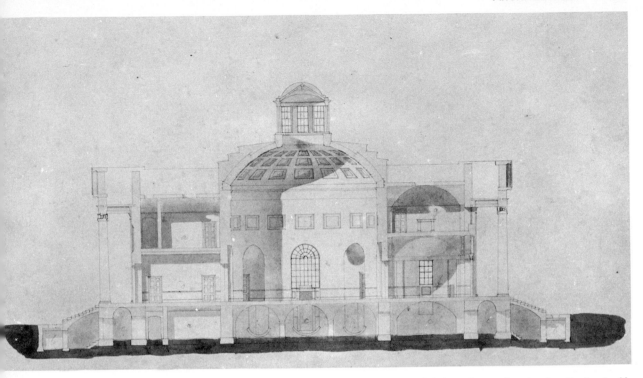

3–16. Interior section, Bank of Pennsylvania (destroyed), Philadelphia, Pennsylvania, by Benjamin H. Latrobe. Detail of watercolor drawing by Latrobe. (The Historical Society of Pennsylvania, Philadelphia.)

curved and rectangular surfaces in the interior is generally unrelieved by ornament except for the occasional use of columns and the sparse formality of panel, soffit, and entablature. The employment of low segmental arches and a continuous entablature at the base of the dome in place of the more usual pendentives enhances the simple geometry of isolated forms playing against one another in a restrained counterpoint.

When Latrobe was called in to supervise the Capitol, the almost ruinous state of much of Thornton's structure required such drastic remodeling that Latrobe practically redesigned the building (incurring Thornton's lasting enmity), keeping only the general conception of the two legislative areas joined by a rotunda. After the burning of the capital by the British in the War of 1812 even Thornton's oval House of Representatives was replaced by Latrobe's semicircular one. Though most of the early work of Latrobe at the Capitol was destroyed, enough of it was

left or was repeated or improved upon in the remodeling to make it worthwhile not to discuss what was, but to confine our consideration of the architect's work in the Capitol to what presently exists. The former House, now Statuary Hall [its former appearance is shown in Samuel F. B. Morse's painting *Congress Hall: Old House of Representatives*, 1821 (PB 307; Illustration 4–42)], is undoubtedly one of the handsomest legislative chambers of the time, both in its grand simplicity and in the elegance of its material, being comparable to similar auditoriums built during the revolutionary era in France. The former Senate (now the Old Supreme Court), the original Supreme Court Room (later Law Library) (AB 118), the Senate Rotunda (AB 117), and the vaulted lobbies joining them are all imaginative in their fine spatial arrangement and in the majesty of their juxtaposition of curved and rectangular forms. Perhaps the most original is the room underneath the former

3–17. Baltimore Cathedral, Baltimore, Maryland, 1804–c. 1818, by Benjamin H. Latrobe. From an old photograph.

3–18. Interior, Baltimore Cathedral, Baltimore, Maryland, by Benjamin H. Latrobe.

3–19. Area under the Rotunda, United States Capitol, Washington, D. C., c. 1809, by Benjamin H. Latrobe.

Senate, which is very bold in conception. Here the simple expression of vaulted structure is combined only with the most forceful of Doric orders, handled in a large and expansive way, and with very little other ornament. Only Soane, in England, was using such original and expressive forms at that time. The area under the great Rotunda (Illustration 3–19), seldom seen by visitors, was meant originally to house the tomb

of Washington, and is another example of Latrobe's grandeur and simplicity of conception. The originality of Latrobe appears in another, though minor, aspect at the Capitol in his design of the "corn cob" and tobacco columns [in the Old Senate vestibule, and Rotunda, respectively, 1809 (rebuilt 1816) (AB 117)] as variants on the acanthus-leaved Corinthian order. These were universally admired, even by Mrs. Trollope, who found occasion to remark in connection with them that "a sense of fitness always enhances the effect of beauty." [8]

The central portion of the Capitol (AB 116) is largely Latrobe's since Bulfinch, who succeeded him, carried out quite faithfully the former's designs, except that he omitted the niches in the Rotunda, unfortunately so featureless without them, and substituted a conventional colonnade with coupled columns (not dissimilar in its graceful proportions to that of the Boston State House) for Latrobe's projected elliptical portico of monumental proportions. Even the more pretentious additions of the dome and the two legislative wings by Thomas U. Walter in the 1850's are in the monumental and powerful neo-classicism originated in this country by Latrobe, though lacking in refinement, for a Roman grandiloquence was substituted for Latrobe's Hellenic restraint. Even though the inconsistencies of design and inconvenience of planning reveal the many hands involved from the beginning, the real distinction and power of the Capitol, especially in its interiors, are largely due to Latrobe. His taste is also prominent in the other most important building in Washington, the President's House, where he brought Hoban's Gibbsian design up-to-date by the addition of two porticos (AB 745, AB 751) in the rebuilding after the British sack of Washington.

Near the White House are two important buildings by Latrobe, St. John's Church and the Stephen Decatur House. The former is one of the less conspicuous buildings by Latrobe. Insofar as it remains the original building—the nave has been lengthened and a new facade added—it is typical in its clearly revealed structural form, coupled with restraint and elegance of detail. The Stephen Decatur House, 1817 (Illustration 3–20), is perhaps more important, for it is the finest prototype of a town house restricted to the cubical form by exigencies of the rectangular city block. But this limitation Latrobe turned into an advantage. The two flat facades joining on the corner in a precise and unornamented edge, the proportions of openings to the total surface, and the importance of the cornice as a final formal accent combine to give

3–20. Stephen Decatur House, Washington, D. C., 1817, by Benjamin H. Latrobe.

the building a massive simplicity which the typical framed houses in the Adamesque style do not possess because of their slimmer proportions and more finely scaled detail. Though less influential than houses of the Decatur type, others by Latrobe were more distinctive as unique examples. Perhaps the architect's domestic masterpiece was the Van Ness House in Washington, unfortunately demolished. This mansion was distinguished for the convenience of its plan and the adaptation of its arrangement to entertainment on the grand scale—largely the purpose for which the house was built. As would be expected in a work by Latrobe, the design of the house was forceful in its expression of the basic volumes and masses of the somewhat complex but unified plan, and was accompanied by the usual restrained ornament suggesting but not quite imitating classical forms, except in the entrance portico where the order is fully treated, its elegance all the more effective because of the reticence of the other detail.

Of Latrobe's other houses, those in Philadelphia, in Richmond, and elsewhere in Virginia in his early years were slightly more conservative in plan and late Georgian in feeling, though as usual displaying an unobtrusive dignity and nicely scaled and restrained detail; those of his later years exhibited more of his personal style. Among his non-domestic buildings the little Louisiana Bank in New Orleans, and the large Merchants' Exchange in Baltimore deserve mention. In the former, the interior is a miniature of the segmentally domed and vaulted ceilings of Latrobe's more prominent buildings, and the exterior is a paradigm of basic simplicity. The Baltimore Exchange, unfortunately torn down fairly recently, was largely Latrobe's though the co-architect was Godefroy, and was a magnificent construction of solid masonry, grand in its exterior massiveness and impressive in its domed interior.

One of the finest of Latrobe's designs was never built, the proposed Central Building of the Pittsburgh Armory, 1814, preserved in one of the architect's beautifully rendered drawings in the Library of Congress (AB 112); an almost Ledoux-like simplicity of mass and plane surface prevails.

Latrobe's career was a spotted one, punctuated with various unfortunate business enterprises into which his capacity of engineer led him. (A survey of his canals and other projects is a fascinating chapter in the early development of the country but not appropriate here.) The professional misfortune of not pleasing President Monroe, which resulted in his virtual dismissal from the superintendence of the Capitol, was soon followed by another loss—the award of the winning design for the Second Bank of the United States in Philadelphia in 1818 to his pupil William Strickland, whose drawings actually owed much to Latrobe (at least this was the latter's conviction).

Latrobe died a man in his prime, in 1820, of yellow fever while he was working on the water works in New Orleans. Though America was deprived of a designer who would have continued to give character to our national architecture, the men whom he had trained in what amounted to the first architectural school in the country—especially William Strickland and Robert Mills—carried their master's tradition into the next period. Mills, for instance, in Philadel-

phia, Richmond, and Baltimore was constructing houses similar to those of Latrobe in their simplicity and boldness of statement during the second decade of the century, though his most distinguished work occurs later and has a clearly Greek Revival accent. This is true also of John Haviland, another Englishman who left his mark on early American architecture, and who was building in the last years of the decade in a Regency fashion not dissimilar to that of Latrobe. But since both Mills's and Haviland's work and influence are chiefly in the next period, it is more convenient to discuss them later.

The work of three other immigrant architects of this period should be mentioned, the Frenchman Maximilian Godefroy and the two Englishmen George Hadfield and William Jay. Godefroy, a trained architect who came to this country in 1804, was the first instructor of architecture in the United States, teaching at St. Mary's College in Baltimore. He is known to have collaborated in the design of the Merchant's Exchange, but to all intents and purposes Latrobe was the principal designer. On the other hand, Godefroy's Unitarian Church in Baltimore, 1817–1818 (AB 103, AB 104; Illustration 3–21), is completely his own, though it reflects the style of romantic classicism which Latrobe shared in a general way with another Frenchman, Ledoux.

3–21. Unitarian Church, Baltimore, Maryland, 1817–1818, by Maximilian Godefroy.

3–22. District Court (formerly City Hall), Washington, D. C., 1820–1823, by George Hadfield. From an old photograph.

The building is basically a domed rotunda inserted in a cube, with just enough of the dome showing to be visible as a partial hemisphere. The clear form of the exterior is given relief not by the usual projecting portico but by the insertion of an arcaded vestibule into the facade, which preserved intact the basic cube—a usage actually derived from Ledoux. In the interior the dome almost joins the arches and the pendentives with no interpolation of an entablature, giving an effect of unusual clarity and boldness. Unfortunately, the functional expressiveness of the design is somewhat marred by the small-scale ornament of the late Louis XVI style, which obscures the structural areas and which would probably have been left undecorated ex-

cept by the soffits or panels, had Latrobe been the architect.

The work of Hadfield [9] and Jay has the dignified and simple monumentality of the generation of Soane and Latrobe, coupled with somewhat more of the graceful elegance of the Regency. Hadfield's City Hall in Washington— now the District Court 1820–1823 (Illustration 3–22)—somewhat neglected by architectural historians, is actually as fine and advanced in design as is much of Latrobe's best work. The building is a vindication of the reputation of a man who had been professionally almost ruined twenty years before because unlike Latrobe, his more tolerant successor, he had refused to carry out Thornton's plan for the Capitol because he said it "could not be executed." [10] The usual emphasis on the ubiquitous classical portico at the center of the building is enhanced and at the same time qualified by wings with facades of monumental proportion, made up of handsome block-like areas of wall enframing a bay with columns *in antis*. Yet the potential heaviness of such a design is mitigated by the fine detailing and the graceful intrusion of arched openings to relieve the prevailing rectilinearity. The best features of both neo-classicism and romantic classicism are combined here with a certain late Georgian gracefulness, creating all-in-all a very distinguished and personal building. Even more individual was Hadfield's remodeling of the Lee Mansion, Arlington House (conceived in 1802 but not carried out until 1824), at Arlington, Virginia. Here the architect designed a portico with a thick-set archaic Greek Doric order, which he used without fluting—a fairly early instance of the Greek order in a domestic building and certainly the first employment of this dramatically impressive early form. The choice of this huge and heavy colonnade to compete successfully with the many porticoed city across the river was a stroke of genius.

Besides a few other houses since torn down and an impressive tomb, Hadfield designed only the old Treasury (1798) which inspired the former State, War, and Navy buildings (all eventually joined together in two E-shaped complexes symmetrically flanking the White House and long since destroyed). Thus only two buildings exist which realize the potentials of a promising architect, trained at the Royal Academy and at Rome, whose early misfortune, in the words of Latrobe, prevented him from taking "the station in art which his elegant taste and excellent talent ought to have obtained." [11]

Buildings by William Jay erected around 1820 in Savannah comprise one of the most distinguished bodies of work by one man in a single city in the United States. The Habersham, Telfair (now an academy), the Owens Thomas House, 1816–1819 (AB 727), and Scarborough (now a school), c. 1820 (AB 728), are thought to be certainly by him, and there are probably

3–23. Branch Bank of the United States (destroyed), Savannah, Georgia, 1819, by William Jay. From an old lithograph.

more. There is considerable variety in the four houses, and each exploits some aspect of romantic classicism in a sophisticated and personal way. What must have been one of the most impressive buildings of the period was Jay's Branch Bank of the United States, 1819 (Illustration 3–23). The old lithograph shows us a building with a strong central mass emphasized by a heavy continuous entablature and a forceful Doric portico surmounted not by a pediment but by cubical blocks repeating the massive central motif. The rather overwhelming monumentality of the whole is tempered by a sequence of arched openings in otherwise unrelieved walls. Such a masterpiece of romantic classicism must have influenced, however indirectly, much of the academic and vernacular architecture of the South in the next period, especially in masonry, as can be seen, for instance, in the surviving buildings in the old commercial area of Mobile, and in the block-like forms of some Georgia plantations.

The importance of such immigrants as Hadfield, Latrobe, and Jay would make it glaringly chauvinistic to suggest that the best American architecture of the period was anything but imported. But though European in origin, it developed under the impact of American conditions of the time. All of these architects, especially Latrobe, were stimulated to a greater monumentality and effectiveness of statement than they might have been in Europe. The need for a national or public architecture of dignity, the relative lack of previous monumental building to stand in the way of the "modern" style, either physically or psychologically, and the sympathy for the supposedly democratic forms of classical antiquity all contributed to this development. Romantic classicism became the basis upon which the outstanding architecture of the next period was based, that of the Greek Revival.

Community Planning

During the period of the early republic the great majority of town and regional planning consisted of an extension of patterns developed by the end of the colonial period—with the addition of a few significant new forms.

The tradition of the dwelling isolated on the large lot in town or countryside in the older settlements was continued by the clearing in the wilderness where the squatter or settler left only a few trees for ornament and shade; and later, further west, by the house standing naked on the prairie. The tendency toward geometric division, seen especially in New England and the Carolinas and further extended to the early settlement of Kentucky and Tennessee, was formalized by the "national grid" suggested by the Land Ordinance of 1785, with its "hundreds" townships of ten-square-mile squares, divided into lots each one mile square. The "wide open spaces" of the West—and even the wide, monotonous boulevards of its cities—take their character from this division.

In the East the grid tradition was also perpetuated as the cities grew. Philadelphia extended its rectangular division west of the Schuylkill after 1802 (*CPB 7) while New York became the most conspicuous example of the urban grid plan, the final form set for the city in the Commissioners' plan in 1810 (*CPB 10). The division into the smaller areas and lots with which we are familiar today led to the further development of the row house so that it became ubiquitous wherever this kind of plan went into effect, that is to say, in most urban areas. Already Philadelphia in the eighteenth century had produced several solutions to the row house; as the practice was taken up elsewhere, architects of the stature of Bulfinch were employed to design them. Beacon Hill in Boston retains a reflection of his ideas (CPB 20), while John McComb, Jr., was the foremost architect associated with this type of dwelling in New York (the houses on the north side of Washington Square remain as examples of the type, though built later). Baltimore is the site of perhaps the most extensive development of the row house. Two of the original groups built in the early nineteenth century remain; one of them, Waterloo Row on North Calvert Street, is an early work by Robert Mills, the follower of Latrobe. Lot sizes, plans, and other features varied somewhat from city to city, but a detailed analysis is not necessary, since in general design they were all similar. A few distinguishing features, however, may be pointed out. In New York a stoop with a cellar entrance under it was common. This was not true in Baltimore, and though sometimes a cellar entrance was used in Boston, the stoop was more often enclosed in a recessed entrance.

In both the country and the city, there was very little variation from the practical mathematics of the grid. A few cities started out with a more imaginative concept, however; Buffalo, for instance, possessed a town plan with avenues radiating from a public square. But it was in Washington that a truly grand conception was introduced by the French architect-engineer, Pierre L'Enfant. The seat of government required the dignity of a fine plan with avenues and openings to exploit the prospects of the important and symbolic buildings—reciprocities of sight, as their designer called them (*CPB 24, *CPB 35, *CPB 36). L'Enfant's plan was a kind of extension of that of Annapolis, ultimately based, as was the latter, partly on Wren's scheme for London after the fire. But L'Enfant's plan derived more from Continental sources, including Versailles, which exploits the triangle as much as the square, especially the configuration of three radiating streets called *patte d'oie* (goose foot; geese have three toes). Though frustrated by circumstances for more than a century, the plan was revived early in the 1900's, and Washington today has a scale, amplitude, and grandeur which enhance its neo-classic architecture and make it one of the most impressive cities in the world.

But Washington was exceptional. Along with the unimaginative acceptance of the grid there was, as well, a general tendency to ignore the possibilities of naturally beautiful sites. At Brooklyn Heights, with its magnificent view over the harbor to Manhattan, the Commissioners had expected the individual purchasers to release voluntarily a small portion of their land for a public esplanade, but they were disappointed. In large cities neither officials nor large landowners like John Jacob Astor did anything for the sake of amenity, as the great landlords in London had done with their open squares, planted and gardened.

This is not to say, however, that the beauty of planting was ignored in the United States. After the original prejudice of the settler against the tree had subsided, avenues of trees were planted to relieve the bareness of the usually rigidly rectangular streets. Views of colonial towns are remarkable for the absence of planting, which begins to appear only in the early 1800's in the form of small elms, maples, and other shade trees. (The more romantic conifers were usually of a later date.) The appearance of residential New Haven (called the "city of elms" until the recent blight) was that of a regularized forest dotted with houses—the result of a deliberate program begun by James Hillhouse in 1790. Litchfield and other Connecticut towns followed suit in what must have been a fairly general movement; from the air, in the summertime, the

buildings of most American residential areas are almost hidden by masses of foliage. The struggle between the practical concept of cleared and rectilinear bareness and an esthetic of variety and contrast of shapes and colors was resolved in the next period when the romantic ideal of a pleasant relation between buildings, especially dwellings, and their natural environment was formulated.

A few other instances of planning besides urban and regional should be noted, colleges and universities and early manufacturing communities being the most conspicuous. The University of Virginia has already been described. Joseph Ramée's design for Union College at Schenectady, New York, is nearly as impressive with its rectangular court and a central Pantheon (executed as a medieval revival building a half-century later) flanked by rectangles and curved arcades (*CPB 11, *CPB 12).

The mill villages of New England, especially in Rhode Island, where textile manufacturing was introduced into the United States in the late eighteenth century, are especially interesting as instances of the earliest planning of entire communities. During the initial stages of the industry the narrow streams of rural New England were sufficient to supply power for small-scale operation, and it was on their banks that the first mill villages were built. These were self-sufficient units; in addition to the mills themselves and the dwellings of the operatives and their families (with housing for superintendents, agents, and sometimes even the owners), they included churches, libraries, schools, and stores. The pleasing appearance of the villages and the presence within them of cultural facilities reflect concern on the part of the owners for the general welfare of the operatives, for both economic and ethical reasons. The conditions surrounding the early textile workers in Great Britain had aroused in the United States actual prejudice against any manufacturing. It was "good business," therefore, to show the public and the prospective workers that pleasant living conditions could prevail. The moral tone of the early republic, too, required of men in responsible positions both the proper conduct of their busi-

Painting

It will be necessary to go into the European background of American painting of this period at greater length than was the case with the eighteenth century; the historical framework into which colonial art fitted was relatively simple by comparison. The art of both Europe and America in these years belonged to the first phase of the modern era. At this juncture in western civilization, so dramatically ushered in by the American and French revolutions, art history is far more complicated than during the seventeenth and eighteenth centuries, when a still somewhat unified hierarchical and traditional society produced works of art and architecture that were easy to categorize in terms of both subject matter and style. Further complicating the situation was the Industrial Revolution, which was already causing the growth of a larger middle class. The consequent weakening of royal, aristocratic, and other traditional authority and the increase of bourgeois influence resulted in the breaking down of the dominance of portraiture (at least in the eighteenth-century Anglo-Saxon world) and in the broadening of taste for other subjects. This is not to say that portrait painting did not remain the most prominent among the figurative arts until the popularization of photography in the 1850's, but genre, still life, and landscape were more conspicuous in the painter's repertoire than before. These subjects, so popular in another bourgeois community, that of seventeenth-century Holland, came into their own again as society in general became more middle-class. Renewed interest in the real world and the familiar was also an aspect of burgeoning romanticism (an attitude more familiar in literature, where it is illustrated in the poetry of Wordsworth).

Landscape, genre, and still life were accompanied during this period by an entirely different kind of painting which had flourished especially during the aristocratic seventeenth century, though almost exclusively on the Continent and hardly ever in England. This was history painting, which was revived not only as an aspect of a romantic nostalgia for the past but as an effective means of presenting political ideologies during this time of social change. The Frenchman Jacques Louis David, for instance, painted propaganda pieces which actually influenced the course of the French Revolution. Later, in the United States, the historical canvases of Trumbull memorialized the American Revolution with figures in contemporary dress, a practice more popular in English history pictures than French wherein the figures were more frequently clad in togas.

In style as well as in subject matter there was a definite break with the past. Though at first a revived classicism in painting as well as in architecture seems more prominent than any other aspect of style at the beginning of the period, it is only superficially more conspicuous and not fundamentally characteristic of the period as a whole. Neo-classicism was only one of a number of manners that existed almost contemporaneously with the beginnings of romanticism, which seems to be its antithesis but with which it has much in common. The word "manner" instead of "style" is used here advisedly, for style in its connotation of a definition of form within a cultural period begins to be less clear at this time. The organic sequence of historical styles from the medieval through the Renaissance to the baroque and rococo seems to have broken off at that point. Thus the modern epoch in its first decades had no easily defined all-encompassing style—or at least if it had, it is not yet discernible to the art historian. Neo-classicism was certainly the most obvious manner (or "style," used in a more limited sense) of this period, and continued to be so for much of the next, especially in architecture and sculpture. The interest in Greek and Roman antiquity which had been initiated in the Renaissance and revitalized during various intervals since (as in Poussin, the French Academy, Palladio, and Lord Burlington), became almost a rage after the discovery of Herculaneum and Pompeii in the mid-eighteenth century. The enthusiasm for ancient art was codified by an esthetic (largely the creation of the first art historian, Johann Winckelmann) which required an almost archaeological imitation in contradistinction to the more or less free inspiration of antiquity prevailing in former revivals. As a result, in academic circles neo-classicism in painting was hardly questioned, at least on the Continent; in architecture it was not challenged anywhere.

But while at first glance neo-classicism seems to be overwhelmingly in the ascendancy, on closer examination a reaction against it can be discerned. Neither the various and exciting world of beginning romanticism nor the broadening taste in subject matter could find appropriate expression in the restrained and cold linearism of neo-classicism. An attempted analysis of the "style" of the period is made more complex, therefore, by both a survival and a revival of the lively, coloristic rococo tradition, especially in England where a painterly technique and dynamic composition still persisted or were revived. In the United States, painting followed this path almost exclusively, in this respect being more influenced by England than by France—a circumstance largely due to the influence of Benjamin West, who taught three generations of Americans in London.

The combination of a romantic attitude with a taste that is generally classical (though often mixed with rococo survival and revival) makes it tempting to use "romantic classicism" as a term which would be as viable for painting as for architecture, thus avoiding the dilemma of a portmanteau stylistic description. Nevertheless, even though the self-contradiction of the term makes it a dangerous one to use in a general history, romantic classicism should be substituted for neo-classicism, with its implications of restriction and unoriginality, as the key stylistic term for the art of this period.

West and His Early Pupils

The story of American painting in the first years of the republic could hardly be told without taking into account the enormous influence of Benjamin West. His studio in London was in fact the first American art school or academy, from 1763 until almost 1820. West's entire professional life was spent in England; he was an intimate of George III and a president of the Royal Academy. It might then be questioned whether he is, properly speaking, an American painter at all. At least some of the originality which made him the initiator of so many of the artistic fashions of his time seems attributable to an individualism fostered by his early frontier environment. But whether this is conceded or not, West is significant in the annals of American art as a painter, English or American (he always called himself the latter), the various phases of whose work directed the course of American art through his American pupils and to a large extent joined it to the mainstream of western art.

Benjamin West was born not far from Philadelphia into a family of Quakers, a group traditionally opposed to the arts. The boy's eagerness to paint impelled him to execute his early work with such primitive materials as the pigments used by the neighboring savages for adorning their faces, and brushes fashioned from a younger brother's hair. Such pertinacity must have been instrumental in persuading his parents to permit him to become an artist. The example of the two second-rate English painters sojourning in the Middle Colonies, William Williams and John Wollaston, formed West's early primitive style, illustrated by the portrait of *Thomas Mifflin*, c. 1758–1759 (PA 114); though his manner has some naïve charm, it lacks the strength of a Feke or an early Copley. But West's accomplishments were sufficient to inspire a group of Pennsylvania merchants to send him to Rome, where he arrived in 1760 to spend three years. His comment that the Apollo Belvedere reminded him of a Mohawk warrior was a notable critical event in this ancient city jaded by years of connoisseurship. All doors were opened to the ingenuous and personable young "savage" and he absorbed the current taste of Rome: the beginnings of neo-classicism, stimulated by the discovery of Herculaneum and Pompeii; the publication of Winckelmann's *History of Greek Art;* the existence of a Roman school of eclectic clas-

3–26.   Benjamin West, *Agrippina Landing at Brindisium With the Ashes of Germanicus,* 1768.   Oil on canvas.   64½ x 94½ inches.   (Courtesy of Yale University Art Gallery, New Haven, Connecticut.   Gift of Louis M. Rabinowitz.)

sicists who emulated the great masters of the Renaissance as well as those of antiquity. This was the cultural atmosphere which a few years later surrounded the young French painter Jacques Louis David. But the example of David, with his previous academic training and his native structural genius, came too late for West to profit by. Instead he was influenced by the weaker eclecticism of Raphael Mengs, a German painter whom Winckelmann admired for illustrating his theories. Mengs had a vapid and empty style accompanied by a technique so smooth that all sense of paint is lost, a lack which is not compensated for by any vigor of drawing, always a virtue of even the driest Davids.

This unstructural and smooth style was part of the classical baggage which West brought back with him to London in 1763. Both the neo-classic point of view and the slick Mengs technique are illustrated in his *Agrippina Landing at Brindisium With the Ashes of Germanicus,* 1768 (Illustration 3–26). Though there is little to recommend this large picture as a work of art, it is significant as a document of the history of taste, for in it West developed the stylistic characteristics of neo-classicism nearly twenty years before the first important picture in the new mode, David's *Oath of the Horaces.* The composition of the *Agrippina* is based on classical bas-reliefs, especially the *Ara Pacis* of Augustus, and antique vases. Its manner is linear and non-coloristic, and its organization is flat and in general parallel to the picture plane —all characteristics of classic art and diametrically opposed to the "painterly," colorful, and dynamic pictures of the current rococo tradition. Equally significant was West's choice of subject, referring as it did to the patriotic heroism of Germanicus at Carthage. West, whose Quaker and provincial moral sensibilities had been offended by the loose and unethical behavior of eighteenth-century Italy, found a rejoinder in the introduction of moral didacticism into his painting, just as David a little later was to inject political propaganda into his. This bourgeois moralizing found favor in the eyes of that eminently middle-class monarch George III, which accounts for West's rapid rise.

No sooner had West achieved the style of the *Agrippina* than his original mind and perhaps his instinct for the main chance made him turn quickly to another kind of subject and manner. *The Death of Wolfe,* 1771 (Illustration 3–27), is the most prominent picture, though not actually the first, to reject the classical trappings of the "grand manner" and to treat a contemporary event as such. The depiction of the scene on the heights of Quebec is realistic in every respect. Even more astonishing is the style, which could be analyzed as baroque. In the composition, with its emphasis upon curves and diagonals, lively color and brush work, and dramatic chiaroscuro, the emotion of the scene is reflected in the excitement of the picture. The strong modeling, the broad handling of individual pas-

3–27. Benjamin West, *The Death of Wolfe,* 1771. Oil on canvas. 60½ x 84 inches. (National Gallery of Canada, Ottawa.)

left little inspiration for the paintings themselves, though there are exceptions, such as the portrait of *Benjamin Franklin,* 1785 (PB 341). The activities of the museum and other business prevented Peale from turning seriously to painting again until 1795. In that year he executed what is perhaps his masterpiece, *The Staircase Group,* 1795 (PB 339; Illustration 3–29), depicting his sons Raphaelle and Titian, the former ascending a curved stair, the latter descending and just about to enter the room. Deliberately conceived as a "deception," the picture was set in the frame of a doorway with an actual step placed before it to project into the room and further the illusion. The painting was apparently successful in its purpose, for on one occasion no less a personage than George Washington was seen to bow slightly to the simulated young men in their simulated stairway. Yet the picture is no mere *tour de force,* but an extraordinarily competent realization of a pair of figures, well-drawn and well-modeled in a very real space subtly depicted with every nuance of light. The figures are caught in the pause of a moment, and yet the balance of legs, arms, and painting stick gives it an almost monumentally static quality. The contrast of light in the face, hand, and knee of young Titian and the deep dark of the shadowed staircase behind and above him is a striking compositional device. Further, the successful depth and mass in the picture are enhanced by careful surface details reminiscent of Copley and the best of the limners. In *The Staircase Group,* Peale finds himself, and deliberately so, for he confessed that he wanted to make an impression with it; he even perfected new technical methods, including the lengthening of his brushes so that he could paint at a distance in order to get the total effect as well as the minute surface ones. The artist once wrote, "Perhaps I have a good eye, that is all, and not half the application that I now think necessary." [12] In this picture he had the motivation to apply himself and also to follow the precept he had so often repeated to his artist-children to "follow nature" and to realize his ideal of a painting "executed so well as to render it a perfect

3–29. Charles Willson Peale, *The Staircase Group,* 1795. Oil on canvas. 89 x 39½ inches. (Philadelphia Museum of Art. George W. Elkins Collection.)

illusion." [13] This concept of artistic excellence, with its overtones of nature being an imitation of God (which was brought back from Rome by West and promulgated to his students), appealed to both the artist and naturalist in Peale and informed his best work.

The continued activity of the museum, the bonanza of the discovery of a mastodon, its exhumation and exhibition, continued to militate against Peale the painter. But once again before he died Peale showed his too infrequently displayed true ability in his self-portrait, *The Artist in His Museum*, 1822 (PB 636). The virtues of *The Staircase Group* are repeated here, but the almost austere clarity and precision of the earlier work are combined with a richer and more painterly technique brought back by Peale's son Rembrandt, in 1802, from study with the later and more colorful West. In this picture Peale paints himself in the act of holding up a curtain which exposes to view the room in Independence Hall where his stuffed birds and Revolutionary portraits are displayed, and affords us a glimpse of the skeleton of the mastodon. A fine wild turkey shot by his son Rubens is in the foreground, together with the gigantic bones of another mammoth.

Peale was a very uneven painter. In the production of more than a thousand portraits and a few other subjects, he seldom realized his potentialities; but when he did, his work was among the best of the painters of his era. Even though lacking in the highest quality, many of his pictures are of great topical interest, as are his portraits of Washington and other leaders of the time, and his delightful genre piece, *Exhuming the Mastodon*, 1806 (PB 345). These reflect the multifarious activities of that "ingenious Mr. Peale" (as West called him when a young student) who played such an important part in the history of the country during its birth pangs, and who was so effective a collector for his own museum—the first in the country and the best for many years—in which he used display techniques that were more than a century ahead of their time.

A word should be added about Charles's brother James, who became a moderately successful portraitist under his brother's inspiration. *Washington and His Generals at Yorktown*, 1786 (PB 349), is a competent document but a little overambitious for the artist's talents. Two other group portraits, *The Ramsay-Polk Family*, c.

1793 (PB 350), and *Self-Portrait With His Family*, c. 1795 (PB 351), show James as an artist with considerably less technical equipment than his brother, but with a certain almost naïve charm.

John Trumbull

The generation of West's pupils during and shortly after the Revolution, including Ralph Earl, Gilbert Stuart, Robert Fulton, and William Dunlap, were temperamentally or deliberately wedded to portraiture. Only one, John Trumbull, was eager to carry on history painting, the more important of his master's leanings. Two circumstances, the great success of Copley and of West himself in this field and the stirring events surrounding the American Revolution, should have prepared the way for a great burst of such work in this country. But only Trumbull took advantage of the opportunity. Actually, he was the only American artist of his generation sufficiently trained and at the same time temperamentally and through force of circumstance in a position to embark on a series dealing with the early history of the nation. Only one other artist had been equally involved in the war and that was Peale, but he was humble about his talents and never even considered such a project. The social prominence of Trumbull and his familiarity with most of the leaders as well as the events of the times gave him virtually a monopoly which would have been not only unprofitable but even unseemly for another to break. Thus, other painters came to maturity but only one other besides Trumbull, John Vanderlyn, received an important commission in this field. Whatever the cause, Trumbull is the painter of the Revolution and on this his fame rests.

The pictures which the public knows and admires in the rotunda of the Capitol are only pale reflections of what might have been. Trumbull's late work, of which these are examples, presents the melancholy picture of a man of real talent, even of genius, against whom circumstances and his own temperament conspired to limit to but eight years his first-rate production, from 1786 to 1794. When government commissions finally came to him, it was too late. This conservative, crotchety Yankee aristocrat, the son and brother of governors of Connecticut, was never sure that a gentleman's proper calling was painting. He therefore dabbled in many other affairs, interrupted his career at the height of his powers to accompany John Jay as his secretary to England, where he remained ten years as Fifth Commissioner to settle the Jay Treaty, speculating the while in old masters and French brandy—disastrously. After unsuccessfully attempting to establish himself as a fashionable portraitist in both London and New York, he finally at the age of sixty-two obtained the commission for the paintings in the Capitol. In his later years Trumbull became a kind of elder statesman of American art. As head of the American Academy of the Fine Arts, his dictatorial policies resulted in the withdrawal of many members and the founding of the National Academy of Design. At seventy-two he gave his pictures to Yale in return for an annuity, designed a building to house them, and lived fifteen more years until his death at age eighty-seven. His remains are entombed under the gallery, replaced now by a later superstructure.

A rather impressive work of his youth shows considerable ability, the portrait of his brother *Jonathan Trumbull, Jr., and Family,* 1777 (PB 438). Quite obviously inspired by Copley, hard, "liney," but rather powerful in its stiff and wooden directness, this picture shows Trumbull to be as good as the best of the school surrounding Ralph Earl. In fact, more than one portrait in Trumbull's early manner has been attributed at various times to both artists.

Study with West and contact in London with the great tradition as seen in the important English artists freed Trumbull's hand from its colonial limitations. The liveliness of the persisting rococo tradition, together with the boldly dynamic baroque composition of West's *Death of Wolfe* were the inspiration for Trumbull's best work, his historical sketches and portraits in the grand manner, represented by *Jeremiah Wadsworth and His Son Daniel,* 1784 (PB 437). Though somewhat marred by the usual Mengs-

West smoothness, such a portrait seems competent enough, hardly deserving the remark by Reynolds, "Tin, sir, bent tin." [14] It may be that this rebuff turned Trumbull further in the direction of developing a more "painterly" and rococo style. At any rate, the small studies Trumbull painted for his historical groups are among the liveliest in the history of portraiture. The face of *Thomas Jefferson* (Illustration 3–30), sketched at his house in Paris in 1787, glows with vitality. The red hair, intense blue eyes, sharp nose, and determined lips of this intelligent, strong, and sensitive face are more convincing than in any other representation of the philosopher-statesman and architect.

The first pictures of the historical series were painted in West's London studio or under his in-

3–30. John Trumbull, *Thomas Jefferson,* 1787. Miniature. Oil on wood. 4½ x 3¼ inches. (The Metropolitan Museum of Art, New York. Bequest of Cornelia Cruger, 1923.)

3–31. John Trumbull, *Battle of Bunker's Hill,* 1786. Oil on canvas. 25 x 34 inches. (Courtesy of Yale University Art Gallery, New Haven, Connecticut.)

fluence from 1786 to 1796: *Battle of Bunker's Hill* (PB 439; Illustration 3–31), *Capture of the Hessians at Trenton,* and *Death of Montgomery in the Attack on Quebec* (PB 440), all in 1786; *The Declaration of Independence,* 1786–1797 (PB 665); *Death of General Mercer at the Battle of Princeton, New Jersey* and *Surrender of Lord Cornwallis at Yorktown, Virginia,* before 1797. (The preliminary study for the *Battle of Princeton* was done in 1787.) *Surrender of General Burgoyne at Saratoga* and *Resignation of General Washington at Annapolis* were not started until 1816, and are much weaker in composition, characterization, and general vitality, having been executed at the time Trumbull began the larger versions for the Capitol. All are in the Yale University Gallery. [A picture of a British victory,

Sortie of the British Garrison at Gibraltar, 1788 (*PB 435), is comparable in quality to the American scenes done about the same time.]

The six American subjects executed before 1797, together with the one British, comprise the best of Trumbull's work. Perhaps their small scale (they were intended as originals from which engravings were to be made) had something to do with their quality. The artist's discouragement following the decline of interest in the Revolutionary subjects after the excesses of the French Revolution and the consequent falling off of subscriptions caused him to turn to other matters until called upon to execute the larger versions of his subjects painted in 1817. By this time his enthusiasm had faltered and his technique had been dulled by the painting of hackneyed portraits and historical, religious, and mythological pictures in West's worst and most pompous manner. Thus the four scenes at the Capitol (as well as the copies now in the Wadsworth Athenaeum in Hartford) are poor reflections of the originals, though they repeat their compositions and are therefore effective at least as decoration.

Trumbull's finest work consists of the small pictures of 1787–1796. Lively in brush stroke, dynamic in composition, and brilliant and fresh in color, they perfectly reflect in their formal elements the spirited action or dramatic situation of the subjects. The best of the rococo style with all its ornamental vivacity is reflected in these little pictures, but the combination of the influence of Copley's accurate eye with Trumbull's own Yankee precision and conscientiousness has introduced the element of fact to compensate for what might otherwise have been merely conventionally decorative formulas. The result is solid, lasting, and rewarding as well as delightfully lively.

Gilbert Stuart and His Followers

Of all the men who studied with West, Stuart was the most consistently competent. Within the strict limitations of portraiture he was unsurpassed in his generation in America and perhaps in the world. Even as a boy in Newport his talent was evident. He was taken at an early age by Cosmo Alexander, a Scottish painter, to Edinburgh where he may have picked up the beginnings of his brilliantly cursory and suggestive style from Allan Ramsay's assistant and follower, David Martin. This painter was the master of Sir Henry Raeburn whose style is closer to Stuart's than is that of any other member of the British school. Stuart returned briefly to America, before the Revolution, on the death of his patron in Scotland, and painted competent pictures, as the portrait of *Mrs. John Bannister and Her Son*, c. 1774 (PB 656), indicates. On his return to England his technique was reinforced by academic training with West, in whose studio he remained until his fabulous early success in London, where he outdid his more famous contemporaries in brilliance. Yet Stuart was not

3–32. Gilbert Stuart, *Mrs. Perez Morton,* c. 1802. Oil on canvas. 29⅛ x 24⅛ inches. (Worcester Art Museum, Worcester, Massachusetts.)

influenced by the eclecticisms or pompous trappings of West or of Reynolds who reintroduced the grand style to England. Stuart said that he always sought reality. But in seeking for a natural effect, his portraits preserve a feeling of immediacy through a brilliantly sketched surety of touch. His is not the tediously reconstructed surface realism of Copley or of the earlier Flemish and Dutch painters, but the suggestion of the quick visual effect which is quite close to the ultimate visual naturalism of the impressionists much later. The lightness and flair of his brush stroke is a last manifestation of the lively rococo style best represented by Gainsborough, whose work Stuart admired (and for which his own has on at least one occasion been taken). This liveliness is enhanced by another practice resembling the technique of the impressionists: a brilliant luminosity achieved by applying the colors directly on the canvas, instead of mixing them on his palette. He is quoted as having said, "No blending, 'tis destruction of pure and beautiful effect." [15] His method of painting bore out the decree, for he would stand off before the canvas, poise himself, and then lurch forward, stabbing the picture with the brush as though it were a knife. The method at its most impulsive and successful can be best seen in the unfinished portrait of *Mrs. Perez Morton,* c. 1802 (°PB 655; Illustration 3–32). Charles Willson Peale, in a letter to his son Rembrandt, after speaking of Stuart says, "Dispatch is absolutely necessary for the painting of portraits, otherwise a languor will sit on the visage of the sitter." [16] Nearly all of Stuart's portraits, no matter how finished they are, retain a luminousness and vivacity. Probably no other artist was as successful in painting flesh, but this is not

3–33. Gilbert Stuart, *Major General Henry Knox,* c. 1810. Oil on canvas. 47 x 38½ inches. (Courtesy, Museum of Fine Arts, Boston. Lent by the City of Boston.)

surprising in a man who loved it so, for he said, "Flesh is like no other substance under heaven; it has all the quality of a silk mercer's shop without the gaudiness or glare, and all the soberness of old mahogany without its deadness or softness." [17] Stuart's portraits glow with flesh tints—and the artist seldom interferes with this sensuous appeal by confusing us with the addition of much else. The majority are bust portraits (it used to be said contemptuously of him in London that he could not paint below the fifth button of the waistcoat), though he was quite capable of painting a monumental full-length portrait of impressive dignity such as the "Lansdowne" *Washington,* 1796, in the Pennsylvania Academy.

Stuart's heads, for all their brilliant surface effect, also have structure, as can be seen in any number of his familiar portraits of famous Americans. The head of *John Adams* (PB 416) is a typical example, or the solid *Major General Henry Knox,* c. 1810 (Illustration 3–33), whose body is so well realized with so little effort. Even his portraits in the aristocratic English tradition are so brilliantly and scintillatingly painted that it is difficult not to admire them in spite of their superficial elegance, as in his portraits of *Joseph de Jaudenes y Nebot* and *Matilde Stoughton de Jaudenes,* c. 1795 (PB 653, PB 654).

Stuart's record of the important figures of his time has a kind of permanence and idealization which makes them almost classic in both the strict and even the stylistic senses of the word, as witness the several Washingtons—not only the "Lansdowne," but the more famous portraits, "Athenaeum," 1796 (PB 421), and "Vaughan," 1795 (PB 420). At the same time the *General Knox* or the superb *Mrs. Richard Yates,* 1793 (PB 419), shows how Stuart can be warm and personal as well. In such pictures as these his excellence in the great European tradition combined with his realistic point of view make Stuart one of the great portrait artists of all time. The question of the relative Americanism in his style is almost irrelevant, for even though the frequent down-to-earth realism of his approach to his sitter is more a native than a British ele-

temporaries and followers who were as much influenced by this tradition itself as by Earl's more sophisticated variation of it. The stylistic similarities in composition, characterization, and manner of painting are obvious in the sequence of five portraits: *Jabez Hamlin,* painted in the 1760's by William Johnston (Illustration 2–50); *The Reverend Ebenezer Devotion,* 1770, by Winthrop Chandler (Illustration 2–51); *Roger Sherman,* c. 1775 (PB 179; Illustration 3–35), and *Benjamin Tallmadge and His Son William,* 1790 (PB 556; Illustration 3–37), both by Earl; and *John Phillips,* painted in 1793 by Joseph Steward (Illustration 3–38). All these pictures reveal a similar, frank realism, an attention to pattern, a sharply modeled linearism, and a tendency to isolate or silhouette the subject. The marked stylistic similarity among these artists and the fact that they lived and worked in Connecticut most of their lives are justification for calling them a Connecticut school.

There is little doubt that Johnston, Chandler, and even to a certain extent John Durand, all of whom worked in Connecticut before the Revolution, were the artistic forerunners of Ralph Earl. It is also very likely that he knew at least the work of Copley if not the master himself. He was thus thoroughly imbued with the local style that originated in the Puritan school of seventeenth-century New England and was carried on by Feke and Copley insofar as they persisted, in spite of themselves, in not being thoroughly English. At the same time, Earl is even more forthright in characterization and realistic portrayal than his predecessors, with the exception of Copley at his best. His portrait of *Eliphalet Dyer* (sometimes attributed to the young Trumbull) in the library at Windham, Connecticut, for example, contrasts greatly with Johnston's portrait of the same man done only about ten years before (Connecticut Historical Society, Hartford). In the earlier picture, Dyer, in his official capacity as a judge in His Majesty's colonial government, is wigged and stands elegantly in a long, flared coat, one hand extended in an expansive and rhetorical gesture. In Earl's picture, Dyer is shorn of his wig and clad in homespun, and sits in a plain Windsor chair

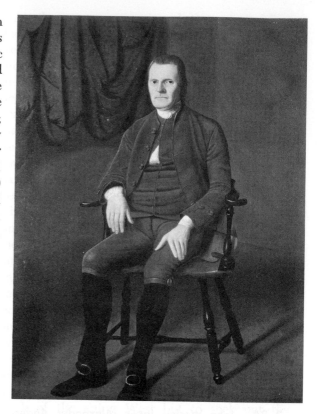

3–35. Ralph Earl, *Roger Sherman,* c. 1775. Oil on canvas. 64⅝ x 49⅝ inches. (Courtesy of Yale University Art Gallery, New Haven, Connecticut. Gift of Roger Sherman White.)

made in Connecticut, with his hands resting naturally on its arms. The king's man has given place to the patriot, a delegate to the first Continental Congress. The Johnston portrait, though flat and "liney," nevertheless reflects an elegance of manner and an attitude typical of English aristocratic painting. In Earl's portrait not only is the style American but the point of view of both artist and subject has become democratic as well.

The full-length portrait of *Roger Sherman,* c. 1775 (PB 179; Illustration 3–35), probably Earl's masterpiece, was painted at about the same time as the *Dyer.* Another patriot, Sherman was a member of the Continental Congress, helped draw up the Constitution, and in the early republic dominated the government of Connecticut for years. In Earl's unforgettable portrait he sits, dressed in homespun, in a Windsor chair, "an old Puritan, as honest as an angel and as firm in the cause of American Independence as Mt. Atlas," to quote from John Adams' diary. Here is seen a direct linear treatment with an emphasis on chiaroscuro, as well as the inexperienced artist's delight in the difficult exploration and solution of the problem of a complex set of objects in space (especially around the legs of the chair and of the sitter), rather than the brilliant surface play of light and color so sure and facile in Stuart. The stiffness and awkwardness of the drawing are not entirely due to the inexperience of the artist; Adams said that Sherman's movements were "stiffness and awkwardness itself." This powerful if somewhat rigid image is the culmination of what we may call an American tradition, both in style

and in point of view, that was now on the very eve of its independence.

Soon after executing this portrait Earl went to England, perhaps not so much out of choice as out of necessity (he was a somewhat slippery patriot, having helped the British forces), and like so many of his countrymen, he washed up on West's doorstep. Undoubtedly Earl lost much of his provincial awkwardness in England, acquiring polish and elegance commensurable with his British contemporaries, as can be seen in his portrait of his English wife, *Anne Whiteside Earl*, 1784 (Illustration 3–36).

Incidentally, in studying Earl's work and as an illustration of the fact that there were English provincial (and Puritan) schools on both sides of the Atlantic, it is interesting to note that Earl's portraits of the Carpenter children, 1799, in the Worcester Museum (*William Carpenter*, PB 555) are in what would be called his "American" manner in contradistinction to his "English" work. The obvious reason for this similarity is that in provincial East Anglia the same taste prevailed as in Puritan Connecticut.

Upon his return to America Earl rejected his English experience and apparently chose deliberately to revert to the provincial decorative realism of his early manner with its emphasis on line and pattern. He even acquired some other aspects of the native school as represented in Johnston, Chandler, and sometimes Copley, not seen before in the *Dyer* and *Sherman* portraits: the complex pattern of floor covering and wall, the shelves of books, and the open windows with views, all used separately or together in many of his subsequent pictures.

From 1778 until 1798 Earl worked throughout Connecticut and in south-central Massachusetts. Among his best portraits are those of *Benjamin Tallmadge and His Son William*, 1790 (PB 556; Illustration 3–37), *Mrs. Benjamin Tallmadge With Her Son Henry and Daughter Maria* (PB 557), and *Judge Oliver Ellsworth and Mrs. Ellsworth*, 1792 (PB 181). All of them are characterized by an ambitious composition in which full-length figures represented standing or sitting are enframed by or placed in a

3–36. Ralph Earl, *Anne Whiteside Earl,* 1784. Oil on canvas. 46⅝ x 37⅞ inches. (Museum of Fine Arts, Amherst College, Amherst, Massachusetts.)

3–37. Ralph Earl, *Benjamin Tallmadge and His Son William,* 1790. Oil on canvas. 78¼ x 54⅛ inches. (Litchfield Historical Society, Litchfield, Connecticut.)

There seems little question that others of the Connecticut school were influenced by Earl or at least experienced a combination of artistic circumstances similar to those that influenced Earl, particularly the example of Winthrop Chandler. Joseph Steward's *John Phillips,* 1793 (Illustration 3–38), seems as predicated on Chandler or even on Johnston as it does on Earl. This portrait of the early benefactor of Dartmouth and of the academies at Exeter and Andover is one of the most impressive in the Connecticut school. The patterned rug, the open window, and the pose of the figure are all familiar props of the group, but the monumentality of the composition, the sensitive modeling in the face, and the characterization of the subject are more remarkable than in comparable efforts by better known painters. The care with which Steward composed his figure in relation to the paneled background and the silhouette of the chair can be proven by an examination

setting of landscape and architectural or other detail, thus affording the artist the opportunity to manipulate bold pattern and design. In pictures of this kind the drawing is linear and firm as in the early *Sherman.* In portraits of a more conventional sort, an English elegance of manner and technique accompanies a rather forthright approach to characterization; even the *Tallmadge* has a certain weakness in drawing that mars a good many of even the best Earls. These negative characteristics, as in the flaccid structure and smooth vacuity of expression in little Charles in the otherwise effective *Mrs. William Moseley and Her Son Charles,* 1791 (PB 558), become more marked in the work of Earl's last two years, when inebriation finally got the better of him.

3–38. Joseph Steward, *John Phillips,* 1793. Oil on canvas. 79½ x 68½ inches. (Collection of Dartmouth College, Hanover, New Hampshire.)

of the surface of the painting, where irregularities indicate the artist's changes. This huge picture (it measures nearly seven by eight feet) is also composed with a nice color balance and contrast which make it an extremely effective decoration. In comparison, Earl's *Tallmadge* portrait is overillusionistic, and Chandler's *Reverend Devotion* is almost absorbed by his books. The *John Phillips* is undeniably Steward's best work. His large picture of *Eleazer Wheelock* (Dartmouth College) is not as fine, and his smaller portraits are very uneven. But painting was only one of Steward's activities. He was a pastor in Massachusetts and Connecticut and his principal occupation was running a museum of curiosities in Hartford, the first to be established after Charles Willson Peale's and almost as extensive.

There was some family connection between Winthrop Chandler and Reuben Moulthrop of New Haven, about whom little is known except through a few documented pictures, one of the best of which is the *Reverend Ammi Ruhamah Robbins*, 1812 (PB 629), in which the silhouetted figure, the Windsor chair, the strong linear design, and the forceful characterization place the painting in the best of the American realist tradition, differentiating Moulthrop from weaker, more inconsistent followers. A portrait of *Bradford Hubbard*, c. 1790 (PB 313), sometimes attributed to Moulthrop, is similar to the best of his work and to a whole group of still anonymous portraits in this productive region. It is beautifully designed to fill the frame yet not crowd it. The brass buttons of the coat contribute to the effective pattern, and the drawing of the face, though emphatic, is sensitive.

Richard and William Jennys, who painted in the Stratford–New Haven area, bring to a climax the strong drawing, hard modeling, and uncompromising precision of the Connecticut school. William, particularly, almost attains the level of a consciously mannered style of great sophistication, exaggerating the characteristics just mentioned into a construction of block-like forms and clear colors which have an almost abstract effect. The portraits of *Major Reuben Hatch* (°PB 606) and of *Mrs. Reuben Hatch*,

3–39. William Jennys, *Mrs. Reuben Hatch*, c. 1800. Oil on canvas. 30 x 25¼ inches. (Lyman Allyn Museum, New London, Connecticut.)

c. 1800 (°PB 606A; Illustration 3–39), are among the best, while four at Deerfield, Massachusetts (The Historical Society), two at the Pennsylvania Academy, and one at the Shelburne Museum in Vermont, *A Gentleman of the Brewer Family*, c. 1800 (PB 606B), are typical.

These lesser men at their best do what Earl *almost* did, carrying his approach a little further into abstract design and hard, angular modeling, something Earl was either afraid to attempt or was too much under the refined influence of West to do. His *Roger Sherman* is still his finest painting.

Elsewhere in Connecticut and throughout New England there were many other interesting known and anonymous portraitists in the quasi-artisan style of the Connecticut school. The prominence of this style in this region probably is attributable to the fact that local tradition was rooted more deeply and for a longer time there than elsewhere and was therefore more resistant to the fashionable painters typified by Stuart. Even in Boston, the very city where Stuart came to live and work, John Mason Furness could paint a portrait like that of *John Vinal*, 1780–1790 (PA 141), a hard and linear picture which in its way is as fine as those by Stuart, but is essentially different and sums up the best of what may be called the vernacular portrait school.

Among some of the more interesting of a large group of pictures in New England similar to those painted by the Connecticut school are two signed simply "MacKay," the portraits of *Hannah Bush* and *John Bush*, 1791 (PB 299, *PB 300), impressive in their directness and decorative power, if somewhat naïve. A few other portraits, not unlike these and more or less related to the beginnings of folk art, have turned up in other parts of the country, as for instance the delightful *Gentleman Farmer*, c. 1815, found in Alabama (Illustration 3–40).

3–40. Anonymous, *Gentleman Farmer*, c. 1815. Oil on canvas. 26⅝ x 21½ inches. (Abby Aldrich Rockefeller Folk Art Collection, Williamsburg, Virginia.)

But these are exceptions, and are evidence pointing either to the predominance of New England in this field or to the fact that little interest has been shown by scholars outside that area.

Artists like Moulthrop, Furness, and even the more conventional Earl may not have been better than their countrymen who returned from abroad with more up-to-date and knowledgeable techniques, but they brought to a peak the archaic tradition of the colonial limner. Their work, like that of their predecessors, appeals to our contemporary liking for flat pattern, linear design, and "expressionistic" characterization.

Most artists and patrons followed the manner of Stuart, either through his influence or that of lesser and forgotten men, mostly Englishmen, who raised the level of academic competence and gradually drove further the wedge between the indigenous local craftsmen and the more conventional artists. This started the cleavage that led to the complete separation of what was to become folk or popular art from the mainstream of artistic effort.

Allston and Vanderlyn

Washington Allston was very different from any of West's other pupils. This aristocratic, Harvard-educated son of a South Carolina planter introduced to American art the whole new world of early romanticism.

Allston's youthful career in Italy and England somewhat paralleled that of West, with one important difference: Allston experienced England before the Continent. Thus, Allston never had to fight the weak Mengs-like neo-classicism of West's early years. At London, in the work of other English painters and in the reformed, later work of West, he learned techniques of underpainting and glazing, and other coloristic effects of the great tradition which had been almost forgotten on the Continent. Allston was delighted with the great Venetian colorists of the Renaissance who reinforced his own romantic predilections. But the classical compositions of Poussin and Claude and the more exciting ones of Salvator Rosa also impressed him, as did the work of more conventional Italian masters. Allston possessed a far more sensitive and

3–41. Washington Allston, *David Playing Before Saul,* 1809. Oil on canvas. 15 x 18 inches. (Courtesy of the Carolina Art Association of Charleston.)

intelligent mind than West or, indeed, than most of his contemporaries. Eclectic as his tastes and accomplishments were, he imbued the best of his emulations with a personal quality of mood that was compelling in its dream-like vision. *Rising of a Thunderstorm at Sea,* 1804 (PB 43), and *The Deluge,* 1804 (PB 44), are inspired by Poussin and by classical composition in general; *The Deluge* has a horrible grandeur ranking it in imaginative power with some early work by the great contemporaneous English painter Joseph Turner, who was influenced by similar sources. *Italian Landscape,* 1805 (Addison Gallery of American Art, Andover, Massachusetts), is a play upon classical architectural motifs and the landscape of the Roman *campagna* where the great Poussin in the seven-

teenth century had arranged and rearranged the beautiful geometry of his nearly abstract compositions. By comparison, Allston's landscape is not too inferior.

Allston's figure compositions are sometimes too static and overworked, showing an inability to accomplish the monumental, which was to be his undoing. But in his small, sketch-like studies, as in *David Playing Before Saul,* 1809 (Illustration 3–41), he achieved a brilliant suggestiveness reminiscent of the best rococo and even the baroque painters in this mode, and, incidentally, far superior to sketches by his master which were probably his inspiration, such as West's *Saul and the Witch of Endor.*

Allston's best work was done in the field of portraiture during the period before his second

3–42. Washington Allston, *William Ellery Channing*, 1809–1811. Oil on canvas. 31¼ x 27¾ inches. (Courtesy, Museum of Fine Arts, Boston.)

return from England in 1818. The unfinished sketch of *Samuel Taylor Coleridge*, 1814 (*PB 49), and especially the earlier portrait of *William Ellery Channing*, 1809–1811 (Illustration 3–42), are extremely rich in their painterly effect, wherein Allston employs tellingly the technical methods of glazing which result in a luxuriance reminiscent of Titian. In the light of such work, it is less difficult to understand how Allston's contemporaries in England could have equated him with that master of the Renaissance. The temperamental sympathy of the artist for the sitters, together with his painterly treatment, combine to place these among the profoundest portraits of the century. Neither the slapdash brilliance of the fashionable portrait school nor the meticulous factualness of the more native school stood in the way of this artist's penetration of the rich and varied means of the Venetian technique. Allston's choice of these two sitters is significant and symbolizes his important place in his generation. Coleridge's position

among the romantic poets and critics of his day is well-known. (It is interesting that he and Allston were friends and mutual admirers.) But Channing's position in America was even more important, for he represented that aspect of romanticism which was implied in Coleridge and which developed into that peculiar phenomenon of which he was a leader: New England Transcendentalism—imaginative, introspective, even mystical.

Unfortunately Allston spent most of his energies on large historical or idealized canvases. But the tradition of history painting was more suited to neo-classicism than to the introspective romanticism of Allston. His lyrical talent was not adapted to the epical demands of many of his subjects, least of all to the huge *Belshasar's Feast* which he began in 1817. He never completed it, though he worked on it until he died under the weight of his artistic and moral obligation to finish it. (His friends and in-laws in Boston had bought stock in it to support him.) An occasional portrait and some small figure pieces, such as *Flight of Florimel,* 1819 (PB 51), attest to the persistence of Allston's talents in other directions, as do his landscapes. In fact, two of the latter are among the finest ever painted by an American, *Moonlit Landscape,* 1819 (PB 53; Illustration 3–43), and *Elijah in the Desert,* 1818 (PB 50). They sum up the distillation of his experience of Europe and the old masters. Neither picture represents a specific place, but each epitomizes an ideal Mediterranean world, a blend of Salvator Rosa, the Venetians, and (in the *Moonlit Landscape*) Poussin and Claude Lorrain. Yet Allston is not eclectic merely, any more than were Tintoretto and Rubens when they combined the influence of their great predecessors into something new and personal. For Allston's pictures were also new in that they were among the first examples of the landscape of mood introduced by romanticism. Though its author was actually describing a painting by Salvator Rosa, what better description of the *Elijah* could be found than this, written by William Hazlitt in 1809: "Such shaggy rocks—such dark and ruinous caves, such spectre-eyed, serpent headed trees, wreathed

3—43. Washington Allston, *Moonlit Landscape*, 1819. Oil on canvas. 24 x 35 inches. (Courtesy, Museum of Fine Arts, Boston.)

and contorted into hideous mimicry of human shape, such fearful visitations of strange light— such horrid likenesses." [19]

The sweep, handling, coloristic richness, and dramatic composition of the *Elijah* have the monumentality and grandeur that Allston sought in his large but empty confections. In a more quietly lyrical mood, the *Moonlit Landscape* is not only equally powerful and colorful but more suggestive of a vague melancholy in the dream-like world it evokes. The shapes and colors recall Allston's own comments on Venetian painting. Speaking of the great colorists he said: "They addressed themselves, not to the senses merely, as some have supposed, but rather through them to that region (if I may so speak) of the imagination which is supposed to be under the exclusive domination of music, and which by similar excitement, they caused to teem with visions that 'lap the soul in Elysium.'" [20]

Allston's technique and subject matter, and the international reputation that accompanied him on his return were instrumental in introducing to America the great tradition of western artistic culture. Perhaps more important was the fact that Allston's work inspired generations of artists who were concerned with the imaginative rather than with the factual. It was Allston who began the polarity which is one of the fascinating aspects of American art, the alternation between the real and ideal, the latter culminating during the nineteenth century in Albert Pinkham Ryder, and in the twentieth in the abstract expressionists. Surely Allston's evaluation of the colorists places him spiritually among the latter, and the vague and amorphous forms of the *Moonlit Landscape* are as suggestive as those of Ryder and our own contemporaries.

Allston was also significant as the first American painter to benefit from the romantic ideal of an artist as seer and genius. After him it became gradually less incumbent on an artist to be a craftsman who played a necessary part in society; he could be a prophet yearning for a remote ideal. Allston either fitted into or played the part of genius beautifully. He so impressed the practical Bostonians who supported him for years without his delivering his product that even as late as 1883 the *Memorial History of Boston* could say of him that "the excess of finer qualities in his nature stood in the way of many of his pictures."

Allston and Ryder are to our painting what Poe, Hawthorne, and Melville are to our literature. Allston was our first romantic, and because of his early career spent abroad he brought the new European movement to the United States a generation before it became endemic. Romanticism in its more conspicuous aspects—literary subject matter, a taste for the mysterious, fantastic, and dramatic, a love of far places and distant times, and a delight in nature—were all present in Allston, and transformed by his genius into something subtly his own. In the next generation these tendencies became more widespread and obvious.

The work of John Vanderlyn, like that of Allston, illustrates the broadening of taste that occurred in the United States during this period. Vanderlyn's career somewhat paralleled that of Allston in that he too was frustrated by a society not quite ready to accept the large historical and allegorical canvases he felt an artist should paint. Like Allston too, the quality of his work was quite uneven; he was at his best an artist of stature, and the only one of importance in his generation whose training had not been either directly or indirectly under the influence of Benjamin West (except at the very first when he studied briefly with Gilbert Stuart). In

1796, Vanderlyn went to Paris for a stay of four years to learn from a pupil of the great David, François-André Vincent. Vanderlyn is thus the only American artist with the exception of Audubon (who painted principally flora and fauna) who underwent the discipline of French neo-classic training in draughtsmanship and in the rendering of convincing structure and form —qualities so lacking in West's teaching. A comparison of a typical portrait done by one of the latter's pupils, such as Pratt or Peale, with one by Vanderlyn will show immediately the difference. The superlative drawing in the watercolor portrait of *A Lady and Her Son*, 1800 (PB 449), or *Robert R. Livingston*, 1804 (PB 452), is something not heretofore seen in the American school. Tight, disciplined, yet graceful and melodious, Vanderlyn's line reflects the form-defining, abstract beauty of the neo-classic linearism of David and his school.

Vanderlyn's skill was early recognized in France. He received the emperor's gold medal in the Paris Salon of 1808 for his *Marius amidst the Ruins of Carthage* (PB 448), a rather empty classicist confection from the point of view of today's taste, and also lacking in those formal qualities of drawing and composition which are characteristic of the French masters. Even less successful is the *Death of Jane McCrea*, 1804 (PB 451), where the hard, linear treatment of neo-classicism is scarcely adapted to the romantic violence of the event depicted. Vanderlyn is far happier in the *Ariadne of Naxos*, 1814 (PB 453; Illustration 3–44), the first nude in American art. The conception and form of this competent and appealing picture is derived from the Venetian treatment of the female nude by Giorgione and Titian, except in the dry manner of painting and in the relatively impoverished color. Had Allston essayed a similar subject, how different the effect would have been! Vanderlyn showed the *Ariadne* together with copies of two Correggio nudes (indicating his further interest in the North Italian colorists in spite of his neo-classic training) in traveling exhibitions which were understandably popular considering their subject matter, unusual in a society whose moral climate was still predomi-

3-44. John Vanderlyn, *Ariadne of Naxos,* 1814. Oil on canvas. 14¼ x 17¾ inches. (The Pennsylvania Academy of the Fine Arts, Philadelphia.)

nantly Calvinist. But painting in the manner of the old masters without the titillation of the nude was not sufficiently in demand for Vanderlyn to set himself up in the style of the French Academicians. He therefore had to resort to devices such as the painting and showing of panoramas. These were a popular kind of informative art, introduced to this country by a European artist in Salem about 1800 and continuing until after the Civil War. Vanderlyn's *Panorama: Palace and Gardens of Versailles,* c. 1820 (PB 454, *PB 455, PB 456), is the only important one still in good condition. As a representative of what was once a significant genre it is a curiosity, but disappointing as a work of art—the praise its recent disinterment has aroused notwithstanding. Mechanically executed, hardly more than hack work, its only virtue is a certain decorative charm which it of course shares with the better French scenic wallpapers of the time.

Vanderlyn was disappointed until nearly the end of his career in not ever having had an official commission such as that given to Trumbull or offered to (and declined by) the aging Allston. When Vanderlyn finally received the commission for the *Landing of Columbus* for the rotunda of the Capitol in 1838, his powers had been frittered away on grandiose schemes typified by his panoramas.

popular English genre and topographical paintings and prints of the period, and is therefore as British in its style as is the work of the contemporary English painters, but the rather bold compositions in Guy's views of Baltimore and its environs give them a more individual quality. The most remarkable example of Guy's work, however, is the late *Winter Scene in Brooklyn,* 1817–1820 (PB 572; Illustration 3–45). This picture resembles the *Tontine Coffee House* in its perspective and its interesting figures, which are silhouetted in lively action against the snow in a manner reminiscent of Breughel's.

It is tempting to say that Guy fitted into the American scene far better than did his other English contemporaries, and that the style he perfected in the United States was derived to a certain degree from his surroundings and not brought over ready-made. Guy's somewhat naïve paintings have a precision and nicety of detail, and a sense of pattern or silhouette which are delightful; the *Brooklyn* picture has also a neatness and rectangularity which fit very well into the somewhat cubic architecture and the sharp light of North America, so different from the rosy mist suffusing Claude's canvases or the ever changing atmosphere of the English climate reflected in English painting. Dunlap said of Guy that his style was "crude and harsh, with little to recommend his efforts." [22] Our contemporary taste would not agree with this dictum.

Landscapes in the artisan tradition continued to be painted on overmantels in Connecticut and elsewhere, but none was as fine as those by Winthrop Chandler. The situation was complicated by the arrival from Naples of Michael Corné who came to paint overmantels and walls as well as panoramas in Salem around 1800, and later in Boston and Providence. These completely competent views in a style which combined late rococo and early neo-classicism are essentially European, and their influence diverted American artists away from the more artisan or "folk" tradition of landscape as decorative wall painting. But before this happened, Ralph Earl executed a few landscapes in the Connecticut convention of Chandler. *Landscape: Looking East from Denny Hill,* 1790's (?)

(PB 182), is probably the best of these, still primitive and unsophisticated in certain respects, with its formal centering and naïve perspective, and not so well designed as Chandler's.

There is almost enough genre in Guy's *Tontine Coffee House* and in his *Brooklyn* picture to justify their being classified in that category. Only two other painters in this period are important enough to be considered at any length in a general survey: Henry Sargent of Boston and J. L. Krimmel of Philadelphia. The latter was a German-born artist who received his early training in his native Würtemburg in a very meticulous technique. This he contrived to combine with an emulation of the genre style of Sir David Wilkie, a print of one of whose paintings he copied. The combination of early nineteenth-century German precisionism and the summary treatment of Wilkie's more painterly genre, derived in part from Charles R. Leslie and similar influences, created a personal style which in Philadelphia before 1820 was said to rival Hogarth's. Most of Krimmel's pictures would hardly bear out this praise, being awkward in composition and pointlessly meticulous in technique in contrast to the consistent style displayed in Guy's precision, which is accompanied by a fine planometric design against which the figures are silhouetted more effectively. Krimmel's masterpiece, however, *Fourth of July in Centre Square,* c. 1810–1812 (°PB 287), is a fairly attractive picture, well composed and with interesting groups of figures which are not as stiff and awkward as those appearing in some other examples of his work. The picture is also interesting as a document of a scene which included Latrobe's handsome pumping station and the *Water Nymph and Bittern* by the sculptor William Rush.

Henry Sargent, a student of West, already mentioned as a portraitist and painter of history pieces, is better remembered by two genre pictures: *The Dinner Party* and *The Tea Party,* 1820–1825 (PB 393, PB 394). These are examples of a talent which should not have been diverted into the activities of a rich Boston merchant, which Sargent was. The luminosity of interior light (shuttered sunlight in one and candlelight in the other) is beautifully recorded. Sargent collected Dutch seventeenth-century genre pictures; his sensitivity to light and his success in realizing objects in it may derive in part from their influence. In any event, the precision of observation in the two pictures and the well thought out perspective and consistent modeling resemble the genre paintings of seventeenth-century Holland more than they do the more cursory treatment of West. The two pictures are very much a part of their time since the fragility, grace, and elegance of the figures and the charming Adamesque rooms reflect Bulfinch's Beacon Hill and its wealthy and cultivated Federalist society.

In so meager a field, it might be well at least to mention the work of a Charleston lawyer and amateur artist who had studied with Allston, John Blake White, who painted pictures that were somewhere between genre and history, concerning events of the Revolution in South Carolina. Some of these are hung in the national Capitol; among them is a delightfully lively little painting, *Miss Mott Directing Generals Marion and Lee to Burn Her Mansion to Dislodge the British.*

In the next period, genre became a popular form for the display of romantic sentiment and produced some of America's finest paintings, for which we are hardly prepared by the scant showing in the first decades of the century.

Still life in the early years of the republic seems to have been the special province of the Peale family, by whose hands it was still competently painted even into our own time.

3–46. Raphaelle Peale, *Still Life,* c. 1820. Oil on canvas. 11¾ x 15 inches. (Courtesy of Wadsworth Athenaeum, Hartford, Connecticut.)

Though Charles Willson Peale had executed some still life before 1810, this branch of painting was not important until Charles's brother James took it up extensively and until Charles's eldest son Raphaelle made it nearly his only concern later in life.

Still life painting was derived largely from seventeenth-century Dutch sources, and even used many of its conventions, such as the plain background, generally dark tonality, and table-top setting. But the often elaborate and complex still life groupings of the Dutch were simplified by the Peales into an almost original formula of paucity and unpretentiousness in the objects, combined with a simplicity of design and clarity of color. The realism of Charles Willson Peale's "deception" technique was especially well adapted to the exploitation of the precision and point of view traditional in this kind of still life. The resulting intensity of vision produced little gem-like pictures in which the observer experiences the beauty of the objects as though they were being seen for the first time. Raphaelle's work is especially successful. He seems to have poured into still life all those creative energies which somehow had never been realized in his portraits, for which he had little talent. His renderings of bunches of grapes, cut melons, glasses, and dew-covered plums are extremely sensitive, with none of the fusty overelaboration of the earlier modes. One of his best, *Still Life,* c. 1820 (Illustration 3–46), featuring the homely parsnip, is a picture of bold formal design, though perhaps more typical is another *Still Life,* done in the same year, which depicts fruit and a wine glass (PB 353).

One of Raphaelle's paintings is perhaps more of a genre picture than a still life, but whatever its classification, it is certainly one of the most individual pictures of the century. The subject consists largely of a sheet, newly shaken out (its folds are still quite evident) and hung on a line; behind it one can spy a naked arm above and bare feet below. There is some evidence that Peale painted it as a joke to fool his somewhat prudish wife, pretending that it was a little nude over which he had thrown a hand-kerchief to hide it from her suspicious gaze. Since the handkerchief was intended to deceive, its technique is extraordinarily realistic; in becoming a sheet in the finished version entitled *After the Bath,* 1823 (PB 354), its precision is all the more effective. The severe rectilinear design—almost like a modern geometric abstraction—and the startling realism of the detail give the picture considerable impact.

Raphaelle Peale's precise particularity links the still life of Copley's *Henry Pelham* (*The Boy With the Squirrel*) to the extensive school of ambitious still life which flourished at the end of the century, of which William Harnett is the best representative.

The Graphic Arts

The graphic arts in the period of the early republic continued in the pattern set in the last years of the colonial era. The reproduction of portraits and views flourished in the medium of line engraving (and the related mezzotint), the technique of which was improved by an influx of foreign craftsmen. Engravings also embellished the pages of the early magazines and annuals. These were not strictly illustrations, but interleaved prints similar in technique to single prints. Soon after its invention, lithography (a reproductive medium wherein a drawing is made directly on stone with crayon or wash and which can be printed as rapidly as letter-press) made its appearance in America in a few examples which were the beginning of what was to become the most popular form of the graphic arts. Woodcut (and wood engraving, which largely superseded it during this period) remained the most popular medium for a while, continuing to be employed in almanacs, broadsides, and the like, and was still executed in the bold and primitive manner of the previous period. But as artistic sophistication spread, such work became rare east of the Alleghenies, though it continued on the frontier as a popular medium of communication, belonging more properly in the category of folk art.

Portraiture and topography continued to be the principal subjects of engraving, most examples being simply reproductions of original drawings which were made for this purpose. The generally high level of skill exhibited in these prints can be seen in such typical examples of J. M. Longacre's stipple engraving after Sully's *Portrait of Andrew Jackson* (GB 136), and Benjamin Tanner's engraving after Hugh Reinagle's *MacDonough's Victory,* 1814 (GB 197). It is, however, in work engraved by the artists who made the original drawing or painting or who executed the design directly on the metal plate or stone (as in lithography) that we see the few examples of graphic art during this period which are, properly speaking, original works of art and not merely reproductions. Charles Willson Peale proved himself a very competent mezzotint engraver in his interpretation of his portraits of *Washington,* 1780 (*GB 156), and *Franklin,* 1787 (GB 157), and Edward Savage's stipple engraving *The Washington Family,* 1798 (GB 187), is as competent a piece of work as can be expected from this only average painter. Rembrandt Peale's *Washington* (from his "porthole portrait"), 1827 (GB 160), is a pleasing example of the new medium of lithography in which tonal values of the painting are sensitively caught.

The topographical engravings in this period were still often executed by the same man who had made the original drawing, so that the work is often fresher and less mechanical than might be expected in a purely reproductive engraving. This is especially true of a series of views of Philadelphia, published in 1800, by William Birch and his son Thomas (already mentioned in connection with landscapes). The engravings after them, however, as examples of print-making, are so subtle, both in their luminosity and in their differentiation of texture, that they deserve mention again under the category of the graphic arts. Typical are the *Bank of the United States, Philadelphia,* 1789 (GB 20), and *Congress Hall and New Theatre,* 1800 (GB 19). The quality of these engravings was not matched by other topographical views in the period, though John Hill's aquatints after paintings by Joshua Shaw in *Picturesque Views of American Scenery,* published in 1819, are as fine as any reproductive engravings after not-too-distinguished originals. The work of the Birches is a worthy precedent for some of the outstanding artistic productions of the next period, especially the topographical views by John Hill's son, J. W. Hill.

Besides Rembrandt Peale's portrait of *Washington,* the only other lithographs of note were a conventional landscape or two: one by Rembrandt Peale (GB 159) and another by Bass Otis entitled *The Mill,* 1819, remarkable chiefly as being the first lithograph to appear in the United States. More interesting is a curious example by Benjamin West, *Angel of the Resurrection,* 1801 (GB 213), which, though produced in London, was the first lithograph by an American. This print demonstrates another facet of West's originality, this time an interest in a new technique, but in style and content it reflects his more pompous manner.

Sculpture

Sculpture as a fine art (as opposed to a craft) was in this period still strongly tied to the artisan tradition; thus it is perhaps artificial to distinguish between the two. In fact, the most prominent figures who could be called sculptors in the conventional sense of the term, Samuel McIntire of Salem and William Rush of Philadelphia, were primarily wood carvers who for the most part executed decoration. It was only at the very end of the period that the indigenous tradition of wood carving was overwhelmed by academic neo-classicism's smooth generalities.

There was considerable neo-classic sculpture in the country during this period, but it was either imported or executed by foreign-born artists. When General Washington was to be memorialized and the new Capitol decorated, there was apparently no one in the country who could produce competent figurative work in stone. Even the decorative carving in the Capitol was done eventually by foreigners, though there were a few competent marble cutters and even executors of busts, such as the Englishman James Traquier and his son Adam, who worked in Philadelphia. At any rate, when the legislature of North Carolina voted a statue of Washington for the state Capitol at Raleigh, they turned to Jefferson for advice. That cultivated connoisseur nominated the idol of the day, the Italian neo-classicist Canova. On the strength of his *Washington* (destroyed by fire in the 1830's), clothed impeccably as a Roman general and holding a scroll addressed to the American people in elegant Tuscan, other Italians were imported under the auspices of Jefferson and Latrobe to work on the Capitol and elsewhere: the two Franzonis, Carlo and Giuseppe, to execute the figures, and Giovanni Andrei to execute the more difficult decorative carving. (The bulk of the elder Franzoni's work perished in the burning of the capital during the War of 1812.) The sculptural decoration, all done under Latrobe's direction and still in place in Statuary Hall, is the work of Carlo Franzoni and several other Italians who came later. These and an allegorical figure of Justice, probably also by Franzoni, in the Old Supreme Court all reflect the same general characteristics of conventional neo-classicism and undoubtedly exerted much influence on the succeeding generation of American sculptors.

McIntire and Rush were too involved in the wood-carving tradition to be more than superficially influenced by neo-classicism. The Salem architect was most at home when he was carving the delicate Adamesque motifs in his exquisite rooms, and undoubtedly also the decorations of the Derby ships. When he worked on a larger scale or in the round he was not so successful. A large medallion of *George Wash-ington,* c. 1805 (SB 28), for an arch formerly in the Salem Common, is hardly more than an enlarged profile cameo, and his bust of *Governor Winthrop,* 1797 (SB 29), is unconvincing and doll-like, though attractive in its repetition of wood-carving devices in the conventions of beard and ruff. Simeon Skillin, Jr., was one of a famous family of ship carvers whose work has been largely lost. The several small decorative figures attributed to Skillin which do remain are disappointing since they reveal to us an essentially folk or artisan craftsman trying to work in an academic vein with absurd, almost grotesque, results, as can be seen in his *Head of Apollo* and *Head of Ceres,* c. 1800 (SB 108, SB 108B). It is to be hoped that the Skillins were more successful in their figureheads than in these mannered little busts, and that their work resembled more that of their successors during the second quarter of the nineteenth century, which is very effective in its breadth of handling and its respect for the medium.

William Rush, the son of a ship carver, was also famous for his figureheads, as attested by contemporaries. But these have disappeared—most unfortunately, for it was said of them: "They seem rather to draw the ship after them than to be impelled by the vessel." [23] Other carvings by Rush which do survive are especially appealing because of the artist's genius in combining the various influences of his artistic environment. Rush was far better able than McIntire to join the vigorous old tradition with the new styles and produce something original and personal. He had studied briefly with an Englishman, and had learned something of neo-classic elegance from Giuseppe Ceracchi, another Italian who had been called to the United States to do a bust of Washington. At the same time Rush must have acquired somewhere a kind of rococo curvilinear decorativeness (which appears even in Canova himself at times), quite adapted to the refinements of wood carving. Another influence which probably also made itself felt in Rush's work was that of the great French realist Houdon, who had done a bust of Washington at Richmond several years before Canova's statue at Raleigh, as well as several others of prominent Americans, which Rush may well have seen.

Rush's wooden figures of *Comedy* and of *Tragedy*, 1808 (SB 129), from the old Chestnut Street Theater at Philadelphia are wonderfully lively, and the gracefully linear garments clinging to their bodies are a combination of classical drapery and rococo sensuous decorativeness. These qualities must have been even more obvious in the wooden *Water Nymph and Bittern* or *Nymph of the Schuylkill* which stood near Latrobe's pump house, as seen in Krimmel's *Fourth of July · in Centre Square* (*PB 287), if we may judge from its metal casting at the present water works, *The Nymph of the Schuylkill*. Rush's *Charity*, c. 1811 (SB 33), and his *The Schuylkill Chained*, c. 1828 (SB 132), are more impressive figures, but retain the character of wood coupled with a rhythm that is not merely decorative. This is also true of his life-size *George Washington*, 1814 (SB 32).

Rush's portrait busts (usually modeled and not carved) are among his most attractive works. The *Marquis de Lafayette*, plaster, 1824 (SB 131), and his *Self-Portrait*, bronze, c. 1822 (SB 30), are marked by an incisive realism indicating great progress over his earlier busts. The *Lafayette* is particularly notable in this respect in comparison with the idealized or grandiose painted portraits inspired by the 1824 visit of the Revolutionary hero. In the portrait of his daughter, *Elisabeth Rush*, terra-cotta, c. 1816 (SB 34; Illustration 3–47), the sculptor shows a sensitive naturalness worthy of Houdon himself, and some of that master's restrained decorativeness as well.

3–47. William Rush, *Elisabeth Rush*, c. 1816. Terra-cotta. Life size. (Philadelphia Museum of Art.)

Rush began as an artisan and ended his career as an artist. This is not true of any other sculptors of the early republic; their work is better discussed under the category of folk or popular art.

Folk or Popular Art

While it is difficult to draw the line between the artisan and the academic artist in such men as Steward and others among the Connecticut school, the amateur paintings by young ladies who followed some theorem or "system" and the decorative work of the Pennsylvania "Dutch" [24] are certainly forms of popular or folk art. But there was also work in this category by those who were professionals (in the sense that they earned their living as craftsmen), who were still, strictly speaking, artisans and not academic artists. Such were the sign painters, gravestone cutters, and the decorators of walls, who, like the majority of the limners, continued to ply their itinerant trades as did the hawkers and peddlers of the time.

Among the various art schools pretentiously advertised by their instructors (often French or English) were those which taught various methods of painting by some ingenious and often purportedly original system. This instruction was supplemented by books, mostly English reprints with detailed descriptions and charts, so that those who were unable to take advantage of actual instruction could have the satisfaction of learning how to do a kind of handiwork which was doubtless thought to be more creative than needlework, yet still suitable for respectable matrons or for young ladies in finishing school. The various stencils, tracing devices, numbered diagrams, and similar shortcuts were little different from the painting sets available today, equipped with ready-made designs and areas numbered to correspond to the color to be applied. The results were more attractive then, however, since the basic design motifs were traditionally decorative and somewhat abstract, and because there was some opportunity to arrange them into varying compositions. Still life, allegories, and landscapes (often with turreted castles and Gothic ruins derived from English source books) were the main subjects, as illustrated in the amusing allegorical landscape *Venus Drawn by Doves,* watercolor on silk, c. 1815 (PB 506). The "mourning picture" also lent itself to somewhat mechanical repetition, using such stock props as gravestones, weeping willows, and grief-stricken maidens leaning against urn-topped tombs. Conventionalized silhouette portraits, in formal symmetrical compositions with schematized perspective, were also produced by stencils and other "systems." Among the most attractive of these are the charming double portraits by Mrs. Eunice Pinney of Connecticut, among which *Two Women,* c. 1810 (PB 29), is typical. Occasionally more spontaneous work turns up, such as the delightful genre scene *The Watercolor Class,* watercolor, c. 1820 (*PB 56), but this is exceptional.

Sign painters, decorators, and carvers of figureheads continued to ply their trades well

3—48. *Ship Figurehead,* possibly from the Commodore Perry, built in East Boston, c. 1820. Original in Mariners' Museum, Newport News, Virginia. Height: 35 inches. Watercolor rendering by Elizabeth Moutal. (Index of American Design, National Gallery of Art, Washington.)

into the nineteenth century, but unfortunately most of the work produced in the first decades has been lost. The examples of wood carving which have survived are in general inferior to the excellent work done a few years later when figurehead carving in particular amounted to a major art form. Two outstanding examples of wood carving, however, indicate the high quality which sometimes must have prevailed: the *Ship Figurehead,* believed to be *Commodore Perry,*

c. 1820 (SB 7; Illustration 3–48), and a bust of *Benjamin Franklin,* c. 1820 (SB 12), which are as sensitive in modeling as is the work of William Rush. (In fact, there is some reason to suppose that Rush may have executed the *Franklin.*) The *Perry,* probably carved for the packet of that name, is a little less academic; but whether it is folk or fine art, it is one of the best busts produced in nineteenth-century America. The subject is sensitively observed, and the character of the medium has been exploited; the quality of the wood has been somewhat enhanced by weathering which exposes the whorls, so beautifully utilized by the carver from the tip of the figure's nose inward as though the form were produced by unraveling a series of palimpsests.

But aside from these exceptional examples (actually far better than the surviving work of the Skillins) only gravestones remain to demonstrate that the craft tradition of the seventeenth and eighteenth centuries continued with some vitality, especially in places isolated from the main centers of advanced taste.[25] The finest stones still appeared in New England where the artisan-craftsman tradition was strongest. In centers like Boston, New Haven, Newport, and Portsmouth (New Hampshire), the decorative vocabulary and elegantly proportioned and incised lettering of the more sophisticated eighteenth-century stones continued, but in more isolated places local schools flourished, resulting in the execution of stones which were even more original than those cut before the Revolution. A variety of interesting examples were produced, especially in Connecticut, the best of which carried on the tradition of the Johnsons. One carver whose name is known, Ebenezer Drake, of Windsor—a contemporary of the younger Johnson—achieved a very personal style in the 1790's. Such a stone as that of Ruth Mather, at Windsor, 1791, designed by Drake (Illustration 3–49), represents a kind of culmination of the extravagant decorative forms of the Connecticut group characterized by sure, precise cutting and the most elegant lettering. At about the turn of the century a group of stones in this style in and around Middletown achieved an

3–49. Ebenezer Drake, gravestone of Ruth Mather, 1791, Windsor Burying Ground, Windsor, Connecticut.

ornamental exuberance which is almost baroque in its bold forms, curvilinear and deeply cut; they seem especially incongruous in Puritan Connecticut.

These stones are the end product of the tradition of the first carvers of Boston, who brought with them English decorative conventions; but another group of stones, again found mostly in provincial Connecticut, are very different. They exhibit such originality of design and sensitivity to the medium of stone that they rank with some of the finest examples of primitive and archaic art anywhere. One of the most interesting is the stone of the Holmes Children in the cemetery at East Glastonbury, Connecticut, 1795 (SB 6);

its procession of profiles is similar in strength of design and solemnity of effect to archaic Greek or Etruscan reliefs. There are many others equally remarkable, most of them found in central Massachusetts and Connecticut and in the Connecticut valley, above Hartford. Among the most interesting are those by the Sikes family in and around Belchertown, Massachusetts, which are characterized by a motif of a head surrounded with geometric and plant motifs treated in a stylized, curvilinear way; and those by the "Carver of Enfield" (Connecticut) whose stone of Joseph Parsons, 1794 (Illustration 3–50), in the Enfield Burying Ground is a powerfully authoritative decorative design.

The gravestones of this period are the last examples of an exceptionally original form of art which was overwhelmed by stock designs of urns and weeping willows and by other sentimental reflections of the academic sculpture of the mid-century.

3–50. "Carver of Enfield," gravestone of Joseph Parsons, 1794, Enfield Burying Ground, Enfield, Connecticut.

PART FOUR

FROM JACKSON TO THE CIVIL WAR

In this period the vast territories acquired in the early days of the republic, increased by the annexation of Texas, the Oregon Territory, and the former Mexican possessions, were rapidly settled with the aid of the steamboat and railroad, and the older sections of the country became more populated through immigration. After the opening of the Erie Canal, New York became the most important link between Europe and the interior of the continent and surpassed Boston and Philadelphia in size; Baltimore as the terminus of the B. & O. Railroad and New Orleans at the mouth of the Mississippi grew for similar reasons. Harrisburg, Pittsburgh, and Albany were big cities by 1825; Cincinnati, Louisville, and St. Louis, by 1830; Rochester, Buffalo, and Cleveland, soon after.

The economy of the North was conducive to the growth of business, industry, and manufacturing, especially iron and textiles, and the clipper ship extended maritime trade. In the rural areas of the East and the Midwest the invention of the reaper brought about a greatly expanded agriculture, while in the South the growth of the slave population and the great plantations was facilitated by the invention of the cotton gin.

The fur trade, the Indian wars, and the cov-ered wagon emerged as symbols of the romance of the country's dynamic expansion; exploration and settlement had their folk heroes in Daniel Boone, Mike Fink, and Davy Crockett. The variegated life of the frontier town, the mining settlements, and the river ports was celebrated by journalists and writers like Mark Twain, and even the War Department reports of western explorations seem livelier than most official documents of the time.

Expansion of territory and wealth was accompanied by a higher standard of living, and with it the security afforded by permanent employment, and the consequent increase in the middle class. The farmer and the wage earner profited from the reform of the election laws and the coming to power of Jackson, whose policies of cheap public lands and *laissez-faire* economy created a new egalitarianism which, combined with Jeffersonian agrarian democracy, brought about the rise of the common man and provided a practical basis for Emersonian optimism.

One of the consequences of economic, geographic, and social expansion was that culture was distributed more broadly—if more thinly—through such agencies as the public school system and the growth of printing and publishing.

A large public was therefore available to the artist and architect, a public with more and wider interests, if somewhat less discriminating than when taste was the prerequisite of gentlemen. This was the period when art, as the mid-century critic Henry Tuckerman put it, was "emancipated from the care of kings and popes, and found sustenance by alliance with commerce and the people." [1] The wealthy merchant-planter continued to be the agent of high culture, even if he was sometimes parvenu. Wealthy patrons of the arts commissioned allegorical paintings, and the latter-day Jeffersons—Southern planters and Northern bankers—designed their own mansions, using the same Greek temples as models. At the same time, more private galleries were founded, and buying was stimulated by a cultural phenomenon of the period, the Art Unions, through which pictures and engraved or lithographed reproductions of them were distributed by lottery to the winners among thousands of contributors. No important new schools were founded,[2] and the growth of great collections and museums belongs to the next period; but every city had its art school and Cincinnati alone produced several sculptors. As facilities for

education and communication increased, a more or less consistent taste was widely disseminated by magazines, annuals, and traveling exhibitions of paintings, and by peregrinating artists themselves who, along with the lyceum lecturers, brought artistic culture to the town and hinterland. Even saloons in burgeoning western towns were in the Greek Revival taste, and every respectable parlor was graced with some marble or alabaster ideal figure on a pedestal.

The wide distribution of generally more academic standards in technique and execution, even if accompanied by inferior conception, naturally made survival more difficult for local schools (like the portraiture school in the Connecticut valley) and for folk traditions (such as the Pennsylvania Dutch). But folk or popular art in the larger sense (that is, not confined to isolated groups) achieved its highest and most significant expression at this time. People who wanted works of art but were not sufficiently familiar with examples of standard academic competence patronized a popular art executed by artists who were largely untrained according to sophisticated or metropolitan standards but experienced in an artisan tradition.

Architecture

In this period the basic formal and functional character of architecture was more obscured than before by the superficial aspects of revivalism. The cavalcade of exotic styles was consistent with that yearning for the remote and bizarre common to both romantic art and literature; it was also consistent with the historicism of the romantic age. Already in the latter part of the eighteenth century no less an authority than Sir Joshua Reynolds, president of the Royal Academy, had stated in his *Discourses* that one of the principles of architecture was "that of affecting the imagination by means of association of ideas."

The Greek was by far the most prominent of the revivals. Actually it was a continuation of

romantic classicism in which Greek details became more conspicuous but which, on a less superficial level, had stylistic and functional aspects transcending mere archaeology. Among the other revivals, the Renaissance (or "Italian villa") style was the closest to the classicism which had dominated the American architectural scene since the early eighteenth century, though its origins were less strictly antique or Palladian. Its greater informality also caused the style to be more adapted to freer planning than other classical styles. The Gothic Revival comprised a more definite break with the past. In its more antiquarian aspects it expressed dramatically the romantic reaction against classicism; in its more vernacular phase, in domestic architecture, it was even better suited to informal planning than was the Italian villa style, due to its greater inherent irregularity and picturesqueness.

With the breaking of the dam of classicistic discipline by the Gothic Revival, a flood of other styles was released. The best architects of the time thought nothing of designing in several styles. Alexander Jackson Davis, for instance, drew elevations not only in the "Grecian" but also in the Gothic, Italian, and even Moorish styles; and when his partner Ithiel Town commissioned a picture from Thomas Cole entitled *The Architect's Dream,* 1840 (PB 138), the subject of the painting is shown lying on the capital of a huge classic column contemplating a scene where Gothic and Egyptian buildings vie with Greek and Roman ones to attract his gaze. Though stylistic variety helped destroy what must have been a pleasingly consistent architectural unity throughout the country, nevertheless the novelty may have been a welcome relief from the ubiquity of classical taste, or what a visiting Englishman called our "bare bold white cubes."

While the excesses of revivalism leave something to be desired from the point of view of "good taste," this is compensated for by a certain naïve originality. It cannot be denied that even the most ludicrous examples of the period, like the "carpenter Gothic" Wedding Cake House in Kennebunkport, Maine (AB 719), have a wry and nostalgic charm.

Was there a basic stylistic coherence under the surface details of revivalism? At first the characteristics of massiveness, geometric formalism, and plane surface seen in romantic classicism are still very clear in the Greek Revival, the Italian villa, and even the early Gothic Revival in spite of its superficial medieval detail, as can be seen, for instance, in St. Peter's, Salem, Massachusetts (Illustration 4–27). About 1840, however, these characteristics gradually became less conspicuous and a profound change began to occur. Not only were Gothic and other exotic revivals more picturesque, but even the classic revivals acquired in the 1850's what might be called a baroque aspect (analogous to what happened to Renaissance architecture when it became more dynamic and sculpturesque in the

baroque period), as can be seen in the familiar example of Thomas U. Walter's additions to the National Capitol which are so different in feeling from the more restrained earlier section.

The stylistic character of architecture at the mid-century could be summed up as "picturesque." Surfaces were more decorated, planes gave way to areas of complex recession and projection, and profiles became more varied; masses and volumes were composed with more contrast, the relation of exterior to interior space was more complex, and plans were less arbitrary and more adaptable to freedom of layout. In all the revivals except the Greek, symmetry gave way to asymmetry both in elevation and plan, and irregularity became the rule rather than the exception. Sir Horace Walpole, one of the first to create a "romantic" building in the remodeling of his house, Strawberry Hill, 1750–1753, in the "Gothick" style, rejected the Georgian because it had too little variety, and admitted of no charming irregularities. He would have been much happier living a century later.

Two factors—the prevalence of revivalism, and the stylistic character each revival shares with each other to a greater or less extent, in spite of differences in detail—make the term "picturesque eclecticism" a popular one with architectural historians. But neither this term nor "romantic" (except in the broadest interpretation) can adequately suggest the other side of the architectural coin: its technological and social aspects, the use of new materials and techniques, and the novel building types demanded by a growing industrialized democracy. The use of iron, first cast and then wrought, made possible the spanning of greater areas, the admission of more light by the reduction of wall surfaces, and the consequent development of industrial and commercial buildings, including the railroad shed, the most dramatic of the new forms. The development of the wooden truss also resulted in novel covering of space, and the invention of the balloon frame greatly facilitated the building of dwellings. A rapidly increasing population needed not only cheap and quickly built housing in the newly settled areas, but apartment and row houses in the cities. The enlightenment and humanitarianism of middle-class society required schools, libraries, museums, hospitals, asylums, and improved prisons. Commercial buildings, warehouses, factories, railroad stations, and great hotels resulted from expansion in business and transportation.

Thus nineteenth-century architecture is more than revivalism in search of a style; it is a combination of this with the practical actualities of the nineteenth century. Indeed, the very variety of revivalism, paradoxical as it may sound, could be said to have acted as a kind of catalyst to turn architecture away from the somewhat arbitrary, formal character of the classic point of view toward a more pragmatic or functional one. While it was taken for granted that past styles should be plundered at will, nevertheless there was often a sense of appropriateness in the choice. This was true not only in the case of the organic relation of building to site—as in the selection of a "pointed" cottage instead of an Anglo-Italian villa for a wooded hillside—but also in matters of design and structure. For example, the Gothic cottage was suited to construction in the traditional and readily available wood framing, and its irregularity was adapted to freedom and openness of planning. It was not primarily an imitation of some hypothetical fourteenth-century dwelling, in spite of its verticality and some superficial detail vaguely derived from medieval decorative motifs. Instead, it was the first step in the development of an indigenous country or suburban house, the direct ancestor of those of Richardson and Wright, and thus one of the first examples of functional or organic architecture. In this connection it is interesting to note that Emerson took into account the organic aspect of architecture—though this is not too strange in the light of his theories of poetry. (Emerson could not abide the Greek Revival Unitarian Church in Concord; he much preferred a good New England barn, and thought the clipper ship the best product of American architecture.)

If it is not perhaps stretching an analogy too far, the polarity of real–ideal, useful in the discussion of the figurative arts, may be suggestive in architecture, using the term "rational" in place of "real." In this way we could say that the "ideal" aspect of architecture was its picturesque or romantic eclecticism, but that the development of new conceptions of plan, structure, and design lying beneath the surface formed its "realistic" or rational aspect.

Finally, what might be called an American tradition as seen in certain formal and pragmatic characteristics of plan, structure, and elevation becomes more evident in this period, especially in folk and vernacular architecture. The "Gothic cottage" exemplifies this tendency: even though a somewhat parallel development occurred in England, the wide eaves, extensive verandas, vertical boarding, and exploitation of the framework in the design of the more developed of such American dwellings went further than in Britain. From the point of view of surface design, a tendency to exploit plane surfaces was perhaps a more clearly indigenous characteristic. (The Swiss architectural critic and historian, Siegfried Giedien, in *Space, Time and Architecture*, singled out the open plan and the plane surface as being the most significant contributions of earlier American building to contemporary architecture.) The adaptation of architectural forms to an abstract series of planes and sharp, well-defined edges is seen most successfully under the rubric of the vernacular Greek Revival, where it becomes a separate style which could almost be called sophisticated, if not academic. The remarkable Swedenborgian House in Cambridge is an example: its facade is an essay in abstract form (Illustration 4–23), and its subtlety is hardly less than that of a twentieth-century non-representational painting.

The situation of the architect, designer, and master builder was far more complex than in previous decades insofar as training and the relevance of source books were concerned—a consequence of the enormous expansion in building as the population spread rapidly across a continent and increased in cities and towns.

In terms of the architectural training of today, no architect in this period could be said to have been properly schooled, until Richard Morris Hunt, the first American architect to study abroad, returned to this country in 1855 from the Paris École des Beaux Arts. Though there were no architectural schools as we now know them, there were schools of architectural drawing, the most prominent being Asher Benjamin's in Boston, where Ithiel Town and Solomon Willard, among others, received some instruction. John Haviland had a school in Philadelphia, and it is known that Maximilian Godefroy taught architectural drawing in Baltimore. There must have been many such "schools"; one existed as far west as Detroit. The Franklin Institute in Philadelphia offered lectures on architecture in the 1830's, and from 1833 to 1842 the old Carpenter Company had a kind of school, where the architect William Strickland was among the instructors.

Two outstanding figures of this period, Ithiel Town and his sometime partner Alexander Jackson Davis, are interesting examples of how relatively easy it was to become an architect. Town, after making a fortune from the invention of a bridge truss, went to draw with Asher Benjamin in Boston, and supplemented this rudimentary training with a fine architectural library. At the American Academy of the Fine Arts in New York, John Trumbull introduced Davis to the mysteries of architectural drawing (the old gentleman had designed the attractive church of Lebanon, Connecticut), after which Davis went to Boston to look at books in the Athenaeum. One of the most interesting buildings of the period, the State Capitol at Columbus, Ohio (Illustration 4–5), was built partly from a design by a painter, Thomas Cole.

As before, many architects developed from the builder tradition as apprentices; but more of them had the opportunity to work during their training period with actual professionals. At first this was rare, since only immigrants like Latrobe were, properly speaking, trained architects. Both William Strickland and Robert Mills, the most prominent members of their profession in their generation, were Latrobe's pupils. But a little later, firms like Town and Davis in New York became veritable schools where young men paid to be taken on as draughtsmen in order to learn architecture. James H. Dakin of New Orleans had worked with the firm, and Francis Costigan of Kentucky and Indiana had had training of a similar kind in Baltimore.

The architect's function in those days was hardly comparable to what is expected of him today. Complex modern structural methods and mechanical equipment did not exist; detail and working drawings, so essential in current practice, were not necessary. An architect or designer could leave most of the work to the builder, who was ultimately responsible for nearly everything except the design which, if he was not working for an actual architect, he could derive from a source book. (This was the case especially before the mid-1840's, prior to the more general appearance of what were later called "architects.") In fact, the majority of the designs were derived from source books, usually varied by the master builder or mason or by the gentleman-amateur, who appeared most frequently in the South, following in the footsteps of Washington or Jefferson.

Even professional designers and architects depended on source books. Richard Upjohn's influential Gothic Revival churches were first based on various collections of views of Gothic edifices and published work by his famous English contemporary, A. W. N. Pugin—sources which he happened to use with more skill than was usually the case.

In the early part of the period, British publications continued to be the ultimate source of styles, but the designs themselves were not so slavishly copied as before. English carpenter handbooks, particularly those of Peter Nicholson, continued to give American builders all they needed to know about structure and joinery. The high standard of carpentry during the period (all the more remarkable because of the unusual structural forms demanded by the various revivalist styles) was largely due to Nicholson's engravings of truss forms, framing types, and the construction of difficult areas such as vaults, arches, and niches, all translated into wood. (This in itself is a commentary on the unfortunate discrepancy between structure and design, a natural result of the eclecticism of the time.) The generally high level of design in the Greek Revival style, however, was due largely to

American source books. Haviland's *Builder's Assistant,* 1818–1821, was the first to introduce the Greek orders in a "carpentry book." The later books of Asher Benjamin, *The Practical House Carpenter,* 1830, and the *Builder's Guide,* 1839, and those of Minard Lafever, particularly *The Beauties of Modern Architecture,* 1835, popularized the style. In fact it could almost be said that the majority of Greek Revival houses were literally designed by these authors. Certainly from their books came most of the details, which were mass-produced by steam planing mills even in remote parts of the country. Benjamin's Doric order, especially in its pilaster form, was the model for at least half of those built, because of its deliberate simplification for execution on wood. Lafever was only a little less influential. Some of his more elaborate plans appeared in as broadly separated places as New York State and New Orleans, but he was not as popular in New England as Asher Benjamin or Edward Shaw. The latter's *Rural Architecture,* 1843, almost equaled Benjamin's later editions in popularity, to judge from the frequency of examples derived from it to be seen throughout New England, especially north of Boston.

Books were equally important for the other revivals. The publications of Andrew Jackson Downing, the landscape architect, went into nearly fifty printings from the 1850's until the late 1880's. His *Cottage Residences,* 1842, and *Architecture of Country Houses,* 1850, were especially influential. Though the earlier books contained some original designs by Downing's sometime collaborator Alexander Jackson Davis, in general they were derived from English prototypes where Gothic and other rural cottage projects had been introduced long before. But in the 1850 book there were several for which the author claimed the distinction that they were "no copy of any foreign cottage." This is indeed almost true, as seen for instance in his use of vertical battened boarding, and the increasing employment of porches and complex bracketed eaves. In the ecclesiastical Gothic Revival, A. W. N. Pugin's publications, especially *Contrasts,* 1838, and *An Apology for the Revival of Christian Architecture in England,* 1843, not only in-

fluenced architects like Upjohn, but led the way in the United States (as they did in Great Britain) toward a more archaeological approach to the medieval styles.

There were, of course, other books besides those of Downing and Pugin which propagandized the other exotic styles. Especially to be noted were Thomas Walter's *Two Hundred Designs for Cottages and Villas,* 1846, which was typical of many more that stole designs from better and earlier publications; and *The Model Architect,* 1852, by Samuel Sloan, whose designs exemplify the excesses of the eclectic exoticism which swept the country as the discipline of the Greek Revival relaxed. Even the soundness of the old builders' tradition could hardly resist the potentialities for carpentry suggested by the plethora of exotic styles in source books such as these. An extreme example of what could happen is illustrated by Maximilian Valson's San Francisco, a river plantation at Garyville, Louisiana, 1849 (AB 736), so garish and ornate that it resembles less a dwelling than a Mississippi steamboat. In this fantastic structure classical columns vie with Gothic windows, which in turn compete with huge Greek ornaments—all tied together in a jumble of brackets and misplaced entablatures.

The confusion of styles, the habit of one architect's designing in more than one of them, the transcendence of them by the vernacular, and finally the existence of a consistent form underlying the superficial modes all militate against the continuation of the use of the framework of revivalism in discussing the architecture of the romantic period. But in such a complexity of factors the Greek and Gothic revivals at least give a certain definiteness. These two styles, then, will be the basis of the discussion (together with some reference to the other modes); the vernacular, folk contributions, and a consideration of new forms and techniques will be treated briefly later.

Late Romantic Classicism:
The Greek Revival

Based on the romantic classicism typified by Latrobe, the Greek was by far the most prominent of the revivals. In Philadelphia it was even called the Greek mania. Greek details spread from Athens, Maine, to Sparta, Georgia. An outbuilding in Jericho, Vermont, was apt to be as Grecian as the facade of a saloon in Tombstone, Arizona. Like the other revivals, the Greek was adapted to every purpose, from Mills's government buildings in Washington to the simple post and lintel construction of warehouses and commercial structures. The continuing need for a public architecture of dignity, and the increasing romantic sentiment for the remote in time and place (accentuated by the courageous war of independence then being fought by the Greeks against the Turks) contributed to the popularity of the manner. Perhaps there was also another reason: a reaction against the overdelicate niceties of the then almost ubiquitous Adamesque style and toward something more solid and basically architectural.

The seedling of the Greek Revival—the romantic classicism typified by Latrobe—found a particularly fertile soil in the United States. Many of Latrobe's details were Greek in origin, as were Godefroy's and William Jay's to a lesser extent, and much of the Greek Revival was often scarcely more archaeologically Greek than the work of this earlier generation. For example, Greek forms were often combined with Roman construction or details, or even steeples; fluting was omitted from columns; entablatures were simplified, either by the omission of triglyphs and mutules or by transforming the three parts of the entablature into three overlapping steps. Even Strickland, one of the stricter adherents to correct detail, had to admit that in his famous bank at Philadelphia (AB 135) it was a difficult task for an architect to preserve *all* the characteristics of a "Grecian temple." He felt it necessary to write (in the *Analectic Magazine,* March, 1819) that certain features of Greek architecture "cannot be applied with their proper effect to places of business, without a consequent sacrifice of those principles which have a constant application to internal uses and economy," a remark almost ridiculously obvious to the twentieth-century reader.

The simplicity and boldness of statement in Latrobe's romantic classicism set the tone for the best of the Greek Revival, which is as free from servile archaeology as is his own work. Restraint, a sense of geometric proportion, and a feeling for flat surfaces characterize the Greek Revival, both professional and vernacular. The style was particularly suited to the tradition of the carpenter-builder, already adept in adapting pattern-book designs to his craft, and to the masons and stone cutters who were stimulated to think in monolithic terms expressed in the simple eloquence of functional post and lintel.

Before turning to the formulators of the Greek Revival, mention should be made of at least one architect who is a transitional figure, John Haviland, an Englishman, like William Jay and George Hadfield, whose work his own resembles. The author of several important buildings in Philadelphia, Haviland's most distinguished is the former Deaf and Dumb Asylum, now the School of Industrial Art in Philadelphia, an impressive edifice notable for the masterly treatment of cubical forms and plane surfaces, unrelieved except by niches and dominated by a central portico where the powerful early Greek Doric order is employed. Haviland is also noteworthy for his prisons, the Eastern State Penitentiary in Philadelphia, 1828–1829 (AB 107), and "the Tombs" in New York, the former designed in a formidable Gothic Revival manner, and the latter in the equally forbidding Egyptian mode. Both buildings were remarkable for the incorporation of the newer penology which involved labor and separate, but not solitary, confinement, and a radiating plan for more efficient supervision.

Willam Strickland and Robert Mills, Latrobe's apprentices and pupils, were the most important of the Greek Revival architects. Strickland was inclined to be more refined in detail and perhaps a little more scholarly in his choice of it than was Mills. He was also a more graceful and elegant designer, as well as basically more eclectic. Mills was less attracted to archaeological sources and much bolder in his forms; to some tastes his work is occasionally even brutal.

Strickland's first important building was the Second Bank of the United States in Philadelphia (later the Customs House), 1818–1824 (AB 135, *AB 137), now part of the restoration of the Independence Hall area. (He won this commission over Latrobe, who achieved only second prize.) Being the first conspicuous building wherein a Greek Doric portico (taken bodily from Stuart and Revet's *Antiquities of Athens*) appears on both facades, its place in the development of later romantic classicism is analogous to Jefferson's Virginia Capitol in the earlier period. Ingeniously planned, lit by lateral windows only, so as not to be inconsistent with the antique custom of the unfenestrated wall at least on the facades, the exterior has little to do with the design except to give it dignity. It bears no relationship to the interior, where only lip service is given to Hellenism in a few details; instead, the grace of almost Adamesque ornament prevails, and even oval forms appear in the plan (AB 134). Furthermore, the axis of the main banking room is at right angles to that of the building, quite inconsistent with the longitudinal axis of the building as a whole.

Strickland's United States Naval Home at Philadelphia, 1826–1833 (*AB 138, *AB 138A), was also well-received because of its conspicuous porticos. It is praiseworthy for the ample balconies or "piazzas" and for the architect's imaginative use of cast iron in their supports. But it cannot compare in composition with Bulfinch's masterpiece, the Massachusetts General Hospital, since there is no relation between the archaeological central motif, the massive, unornamented end blocks, and the finely scaled detail of the porches and their attenuated supports.

4–1. Philadelphia Exchange, Philadelphia, Pennsylvania, 1836, by William Strickland. Watercolor drawing by Strickland. (The Historical Society of Pennsylvania, Philadelphia.)

4-2. State Capitol, Nashville, Tennessee, 1845–1859, by William Strickland. From a photograph taken during the Civil War by B. N. Barnard. (Library of Congress.)

Strickland's most remarkable building is the old Philadelphia Exchange of 1836 (AB 133; Illustration 4–1) a graceful accent in the older section of Philadelphia and, happily, part of the large-scale restoration of that area. It is fairly conventional in its ground floor, where simple post and lintel construction is employed. But the upper part of the building is unusual in having a curved facade around which sweeps a file of engaged Corinthian columns which repeat in larger dimensions the crowning cupola, a copy of the fifth century B.C. monument to Lysocrates in Athens. Derivative though this motif is, it is used with originality, and offers scope for the elegant refinement of Strickland's taste.

A more conspicuous, if less successful, building is Strickland's State Capitol, in Nashville, Tennessee, 1845–1859 (AB 209; Illustration 4–2). Like Jefferson's Capitol it is a temple-shaped building, crowned prominently with the same motif which Strickland employed on the Exchange (more correct for a Greek temple, since the monument is also Greek; but no Greek would have combined the two forms). The juxtaposition is completely arbitrary, for the tower has no reflection in the interior. Though Strickland deserves credit for an attempt to find an expressive or symbolic motif other than a dome, the latter is more satisfactory, as subsequent usage has proved.

The work of Robert Mills reflects a less refined taste than Strickland's, but Mills's more forthright structures seem more consistent with the Greek Revival as it developed in the United

4–3. Patent Office (now the National Collection of Fine Arts and National Portrait Gallery), Washington, D. C., 1836–1842, by Robert Mills. From an old photograph, before changes in 1936.

States. Mills set out to be a professional architect, grounding himself with a thorough classical education and studying and working with both Jefferson and Latrobe. Mills's earnest example became a standard for other government architects for years to come.

The early work of Mills is as transitional as that of Haviland, and consists principally of houses in Richmond, Virginia (including the Brockenborough House, the "White House of the Confederacy," 1814), and large auditorium-like churches, such as the Monumental Church in Richmond, 1812, designed to accommodate the large crowds of Protestant revivalism.

Mills first hit his stride with the Records Office at Charleston, the so-called "Fireproof Building" (now the South Carolina Historical Society), 1822–1827 (AB 202). It is instructive to compare the proposed design for the facade with that of the executed building. The Adamesque, gracefully curved stair in the drawing has been replaced by one with right angles, which is much more consistent with the rectangularity of the building as a whole. More significant are the elimination of fluting in the columns of the portico, and the replacement of the pediment with a kind of sloped parapet. These elements simplify the building and give it a somewhat austere quality and a more powerful effect. The Doric detail here (as also in the Richmond Monumental Church) is considerably modified from the academic Greek, especially in the entablature. The resulting effect is simpler, stronger, and more related to the rationale of masonry than to the somewhat arbitrary conventions of Greek architecture, whose stone forms derived ultimately from a more ancient wooden construction. This relative freedom from archaeological bias and the tendency to design in heavy, block-like forms with sparse ornamentation are true of most of Mills's government buildings: the smaller ones, like the custom houses at New Bedford and Newburyport, or the larger ones in Washington, such as the old Patent Office (now the National Collection of Fine Arts and the National Portrait Gallery), 1836–1842 (Illustration 4–3), which though incorporating ideas and additions by other architects is essentially of Mills's design. This building epitomizes Mills at his most characteristic as far as its general effect is concerned: either grand in its austere and forthright dignity, or "stodgy" and heavy-handed—depending on one's taste.

Less characteristic but more generally appealing because of its magnificent yet graceful colonnade is Mills's Treasury Building, 1836–1842 (AB 125; Illustration 4–4), which still holds

4–4. Detail of colonnade, Treasury Building, Washington, D. C., 1836–1842, by Robert Mills.

its own in scale and size and has not been overwhelmed by any subsequent building in Washington. Here Mills showed he could be as correctly classical as Strickland and as graceful, while retaining his own impressive strength and monumentality. An illustration of Mills's subtlety as a designer is the fact that the great length of the lateral colonnade is not monotonous, partly the consequence of his choice of the Greek Ionic, rather than either the overelaborate Corinthian or the too direct Doric.

Mills's government buildings are notable for their practicality and the expressiveness of their masonry construction. Efficiently planned even for the complexities of modern business, uncomplicated in articulation and structure, and therefore presenting little maintenance problem, they are built as solidly as Roman buildings and, save for nuclear disaster, will last as long. In one of them, the areas vaulted by Mills survived a severe fire after the Civil War, in contrast to the iron-supported roofs and floors of the later sections of the building, which were destroyed.

Even in the architecture of monuments Mills excelled. One of the most prominent of American symbols is the Washington Monument, begun in 1833 (AB 122), the conception of Mills. Of course obelisks existed before, but not even the wealth and labor available to the Pharaohs could have produced one of this height. Originally designed to rise from a substructure of Doric columns, Mills himself probably [3] eliminated this base, permitting the simple eloquence of the four-sided shaft to speak for itself.

Both Mills and Strickland tackled problems germane to their age, and solved them ingeniously within the framework of the mid-century's preferred revival style, but Mills was bolder, and his forms better expressed structure and function.

Mills set a standard of honest workmanship, solid, permanent construction, and impressive, simplified classical forms which inspired a public architecture equal to that of any other country; he established a tradition carried on in the next generation in the work of Thomas Walter and Ammi Young, also government architects. Some may regret the stranglehold of classicism on government buildings in Washington, but romantic classicism and the Greek Revival have given a monumental consistency to the capital which, though anachronistic now, is still expressive of the spacious dignity which L'Enfant, Latrobe, and Mills meant to symbolize the greatness of America. Mills's buildings are among the best of the period from any point of view but particularly in the context of his age, for he used archaeology with discretion and created new forms suggested by its great past but adapted to the uses of his time and even of today.

The importance of Strickland and Mills in the first generation of the Greek Revival (though both also occasionally worked in the other re-

vivals) was probably not rivaled by anyone else, but the influence of Ithiel Town and Alexander Jackson Davis, who for a while worked together as a firm, was nearly as great.

It is difficult to determine which one of the partners was most responsible for the individual buildings among the many the firm designed. Town was not the draughtsman that Davis was; his genius was in construction rather than in design.

The most conspicuous of the firm's early buildings is the Subtreasury on Wall Street, formerly the Customs House, 1833, where the temple-like portico is one of the first prominent Greek examples in the city. (The interior was designed by another architect.)

4–5. State Capitol, Columbus, Ohio, 1839–1861, by Ithiel Town and others.

On the basis of such work, Town and Davis were commissioned to design a number of state capitols. Some, like Town's Connecticut Capitol at New Haven [4] (destroyed) followed the pattern of Jefferson's at Richmond; others were like Bulfinch's domed Massachusetts State House; and some combined both prototypes, as in the old Indiana Capitol, a temple with a dome. The most successful and original was that at Raleigh, North Carolina, 1833–1840 (AB 734), where a geometric, block-like form, combined with projecting porticos and a dome, encloses an interior area that has a nice spatial relationship to its covering. The exterior of the building is chiefly distinguished by repetitive rows of pilasters with scarcely projecting capitals which, because of their low relief, do not interfere with the impression of solid mass.

A treatment very similar to that of the side elevations of the North Carolina Capitol is seen in what is perhaps the most remarkable building of its kind in the country, the State Capitol at Columbus, Ohio, 1839–1861 (Illustration 4–5). Though designed by a number of hands (the first prize was won by a local architect; the third, by Thomas Cole, the landscape painter), Town and Davis had the task of pulling together the final solution, and must also have inspired at least two of the designs considered, since rows of pilasters like those at Raleigh comprise an effective part of the total effect. Davis certainly lowered the basement or base upon which the order rests, thereby contributing greatly to the building's impressive simplicity. The conception of four recessed Doric porches, however, was not by the firm. These and the block-like shape and low dome were part of the original design, one of the most imaginative of the time, a conception which retains intact the geometry of the basic cube but varies it with an alternation of flat pilasters and non-projecting colonnades.

Town, sometimes together with Davis, was responsible for a number of important residences which were among the finest in the country and which became prototypes for many that followed.

One of the first temple-fronted houses (that is, not with projecting portico, as at Jefferson's

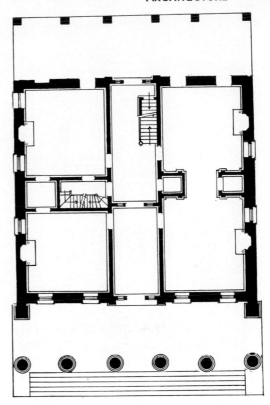

4–6. Original plan of Russell House (now Honors College, Wesleyan University), Middletown, Connecticut, 1828. (Adapted from *Great Georgian Houses of America*, Architects' Emergency Committee; New York: 1933.)

Monticello, but with the entire facade prefaced by a colonnade, usually pedimented, as at the Richmond Capitol), was the Russell House (now Honors College, Wesleyan University), Middletown, Connecticut, 1828 (AB 225; Illustration 4–6). This magnificent residence is notable for its monumental scale and spacious interiors, but even more so for two aspects of its plan: a double parlor where two rooms (usually, as in this case, on the longitudinal axis) are partially joined by an opening that is much wider than an ordinary door; and secondly, a colonnade on the rear facade (since closed in). The first initiated a trend which became particularly popular in New York City, largely through the example of Town and Davis themselves (see

4–7. Bowers House (destroyed), Northampton, Massachusetts, 1825, by Ithiel Town. From an old print.

Illustration 4–10 and accompanying text). The second became popular in the South, for it provided an additional shaded area and further cross ventilation.

Another important house, both intrinsically and from the point of view of precedent, was Town's Bowers House (destroyed), 1825, in Northampton, Massachusetts (Illustration 4–7). Its central block was prefaced by a temple portico like that of the Russell House, but it was graced by colonnaded wings as well, though the columns were in fact not columns at all but four-sided piers—a Greek Revival usage which became nearly as popular as the column itself for support. An unusual (and seldom imitated) feature of the Bowers House is the absence of a central hallway and door (the building was entered through a wing), thus permitting a double parlor parallel to the facade and not at right angles to it.

Less imitated than the Bowers and Russell houses, but equally distinguished, are Town's own house in New Haven (lately part of the Yale University Press), 1836, and the Alsop House in Middletown, Connecticut (now incorporated in the Davison Art Center of Wesleyan University[5]), 1838 (Illustration 4–8). Both are by Town alone. The central portion of each house is an essentially simple block without peristyle or even pilaster strips. This area is flanked by wings with peristyles formed by piers. Both are similar in interior plan to the Bowers House; that is, they are entered through one of the wings, again permitting double parlors parallel to the facade. Since the Town House has been considerably damaged by remodeling for non-residential purposes, the completely restored Alsop House must to a certain extent represent both structures. There is little detail except the wide eaves, which replace the usual entablature. The almost mathematical severity and planometric elegance of the structure itself are countered by a porch supported by delicately scaled and detailed iron work, and by areas decorated with wall painting consisting of a frieze of swags and simulated antique statues in niches. The house is remarkable also for its interior painting, including further *trompe l'oeil* statues, and decorative motifs taken from Raphael and Piranesi, comprising altogether the most elaborate program of decoration in American domestic architecture before the Civil War. If the Alsop House is by Town, he and his cultivated clients created here an epitome of the Greek Revival in a simplified and pared-down version which in its spirit is very close to romantic classicism, and in its decoration is a late exemplification of neo-classicism in general.

Various town houses (since disappeared), which also exerted considerable influence, were designed by Town and Davis in New York. More interesting than the usual archaeological

4–9. Brevoort (de Rham) House (destroyed), New York, New York, c. 1835, by Alexander Jackson Davis. From an old photograph.

4–8. Detail of Alsop House (now Davison Art Center, Wesleyan University), Middletown, Connecticut, 1838, attributed to Ithiel Town.

solution was the adaptation of the eloquent simplicity of Latrobe's Decatur House to Davis' Brevoort (de Rham) House, c. 1835 (Illustration 4–9), once at Fifth Avenue and Ninth Street, New York. A very correct and exquisitely detailed portico was displayed against the elegant plainness of a wall on which elements replacing the pilasters and entablature were stripped down to panel form. The grandeur and dignity of this house and another, the destroyed John Cox Stevens House, 1845, made the firm's urban dwellings precedents for similar houses throughout the country. The interior of the Stevens House, with its double parlor, is shown in a typically refined rendering by Davis (AB 102; Illustration 4–10).[6] Town and Davis were also active, with Martin Thompson, in designing in New York slightly less pretentious row houses, since destroyed but of a type still represented by those on the north side of Washington Square. An excellent example of this kind of house, though not by Town and Davis, is the Old Mer-

4–10. Parlor of the residence of John Cox Stevens (?), New York, New York, 1845, by Alexander Jackson Davis. Watercolor drawing by Davis. (Courtesy of The New-York Historical Society, New York City.)

chants House, 1831, on East Fourth Street; the interior finish is particularly fine, and the house is furnished in the style of the period. More unusual were the apartments of joined residences designed by Town and Davis, represented today by a surviving section known as "Lafayette" or "Colonnade" Row, 1836 (*CPB 21, *CPB 22), near Cooper Union, a complex whose design was united by a Corinthian colonnade nearly a block long.

Before deciding on a design for the Ohio Capitol, the commissioners traveled east to consult with "the most eminent architects and men of taste" in Philadelphia and New York—and

Boston. Though this city did not have the nationwide influence of the other two centers, there existed in it a strong local school which, because of its less academic and more functional character, had considerable originality and exerted influence wherever Quincy granite was exported.

Though long faithful to the graceful Adamesque style of Bulfinch, Boston's high level of cultivation, including its classical proclivities (symbolized in such institutions as the Athenaeum), made it especially receptive to the Greek Revival. Bulfinch's use of granite in the Massachusetts General Hospital, and elsewhere, also had a great deal to do with the stimulation of interest in the geometric simplicity of romantic classicism, which prepared the way for its extension in the Greek Revival in the hands of younger men like Alexander Parris, Solomon Willard, and Isaiah Rogers, who filled the vacuum left by Bulfinch's removal to Washington.

After a decade of designing distinguished houses in Portland, Maine, Alexander Parris came to Boston. His first notable work there, the Sears House (now the Somerset Club), 1816 (AB 128), though it incorporates the graceful curves of his and Bulfinch's early style in the bay windows, otherwise possesses an unadorned simplicity that is largely the consequence of the use of granite. The facade of St. Paul's, 1819, the Episcopal cathedral of Boston, on Tremont Street, displays a temple front of such elemental simplicity in its granite construction (the unfluted shafts of its portico are topped only by the simplest capitals and residual entablature) that it was once jeeringly called a "collection of grindstones."

More acceptable was Parris' Unitarian Church in Quincy, 1828 (Illustration 4–11), perhaps his masterpiece and one of the finest of Greek Revival churches. Here the Wren–Gibbs formula for facade and tower is reduced in monolithic construction to the basic forms of romantic classicism, relieved only by the most chaste and correct Greek detail. Parris' Quincy or South Market, designed in 1823 (*AB 126, AB 127), is an impressive example not only of the dignity which can be given a public building by Greek Revival design, but of the adaptability of the style to any purpose. A huge edifice with Doric porticos, the central block is crowned with an elegant saucer dome which gives a pleasingly graceful accent to a long and rectilinear structure which would otherwise be monotonous. The stonework is distinguished and original; the fine courses of hewn granite are adapted to a basically classical form; the direct statement of masonry is exploited, and academic correctness is qualified by such practical changes as the penetration of the entablature by the fenestration of the second story.

Powerful granite construction of this kind was made possible by the opening of the Quincy quarries by Solomon Willard, who devised

4–11. Unitarian Church, Quincy, Massachusetts, 1828, by Alexander Parris.

machinery and railroad cars for the extraction and transportation of the huge blocks used in the buildings of Parris, and others.

Willard's own buildings most effectively brought out the massive dignity inherent in the Greek Revival as interpreted in monolithic granite. Unfortunately, of his important buildings, only some structures at the Charlestown (Massachusetts) Navy Yard remain. The rest have long since disappeared and with them a reputation that deserves to be revived. Willard's lesser structures, such as the Norfolk County Court House at Dedham, Massachusetts, and the Town Hall at Quincy, Massachusetts, are still standing, and even these have the forceful statement of his style at his best, as seen in old prints. The finest and most typical of Willard's buildings was the Suffolk County Courthouse, Boston, 1845 (Illustration 4–12). This remarkable edifice, each facade displaying a monolithic portico, could be likened to a great piece of granite with windows and doors cut into it, as though into the "live" rock. Little detail interfered with the directness of this treatment; there was no projecting molding, let alone sill or lintel. Openings were simply interruptions in the otherwise continuous courses of granite. Like Mills, Willard could be original in his employment of a basically Greek formulation as an expression of civic dignity.

Among the most interesting of the granite structures in Boston are the warehouses and commercial buildings in the old waterfront district, which give this area an unexpected and perhaps even unintended grandeur. The block-like massiveness and cubic strength of these buildings, such as the Union Wharf Warehouse,

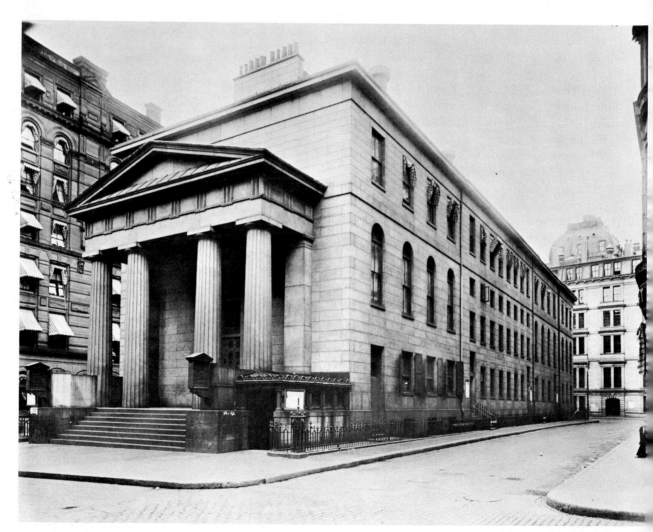

4–12. Suffolk County Courthouse (destroyed), Boston, Massachusetts, 1845, by Solomon Willard. From an old photograph.

4–13. Union Wharf Warehouse, Boston, Massachusetts, 1846, by Gridley J. F. Bryant.

1846 (AB 301; Illustration 4–13), and others by Gridley J. F. Bryant, derive not only from the use of monolithic material but from the relative absence of revivalist detail, since it was not felt necessary to adorn buildings which were merely practical. An even more interesting aspect of these buildings is their basic method of construction: the Greek post and lintel is reduced to its logical and essential function as an unadorned pier supporting a great architrave beam, a motif repeated in a general way in the fenestrated areas above. Thus the two basic components of Greek architecture, its cubic mass and its post and lintel construction, are often better illustrated in these practical buildings than in their more pretentious counterparts which display archaeological detail. In any event, these utilitarian structures, almost lacking in academic character, are as much a part of the period as are their more correctly eclectic contemporaries.

Certainly the impetus for the development of buildings of this kind was given by the large and original treatment Parris gave to the lateral facades of the Quincy Market, and more clearly by the work of Willard. Similar buildings exist in many of the commercial districts of the eastern seaports. Their development may have occurred separately and simultaneously, since this simplified post and lintel construction became the logical interpretation of the general stylistic character of the Greek Revival in terms of rational building, once large enough stones could be quarried and transported.[7]

Whatever its origins and distribution, the granite commercial style of Boston was an important architectural development, not only for its own powerful and logical form but as a prefiguring of future development. Richardson's revival of it in his late commercial buildings (notably the Harrison Avenue Ames Store in Boston) may well have influenced Louis Sullivan in his expression of the cage form of the steel frame, basically so similar to simplified post and lintel construction.

Among the academic architects in the second generation, probably Thomas U. Walter is the most important. Though a student of Strickland, his personal style is closer to that of Mills, for a number of his buildings in and around Philadelphia have a solid and direct dignity which recalls the earlier architect, as for example, the Eye Hospital, Preston's Retreat, the First Universalist Church, and the Crown Street Synagogue. Walter's best known work, however, is Founders' Hall, the main building of Girard College, Philadelphia, c. 1833–1847 (AB 162, AB 164; Illustration 4–14). When this building is glimpsed for the first time, the sight of yet another temple is apt to arouse a feeling of boredom in the observer. Ancient fane it surely is; but the scale, the proportions, and the materials are so handsome and impressive that strong feelings about appropriateness, function, and originality are temporarily anesthetized. No photograph can do justice to the tremendous peristylic mass rising majestically above the now semi-slum region and completely dwarfing human beings. The relations of all the parts to one another are satisfactory, though there has been criticism of its length versus its breadth— but these dimensions were determined by the founder's will. The use of the finest marble and of masonry construction throughout corroborate the fact that no expense was spared. The mag-

4–14. Detail of colonnade, Founders' Hall, Girard College, Philadelphia, Pennsylvania, 1833–1847, by Thomas U. Walter.

nificent interiors, with their beautiful detailing (especially in the stairways) and their masonry vaulted and domed ceilings, are in no way disappointing after the initial impact of the exterior. Strickland's Second Bank of the United States seems tentative and almost shoddy in comparison with the majestic authority of this building.

Founders' Hall is eclectic, inconvenient, cold, and echoing. In a word, it is an unfunctional building, except as a monument to the arbitrary whims of two self-willed men, Stephen Girard, the founder, and Nicolas Biddle, the principal trustee, who insisted on the temple form (Walter's original design was less archaeological and more functional). Founders' Hall is, nevertheless, architecture of the highest formal and structural quality, and doubtless the masterpiece of the Greek Revival in its most academic phase. Nicolas Biddle can almost be forgiven his hyperbole when he announced that Philadelphia possessed the most beautiful building then standing.

Walter's other, more characteristic talents are seen in the simplicity of the other Girard College buildings (AB 151) and their relationship to one another and to the temple in their midst as part of a total complex. Since this arrangement was also prescribed in the will, the architect's solution within these limitations is all the more remarkable.

Walter's additions of the Senate and House wings and the central dome to the National Capitol, between 1855 and 1865, take us out of the Greek Revival into the period of decline marked by more extravagant eclecticism and less restrained taste. The Roman detail is ostentatious and the dome is inescapably cast iron painted to resemble masonry. Yet withal, the magnificent conception of the whole reflects the compositional mastery of a great architect—not the least part of his achievement was the incorporation of Thornton's, Latrobe's, and Bulfinch's earlier work.

Among the architects of the second generation who were influenced by the Boston masonry tradition were Ammi B. Young and Isaiah Rogers. Young, said to be a pupil of Parris, interpreted the Boston style in an unusually stately and academic way in the Boston Customs House, the original part of which (now the base of the present tower), built from 1837 to 1847, combined severe granite surfaces with correctly detailed Greek Doric porticos. Young's later work as Treasury Architect, though reflecting the broader eclecticism of the midcentury, carried on the solid structural statement of the architect's Boston years. Rogers also introduced the Boston granite style into other parts of the country; his facade of the Third Merchants' Exchange in New York (incorporated into the larger fabric of the present First National City Bank Building in lower New York by McKim, Mead & White) reflects somewhat the strong statement of his Suffolk Bank (destroyed) in Boston.

Rogers is particularly noted for his large hotels. Landmarks in luxury hotel design and among the most impressive structures of the era, they represented as fine an integration of function and style as was found in the commercial buildings of the era. The first of these, the Tremont House, 1828 (Illustration 4–15), in Boston, was in fact the first great modern hostelry. The grand and simple facade reflects the architect's feeling for monumental granite construction, which he undoubtedly absorbed in Willard's office, where he was trained. The grace in the detail of the porch and the slightly curved bays of two of the reception rooms, however, have a quite different effect. An entrance rotunda with engaged columns and a spacious dining room surrounded by a free-standing colonnade were typical of the hotel's sumptuousness. A plan designed for great convenience and ingeniously adapted to the irregular site, and the first large-scale use of water closets and other fixtures (made possible by improvements in water supply, plumbing, and sewage disposal), together with its pervading opulence, made the Tremont House a prototype in luxury hotel design, and brought fame to its architect. The Astor House in New York was the most notable of a number of hostelries designed by Rogers which were strung across the United States east of the Mississippi from New Orleans to Bangor.[8]

Other architects too numerous to mention executed distinguished buildings in New England; the influence of some went further. Among the most prominent were Elias Carter of Worcester, Massachusetts, and Russell Warren of Providence, Rhode Island, both of whom worked in the South. Warren, with James Buklin, built one of the most interesting surviving examples of the Greek Revival, the Arcade in Providence, 1827–1829 (AB 166, AB 167). Though it derives from Haviland's similarly skylighted and dignified Arcades built in Philadelphia and New York early in the century and based on European prototypes, it is more ambitious in scale

4–15.   Tremont House, Boston, Massachusetts, 1828, by Isaiah Rogers. From a watercolor by George Harvey. (Courtesy of the Boston Athenaeum.)

and more successful in design. Furthermore, it is preserved and in use, the only remaining example of its kind. Two facades dignified by Ionic colonnades facing on two business streets connect a glass-covered shopping area. This open, spacious volume is lined with three tiers of shops, the two upper stories of which open onto balconies. The whole design is tied together by stairways and railings of iron with patterns freely derived from Greek motifs.

The Greek Revival architecture of Providence as a whole deserves more than this brief notice. Baltimore too, once an almost consistently Greek Revival city, as seen in *View of Baltimore City,* 1850 (Illustration 4–16), could be treated at

length, along with several other cities. New Orleans, however, is more interesting than most of them, and a cursory mention of some of its buildings will serve as a further illustration of the scope of the Greek Revival. The enormous wealth of the region of which it was the center (in 1860 Louisiana had the highest per capita income in the nation, an impressive statistic, even discounting the fact that slaves were not counted) contributed to the flourishing of building, while its semitropical climate gave it a regional distinction. Many of the houses in the *Vieux Carré* and newer areas were designed or built under the influence of James Gallier, Sr., who had worked closely with Minard Lafever,

4–16. *View of Baltimore City,* Baltimore, Maryland, 1850. Lithograph by Sachse and Sons. (Courtesy of the Hambleton Collection, Peale Museum, Baltimore, Maryland.)

and by Charles and James H. Dakin, the latter of whom had practiced with Town and Davis. Variations on the conventional Greek Revival of these mentors, and typical of New Orleans (and of the South in general), were the houses with a porch and a gallery above supported by a colossal order or by two superimposed ones. Even more regional were the great number of dwellings and apartment houses (as at Baltimore and Charleston), such as the Le Prète House, 1835 (AB 299), which were covered with a proliferation of metal porches. The Pontalba Building, 1851 (AB 179), formerly ascribed to James Gallier, Jr., but now given to Henry Howard,[9] the designer of some famous plantation houses, holds its own in the company of the cathedral and the Cabildo on Jackson Square. Its monumental construction and boldly proportioned blocks of brick are relieved by

finely detailed Greek ornament and tiers of richly decorative iron balconies which enhance the mass and at the same time are consistent with the balconies of the nearby buildings of the quarter.

The public buildings of New Orleans are appropriate to its importance. The City Hall, 1845, by James H. Dakin and James Gallier, Sr., is a gracious and correct design, while the Customs House, 1849–1865, by A. T. Wood, is more original, a huge and severe granite mass with a splendid skylighted interior, surrounded by colossal engaged Corinthian columns (AB 170, AB 171).

Distinguished examples of the Greek Revival are distributed throughout the country and not isolated exclusively in important centers of building. Among the most rewarding examples

4–17. Kennebec County Courthouse, Augusta, Maine, c. 1845.

are county courthouses, city halls, and state capitols, many by relatively unknown designers. Indiana is especially rich in the former. The Kennebec County Courthouse at Augusta, Maine, c. 1845 (Illustration 4–17), is an interesting variation in monolithic granite that adapts the stocky proportions of the facade of Bulfinch's Capitol in that city, reducing them to almost elemental shapes—a local variation in native Hollowell granite of the similar development in Quincy granite in Boston. The City Hall and the State Capitol at Jackson, Mississippi, are simplified versions of the North Carolina State Capitol by Town and Davis. Perhaps both of the buildings in Jackson, and more certainly the latter, are by William Nichols, who may have designed some of the more distinguished residences and plantation houses in and around that city and in the Natchez Trace. College buildings are another type in which the

Greek Revival flourished, continuing an American development begun with Jefferson at the University of Virginia and Ramée at Union College. Washington and Lee at Lexington, Virginia, has an ambitious group with porticos and colonnades modeled after Charlottesville. The University of South Carolina at Columbus has handsome academic buildings by Mills, and the University of North Carolina has somewhat more finished and refined examples by Davis, or Town and Davis, as does Davidson College in the same state.

Two other public buildings are most unusual. The first is the huge Asylum (now a State Hospital) at Utica, New York, 1838 (AB 155), said to have been designed by the chairman of its board of trustees. This impressive structure is notable for its giant colonnade, larger in scale than any similar structure in Europe or America. The second building, actually a complex of buildings, is the Fairmount Water Works Pumping Station on the Schuylkill River at Philadelphia, 1819–1822 (AB 105), apparently much admired in its day, to judge from the numerous representations of it—for instance, in a painting by Thomas Birch, 1821 (PB 88), and an engraving after Thomas Doughty, c. 1825 (GB 98). Though generally ascribed to an engineer named Frederick Graff, it is thought to exhibit enough of the characteristics of Mills's style to be ascribed tentatively to him. The adaptation of a studied formality, graced with classical Greek detail, to an engineering project is a further instance of the congruence of architect and engineer which was not to be disrupted until later in the century. (The vaults of Mills, his bridges and other engineering programs, and similar projects by Strickland are further confirmation of this point.)

Innumerable local masons and carpenters adopted the proportions and detail of the Greek Revival, and applied them to the traditional Wren–Gibbs formula for town halls, churches, and meetinghouses—just as Parris had done in his Unitarian Church at Quincy. Vermont and coastal Maine, areas less changed by industrialization than some others, preserve quite a number of examples. The temple-porticoed brick

Congregational Church at Charlotte, Vermont, c. 1840 (AB 701), or the bolder and simpler Congregational Church built at the same time at Orwell, Vermont (AB 668), with its recessed portico, are quite typical. Such structures, in brick with wood trim, were matched by those in the more popular material of wood, which was nicely adapted to the neatness and precision of the Greek Revival style, as seen in the Congregational Church at Madison, Connecticut, 1838 (AB 710), with its impressive colonnade and tower—as fine a structure in its way as Parris' church at Quincy, from which it partially derives. More typical and less pretentious, and therefore all the more adaptable to wood, is the church at Slatersville, Rhode Island, c. 1840 (AB 334), from which it is not too much of a step to the vernacular.

Little has been mentioned so far about domestic architecture except in the case of Town and Davis, whose work in this instance, as in others, was prototypical. This building type is of course the most numerous, and thus for practical reasons can only be discussed generally and categorically with regard to plan and elevation; a few unusual and distinguished examples will be singled out.

The attached row house of the urban centers is the most consistent form of domestic building. It is long and narrow in plan, due to the exigencies of the city block; has an entrance and stair hall to one side, flanked on each floor by a single room opening to the facade and the rear; and sometimes includes a service wing added to the rear. Differences between examples in various cities are small, due to the prevalence of the grid plan in most of them, though distinctions between types in various cities can be made. (In New York, for instance, the main floor is entered from the street by a stoop or short flight of stairs, whereas in Philadelphia the main floor is more often entered directly from the street.) New York formerly possessed the largest number of row houses in the Greek Revival style, some of which still exist, notably those on the north side of Washington Square. But the largest group remaining are on Beacon Hill in Boston, and comprise the most consistent survival of early nineteenth-century urban domestic architecture in the country (including, of course, many examples from the early republic). They are especially attractive because of their hillside site and the presence of Louisburg Square, and they are preserved by strict zoning regulations.

There was, of course, greater variety in the larger city houses than was usual or possible in the row house. Aside from the dwelling isolated in a large lot, which is an urban instance of an essentially suburban or country residence, the house covering two or more lots is the nearest to the row house. The ampler houses in the neighborhood of Mount Vernon Square in Baltimore are among the finest of these. Similar houses exist in other cities—Richmond, for example—but are now mostly in blighted areas. Most of those built in New York have disappeared, but the handsome Brevoort (de Rham) House (Illustration 4–9) (attributed to Davis), though destroyed, is important enough to mention once again since stylistically it is an outstanding example of the development of the Latrobe-derived combination of an isolated area of refined detail contrasted with plain surfaces and a simple cubical mass. A facade such as that of the Brevoort House led the way in domestic architecture to a kind of quintessential Greek Revival formulation (analogous to that seen in the commercial architecture of Boston), in which the pilaster strips and entablature were reduced to their simplest form.

Houses of this type could be either situated in rows or isolated from one another on lots of various sizes, and were therefore suited for urban building. Less adaptable were the houses with temple-like porticos or those with wings, which required a certain amount of perspective in order to be properly seen; they were more suited to larger city lots, suburban areas, or the country. The most popular type was that exemplified by Town's temple-fronted Russell House; less pretentious versions are the Ralph Small House, built in the early 1830's in Macon, Georgia (*AB 143), and said to be by the Worcester architect Elias Carter, and the Mrs.

F. J. Dodd House in La Grange, Georgia, 1845 (*AB 731), possibly by Phillip Greene. The peristyles of both buildings are without pediments, a characteristic of southern houses generally and of Carter's houses in Massachusetts.

Vying in popularity with this free-standing type was the house whose central block was flanked by colonnaded wings (with either columns or antae), seen mostly in the North and West. Town's Bowers House (Illustration 4–7), if not the earliest example of this type, was one of the most distinguished (unusual only in that it is entered from one of the wings). The Wilcox–Cutts House in Orwell, Vermont, 1843 (*AB 111), attributed to James Lamb, is a more than usually pretentious variant of this type, with its giant temple colonnade projecting further than was customary. There were modifications of the design, the most important being the omission of colonnades from the wings. Less frequent was the house where the central block was astylar (without columns) while the wings retained colonnades, like the Alsop House (Illustration 4–8). An interesting departure from the usual plan is the impressive mansion Fatlands, in Audubon, near Valley Forge, Pennsylvania, 1845 (AB 160), which has only one astylar wing (though the other was obviously planned) to which is attached a small block with a temple portico, about half the size of the principal one which dignified the central block. (Unfortunately this house has recently been somewhat altered.) Another popular type, though less so than in previous decades, was that with a giant portico projecting from the central area of the facade (as at Monticello); in the North it usually had a balcony but in the South, as at Stanton Hall, Natchez, Mississippi, 1851 (AB 726), no balcony was added.

The two most popular types of the large houses of the South, both in the towns and on the plantations, were characterized by giant colonnades, either restricted to two opposite sides of the house, as at D'Evereux, Natchez, Mississippi, 1840 (AB 720), or completely surrounding the house (Illustration 4–19). Among the examples with balconies is Oak Alley, near Vacherie, St. James Parish, Louisiana, 1830–

1839 (AB 154A); among those without are the Henry Grady House, Athens, Georgia, 1845 (*AB 732), and the President's House at the University of Georgia, Athens, 1854–1855 (AB 733).

There were some houses which, though technically without peristyles, were not astylar, for various combinations of engaged columns and pilasters were used to decorate facades. An example is the Wooster-Boalt House, Norwalk, Ohio, 1848 (*AB 161).

As would be expected, there are many houses atypical in plan and composition, some as distinguished as they are unusual. Among them are two of the finest in the country, the addition by Philip Hooker to Hyde Hall, 1833 (AB 108; Illustration 4–18), on Oswego Lake near

4–18. Addition to Hyde Hall, near Cooperstown, New York, 1833, by Philip Hooker.

Cooperstown, New York, and the Alfred Kelley House in Columbus, Ohio, 1835–1838. The first is a part of a great manorial estate in upper New York, the other a mansion in a growing midwestern city, then only a frontier town. One is by an important architect (more famous for his work in the style of the early republic), the other by a gentleman-amateur, the owner. The addition to the earlier building at Hyde Hall, consisting principally of two large drawing rooms, is notable especially for its facade. Here the order has been stripped of all excess detail and reduced to its basic masonry forms; the walls and fenestration are equally simple. Though more lip service is paid to the order here than in the more vernacular granite style of the Boston commercial buildings, the effect of the use of large, cut stones and monolithic columns is similarly monumental. This forthright use of masonry is combined with a refined sense of proportion in the composition of the parts, here recalling or summarizing the spirit if not the letter of Greek forms.

The Kelley House is equally monumental in its solid masonry, but far more impressive in its scale. One of the great mansions of the period, it is graced not only by a projecting portico on one facade, but by recessed porticos on the three other facades, creating a quite unconventional but ingeniously roomy plan. Kelley, a wealthy contractor and builder of canals and locks, knew stone and appreciated its potentialities. The ten columns of the exterior were brought by canal boat with the rest of the imported sandstone, and put together in one of the grandest masonry piles in the domestic architecture of the country. The superb detailing of the orders and the elegant proportions of the house as a whole show a man of taste (a New Haven paper called Kelley the "proudest Nabob in the West" [10]) while the monumental yet elegant massing of the building and its fine stone work show the mason and the engineer.

Among the better known architects (besides Town) noted for their important or unusual houses was Strickland, who built at least two distinguished mansions in and around Nashville, the most notable being Belmont (now

Acklen Hall), at Belmont College, Nashville, Tennessee, 1850 (AB 139, AB 140, AB 142). The facade of this unusually pretentious town house displays not only a projecting portico with a colossal Corinthian order, but also two one-story porticos on either side. This innovation, together with the overelaborate detail, is much more mid-century than is Strickland's work in general, suggesting the collaboration of Strickland's architect son. The great scale of the entrance hall, with its free-standing columns and divided stairs, and the ballroom, which is graced by a double colonnade, are similar to another great house west of the Alleghenies, Picnic House (the William Croghan House), in Pittsburgh, c. 1835 (AB 149, AB 150, *AA 150A), the ballroom of which is surely one of the most elaborate and academically detailed interiors in the Greek Revival style.

In the foregoing discussion of domestic architecture it has seemed practical only to typify and illustrate with a few examples. There is a group of houses, however, which should be dealt with a little more in detail (though a few of them have already been mentioned as illustrations of types) since, as well as being intrinsically interesting, they comprise a development which is unique in the United States.

A few distinguished examples in the Greek Revival style were built in the older slave states, such as Berry Hill in Virginia, a magnificent temple-fronted example, flanked at a considerable distance by two charming smaller temples; or Doughregan Manor, the Carroll estate near Ellicott City, Maryland, an astylar variation on the usual block-like type, further lengthened by wings in one of which is a chapel. The Manor is an exaggerated late example of the extended plan common in the South since the eighteenth century. The Greek Revival was particularly adapted, however, to the newer areas of the Deep South, which were: first, the lower Mississippi valley from Natchez down to New Orleans and its vicinity, especially in the Feliciana parishes south of the Mississippi line, and along both sides of the river from Baton Rouge to the metropolis, that is, the "Grand Parade"; second, the Louisiana parishes west of the Mis-

4–20. Gaineswood, near Demopolis, Alabama, 1842–1850, by Nathan Bryan Whitfield.

General Whitfield. William Cooper of Savannah, for instance, is said to have built a number of plantation houses around Darien, Georgia; and in 1845 James Clarke Harris designed Malmaison (the residence of the last chief of the Choctaws east of the Mississippi), in Carroll County, Mississippi, a porticoed building whose classical dignity is compromised by the beginnings of jig-saw work. The architect Henry Howard of New Orleans is known to have designed three of the most distinguished plantations in the South (all unfortunately destroyed). Two of them erected in about 1845, Madewood, and Woodlawn (Illustration 4–21), on the Bayou Lafourche, in Assumption Parish, were fairly academic in detail, parading magnificent Ionic porticos. The main body of the buildings, however, was supplemented by subsidiary additions which in their gabled geometry and their position at right angles to the central block showed again, as at Gaineswood, that it was not magniloquent classicism alone but composition as well which distinguished the finest plantation houses.

Howard's third great mansion, Belle Grove, 1858, formerly on the west bank of the Mississippi near Port Allen, was perhaps the most magnificent of the Louisiana plantations. [It is illustrated frequently, having appealed to a number of photographers, including Edward Weston (*F 96).] Large in scale and massing, varied in plan, rich in decoration, and designed with several porticos of different heights, a curved bay area, and wings, it represents the last phase of classical revivalism in its use of varied classical sources (including Italian Renaissance and baroque), its asymmetrical plan, and the opulence of its decoration. The destruction of this mansion (and others by Howard) through neglect typifies the undeserved fate of many more on the river and the bayous—ignored, rotting away, and often surrounded by oil wells. Too few, like Oak Alley, are preserved privately or, like Buen Retiro, through public action.

Another late example showing an elaboration of ornament (though retaining a conventional plan with a giant projecting portico, as we have seen) similar to Belle Grove is Stanton Hall. More impressive, and comparable to Belle Grove in heaviness of detail and complexity of plan, is Rattle and Snap, 1845, the old Polk estate near Columbia, Tennessee, on the Natchez Trace. One of the grandest of the southern mansions, its scale and proportions are characteristic of the Tennessee plantations, which were more influenced by the extravagant manner of the lower Mississippi than by the more restrained and conventional examples in nearby Kentucky.

In a survey necessarily limited in detail, perhaps the foregoing sampling of the more distinguished or typical buildings will suggest to the reader the wealth of architecture in the Greek Revival style, and will stimulate him to the discovery and appreciation of buildings in his own vicinity or in other areas where his curiosity might lead him.

The influence of individual architects and of centers of design such as Philadelphia, New York, Boston (and to a lesser extent Baltimore, where there were followers of Latrobe and Mills), together with that of the carpenter handbooks, carried the Greek Revival everywhere, giving a consistent character to the American scene and justifying Talbot Hamlin's remark in his *Greek Revival Architecture in America* that the Greek Revival is America's national style. In any event, the meetinghouses and academies, the mansions of planters and ship captains, and the houses of industrious mechanics still exist as they did a hundred years ago in a succession of places largely unspoiled by the unplanned tawdriness of much of the contemporary scene. They evoke the earlier days of the republic, the time of the lyceum, of oratory and literature; and, in maritime New England, they bring to mind the days when the Yankee character was conditioned by an economy of "wind, wood, and water," when Yankee ships were known 'round the world, and half America was built with lumber out of Bangor.

Before taking leave of the Greek Revival, a summary statement should be made about one of its most significant aspects: the vernacular, as opposed to the academic. It has already been noted how the Kennebec County Courthouse in

4–21. Woodlawn (destroyed), near Napoleonville, Assumption Parish, Louisiana, c. 1845, by Henry Howard.

Augusta, Maine, is a reduction to simple masonry terms of the essential shapes of Bulfinch's Capitol in the same city, and how close the church at Slatersville, Rhode Island (AB 334), comes to being in the vernacular. It is only a short step to such a structure as the Chestnut Hill Baptist Church at Exeter, Rhode Island, 1838 (AB 333), in which the Greek orders have been minimized to a carpentry of almost pure geometry. Such developments can be accounted for by the feeling for the limitations and potentialities of stone and wood on the part of traditional craftsmen who were not trained architects. But characteristics which could hardly be called academic have also been noticed in some of the structures by Mills, Willard, Parris, and even Town and Davis. Mills by his direct expression of plan and masonry construction contributed a simple formal grandeur to his buildings; Parris and Willard stripped down the orders to their basic components; and Town and Davis took the romantic classical norm of Latrobe and reduced it to an even sparser elegance in such buildings as the Brevoort House. The economy of means which was natural to Parris and Willard, who were engineers and stone masons as well as architects, helped create a style that was well adapted to the designs of the anonymous masons who erected the commercial buildings and the warehouses in the maritime cities—a simple post and lintel style which proved a practical formula from Down East villages to the river towns of the West and the new cities on the Pacific coast. The block of stores at Slatersville, Rhode Island, 1855 (AB 335), is typical. A similar architectural spirit in domestic building can be seen in urban housing blocks, one of the most handsome examples being the John Neal Houses, Portland, Maine, c. 1836 (Illustration 4–22). There, granite is used as beautifully as in Parris' Quincy Market and with as fine a sense of style in the adaptation of the rectilinear austerities of the Greek form to panel, sill, and lintel in an unacademic but nonetheless elegant and functionally expressive solution.

The carpentry tradition, so strong in the United States, played an even more important

4–22. Facade, John Neal Houses, Portland, Maine, c. 1836.

part than masonry in the development of an indigenous Greek Revival. We have seen how in the eighteenth century the builder of the Brooklin (Connecticut) Meetinghouse, for instance, achieved an entirely different effect from that arrived at by Joseph Brown in the contemporaneous Gibbs-derived design of the Baptist Church at Providence. The carpenter-builder at Brooklin adapted detail and proportion more honestly to wood, and simplified surfaces for the same reason, achieving a total effect more dependent on proportion itself and on the nicety of the joinery of flat planes than on correct academic detail. An analogous development has been seen in the Adamesque house where the adaptation of late Georgian decoration and slim proportions became more attenuated and "edgy" in the wooden versions of the style in this country. The carpenters of the Greek Revival were even more successful in reducing the classical vocabulary to treatment appropriate to wood. Most of the simpler dwellings of the period in New England and elsewhere reflect this process. Many of them employ the Doric pilaster order in Benjamin's *Practise of Architecture* (1833) and reduce its already simplified form to emphatic basic terms. Two Greek Revival houses on Cape Cod, of about 1850, one at Wellfleet (AB 705) and the other at Eastham (AB 707), can be taken as typical in this respect. The neatness, precision, and economy of form—the "shipshapeness"—of houses such as these can be attributed to the fact that they were built by "housewrights" who were also shipwrights.

A more sophisticated example is the Swedenborgian House in Cambridge, Massachusetts, c. 1845 (Illustration 4–23); its nicety of proportion would almost indicate a deliberate stylization of the vernacular.

The non-domestic architecture in the vernacular Greek Revival is equally individual. Even a fairly academic building such as the Baptist Church of Sedgwick, Maine, built in the 1840's (Illustration 4–24), shows some deviation from the prototype from which it was taken, an engraving in Benjamin's *Practise of Architecture* (Illustration 4–25). (In a copy of the book now in the possession of the descendants of the builder, the engraving is marked with the indi-

4–23. Swedenborgian House (Harvard University), Cambridge, Massachusetts, c. 1845.

4–24. Baptist Church, Sedgwick, Maine, 1840's.

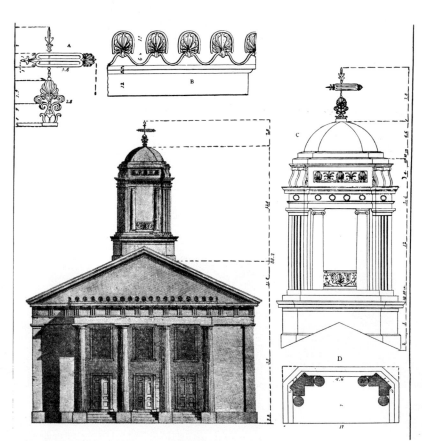

4–25. Elevation of a church from Asher Benjamin's *Practise of Architecture* (New York: 1836).

4–26. Congregational Church, Higganum, Connecticut, c. 1845.

penter and joiner. On a larger scale, masons and stonecutters were stimulated to think in monolithic terms and in the simple grandeur of post and lintel. Not only is the American Greek Revival interesting for its intrinsic beauty, but it is significant in the historical development of American architecture. Post and lintel construction in Boston and Philadelphia is in the background of the development of the expressive design of the tall building hinted at in Richardson's late work and formulated by Sullivan; and the plain surface and subtle play of geometric form are part of an indigenous tradition whose later manifestations in Sullivan and Wright contribute to the flavor of the contemporary International Style.

The Gothic Revival

Though examples of the Gothic style were less numerous than those of the Italian Renaissance or "villa" style, the picturesqueness of the Gothic made it, after the Greek, the most conspicuous of the revivals. As early as 1846 the popular designer and propagandist Andrew Jackson Downing announced that "the Greek temple disease had passed the crisis," [11] and in 1843 a Gothic design had been substituted for the Doric one planned for the chapel of the famous Mount Auburn Cemetery in Cambridge, Massachusetts.

The Gothic is the revival most compatible with romanticism, marking a reaction against classical canons and reflecting the new interest in the Middle Ages and the revival of established religion.

At the very beginning of the century Chateaubriand in his *Genius of Christianity* had said that it was impossible to enter a Gothic church without "experiencing a kind of thrill accompanied by a vague sense of the divine." By the 1840's, to want to live in a sham medieval environment, a "Scottish baronial" manor, or a "Norman cottage" was as natural as reading Sir Walter Scott, and, at least among Catholics and Episcopalians, it became almost spiritually binding to build church edifices in a medieval style.

In its earliest phase the Gothic amounted to little more than the superimposition of vaguely

cations of changes which he carried out.) The actual building is bolder and more forthright than the original design, especially in the tower and in the base that has been added, both of which exploit the planometric possibilities inherent in traditional wooden construction. Further reduction to basic geometric forms can be seen in such an example as the Congregational Church at Higganum, Connecticut, c. 1845 (Illustration 4–26). Though at first such a structure may seem uneducated and crude, even the most academically prejudiced taste should be impressed by its beauty, which is unconventional but no less striking.

The interaction between professional or academic architecture and the vernacular with its traditional adherence to local materials and usages is the principal factor that differentiates the indigenous Greek Revival from the international classicism of the more archaeological examples of the style. The resulting clean and simple masses, the plain surfaces and planometric play of form which characterize the American Greek Revival became a formal language not only useful to the professional but peculiarly adaptable to the traditions of car-

medieval detail on basically classic forms, at first in a naïve way that produced almost rococo decoration. Later, a greater archaeological accuracy in detail and in structure created a more genuine Gothic Revival, especially in ecclesiastical architecture. Here, eclecticism was combined with a greater sensibility for the organic relationship between structure and form that prevailed in the original Gothic architecture of the thirteenth and fourteenth centuries. With the rejection of such easy effects as vaults of lathe and plaster, a usage common in the earlier phase of the revival, structural honesty began to be equated with morality. (The final formulation of this point of view was made by John Ruskin, whose confusion of esthetics and ethics was a typical Victorian trait.) Yet the concern with honesty in the expression of structure, though not the central point of the criticism of the time, gradually drew the attention of builders and the public to an interest in basic principles of architecture as opposed to merely surface ornament. So it is that we must look beneath the "crockets and finials" of Gothic revivalism to something more significant. Ideals of structural morality found their most significant expression in domestic architecture, where Gothic and other medieval revivalist designs were adapted to wooden structures, to create forms as romantic as those of the past; but these houses were also the result of the circumstances of the time, not merely an arbitrary imposition of associative detail on basically classic forms, as in the earlier phase of the revival. In a word, though the Gothic is often merely picturesque, it can be functional and organic as well, like its namesake of the thirteenth century.

In the discussion that follows, the early, superficial phase of the revival (spelled "Gothick" by its proponents in the eighteenth century) will be considered first, then its more archaeological phase, and finally its adaptation to a more functional or organic concept, especially in domestic architecture, to be treated further in the section on the progressive aspects of the small house.

Soon after Sir Horace Walpole bedecked his basically Georgian house with quaint Gothicisms borrowed from Batty Langley, the "Gothick" made its appearance in the United States. Jefferson had a pavilion in the style at Monticello, and Latrobe's first design (and the one he preferred) for the Baltimore Cathedral was in what its author considered the Gothic style. Godefroy's Chapel for St. Mary's Seminary, 1806 (AB 246, AB 247), also in Baltimore, is a charming confection, with a facade covered with vertical accents and points and an interior which is equally superficial in its Gothicisms.

The first important church to be built in the early phase of the revival was Trinity Church in New Haven, 1816, designed by Ithiel Town only four years after Benjamin's Center Church and two years after Hoadley's United Church had been erected on the same New Haven Green. The pointed windows, castellated towers, and imitation plaster vaults of Trinity (all the more conspicuous in contrast with its classical neighbors), must have been startling in conservative New Haven. But even these Gothic features and picturesque details, taken from a popular early source book on York Cathedral ("to relieve the tameness of the walls," as one contemporary commentator put it [12]), do not change the basically cubical form of the building, an effect to which the massive, rugged walls contribute. Trinity was only the most conspicuous of similar fundamentally classical buildings with Gothic trim (Strickland's St. Stephen's in Philadelphia, 1829, is another). But it was in a sense prototypical: its massive simplicity was the model for numerous others which in the Boston and Salem areas assumed an even more monumental character in the hands of architects of the Boston granite school, as in the Bowdoin Street Church (now St. John Evangelist) in Boston, c. 1831, by Solomon Willard, and the North Society Unitarian Church in Salem, 1837, by Gridley J. F. Bryant. St. Peter's in Salem, 1836 (Illustration 4–27), though its architect is unknown, perhaps typifies the style at its best. The "antediluvian ruggedness" [13] of these buildings is relieved only by pointed windows, very simple crenelations, and occasional quatrefoil openings. As a rule, these churches are also basically rectangular, not cruciform, they often lack a chancel, and they do not have masonry vaulting.

from which it originated, and can be given a character that derives from local circumstance which is, in this instance, composed of the tradition of the four-square New England meeting-house and the granite school tradition of Boston.

While these not very sophisticated varieties of early Gothic revivalism persisted well into the 1840's in the United States, in England complex plans and massing appeared somewhat earlier. Even the designs for the Commissioners' churches, issued after the Act of 1818 in England, were seldom as rectangular as those of the granite style in eastern Massachusetts. Since the "preaching box" auditorium of New England never completely replaced the plan characterized by aisles and chancels, traditionalism was further stimulated by the publication of A. W. N. Pugin's *Contrasts,* in which the Eng-

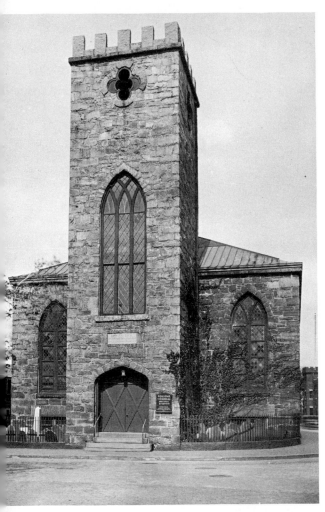

4–27. St. Peter's Church, Salem, Massachusetts, 1836.

A development similar to that in the early masonry churches occurred simultaneously in those of wood, as in the quite "classical" facade of the Baptist Church, c. 1835, in Kennebunk, Maine (Illustration 4–28). Wooden Gothic churches were on the whole, however, somewhat more picturesque, since the decorative forms and motifs of the Gothic style, especially the tracery and the steeple, were more easily imitated in wood. On the whole the masonry buildings are more noteworthy than these "carpenter Gothic" examples, since they exemplify the fact that revivalism can be adapted to a formal expression very different from the style

4–28. Baptist Church, Kennebunk, Maine, c. 1835.

lish architect dramatized in eloquent drawings the varied charm of medieval buildings in contrast with the cold, dry impersonality with which he deliberately endowed his classical ones.

Though at first Pugin himself was more interested in effect than he was in an understanding of the fundamental relation between structure and form which is finally the esthetic of Gothic architecture, the more he learned about medieval buildings the more he came to realize the importance of structural integrity. The ideas of Pugin, combining eclecticism with a more fundamental understanding of the Gothic, had great influence in Catholic and Anglican circles (Pugin was himself a Catholic convert) at a time when the revival of Christian devotion and liturgy, typified by the Oxford movement, was so great. The Oxford movement itself put great emphasis on "Christian art," and the Camden Society at Cambridge (later the Ecclesiological Society) devoted much of its attention to reforms in both ritual and architecture, largely inspired after 1840 by Pugin himself. *The Ecclesiologist,* the publication of the latter group, which first appeared in 1841, had considerable influence in the Anglican Communion on both sides of the Atlantic, an influence which soon permeated other Protestant denominations.

The change after 1840 in the American Gothic Revival was inspired by English precedent. This was due not only to the immigration of some English architects to this country, but more specifically to Pugin himself, directly or indirectly. Richard Upjohn, for instance, developed into the most important Gothic Revival architect in the United States, but only after becoming familiar with Pugin's work of the late 1830's and early 1840's.

Pugin's churches, aisled structures with deep chancels adorned with spired towers and sometimes with a porch, were conspicuously varied and asymmetrical in design, a fact which appealed to the increasing taste for the irregular and the picturesque. Such prototypes by Pugin himself and by his contemporaries were very influential in both Great Britain and America, and gave the Gothic Revival in both countries a character which distinguishes it from that of

4–29. Trinity Church, New York, New York, 1839–1846, by Richard Upjohn. Drawn by Upjohn, lithographed by Forsyth and Mimée (detail).

the Continent, where medievalism made its inroads later.

Upjohn's Trinity Church, New York, 1839–1846 (AB 263, AB 264, AB 265, *AB 266; Illustration 4–29), was inspired by Pugin's St. Marie's, Derby, with its symmetrically placed tower. It is the first important paradigm for the more correct Gothic Revival of the mid-century, being characterized by aisles without galleries, vaulted ceilings, and archaeologically correct detail. (It is a great pity that the vestry overruled the architect's desire for a masonry vault at Trinity. What appears to be one is a sham—a circumstance which Upjohn did not allow in his later churches, in which, if masonry was not permitted, he preferred to employ wooden trusses, an equally authentic English medieval usage.)

ceptable to contemporary taste, in spite of its unavoidable eclecticism.

Upjohn became the most important ecclesiastical designer in the country, and remained so into the 1860's. Among his most outstanding churches are those in which the roof is frankly of wood. The most impressive example of these is the First Parish Church at Brunswick, Maine, 1846 (AB 282; Illustration 4–31), where the organization of arches, braces, struts, and hammer beams forms a fascinating maze. This complex system of support was necessitated by the vast area to be covered, since the Congregational parish retained the Protestant tradition of the open meetinghouse plan and rejected side aisles, which would have narrowed the central area and thereby have made the roofing problem less difficult. Though this factor prevents the ele-

4–30. St. Mary's Church, Burlington, New Jersey, 1845, by Richard Upjohn.

If Trinity is a church of Gothic design suitable for a city, St. Mary's, Burlington, New Jersey, 1845 (Illustration 4–30), is the country church *par excellence,* comparable with the best Gothic Revival on either side of the Atlantic. Except to the trained eye, Upjohn's low-lying building with its tapered masonry spire could easily be taken for an English parish church. The dependence for this effect on the masonry itself rather than on bookish details holps to make St. Mary's more than usually ac-

4–31. Interior, First Parish Church, Brunswick, Maine, 1846, by Richard Upjohn.

gant and neat solution seen in some of Upjohn's other wood-roofed churches, as at St. Stephen's, in Providence, 1860, the wooden members at Brunswick are not decorated as at St. Stephen's, their inherent complexity being sufficiently picturesque to require no further ornament. The relation of empty, covered space to the labyrinth of the interpenetrating supports of the steeply pitched ceiling is very dramatic. This revival of medieval framing is singularly appropriate in a region where it had actually survived in examples like the Old Ship Meetinghouse at Hingham, Massachusetts, and in a simpler form at nearby Alna, Maine.

Whether Upjohn realized the remote affinity of his roof with the traditional wooden architecture of New England we cannot know, but he was surely aware of the latter when he chose the vertical board and batten for the external walls of the Brunswick structure (AB 282). The exterior is medieval enough with its pointed windows, its buttresses (partially bracing the heavy interior roof framing), its roof line spiced with pinnacles and crenelations, and its well-proportioned spire (until a recent remodeling after hurricane damage). Throughout the Brunswick church, Upjohn's early training as a cabinet maker came to the fore in his realization of the possibilities inherent in the indigenous habit of using wood. Though the use of board and batten was by no means unique for that date, Upjohn was the first professional architect to adapt what amounts to a vernacular method to a more pretentious building such as this.

The contemporaneous First Parish Church at Ipswich, Massachusetts, 1846, is a simpler and smaller version of the Brunswick church, a little more vernacular and "carpenter" in character, and the best of a type that may have had some influence on Upjohn's thinking.[14] In a later version of a board and batten church which Upjohn published in his *Upjohn's Rural Architecture* (1852), and in a number of similar examples such as St. Luke's, Clermont, New York, 1857 (*AB 269), he reduced the Brunswick building in size and simplified its details, omitting all ornament except the pointed arches in the window. A similar example, not as sophis-

4–32. Detail, Grace Episcopal Church (destroyed), Bath, Maine, 1852.

ticated but related more to the vernacular, was the recently demolished Grace Episcopal Church in Bath, Maine, 1852 (Illustration 4–32), in which the adaptation of Gothic to the rationale of carpentry was even more remarkable. Though basically similar to Upjohn's design, no quarter was given to any element not easy to execute in simple carpentry. Windows, for instance, were of course pointed, but were topped simply by a triangle, not a curved board, and the buttresses were frankly triangular.

The chief rivals of Upjohn as designers of Gothic churches were John Notman and James Renwick. The former, an Englishman, executed some charming churches in a restrained, nicely proportioned fourteenth-century style, the best being St. Mark's, Philadelphia, 1850, a more pretentious urban example of Pugin's later style than is Upjohn's St. Mary's, at Burlington, New Jersey. But Renwick's Grace Church, 1845–1846 (AB 253), and St. Patrick's Cathedral, 1858–1879 (AB 740, *AB 740A), both in New York, are among the most famous in the country. Renwick was more daring in the use of masonry than was Upjohn and did not depend on wooden ceilings to the same extent. Perhaps less accurate in Gothic detail than Trinity, Grace Church has genuine vaults, a picturesque profile, and a steeply pitched spire. St. Patrick's was the first church in the United States in which the influence of French Gothic was conspicuous. The careful detail, refined proportions, and spacious interior are quite reminiscent of genuine medieval Gothic, in spirit if not precisely in letter.

There are a number of church edifices throughout the country which are quite different from those by Notman, Renwick, and Upjohn and are usually more vernacular or less discriminating in their combination of eclectic sources. One group, consistent with the growing feeling for the picturesque, chose to imitate the most extravagant of late English Gothic forms—the perpendicular style—characterized chiefly by complexly ribbed vaulting. Outstanding among these is the Unitarian Church, in Charleston, South Carolina, 1852–1854 (AB 252), by Francis D. Lee, an architect who worked in several exotic modes. Though the former Yale College Library (now Dwight Chapel), 1842, by Henry Austin, was not built as a church or chapel it is so thoroughly ecclesiastical (as was the case with the older Harvard College Library, since destroyed) that it can be considered in that category. A rather imaginatively conceived variation on the English perpendicular style, the emphasis in its design lies in its height and its dramatic facade (whose principal element is a large window framed by two turrets) rather than in its complex vaulting. A number of American churches, incidentally, beginning with Strickland's St. Stephen's, are similarly inspired.

Though the Gothic was most appropriate for ecclesiastic edifices, there are other non-domestic structures, besides libraries, to be noted. A few town halls and state capitols essayed the new style, though it never became as popular as the less picturesque Greek Revival, which was better adapted to civic dignity. The sham medievalism of these buildings was nicely summed up by Mark Twain in his description of the then state capitol (still preserved as a state monument) at Baton Rouge as "a white-washed castle with turrets and things—materials all ungenuine within and without, pretending to what they *are* not." [15] Haviland in his Eastern State Penitentiary, Philadelphia, 1823–1829 (AB 107), clad this rationally planned and basically romantic classical structure with the towers and crenelations of a Gothic castle, setting a precedent for a succession of similar fortress-like edifices, not only prisons [Richardson's Allegheny County Courthouse and Jail at Pittsburgh (Illustration 5–17), built a half-century later, is an outstanding example], but also armories and forts whose military purposes were enhanced by the recall of medieval castles.

Though domestic architecture in the Gothic Revival was not nearly as popular as that in the Greek mode, a number of large houses were built in the medieval style, as well as numerous smaller ones, more usually called cottages since they were often suburban or rural. In the field of the larger, more pretentious houses in the Gothic manner, Upjohn was one of the first to excel. On the basis of a small Episcopal Church in Bangor, Maine—St. John's, which preceded Trinity by a few years—Robert Hallowell Gardiner, the squire of Gardiner, Maine, asked Upjohn to design the rebuilding of Oaklands (which had been burned in 1835) in the Gothic taste. Perhaps the client was not so eager for authenticity as was his architect, for he remarked somewhat petulantly in his memoirs that Upjohn had introduced hammered stone and battlements, which were the cause of endless trouble and expense ever since. Though Oaklands (Illustration 4–33) is still somewhat classically regular in plan, it is turreted, castellated, and decorated with Gothic-derived detail within and without. Its romantic castle-like appearance is enhanced by its fine site and by the grove and dell-like gardens which surround it. The mansion is situated in the best position to command a fine view down the Kennebec, for Mr. Gardiner and a friend "familiar with the country residence of English gentlemen," spyglasses in hand, went climbing trees to find the best prospect before choosing the site. In this respect, Oaklands, though a fairly early residence in the Gothic style, is typical, for "Gothick" architecture was a most appropriate accompaniment to that tradition of landscape architecture which had flourished in England during the eighteenth

4–33. Oaklands, Gardiner, Maine, 1836, by Richard Upjohn.

century under the great landscape architect Humphrey Repton, a relationship which was popularized a little later in America by Downing.

Meanwhile, another influential designer, Alexander Jackson Davis, was at work in the Gothic, a style for which he nearly gave up the Greek. As a matter of fact, his drawing for Glen Ellen at Towson, Maryland (AB 243), a house designed for the heir of the Gilmore fortune in Baltimore, was executed as early as 1832. More "showy" than Oaklands it was also basically far more symmetrical and ordered, but with its share of Gothicisms.

Though subsequent examples increased in picturesque effect, none of Davis' designs for large houses, executed or not, lost the basic classical plan and massing; Upjohn after Oaklands became increasingly free in both plan and composition. This is particularly evident in his Kingscote, Newport, Rhode Island, 1838 (*AB 258A, AB 259, AB 261, AB 262)—one of the first Newport "cottages," which are, in fact, mansions—a building that is unbelievably complex in both plan and decoration and would surely satisfy the most ardent nostalgia for the medieval.

Elaborate dwellings such as these, often employing forms derived from larger-scaled ecclesiastical architecture and creating effects which are more like stage sets than buildings, existed all over the country. Even in the South the planters' penchant for the grandiose was occasionally satisfied by the Gothic instead of the Grecian, as in the absurd wooden castle at Aberdeen, Mississippi, or Afton Villa, St. Francisville, Louisiana, 1849 (*AB 651).

But these large houses were exceptional residences; naturally there were less pretentious ones in the Gothic style, many of them inspired by Downing's several publications. Some of them, to be discussed in another connection, were unusual in their simplicity and their almost modern character. But most were characterized, at least superficially, by excessive ornateness, especially in porches and roofs (particularly the carpentry attached to the eaves, called verge or barge boarding).

Beneath the romantic panoply of "pointed," "English," "Tudor," and "rural" Gothicisms, the basic reason for the popularity of the Gothic Revival as the style most appropriate for the small and medium-sized house was that its irregularity and asymmetry made the Gothic a more convenient and adaptable plan than would have been possible with a more formal style such as the Greek Revival. At the same time, its picturesque profile and its usually wooden structure were esthetically related to the suburban or rural environment which, if not already wooded, soon would be if the recommendations of Downing and others who popularized the Gothic cottage were followed. Such examples as the medium-sized Oakes Angier Ames House, North Easton, Massachusetts, 1854 (AB 257), and a smaller one in Salem, Massachusetts, c. 1845–1850 (*AB 642), both inspired by Downing, illustrate these various characteristics, while at the same time the ample proportions, wide eaves, and porches give them an air of comfortable country living.

Downing's publications carried in their pages designs by others as well as himself, most notably Davis who also executed a number of excellent small houses, in which he was less restricted by his essentially classical habits of thinking than in his larger dwellings. Davis' "A Cottage in the English or Rural Style" from Downing's *Cottage Residences,* 1842 (AB 245), is as open and free in planning as are Downing's,

and as varied in profile and detail—characteristics found in several he executed in about 1860 for Llewellyn Park in North Orange, New Jersey, one of the first planned suburbs or garden cities (*AB 272). More romantic is Llewellyn Park's curious round Gatehouse, 1853–1869 (*CPB 43), with its conical roof and bay windows. It is like no known medieval prototype but is surely a delightful notion of what might have been.

Except for their medieval detail and excessive picturesqueness of composition, Davis' less exotic houses at Llewellyn Park and those inspired by Downing are nearly twentieth-century in their openness of plan and their relationship to the environment, as well as in their simple framing, which is expressed in the total feeling of the design even under the medieval excrescences. (Other houses by Downing in the Gothic style and those by some of his contemporaries and successors are not as obviously revivalistic, and will therefore be included in the discussion of the small house.)

There were many dwellings in what might be called a "carpenter Gothic" vernacular, which frankly exulted in their pseudo-medieval picturesqueness. An outstanding illustration of this tendency is the Wedding Cake House in Kennebunkport, Maine, c. 1850 (AB 719), one of the most delightful flights of a carpenter's fancy. A sober box of an 1820 house has been completely covered with misunderstood Gothic ornament said to be derived from a sea captain's memories and sketches of Milan Cathedral, which had impressed him during a visit to that city from some Mediterranean port.

Rural carpenters all over the country rose to the challenge of the verge board, bracket, and eave; the invention of the scroll saw freed their inventive fancy further. Dwellings from raw mining towns in Colorado (AB 324) to campmeeting cottages in Massachusetts added color and liveliness to the American scene and partook of a "folk" character which was in its way as characteristic of the 1850's and 1860's as the more solemn restraint and sense of proportion of the last phase of the Greek Revival had been of the earlier decades.

Italian Renaissance or "Villa" Revival

Of all the revivals, except the Greek, the Italian Renaissance style was the least exotic, being yet another variation on the classical theme; however, in its more picturesque "villa" phase it was as adaptable as any other revival to the freedom of plan and composition preferred during the mid-century. As Downing, describing one of his Italian villas, put it, "the Grecian had an elegant simplicity, the Italian had an elegant variety." At its most conventional, usually in non-domestic architecture, this manner has all the dignity of earlier, classically derived styles, differing chiefly in that the detail of the orders originated in the Italian Renaissance rather than in antiquity. The use of the mode in both England and America was given impetus largely by the work of Sir Charles Barry whose Manchester Athenaeum and London clubs of the 1830's were the first conspicuous edifices deriving from Italian Renaissance prototypes. These buildings were characterized by their astylar facades crowned by the oversized cornices of the Florentine fifteenth-century palaces, and by a severity relieved by quoining, by somewhat overemphasized rustication, and by other details. Several important buildings in the United States were influenced quite directly by Barry's buildings. The earliest example, the Philadelphia Athenaeum, 1845–1847 (AB 374), by the English-born architect John Notman, follows them most closely and is the outstanding example of the type in America. The Boston Athenaeum of 1847, designed by the then amateur Edward C. Cabot, is an impressive and larger building. Though not so skillfully composed as its Philadelphia counterpart, it has a massiveness characteristic of the Boston Greek Revival school though executed in brownstone, as was the Philadelphia Athenaeum. The Peabody Institute in Baltimore (that is, the first three bays on the right; the remainder is a later addition) by another Englishman, E. G. Lind, is more in the Barry–Notman tradition, and seems a little more correctly Renaissance than its two predecessors, even if it is relatively late.

The Renaissance manner—ornate but still dignified—was especially well adapted to the commercial building and business block, as can be observed in many older "downtown" sections; in San Francisco, for instance, Renaissance buildings such as the Hotalung Building, 1860, are among the city's oldest edifices.

But perhaps the happiest usage of the Renaissance style was in the city residence, either incorporated in a block or as a detached mansion, since its basic classicism did not involve too great a break from the Latrobe-derived Greek Revival house. The area in and around Mount Vernon Square in Baltimore is especially rich in examples of the first type, some of them by Jacob Small; among the most distinguished and correct examples of the detached type are two houses in Providence: the Tully-Bowen house by Thomas Tefft, and the Thomas Hoppin House, 1853, by a little-known architect, Alpheus Morse.

The "Italian villa" style (as distinguished from the Renaissance Revival proper), with its towers, irregularity of plan, three-dimensional variety, and asymmetry, seems hardly Renaissance in origin. As a matter of fact, it derives less from actual buildings than it does from the oddly shaped edifices that appear in the seventeenth-century landscape paintings by Claude, Poussin, and Rosa. It is thus a style literally "picturesque" in origin. "Italian villa" is further characterized by an elaborate, decorative vocabulary derived in general from the Italian Renaissance, but one in which the classical brackets and consoles employed to support cornices were emphasized and exaggerated in form and scale, as was consistent with the taste for varied and dramatic effects.

This less conventional form of Renaissance Revival was brought to the United States by Notman, whose house for Bishop Doane, 1837, in Burlington, New Jersey, on the banks of the Delaware, was the first of the type to be erected (though the always *au courant* Davis had designed one in 1835), and became the forerunner of an extremely successful type which had already been popularized in England by Osburne House, Queen Victoria's huge villa on the Isle of Wight.

Downing published a "Villa in the Italian Style" in his *Cottage Residences,* 1842 (AB 357), which is relatively conservative in its lack of the more elaborate decoration common a few years later in his own designs as well as in those of others. Davis' John Munn House (now Dowling Hospital), Utica, New York, 1854 (AB 356), is an unusually fine example in which the architect exploits with great monumental effect the possibilities of the three-dimensional play of projecting and receding masses inherent in the irregular and asymmetrical plan. Upjohn also executed distinguished examples of the Italian villa. His King Villa (now People's Library), Newport, Rhode Island, 1845–1847 (Illustration 4–34), is much freer in plan and composition than anything Davis did in this manner. Though heavy and massive, like Davis' Munn House, and with large plain surfaces, it is far more picturesque in its ornament, whose elaborateness and somewhat brutal scale are more typical of the style in its later and more popular phase. Upjohn also takes greater advantage of the possibilities inherent in the irregular and asymmetrical composition to create a more informal and open plan.

4–34. King Villa (now People's Library), Newport, Rhode Island, 1845–1847, by Richard Upjohn.

Henry Austin of New Haven, as a follower of Ithiel Town, naturally found himself happy in the still somewhat classic "Italian villa" style. His Norton House of about 1849 in New Haven (AB 353) is a fairly restrained example; but his Morse House (Victoria Mansion) in Portland, Maine, 1859 (AB 717, AB 718), is one of the best examples of the "Italian villa" in its mansion form. Here baroque and other exotic details are added to Renaissance ones to create one of the grandest and most luxurious houses of the period. The lavish interiors are excellent illustrations of the florid and heavy forms which began to overwhelm the remnants of classical restraint at the end of the period.

The Romanesque and Exotic Revivals

It is not always easy to distinguish the Romanesque Revival from the "Italian villa" and other classically derived styles, because, like them, it uses the rounded arch as distinguished from the pointed arch of the Gothic. But the Romanesque historically preceded the Gothic and, like it, is a medieval style, characterized by detail which is adapted to an irregular and varied composition and is not classical. Structures in this style are as picturesque as the Gothic, though they are more massive in effect.

These stylistic characteristics were put to good use by James Renwick in one of the most dramatic structures derived from medieval sources, the Smithsonian Institution in Washington, 1846–1855 (AB 255). Here Renwick brought out the inherent possibilities of the Romanesque, capitalizing on the massive, expressive vigor of its rugged grandeur, arranging the parts of the building like some medieval castle with a tower, a vaulted hall, and a chapel—an incongruous housing for exhibits that are largely scientific. The Smithsonian is perhaps the most conspicuous monument of the Romanesque Revival in America, flaunting its brash romanticism in the midst of the classical Washington of L'Enfant, Latrobe, and their successors. The few other important examples of the style are more conservative; Upjohn's Utica City Hall, 1852–1853 (*AB 387), has something of the majesty of an early Italian Romanesque church

but with a simple campanile. The masterpiece of the style, unfortunately destroyed, was Union Depot, Providence, Rhode Island, 1848 (Illustration 4–35), by Thomas Tefft. A two-towered structure with long radiating wings encompassing the multifarious functions of a railroad station, its complex design was unified by a decorative formula of quite archaeologically correct motifs derived from the arcades, pilaster strips, and corbel tables of the Lombard Romanesque of the twelfth century, all arranged with great refinement.

Until it became an expressive instrument in the hands of Henry Hobson Richardson after the Civil War, the Romanesque was never a popular revival except in one field, that of brick industrial architecture, where the simplicity of its basic forms was particularly well adapted to the monotonous sequence of bays and fenestration of the larger mills, which was relieved and accented by the pilaster strip, a prominent element in Romanesque design.

Besides the Italian and medieval revivals there were several other styles in the repertoire of eclecticism, principally the Egyptian and Mohammedan—the last variously designated as "Indian," "Persian," and sometimes "Byzantine." There were even "Chinese" buildings. To discuss them all would be a formidable task and somewhat pointless in a survey such as this, since, unlike the Greek and Gothic revivals, the exotic styles led to few significant future developments.

Perhaps the most outstanding example of eclectic exoticism was P. T. Barnum's Iranistan, built by the great showman at Fairfield, Connecticut, close enough to the tracks of the nearby railway for all to see. A huge bulbous dome of Mohammedan origin, and detail from the same general source competed for attention in a building utilizing tiles and iron among other materials. The structure has long since disappeared. Samuel Sloan's Longwood, near Natchez, Mississippi, 1860 (AB 381), is still standing (though it was never finished after the Civil War interrupted its builders), and is illustrated as Design No. 1 in Sloan's *Model Architect* (1852). Its odd shape, many verandas, bulbous dome, horse-

4–35. Union Depot (destroyed), Providence, Rhode Island, 1848, by Thomas Tefft. From an old photograph.

shoe arches, and Italian and "bracketted" detail comprise a confection nearly as strange as Iranistan.

Motifs which are vaguely Moslem or Moorish in origin appeared elsewhere (the horseshoe arch is frequently combined with medieval-derived detail), often in the most unlikely places. Francis D. Lee used them in the Fish Market and the Farmers' Exchange Bank in Charleston, South Carolina, 1853 (AB 370, •AB 370A), where he also employed a strange polychromed form of mixed Arab and Spanish baroque origin in the window enframements of a building that is now the St. John Hotel. Henry Austin also used Mohammedan motifs, which he often combined with Egyptian or with even more bizarre details.

Of the non-European styles, the Egyptian was the most popular, deriving its impetus from the Napoleonic campaigns, which aroused the curiosity of the occidental world in this ancient culture. Motifs derived largely from Dominique-Vivant Denon's *Voyages* (1802) and from earlier sources, including Piranesi, became part of the European decorative vocabulary, particularly in France where Egyptian motifs vied with Imperial Roman ones in the French Empire style.

In America the Egyptian was at first used only superficially as applied decoration (as was the case with the early Gothic Revival), and never to the extent that it was on the Continent. The powerful and massive grandeur of the Egyptian manner was adaptable to the character of romantic classicism and consistent with that of the Greek Revival, involving little more than the slanting of the main structural mass to recall the shape of the ancient pylon and the substitution of Dominique-Vivant Denon's detail for Stuart and Revet's and Benjamin's. John Haviland's "Tombs" prison in New York City, mentioned earlier, demonstrates well the expressive power of the Egyptian Revival, as does Strickland's Downtown Presbyterian Church in Nashville, Tennessee. Surely one of the most curious structures in America is the Presbyterian ("Whalers' ") Church at Sag Harbor on Long Island, 1844 (Illustration 4–36), by Minard Lafever. Until the 1938 hurricane, an almost fantastically shaped tall steeple capped a building whose form recalls the pylons of the Nile (but which is constructed of wood, a most inappropriate material in which to imitate that ancient architecture) and ostensibly symbolizes Solomon's temple. The direct statement of the Egyptian obelisk was particularly suitable for monuments in an era when the eloquent simplicity of romantic classicism prevailed, as in Mills's Washington Monument, and in Willard's Bunker Hill Monument at Charlestown, Massachusetts. The traditional association of Egypt with ancient mystery, wisdom, and an aura of sublimity appealed also to the romantic sensibility. Thus the Egyptian Revival was considered particularly suitable for funerary architecture, and was employed not only for tombs but most effectively as entrance gates to cemeteries, as in Henry Austin's design for the Grove Street Cemetery at New Haven, 1845.

The Egyptian style was also adaptable to more functional uses, in the pylon supports of early suspension bridges, which were necessarily weighty, and in early commercial buildings. The basic post and lintel of Greek architecture is not much different from Egyptian, and the substitution of Egyptian ornament for Greek was essentially incidental, as in the impressive Pennsylvania Fire Insurance Company Building, 1838 (*AB 156), in Philadelphia.

There were aspects of mid-century architecture which could be said to transcend revivalism though remaining part of it. The work of architects like Mills and Willard, for instance, looked forward to the plain surfaces and simple

4–36. Presbyterian ("Whalers' ") Church (steeple destroyed 1938), Sag Harbor, Long Island, New York, 1844, by Minard Lafever.

masses of modern architecture, and the relaxation in formality of plan and composition in the Gothic and Italian Revival house was the first step toward the open plan of today. But there were other aspects of the architecture of the period which had greater implications for future development or do not quite fit into revivalistic categories: the further development of the small house into an almost contemporary type; new materials and new uses for older ones; new building types (often, however, still largely restricted by revivalism); and finally the interesting "folk" art of the sects, which, though not prophetic of technical advance, was distinguished in design, being freed almost entirely from revivalism and therefore contemporary in form if not in technique.

The Small House: Progressive Aspects

In many cases the small or medium-sized house of the various revivals developed in a quite different way from the more conventional examples of the modes that inspired them, becoming almost free of eclecticism. Because of the originality which the best of them achieved at the end of the period, they comprise one of the most important phases of American domestic architecture.

The detached house in the city (or preferably the suburb, small town, or the country itself) has been an American ideal since the seventeenth century, when the dwelling of the yeoman was adapted to the New England settlements, and continues in our own day, when the "development" flaunts its "ranch" houses on their quarter-acre lots. During the romantic period in America, this ideal received its greatest impetus from two sources: the love of nature, one of whose expressions was an enthusiasm for rural architecture, first in England and then in America; and the combination of the agrarianism of Jeffersonian democracy with the egalitarianism of the Jacksonian era.

The small country house was first of all an English enthusiasm deriving partly from the informal landscape gardening tradition of the late eighteenth century and the Regency. In adapting architecture to rural living, every inspiration the vocabulary of current eclecticism could supply was utilized, from "Anglo-Grecian" to Moorish. The irregular plan and massing, the arcades, wide cornices, and conspicuous consoles of the Italian villa style; the bay windows of the "Tudor"; the quaint asymmetry and verge boards of the "pointed" cottage; the irregular and rustic forms of the "Swiss chalet"—all adapted themselves to a development in America which became increasingly indigenous in character. The drier and warmer weather of America (at least in summer), and the tendency to a greater informality in living tended to adapt the foreign prototypes to more openness and flexibility of plan. Furthermore, the prevalence of wood construction led to an increasing tendency to express this basic fact in the design. Andrew Jackson Downing was the first American propagandist of the small house and remained its most popular spokesman. The majority of the designs in his publications, both by himself and by other American architects (he employed Davis from the beginning, and the Englishman Notman contributed drawings later), show an ultimately English origin. But some do not. In his *Cottage Residences* (1842) he claimed that a number of them were "no copy of any foreign cottage." Two of the most outstanding in this respect were Designs V (AB 244) and VI (Illustration 4–37), "A Cottage Villa in the Bracketed Mode"—the wooden version; and "An Irregular Villa in the Italian Style, Bracketed." The former, described by Downing himself as "so simple in construction and so striking in effect," exhibited enough picturesque eclecticism to suit the taste of the time, but did possess qualities which were different from the English prototypes. Downing considered the design to be suitable for North America because it was easily constructed in wood; the wide projecting eaves were designed to protect the walls and, in the South, to serve as shelter from the sun. Downing highly recommended tongue and groove boarding covered with a strip, that is, batten boarding (*AB 313). The cottage villa, like most of Downing's houses, has a conspicuous "umbrage," the current eu-

and wide eaves are also beautifully incorporated in the composition of this sophisticated example of the resort house.

These cottages and smaller houses by Downing, Davis, Wheeler, and others, with their open plans, marked relationship to the environment, and reflection of structure in the design, became very much a part of the American resort and suburban scene and a prediction of contemporary domestic architecture, particularly of the theories of Frank Lloyd Wright who would find it easy to describe them with his favorite term of approbation, "organic."

There is one curious aspect of these houses, however, which is anomalous: the fact that the balloon frame (discussed in the next section), which was beginning to be popularized in the 1830's, was not used in their construction. This is probably because the new method was associated with cheap and rapid building or because the actual framing members had the appearance of being relatively insecure. Therefore the balloon frame was not consistent with the dramatically expressed structure that was part of the esthetic of the houses under discussion. It is paradoxical that the organic reflection of structure which is so modern in these houses should also be an expression of a building method that is so traditional.

New Methods and Materials; Newer Building Types

The balloon frame was exploited as a building method but was not a distinguishing feature of architecture during this period; later, when it became the accepted method of framing, its basic form was usually hidden by the eclectic detail of the post-Civil War era. (The better houses, such as those of the "stick" and shingle styles, were still constructed in the older method for much the same reasons as the earlier houses in which the new method was ignored.) Nevertheless, as a sociological phenomenon as much as an architectural one, the balloon frame cannot be ignored. This system of construction replaced the simplified heavy English mortise and tenon frame with slenderer elements that were nailed together and braced diagonally at places of

greatest stress, as shown in a "Diagram for Balloon Frame" from William Bell's *Carpentry Made Easy; or, The Science and Art of Framing in a New and Improved System*, 1858 (AB 288), and in "Diagonal Ribs for Vertical or Battened Siding" from *Woodward's Country Homes*, 1865 (AB 309). Mentioned favorably by Gervase Wheeler in 1855 and described as "particularly intended for the new settlers" it was in common use during the 1840's, having been first employed in St. Mary's Catholic Church in Chicago, in 1833. It would have been impossible to have constructed with the older method the enormous number of dwellings which were put up in the mushrooming towns of the West. In fact, the balloon frame can be thought of as partially responsible for the rapidity of the expansion of population beyond the Mississippi. The daguerreotype *View of San Francisco*, c. 1855 (Illustration 4–73), indicates how urban growth was expedited by this method of building, which turned a Mexican frontier outpost into a flourishing city only a few years after the discovery of gold in the area. Such must have been the appearance of Chicago fifteen years before, and of a hundred other places. The balloon frame, when covered with simple clapboarding and little detail—and that usually vernacular Greek Revival—did contribute toward a kind of volumetric simplicity characteristic of these houses, but one soon to be replaced by the greater elaboration of the 1860's and 1870's.

Besides the invention of the balloon frame at the end of the period, other developments in the use of wood should be mentioned in passing. Ithiel Town's patented lattice trusses for highway bridges (*AB 293A) made longer spans possible, and was the method used in the then nearly ubiquitous covered bridge, a few examples of which still remain, as the one designed by F. Smith at West Cornwall, Connecticut, 1841 (AB 337). Other elaborate truss forms were used in oversized barns and storehouses, such as the tobacco barns of the Connecticut Valley (*AB 326), while builders and engineers evolved even more complex roofing forms to cover large areas such as the assembly halls of the community groups, notably the huge Mormon Tabernacle, and railway sheds. But these late developments in wooden framing, however remarkable, were soon succeeded by the development of metal, which could be used to span large areas more efficiently.

Though steel was not invented until the end of the period under consideration, iron did come into general use. Cast iron columns had been used to supplement framing and masonry walls before the 1840's, when both iron columns and beams were almost universal in mills, factories, and commercial buildings. Heavy machinery could be better supported, and larger areas were freed for use than was possible in conventional frame and masonry structures. Iron columns were employed openly by Strickland in his Naval Home in Philadelphia, 1827–1832 (*AB 138), and Ammi B. Young used conspicuous iron columns and beams in his government buildings of the 1850's, as at the Providence Customs House. Walter used iron framing in the new wing of the old Patent Office, but here it was hidden; the Greek pilasters supported nothing, since both the walls and the roof were of iron only faced with Greek detail in other material, whereas in the older part of the building by Mills the pilasters actually helped support the fine masonry vaults. (The break between architecture and engineering within a generation is dramatically symbolized in the two parts of this building. Both disciplines were one in Mills's section; but in Walter's the division between them had taken place. It is interesting to note that Mills's thin vaults of hydraulic cement and stone survived the fire of 1877 while Walter's iron collapsed in a chaos of twisted metal.)

Iron supports made possible greater areas for fenestration in masonry buildings, since they helped free the walls from their exclusively bearing function. This development was not exploited in design until later, however, since the resulting insubstantial appearance was inconsistent with the taste of the mid-century, which preferred more massive forms.

Closely related to the freeing of the wall was the development of the iron facade. Haviland designed one as early as 1825, a pleasant romantic classical pastiche that in no way exploited the possibility of greater openness inherent in the use of the material. This was not done until James Bogardus, neither an architect nor an engineer but an iron manufacturer, built several buildings using cast iron members in their facades to supplement the iron frame so that greater areas for fenestration were made possible, as in the Cast Iron Building, Washington and Murray Streets, New York (AB 289), and Harper and Brothers Building, 1854 (*AB 290), in the same city. Others soon followed, though not all by Bogardus. Among the finest and most typical were the Haughwout Building in New York, 1857 (AB 291), and the Cast Iron Building (now Robins Paper Company) in Baltimore, c. 1870 (AB 306). The Z. C. M. I. Department Store in Salt Lake City, Utah, 1868 (AB 305), is one of the most effective of the early buildings of this kind, unusual in the relative lack of heavily picturesque ornament. Yet the prestige of older designs based on the technique of masonry was difficult to overcome. This, and the mid-century taste for the massive and bold, frustrated the natural tendency of the combination of iron and glass to create a light and airy design. Since it was as easy to cast in metal an elaborate eclectic facade as it was a simple one, the esthetic of the relation between function and design was usually ignored. The metal frame of the pre-Civil War era succumbed to the heavy applied ornament of both the masonry and the iron facades, not to emerge again until the 1880's in Chicago.

There was another kind of building, however, in which the open effect of the combination of iron and glass was more difficult to efface, and that was in the large shed for exhibition purposes or for railroad depots. This structural method, used first in conservatories, was employed by Sir William Paxton in the Crystal Palace built for the Great London Exposition of 1851, a building with a new kind of space indefinitely extendable by means of a grid of regularly spaced parts, mass-produced and easy to assemble. Employed in America in the short-lived Crystal Palace in New York, by Carstensen and Gildemeister, 1853 (*AB 650), and in smaller exhibition halls and conservatories, its chief use was in railroad stations.

Iron naturally succeeded wood in the construction of bridges in the truss system, but this method was gradually replaced by cables as the main support. Some examples are the Bidwell Bar Suspension Bridge, 1856, at Oroville, California, built by the Starbuck Iron Works, Troy, New York, and John Roebling's bridge (since destroyed) at Niagara Falls, 1852, which was the prototype for the first of the really great spans, his Brooklyn Bridge of 1867.

One other use of iron, somewhat related to the cast iron facade, should be mentioned: the great dome of the United States Capitol designed by Walter. Inspired by a similar use in the dome of St. Isaac's in St. Petersburg, Russia, built in 1842, the structure, in its proportion and its bold silhouette, is a commanding symbol of government. If its imitation of masonry is not "honest" to the purist, at the least it is expressive.

Among the many building types of a rapidly developing society, several new ones such as the large hotel and the prison have been noted in passing. Others—commercial architecture, mill architecture, and a completely new type, the railroad station—require more comment. Nearly all of these buildings were revivalist (a fact almost unavoidable in the romantic age), but occasionally a combination between the function of the building and its superimposed style resulted in an example of distinguished architecture which was not strictly (or merely) revivalist.

Of course many commercial buildings were as eclectic as the contemporary mansions. An occasional Romanesque and many Renaissance business palaces are still to be seen on lower Broadway in New York and lower Chestnut Street in Philadelphia (one in Philadelphia was designed by Notman). As the century advanced, the architectural ornament of these buildings in general became more elaborate. Only the commercial buildings of the Boston granite school and its counterparts elsewhere preserved an almost non-revivalist aspect. The Jayne Building in Philadelphia, 1849 (AB 608), by William L. Johnston, was one of the most interesting of these edifices. Though its detail was Gothic, the structure (with the exception of its ornate tower)

belongs basically to the post and lintel granite type, and is unusual in that it reaches a height of seven stories (without the tower) and thus prophesies the skyscraper. (Only one other building, the destroyed and almost forgotten Boston Exchange Coffee House, 1808, had an equal number of stories.)

Mill architecture comprises one of the most interesting aspects of the building of this period. The earliest examples in New England carried on the pattern typified by the brick mill at Harrisville, New Hampshire, 1822 (CPB 14E), but as textile manufacturing became more extensive in the scale of its operations, the buildings became much larger, as at Lowell and Lawrence, Massachusetts. The large brick masses of these structures remained largely free of revivalism, quite unlike mills elsewhere in the country; in Charleston, South Carolina, for instance, Bennet's Rice Mill, 1844, is a great Palladian edifice designed by an architect, its appearance hardly expressing its function. When the Merrimac Mills were erected in Lowell in 1847 an architect was called upon to design only the belfry; otherwise the building was the product of engineers. A typical New England example known to have been executed by an owner-engineer, Zachariah Allen, the Allendale Mill at Centerdale, Rhode Island, 1822, is one of the handsomest buildings of its type. It has clear-cut, massive simplicity, and every feature is clearly expressive of a function, with no "nonsense" added. Buildings of this sort, both mills and housing for operatives, are among the most impressive examples of architecture in this period, incorporating the cubic simplicity of the indigenous warehouse and farmhouse within the similar basic esthetic of romantic classicism and the vernacular Greek Revival.

Not until the 1850's did the desire for a more pretentious appearance influence mill architecture, though those styles were favored (such as the Italian Renaissance and Romanesque) which could be applied with the least disturbance to the basic structural function. Zachariah Allen, for instance, when he designed and built his new Georgia Mills (now Industrial Tool and Machine Company) at Georgiaville, Rhode Island, 1853 (AB 304), feeling it necessary to be more showy than in his Allendale Mill, chose the Italian Renaissance. But the addition of pilaster strips, an entablature, and a large-scaled pediment with arched windows hardly changed the fundamental mill form. One of the finest groups of buildings in New England, industrial or otherwise, the Georgia Mills (even with their later additions above the top floor, which destroy the sweep of the pedimented gables) have a simple grandeur of masses arranged in rational grouping, and a majestic rhythm of alternating pilaster strips and windows—all arranged with an impeccable sense of proportion (perhaps resulting from an efficient interior arrangement), and crowned by the formality of the fenestrated pediments.

Many mills retain something of the earlier simplicity of the type in spite of the turn to more explicit revivalism in which picturesque eclecticism is very successfully blended with functionalism. The Romanesque details of pilaster strip and corbel table are particularly adapted to brick, as in many later Rhode Island mills. Here the surface decoration is applied with considerable refinement to large, grandly conceived buildings, some of which, because of the high quality of their design, have been attributed to Thomas Tefft—as, for instance, the White Rock Mill, Westerly, 1849 (AB 304A), or the Eagle Screw Company in Providence. The sturdy solidity of form and the decorative elements of Romanesque brick architecture were most happily adapted to industrial building. The White Rock Mill is especially interesting in the width of its windows and the narrowness of its pilaster strips, exploiting in a quite conscious design the evident fact that masonry walls are supplemented by an iron framework within. This building is therefore prophetic of later and more frankly functional industrial architecture.

These are only a few of the mills which dot the New England countryside and give it considerable architectural character, particularly in Rhode Island, the valleys of western Connecticut and Massachusetts, and along the streams of Vermont and New Hampshire. Unlike the seaboard cities in which the textile industry was transformed by coal-produced steam, these old

water-powered mills were not replaced by the later large-scale industrialization. But even in coastal towns like New Bedford and Fall River, and in others where the industry was already too firmly established to languish after it outgrew the available water power, there remain remnants of the pre-Civil War mill complexes in the midst of gargantuan later factories.

Where they have not been overwhelmed by later developments (as at Manayunk and Conshohocken on the Schuylkill River near Philadelphia), early mill buildings comprise one of the most important and neglected aspects of American architecture. The simple functionalism of their vernacular tradition of cubic simplicity in wood or brick in New England, and fieldstone in Pennsylvania, is well-planned and dignified. They are hardly touched by revivalism; but when they are, their designs are adapted to the simpler aspects of romantic classicism or of the Greek, Italian, and Romanesque revivals.

The same cannot, unfortunately, be said of the railroad station, which as a type did not integrate as well with revivalism or even emerge clearly as a separate entity until later in the century. At first the station was frequently either a circular or octagonal building like a toll house on a pike, or a Greek temple one third of which was taken up by the track which emerged between columns on the facade. A little later two types were most frequent: the terminal with an impressive revivalist facade, a frontispiece revealing in no way what lay behind it; or an equally revivalist building which was not a terminal but a way station and therefore parallel to the track, but which, because of this, offered more opportunity for an integrated design (this was the case in Tefft's Providence Depot). All the stations of this era have disappeared, but two of them, both way stations like Tefft's, should be remembered. One, Henry Austin's Union Station, New Haven, 1848–1849, was not unlike the Providence Depot in its integration of complex function with design; it was also one of the most fantastic eclectic excursions in American architecture, combining principally "Italian villa," Egyptian, and Mohammedan elements. The second, Gridley J. F. Bryant's Boston and Maine Depot

4–39. Boston and Maine Depot (destroyed), Salem, Massachusetts, 1847, by Gridley J. F. Bryant. From an old photograph.

at Salem, Massachusetts, 1847 (Illustration 4-39), was only recently destroyed. In spite of a somewhat frivolous eclecticism including elements of Romanesque, Gothic, "castellated," and even "Italian villa," Bryant's characteristically dramatic statement appeared in the building itself and in the exterior arches behind which was the largest span of metal and glass up to the time of its building.

The Architecture of Sects

What might be called a form of "folk" architecture, to distinguish it from the vernacular forms of the academic, is that erected by sects which were isolated for one reason or another from the society by which they were surrounded, either because of recent foreign origin or, if native, because of their extreme differences of religious belief. Of the first group the Rappists or the Harmonists were typical; of the second, the Shakers and Mormons. Though the architecture of these groups is not as significant in the mainstream of architectural development as that of some others, it is of considerable interest since its methods of construction were often unusual. The standards of beauty which inspired it were not eclectic, because in most cases the religious tenets of its builders restricted display or show. At the same time (like vernacular architecture) the buildings of the sects act as a kind of basic stylistic barometer of the time, since they are usually unencumbered by the more obvious trappings of revivalism.

George Rapp, when he came with his group from Germany to Harmony, Pennsylvania, in 1804, built in the German style of the late eighteenth century. Very little of this construction remains; but after a decade in New Harmony, in Indiana, he returned to a site near the original Harmony and founded Economy (now Ambridge) where he and his adopted son Fred were in charge of the erection of a series of buildings, many of which remain. This self-supporting and industrious community built many structures designed for various activities such as cotton-spinning, brick-making, and distilling. The half-timber construction of the German countryside, expressed in large buildings of great simplicity, is particularly noticeable in the storehouse and granary at Ambridge, 1826 (*AB 330, *AB 331).

Even more original are the Great House (Rapp's home), the Feast Hall, and the Church, all distinguished for their boldness of statement and size. The Church is unusual for its curved eaves and slightly curved roof—influenced by the German baroque—but the most original building of the group is the Feast Hall which contains an especially fine "gathering" room, covered by the large sweep of a low segmental vault within a conspicuous hip roof, undoubtedly concealing an elaborate truss system.

Later buildings were erected at New Harmony, Indiana, after the influence of Robert Dale Owen succeeded that of Rapp, but these, though large, are more conventional than those in Economy.

The Shakers, too, were notable for the size of their structures, a characteristic shared by all such groups, since community meeting and housing were the focus of their religious and social life. The multistoried dwellings for communal housing and the huge barns to take care of the community's herds were the most interesting of the Shaker buildings, though the meetinghouses were also distinctive. The latter were characterized by four entrances (one each for the female and male "clergy" and the sisters and brethren) and by a huge, arched rainbow roof, the shape of which was repeated over the doorways, as can be seen at New Lebanon, New York. The multistoried dwellings—which were in fact dormitories for the four groups—were notable for the concentration of work areas and functional features, as seen in the communal closets and the arrangement of rows of beds, tables, and other furniture. Emphasis was upon convenience, neatness, and functional simplicity (Illustration 4–40). (It is interesting to realize that much of the inspiration for contemporary Danish furniture, so similar to that of the Shakers, came from the products of that group.) The mechanical ingenuity in furniture and small equipment was also present in the planning and arrangement of the communal laundries and other functional buildings, especially the barns. The one at Hancock, Massachusetts, is related to a hillside in such a way that the hay can be taken in at one level and thrown down to the stock on a lower one. This great structure of stone and wood (Illustration 4–41) is surely one of the finest and most ingenious examples of the round barn—a basically much more functional form than the conventional rectangular one, since it permits the stock to be fed around a common manger. The masonry walls, the cupola for ventilation and light, and the complex interior joists radiating from the central chute combine to make this one of the architectural achievements of the century in structure and design—be it academic, vernacular, or folk.

The organic harmony between the appearance of the object and its use, a basic principle of good design today, was realized in the nineteenth century perhaps better among the Shakers than anywhere else. The simplicity, order, and clarity of their work, the eschewing of decoration, and the pride in craftsmanship are the direct results of their religious tenets: communism, lack of ostentation in living, and belief in utility and work. Timothy Dwight, President of Yale and a staunch Congregationalist who could hardly have approved of the Shakers, was sufficiently struck by their virtues to have remarked that whatever they did they did well. The balanced directness of the Shaker structures, the symmetrical arrangement of the interiors, the austere and dignified forms, and the superb craftsmanship illustrate a distillation of the honest vernacular born out of romantic classicism and the Greek Revival and carried much further, per-

and even over the dramatic heights of the new city of San Francisco. Overcrowding in the older cities and the absorption of open space in the newer towns led to the gradual deterioration of the urban environment and to traffic problems, which stimulated various solutions such as elevated railways as early as 1848 in New York City (CPB 28).

Though the general situation in urban planning left much to be desired, there were, of course, exceptions in certain cities where a combination of local tradition and community foresight on the part of responsible persons put long-range amenity before short-range profit. These factors existed, not surprisingly, in the older cities of the East where in several instances circumstances contrived to preserve certain areas which still serve as touchstones to the best aspects of urban areas as they existed in the earlier part of the nineteenth century throughout America. Among the most notable are Beacon Hill in Boston, the neighborhood surrounding Brown University in Providence, the section whose center is Mount Vernon Square in Baltimore, and the *Vieux Carré* in New Orleans. A few streets in Philadelphia and several houses near and on Washington Square in New York also preserve some of the former character of these metropolises.

Perhaps the most conspicuous reaction against the abuses of the city as it developed in the mid-nineteenth century was the creation of large parks where extensive areas of still rural character were set aside as a form of public philanthropy to alleviate urban congestion. Fairmount Park in Philadelphia, 1855, was the first of these. It was soon followed in 1856 by Central Park in New York (CPB 63), designed by Frederick Law Olmsted, Sr. (with the help of the architect Calvert Vaux). Central Park was remarkable for the integration of its formal axial plan (appropriate for the idea of a great city) with the informal and naturalistic principles of romantic landscape design. It was even more noteworthy for the exploitation of the terrain and of such natural amenities as ponds, and for the siting of roads and paths in such a way that they followed natural contours. Also remarkable was the introduction of such devices as the underpass for the control of cross-traffic.

Other parks by Olmsted were soon to follow, notably Prospect Park in Brooklyn and Golden Gate Park in San Francisco, the latter a praiseworthy civic act in the early history of that city which has lent a great deal to its present distinction.

There were two outstanding exceptions to the generally unplanned and irrational growth of most urban areas. The first is what may be called the Utopian community; the second, the mill town, developed into more complex forms by the advancing technology of the Industrial Revolution. Though the communities of the first group have much of intrinsic interest and beauty —the pleasant openness and the efficient yet non-mechanistic planning of such towns as New Harmony, Illinois, the Rappite Community at Ambridge, Pennsylvania (CPB 105), the Oneida Community in New York, and those of the Shakers—they were too restricted by the tenets of the various sects which built them to be more than the odd exception. They were also too basically communistic to be prototypes for the kind of community planning required by a capitalist and individualistic society. The only exception to this rule was the regional planning of the Mormons in Utah, which was paternalistic or dictatorial as opposed to communal. The whole territory was developed according to a carefully worked-out economy. Yet together with this practicality there prevailed an equal sensibility for esthetic values which was expressed in such ways as variations on the grid, the placing of houses at various orientations to each other, and, in Salt Lake City, the incorporation of streams into the city plan and the laying out of broad avenues.

The textile mill towns of the second and third quarter of the century were not as idyllic as those of the first quarter, but none of them reached the tawdriness of the later coal and other mining towns. After the early development in Rhode Island of small-scale manufacturing powered by small streams, the center of the industry shifted to northeastern Massachusetts where the increased power afforded by larger streams permitted the production of larger quantities of sheeting and shirting. Consequently, because a much greater number of operatives were required, individual dwellings in the villages were succeeded by semidetached or row houses as well as by boarding houses to accommodate the farm girls who were induced by good pay, pleasant physical surroundings, and appropriate educational and moral atmosphere to work in the mills. The city of Lowell, Massachusetts (CPB 19), was particularly notable for the high standard of its architecture in both mills and housing, and also for the integration of these structures with other community buildings, churches, schools, and the residences of managers and foremen. Parts of Lowell are still handsome because of the neat cubical character of its consistently brick architecture stretched along the river and canals which, like the streets, were often bordered by elms.

When steam power succeeded water power, many of the old textile towns continued, as did the paternalistic pattern of ownership, though new towns also appeared. White Rock, Rhode Island, 1849 (CPB 31), is an interesting surviving example of the latter, notable for its axial plan connecting the mill, lyceum-school, and company store with single and duplex housing, dormitories, and boarding houses. Greater productivity and the consequent need for cheaper labor, caused by increased competition, forced the owners to be interested only in a sufficient margin of profit to keep in business, thus eliminating the "fringe benefits" of paternalism. As a consequence the older towns like Lowell and the somewhat later ones like Lawrence, Massachusetts, Nashua and Manchester, New Hampshire, all on the Merrimac River, and Chicopee and Holyoke, Massachusetts, on the Connecticut River, lost their character as integrated communities. Later towns like New Bedford and Fall River in Massachusetts (situated closer to the source of their power, coal), and the factory towns along the Schuylkill River in Philadelphia and its environs are impressive architecturally because of the style and grandeur of the mills, but no longer because of the quality of their community planning.

Painting

If neo-classicism can be accepted as a stylistic term embracing the most important aspect of the art of the Federal period, the concept of romanticism is equally applicable for the succeeding decades. Yet the word has too many meanings (one scholar has said that there are at least forty definitions) to permit its use without some discussion of its application to the art of the United States in this period, from the point of view of both attitude and style.

Romanticism as an attitude of mind implies these antitheses: a concern with the imaginative, with the "ideal" (not the generalizing idealism of classicism, but the intense personal experience as opposed to a group experience); and an equally profound concern with the real, the particular. Unlike neo-classicism, romanticism is emotional, but it can be both unspecific in its imaginative suggestiveness, and expressive of intensity of feeling in the precisely described particular object or incident.

Similarly, romanticism as a style seems to be characterized by two contrasting techniques: the broad and impetuous handling of paint for the more immediate expression of emotion; and secondly, the meticulous depiction of specific detail.

Earlier in the century the work of the Peales illustrates the "real" aspects of burgeoning romanticism, while that of Allston reflects the "ideal." Furthermore, Allston's work is typical of "ideal" romanticism in its literary reference: nostalgia for the past and enthusiasm for the exotic and faraway.

On the whole, however, the more realistic aspect of romanticism prevailed in the United States, or at least motivated the best pictures, as judged from the perspective of the twentieth century. The unpretentious landscapists, such as the "luminists," are now more appreciated than their bombastic colleagues of the Hudson River school, and the factualness of a George Caleb Bingham appears today more compatible with artistic worth than the allegories and sentimental genre pieces which were formerly so popular.

The romantic movement coincided with America's era of greatest social and economic expansion. Increasing prosperity, general improvement of the standard of living, Jacksonian egalitarianism, and the potentials of the frontier combined to bolster a native optimism. Various facets of America's dynamism, including the excitement of the opening of the West, were sufficient inspiration for romantic subject matter without dependence upon the exoticism of foreign lands and the remote past or upon stimulation from the more melancholy and sometimes morbid aspects of European romanticism. There was little place in American art for the introspection of a Delacroix, or an Allston. This is not to say that the "ideal" did not have its place in American romanticism, but on the whole it was less significant than the "real." There was only one prominent artist, John Quidor, who was inspired directly by literature, and the lyrical ideal romanticism of Allston at his best was carried on by rare artists like William Page. On the other hand, certain less attractive aspects of European ideal romanticism were reflected— even exaggerated—in American art of this time. Among these could be cited the transformation of genuine emotion into sentiment,[16] especially in sculpture and in genre painting, and the injection of pretentious religious or moral content into various kinds of painting, especially landscape, a phenomenon which is nicely summed up in the words of one of the most prominent landscapists of the period: "The external influences of this our dwelling place is fraught with lessons of high and holy meaning only surpassed by the light of Revelation." [17] This attitude in its more elevated aspects is closely identified with the pantheism of New England Transcendentalism (which derived ultimately from German idealist romantic philosophy), reflected in Emerson's poetry and essays and, in a more naïve way, in the nature poetry of Bryant. It was no accident that a picture representing two men in silent communion with nature, painted by the greatest of the German romantic landscapists, Casper David Friedrich, was paralleled in the United States by Asher B. Durand's *Kindred Spirits* (Illustration 4–50). Indeed, any grand or touching aspect of nature, no matter how unimaginatively or bombastically painted, would move a viewer to an almost religious enthusiasm, a fact which must be taken into account before the popularity of the landscapes of the Hudson River school (many paintings of which today seem to be so full of extra-artistic reference) can be understood.

From the expression of religious sentiment in art it is an easy step to artistic moralizing, a critical point of view which achieved its most eloquent expression in the writings of John Ruskin, who was much read in America. The recognition of the confusion of ethics and esthetics (the "ethical fallacy" in criticism, wherein a work of art, besides being pleasing or beautiful, must reflect and influence the moral tone) is useful when we look at the many little moralizing genre pieces of the time or contemplate the grandiose series on civilization and life by Thomas Cole.

To turn from the attitude of the artist in relation to his subject matter to the problems of technique or style, the most outstanding characteristic of American painting in this respect is the prevalence of the realistic and detailed as opposed to the ideally generalized (even when combined with ideal subject matter). The meticulous technique of the early English pre-Raphaelites (whose realism was much approved by Ruskin) and the school of Düsseldorf in Germany (which succeeded London in this period as the most popular place for Americans to study art abroad) found a fertile soil in a country where there already existed a tradition of precise representation which had flowered in Copley and been continued in the work of the Peales. In any event a precise literalness of treatment, whether European or native in origin, often accompanied an equally particular attitude toward subject matter reminiscent of Emerson's attitude in his *American Scholar:* "The meal in the firkin, the milk in the pan, the ballad in the street, the news of the boat."

In conclusion, it should be said that to draw a line between "real" and "ideal" romanticism is to risk the danger of all generalities, for often in the same artist real and ideal appear in various combinations, and religious or moralizing subjects are realized in a meticulous technique. Emerson himself, in so many ways the best and most typical of the creative Americans of his time, exemplifies the dualism of this period. He cries out for a poetry which will do justice to America in all her various aspects, which he lists very specifically, yet in his essay *Art* he asks the landscape artist to omit the details and to give us only the spirit instead—"the suggestion of a fairer creation than we know." But Emerson resolves the dualism too, for in another place he writes, "There are two powers of the imagination, one that of knowing the symbolic character of things and treating them as representative, and the other is practicing the tenaciousness of the image, cleaving into it, letting it not go . . . [making it] as palpable and objective as the ground on which [the poet] stands." [18] Such a comment surely can apply to the work of artists like George Tirrell in landscape, Bingham in genre, and to all the best of the unpretentious, observant, yet sensitive realists of the period.

Samuel F. B. Morse

The figure of Samuel F. B. Morse is a useful one with which to start the discussion of the painters of this period. He is a link between it and the early republic (much of his work falls chronologically in the earlier era), and he essayed nearly every genre and every stylistic manner prevailing at the time, and usually with distinction.

The young Morse accompanied Allston to London in 1811 on the latter's second trip there, and studied with West as well as with Allston himself. His early painting of the *Dying Her-*cules, 1813, and his sculpture of the same subject, done in the same year, reflecting the excessive musculature of the Hellenistic Farnese *Hercules,* show both the influence of Allston's neo-classic bias and the artist's own more dynamic taste. Morse returned to America in 1815, saturated not only with classicism but also with the work of the more painterly and romantic Italians, "ambitious to rival the genius of a Raphael, a Michelangelo or a Titian." [19] But no commissions came. Instead he gained a precarious living in Charleston, South Carolina, and in New York as a portraitist, in which field he was soon the equal of Sully.

Among Morse's most charming portraits is that of his wife, *The Muse: Susan Walker Morse,* 1835–1837 (PB 628), which displays the fine painterly handling of the English school, a talent which brought him two important commissions from New York City, a portrait of *President Monroe* and one of the *Marquis de Lafayette,* 1824 (PB 308), the last painted on the occasion of the latter's triumphal visit to the United States. Both pictures are very competent examples of the "official" portrait, the *Lafayette* in particular being brilliant in its composition and color, and painted with sweep and enthusiasm which are conveyed in rich brush work. Far from being a hack portrait, the picture shows that the artist was obviously moved by the character and personality of his famous sitter. More remarkable than Morse's single portraits is the "group portrait," *Congress Hall: Old House of Representatives,* 1821 (PB 307; Illustration 4–42), which would be noteworthy if for no other reason than for the amount of labor expended in its execution. For this painting Morse executed eighty-eight small portraits of members of Congress and the Supreme Court and of other individuals (including his father and a Pawnee chief, shown in the balcony), working from dawn for an average fourteen-hour day, sketching portraits in the morning and evening and solving problems of perspective and the like in the intervening hours. Though the primary purpose of the painting was to exhibit to the public a faithful representation of the "National Hall," as the printed description

4–42. Samuel F. B. Morse, *Congress Hall: Old House of Representatives,* 1821. Oil on canvas. 87 x 131¼ inches. (In the Collection of the Corcoran Gallery of Art, Washington.)

states, it is far more than a mere record of the personages and of Latrobe's fine architectural design. Rendered in a subtle lamplight calculated to bring out all the richness the architect meant the great hall to have, space and enclosing architecture were realized in a very convincing way with muted contrasts of light and dark and with varied and decorative color. The picture is one of the most consistent achievements of realistic representation of the century, but it failed as a money-making exhibition piece because it was not as ideal as West's traveling allegories and Rembrandt Peale's *Court of Death.* *Congress Hall* had no program other than to be a record; it failed because it was too forthright and matter-of-fact for a romantic age.

Morse did attempt one other similar picture, however, the *Exhibition Gallery of the Louvre,*

1833 (PB 311), a monumental composition in which the artist is equally sure in his grasp of space and atmosphere. Incidentally, this picture also demonstrates the painter's extraordinary sensitivity for the history of taste; each of the pictures by the old masters is most effectively suggested in Morse's own canvas by a kind of shorthand that grasps the essence of each master's personal style and of his period.

Morse essayed a number of landscapes which, in their sketch form, are often fresh in handling and unpretentious in treatment. But in their further development too often they become somewhat mechanical and grandiose, as in *Niagara Falls from Table Rock,* 1835 (PB 312) —a well-composed and impressive picture nevertheless. Morse swung from realistic landscapes of this sort to ideal and even allegorical ones, thus encompassing the landscape taste of the romantic era. One of the most satisfactory is the *View from Apple Hill, Cooperstown, 1828–1829* (*PB 310; Illustration 4–43), a remarkable blending of Allston's idealism with an American matter-of-factness. The compositional conventions of classical landscape are combined with a pellucid atmosphere which illuminates a typically American scene, including buildings rigidly parallel to the picture frame and precisely geometric.

Morse is representative of his period in his portraiture, which is varied and excellent, and in his landscape. But in his emphasis on the real as opposed to the ideal in its more pretentious aspect, he points toward the richer realism of Winslow Homer and Thomas Eakins and away from the false sentiment of much of the painting of his own time.

Portraiture

Morse can be included with Sully as one of the outstanding portraitists of this period and perhaps the best. He was not seduced by the easy facility of the Stuart formula nor by the desire for mere verisimilitude which overwhelmed much portraiture in the mid-1840's. Morse ceased to produce significant paintings around 1835, when photography and the invention of the telegraph began to absorb his interest. Sully, though his work at its best during this period (as in his *Queen Victoria* portrait) compared in quality with his earlier years, changed little in his essential character. But mid-century sentimentality combined with the influence of Sir Thomas Lawrence's technique (which Sully saw in 1832), more summary and suggestive even than Stuart's, resulted in his

4–43. Samuel F. B. Morse, *View from Apple Hill, Cooperstown,* 1828–1829. Oil on canvas. 22⅜ x 29½ inches. (Collection of Mrs. Stephen C. Clark. Photo courtesy of the New York State Historical Association, Cooperstown, New York.)

characterization becoming too vapid and his effects too easy.

The great age of portraiture was before 1825. In the second quarter of the century and later there was certainly competence, and a great deal of it, but very little more. Any large collection of portraits of the time, such as that at the New York City Hall or the New York Chamber of Commerce, has a monotonous level of consistently good workmanship, the cumulative effect of which is an aggregate dullness. Only the exceptional portrait by a conventional artist, or the unusual portrait by an artist out of the mainstream (often anonymous and sometimes approaching the category of "folk artist") is sufficiently arresting to attract the attention of twentieth-century taste.

Portrait painters flourished throughout the country, in the new West and the new "cotton South," as well as in the older communities of the seaboard where the most proficient artists worked. Most of these were the inheritors of the Stuart–Sully tradition and, in some cases, their students. At the same time there were other portraitists who began to paint with a meticulousness that rivaled the new medium of photography with which the portraitist had soon to compete.

Among the painters who represent the former tradition, John Neagle is probably the best. Like so many painters who later became academically competent he started in the artisan tradition, in this case as a coach and ornamental painter. But he later learned how to paint in a more conventional way from the example of Charles Willson Peale and from Sully, whose stepdaughter he married. Neagle's portraits show how brilliant and at the same time how easy the Stuart manner could become in the exploitation of the painterly formulas. His most famous picture is *Pat Lyon at the Forge,* 1829 (PB 326), unusual for its era in approaching an almost genre treatment. The egalitarian climate of opinion is reflected in this representation of a working man—even if one of considerable local fame. (Lyon was the original village blacksmith of Longfellow's poem.) Bold in composition, the picture has a directness that is some-

what blurred by an almost too colorful and dashing technique—at least for so earthy a subject. But in other portraits this elegant technique stands Neagle in good stead, as in that of the architect *William Strickland,* 1829 (PB 322), and in his portraits of children, as in *Matilda Washington Dawson,* 1829 (*PB 325), and especially in the charming sketches of Indian papooses done in the neighborhood of Lake Huron. Sometimes Neagle overcomes the easy generalities of the Stuart–Sully formula by a directness of observation and a solidity of construction often lacking in his mentors, qualities which appear in such a picture as that of *Henry Clay,* 1843 (PB 631).

Like Neagle, Chester Harding became a prominent painter in spite of the anti-artistic prejudice of the frontier society from which he came. (In his early years as a portraitist his grandfather took him aside and said: "Chester, I think it very little better than swindling to charge forty dollars for one of those effigies." [20]) Yet, from being a backwoods chair maker, tavern keeper, and even a peddler, Harding rose by sheer determination to eclipse Gilbert Stuart in Boston and to become the darling of the British aristocracy. An uneven painter, his best pictures are workman-like, neither slapdash nor overfinished, and are honest with a kind of Jacksonian directness. His *Amos Lawrence,* c. 1845 (PB 202), a portrait that is considered one of his best, is typically solid, well-realized, and unpretentious, though the importance of the textile magnate who was the subject is not discounted. But to compare it with Copley's portrait of an earlier Boston businessman, Nicolas Boylston, is to discover that in spite of a greater realism, achieved by means of the combination of painterliness and careful observation, the mixture is not as satisfying as the unpainterly hardness of Copley, which, for all its meticulousness, is more consistent in its retention of line and pattern. Copley's realism may be said to be "magic"; Harding's, merely matter-of-fact.

The work of Francis Alexander is somewhat outside the Stuart–Sully tradition, for he added to the influence of Sully that of Allston, which (probably inspired by Allston's example) he supplemented by the study of the great Venetians. Consequently his portraits, like that of *Mrs. Jared Sparks,* c. 1830 (PB 42), have a richness of color and subtlety of technique which differentiate them at least in style from most contemporaneous portraiture.

The technique represented at its weakest by Sully's pretty imitators and at its best by Neagle was gradually superseded by a style characterized by a growing meticulousness that was further stimulated by the influence of the camera. To this invention can also be attributed the harsh contrasts of light and dark, the hard and lifeless shadows, the darkening of the palette, and even the stiffness of the daguerreo-

type pose (necessitated by the long period of time required for exposure, during which the head was held in a clamp). Artists like Henry Inman, also a prominent genre painter, and Charles Loring Elliott, the author of some seven hundred portraits and acclaimed in 1850 as the leader of his profession, typify the gradual change from the painterly to the photographic. Their earlier work is represented by the somewhat sentimental *Georgianna Buckham and Her Mother,* 1839 (PB 252), by Inman, and their later by Elliott's *Mrs. Thomas Goulding,* 1858 (PB 190), in which a dead level of competence is comprised of careful observation, meticulous realism, and a mechanically smooth technique but not much formal organization or sensuous appeal.

Similarly solid and equally influenced by the camera, but saved from mere verisimilitude by a grasp of form derived from study in Paris and by some insight into character, is the work of George Healy and Thomas Hicks. Healy's *John Tyler,* 1851–1864 (PB 586), and Hicks's *Hamilton Fish,* 1852 (City Hall, New York), are typical of the best of the portraits of the mid-century; yet in spite of the dignity of these figures, substantially realized in convincing space, both seem pedestrian in comparison with a portrait like Morse's dashing *Lafayette.*

In sum, the conventional portraiture of this period, beginning with the tradition of Stuart and Sully, was soon overwhelmed by its own facility. At first rescued by realism only to be later engulfed by it, it resorted to the camera's aid but finally succumbed to photographic imitation.[21]

More esthetically rewarding than most of the conventional academic portraits of the time are those out of the mainstream, usually pictures recently rediscovered. These are the work of artists who were original to the point of being eccentric in a conventional field, or by those who were so provincial or stubborn that they never quite gave in to what was popularly expected of them.

Among the first group, William J. Hubard of Virginia can be singled out. His portraits of *John C. Calhoun,* c. 1830 (Illustration 4–44),

4–44. William J. Hubard, *John C. Calhoun,* c. 1830. Oil on canvas. 19½ x 14⅝ inches. (In the Collection of the Corcoran Gallery of Art, Washington.)

and *Horatio Greenough in His Studio in Florence*, c. 1838–1839 (PB 247), are unusual in composition, dramatic in lighting, and moody in feeling. Calhoun sits isolated and small in the center of a large room, in the darkening shadows; Greenough is represented brooding and sinister-looking in the depths of his Florentine studio. There is neither the usual facility of paint nor the meticulous detail of most of Hubard's contemporaries, nor, in fact, is there much of their general academic facility, but these are compensated for by a mood of melancholy rare in American romanticism.

William Page was another artist who infused his portraits with a quality which is less matter-of-fact and more imaginative than most of his contemporaries. Indecisive in his art as in his life (he studied for the bar, became a minister, and was married three times), he experimented with various techniques from the most precise to the most suggestive—though the influence of Allston and, through him, of the great Venetians, was the most persistent. Page's early portraits have something of the melancholy quality of Hubard's; his later ones are not only infused with darkly rich and glowing color, but also with forms which are evocative beyond the objects they represent. Page's study of Raphael's abstract design, in which he found representation to be subordinate to the basic curvilinear repetitions of the design (which he called the "soul" of the picture), undoubtedly had much to do with the formal power of his own best work.

By the time the artist executed his affecting portrait of his last wife, c. 1860 (PB 332; Illustration 4–45), he had perfected a rich Venetian coloristic technique and managed to imbue the composition as a whole with a strength of design which is more than mere likeness. At the same time he utilized the camera as an aid to accuracy, as he freely admitted, but with a much different effect than did most of his contemporaries, who failed to combine photographic factualness with Page's evocative shapes and glow of subtle color. The heavy form of Mrs. Page, her intent gaze, the static composition, the shape of the Coliseum in the background

4–45. William Page, *Mrs. William Page*, c. 1860. Oil on canvas. 60¼ x 36¼ inches. (Courtesy of the Detroit Institute of Arts.)

repeating the shape of the bonnet, the accurate visual detail, and the envelope of sun-filled air unifying form and color—all combine to make this one of the finest portraits in American art between Copley and Thomas Eakins.

Among the more provincial or retardataire artists who did not succumb to current fashion but who were nevertheless too academically competent to be called folk artists are a number of anonymous portraitists represented by such pictures as *Captain Nicolas Broughton,* c. 1830 (*PB 55), which combines the academic competence of the second quarter of the century with the pattern and linearism of the earlier provincial style. This is true also of a remarkable painter, Henry F. Darby, whose *Reverend John Atwood and His Family,* 1845 (Illustration 4–46), a picture of great size and powerful abstract design, is almost an apotheosis of this older tradition, brought up-to-date with the addition of academic competence in drawing,

anatomy, perspective, and technical brilliance. Similar in some ways, though not as powerful, is another group portrait by George Hollingsworth, *The Hollingsworth Family,* c. 1850 (Illustration 4–47), only recently identified. But the painting has another quality which gives it further individuality: a mood that can be one either of brooding solemnity or of repressed tension, depending on the response of the viewer.

The unusual character of pictures of this sort is matched by few other portraits of the period.

4–46. Henry F. Darby, *Reverend John Atwood and His Family,* 1845. Oil on canvas. 72 x 96¾ inches. (Courtesy, Museum of Fine Arts, Boston. M. and M. Karolik Collection.)

4–47. George Hollingsworth, *The Hollingsworth Family*, c. 1850. Oil on canvas. 42 x 72 inches. (Courtesy, Museum of Fine Arts, Boston. M. and M. Karolik Collection.)

This fact bespeaks a situation, touched on earlier, wherein the conventional artist was well thought of and the more individualistic one neglected, only to be rediscovered in our time by sensitive collectors and to be reappraised by critics and museums—as the existence of the M. and M. Karolik Collection at the Museum of Fine Arts, Boston, so brilliantly testifies.

Landscape Painting

In the second quarter of the nineteenth century, landscape became the most popular form of painting not only in America but also abroad, particularly in northern Europe and in England. Yet in the United States, stimulated by patriotic self-awareness and by the extent and variety of the terrain, it flourished to an extent hardly equaled elsewhere. Literature helped prepare the ground. James Fenimore Cooper emphasized the setting of his novels, describing various scenes with great exactness. The nature poet William Cullen Bryant was one of the most popular in the English language, and even Washington Irving, though he preferred Europe for the richness of its accumulated treasure, said that an American need never look beyond his own country for the sublime and beautiful.

The tradition of the topographical English landscapists, like that represented by the Birches, father and son, began to weaken about 1825. Two later British immigrants, George Harvey and the Irishman William Wall, made pictures to be engraved which were a little less conventional than before in their emphasis on the picturesqueness peculiar to specific places. It is not surprising that the cataracts and twisted trees of the Catskills made their appearance by 1830.

It is no accident that the first group of landscape painters who can be thought of as comprising a school should be called after Hudson's noble river, of which Adrien Van der Donk had already remarked in 1654, "Here the painter can find rare and beautiful subjects for his brush." [22] The Hudson, especially after the opening of the Erie Canal, was America's most traveled river during a time when water transportation far exceeded that by land. But the painters of the Hudson River school were by no means confined to its shores. The cataracts and gorges of the White Mountains were almost equally attractive, and by the 1860's the grandeur of the West had stimulated landscape artists to huge feats of dramatic and coloristic prowess.

The artistic results of all this enthusiasm, however, do not come up to one's expectations, for American landscape painting of this period, when contrasted with that of the English of the same time, is found somewhat lacking. John F. Kensett's *Coast Scene with Figures* (Illustration 4–51), for instance, when compared with a typical painting by one of the great English landscapists of the romantic school such as Constable or Turner, is characterized by meticulous detail, brash color, painstaking handling of paint, and a harsh, smooth surface. Though these characteristics can be exploited in paintings of considerable stylistic interest, as in the case of the "luminists" (Illustrations 4–57, 4–58, 4–59), they are in general less attractive than the broad and painterly treatment, rich coloristic effects, and spontaneous immediacy of the English.

The reasons for the wide dissimilarity between American and English landscape are fairly obvious. First of all, the beginnings of American landscape derived from conservative English tradition which had been brought to the United States long before the flowering of the romantic school in England—a tradition which the English themselves had meanwhile gone beyond. A more important reason is that Americans of this period no longer studied in England, preferring Continental schools, especially German. Consequently, the painterly tradition (essentially a survival from the rococo), which had enlivened the work of Trumbull and Stuart and which was one of the principal ingredients of the newer English landscape school, was virtually unknown to American artists of this generation (except through the medium of engraving whose finicky lines were by their very nature the antithesis of the easy and broad handling of the originals). Instead, American landscape painting reflected the meticulous treatment and hard handling of the German schools, particularly that of Düsseldorf, where an almost mechanical verisimilitude was taught and practiced. Finally, many of the first generation of American landscapists came from the artisan tradition or were professional reproductive engravers, with the consequence that they were self-trained as landscape painters. Both these circumstances oriented the whole technical direction of the school toward the detailed and literal (a tendency furthered by the Düsseldorf training of the next generation). Thomas Doughty, the precursor of the Hudson River school, and Thomas Cole, its most famous member, were self-taught; and Durand, perhaps the most influential of the group, was first an engraver, as was Kensett.

Before discussing the individual artists, one characteristic of American landscape which was not shared to an equal extent by the English and Continental schools should be touched on and explained: a tendency toward a large scale and a grandiose, panoramic point of view. The size of the country and the spectacular nature of much of its landscape doubtless contributed toward this development, but more important was the influence of the panorama itself. This curious form of art, part instruction and part entertainment, became more popular in the United States than abroad, perhaps because its "educational" nature appealed to the prevailing desire for self-improvement. Soon panoramas became cycloramas, and some even moved on rollers; and these became dioramas in which the shifting of lights and backgrounds changed the seasons and the time of day, and gave effects as "educational" as "3-D" films. Some of those that moved were allegedly three or more miles long. Appropriate to these dimensions were several of the Mississippi; the most famous was by John Barwood who was commanded by Queen Victoria to show it to her in a private session at Windsor. The only significant remains that survive from this once popular art are fragments from an effort by John Egan, now in the University Museum at Philadelphia, depicting the mounds of the Mound-Builder Indians. As in the case of Vanderlyn's panorama, what we can see of this leaves us with not much regret for what has been lost. Though today the panorama seems more a sociological phenomenon than an artistic one, its influence is quite clear in such a picture as Cole's *The Oxbow (the Connecticut River Near Northampton)*, 1846 (Illustration 4–49), and in much of the work of Albert Bierstadt, Frederick Church, and Thomas Moran.

Thomas Doughty is often thought of as the founder of the Hudson River school. He was certainly one of the first to strike the note of ideal sentiment, derived somewhat from Allston, which was to be a characteristic of the school. This quality he combined with the composition and conventions of the English immigrant landscapists, carried out in a technique largely derived from the reproductive engravers, though with more liveliness than would be expected. *In Nature's Wonderland*, 1835 (PB 150), and *In the Catskills*, 1836 (PB 538), are typical of his work which, in spite of its undigested conventions, and partly because of them, has the seminaïve charm of the largely self-taught artist. Later, as seen in *Landscape, House on Cliff above Pool* (PB 148), Doughty became more specific in his locale and more naturalistic, under the influence of the seventeenth-century Dutchman, Jacob Ruisdael, whose paintings had impressed him during a trip to Europe.

On the whole Doughty's work never became as rhetorical in its sentiment nor as picayune in its realistic detail as did that of others of the Hudson River school. There is a certain charm in Doughty's unpretentious poetry in spite of its technical deficiencies.

Thomas Cole and Asher B. Durand can be said more properly to be the founders of the Hudson River school, though Doughty's poetic idealization strongly influenced Cole and his tendency toward the meticulous was shared by Durand.

Cole struggled to become a painter with the same determination as Doughty and, like him, was largely self-trained. Apprenticed as a boy in England to an engraver of calico designs and later to a wood carver, when he came with his family to western Pennsylvania in 1823 he was so fired with enthusiasm for the wild American landscape that he started to paint immediately. Cole's sketches of the Hudson valley region, which he did a few years later, attracted the attention in New York of old Colonel John Trumbull in 1825, and from this time on Cole was consistently successful in the sale of his dramatically drawn and tinctured pictures, many of them composed of elements he had sketched while "his heart had been wandering in the Highlands and nestling in the bosom of the Catskills," to quote his biographer.

Cole's relatively early *In the Catskills*, 1837 (PB 137), shows a close resemblance in composition and treatment of foliage to the contemporaneous work of Doughty, but it is much larger, though not so dramatic as some of his later and more typical works. In the latter the artist employs many of the stock-in-trade motifs and effects of the seventeenth-century Italian painter, Salvator Rosa—as did many another, including Allston, especially in his *Elijah in the Desert*. But in contrast to the earlier American painter, Cole's use of gnarled skeletal trees, turbulent clouds, and tossing foliage is actually much less genuinely expressive. The addition of dramatic atmospheric effects to these motifs recalls the work of Turner, but Cole's relative lack of training prevented him from ever attaining the great Englishman's magnificent glowing transparencies of glaze upon colored glaze. Yet Cole's most successful pictures of this kind, such as *Tornado*, 1835 (Illustration 4–48), and *Landscape With Tree Trunks* (PB 132), are not only imaginatively powerful but exhibit considerable freedom of brush work—qualities which preserve in these more finished pictures some of

4–48. Thomas Cole, *Tornado,* 1835. Oil on canvas. 46⅝ x 64⅝ inches. (In the Collection of the Corcoran Gallery of Art, Washington.)

the spontaneity of his sketches. Cole's *The Oxbow (the Connecticut River Near Northampton),* 1846 (PB 528; Illustration 4–49), is more typical. Representing a huge panorama arched over with a spacious and agitated sky, the picture has a sweeping curvilinear composition, and dramatic contrasts of light and dark which are reminiscent of the baroque. On the other hand, it is meticulous in treatment, hard in color, and stingy in brush work when compared with the landscape painting of the seventeenth century and of the English romantics.

Cole's later work, much of it done in Europe in the 1840's, shows little change derived either from personal growth or from the stimulation of new environments. For Cole did not go to Europe to improve his style or technique, but to find "nobler subjects." Such pictures foreshadow the work of his followers and younger contemporaries who wandered over the surface of the earth in the search for that grandeur which they were incapable of producing from within themselves.

Asher B. Durand was a very different artist from Cole. Though his *Kindred Spirits,* 1849 (PB 157; Illustration 4–50), representing Cole and the poet Bryant contemplating a wild and sweeping landscape, is infused with Cole's

4–49. Thomas Cole, *The Oxbow (the Connecticut River Near Northampton),* 1846. Oil on canvas. 51½ x 76 inches. (The Metropolitan Museum of Art, New York. Gift of Mrs. Russell Sage, 1908.)

idealistic awe in the presence of nature, it is far more painstaking and essentially less pretentious. In fact, much as Durand admired Cole, he considered his mannerisms and technique slipshod. Certainly, in comparison with Durand, Cole did generalize. His procedure was as far as possible from that of the literal-minded Durand. He seldom painted a subject immediately, but waited until the "great features . . . whether the beautiful or the sublime . . . dominated his mood." [23] As a consequence there prevails a pictorial generality not sufficiently bolstered by the kind of observation that preserves the structure of his early work, which was more closely derived from detailed sketches.

Durand wrote in the magazine *Crayon* (which also published Ruskin's *Modern Painters,* wherein the author appeals for a literal transcription of nature) that a difficult truth was preferable to an easily expressed falsehood. But most critics would not find this "difficult truth" worth approaching in Durand's excessively laborious way. In the long run, *Kindred Spirits* or a more typical picture, *The Old Oak,* 1844 (*PB 154), for all their marvelous particularity, are somewhat boring because of the undifferentiated labor lavished on each part. Yet occasionally a quality of light which is quite fresh and pleasing is seen in some of Durand's work, such as *Catskill Clove,* 1866 (PB 158), which mitigates the detail and grandiosity characteristic of his work and of the school as a whole.

Durand's training as an engraver, his honest if pedestrian attitude, and his practice of drawing and painting from nature combined to form an influential body of work which was salutary in spite of its meticulousness, for it compensated for the more cursory and easy effects which the example of Cole alone could have exerted on the school. Both Cole and Durand together influenced most contemporaneous and subsequent landscape painting.

Before taking up Cole's immediate followers, whose careers began later in the mid-century, the work of some earlier artists, both those belonging to the Hudson River school and those not so closely connected with it, should be discussed. John F. Kensett is similar to Durand in

4–50. Asher B. Durand, *Kindred Spirits,* 1849. Oil on canvas. 46 x 36 inches. (Courtesy of the New York Public Library.)

his respect for fact and his rejection of the pretentious and grandiloquent. An engraver, like Durand, he accompanied the latter to Europe to study the works of landscape artists, though his style was not much affected thereby. In fact, Kensett's manner of painting hardly changed in a long and prolific career, but the variety of his subjects and composition did; consequently he is the least monotonous of the Hudson River group. Though critics have remarked on a certain luminosity or misty airiness in his work, as can be seen especially in some of his Newport sketches, on the whole this quality is obscured by a hard, glassy smoothness of brush work and surface and by a too painstaking treatment of detail, especially in foliage. These characteristics can be seen in *Coast Scene With Figures,* 1869 (PB 609; Illustration 4–51), and in another typical but later painting that shows little change or development, *River Scene,* 1870 (*PB 282). It must be admitted, however, that Kensett's meticulousness and hard light do possess a somewhat magical effect, as seen in the wooded interior in *Cascade in the Forest,* 1852 (PB 278), and in the far-stretching spaciousness of *Third Beach, Newport,* 1869 (PB 281). This last picture, though still full of detail, has some of the atmosphere, if not the painterly dash and pleasanter color of the artist's smaller, less ambitious sketches.

Sanford R. Gifford is not unlike Kensett in his occasional sensitivity to the quality of light, as seen in *In the Wilderness,* 1860 (PB 194), a picture that possesses a quite personal mood. These qualities can be seen also in some of the landscapes Gifford executed before his artistic judgment was impaired by the desire to imitate the grandeur of Church and Bierstadt, as in his *Kaaterskill Falls,* 1862 (*PB 195).

Jasper Cropsey often shows a freer touch than either Kensett or Gifford, and was less stingy with his pigment, both in its application and intensity. At its best his color is lively and exciting, as in the *View of the Kaaterskill House,* 1855 (PB 145), one of the most convincing of the early representations of the brilliant autumnal foliage of the Northeast. This relatively un-

4–51.   John F. Kensett, *Coast Scene With Figures*, 1869. Oil on canvas. 36⅛ x 60¼ inches. (Courtesy of Wadsworth Athenaeum, Hartford, Connecticut.)

pretentious picture is less typical than the more dramatic *Eagle Cliff, New Hampshire*, 1851 (PB 532), in which the acid harmonies and contrasting hues are not dissimilar to those used in the then newly invented chromolithography.

Before proceeding to the second generation of the Hudson River school, note should be made of a humbler painter, George Henry Durrie, who is more interesting today than many of his more famous contemporaries. Durrie's work represents a conventional and backward-looking technique, and a point of view somewhat related to the simple naïveté of the folk artist. Furthermore, it was particularly suitable for reproduction in lithography, a medium which had begun to supersede engraving. His Connecticut farm scenes, depicting the then rural areas around New Haven, were duplicated by the lithograph publishers Currier and Ives, and had much to do with the creation of the popular

stereotype of the old New England of solid country folk, which is still perpetuated by the illustrator Norman Rockwell. Durrie's subjects, such as *Farmyard, Winter*, 1862 (PB 541), have a certain authenticity, in spite of being painted with a rococo decorative charm, for they display a keen observation of rural architecture, changes of season, and the various tasks and activities of the farmer's day.

The most famous of the second generation of landscape painters were Bierstadt, Church, and Moran. Albert Bierstadt is perhaps the most impressive artist of the Hudson River school. His technical competence in the recording of visual reality outstripped that of all the others, and he did not strain as hard as did Church and Moran for exaggerated effect. Born in Germany but brought up in the United States, he returned to study at Düsseldorf where he acquired the necessary equipment to handle every variety of appearance that nature could possibly present to him. In 1858 and in 1863 he went on expeditions to the Rockies, and the pictures painted on these trips made him one of the wealthier men of his generation. Grandiloquent canvases of panoramic space and accurate detail followed one another from his easel—dramatic in composition, scientific in their rendering of the geology, flora, fauna, and meteorology of the great West. These vast paintings not only instructed the observer, they also aroused in him awe in the presence of God's creation and gratitude for His generosity in giving all this for Americans to exploit, and at the same time touched his sentiment with references to the passing of the Indian and the buffalo. Bierstadt's canvases were big enough and sufficiently brilliant in color to be noticed even in rooms filled with florid carpets, draped and tasseled mantelpieces, potted plants, marble busts, prismed chandeliers, overstuffed furniture and overdressed women. They were finicky enough in detail to be consistent with the lace, antimacassars, and other gewgaws of the age. Furthermore, Bierstadt's high-keyed color somewhat compensates for the overattention to detail which in most pictures of the Hudson River school is all the more oppressive because it is accompanied by a gloomy palette. Among the most impressive of these pictures (and it must be admitted they are certainly that) are *In the Yosemite Valley,* c. 1867; *Last of the Buffalo* (PB 69); and *The Rocky Mountains,* 1863 (PB 75; Illustration 4–52). Not quite so large, but otherwise typical, is *Thunderstorm in the Rocky Mountains,* 1859 (PB 71).

Less impressive in scale, but more so in final artistic merit, are Bierstadt's sketches and the small pictures related to them, such as *The St. Lawrence River from the Citadel, Quebec,* after

4–52.   Albert Bierstadt, *The Rocky Mountains,* 1863. Oil on canvas. 73¼ x 120¾ inches. (The Metropolitan Museum of Art, New York. Rogers Fund, 1907.)

1880 (PB 510). It is in these that the subtler dimensions of his artistry are shown. The Karolik Collection at the Museum of Fine Arts, Boston, possesses a number of Bierstadt's sketches, including several from the artist's Rocky Mountain trips. Some of the latter—for instance, *Indian Camp* and *Indians near Fort Laramie*—demonstrate that Bierstadt could be spontaneous and summary and at the same time sure in drawing and subtle in color. These small pictures seem to burst like drafts of sunlit air into the dark, stuffy world of his other paintings and those of his contemporaries, with their oppressive detail, dull tonality, and heavily gilded frames. It is a relief to know that pictures like these were possible, and that the explorations of two generations of landscape artists resulted in more than the monuments of uninspired workmanship which most of them left.

Frederick Church and Thomas Moran combined the idealized landscape of the Cole tradition and the meticulous handling of Durand and of the Düsseldorf group with the mid-century passion for bigness. Church was in fact a pupil of Cole, but during Cole's last years his technique had begun to take on some of Durand's precision and to lose the charm of his earlier, more suggestive and decorative brush stroke. Church achieved in his method "a most photographic imitation of the natural objects and effects," as a prominent critic wrote in praise. As a matter of fact, he and many another of the explorer-painters took their cameras with them. It is instructive to compare the early camera work of the pioneers of western photography, Timothy O'Sullivan and William Jackson (F 37, F 49), with the hand-painted replicas of nature by Church, Bierstadt, and the rest. The obvious artistic superiority of the photographs over the paintings can be explained in terms of the media involved. A photograph is much more effective than is a painting in the recording of detail and registration of values, factors which are supplemented by the impact of reality caught precisely in a unique moment of time. The imitation in painting of these photographic effects, even with the addition of color, is not enough.

Church, like Bierstadt, might be remembered as a better artist if his sketches (now preserved in the Cooper Union, New York), not unlike Bierstadt's in their freshness and lack of pretension, were better known. But his enormous canvases appealed to the taste of the time, and he prospered. Church's ambitions were as sizable as his pictures, each square inch of which is covered with an industry that might be called compulsive. Motivated by the German naturalist von Humboldt's recommendation that landscape should be presented with a scientific factuality, Church painted scenes and natural phenomena throughout the globe. The results of his keen observation are not without their instructive value, and the artist seasons his otherwise too factual appeal with a dash of the dramatically strange and exotic.

Church composed with skill, even though he used the stock formulas of arrangement derived ultimately from Claude. But he had to compose well, otherwise the observer would be sunk in a quagmire of unreadable data. Church at his most bombastically characteristic is seen in pictures whose subjects range from the Catskills —as in *Scene in the Catskills,* 1851 (PB 119), which he makes even more dramatic than Cole —and *Niagara,* 1857 (PB 123), appropriately grandiloquent and huge in size, to *The Mountains of Ecuador,* 1855 (PB 524), and *View of Cotopaxi,* 1857 (PB 125), one of several versions of the subject.

Thomas Moran, a late follower of Church, added more Turneresque and glowing colors and dashing brush work to Church's meticulousness. Two huge canvases, *Grand Canyon of the Yellowstone River,* 1893–1901 (PB 627A), and *Cliffs on the Upper Colorado River, Wyoming Territory,* 1882 (PB 627), are conspicuous monuments to the artist's industry and to the taste of a period which too often confused quantity with quality—a tendency which increased in the period after the Civil War, when these pictures were painted.

Among the artists less famous in their day than Church and Bierstadt, but more appealing in our own time, is Worthington Whittredge. After the struggle from the frontier to the city (in this case, Cincinnati) typical of so many artists, and after the usual bout with portrait painting, Whittredge went abroad and studied for a while at Düsseldorf. Though he succeeded eventually in sloughing off this rigorous training and its concentration on detail, it was a difficult task, and he never quite achieved the freedom one feels he was striving for. Perhaps it was as much the spirit of the time that prevented Whittredge from attaining his potential goal, for he stated that he took only what he wanted from Düsseldorf. Though his European paintings are not outstanding or very different, they are a little more painterly and sketch-like than those of most of his contemporaries. Whittredge's style developed gradually from the typical detailed and dry technique of his generation into a very bravura handling, and (after the artist's return from Europe) was accompanied by simple, unpretentious subjects. When he went West on an army expedition, the dramatic country made little impression on him! Instead, Whittredge preferred the subtler charms

of the East, especially New England. Even Whittredge's early depictions of the Catskills, such as *The Crow's Nest*, 1848 (PB 487), and his subtly illuminated *Deer, Mount Storm Park, Cincinnati*, before 1850 (PB 489), are modest in scale and treatment and indicate how basically different he was as an artist. In Whittredge's handling there is more liveliness and a more interesting and subtler illumination than usually appears in the painting of the time. He himself said of the Hudson River painters as a whole that "they never got beyond a literal transcript" and that their work was seldom anything more than "carefully painted studies of the most commonplace subjects without the slightest choice or invention." [24]

Whittredge's *Home by the Sea*, 1872 (PB 491), and two smaller versions of the same subject, one in the M. and M. Karolik Collection at the Museum of Fine Arts, Boston (Illustration 4–53), and the other at the Los Angeles County Museum, represent the artist at his

4–53. (Thomas) Worthington Whittredge, *Old Homestead by the Sea*, c. 1872. Oil on canvas. 22 x 32 inches. (Courtesy, Museum of Fine Arts, Boston. M. and M. Karolik Collection.)

best. Painterly in technique, fresh in color, vivacious in brush stroke, Whittredge in these pictures almost approaches the breadth and luminosity of early impressionism, especially in his use of highlights to give sparkle. Modest and indigenous in subject, these pictures well illustrate the artist's feeling that an American artist should steep himself in his native environment and not spend his artistic energies elsewhere. The broad sweep of sky, salt marshes, and sea, the gambrel-roofed, shingled farmhouse, the rocks and ancient apple trees are redolent of the New England coast.

Before turning to the "luminists," certain other artists should be considered. One, George Inness, is a painter whose early work is related to the landscape of the pre-Civil War period (his subsequent work belongs to a later era, and is discussed in Part Five). Others like George Loring Brown or David Johnson are outside the main current of the Hudson River school, their significant work being more closely related to the "luminists."

The early work of George Inness is not unlike that of Doughty, and for a good reason. He learned to paint under the French émigré Régis E. Gignoux, whose late rococo mannerisms resembled the conventionalized work of the retardataire English landscapists who inspired the earlier artist. But Inness soon discovered in himself an originality which places him head and shoulders above most of his contemporaries. Furthermore, he was stimulated by other sources than the usual ones for his period. He was among the first of the Americans to discover the virtues of the French landscapists of the Barbizon group, whose work was partly inspired by the Dutch realistic landscapes of the seventeenth century. Combining this influence with a native freshness and airy sparkle presaging the near-impressionism of his later years, he painted a number of pictures not only pleasing in these aspects, but free from both the idealizing rhetoric of Cole and the tedious specificity of Durand. He did, however, share Durand's realism, and followed his advice to

paint out-of-doors. The best of his early pictures are *Delaware Water Gap*, 1861 (PB 258), and *The Lackawanna Valley*, 1855 (PB 256; Illustration 4–54), extraordinary in their fresh, luminous quality. In the latter picture it will be noticed that Inness has no qualms about introducing railroad engines and roundhouses in a landscape which his more romantic contemporaries would have considered desecrated by such intrusions (though it must be admitted that the picture was commissioned by the Delaware Lackawanna and Western Railroad). There is something of the panoramic point of view in these paintings, a characteristic further illustrated in *Peace and Plenty*, 1865 (PB 260), the climax of his early work. This picture is also enormous in size, like those of the Hudson River school, but with more justification. The subject itself is epic, since the painter was celebrating in it the conclusion of the Civil War and perhaps also the victory of the North. Furthermore, its clear and spacious composition is much more monumental and better organized than most of those by Bierstadt, Church, and the rest. The picture has a real grandeur without relying on compositional props, meretricious detail, and exaggerated color. *Peace and Plenty* —a lush New England scene bathed in the fresh sunlight of a summer's day—is a fitting climax to the landscape painting of the period for it combines scale and rhetoric with a genuine painterly richness and breadth.

George Loring Brown is the only prominent landscape painter associated with Boston in this period, and is thus not to be included with the Hudson River group. In fact, like Alexander in portraiture, Brown in landscape reflects the particular Boston phenomenon of the specific influence of Washington Allston. Inspired by the older artist's copies of Claude and his original variations on Claude's themes, Brown spent most of his life in Italy where he painted conventional classical landscapes in such number that he was nicknamed "Claude" Brown. But after his return to Boston in 1862 he began to paint quite differently, perhaps under the influence of North American light, but more probably stimulated by a group of mid-century

4–54. George Inness, *The Lackawanna Valley*, 1855. Oil on canvas. 33⅞ x 50¼ inches. (National Gallery of Art, Washington. Gift of Mrs. Huttleston Rogers.)

Italian painters, the "Macchiorelli," who had developed a proto-impressionist point of view with no apparent contact (at least in the early years) with the predecessors and early practitioners of the movement in France.[25] In any case, two of Brown's pictures, *Medford Marshes*, 1862, and *The Public Gardens, Boston*, 1869 (Illustration 4–55) (both in the M. and M. Karolik Collection, Museum of Fine Arts, Boston), have a brilliant, cursory, but richly pigmented suggestion of space and atmosphere which is remarkable, considering their date.

David Johnson, who was at first an unpretentious painter with a personal kind of intense realism, later succumbed to the grandiosity of Cole and Church, which he was little equipped

by temperament to emulate—a factor that perhaps accounts for his not very great reputation. He is being reconsidered here in preference to a number of similarly obscure but worthy landscapists of the period, because of the individual charm of his early work, a quality which almost justifies his inclusion in the "luminist" group. The merit of this early work consists largely in being free of the false sublimity of Cole and Church, and of the engraver-like precision of Durand and the Düsseldorf meticulousness that supplemented it. His *Old Mill, West Milford, N. J.*, 1850 (Brooklyn Museum), is depicted in a clear, strong light unblurred by the rose-colored glasses of sentimentality, and shows no hint of either the grandly or the quaintly

4–55. George Loring Brown, *The Public Gardens, Boston,* 1869. Oil on canvas. 18 x 30 inches. (Courtesy, Museum of Fine Arts, Boston. M. and M. Karolik Collection.)

picturesque. The subject is among the most ordinary, not to say "ugly," chosen by an American landscapist during this period. Even more remarkable is his *North Conway, New Hampshire.* Though in general the picture has the spectacular subject matter expected of the site, its central portion (Illustration 4–56) is more original, representing a group of box-like, sharp-edged buildings related to each other in the geometry characteristic of a New England village seen on a bright, crisply clear day, and bathed in a crystalline luminosity.

At least one critic, J. J. Jarvis, looked seriously at such unassuming work as Bierstadt's sketches and asserted: "In the quality of American light, clear, transparent, and sharp in outline, he is unsurpassed."[26] Today we are inclined to agree with this somewhat eccentric critic who was often far ahead of his times. The fact that he singled out "American light" for special

4–56. David Johnson, detail of *North Conway, New Hampshire,* n. d. Oil on canvas. 16 x 23 inches. (Courtesy, Museum of Fine Arts, Boston. M. and M. Karolik Collection.)

comment is as remarkable as his appreciation of Bierstadt's casual sketches. A few other instances of similar awareness can be pointed out, such as in the Englishman George Harvey's proposal to execute a watercolor series entitled "Atmospheric Landscapes of North America," and the remarks of Charles Dickens, who found our light so different from that of Britain, with a quality that makes things "bright and twinkling" and "every sharp outline . . . a hundred times sharper than ever" [27]—a characteristic which he felt to be consistent with our "prim" architecture. No one would deny that each region has its own special appearance, and that light is the ambiance in which this is perceived. The pictures of the French impressionists are filled with the radiance of the Île-de-France, and the atmospheric freshness and transparency

of English landscape painting would have been unthinkable without the varied and subtle changes of English weather. To deny the existence of the quality of American light would be to deny something basic to the visual environment in which the American artist lived. Bierstadt certainly exploited this quality in his sketches, if not in his larger paintings. Whittredge was partially aware of it, at least in his seaside landscapes, as were lesser men like David Johnson in his earlier phase. But it remained for the group whom John I. H. Baur of the Whitney Museum has christened the "luminists" to exploit fully the special character of American light.

The two most prominent artists of this group are Fitz Hugh Lane and Martin J. Heade. Lane spent most of his life in a house overlooking

4–57. Fitz Hugh Lane, *Southwest Harbor, Maine*, 1852. Oil on canvas. 32 x 40 inches. (Courtesy of Mrs. Pierrepont Johnson, Newport, Rhode Island.)

Gloucester Harbor, painting that varied scene and its environs on Cape Anne; he also worked Down East in Maine (and possibly in New York and Puerto Rico). He was undoubtedly greatly influenced by an artist of English origin, Robert Salmon, who painted pictures of Boston Harbor, such as *Boston Harbor from Constitution Wharf*, c. 1829 (PB 646), which were not especially unusual except for their concentration upon the horizontal and vertical accents of ships' rigging—a characteristic which may account for Lane's emphasis on almost mathematical structure in his work. The light in some of Salmon's pictures, as in *South Sea Whale Fishing*, 1831 or 1835 (PB 392), which is quite clear and luminous, may also have influenced Lane. Lane's light, however, is remarkably subtle, achieving in Baur's words a "magic quality," and an "unearthly clarity . . . or enveloping tones of dusk."[28] Lane's hard, smooth finish is perfectly appropriate to express his sensibility for infinite nuances of tonality, and to describe the detailed texture of objects upon which the light plays. This precision of treatment is also consistent with his utterly static and almost abstractly geometric compositions.

Among the examples of Lane's extraordinary work, *Ships in Ice off Ten Pound Island, Gloucester*, 1850's (*PB 295), and *Owl's Head* are the most impressive, though *A Maine Inlet* (PB 615) and *Fresh Water Cove from Dolliver's Neck* (PB 616) are nearly as fine. (All are in the M. and M. Karolik Collection, Museum of Fine Arts, Boston.) *Southwest Harbor, Maine*, 1852 (Illustration 4–57), exhibits Lane's peculiar qualities perhaps better than any other.

Heade was a more versatile painter than Lane, and less consistent. In fact, some of his later landscapes do not fall so readily into Baur's category, being painted more broadly and conventionally, though possessing many "luministic" effects. [Others, not landscapes at all, consist of very detailed still lifes and pictures of South American birds—as in *Humming Birds and Orchids* (PB 214)—wherein the technique is precise to a degree hardly surpassed by today's "magic" realists.] However, a number of Heade's landscapes can certainly be described as "luministic." Though sometimes more dramatic and mysterious than those of Lane, Heade's pictures have the same subtle effects of atmosphere, precise treatment, and smooth

4–58. Martin J. Heade, *Approaching Storm: Beach Near Newport*, c. 1860. Oil on canvas. 28 x 58¼ inches. (Courtesy, Museum of Fine Arts, Boston. M. and M. Karolik Collection.)

4–59. George Tirrell, *View of Sacramento, California, from Across the Sacramento River*, 1855–1860. Oil on canvas. 27 x 48 inches. (Courtesy, Museum of Fine Arts, Boston. M. and M. Karolik Collection.)

finish. In addition, they resemble Lane's pictures in their almost mathematical formality, a quality underscored by their long, narrow format, with an emphasis on the horizontal accent. The moodiness suggested in Lane's canvases is also present in Heade's, which are equally static, mysteriously still—a quality seen even more effectively in a few drawings, as in *Newburyport Marshes, Twilight* (GB 94B). But in two extraordinary paintings Heade achieves effects which go beyond Lane's. In these he combines his precisionist technique, his decided horizontality, and his preoccupation with light and atmosphere into a synthesis as haunting and strange as in any American pictures of the nineteenth century. *Approaching Storm: Beach Near Newport*, c. 1860 (PB 582; Illustration 4–58), is the more impressive of these two. Here the hard, glassy waves beat ominously on a lunar shore whose unearthly sand and pinnacled rocks are lit by an eerie electric brightness clashing against a darkening acid sky. A few sails on the horizon are scudding to cover

before the onslaught of the storm, a very terrestrial business in the midst of this ghostly scene. The combination in this picture of a precisionist and realistic technique (which paradoxically seems to transform the real world into an unreal one), vast perspectives, and the juxtaposition of the dream-like with the normal is characteristic of some surrealist painting of our own time, notably that of Salvador Dali during the 1930's. *Storm Approaching, Larchmont Bay*, 1868 (private collection), has something of the same quality. Though these two pictures stand alone in their mysterious intensity, Heade's compositional and stylistic peculiarities make the majority of his other landscapes, even the most mediocre, somewhat distinguished.

Baur rightly includes other painters in his category of "luminists," though these are of less significance in a general survey. George Tirrell's *View of Sacramento, California, from Across the Sacramento River*, 1855–1860 (PB 664; Illustration 4–59), is an isolated example by an artist about whom almost nothing is known except the signature on this one canvas. It is not only notable for a luminous tonality and a skillful composition in the general sense, but it is further remarkable for its color and arrangement of forms within the total picture area. The color is subtle in its contrast and harmony of warm and cool hues, arranged in a sequence from rose to ochre on the warm side of the palette, and, on the cool side, from a blue to green, but with overtones of rose in the blue, and of ochre in the green. The treatment of the objects is meticulous, as is the case with the other "luminists," yet the artist's effort is not spent on minutely undifferentiated detail, but upon the definition of form in outline (that is, the edges of objects themselves and of their shadows), upon the interplay between these lines and the forms isolated by them, and their final, precise arrangement in a series of receding planes parallel to the picture plane. It is thus clear that another quality besides the treatment of light and color distinguishes this picture: its composition. For, the peculiar character and charm of Tirrell's painting depend not only on the treatment of light itself, but on the combination of this with a geometric composition of sharp-edged and precisely delineated objects. Lane's pictures, and to a lesser degree Heade's, share these characteristics with Tirrell's. Thus the term "luminist" is not quite accurate, for it emphasizes only one of the characteristics of this kind of painting—its quality of light—while neglecting the precision of the forms which are gelled in the surrounding ambiance of glassy luminosity. By whatever name they are tagged, these "luministic" pictures are a far more indigenous manifestation of landscape painting than the Hudson River school, for they derive more from their immediate environment than from conventional composition and ways of seeing.

For this reason, it is perhaps not strange that closer parallels can be discovered between the "luminists" and the best of the folk landscapists, who are indigenous almost by definition, than between the "luminists" and the academic landscapists. Paintings by Tirrell and Lane are stylistically nearer to those by Thomas Hicks (PB 20) and J. D. Bunting (PB 517) than they are to Cole's and Durand's, as can be seen even in the most casual comparison.

In the wake of the discovery of artists like Tirrell and the re-evaluation of those like Lane, a number of other talents have come to light. Among them is the Negro artist Robert S. Duncanson whose Ohio paintings, such as *Blue Hole, Flood Waters, Little Miami River,* 1851 (PB 540), combine the conventional classical composition and decorative detail of the early part of the century with a pleasantly naïve sense of the dramatic. Another is George Bacon Wood, whose landscapes, barn interiors, and genre scenes (concerned with children, fish houses, and dories) are suggestive of the earlier work of William Mount in composition and premonitory of the early Winslow Homer, whose fresh color and painterly technique are similar to Wood's. Henry Walton, known principally for his lithographed views of places in central New York, was also an interesting painter nearer to the "luminists" than to the Hudson River school, if perhaps less conscious of his design and less academically competent. His landscapes are reflected in such a lithograph as *East View of Ithaca, New York,* 1837 (GB 205), which, in its sweep and dramatic sky is conventional enough, but in its composition, detail, and quality of light is quite "luministic." Walton is typical of a whole group of artists whose paintings or drawings have been largely lost, since they were originally intended for reproduction. Some of these topographical artists are as interesting as Fitz Hugh Lane (who in fact often painted views to be reproduced), or as Tirrell, the composition of whose *View of Sacramento* is very similar to the engraved or lithographed city-scapes of the period, suggesting that this may have been its original purpose. Since only a few of the original works of these artists still survive—among them a handsome watercolor by J. W. Hill, *Broadway and Trinity Church,* 1830 (GB 101)—it will be more convenient to discuss them in the category of the graphic arts, by which means they were reproduced, bearing in mind, however, their interrelation with landscape painting.

Ideal and History Painting; Painting Inspired by Literature

Ideal painting was characterized by a concern with classical and historical subject matter in the grand manner on the one hand, and a romantic interest in the remote and exotic on the other. It did not flourish in the United States. Allston's retrospective exhibition of 1839 in Boston contained pictures illustrating both of these aspects of romanticism; yet in spite of the unusual praise it aroused, the show did not stimulate a notable revival of interest in Allston's subject matter. Ideal painting languished in spite of efforts to keep it alive by the purchase of casts from antique sculpture by academies and athenaeums and by half-hearted government commissions. Samuel F. B. Morse's classical pictures executed in London were admired when he returned with them to the United States, but were not bought; nor was he ever given a commission to execute anything in the grand manner. The spirit of the age was not sympathetic to this kind of painting, an attitude which was reinforced by Allston's inability to finish *Belshasar's Feast* and by the artistic failure of the monumental paintings in the rotunda of the National Capitol by Trumbull. There was thus very little in painting to compare with the neo-classical ideal in sculpture, which remained the chief source of inspiration and taste for that art until after the Civil War. Only Cole's allegories and Daniel Huntington's equally sermonizing pictures were in any way popular, and this was due largely to their sentimental moralizing.

W. S. Mason and Henry Peters Gray were among the few painters who continued in the vein of Allston and of Vanderlyn's *Ariadne,* and who paralleled in paint the neo-classic formulas of the sculptor Hiram Powers, whose *Greek Slave* was so popular. Gray's *Greek Lovers* (The Metropolitan Museum of Art, New York) and *Judgment of Paris* (Corcoran Gallery, Washington) have the appearance of blown-up cameos and are only a little less dull than the work of any of the painters who carried on the losing battle of neo-classicism. Mason at least avoided Gray's lackluster smoothness of finish and endowed his small mythologies with an almost rococo charm and pretty sensuality, as in his little *Venus and Cupid* (M. and M. Karolik Collection, Museum of Fine Arts, Boston).

The work of Daniel Huntington, enormously popular in his day, is stylistically related to neo-classicism in its smooth handling and large size, though in subject matter it is more romantic. Typical is his *Marcy's Dream* (The Metropolitan Museum of Art, New York), illustrating a scene from *Pilgrim's Progress,* a canvas which is a descendant of West's large religious pictures, though its sentimentality places it in the mid-century. Such pictures, and hundreds of competent portraits, made Huntington one of the most respected artists of his day, if one of the dullest to our eyes.

Only two painters of real distinction were drawn to ideal painting as such, as distinguished from either "history" or sentimental literary anecdote: William Page and Thomas Cole. Page, whose occasional portraits have already been mentioned, produced even fewer ideal pictures, but these were as provocative as his portraits. Even more a theorist and less a painter than Allston, the quality of Page's mind and personality had an effect on his contemporaries similar to that of the older man, and likewise much more was expected of him than he actually produced. Page studied the Venetian-derived glazing of Allston in Venice itself, spending four years on a careful copy of Titian's *Venus of Urbino.* He was also eclectic in the sources of his figures, deriving them from antique and Renaissance precedent. Sometimes his drawing is awkward under the rich veils of color, and in some instances he is even ludicrous in his straining for a significant statement. But in one or two pictures, certainly in the *Cupid and Psyche,* 1843 (PB 330), there is a mysterious twilight and a brooding solemnity which, though somewhat reminiscent of Allston, are quite personal, and serve to make him a link between the earlier artist and Albert Pinkham Ryder. The almost melancholy half-light of rich and subtle glazes and of massed shapes against an empty landscape give the painting

4–60. Thomas Cole, study for *Voyage of Life: Manhood*, 1842. Oil on canvas. 12⅛ x 17 inches. (Courtesy of Smith College Museum of Art, Northampton, Massachusetts.)

what Page would have called its "soul," with a life of its own, its forms derived from reality but transformed into something that transcends mere resemblance. Shackled with theory, producing little (and much of that ineffectual), Page nevertheless in his few works which do succeed painted pictures that to our eyes are among the most intriguing of the period.

Thomas Cole's series of "cosmoramas," on the other hand, are less interesting as works of art, no matter how curious they are as examples of the taste of the time. The romantic fascination with death, with the passage of time, and with the rise and fall of civilizations (which came with the realization that conventional biblical time was not accurate and that even the historical past stretched back many centuries before the creation in Genesis) inspired these series

of huge paintings, the most notable of which are the *Course of Empire,* 1833–1836 (PB 128), and the *Voyage of Life,* 1842 (PB 133, PB 139, PB 140, PB 141; see also Illustration 4–60). Commissioned by cultivated men, admired and reproduced in countless engravings, the only conspicuous pictures, in a Protestant culture, which could be called even remotely religious (the *Voyage of Life* was intended for a "meditation room"), these canvases bristle with extraneous reference, and are so rhetorical and sententious that it is difficult to discern their artistic merits. They are further marred by a too vivid and unorganized color, intrusion of detail, and an oily slickness of texture; but a dramatic grandeur both of concept and composition breaks through their bombast and pretentious size. Perhaps it is the baroque spaciousness and atmosphere and the dynamic composition which rescue the huge canvases from bathos. These more attractive qualities, which are almost overwhelmed in the finished works, are seen in undiluted form in the sketches, where the shapes, color, and brush work are united in a statement where means and effect are more successfully integrated. The study for *Voyage of Life: Manhood,* 1842 (Illustration 4–60), for instance, has all the pictorial essentials of the final work (PB 140) without its glossy finish and overconscientious detail. Cole felt that *subject* was the essential part of painting and that chiaroscuro, modeling, and color were but "food for the gross eye." [29] The final failure of these pictures, in spite of their virtues, lies in the dichotomy, which the artist never resolved, between the didactic subject and the sensuous means used to make it palatable.

History painting, too, became moribund at the end of the period, after the last great impetus given to it in 1836 by the commissions for four pictures to complete the cycle begun by Trumbull in the rotunda of the Capitol. One was given to the aging Vanderlyn, one to Walter Robert Wier, another to John Gadsby Chapman, and the last to William Henry Powell (after Inman died). Wier and Chapman were basically illustrators, and Powell was a barely competent painter from the Midwest, appointed for political reasons. None had any idea of the demands of wall decoration. The Trumbull pictures were at least consistent with each other in scale, and adjusted to the proportions of their architectural setting. The others are not only inconsistent with the Trumbulls in the size of their figures, but with each other. They abound in meticulous detail and have little or no simplicity and grandeur of statement, but instead are conglomerations of nearly unreadable incident. They are in fact enormously enlarged illustrations more suitable for engraving as decorations in the magazines and gift or "token" books of the age than for the ornamentation of walls. Furthermore, they are full of the empty histrionics of gesture, the "factual" trappings of costume, and other detail which is as meretriciously realistic as the meticulous treatment. Vanderlyn's picture offends with

the rest, and is perhaps the worst but fortunately the last prominent manifestation of the smooth facility of the Mengs–West tradition in paint.

Other large and conspicuous decorations in the Capitol are simply further examples of "swollen easel pictures," to use Virgil Barker's happy phrase. But one of them has an academic competence and even a certain vitality, if not beauty: *Westward the Course of Empire Takes Its Way,* by Emanuel Leutze. This painter, who was born in Germany and who returned there to study after spending his youth in the United States, had already sent back a painting which was to become part of American patriotic iconography: *Washington Crossing the Delaware,* 1851 (The Metropolitan Museum of Art, New York). This huge picture with its carefully rendered uniforms, weapons, and ice blocks had an enormous success with a public still naïvely fascinated with verisimilitude. *Westward the Course of Empire* is larger and filled with even more incident, and like the other Capitol paintings was totally unsuited for wall decoration. Unorganized as the picture is with its cluttered composition, its gesturing figures, and its acid hues, it nevertheless conveys a certain vigorous urgency. Perhaps the sketch, 1861 (PB 618), reflects better the artist's first enthusiasm than does the finished result. At any rate, the smallness of the scale is more appropriate to the essentially easel character of the concept.

History painting gradually degenerated into a kind of genre in historic dress, and faded out into a sentimentality suggested by such a title as *Washington Receiving His Mother's Blessing,* a saccharine picture by Powell (Senate House Museum, Kingston, New York).

Painting inspired by literature, an important branch of European romantic art practiced by such talents as Bonington in England and Delacroix in France, enjoyed much less popularity in America, with the exception of the work of John Quidor. [30] This artist's variations on themes suggested by Washington Irving transcend the charming whimsy of the author, which seems almost pedestrian in comparison. Quidor's liveliness and fantasy are actually far closer to Poe

4–61. John Quidor, *The Money Diggers,* 1832. Oil on canvas. 16¼ x 21½ inches. (Courtesy of The Brooklyn Museum, Brooklyn, New York.)

in their dream-like, even nightmarish, quality, and make of him one of the most original American painters of the nineteenth century. Never popular, Quidor had to support himself by artisan and other work. His style had none of the slick technical polish and superficial realism expected by the contemporary public, but was bold and dashing in brush work, almost expressionistic in drawing, and strong in composition.

Quidor's best known work comes from two periods, the first beginning in 1828 and lasting for a decade, the second beginning after 1856 and lasting for another decade. *The Money Diggers,* 1832 (PB 638; Illustration 4–61), can

be taken as typical of his early work, and the *Voyage to Hell Gate from Communipaw,* c. 1866 (PB 372), is representative of his last period. The difference between the two lies principally in the modeling, color, and application of pigments. The early work is strongly modeled in sculpturesque form emphasized by exaggerated chiaroscuro, though relieved by brilliant strokes of color which are sometimes almost impressionistic in handling. The later work is almost monochromatic, the paint applied with glazes, the forms drawn in suggestively with the wet brush. Otherwise the two pictures share an exaggerated and expressive drawing of the figure, a dynamic composition, and an air of unreality or fantasy. In *The Money Diggers* the terror of the robbers is wonderfully expressed in the strongly modeled figures, while their excitement is reflected in the twisted branches of a dead tree. The dark hole in the earth and the brilliant bonfire are other elements in a well-organized and dynamic composition. In *Voyage to Hell Gate* the design is equally lively, the boat being blown by a smart wind which whips the sail and the branches of the trees on shore, while the little figures on board gesticulate violently. All of this complexity is suggested with the greatest economy of means.

In both of these pictures, and in the *Battle Scene from Knickerbocker's History of New York*, 1838 (PB 637), which brims with an almost caricatured ridiculous activity, there is a strong influence from Dutch and Flemish genre painting, though the English caricature tradition from Hogarth to Thomas Rowlandson and George Cruickshank may also have played a part.

Typical of Quidor at his best, and showing characteristics of both periods (though painted at the beginning of the second period), is *Wolfert's Will*, 1856 (PB 371). The strange illumination shimmering over Wolfert's bed linen and night dress, the whirling accents of the composition, and the almost burlesque gestures and expressions transfer the meaning of Irving's story to another plane. Here is seen the broad humor of much of Quidor's work, together with the effective modeling that survived from his earlier period, and the expressive drawing and subtle glazing of the later one.

Imaginative in conception, bold and expressive in technique, lively in composition, and with a very personal and original style, Quidor's work is far superior to that of most of his storytelling contemporaries, which is marred either by a pedestrian realism or obvious sentimentality.

Genre

Though "ideal" romanticism seldom succeeded in America except in the mixture of dream and landscape in Cole's "cosmoramas," the ideal, when it was combined with genre inspired by

foreign places and by literature, was more conspicuous. But little of it is distinguished. One exception is William Page's *The Young Merchants* (*PB 327), depicting two Italian street vendors, a boy and a girl. The figures are strongly but subtly modeled in an atmosphere of richly colored luminosity, painted with glazes and impasto in an "old master" way, and the picture as a whole is infused with the artist's peculiar moodiness. However, by the 1840's the classical ruins and strained allegories began to be replaced by subjects drawn from the American scene. Among those appearing in the popular gift books and annuals as early as the mid-1830's were engraved versions of genre subjects by William Sidney Mount.

Mount was the first painter to succeed conspicuously in a field which had heretofore been considered inferior to other branches of painting, and he can therefore be thought of as the chief initiator of the genre school, which flourished from the 1840's onward. Only one other artist before Mount was anywhere as notable in the field, and he was primarily an illustrator: David Claypoole Johnston, whose droll imitations of the English caricaturist Cruickshank are worthy of note because of their engaging humor and clever, if overexaggerated, drawing. Though Mount was undoubtedly aware of Johnston, if not indeed of Cruickshank, and derived encouragement from their popularity, a far more likely source of inspiration for Mount's work consisted of engravings after the English genre painters, in particular Sir David Wilkie and the American-born Charles R. Leslie, both painters of semiliterary anecdote, and George Morland, famous for his horses and his stable scenes.

The popularity in America of this kind of painting may have been reinforced by the consequences of Jacksonian democracy; but the rising middle class in Europe had also imposed its taste for the familiar and anecdotal, especially in the Germanic countries where a meticulous technique and a familiar point of view (derived partly from Dutch seventeenth-century genre) flourished, particularly at Düsseldorf, where so many Americans studied. For Mount, the same Dutch inspiration was probably a strong incentive. There were many Dutch genre paintings in New York—some actually brought over in the seventeenth century—and no less a mentor than Allston had urged Mount to study the work of two Dutch artists, Adrian Van Ostade and Jan Steen.

Whatever were the influences, the trend of the times turned Mount from his early essays in history painting toward a point of view far more sympathetic to his own nature. He stated in 1846: "There has been enough written on ideality and the grand style in art, etc. to divert the artist from the true study of natural objects."[31] Perhaps this last phrase is the key to Mount's becoming the first important, and perhaps the best, genre painter in the history of American art. It was the familiar world of experience which he loved and which naturally predisposed him to the unpretentious in subject matter, without the addition of allegory, sentiment, didacticism, or other commentary. This is not to say that Mount did not relish telling a story—he would not have belonged to his century if he did not. But he told his own stories. As one of his contemporaries said of him, "He is peculiar in the habit of tasking his own mind for his subjects, so that you never see him illustrating the pages of any writer, historian, poet or wit."[32] Mount's subjects are taken, instead, from his Long Island rural experience: country dances, horse trading, Negro fiddlers, and the activities of country children.

Mount's first essay in genre was the *Rustic Dance*, 1830 (M. and M. Karolik Collection, Museum of Fine Arts, Boston). Though poor in drawing and composition, it was immediately liked. The public was ready for it and the young artist's work was in demand from then on. Mount soon gave up the somewhat caricature-like style of this picture, derived from Cruickshank and Johnston, for a more personal approach, and after a few story-telling subjects in the sentimental English tradition he hit his stride in such subjects as *Bargaining for a Horse*, 1835 (*PB 314). Mount's best works were painted in the years from 1845 to 1858, and from these, four paintings may be singled out as among the finest and most characteristic: *Eel Spearing at Setauket*, 1845 (PB 317; Illustration 4–62); *The Power of Music*, 1847 (PB 318); *Boys Caught Napping in a Field*, 1848 (PB 630); and *Banjo Player*, c. 1858 (*PB 321; Illustration 4–63). Mount's expressive figures and bold, effective composition are seen especially in *The Power of Music*, where assorted rustics are depicted reacting in each one's individual way to the music of a youthful fiddler in a barn. In *Boys Caught Napping*, the luminous light, rich color, and fine paint quality of Mount's technique are unusually clear, as well as his solid drawing and effective modeling. This competence derives largely from the artist's own self-education, supplemented by drawing from casts at the National Academy and undoubtedly by further instruction by its director, Samuel F. B. Morse, for Mount's transparent thin glazes and brilliant highlights show an understanding of the fundamentals of the great tradition in painting. Mount was also an avid student of the techniques of the old masters, and an experimenter in various methods and materials, even using Long Island earth for some of his colors. The rich, though never too bright, color of his works and the state of their preservation after a hundred years give evidence of Mount's careful technique.

In *Eel Spearing*, the figure of the colored woman in the act of spearing is not only cleverly drawn but monumental; the depiction of the surrounding air and the spacious landscape is not merely painterly but suffused with a luminosity as subtle as that of Fitz Hugh Lane or George Tirrell. The grand and simple figures silhouetted against the limpid stillness of the water, and the heat-filled, heavy summer air are wonderfully realized. The boat, the figures, and the straight lines of oar and spear are isolated against a background rigidly parallel to the picture plane, in an arrangement as monumental and spacious as that of a Renaissance picture. Even more remarkable in composition is *The Banjo Player*, in which Mount achieves an effective simplicity which seems almost deliberately geometric. Here, some years after *The Power of Music*, he has eliminated the listeners; all that remains are the barn and the solitary musician. There is evidence in the canvas that

4–62.   William Sidney Mount, *Eel Spearing at Setauket*, 1845.   Oil on canvas.   29 x 36 inches.   (Courtesy of the New York State Historical Association, Cooperstown, New York.)

Mount painted out several figures before arriving at the present solution, a fact which suggests that he was quite aware of the almost abstract beauty of a composition made up principally of the simple shapes of the barn, the geometry of its framing, and the pattern of its door. The luminous richness of paint, the precise but unobtrusive detail, together with the extraordinary composition make the picture one of the masterpieces of American art. Here the painterly tradition seems to have been combined with two indigenous qualities: the achievement of a clear

luminosity of atmosphere, and a realization of planometric composition.

One more picture by Mount should be mentioned, *Long Island Farmhouse*, after 1854 (PB 320; Illustration 4–64), his only completed landscape among a host of charming, almost impressionistically painted sketches [such as *Landscape With Figures*, 1851 (*PB 319)]. Imbued with the translucent light and brilliant touch derived from the artist's practice of painting out-of-doors, the *Long Island Farmhouse* is a sensitive record of a particular place, time of day,

4–63. William Sidney Mount, *Banjo Player*, c. 1858. Oil on canvas. 25 x 30 inches. (Courtesy of the Detroit Institute of Arts.)

and year. Its subject is a typical "salt box" dwelling of eastern Long Island depicted in the light of an afternoon sun which casts along the ground the long shadows of a sensitively drawn tree. A rail fence in the foreground, parallel to the viewer, frames the geometry of dwelling, barn, and outhouse. The affectionate precision of the buildings' detail, which describes the wear and decay of two hundred years' time, makes the barely glimpsed children almost unnecessary for the sense of warm humanity suffusing the whole picture.

Mount's native quality and originality must have been recognized even in Europe, for a Paris lithographic firm distributed his work there, and even offered to finance him on a trip to Europe —circumstances not paralleled in the case of any other American painter of the period. Mount preferred to stay in his own countryside. His stubborn liking for his native place and its rustic inhabitants, and the unpretentious directness of his observation of them contribute to the quality of his best pictures, separating them from the work of many of his contemporaries, which is confused with references to ill-digested moral and literary ideas.

The success of Mount encouraged others to take up genre painting devoted to the familiar and anecdotal. Much of it was technically inept, exposing the artists' lack of training, or, if fairly competent technically, it was too obvious or sentimental in content.

The ablest and most interesting of the genre painters, aside from Mount, were David Gilmour Blythe and Richard Caton Woodville. Blythe, a frontier artist who flourished in and around Pittsburgh, was self-trained but undoubtedly in-fluenced by the paintings he saw in Boston, Philadelphia, and Baltimore while he was a ship's carpenter from 1837 to 1840. He improved on the thin and acid caricature of Johnston by a quite serious study of the Flemish and Dutch genre masters of the seventeenth century, par-ticularly Van Ostade (from whom he must have derived his gross, solid figures and bold chiaro-scuro), and Adriaen Brouwer, whose brisk and easy brush stroke with its power of broad sug-gestion of action and space stood Blythe in good stead in his satirical commentary on the ab-surdity of human ways. Typical examples of

4–64. William Sidney Mount, *Long Island Farmhouse*, after 1854. Oil on canvas. 21⅞ x 29⅞ inches. (The Metropolitan Museum of Art, New York. Gift of Louise F. Wickham in memory of her father, William H. Wichham.)

Blythe's work are *Pittsburgh Post Office* (Carnegie Institute, Pittsburgh), showing a crowd struggling at the general delivery window, and the lively *Art Versus Law* (PB 90), broad, obvious, but powerful.

Woodville, of all the American genre painters except Mount, had the greatest reputation and was certainly better trained academically than most. He studied at Düsseldorf, hoping to acquire the kind of technical accuracy he had admired in the Dutch paintings he had seen in the Gilmore collection in his native Baltimore. His *War News from Mexico*, 1848 (PB 684), exhibits his technique at its most impressive to the layman. Representing a group on the steps of a hotel listening to the voice of the reader of a news sheet, the picture has nothing one can complain of except its theatricality. Woodville's *Politics in an Oyster House*, 1848 (PB 497), is simpler in composition and the gestures of its characters are less rhetorical. Remarkable for deft imitation of reality and for an effective grouping of figures in an interior, *The Card Players*, 1846 (PB 496), has some of the simple dignity of the best Dutch genre work, yet is spoiled by a rhetorical exaggeration of the event which takes it out of reality onto a stage, and by an attention to detail which is often merely trivial in spite of its clever handling.

Among a host of less competent painters, there were artists like James G. Clooney and Albertus D. O. Browere in New York State, and James Henry Beard in Ohio, who painted amusing commentaries on country and small town events in an exaggerated, almost Cruickshank, fashion which covered up a certain amount of academic incompetence. The New England genre painter Jerome Thompson had more individuality. Primarily a portraitist, as were so many artists whose principal income was derived from this stable market, Thompson was the author of two rather unusual group portraits crowded with incident, *The Picnic. Near Mt. Mansfield, Vermont* (PB 432) and the more competent *A "Pic Nick" in the Woods of New England* (PB 431). Thompson executed these after his return from a trip to England in 1852, where he had studied the works of Hogarth and of contemporary English genre painters. But in comparison with work by Sir John Millais and William Mulready, Thompson seems provincial and inadequate, though ultimately more competent than most of his American contemporaries.

There were other genre painters who were definitely more "ideal" than "real," suffusing their stories and commentaries on life with sentimentality, and painting with a kind of decorative prettiness recalling the rococo, a manner which had never died out in the technique of engraving; the eighteenth-century treatment of scintillating light, intricacies of foliage, and texture of stuffs persisted well into the nineteenth century and must have influenced the technique of painting itself. Perhaps the most popular of the genre painters of this kind was Lily Martin Spencer, whose pictures appealed to the sentimental tastes of her generation much as did the poems of her contemporary, the prolific Lydia Sigourney, and appeared as engravings in the same gift books.

The successful portraitist Henry Inman, an artist of greater skill than Mrs. Spencer, was perhaps the most competent painter of sentimentally "ideal" genre. His prettified school children, represented in several pictures, purport to portray the rough and tumble of rural American childhood, but the treatment is so dainty that his boys appear to be slightly older cherubs by Boucher, their faces rouged with theatrical makeup, dressed up in costumes from some stage box labeled "ragamuffin." This falseness, no matter how painterly and decorative, was all too frequent in an era when the women's magazines and annuals played such an important role. It is a relief to turn to the more real boys of Mount, or to a rather impressive picture, *Buffalo Newsboy,* 1853 (*PB 297), by Thomas Le Clear, who transcended his usual mediocrity in an interpretation remarkable for its relative lack of sentimentality.

Some of the best genre painting was devoted to the frontier, the Indian, and the opening of the West. The novelty and excitement of these indigenous subjects largely replaced themes drawn from the ancient and medieval past or the exotic lands of the Near East or North Africa, which were among the principal sources of inspiration for European romantic art.

Of all the aspects of the West which appealed to the imagination, the subject of the Indian was the most fascinating. The red man was a romantic creature, whether idealized as in the pages of the novelist James Fenimore Cooper, or more realistically treated as in those of the historian Francis Parkman. Both points of view are seen in the work of George Catlin, one of the earliest and perhaps the most interesting of the painters who concerned themselves with the Indian. As a young portrait painter in Philadelphia, Catlin, greatly impressed with the sight of three Indian braves on a visit to Philadelphia, embarked on an ambitious project to record all the tribes between the Alleghenies and the Pacific. From 1829 to 1832 he visited forty-eight of them and made innumerable paintings and drawings, many of which were engraved and published in his *North American Indians* (1841). These pictures, consisting of individual portraits, groups of figures, and landscapes with figures, comprise an invaluable ethnological and anthropological record. Though not often very convincing from the point of view of academic competence in drawing, perspective, or anatomy (Catlin was largely self-taught), nevertheless many of his paintings have an immediacy which makes them more than merely informative. His portraits, though a little naïve, brim with a feeling of authenticity, as in *One Horn. A Dakota (Sioux) Chief*, 1832 (PB 102); the lithographed figures in his published work and in single prints have a certain decorative power as well, typified in *Osceola of Florida*, 1838 (GB 47). Catlin seldom gave convincing life to his depictions of dances and other ceremonies, but his hunting scenes have considerable vigor, as in the lithograph *Buffalo Hunt: Chasing Back*, 1844 (GB 48). His landscapes have a certain sweep, and the excitement of a newly discovered world is communicated in the freshness of a somewhat naïve point of view, as in the *Upper Missouri: The Grand Detour*, c. 1832 (*PB 103). Figures move over them with liveliness, and are composed with a sense of decorative pattern, as in *Buffalo Chase in Snowdrift*, late 1830's (PB 518).

Catlin was preceded in the field by only two artists, Charles B. King, whose *Young Omahaw, War Eagle, Little Missouri and Pawnees*, 1821 (*PB 283), is more academically competent and less immediate than Catlin's portraits, and Peter Ruidesbacher, who was the first to make a consistent business of painting Indians, which he did from 1821 to 1826 in Minnesota and the Dakotas.

Two other artists, Alfred Jacob Miller and Charles Bodmer, who followed Catlin, were notably better than the self-taught Ruidesbacher, and had a greater facility than Catlin, being academically trained. The first studied at the École des Beaux Arts in Paris, and brought back an ornamental style which was a kind of survival of the rococo, and thus singularly inappropriate for the portrayal of the savage and of the wild frontier. A six-month trip to the West in 1839 with Sir William Drummond Stewart, a Scot sportsman, gave Miller enough material to work over until well into the 1870's. The sketches from his 1839 trip are lively, if somewhat overdecorative, and therefore more attractive than the finished paintings of the later years, as illustrated in *Beating a Retreat* (*PB 699). Miller was at least competent as a draughtsman, if not original; Bodmer could hardly draw adequately. This third-rate Swiss artist accompanied for two years the expedition of the German naturalist, Maximilian, Prince of Wied, and supplied illustrations for his patron's *Journey into the Interior of North America* (1839). Though his animals are portrayed more convincingly than Miller's, most of his relatively incompetent drawings were considerably improved by being engraved in aquatint by other hands. Consequently his aquatint *Indians Hunting the Bison*, 1843–1844 (*GB 24), is not only informative but convincing.

John Mix Stanley, though self-trained, was a better artist than Bodmer and superior to Miller as well. Though his work is often sentimental and shows evidence of the amateur in his figures and his treatment of perspective, some of his pictures, especially the landscapes, have scope and spaciousness. These qualities also infuse his figure pieces (usually combined with landscape) with the awesomeness of the great West,

4–65. John Mix Stanley, *Chinook Burying Grounds,* c. 1860. Oil on canvas. 9¼ x 14¼ inches. (Courtesy of the Detroit Institute of Arts.)

as in his *Indians Playing Cards,* 1866 (PB 413). A few small compositions (probably sketches) in the Detroit Institute have a certain impressive simplicity of design and even considerable subtlety, a fact which makes more regrettable the loss of the bulk of his finished pictures in a fire in 1865 at the Smithsonian Institution. *Chinook Burying Grounds,* c. 1860 (Illustration 4–65), is a quite moving document representing Stanley at his best, and is far superior to his later, more sentimental or melodramatic works which survived the fire.

Seth Eastman, who learned to draw as part of his officers' training at West Point, tried out his initially meager abilities in sketching Indians when he took command of Fort Snelling in the Minnesota Territory. His first important work, the illustrations for the epoch-making six volumes of Schoolcraft's *Indian Tribes of the United States,* are marked by a too deft mannerism and an overdramatic treatment which make his Indians seem more like those in Longfellow's *Hiawatha* than the actual ones discussed in the pioneering work in anthropology, which inspired

the poem. Eastman's later work is far more genuine in feeling and reflects a longer absorption in Indian matters. His *Sioux Indians Breaking Up Camp,* c. 1848 (°PB 565), and *Mourning for the Dead,* 1849 (°PB 184), for instance, are worthy visual companions to similar scenes described by Parkman in his *Oregon Trail.* One of Eastman's best pictures is the *Lacrosse Playing Among Sioux Indians,* 1857 (PB 186), in which the space is real, the drawing relatively accurate, and the color as lively as the action portrayed.

Perhaps the most interesting of the Indian painters, and the last to flourish before the Civil War, was a German, Charles Wimar. His Düsseldorf training gave to his dramatic and picturesque paintings (done around 1860) a convincing realism generally lacking in his less academically trained contemporaries. In Wimar's case, the meticulous, all-inclusive detail of the German school was considerably mitigated by a personal style in which monumental and simplified figures are arranged in planes in well-organized, almost Renaissance compositions. These qualities are seen at their best in *Buffalo*

Hunt (Washington University, St. Louis) and *Buffalo Dance*, 1860 (PB 682; Illustration 4–66). In the latter, a ceremony of the Mandan Indians, which often continued for two or three weeks unceasingly until the buffalo came, is being observed, in the light of the moon and a fire, by an intensely still and expectant audience watching every step of the magic of the ritual. It is a composition in which a large number of figures and a variety of activities have been organized into an impressively unified whole. Both the treatment of figures and the composition are more reminiscent of the work of another St. Louis artist, George Caleb Bingham, than of Düsseldorf, suggesting the influence on the German artist of Bingham, one of the most powerful and interesting painters in the history of American art.

The life of the frontier in general was nearly as fascinating as that which concerned the Indian specifically. Bingham was its principal and most impressive recorder, but naturally other artists were involved. Among them was Charles Deas, whose *The Death Struggle*, 1845 (PB 534), and *Prairie Fire*, 1847 (PB 535), are melodramatic incidents expressed in a rhetorical style of considerable academic competence. However, they have none of the final assurance which raises Wimar's and, above all, Bingham's paintings beyond mere topical commentary to the category of important works of art.

Yet Bingham had his technical deficiencies. There is sometimes a certain awkwardness in his proportion, and his figures are not always convincing in articulation or movement; occasionally his rendering of emotion is as naïvely overdrawn as the stage performances on the early showboats must have been. Bingham studied only three months at the Pennsylvania Academy and certainly was not influenced by the painterly and fluid style of Sully or Neagle in Philadelphia. Unlike Mount, he turned his back on this tradition and developed his own manner through a kind of dogged transcription of what he observed. In this he is like Copley, who evolved his own style because he knew only engravings of the pictures in the tradition to which Sully

4–66.   Charles Wimar, *Buffalo Dance*, 1860. Oil on canvas. 24⅜ x 48 inches. (Courtesy of the City Art Museum of St. Louis.)

belonged as a latter-day descendant. Bingham's careful and precise drawings reflect the diligent effort that he substituted for the easy suggestiveness of the Stuart–Sully formula, which by this time was running thin. Many of his more successful studies (in the Mercantile Library, St. Louis) of flatboatmen, farmhands, Negroes, and respected citizens display a sensitive grasp of what Degas later called the essential "gesture" of the figure as a whole, and are the basis for the more convincing persons in his paintings. The solid, well-realized figures in the *Jolly Flatboatmen, No. 2*, 1857 (PB 85), the crowds in *The Verdict of the People* (Illustration 4–68), the characteristic attitude of the fur trader at his oar and the boy leaning on the cargo in the *Fur Traders Descending the Missouri* (Illustration 4–69), or *The County Election*, 1851–1852 (PB 81), all show the exacting draughtsmanship that Bingham expended on the human body. Occasionally his figures even have a grandeur and relaxed grace reminiscent of the Renaissance as, for instance, in the meditative boy in the left foreground of *The Verdict of the People;* or a powerful, almost abstract simplicity as in *Daniel Boone Escorting a Band of Pioneers*, c. 1851 (PB 83). Bingham's composition, both in the surface design and the arrangement of three-dimensional space, is especially successful. A good illustration is the roughly triangular shape of the group of men in *Raftsmen Playing Cards*, 1851 (PB 79; Illustration 4–67). The group of figures is isolated against a background consisting largely of the two triangles formed by land and river. The observer's eye is led toward the group by the diagonal shapes of the raft in perspective, but stopped by the placing of the bench parallel to the picture plane. A symmetry

4–67. George Caleb Bingham, *Raftsmen Playing Cards*, 1851. Oil on canvas. 17 x 21 inches. (Courtesy of Paul Moore, Minneapolis, Minnesota.)

4–68. George Caleb Bingham, *The Verdict of the People*, 1854–1855. Oil on canvas. 46 x 65 inches. (Courtesy of the Boatmen's National Bank, St. Louis.)

which might otherwise be boring is relieved by the angle formed by the stick at the lower right, and by the fact that the actual apex of the composition is a little off-center. This surface pattern is accompanied by an equally subtle three-dimensional organization. The group of boatmen forms a kind of pyramid, yet at the same time a volume is created by the curved figures of the two men at the side and the slightly bent form of the man leaning on the pole.

It has been pointed out that Bingham must have known engravings after the old masters, since the pyramidal grouping in such a picture as the *Raftsmen* is very much like that employed by Raphael or Poussin. Other devices,

such as the enframement of open space by architecture, employment of alternating areas of light and dark, both especially notable in *The Verdict of the People*, 1854–1855 (Illustration 4–68), and the grouping of figures and objects in relation to a series of planes parallel to that of the picture itself, also derive from traditional compositional practices, as does the obvious use of balance and symmetry in general. More subtle, though also traditional, is Bingham's use of deliberate asymmetry, as in *Shooting for the Beef*, 1850 (PB 78), in which the group of men on one side is balanced against open space on the other. Some of these characteristics, notably parallelism to the picture plane, are seen in the

4–69. George Caleb Bingham, *Fur Traders Descending the Missouri*, c. 1845. Oil on canvas. 29 x 36½ inches. (The Metropolitan Museum of Art, New York. Morris K. Jesup Fund, 1933.)

unforgettable *Fur Traders Descending the Missouri*, c. 1845 (PB 76; Illustration 4–69), one of the most impressive compositions in American art, depicting a man, a youth, and a little captive bear drifting down the stream in a dugout canoe, all mirrored in the smooth surface of the water and silhouetted against a backdrop of a mist-shrouded, heavily foliaged island and a barely visible, more distant shore. In this picture the peculiar quality of Bingham's light is seen at its best. The effect is not unlike that in some of Mount's pictures, though the means are very different, the paint being applied more smoothly and thinly. The suggestion of the humid air of the river-bottom country gives to the summer day on the Missouri a timelessness similar to that on Mount's river in *Eel Spearing at Setauket*. This strange and at the same time evocatively familiar light dims the distance in the afternoon heat, yet picks out with mirror-like accuracy objects nearer at hand. It can also be seen in the *Fur Traders* that Bingham is a colorist of no mean ability—if a somewhat unsubtle one—for he uses color as directly as he draws. The intense blue-green and red of the shirts sing out in the midst of the lower-keyed background, and re-echo in the warm glow of the sun-filled humidity and the cool, pale green water. Color is also an important part of the formal organization of Bingham's pictures, as seen in *The Verdict of the People* where the unification of so much visual material is aided by the use of small areas of intense color which reverberate in other larger, less brilliant, ones.

In drawing and composition, Bingham's work has been compared with justice to that of the great traditional artists of the past, but the individual character of his paintings is only enhanced by these qualities, which have been universal in great art since the Renaissance. For it is the intensity of Bingham's involvement in the subject that finally makes his work sincerely original and not eclectic. An interesting manifestation of this intensity can be seen in the quality of the detail which in a reproduction is hardly evident, especially since the all-over design is usually so impressive. The careful observation of the texture and color of a torn shirt or the striation of a rock reflects the artist's involvement in the matter-of-fact. This quality, combined with the splendid generality of his conception of the total object, be it figure or rock, and the all-inclusive clarity of his composition, create a personal style which is not only American but universal.

Though no one artist could really do justice to Emerson's expansive evocation in *The Poet* of the American scene with its "banks and tariffs, the newspaper and the caucuses, Methodism and Unitarianism . . . our log rolling, our stump and our politics, our fisheries, our Negroes and Indians . . . the northern trade, the southern planting, the western clearing, Oregon and Texas," Bingham succeeds in projecting at least one facet of this America, and one of its most interesting.

In a word, Bingham had that "meat and dagger" for which Emerson was searching in the American artist.

The work of John James Audubon is difficult to place in any airtight category. A zoologist interested primarily in the documentation of bird and beast, he was similar in motivation to the artists who recorded the Indian and the frontier, and as such presents another facet of American romantic art inspired by the vastness and variety of North America. Audubon's work is the culmination of that of a number of artist-naturalists before him, his most famous immediate predecessor being Alexander Wilson. [The work of the latter, who flourished in the first decade of the century, would be more famous if it had not been overshadowed by that of his successor. A typical example of Wilson's competent work, engraved by Alexander Lawson, is *Blue Jay, Goldfinch and Oriole*, 1808 (GB 131).] Though Audubon's main purpose was doubtless scientific accuracy, his drawings are first of all works of art, for his subjects are sensitively observed and beautifully recorded in compositions which are masterpieces of decorative design as well.

In spite of study in his youth under Jacques Louis David in Paris, where he must have learned his precise and elegant delineation, some of Audubon's earlier drawings were a little awkward, and his creatures not too well articulated. This was also the case in his early portraits, which have an almost "folk" naïveté, and in his early landscapes, represented by *Natchez, Mississippi*, 1822 (PB 64).

As Audubon's experience grew, his work became surer and subtler, and by the time he had embarked in earnest on his *Birds of America* in the 1820's, he was a master of his genre. Through his own efforts at finding subscribers, the work was published in a series from 1827–1838, with plates engraved in aquatint mostly by Robert Havell, Jr., in London, and hand-colored. In all, there are 435 plates illustrating 1,065 birds ranging in habitat from Labrador to Florida, from the salt marshes of the Atlantic seaboard to the western tributaries of the Mississippi. So many specimens would be monotonous in the hands of a lesser artist, but Audubon enlivens the series with all kinds of variety of movement and

4–70. After John James Audubon, *Noddy Tern* from *Birds of America*, 1827–1838. Colored aquatint by Robert Havell, Jr. 12½ x 19¼ inches.

background. Birds scurry, fight, peck, and cry; owls gaze at us with great unblinking eyes; cranes stalk the cane brake; the Arctic tern dives on some watery prey; the herring gulls swoop and sail around each other, their silhouettes expressing vigorous action and at the same time forming a bold design (GB 91). Sometimes the decorative quality can be very subtle, as in the *American Gold Finch* (GB 86) darting among the pointed-leaved and furry-flowered thistle; or very luxurious as in the marauding *Blue Jay* silhouetted against the forms of a dead branch entwined with a flowering vine. At other times the design may be very bold, as in the svelte black *Noddy Tern* (Illustration 4–70) perching on a dead branch against the background of an austere northern coast of cliffs and pointed mountains, and turning its head gracefully backward. Audubon's feeling that his birds should be represented as nearly life-size as practicable

caused him to choose the format of the elephant folio. This gave his larger specimens an impressive monumentality, as seen in the almost overwhelming *Turkey* or the *Whistling Swan*, and at the same time gave to his smaller birds a most ornamental effect, included as they are in an interesting arrangement of plants and other objects which fill up the space of the page, as in the complex forms of trumpet vine and flowers among which dart the *Ruby-throated Hummingbird* (GB 88).

Though the engravings on the whole do adequate justice to the original watercolor drawings, the latter (most of them in the New-York Historical Society) are a revelation in their exquisite line and delicate color, as in the extremely decorative *Black-Billed Cuckoo* (PB 60), the strongly designed *Gyrfalcon* (PB 61), and the *Purple Grackle* (PB 62) eating corn kernels among the bold shapes of cornstalk and leaf.

Quadrupeds of America was published in 1845. Though the drawings for this were on the whole not so fine as those for the earlier *Birds* (Audubon's two sons, Victor and James W., assisted him in the later book, as well as in some of the last plates in the earlier publication), many of them are equal in quality. Among these are the *American Porcupine,* 1842 (PB 63), and the *Virginia Deer,* sometime between 1838 and 1851 (PB 65).[33]

The Graphic Arts

Print-making during the period between 1825 and the Civil War followed generally the precedents set earlier in the century. The reproduction of portraits and views continued to be the chief occupation of the engraver, though his repertoire was augmented by other subjects, principally ideal and genre. Asher B. Durand's engraving (supplemented with etching) after Vanderlyn's *Ariadne,* 1835 (GB 71), is one of the more sensitive interpretations of a painting, though other examples after Mount (*GB 36), Bingham (GB 65), Krimmel (GB 130A, GB 133), and Woodville (GB 127) testify to the high technical level that prevailed among the more competent craftsmen. Reproductions of paintings (or more frequently of drawings, as in the case of two studies by Mount reproduced in the pages of the *New York Mirror*) were also executed in the more popular and less expensive medium of wood engraving, often interleaved in the pages of magazines, though engraving and aquatint (which had largely replaced mezzotint for the reproduction of tonal passages) were still preferred as more appropriate for the gift books and annuals. Later in the period, lithography, usually associated with the popular print, was employed for the more respectable purpose of reproducing paintings, reaching a degree of considerable tonal refinement in portraiture (*GB 145) and other subjects, including genre (*GB 189B). Large prints such as those after Bingham were sold, raffled, or given as prizes or premiums by the art unions.

In this era there was an increase in the amount of original graphic work, that is, prints engraved or lithographed by the artist who executed the original drawing or painting, or who engraved or etched his conception directly on the plate or drew it on the stone. Among these are several by artists better known as painters. Examples are *The Good Shepherd,* 1849 (GB 54), a colored lithograph by Thomas Cole, who translated the mood of his ideal landscapes into an effective graphic design; or the lithographs (already mentioned) executed after their drawings by the Indian painters Catlin (GB 47, GB 48) and Bodmer (*GB 24). David Gilmour Blythe at the end of the period executed a complicated composition in color lithography, *President Lincoln Writing the Proclamation of Freedom,* 1864 (GB 23). The lithographed portraits by William Henry Brown (GB 32, *GB 33) are essentially only a translation of the old-fashioned silhouette, though charmingly done.

Only one artist who was primarily an original print maker (not a painter or draughtsman trying his hand at prints) is worth mentioning: David Claypoole Johnston, the author of a series of etched genre subjects (gathered together in a group entitled *Scraps*) drawn in a lively caricature style derived from the English artist Cruickshank.

Most of the topographical painters and draughtsmen whose work was executed largely to be made into prints were also graphic artists, sometimes engraving or lithographing their own work as well as that of others. Thus, their production as artists is difficult to isolate from the work of the more exclusively reproductive craftsmen, since much of their original work has been lost and therefore is known principally through prints. These prints, however, when engraved by themselves, can be considered original works of art in the conventional sense, and not mere reproductions. The topographical artists derived their quite conventional treatment from the tradition represented by the Birches and the other English landscapists who came to the United States early in the century; Thomas Thompson's lithograph *The Battery and Harbor, N. Y.,* 1829 (GB 198), is typical. This tradition was strengthened by the arrival of other Englishmen, particularly William Bartlett. [Bartlett's drawings for N. P. Willis' famous *American Scenery* (1839) were the source of hundreds of copies ranging from folk art to professional and giving rise to the attribution of many landscapes to Bartlett.] William J. Bennett is the most typical and the most competent of the Englishmen, both as an original draughtsman and as an engraver, for he exploited all the technical dexterity which had been developed in England to convey the subtle atmospheric effects of the landscape painting of the period. Bennett's views and city-scapes have a brilliance hardly excelled by his own technique in engraving them. His panoramic landscapes have some of the grandeur and varied weather of Turner, as in *West Point from Phillipstown,* a colored aquatint, 1830 (GB 10), and his nineteen views of American cities (also in colored aquatint) executed between 1831 and 1838 are considered the finest of their kind. *Boston from City Point Near Sea Street,* c. 1832 (GB 7), is an excellent example of the latter. These beautifully executed prints are far superior to the relatively amateur lithographed views by John H. Bufford, whose *College of Princeton, N. J.,* c. 1836 (*GB 34), is almost naïve, or to those by George Lehman, whose *Merchants' Exchange,* also a lithograph, 1835 (GB 132), is equally lacking in drawing and perspective. Even Alexander Jackson Davis' lithograph of *Yale College and State House,* c. 1832 (GB 63), is relatively unsophisticated. The drawings of Hugh Reinagle, lithographed by various artists (*GB 144B, *GB 165), are typical of a general level of pedestrian competence, as are views by the landscape painter Thomas Doughty (*GB 98) and others engraved by the Englishman John Hill. Conventional genre-filled views (not unlike Guy's *Tontine Coffee House* in composition) were popular, such as the

aquatints by John Rubens Smith (GB 190) among others (GB 116). *Baltimore and Calvert Streets, Baltimore,* c. 1835 (GB 178), a chromolithograph published by Sachse and Company, is typical of these lively and overbusy prints, while Sachse's later *View of Baltimore City* (Illustration 4–16), more carefully and statically composed, exhibits some of the conscious geometry which, when combined with a subtle luminosity, distinguished the best of the city views, whether engraved, aquatinted, or lithographed. The work of J. F. A. Cole, as exemplified in the colored lithograph *New Bedford, Massachusetts,* c. 1858 (GB 51), is almost as attractive in these respects as some of Fitz Hugh Lane's lithographs after his own paintings, as for instance his *View of Castine, Maine* and *Gloucester, Massachusetts.*

The best and most original artist in the field of the topographical view and the city-scape was J. W. Hill. Trained by his father John Hill, J. W. Hill employed his parent's expert technique to good advantage in reproducing not only his own work, but that of others, which he did as competently as Bennett. But unlike Bennett, who could give an air of style and competence to prints after the crudest drawings, Hill was far more interested in engraving his own views. Though some of Hill's more conventional work is not as fine as the generally high standard of Bennett's as a whole, it is even bolder in atmospheric effects and more dramatic in composition. In Hill's city panoramas and his less pretentious views, however, he is more original than Bennett, and he turns away from the dependence on decorative foliage and subtle atmospheric effects which by the 1840's had become a tiresome formula. Hill's two famous views of New York, *New York, from Brooklyn Heights,* an engraving and colored aquatint engraved by Bennett, 1836 (GB 11), and *New York, from St. Paul's Chapel, Looking Southeast,* engraved by Henry Papprill, 1848 (Illustration 4–71), in the same mixed medium, are magnificent panoramas which reject the more conventional distant view framed in accessories, and concentrate instead on the matter at hand: the geometry of the American city-scape itself.

4–71.   After J. W. Hill, *New York, from St. Paul's Chapel, Looking Southeast,* 1848. Engraving and colored aquatint by Henry Papprill.   36½ x 52⅜ inches. (Courtesy of Prints Division, New York Public Library.)

The first of these prints, when looked at casually, seems full of the usual atmospheric and pictorial devices, executed with great skill, and similar in effect to the best of the originals by Bennett and other Englishmen. But a closer examination of the print shows a sensitivity for the prismatic forms of the American scene, not only in the fairly obvious shapes of the Brooklyn foreground, but also in the distant buildings of Manhattan. This characteristic in Hill's work had already appeared in his four watercolor views of the Erie Canal done from 1830 to 1832, in which the artist minimized the wallpaper-like decorative quality typical of Bennett and his contemporaries, and concentrated instead on the planometric forms of buildings seen in a luminous clarity. *New York, from St. Paul's Chapel,* the best of Hill's city views, is an epitome of the complex architectural view: an arrangement of mathe-matical forms—walls, roofs, streets of all shapes and angles—enlivened with people, traffic, and lettered advertisements. This complicated variety is held together by an authoritative design which leads the eye great distances in several directions and back again in a most rich and satisfying abstract composition.

Hill's later work (such as the *View of Richmond,* 1852, and a series representing smaller American cities, published in the 1850's, some of them in the magazine *Ladies' Repository*) was reproduced by lithography rather than by aquatint, and therefore loses some of its refinement, but the basic precision and clarity are still there. Hill, even when compared with Fitz Hugh Lane in this field, is consistently better, for only the latter's *View of Castine, Maine,* reproduces the precision and luminosity of his paintings. Hill, Bennett, and Lane stand head and shoulders over the majority of the popular depictors of cities, typified by the prolific E. Whitfield, who too easily succumbed to the mannerisms of the English school.

The popular lithographs of the period were less professional on the whole than the usually competent city views, though there were exceptions. Generally speaking, the lithographs published by Currier and Ives approached more the character of folk art, though the basic rules of perspective and anatomy were at least given lip service. Lithography, because it offered greater economy of labor in drawing and printing than the other graphic arts, became a genuinely popular medium, especially after the introduction of color (chromolithography) made it even more attractive.

Currier and Ives, whose boast "printmakers to the American people" was quite justified, supplied a huge market with representations of every kind of subject ranging from the informative to the most sentimental. These lithographs (and those of other publishers) comprise an eloquent record of the far-ranging interests of this mid-century generation on the threshold of modern industrial society, a generation bursting with energy and adventurousness, exploiting the land and its products, enjoying comfort and even luxury, but still motivated by the ethical, religious, and social sentiments of an earlier time.

The opening of the West (GB 150B), steamboat races, and shooting for the beef competed as subject matter with sailors' homecomings and Thanksgivings with grandmother in the country. News events, famous personages, race horses, and side wheelers were recorded. Some of the most exciting and typical subjects involve the depiction of movement, reflecting the dynamism of American life: the building of the Pacific railroad, speeding horse-drawn sleds (*GB 6, *GB 127B), elegant equipages cantering through a park, horse races (*GB 64B), and the contests between the Mississippi steamboats (*GB 151), in which the artists exploit the drama of the huge fires and the spark-filled smoke against the night sky. Prints involving speeding trains (GB 149B, GB 149C) were very popular, and those depicting clipper ships (GB 155), especially Donald McKay's famous *Flying Cloud* (GB 37), *Red Jacket* (GB 154), and *Nightingale* (GB 153), are among the most attractive.

Important as these popular lithographs may be as social documents, and as quaintly decorative as they are to twentieth-century eyes, they are on the whole hardly impressive as works of art. Most of the more naïve prints are technically too overdramatic or sentimental and just a little too academically competent to be genuinely folk art, though some approach the latter in bold decorative design.[34]

Photography

In this period photography made its first appearance among the arts, yet some of the products of these early years are of exceptionally high quality. Portraiture and views, mostly urban, were the principal subjects of the early photographers, since the length of exposure required precluded the recording of action. "Art" photography—elaborately composed photographs in imitation of sentimental or moralizing genre painting—had not yet developed to any significant extent. This is not to say that a dichotomy between respect for the photograph considered as

a direct image of reality and its manipulation by hand work or other adjustment had not already begun in the 1840's. But, at least in this period, the "art" photograph is too absurd or undistinguished to be taken very seriously today in comparison with what has since come to be called "straight" photography.

The first photographic method to be introduced commercially was the invention in France by Louis Jacques Mandé Daguerre of the daguerreotype in 1838–1839. Studios for the taking of daguerreotypes (or their variants, ambrotypes and tintypes) sprang up all over Europe and the United States during the 1840's and 1850's. These early processes permitted only one image, the positive produced on the metal by its exposure to light and subsequent processing. Shortly afterward, the collodion or wet plate, which was a negative permitting the printing of more than one positive, came into use. Though some distinguished photographs were made by all of these processes, the daguerreotype was most adapted to the recording of reality with the greatest precision of detail and range of tone. Among the outstanding daguerreotypes made before the Civil War are those by the Boston firm of Southworth and Hawes, exemplified in their portraits of *John Quincy Adams* (F 65) and *Lemuel Shaw*, Chief Justice of the Massachusetts Supreme Court, 1851 (F 69; Illustration 4–72). Adams, old and frail, is shown sitting in his Quincy house; his refined and intellectual face is sensitively recorded. Shaw, massive and impressive, is portrayed strongly modeled in a shaft of light which dramatizes his powerful head and his bulky figure in its unpressed suit.

Nearly as fine is the work of Mathew B. Brady (later famous as the photographer of the Civil War), who began daguerreotyping in 1854. His portrait of *Justice Richard Montgomery Young* of the United States Supreme Court has the impact of a real presence. Daguerreotypes such as these are completely untouched by the prettifying effects of today's portrait photographer, who all too often perverts the basic truth of the lens into an ideal image. Comparable to the very best work by painters in the brilliant Stuart–Sully tradition or by eccentrics like Hubard and Page, these early photographs are outstanding examples of portraiture, psychologically penetrating and formally satisfying.

There are other portraits which are nearly as fine as those by Brady and Southworth and Hawes, partly because of the photographers' lack of pretension, as in the touching *Woman and Child* by an unknown photographer, c. 1850 (F 2). A daguerreotype of the painter *Asher B. Durand*, also by an anonymous photographer, c. 1850 (F 1), is less arresting, and therefore more

4–72. (A. S.) Southworth and (J. J.) Hawes, *Lemuel Shaw*, 1851. Daguerreotype. (The Metropolitan Museum of Art, New York. Gift of Edward S. Hawes, Alice Mary Hawes, Marion A. Hawes, 1938.)

typical of the usual product of this popular art; the bulk of the earliest photographs (F 5, F 30, F 59) are more interesting as documents than as works of art. Besides portraiture there are a few interesting examples of what might be called genre, the best being by Southworth and Hawes. Not quite as impressive as their portraits, they are nonetheless more than mere documents. Among them are *Classroom*, c. 1850 (F 68), and *Operating Room of the Massachusetts General Hospital, Boston*, c. 1850 (F 66), in which an operation is simulated for the photographers.

After portraiture the most extensive branch of photography in the early decades of the art was landscape or "view" photography. Only a few interesting views surpass the level of technical competence represented by the typical

4–73. Anonymous, *View of San Francisco*, c. 1855. Daguerreotype. (Collection American Antiquarian Society, Worcester, Massachusetts.)

Philadelphia Exchange by W. & F. Langenheim, a calotype, c. 1849 (F 42). Among them is Southworth and Hawes' *Cunard Liner "Niagara" in Dry Dock, Boston*, c. 1850 (F 67). One of the most impressive, however, is a *View of San Francisco*, c. 1855 (Illustration 4–73). The striking composition of this anonymous photograph is quite clearly the result of the careful placing of the camera so as to emphasize the geometry of buildings arranged parallel to the picture plane. At the same time diagonal accents or other devices to lead the observer into the picture, and decorative elements, such as enframing foliage, are studiously avoided. In this unpretentious but skillfully composed record can be observed the basic style of a way of seeing which is characteristic of other representations of the American scene executed in painting and the graphic arts during the 1840's and 1850's, especially in the work of those least influenced by academic conventions, as for instance in the landscapes of Fitz Hugh Lane, George Tirrell, and J. W. Hill.

A series of photographs comprising a panorama of the Cincinnati waterfront in 1848 by the firm of Fortayne and Porter is also worth mentioning for its composition (which is quite similar to Tirrell's *View of Sacramento*). Alexander

Hesler's views of Chicago and Galena, Illinois, taken in the late 1850's are equally arresting. (His portraits might also be noted, especially a portrait of Lincoln in 1860, at the Chicago Historical Society.)

Directness, honesty, contrast of black and white, subtlety of value, and recording of detail make these unpretentious records of persons and places among the most gratifying in the history of the medium of photography.

Sculpture

Academic sculpture of the mid-nineteenth century is not one of the most esthetically rewarding phases in the history of American art. The combination of a neo-classical approach with sentimentality, meretricious realism, mechanical dexterity, and a general lack of broad technical training leaves little to admire in the results. Only a few sculptors escaped the tiresome consequences of this combination, either because they had a little more training or were not seduced by that "paltriness" or "trumpery of the theatre" which Emerson so rightly associated with the sculpture of his time.

Yet we must be careful not to follow the temptation to condemn a whole school merely because the taste of our own era is out of sympathy with its artistic ideals. If Allston can be praised for bringing a broader and more European taste to America (and this by means of some pictures which, it must be confessed, are not among the greatest), surely the introduction of an internationally respected manner of sculpture cannot be discounted, especially since American work in the medium compares well even with that of the European leader of the movement, Bertel Thorvaldsen, and is on the whole better than that of the most famous English exponent of the style, John Gibson.

The discussion of the sculpture of this period could well start with John Frazee and Hezekiah Augur, who began as craftsmen and are therefore transitional from the period in which the art was dominated by men who were primarily ornament and figurehead carvers and sculptors only secondarily. The importance of Frazee as a pioneer is indicated by the naturalism of his portrait renderings, a characteristic which per-

sisted in some of his successors and happily preserved their products from being totally engulfed in the general, smooth vacuity characteristic of the medium as a whole during this period. It is possible that the precedents for this realism were the powerful bronze busts based on life masks of famous Americans by John H. I. Browere, among them the *James Madison, Aged Seventy-Four*, 1825 (SB 36), and the arresting *John Adams, Aged Ninety*, 1824 (SB 35).

Though neo-classical convention required Frazee's merchants and businessmen to be draped in togas, they are otherwise strikingly life-like. This is partly due to the fact that their three-dimensionality is exaggerated and their features almost caricatured, qualities of expressive abstraction which mitigate their literalness. Frazee's *Self Portrait* in bronze, 1829 (SB 116), is simpler and more direct than some of his other work, though his *John Wells*, 1824 (SB 40), is effective. A number of Frazee's busts in the Boston Athenaeum, such as that of *Thomas H. Perkins*, 1834 (SB 39), are equally convincing, in considerable contrast to the greater idealization and even prettiness of the majority of stone visages of the next decades. Two exceptions among these, however, may be noted: Edward Brackett's bust of *Washington Allston*, 1844 (SB 69), and S. V. Clevenger's bust of *Henry Clay*, 1842 (SB 70).

Hezekiah Augur, who began his career as a cabinet maker in New Haven, was not impelled into sculpture by a desire to be more natural, but by the inspiration of classical statuary as represented by a cast of Apollo brought back to New Haven by Samuel F. B. Morse. Augur's most famous works, *Jephthah and His Daughter*,

1828–1832 (SB 42)—two statues complementary to each other—though appearing rather like earlier decorative wood carving to our eyes, must surely have been thought to be classical by their creator, who spent considerable effort on the rendering of the armor and other antique details.

Both Frazee and Augur are more pleasing to modern taste than many of their more sophisticated successors. Both also point to the immediate future of sculpture—Augur with his classicism, and Frazee with that realism which sometimes infuses even the most neo-classical works with at least a certain pale vitality.

This meager and inauspicious beginning hardly prophesied the great torrent of sculpture that inundated the country in the late 1840's and the 1850's. During the first quarter of the century, native American sculptors were considered hardly more than artisans, but by 1856 a critic was able to proclaim that we could rejoice in a Phidias of our own, Thomas Crawford. A great- deal had happened meanwhile as a background to such a claim. *The Greek Slave* (Illustration 4–75) by an American, Hiram Powers, was the sensation of the London Exposition of 1851, and *Cleopatra* (Illustration 4–76) by William Wetmore Story, another American, in the Exposition of 1862, became nearly as famous. The *Greek Slave* made a triumphal tour of two continents and it was generally conceded, certainly in the United States, that the genius of American sculptors led the rest of the world. Florence and Rome were full of American sculptors. Cincinnati alone nurtured six prominent practitioners of the art, and every American city had its quota.

How can this vast increase in the popularity of the art be accounted for? There are several reasons. First, the always present demand for portraiture was met by a medium and style which in this case possessed the virtues both of permanence and of the respectability lent by classical precedent. Second, the art which had so conspicuously graced the republics of antiquity was felt to be the most appropriate one for the modern republic. This sentiment could hardly have been better expressed than by Thomas Crawford when he wrote: "I look to the formation of a pure school of art in our glorious coun-

try. We have surpassed already the republic of Greece in our political institutions, and I see no reason why we should not attempt to approach their excellence in the Fine Arts which as much as anything has secured undying fame to Grecian genius." [35] In Boston, that self-conscious "Athens of the West," steps were taken early to promote the sculptural art, and other cities later became equally active. Casts were imported, exhibitions were held, and promising young carvers were sent on trips to Italy. A third reason for the popularity of sculpture was the demand for sepulchral monuments in the large park-like or garden cemeteries newly instituted to replace the unsanitary churchyards and crypts, as at Mount Auburn in Cambridge, Massachusetts, Laurel Hill in Philadelphia, and Greenwood outside New York.

Before discussing individual sculptors, it might be well to inquire into the ingredients which the work of most of them had in common and which at the same time contribute to their distastefulness today: the obvious lack of understanding of sculptural quality, the sentimentality laced with various degrees of realism, and the smooth surface and mechanical dexterity—bypassing for the moment the quality of neo-classicism which they all shared, and which is the most obvious to account for. The absence of sculptural feeling is due largely to the lack of any training of consequence. Ornamental stone carving for architecture and gravestones was the chief source for the enlisting of talent in the field, but gentleman-amateurs with a taste for the fine arts, makers of effigies, and fashioners of horrendous murder scenes for wax works also supplied the ranks. In any case, hardly a single prominent sculptor of the era had the kind of training which sculptors in former times acquired through apprenticeship to a master.

Closely coupled with lack of a tradition and scarcity of training was the reliance on other works for inspiration, a practice which often came close to being outright plagiarism. One of the reasons for the popularity of Italy as a place for sculptors to work was that the whole peninsula was an inexhaustible mine of figurative motifs and poses. The esthetic of neo-classicism was still strong enough not only to condone such borrowing but to recommend it. If a subject which had not been dealt with by the sculptors of antiquity had to be executed, such as Crawford's American Indian on the Capitol pediment, the sculptor had to do little more than find a classical figure in a lugubrious pose and, in this case, put feathers on its head. Such "borrowings," together with so little experience with the actual model, contributed much to the emptiness of the marble pieces of the period.

The quality which is perhaps least appealing to modern taste in this sculpture is its sentimentality, which, combined with the idealization of neo-classicism, produced so often what Albert Ten Eyck Gardner calls an "expression of adenoidal vacancy which was taken for sublimity." [36] This "sublimity" (a quality also referred to frequently as "dignity") was something the pagan Greeks were supposed not to have possessed, and was believed to be present in modern sculpture by virtue of the sculptors' suggestion of the human soul, something which was only possible after the introduction of Christianity. What was sought, according to Powers, was the "awareness of the heart, rather than of the mind." [37]

The attitude toward the nude is an excellent gauge of the sentimentality of the age. Already somewhat sterilized by the impersonality of the smooth white stone, the nude was, as Henry James says, "so undressed yet so refined." [38] But even so, in this morbidly squeamish age the nude was looked at askance unless garbed with some lofty sentiment, such as the chain which makes the *Greek Slave* an unwilling exhibitionist.

Often combined with idealization was a surface realism which the mid-nineteenth-century artist found hard to resist, even though it was hardly consistent with neo-classic generality. This is illustrated particularly well in the precise treatment of the threads in the garment of Crawford's *Armed Freedom*, though the statue was placed on the very top of the Capitol dome, far from scrutiny. In this connection, Gardner quotes the remark of the Empress Frederick of

Germany that Harriet Hosmer "had a genius for toes." Such inconsistencies as these only added to an esthetic confusion already confounded by simultaneous borrowings from several classical sources.

Another somewhat unattractive quality which these sculptures flaunt is their mechanical smoothness—their "white moonlight," once so admired. This quality was achieved principally by an uncanny skill in doing away with all feeling for the stone on the part of the Italian stone cutters who executed the statues from the sculptors' clay models. But Yankee ingenuity introduced gadgets which made the stone cutters' task even easier. Hiram Powers invented tools that achieved surfaces compared by his contemporaries to those of Praxiteles. Hawthorne, however, was more critical in *The Marble Faun* when he described a piece of marble as being "hand finished by some nameless machine in human shape." [39] No person was considered really cultivated unless his drawing room was graced with an "ideal figure"; consequently the sculptor's assistants were kept busy with mechanical repetitions which were much facilitated by gadgets for more efficient pointing and finishing. One writer described the following scene in the studio of Randolph Rogers in Rome: "I went once to his studio and saw seven Nydias [the blind girl of Pompeii] all in a row, all listening, all groping, and seven marble cutters at work, cutting them out." He added, "It was a gruesome sight." [40] One of the seven, executed in 1859, is now in the Metropolitan Museum (SB 59).

There are, of course, exceptions to any generalizations about this period. An occasional piece by one of the overpraised masters and the entire work of some sculptors were completely different from the spirit of the age.

Among the many sculptors who went to Italy, the most famous in their day, in terms of both commissions and reputation, were Greenough, Powers, Crawford, and Story.

Horatio Greenough was the first of the expatriates, indeed the first American, to study the art of sculpture abroad, and also the first to receive commissions of importance. Of a distinguished Boston family, he was directed toward an interest in art through the influence of Washington Allston, and made his earliest attempts at sculpture by copying casts in the Boston Athenaeum. After graduating from Harvard in 1824 he went to Italy where he remained, except for two years early in his career, until the year before his death. As was so often the case, Greenough's first commissions were busts, but their generality lacks the bold realism and the occasional saving literalness of Powers and Story. But something of the loftiness of idea which infused Allston was present in Greenough at his best; this is seen most effectively in his monumental, if derivative *George Washington,* 1833–1841 (SB 45; Illustration 4–74). There is a good deal to mock in this depiction of the practical American half-naked in a sheet, pointing pointlessly to the sky, and seated in the irrelevant pose of Phidias' Olympian Zeus; it was even ridiculed in its own day. But it is in its way more monumental than anything by Canova or Thorvaldsen. Although Greenough had studied with the latter, he had more native force and sense for the truly glyptic than the Danish sculptor, and he had trained himself as a stone cutter at the Carrara marble quarries. Furthermore, he had studied anatomy with a Boston surgeon. As for the choice of Washington's pose, this was consistent not only with neo-classic taste but with the conception of an apotheosis, not a portrait, of the father of the country. It must be remembered that the *Washington* was meant for the rotunda of the Capitol, where its scale and massiveness would have enhanced the great emptiness which almost demands such a dignified figure. The statue was removed at Greenough's own request (he felt that the light falling on it from above gave it a false and constrained effect), and it was placed in the Capitol grounds from whence it was later removed to the Smithsonian Institution. Instead of being placed under a classic dome and surrounded with ample space where its monumental majesty would be evident, it has been forced into the constricted space of Renwick's medieval apse, and looms ludicrously

4–74. Horatio Greenough, *George Washington,* 1833–1841. Marble. Height: 11 feet, 6 inches. (Courtesy of the Smithsonian Institution, Washington.)

out of the pseudo-religious gloom amid the scientific and ethnological clutter—hardly an environment to bring out its best points.

Greenough's other important work, also commissioned for the Capitol, is *The Rescue,* 1837 (SB 44), which is at least better than the *Columbus* by the Italian Luigi Perisco on the other side of the main stairway. There is not much more to recommend it, however, beyond its convincing anatomy. Completely unorganized as a group composition (Greenough could cope better with the single figure), the woman and child are isolated from the man who is pinioning the arms of an Indian about to attack them. There is also a dog (showing a "singular impartiality," as one critic put it [41]) which is not integrated in the composition in any way.

Thomas Crawford arrived in Italy about a decade later than Greenough. Of humble origin, barely educated, he came to sculpture by the most normal route of rising from an artisan's position. Apprenticed first to a wood carver, and later working with Frazee and his partner in their stone cutting establishment, such a technical background should have equipped Crawford for a more solid accomplishment than Greenough's. But even added training with Thorvaldsen failed to do this. Perhaps Greenough's intellectuality and broader liberal education had something to do with his greater artistic success. Crawford's fame was pressed upon him to satisfy the need for another American sculptor of note besides Greenough. A writer in 1842 prophesied, with something of a challenge in his tone: "He will be the first of *modern* sculptors; now an American may well rival Phidias." [42]

Crawford's equestrian *Washington Monument* on the Capitol grounds at Richmond, Virginia, 1858 (SB 115), is just barely balanced on the brink of a pedestal that is completely inadequate in scale and dimension. At the National Capitol, besides the *Armed Freedom* on the dome, which is both grandiloquently ideal and minutely realistic, Crawford executed the pediment and the bronze doors of the Senate wing. The theme of the pediment, the "Past and Present of America," is appropriate to the poetic vagueness of a neo-classical concept, but some individual figures are treated with anything but generality, such as the realistic wood chopper, who is juxtaposed with an idealized "America" and a Hellenistic nude in the guise of the poor Indian whose feather-covered head is bowed not only with melancholy but seemingly with the weight of the cornice. Such inconsistencies are not helped by a lack of unified design that is incredible in a man who must have been acquainted with similar compositions from the Renaissance and from classical antiquity. Crawford's Senate doors, c. 1850–1866 (SB 57), are

better; at least their narrative can be followed, since they are somewhat organized, though in a very obvious way. There is an advantage in the simplified unity and relative lack of detail of the figures, since there are so many of them. However, compared with bronze doors of the Renaissance and other eras, these by Crawford hardly deserve mention, a comment which can apply equally to Randolph Rogers' doors for the Capitol rotunda, though they are a little less pretentious in what they attempt.

Hiram Powers was perhaps the most famous of the American sculptors who lived in Italy, largely by virtue of the extraordinary success of his *The Greek Slave*, 1843 (SB 48; Illustration 4–75). Born a Vermont farm boy, he moved with his family to Cincinnati, where he began his career as the chief talent behind the wax figures and automata in the Western Museum in that city. The same ingenuity accompanied him in his later trade of sculpture, to which he was led by his wax-work ability to strike off a likeness. On the way to Italy he stopped off at Washington to model President Jackson. This bust, *General Andrew Jackson (1767–1845)* (SB 47), executed later in Florence (he never left Italy after his arrival in 1837), is not only his best, but also among the finest by any sculptor in these years. Realistic and honest, it represents the canny old warrior in a forthright way—even without his false teeth. Powers' busts of other famous Americans are not as honest and direct, and were accompanied by a succession of ideal Persephones, Faiths, and other allegorical or mythical females, all less than pleasing to modern tastes in their alabaster vacuity. *The Greek Slave* struck just the note of titillation consistent with Puritan modesty. Its idealization gave it an almost neuter quality; as Hawthorne (who was discomfited by nudity) said, "It could borrow no merit in chastity, being really without sex." Clergymen banded together to give it a "character" (to use Gardner's term) for publicity purposes during its worldwide exhibition. Perhaps it was the tension between the "real" and the "ideal" which made it so fascinating: the care lavished on the detail of the tasseled mantle cast aside on the tree trunk, and on the little cross

4–75. Hiram Powers, *The Greek Slave*, 1843. Marble. Height: 67 inches. (In the Collection of the Corcoran Gallery of Art, Washington.)

and chain laid on it, was matched by the generality of the marble flesh, finished to the last possible degree by Powers' own inventions. Another important reason for the statue's success was the literary sentiment embodied in the subject—a Christian female prisoner taken by the Turks from a Greek island, stripped and chained

to be sold in a public place—a situation which inspired no less a poet than Elizabeth Barrett Browning to verse.[43]

The success of this statue initiated a succession of female figures which sprang from Powers' "teeming fancy," the *California,* 1858 (SB 46), perhaps being the best. All were influenced by the famous Venus di Medici in Florence, a Roman copy of a lost Praxiteles original, and were ennobled by that emptiness of expression which Powers never wearied of explaining as being so much more spiritual than that of his pagan prototypes.

William Wetmore Story, unlike the "ingenious Yankee mechanics" Crawford and Powers, was a Boston "Brahman" as was Greenough. A successful lawyer, only chance led him to sculpture, for when the community desired a memorial at Mount Auburn to his distinguished father, a Supreme Court justice, it turned to the son, who was known to have some interest in the art. The younger Story naturally went to Italy to prepare himself for the commission. Soon acquiring an apartment in the Palazzo Barbarini in Rome, he stayed there until his death, basking in luxury and early fame, the friend of the great and talented from the pope himself to the Brownings. Playwright, poet, collector, host, he always remained a dilettante in many things, and perhaps most of all in sculpture. Even Story's admirer, Henry James (who wrote an entire book about him), had to confess that he "was not with the last intensity a sculptor. Had he been this, he would not, in all probability, have been also with such intensity so many other things." [44] How much Story's wealth, social position, literary achievement, and renowned general cultivation had to do with his reputation it is hard to say. There is at least no question that he was generally more competent than his predecessors who, James says, were still "wearing the fetters of the academic sylphs and heroes equally without temperament or attitude, pomp or circumstance." [45]   Although Story's fame rests largely on a series of grieving females who appealed strongly to Victorian taste —Cleopatras, Medeas, Libyan Sybils, and weeping Jerusalems—nevertheless they have more dignity than Powers' ambiguous nudes. In fact they almost measure up to James's pomp and circumstance and have rather less than usual of what Emerson called the "paltriness of sculpture." At least "the so interesting statue" of *Cleopatra,* 1869 (Illustration 4–76), as James called it, deeply impressed Hawthorne, who used it as the catalyst for a key situation in *The Marble Faun,* where he describes its "marvelous repose, the repose of despair . . . and yet, such was the creature's latent energy of fierceness, she might spring upon you like a tigress. . . . Her face was a miraculous success." [46] (Our contemporary critic Ten Eyck Gardner feels differently, for he includes *Cleopatra* with Story's other prostrate females when

4-76. William Wetmore Story, *Cleopatra,* 1869. (Replica of the 1858 version.) Marble. Height: 56 inches. (The Metropolitan Museum of Art, New York. Gift of John Taylor Johnston, 1888.)

he says, "Very few of his effigies had sufficient vitality to stand upright—they recline heavily draped against their self-generated cold." [47]) In the long view, perhaps Story's works will be more seriously considered than those of most of his contemporaries. At least they are seriously monumental, if a little ponderously so, and not too sententious in spite of their subjects. They partake of the earnestness of the period, and in their heavy, overdraped quality are consistent with the overstuffed and cluttered but nevertheless impressive interiors of the time; they look well, brooding in the semi-darkness of smoke-stained neo-classical porticos in northern industrial cities.

There were many other "Italian" neo-classical sculptors during this period, whether they lived in Italy, as was more than likely the case, or not. Among them was Randolph Rogers, whose *Nydia* and bronze doors at the Capitol have been noted, and Richard S. Greenough, the younger brother of Horatio. But the most famous was Harriet Hosmer, whose claim to fame is perhaps more dependent on her career as a kind of original Boston "blue-stocking" than as a sculptress. Her feminist leanings attracted curious attention and her individual and lively person won her many famous friends. She led a kind of Henry Jamesian existence in extended visits to English country houses, combining business and pleasure in the process of acquiring commissions. Her "tom-boy" originality, however, was not transferred to her sculpture. She chose to study with the English sculptor John Gibson, the most confirmed neo-classicist of his generation, who had the somewhat dubious advantage of having studied with *both* Canova and Thorvaldsen. In her choice of subject she took into account Victorian taste with a Yankee acumen similar to Story's, whose formula of grief-stricken women she followed with great success, as in her *Beatrice Cenci,* 1854 (SB 64).

The most attractive Italianate sculptor of the later generation, and perhaps superior to any of them, is the relative latecomer William Rinehart. Though his best work was executed in the 1870's, just before his death, it is completely within the spirit of Italian neo-classicism. His nude *Clytie*, 1872 (SB 67), is both warmly felt and sculptural, in comparison with which *The Greek Slave* is like the work of "a conscientious beginner," as Lorado Taft put it. His *Latona and Her Children*, 1874 (SB 65), is one of the few "ideal" pieces which has sculptural unity. In this group, rounded forms curve in and around each other with a somewhat rococo delicacy to create an elegantly graceful whole, and the children and the mother are modeled with some sensitivity. The only conspicuous neo-classic conventions are the smoothness, the idealized features, and the too generalized limbs.

Of the Americans who remained at home or returned from Italy, some were relatively naïve and untrained men whose productions may not be great, but who exemplify considerable inventiveness and Yankee ingenuity. One of the most remarkable was Clark Mills, whose *Andrew Jackson* at Washington, 1853 (SB 71), was the first equestrian statue in the United States, preceding Crawford's *Washington* at Richmond by a few years. The sculptor successfully attempted a lively pose with a rearing horse cleverly balanced on its hind legs, a mechanical achievement of the first order, especially when it is realized that Mills knew no actual sculptural precedent, only engravings. Mills's vigorous handling of the problem is more successful than Crawford's (even though that sculptor was acquainted with the ancient equestrian statue of the Emperor Marcus Aurelius at Rome, and had the benefit of the assistance of the whole Roman confraternity of sculptors and casters). Mills's equestrian *Washington*, at Washington Circle in the capital, is also a competent performance, representing the general in the act of reining in his horse.

Henry Kirke Brown and Thomas Ball were also famous for their equestrian work. Brown's *Washington*, in Union Square, New York, 1853–1856 (SB 72), is a vital and solid statue, without the dexterity of Mills's, but with more monumentality. It is perhaps the most dignified (and the closest to the Marcus Aurelius) among the

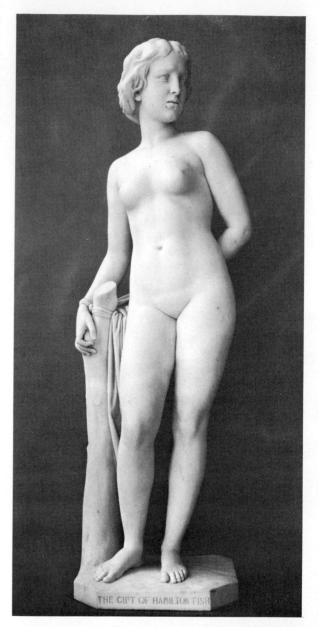

4–77. Erastus Dow Palmer, *The White Captive*, 1859. Marble. Height: 66 inches. (The Metropolitan Museum of Art, New York. Gift of Hamilton Fish, 1894.)

several equestrian representations of the father of the country, though Ball's version in the Public Gardens in Boston is almost as successful in its conscientious realism.

It would be easy to place Erastus Dow Palmer among the most neo-classic group of sculptors because of the superficial resemblance of his popular nudes to those by Powers, Rinehart, and others. Yet his *The White Captive*, 1859 (SB 61; Illustration 4–77) is far more natural and winning than Powers' *Greek Slave*, and not so mechanically smooth. The *Captive* possesses a body with organic articulation, and flesh with some warmth. Although Palmer had no training in academic sculpture in Italy or anywhere else, the artisan tradition served him better than it had Crawford, perhaps because he had more inborn talent. Originally a master builder and designer, a chance contact with cameo carving in his leisure led Palmer eventually to sculpture. As successful as his contemporaries in Florence and Rome, he carried on a kind of sculpture factory in provincial Albany, New York, especially in portrait busts which possess some of the same saving realism with which his nudes are enlivened.

Contemporary taste may well find it difficult to discriminate among Powers' *Slave*, Rinehart's *Clytie*, and Palmer's *Captive*; but there are two sculptors, John Rogers and William Rimmer, who are completely distinguishable from the rest—the first was extremely popular, the second ignored and hardly remembered until our own time. Originally an engineer, John Rogers, though he studied briefly in Italy, was influenced only by the *tour de force* realism of the Italian stone cutters and not at all by their neo-classic idealization. Whatever sculptural virtues he may have lacked, he was always consistent in his realism, which is startling in its descriptive verity. Rogers' various genre groups dealing with everyday subjects, like *Checkers up at the Farm*, 1859, 1877 (SB 79), and with themes taken from the stage, national politics, and the Civil War, like *Wounded to the Rear*, 1864 (SB 78), are hardly great sculpture, but their down-to-earth reporting and their lack of pretension make them a welcome antidote to the work of the neo-classicists. The realistic competence of the "Rogers groups" places them above the naïveté of folk art, yet their appeal was genuinely popular. Sales of plaster copies of Rogers'

groups amounted to 100,000 in number. As popular commentaries on the America of the mid-century and Civil War period, they are to sculpture what Currier and Ives lithographs are to the graphic arts.

No less skillful than Rogers, William Rimmer was more than a mere imitator of nature, for he possessed the plastic qualities associated with great sculpture to a degree shared by none of his American contemporaries. Though only a few of his works survive, these display an anatomical knowledge and expressive power which are emphatic. A jack-of-all-trades, Rimmer was

4–78. William Rimmer, *Falling Gladiator*, c. 1862. Bronze. Height: 62¾ inches. (Courtesy, Museum of Fine Arts, Boston.)

principally a medical doctor and not until 1855 did he commence to work seriously in sculpture. A lecturer on anatomy in Boston, and later director of the School of Design for Women at Cooper Union, New York, his teaching was an important influence among the next generation of artists. Rimmer's knowledge of anatomy and of the materials of stone and bronze was far greater than that of most of his contemporaries, whose work seems flaccid and superficial in comparison. At the same time, Rimmer had considerably more emotional depth, a quality seen already in his early *Despair, Seated Youth,* executed in gypsum, 1830 (*SB 127). Though *The Dying Centaur,* a bronze statuette, 1871 (SB 52), and *Falling Gladiator,* a bronze made in 1900 from an original plaster of about 1862 (SB 50; Illustration 4–78), are classical in subject matter, their strength and expressiveness exceed any of the works by contemporary Italianate American sculptors. Rimmer's *Fighting Lions,* another bronze, cast in 1907 from an original plaster of about 1871 (SB 51), has a vigor and violence comparable to the work of the greatest of the sculptors of animals during this era, the Frenchman Antoine Louis Bayre. The granite *Alexander Hamilton Monument,*

on Commonwealth Avenue, Boston (SB 126), is very different from Rimmer's other works in the static dignity required of the subject, but it shows an appreciation for the character of his medium, a quality completely ignored in the mechanically refined stone surfaces of his contemporaries.

It may seem that too much space has been given to the generally unrewarding subject of the sculpture of this period, but as an artistic and social phenomenon this phase of American art history has some significance. The hold which neo-classicism had over American sculpture was so strong that it compelled even Greenough (whose pregnant theories on form and function are among the most important esthetic ideas of the nineteenth century) to adhere to its principles in his own creative work. Likewise, the fascination with the old world, which seduced so many sculptors of the school to live abroad (and convinced William Wetmore Story that Allston was wasting his genius in the cultural desert of New England), was the first conspicuous manifestation of an attitude which had grave consequences for American art and artists, many of whom became expatriates.

Folk Art

It has been pointed out earlier that it is somewhat difficult to divide academic from folk art in this period, since the artist and artisan were still often closely related. Part of the charm of a painter like Earl, for instance, lies in his combination of a somewhat naïve (or provincial) sense of pattern and line with an otherwise sophisticated manner. But during the second quarter of the nineteenth century, the tradition and techniques of academic painting permeated the country so generally that it was only the very naïve or provincial artisan who was unaware of them. A Frothingham or a Neagle turned from coach painting to depict visages, not in a still linear flat and decorative way, but

in the manner of Gilbert Stuart. Some, like Erastus Field, remained in the old artisan tradition, unaware of or unmoved by the other. But it was impossible for this situation to persist for long; the growth of technology and communications made both the native folk art tradition and that of isolated enclaves (like the Pennsylvania "Dutch") continuously less able to withstand the realism and sophistication of the rest of the country's art. Furthermore, the "popular" aspect of folk art, that is, its fulfillment of certain artistic needs among large groups, was undermined by the appearance of photography, inexpensive lithographs, multiplied iron castings, and other products of the machine, thus making obsolete the work of the popular painters of portraits and landscapes and of the carvers in wood and metal. For these reasons, the period in which folk art flourished was from about 1825 into the 1850's.

It is important to bear in mind the distinction, made in the earlier discussion of folk art, between the amateur and the professional. Most of the best folk artists were professionals. Though the genteel "cut-outs" and pastels by ladies and young girls sometimes resulted in something of interest [as in the typical *Basket of Fruit*, watercolor on velvet, 1840 (PB 5)], the products of the professional itinerant portraitist or wall painter and of the figurehead or shop sign carver are usually more important. Both amateurs and professionals were naïve and similar in style, but they differed in skill. Within the limits of their tradition, whether it was sign painting, tin smithery, or wood carving, the professionals were highly trained and sophisticated. For these traditions were no less exacting than academic ones; they were just different.

Unlike folk painting, much wood carving and metal cutting was done without competition from professional academic work. The weather vane (until the invention of metal castings) and the billethead were not lesser, cheaper, or more naïve "fine" art. They fulfilled a utilitarian and artistic need that was not met better or differently elsewhere.

It is unfair to judge folk art as unskilled imitation of fine art, because at its best and most typical it was not. The folk artist was not necessarily any less an artist than his academic counterpart; his taste had simply not been affected by the main artistic currents of his time. The results of his efforts are often without distinction, as might be expected of uneducated persons with no acquaintance with the standards of the fine arts. But frequently the naïve eye sees more directly and intuitively than the academically trained one, and the result is often a more effective expression. Even the less interesting folk artists had an esthetic advantage over their more conventional contemporaries in that they possessed the craftsman's feeling for his medium and his tools, and a sense of the ap-

propriate use of each wherein its limitations are respected and its possibilities exploited. Almost any passable figurehead is more satisfactory in this respect than a piece of neo-classic sculpture which shows little sensitivity to either medium or tool. In folk art there is also an interplay between the treatment of the material and a concern for design, rhythm, pattern, and other abstract qualities which are hampered by a primarily realistic point of view. These two factors —the realization of the importance of the medium and the persistence of an abstract tradition—comprise the secret of the charm of most folk art; for even its less impressive examples generally have balance, organization, and some sense of exploitation of material which the conventionally more competent "fine" art of the period often lacks.

A distinction of quality should always be made between folk art which is merely quaint and curious and that which has real artistic merit. A sentimental or antiquarian delight in any artistic object from the American past is worthwhile from the point of view of social history, but it should not influence critical judgment. To consider every theorem-produced basket of fruit by some schoolgirl or every formula portrait as worthy of being called a work of art simply because it is not academic is doing a disservice to the rising appreciation for folk art of real merit. It is unfair to pass judgment on folk art in terms of academic art, but by the same token, when folk art deliberately sets out to imitate academic art we are forced to judge it in the latter's terms. For instance, only a misguided fascination with the quaint would permit a much admired primitive picture like Edward Hicks's *Penn's Treaty* to be judged as a work of art in the same terms as its prototype by West, which is a very competent performance by the President of the Royal Academy in the tradition of the best academic art—even if it is pedestrian and dull and not nearly so much fun as Hicks's casual version of it. To condone Hicks's treatment of the subject is like admiring a misquotation, or setting up a parody of some great piece of writing as being better than the original. But when Hicks executed something from his own observation or memory, as in his *Residence of David Twining, 1787* (Illustration 4–82), or rearranged motifs from several sources in his inimitable way, as in his several *Peaceable Kingdoms* (PB 21), the result is individual and esthetically convincing. When works of folk art have this quality, they are not only sociological documents but intrinsically works of art.

In a field in which there are so many hundreds of examples—folk art is, after all, also popular art—it is perhaps better to concentrate on examples which are readily available in public collections. This is not only more convenient, but in doing so we benefit from the sum of professional judgment on folk art, which only began to be collected as recently as thirty-five or forty years ago, when qualities of design as opposed to mere realism became sufficiently accepted to be extended backward in a re-evaluation of our artistic past.

Painting

Until the invention of the daguerreotype put the effigist out of business, portraiture was the most popular form of folk art. It is therefore a field of enormous dimensions, made more complex by its degree of relationship to past (both folk and academic) and to contemporaneous production.

The old limner conventions died hard. Erastus Salisbury Field of western Massachusetts can be taken as an example of an artist who tried to break away from a local tradition and become more sophisticated, but who only partially succeeded. In a series of excellent portraits such as his *Portrait of Mrs. Joseph Moore (née Almira Gallond)*, c. 1840 (PB 700), he carried on the Connecticut valley style of linear accent and flat pattern even after he had taken pains to become more up-to-date by spending three months in New York looking over Samuel Morse's shoulder as he painted the *Lafayette*. Yet nothing in Field's pictures is very different from those of his provincial prototypes except a greater freshness of color. Field's group portrait of *Joseph Moore and His Family*, c. 1840 (*PB 694, *PB 695; Illustration 4–79), can be

taken as an excellent example of his work and, when compared with the contemporaneous Darby or Hollingsworth group portraits (Illustrations 4–46 and 4–47), illustrates well the basic differences between folk and academic portraiture.

A comparison of Field's *Girl Holding Rattle*, c. 1835 (*PB 17), with two similar subjects, one by an anonymous artist, *Girl in Garden*, c. 1840 (*PB 11A), and the other by Isaac Augustus Wetherby, *Mary Eliza Jenkins*, 1843 (PB 37), underscores the persistence in Field's work of characteristics of the Connecticut valley school, still not too distinguishable from the academic art of the first quarter of the century, and, in comparison with Hollingsworth or Neagle, definitely more backward-looking. *Girl in Garden*, with its flat pattern and consequent decorative charm, is more naïve than Field's *Girl Holding Rattle*, while *Mary Eliza Jenkins*, though still strong in silhouette and conspicuously patterned, is very rounded indeed, an obvious emulation of academic models. The result is far less stylish than in Field's painting because it is a compromise, or rather an unresolved conflict between an inherent older folk tradition and a desire to be more realistically convincing. The same conflict, which was the predicament of many folk portraitists, is apparent in the *Portrait of Jasper Raymond Rand*, c. 1845 (PB 10), by Joseph Whiting Stock. Stock, whose work has been identified from among the vast number of still anonymous folk artists (he executed 900 pictures between 1832 and 1846), was a contemporary of Field and worked in the same area, western Massachusetts.

A more satisfactory compromise from the esthetic point of view (at least their pictures are more attractive to present-day taste) was made by other portraitists who managed to introduce enough convincing realism in their modeling to suit their patrons, yet retained the linear charm and sense of pattern of the limner tradition. Examples are the bust *Portrait of a Young Lady*, c. 1830 (PB 8), by an anonymous portraitist; a full-length figure, *Miss Tweedy of Brooklyn*, also done by an anonymous artist in the second quarter of the nineteenth century

4–79. Erastus Salisbury Field, *Joseph Moore and His Family*, c. 1840. Oil on canvas. 82¾ x 93⅜ inches. (Courtesy, Museum of Fine Arts, Boston. M. and M. Karolik Collection.)

(*PB 7); and especially the charming portrait of *Woman With Sewing Box*, c. 1830 (Illustration 4–80), sometimes attributed to Erastus Salisbury Field, which retains both the clarity and the strong design of the Connecticut school.

Among the most attractive of the known painters of the group are Ammi Phillips (some of whose work has been attributed to the Kent limner), and I. J. H. Bradley, whose work appears in several well-known private collec-

tions of folk art. Notable for the care with which he painted accessories like flowers, plants, and the musical instruments which appear in several of his portraits, Bradley's work is also distinguished for the pattern and design common to most folk art, and for an unusual intensity of facial expression, which is often arresting. One of his best known works is *The Cellist*, 1832 (PB 12), in which the shapes of the cello, piano, and sheet music, and the black-and-white contrast of the performer's dress suit and lively silhouette are combined to make up one of the most engaging pictures of its type—naïve, yet appealing for its directness and its very lack of easy painterly flair.

The majority of folk portraits came from the newly opened West; a few, from the rural regions of New England: Maine, western Massachusetts, the Connecticut valley, and Nantucket. J. S. Hathaway and William Swain in Nantucket, and R. B. Crafft in Indiana may be taken as typical. Such artists carried on the limner tradition, but more naïvely, often being unable to draw, for instance, the hand. Their pictures are a little too bold in pattern, awkward in modeling, and obvious in their attempt to imitate academic composition. Yet often, by chance or instinct, or because their effects did not come as easily as to the trained artist, these portraitists were able to grasp a psychological intensity unknown in the work of others. Dickens, with some ridicule and yet with considerable insight, describes in his *American Notes* a pair of such pictures in the front parlor of a house in Belleville, Illinois: "Both looking as bold as lions and staring out of the canvas with an intensity that would be cheap at any price."

There were other popular artists, even less academically skillful, who worked by formula, thus achieving cheaper though still satisfactory likenesses. The most common of these prepared their canvases with conventionalized figures as a preliminary to adding the individual heads. This procedure was a convenient device for the itinerant artists, of whom there were many plying their trade. Naturally there is considerable variation in quality among such pictures, but the best are marked by a continuation of the flat, linear treatment of the figure. Interesting variants of this general type are drawings and watercolors of faces and figures in silhouette, deriving from the more academic silhouettes done earlier in the century by the French emigré C. B. J. Fevret de Saint Memin, typified in his *Portrait of Thomas Jefferson*, c. 1804 (GB 179), and by the Englishman Dr. James Sharples. Among the most attractive of these are the double portraits of couples, sometimes with one

4–80.   *Woman With Sewing Box (Miss Appleton of Ipswich, Massachusetts?),* c. 1830. Oil on canvas. 51⅝ x 42½ inches. (Abby Aldrich Rockefeller Folk Art Collection, Williamsburg, Virginia.)

or more children added, by Joseph Davis of New Hampshire, who worked also in western Massachusetts. His *James and Sarah Tuttle,* 1836 (PB 14), is typical of his compositions. The patterned floor, textured furniture, and abstract treatment of accessories and figures are basic elements in all his pictures, upon which he makes slight variations of feature and characterization. A more sophisticated version of Mrs. Pinney's similar formulations of earlier in the century, Davis' work is closely related, like hers, to the decorative tradition of the time as seen in carpets, painted floor-cloths, and wall paintings.

To conclude this necessarily cursory survey of an enormous field, a brief outline of the life and work of William Matthew Prior, a typical folk or popular portraitist whose prolific work has been somewhat documented, may shed light on the subject as a whole. Prior's life can be traced from Bath and Portland, Maine, to Boston, where he settled in 1847. From there he journeyed as far as Baltimore, but worked mostly in the Fall River–New Bedford region in Massachusetts, traveling at first by wagon and later by railroad. Prior had more than one manner, the choice of which was controlled by the price. One of these—the most popular—he described thus in an advertisement: "Persons wishing for a flat picture can have a likeness without shade or shadow at one quarter price." [48] Prior's pictures of this kind show an admirable economy of means, a very sophisticated version of the line and pattern traditions of the earlier limners. But Prior could also paint in a manner not uninfluenced by Gilbert Stuart (he named his

4–81. William Matthew Prior, *Mrs. Nancy Lawson*, 1843. Oil on canvas. 30 x 27 inches. (Courtesy Shelburne Museum, Shelburne, Vermont.)

eldest son after him, as a token of admiration). He often combined the two styles, using a quite sophisticated version of the limner tradition of symmetrical arrangement, conventional poses, and flair for pattern, while at the same time employing the broadly painted Stuart–Sully tradition, but with none of its facile mannerisms. A typical picture is his portrait of the wife of a Negro minister, *Mrs. Nancy Lawson*, 1843 (Illustration 4–81).

The professional folk artist, as opposed to the amateur, was principally concerned with portraiture. Landscape, still life, genre, and ideal subjects were more often done by the amateur, though a few men like Prior did dabble in landscape as well. Edward Hicks essayed nearly all of these types. Called "the most distinguished popular artist of the early nineteenth century" [49] in an exhibition of American art in Paris, he is undoubtedly the most conspicuous of American folk artists. Besides being a painter he was a prominent Quaker throughout his life, assisting his cousin Elias Hicks in the latter's division of the Hicksite from the Orthodox Friends. Except in moments of enthusiasm, his opinion of painting was not high, as would befit a Quaker. He wrote: "It appears clearly to me to be one of those trifling insignificant arts which has never been of any substantial advantage to mankind." [50] He was probably referring to the fine arts and not to the useful ones, for Hicks was mainly a carriage painter, though he also painted wagons, street signs, "winser" chairs and settees, fireboards, chimney boards, milk buckets, clock faces, and "cyphers on gigs."

Hicks's best paintings are those in which he has been moved profoundly by some scene or memory of actuality, as in his few unpretentious Bucks County (Pennsylvania) landscapes. The best of these is *Residence of David Twining, 1787*, c. 1845–1848 (PB 20; Illustration 4–82), a picture in which accurate notation of fact, clean-cut edges, linear refinement, and geometric neatness seem indigenous. Such a picture will stand up with the best in American primitive art. But the potpourri of derived motifs and of figures in Hicks's other pictures

4–82. Edward Hicks, *Residence of David Twining, 1787,* c. 1845–1848. Oil on canvas. 27 x 32 inches. (Abby Aldrich Rockefeller Folk Art Collection, Williamsburg, Virginia.)

—*Penn's Treaty* (after West), *The Declaration of Independence* (after Trumbull), the *Landing of Columbus* (after Chapman), and even the various versions of his famous *The Peaceable Kingdom* (PB 21)—can hardly have more than a kind of engaging naïveté. Some of Hicks's artistic prominence is undoubtedly due to his fame as a person, a fact which preserved knowledge of the authorship of his pictures while the work of others equally good or better has been neglected or remains still shrouded in anonymity.

The majority of folk landscapes are more or less faithful copies of engravings (often from magazines or gift book annuals) after well-known landscape painters. The relative merit of these efforts lies in the artists' largely unconscious ability to retain a "folk" or popular facility for seeing things conceptually and in large rhythms and patterns—that is, in a way not influenced by the professional artists' "correct" way of seeing, with its logical perspective. The sometimes fortuitous results vary. One of the most delightful examples is an anonymous painting, *Meditation by the Sea*, 1850–1860 (PB 504; Illustration 4–83), obviously inspired by Kensett's *Coast Scene with Figures* (Illustration 4–51) or an engraving from it or from Heade's *Approaching Storm: Beach Near Newport* (Illustration 4–58), to which it is actually closer in mood. The absurd bearded figure standing in a Napoleonic attitude before a conventionalized sea is a little ridiculous, but the spaciousness and the meticulous treatment bring to mind Salvador Dali's dream-like seascapes, though this picture has the virtue of innocence and lacks the somewhat meretricious deliberateness of the Spanish pseudo-surrealist.

Erastus Salisbury Field's *Garden of Eden*, 1860's (PB 18), is a potpourri of motifs from the Hudson River school and British sources (known through engravings) put together with a naïve charm analogous to that of Hicks in similar pictures, but more knowing technically in its amateur perspective. Even more unsophisticated is L. Whitney's *American Landscape* (PB 38), which is typical of many similar paintings wherein pattern and design are not restrained by the necessities of correct perspective or by logical relationships of position and scale.

The topographical view and city-scape were equally adaptable to popular or folk treatment. In such paintings as *A Street in Brooklyn*, c. 1840–1860 (*PB 9), it is not surprising to see an exaggeration of a native tendency to flat planes, linear emphasis, and precise detail, traits

4–83. Anonymous, *Meditation by the Sea*, 1850–1860. Oil on canvas. 13½ x 19½ inches. (Courtesy, Museum of Fine Arts, Boston. M. and M. Karolik Collection.)

4–84.   J. D. Bunting, *Darby, Pennsylvania, After the Burning of Lord's Mill,* 1840–1850. Oil on canvas. 42 x 51¼ inches. (Courtesy, Museum of Fine Arts, Boston. M. and M. Karolik Collection.)

which are more restrained in the academic work of its kind by representational conventions. An equal emphasis on the geometric is seen in many of the more naïve panoramic views, done in emulation of the correctly drawn lithographic bird's-eye views of towns and cities so prevalent from the 1840's onward. Among these are some by Joseph H. Hidley (wood carver, portrait painter, and taxidermist), whose lithographed *View, Poestinkill, N. Y.,* c. 1860–1870 (CPB 56), demonstrates an eye for detail and form which gives it singular style. Of the pictures that show

the native qualities of design in the flat linear tradition, perhaps a large canvas by J. D. Bunting, postmaster of Darby, Pennsylvania, entitled *Darby, Pennsylvania, After the Burning of Lord's Mill,* 1840–1850 (PB 517; Illustration 4–84) is the most impressive. In spite of the inadequacies of perspective and scale in this picture (seen, for instance, in the relation of the figures to the buildings), the logic of the design as a whole is convincing in the forceful consistency of its style, so rectilinear and plano-metric. In such a picture as this, and in Hicks's

Residence of David Twining, can be seen a resemblance not only to some contemporaneous academic work [such as Mount's *Banjo Player* (Illustration 4–63), with its concern for geometric pattern], but also, within the broadest stylistic reference, to contemporaneous vernacular architecture.

Genre scenes are fewer and more variable than portrait and landscape. Typical of one kind is the amusing *The Quilting Party* (PB 2) by an anonymous artist, filled with figures and incident narrated with a liveliness not restricted by the requirements of correct anatomy and perspective. Another kind of genre, which could be described as portraits of interiors with figures, seems exclusively a folk art phenomenon and by its nature demonstrates, as do the amateur city-scapes, a natural feeling for the geometric and precise. The tradition began earlier in the century, as seen in the *Portrait of Elizabeth Fenimore Cooper,* by "Mr. Freeman," 1816 (PB 4), representing the old lady seated isolated in the middle of the living room of her mansion. A particularly attractive example is Joseph Warren Leavitt's *House of Moses Morse, Loudon, N. H.,* c. 1825 (°PB 22; Illustration 4–85). The tradition persisted well into the later

4–85. Joseph Warren Leavitt, *House of Moses Morse, Loudon, N. H.,* c. 1825. Oil on canvas. 7 x 9 inches. (Collection of Nina Fletcher Little, Brookline, Massachusetts.)

decades of the century, at least in the work of Ella Emory, who represented the interior of the Peter Cushing House, Hingham, Massachusetts, in paintings done around 1878 (°PB 15, PB 15A).

There is a whole category of pictures which are chiefly landscapes but wherein the figures and either "ideal" or topical commentary are more important than the recording of place. Most of them are anonymous, uncraftsmanlike, and probably the work of lady-amateurs of poetic sensibility, expressing their loneliness or pining in the wilderness for a more metropolitan life. Many such pictures have the usual decorative charm associated with better folk art, and a kind of lyricism made up of a pastiche of conventional romantic bits and pieces, much like the poetry of Edgar Allan Poe. The well-known *Runaway Horse,* 1840 (Whitney Museum, New York), is typical in its evocation of mood in the dream-like near-moonlight which illuminates a bridge, a group of people sojourning in boats near the shore, and sailboats in the distance, as well as decorative trees enframing the scene, and a wonderful black horse (taken from the weather vanes of the period) being chased by a coach dog. Currier and Ives lithographs and other popular prints were often sources of such motifs. More realistic pictures depicting buffalo hunts, speeding trains, and racing steamboats were common; their excitement was projected by an exaggeration of the more correctly realistic action depicted in the prints from which they derived.

Sculpture

It is a relief to turn from what Henry James called "the white marmorial flock" of the academic sculpture of this period to its less pretentious counterpart among the folk arts. Though much of it is very close to craft work, which is not the subject of this book, such sculpture as weather vanes and decorative roosters is of justified interest because it is today often more esthetically satisfying than the bulk of the marble pieces which were formerly more artistically acceptable. A vigorously decorated rooster is a far happier denizen of a museum at present than a Persephone that has long since been relegated to the corridors leading to the institution's rest rooms.

The bulk of this carving and metal work was not in competition with conventionally superior performance, as was folk painting, and could therefore develop in its own way and within the framework of its own standards. This is seen most clearly in weather vanes and other domestic decorative carving. A few carved roosters are still greeting the dawn high on their original perches (what one sees mostly nowadays are the mass-produced ones which began to be manufactured in the 1840's), but the best are in collections; their vigorous contours, some in metal, some in wood, are exemplified by the quite primitive but decorative wooden *Cockerel*, c. 1830 (*SB 101B), or the later *Rooster*, c. 1850 (SB 18), of cast and sheet iron.

Free-standing wooden roosters (not weather vanes) and eagles, the popular national symbol, exist in quantity. At the Kittery Point Navy Yard in Maine, opposite Portsmouth, New Hampshire, in the Civil War era, a carver by the name of Bellamy executed large, elegant eagles for figureheads, and smaller, more graceful ones for billetheads and public buildings. Many may now be seen in public collections. Two fine examples (one found in Portsmouth itself) at the Shelburne Museum, Shelburne, Vermont, if not actually by Bellamy, reflect his style (SB 13, SB 206). There is a Bellamy eagle in the Rockefeller Folk Art Collection at Williamsburg, which also possesses perhaps the finest carved bird of American provenance in any collection, an *Eagle* done in about 1830, clutching a ball in its talons, screaming, and about to flap its wings (Illustration 4–86). It is supposed to have been the sign of the Eagle Tavern in Pawtucket, Rhode Island. Each feather, though inevitably somewhat conventionalized and repetitive, is carved in individual high relief and in a different dimension. Its carver obviously possessed feeling for wood and for his chisel and other tools. Some beautifully simplified duck decoys, masterful reductions to basic form, can also be seen at Williamsburg, and at the New York State Historical Association at Cooperstown, where a *Canada Goose* (SB 102) is among the

4–86. Anonymous, *Eagle,* from Pawtucket, Rhode Island (?), c. 1830. Wood. Height: 56 inches. (Abby Aldrich Rockefeller Folk Art Collection, Williamsburg, Virginia.)

best. The Rockefeller Collection is not only rich in the field of carvings, but also in that of cut metal. Of the latter there is an especially beautiful coiled *Snake* in cut iron, c. 1830 (*SB 101A), with a fine darting tongue and a hole for an intent serpent's eye. Fine metal weather vanes of this kind are matched by wooden ones of all sorts, and are similar to a splendid sheet iron *Pheasant* (SB 9), a trade sign done early in the century. Other weather vanes such as a wooden *Sea Serpent* and a *Bull* (SB 104, SB 105) are indicative of the wide range of the carvers' abilities from relative naturalism to fantasy. A carved *Whale* in silhouette (Illustration 4–87), still in

4–87. Anonymous, *Whale*, from barn of farm at Little Compton, Rhode Island. Wood. Length: c. 36 inches. (Index of American Design, National Gallery of Art, Washington.)

place on the shed of a salt-water farm at Little Compton, Rhode Island, shows at their best the rhythmic qualities and the feeling for material found in this unpretentious and instinctively decorative art.

Ship carving comprises the most impressive sculpture of the period. Relatively few figureheads have found their way to public or private collections, yet during the clipper-ship era an incredible number of figureheads, stern pieces, and other decorative carvings were produced. Nearly all were executed in New England, and, except for Newburyport and Boston, most of it was done Down East, for in the 1840's and 1850's Maine built more than half the ships, barks, and brigs produced in the whole country. While Maine-born academic sculptors were busy in Italy executing their sentimental neo-classicisms [Paul Ackers' *Dead Pearl Diver* (Sweatt Memorial Museum, Portland, Maine) is typical], their stay-at-home contemporaries were turning out a spate of ship carving which possessed better basic design and certainly more feeling for the medium than existed in all the American studios in Rome and Florence. But of the reported one thousand figures by Colonel Charles A. L. Sampson's firm in Bath only four are now known; of the five hundred by William Southworth of Bath and Newcastle, apparently not one remains. The work of Harvey Counce of Thomaston, one of the most productive and reputable carvers Down East, is remembered by a lone stern piece which now graces a melancholy

and deserted sail loft in Thomaston. Thomas Seavey, the best-known carver of the then flourishing port of Bangor, is known today only by his trade sign and one figurehead.

Figureheads exhibited today at such museums as the Mariners' Museum, Newport News, Virginia, the Old Dartmouth Whaling Society, New Bedford, Massachusetts, the Marine Historical Association, Mystic, Connecticut, the Rockefeller Folk Art Collection, Williamsburg, the New York Historical Association at Cooperstown, the Shelburne Museum, Shelburne, Vermont, the Boston Museum, and the Addison Gallery at Andover, Massachusetts, are of course variable in quality, but all are characterized by a vigor of design and an expert handling of the medium which make them esthetically rewarding objects. In general it may be said that realism is more prominent in them than classical emulation, but this realism is tempered by the soft pine from which most of the figures were cut. The hardwood of the English and the Continental figureheads lent itself to more meticulousness and at the same time less ease in the handling of large surfaces and planes. Pine in the hands of American carvers flowed with an easier grace and resulted in a more effective sense of the whole.

The *Classical Figure,* c. 1830 (SB 202), is an early, delicately carved example, as is the more elaborate *Woman in Yellow,* c. 1835 (SB 215). The *Lady With a Scarf,* c. 1850 (Illustration 4–88), a figurehead-like piece which was the shop sign of Isaac Fowle, one of the most prominent successors of the Skillins, can be taken as representative of the more active figureheads. The sweep of the heavy Victorian garments, the direct marks of the chisel, the solidity in the figure, and the evidence of a stiff wind make this one of the best examples of the period. The broader treatment of the figurehead *Twin Girls,* c. 1860 (Marine Historical Association, Mystic, Connecticut), indicates the growing trend toward more simplified forms. But these girls are stolid and static when compared with the windblown *Lady With a Scarf* or with the figureheads (in private collections) carved by Colonel Charles Sampson as late as the mid-1870's for the *Belle of Bath* and the *Western Belle,* famous

4–88. Isaac Fowle, *Lady With a Scarf,* figurehead (trade sign), c. 1850. Original in Bostonian Society, Old State House, Boston, Massachusetts. Wood. Height: 74 inches. Watercolor rendering by Elizabeth Moutal. (Index of American Design, National Gallery of Art, Washington.)

from Portland, Maine, to Portland, Oregon. Both lean forward precariously: the long bowsprit of the clipper ship allowed no pedestal for more static forms, as did the earlier vessels. In considerable contrast to these typical contemporaneously garbed figures is a rare classical figure by Thomas Seavey made for the bark *Minerva,* c. 1850 (Illustration 4–89). Comparison with the marble goddesses of the "Italian" Yankee sculptors is inevitable. A certain similar smoothness does emerge in both but the *Minerva* has a feeling for the wood, which has now been enhanced by weathering that has removed the paint and revealed the grain so nicely exploited by the carver.

Male figures were often utilized as figureheads and a variety of Indians, sailors, and statesmen have survived. A *Sailor* found somewhere in Maine and now in the Sewall Collection in Bath, Maine, is one of the simplest and most direct. It is considerably more successful than the *Andrew Jackson* carved by Laban S. Beecher of Boston for the frigate *Constitution* in 1834 (SB 14), in which the attempt at complex anatomy and drapery is less pleasing than the broader, more effective handling in the *Lady With a Scarf* and others.

Some figureheads were made in the form of busts to be placed on the prows of the earlier ships, and occasionally on later ones, though the sweeping forms of the *Belles* from Bath exploited the decorative possibilities of the great clipper bow to greater purpose. One of the finest figureheads in point of refinement is the magnificent *Commodore Perry* (see Illustration 3–48). More typical, and indeed more appropriately simplified for its place high up on the ship is the turbaned Oriental for the ship *Asia* (*SB 144), which is modeled in broad planes and with effective conventionalizations.

There was other work connected with maritime carving which was not necessarily sea-going. Among the most delightful pieces of early nineteenth-century folk sculpture is the chunky little figure of a *Navigator* (SB 10) holding a huge sextant, a piece of wood carving reduced to the essential shapes of its subject. Used as a shop sign for a ships' chandlery, it is probably older than the more forceful and exaggerated *Mariner With Sextant,* 1830–1840 (SB 211), another shop sign.

When figurehead carving began to taper off in the late 1850's and early 1860's, many carvers turned to Indians and other subjects appropriate for tobacco shops. An exceptionally fine early example representing an *Indian Trapper* (Rocke-

4–89. Thomas Seavey, *Minerva,* figurehead (trade sign), c. 1850. Wood. Height: 57 inches. (Bangor Historical Society, Bangor, Maine.)

feller Folk Art Collection, Williamsburg), is, in all probability, by a figurehead carver, for the flowing contours, the bold and practiced strokes, and the traces of flat areas of rich color suggest the ship carvers' art. An even more arresting carving is that of an *Indian Squaw* (SB 11A), said to have been made by an African slave. This extraordinary figure seems to be some kind of presence, not a mere piece of carved wood, and is more suggestive of primitive than of folk art.

Not only tobacconists, but other shopkeepers ordered free-standing figures as shop signs: Indians, sailors, firemen, Highlanders, popular celebrities ranging from Daniel Webster to Jenny Lind, and such allegorical figures as Liberty and Uncle Sam. Typical are *Chief Black Hawk* (SB 216), quite refined and elaborate; the cruder but more effective *Lady of Fashion* (SB 101D); and the jaunty *Sailor* (SB 20). Among the figures which were neither figureheads or shop signs is a very curious example, a quite elaborate and picturesque carving which hung above the Kent County Jail in East Greenwich, Rhode Island (SB 8). Others seem to have been carved for their own sake, like academic sculpture. Among the best of these is a *Dancing Negro,* 1825–1850 (SB 210, *SB 210A), from Charleston, South Carolina, very convincingly lively but still preserving the quality of carved wood. It is all the more vivacious when compared with *Clog Dancer, "Jim Crow,"* of approximately the same date (SB 205) (a representation of T. Rice, "The Original Jim Crow"), which is a far more conventional dancing figure. Equally wooden in feeling, but more dignified in its rigid pose, is the life-size image of the *Reverend Campbell* (SB 213), a Negro preacher on the estate of Allan Pinkerton, the famous detective, at Onarga, Illinois. Carved by a Chicago maker of cigar store Indians, it represents the clergyman in a long, brilliantly red plush coat like that of a Chicago doorman, bought by Mr. Pinkerton to impress the recently freed slaves with the importance of their spiritual advisor. The area of intense red, contrasting with the coal-black shoes, umbrella, Boston bag, and glistening black face, all combined with the reduction of the complexity of this figure to the large shapes and rhythms of a really sculpturesque conception, make this a remarkable piece of wood carving.

Portraiture as such was rare in folk sculpture. Among the best are four by Alexander Ames, which are realistically painted as well. The *Bust of a Woman,* for example, c. 1840 (*SB 101C), is strong and sure in carving, and is a convincing image of a person. The *Head of a Boy,* 1847 (SB 107), is even finer and subtler; it is a more direct and simpler piece. The head is beautifully modeled in interlocking planes; the gaze is intense under the youthful yet almost fierce eyebrows, and the serious, full lips are enhanced by a delicate color, creating an image equal in expressiveness to the best folk portrait paintings.

An ideal life-size standing portrait of *Lafayette* by the genre painter David Gilmour Blythe, 1845 (SB 37), is a curious figure. Though by an artist who trained himself to an almost academic standard in painting, the *Lafayette* has more stiffness than the wood carvings executed by typical folk artists, probably because the medium was relatively unfamiliar to Blythe. But for all this, the figure has a formidable presence and can be counted as one of the more impressive pieces in the field of folk or popular sculpture.

One other outstanding portrait—or rather, interpretation of a personality—is the *Henry Ward Beecher*, c. 1840 (SB 101; Illustration 4–90), whittled by a Mr. Corbin of Centerville, Indiana, a farmer who had been inspired by the great preacher on one of his swings through the Midwest. In spite of the ridiculous anatomy, the tiny hands, and the strained pose, the little figure has a more intense feeling than most academic work of the period, and a far greater sense of the medium and what can be done with it and with the tools proper to it.[51]

The Folk Art of Isolated Groups

Various isolated religious and racial groups produced a form of art which, understandably, belongs to neither the academic nor folk traditions which surrounded them, though it is not entirely unrelated. Among these groups were the Pennsylvania "Dutch." The German settlements in southeastern Pennsylvania, founded by religious groups in the eighteenth century, persisted in a separation from their environment which has lasted in some instances until our own time, and naturally produced an art which until the 1850's was a continuation of German folk art. Most of it appears in the form of decorative art; the medieval motifs of central European popular ornament have given a distinctive character to Pennsylvania Dutch furniture, ceramics, textiles, and other objects. The bold abstract design and vivid colors equal and in most cases excel the much rarer analogous designs remaining from

4–90. Corbin, *Henry Ward Beecher,* c. 1840. Wood. Height: 21½ inches. (Abby Aldrich Rockefeller Folk Art Collection, Williamsburg, Virginia.)

seventeenth-century New England which were, of course, derived from similar ultimately medieval sources. In the non-decorative arts, the work of the Pennsylvania Dutch is largely confined to "fraktur" (from the German *Frakturschrift*), an adaptation of central European manuscript illumination based on Gothic script. In the eighteenth century it appeared at its best and most elaborate in the products of the Ephrata Writing School, the culminating achievement of which was the hymnal of 1747, *Die Turteltaube,* by the Brethren and Sisters, done in a procedure similar to that of the medieval illuminators. (The nineteenth-century historian of the Ephrata group says of the hymnal that it was artless and simple, "but something wonderful shone forth from it, for which no name can be found.") The decorative motifs—roses and lilies, hearts and turtle doves, pelicans, nightingales and eagles, stags and unicorns, and, finally, the stars and the sun—of this book, and of other products of Ephrata and of similar isolated German communities elsewhere, were religious symbols. Most of the later fraktur work is also religious and was executed either in connection with birth or baptismal certificates or biblical quotations. Two frakturs now in the Philadelphia Museum are early and elaborate examples still reflecting the character of the *Turteltaube:* a biblical quotation *Halted euch nicht selbst for klug,* 1798 (*GB 170), by Christian Strenge, and *The Thirty-Fourth Psalm: Ich will den Herrn loben,* 1801 (GB 167), by George Geistweite. One of the most common uses of fraktur was in elaborate birth certificates such as that by Heinrich Otto, 1782 (PA 147), which is very much in the manner of the biblical verses. These certificates became less heavily ornamented and more delicate as the tradition was continued by schoolteachers and itinerant penmen, as in an example by Francis Portzline (*PA 148); as exercises in ornamental penmanship they are extremely decorative in their calligraphic elegance. Some of this calligraphic quality, as well as their bold design, is continued in the certificates executed in combination woodcut and stencil, as in a baptismal certificate of 1826 (GB 168). But on the whole these prints are cruder than the drawings and watercolors, though still extremely decorative, as in the earlier woodcut *Adam and Eve,* c. 1820 (GB 168).

The folk tradition which produced such effective illumination and flat decoration had its counterpart in sculpture. The human figure was infrequently treated (and crudely when it was, as was the case in painting), but some delightful animals and birds—usually doves and eagles—came from the hands of the Pennsylvania Dutch carvers, ranging from the conventions of painted wooden toys, bold and whimsical in design (SB 222), to the realism of a small, magnificently alive carved *Stag* by one Reber of Lehighton, Pennsylvania (SB 223). Another outstanding example is an especially fine life-size eagle originating in Lancaster County, Pennsylvania, during the first quarter of the century (SB 16).

Perhaps the best wood sculpture was done by Wilhelm Schimmel, a German immigrant who carved and whittled for his food and lodging among the Pennsylvania Dutch from about 1860 to 1890. Though his work is late, it is a vigorous conclusion to a long folk tradition. The Henry Francis du Pont Winterthur Museum, Winterthur, Delaware, has a large collection of Schimmel's eagles, remarkable for their strong silhouettes and for the way in which the decorative possibilities of the tool marks in the wood are exploited, as, for instance, in the use of a sawtooth device for the feathers of the body and a more rectangular edge for those of the wings.

Pennsylvania Dutch gravestones are as decorative as those of seventeenth- and eighteenth-century New England, though they are usually more crudely or vigorously carved; they derive from a more permeating and persistent folk tradition which lasted well into the nineteenth century. In general the motifs repeat those of the furniture and decorative arts, but because of their deep relief they have more impact than flat decoration, no matter how effectively colored.

Though in no way related to the Pennsylvania Dutch, the religious sect known as the Shakers similarly isolated themselves from their surroundings, with the consequence that their art is equally distinctive. However, the work of the Shakers is not part of a continuous folk tradition, but a quite independent development which, because of its format and medium, bears considerable superficial resemblance to the frakturs. As original as their architecture, the art of the Shakers (which consists mostly of what are called inspirational drawings, executed in pen with delicate color added) is inevitably somewhat influenced by the general ambiance of folk art; that is, its motifs are those which persisted in the decorative arts in areas and social groups not yet influenced by the classicism which accompanied Georgian and neo-classic taste. (Abstract or stylized naturalistic forms, ultimately medieval in derivation, persisted longer in textiles and wall decoration, for instance, than elsewhere.) An excellent inspirational drawing showing these design characteristics is one by Father James (for Jane Blanchard), *A Type of Mother Hannah's Pocket Handkerchief*, 1851 (*PB 702). The *Tree of Life*, 1854 (*PB 704), is bolder but still very complex and refined in its exquisite drawing and color. The *Emblem of the Heavenly Sphere*, a gift from Mother Ann, 1854 (*PB 703), is typical of another type of Shaker inspirational drawing characterized by diagrammatic arrangements of symbols or emblems with various legends.

These extraordinary drawings are typical of a whole group distinguished by a conceptual and artistic imagination unfettered by the nearly ubiquitous representationalism surrounding it, and inspired by an intense religious dedication.

Like the Pennsylvania Germans, the Spanish-Americans (whether of European or mixed Indian blood) in the Southwest, Texas, and California were isolated by language and culture from the nation within whose boundaries they were included after the Mexican War. They produced a decorative art of considerable charm, deriving ultimately from Spanish Renaissance and baroque forms; its quality and vitality are a distant and late manifestation of the art of the counter-reformation in Catholic Europe.

In centers of Spanish colonial penetration such as San Antonio, Texas, and San Xavier del Bac near Tucson, Arizona, where craftsmen from Mexican metropolitan centers executed architectural carving during the eighteenth century, it is not surprising that equally accomplished artists worked in the figurative arts as well. The figures of saints on the facade and interior of San Xavier typify the best of this work, which is a competent though provincial reflection of the sculpture of seventeenth-century Spain, such as that of Alonzo Cano, which is emotional but not too sentimental. Some sculpture was actually imported from Mexico, as, for example, the elaborately carved and polychromed limestone altarpiece in the Church of Christo Rey in Santa Fe, New Mexico, 1763 (*SB 158), carved in the excessively baroque style of Zacatecas, Mexico, from which it came. The painted reredos in the Church of San Miguel at Santa Fe, 1798 (*PA 153), reflects a similar standard, somewhat sophisticated though still provincial, as does a plaster relief on wood, *Nuestra Señora de la Luz,* c. 1760–1780 (SB 220). Such works undoubtedly had some influence, as is evident in the rather complex and provincial baroque painting, *Nuestra Señora de Guadalupe* (PA 156). In remoter places farther from Mexican centers, especially as contacts with outlying regions languished after independence from Spain, work became more primitive, naïve, and original. When craftsmanship deteriorated in representational skill, it gained in boldness of design and expressive power, as seen in a *Holy Trinity* in wood and gesso, c. 1800 (SB 151), which is wonderfully naïve and direct, and in the painted retables of many New Mexican churches. Those at Laguna and Ranchos de Taos, and especially some at the early nineteenth-century Santuario de Chimayo are typical in their combination of Spanish baroque exuberance and Indian boldness. The retable by José Aragón (of Chamisal), 1824–1835 (*PA 159), reflects the style and character of those which are still in place, in its crude but immensely colorful and dynamic decoration, peopled with expressive figures.

Though the sculptured saints at Chimayo, 1825–1835, are more elaborately baroque than most work done that late [as the *San Rafael Arcángel* (*SB 157)], in general both painting and sculpture became even more expressive and original with the increasing isolation of the area from Hispanic culture after its annexation by the United States. This work could be called actually indigenous, since geographic, cultural, and political circumstances combined to create a situation unique to that part of the world. Certainly the art of the Spanish-Americans, in New Mexico particularly, is among the most esthetically interesting and emotionally expressive within the confines of the United States, though it has no

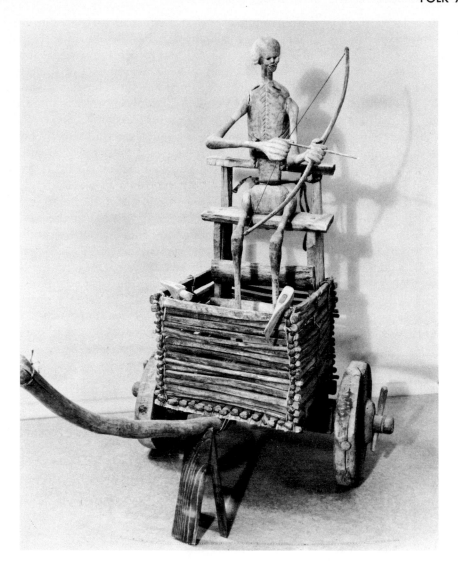

4–91. Anonymous (perhaps a member of the Lopez family, Cordoba, New Mexico), *Carreta de la Muerte (Death Cart),* c. 1850 (?). Wood. Height: 51 inches; figure: 36 inches. (Taylor Museum, Colorado Springs Fine Arts Center, Colorado Springs, Colorado.)

connection whatsoever with the almost totally Anglo-Saxon-derived culture of the rest of the country.

The *Santos* (images of saints in any medium) and *Bultos* (figures carved in the round) of New Mexico were the work of *Santeros* (makers of saints' images), many of whom belonged to the Catholic *Penitente* parishes in New Mexico; this sect was known for the physical violence of

its self-inflicted penances during Passion Week. The emotionalism of the *Penitentes'* fanaticism was reflected also in their images, reduced from the Cano-like representationalism of the previous century to a bold expressionism in almost abstract form. Those working at Cordova, New Mexico, were among the most expressive and vigorous *Santeros.* The reredos by José Rafael Aragón (of Cordova) done between 1825 and

1850 (PA 3) is a large painting belonging to this school. More typical are a number of sculptures—a *Bishop* (SB 153), a *San Antonio de Padua* (SB 152), and especially a *Nuestra Señora de Guadalupe* (SB 219), from Rancho de San Antonio (all in the Museum of New Mexico, Santa Fe)—which are very effective folk translations of Spanish baroque prototypes.

A number of small paintings, represented by *A Flight into Egypt* (PA 2), a *Holy Family and Holy Trinity* (PA 155), a *San Juan Nepomuceno* (PA 157), and the *Santo Niño de Atocha* (Museum of New Mexico, Santa Fe), are forceful and expressive. This is especially true of *Veronica's Veil*, from the Rio Grande valley (*PA 154), which is almost as effective in its intense religious feeling as the *Santos* of the *Penitente* parishes, especially the crucifixes and the figures of Christ as Man of Sorrows. The heads of some of these suffering Christs have the powerful effect of early medieval wood carving, boldly cut (as though almost slashed with the knife) and forceful in strongly modeled contrasting planes. The impact of these figures is partly explained by their having to be seen while in motion and often from a distance (they were carried in processions). Some of the most effective of the images traditionally borne in this way were angels and figures of Death, usually represented as riding in a cart or *carreta*. One of these *carretas de la muerte*, c. 1850 (?) (Illustration 4–91), said to be from Cordova, New Mexico,[52] is preserved at the Taylor Museum in Colorado Springs; another is still in the sacristy of the remote church at Las Trampas in the hills northwest of Santa Fe.

Sculpture of *Santos* and *Bultos* continued vigorously late into the century, as in the simple and expressive *St. Francis of Assisi*, c. 1875 (SB 147), and has persisted almost until our own time.

PART FIVE

FROM THE CIVIL WAR TO 1900

The forces for political, economic, and social change that originated in the romantic age exploded in the Civil War and its aftermath. The victory of the North was a victory for industrialism. The defeated South played almost no significant part in the postwar period; certainly its contribution to the arts was negligible except in letters. Thus the plains states and the West succeeded the South as heirs to the agrarian point of view both politically and culturally. The war itself accelerated the growth of industry and big business. Capital which had been amassed in the financing of the northern armies was invested in railroads, manufacturing, and the exploitation of raw materials. Corporate enterprise became the most efficient economic system, represented in the huge railroad combines, in industry in general, and in concomitant banking and insurance.

The wealth of the country increased almost by geometric progression. In 1893 the United States was richer by thirty billion dollars than it had been in 1883. Towns grew and cities became gargantuan; rural areas began to be depleted. In 1890 New York City had over a million inhabitants, and Chicago's population reached that number soon after. When there were no longer sufficient native Americans to supply the expanding labor markets, foreigners were induced to emigrate; between 1890 and 1900 more than five million came to the United States.

The physical effects of this enormous growth changed the country from an idyllic, pastoral America to a smoky, industrial one. Railroads covered the country, exerting economic control, making or breaking towns and cities, changing the whole scale and character of the landscape by the introduction of speed and by disregard for natural configurations (much as the superhighway does today), spoiling the littorals of rivers and lakes, and creating slums in the most naturally beautiful and salubrious urban areas. On the other hand, the railroads created the growth of suburbs and resorts and were the instrument for a greater appreciation of the more dramatic natural wonders of the country. Finally, together with the telegraph and the telephone, the railroads shortened distances and brought about greater conformity and fewer regional differences.

Though the recent immigrants lived in abject poverty, and many among the agrarian population, both in the East and in some of the newer settlements of the West, were economically depressed, the general standard of living rose, and individuals with great fortunes were not uncommon. This was the age when the slum dweller and the mortgaged homesteader existed almost side by side with the prosperous middleman and the "robber baron." Big business and those who fattened on it were in the forefront of political and cultural activity; at the same time, reaction against its abuses and disaffection for its subjugation of the old agrarian democracy found expression in political and social reform, in the rise of labor movements, in the thinking of radicals like Thorstein Veblen and Henry George, and in the movement represented by the Populist and Progressive parties.

In this period the United States changed as much culturally as it did physically. The old idealisms had been consumed in the passions of the war; the puritanical concepts of individual initiative and industry, bolstered by the optimistic aspects of Emersonian democracy, had been distorted into a materialistic doctrine derived from the evolutionary philosophy of Herbert Spencer, in which free and even vicious competition was at least tacitly approved as an aspect of the survival of the fittest. Disillusionment, together with crass materialism, contributed to the rape of half a continent by selfish interests and to the venality and corruption of big business and politics as exemplified in the Erie scandal and the Tweed Ring. In the pragmatic world of "operators" like Jay Gould and Jim Fisk, the Boston transcendentalist was as out of place as the antebellum southern gentleman. It was a world in which exploitation was progress, a world in which one financier, pulling himself out of the crash he helped to produce, said, "Nothing is lost save honor." [1]

Conspicuous spending in the arts was now more the concern of the parvenu than of the gentleman. The newly rich set out to purchase culture as they would an interest in a corporation, and the result was an ostentatious eclecticism. European art was bought in preference to the native product and European period styles were aped with ludicrous lack of sophistication in an effort to bring an appearance of respectability to often ill-gotten gains. Commercial buildings, for instance, were covered with borrowed adornments, and mansions of bastard stylistic lineage were filled with trophies of European travel. Stockyard kings lived in Rhenish castles and the children of an illiterate former Brooklyn ferryman lived in French *châteaux* and Italian *palazzi*. As architecture became increasingly elaborate and stylistically incongruous, the interiors required equally pretentious pictures which, if they were not European, were in the grandiose Hudson River tradition or were examples of sentimental genre. What was by this time becoming more genuine in American painting was ignored.

The most typical art and architecture of the postwar era were of the sort just described, but far more significant was the work of those artists who were little influenced by the taste of the new plutocracy or who deliberately revolted against it. Landscape and genre, for instance, still followed the opening of the West, recording the magnificence of the country itself, the new settlements by disbanded soldiers and homesteaders, the ways of the Indian and the "bad man," and the conflict between cowboy and farmer—the beginning of a national legend. The art of photography found some of its most eloquent material in the West, ranging from the recording of the progress of the Union Pacific to the discovery of the ancient cliff dwellings in the Canyon de Chelly. More interesting was the art which was produced as a reaction to the new industrial and parvenu world. In architecture the retreat from the city and the factory to the summer resort and the suburb was reflected in the further development of the non-urban American house, reaching, in the hands of Henry Hobson Richardson and some of his contemporaries, an almost modern form in the so-called shingle style. In painting the revolt was reflected in a nostalgic attitude toward rural America, which was fast disappearing, and toward those regional differences which were rapidly being minimized by more efficient communication—factors which led to a similar development in the "local color" school of writers. Artists like Winslow Homer celebrated this world of rural countryside, seashore, and forest, the land of farmer, fisherman, and vacationist. But more often the painters merely sentimentalized their subjects with a kind of spurious quaintness. The appeal of the romance of the West, for instance, was not matched by interest in such subjects as the hopelessness of the exploited midwestern farmer, the plight of his hard-scrabble eastern cousin, or the bestial conditions of the tenement dweller. The gayer, more optimistic aspects of American life usually appealed to the genre artist, just as they did to novelists like William Dean Howells, who succeeded the more profound Herman Melville and Nathaniel Hawthorne.

The most extreme form of revolt against the American environment was manifested in the actual expatriation of many artists, some of them among the best the country had produced, who, like Mary Cassatt and James McNeill Whistler, fled from the materialism and venality of the postwar era, typified by the Grant Administration—an environment which Henry Adams said no sensitive nature could regard without a shudder. If an artist was unable to go to Europe he at least tried to come to New York, rather than "rot," as one of them said, in a midwestern studio. A far cry from the age of George Caleb Bingham! For the majority of those artists who did remain at home there was little relationship between their work and the American scene except on a superficial genre or illustrative level. But the best of them were sufficiently aware of their own identity to be themselves, and did not require the artificial stimulus of an exotic environment. Winslow Homer and Thomas Eakins, for instance, acquired their technical knowledge from Europe, but the essentials of their art derived from the American environment.

Another form of revolt against the more vulgar aspects of the prevailing materialism appeared in the late 1880's and the 1890's, partly as a result of the natural propensity of one generation to rebel against its predecessor. But this reaction was a mixed blessing. Although uncouth and vulgar, the post-Civil War generation had possessed a vigorous vitality. It had no real culture. But the next generation had too

much, or was too self-conscious about what it had, imitating Europe slavishly and falling prey to the snobbery of "good taste." The vitality of the culture that had produced the shingle style and the skyscraper was almost overwhelmed by gentility. The prominent firm of McKim, Mead & White, for instance, turned away from successful cultivation of the shingle style to an imitation of palaces from the vanished age of the Renaissance courts. "Good taste" vitiated the talents of many painters and sculptors as well, especially in ideal subjects, warping the native realism of a Saint-Gaudens, for example, into mere prettiness. A particularly good illustration of gentility in the figurative arts at the end of the century can be found in the treatment of women, both allegorical and actual. The almost sexless creatures who sit in sculptures at the entrances to college libraries and drift through paintings on the vaults of state capitols and courtrooms are characterized by a reticent idealism—as an admirer described Saint-Gaudens' angels. If they are not ideal females but real persons, they are such gentlewomen that we are urged by a contemporary critic to stand uncovered before them—that is, with our hats off.

The earnest struggle for culture in the 1850's (which caused a commentator to describe Boston as one large lecture hall) was succeeded by the more pretentious purchase of it in the 1860's and 1870's, and by sheer snobbery in the 1890's, when dead styles and dead techniques were not even exploited as in earlier eclecticism, but merely copied. The World's Fair at Chicago in 1893 symbolized the victory of the genteel tradition. In the city where the most original and creative architecture of the time had been developed, a white plaster mirage of classical design decorated with equally academic figures so impressed a generation with its false grandeur that the advance of architecture was retarded for two or three decades.

The position of the artist in the postwar period was much less secure than it had been. In spite of the general increase in wealth, artists were not as extensively patronized as before, for several reasons. Before the Civil War, the artist, consciously or unconsciously, was a part of the culture that produced him. A Mount or a Bingham was thoroughly integrated with his environment, and his patrons realized this. In the post-Civil War period the artist was often out of tune with the prosperous middle-class world. He turned into himself, like Ryder; went his own way, like Eakins; or went abroad, like Whistler. The last course was generally the most profitable for the artist, for many newly rich patrons of the arts, unsure of their tastes, limited their purchases to either the works of European artists or those of Americans living abroad, whose residence there lent them a patent of respectability. The stay-at-homes, and especially the artists among them who persisted in their non-conformity, were unlikely to receive patronage, yet they were often actually the best. Another cause for the less secure position of the artist was the gradual usurpation of portraiture by photography. But whatever the reasons, many young American artists who left the country to study abroad just after the Civil War, when their profession was still thriving, returned in later years to a life of insecurity. The more fortunate among them were employed in the decoration of government buildings and other public edifices; banks and even office buildings, particularly at the end of the period, were lavishly decorated. The liturgical revival and the re-emphasis on decoration in the churches, especially the Episcopalian, provided another means of employment. Illustration and the reproductive graphic arts became a source of income for the artist as magazine and book production multiplied.

Many artists and architects still received training abroad. It was almost mandatory to study in Europe, where Paris and Munich succeeded Düsseldorf as centers of instruction in painting. In America the National Academy of Design continued as an active force (a life class was organized there in the 1870's), but it was soon supplanted by the Art Students' League of New York, founded in 1875. Thomas Eakins reorganized the Pennsylvania Academy in the same decade, introducing rigorous life and anatomy classes, and in the process created what we would call today the first actual professional school. In 1877 the Society of American Artists was founded and through its influence the Munich theories and practices were promulgated. Watercolor and etching societies gave a more professional stamp to those particular fields. A great many artists studied with individuals rather than in schools. The two most important artist-teachers were Richard Morris Hunt (with whom La Farge, among others, received training and inspiration in the 1860's), and William Merritt Chase in the 1870's and 1880's.

For architectural training the student went to the École des Beaux Arts in Paris if he possibly could, though the Massachusetts Institute of Technology opened an architectural school in 1866. But the apprentice system was still the most effective way to receive architectural training. Frank Furness, for instance, worked with Hunt, and Louis Sullivan with Furness; Stanford White received his training in Richardson's large firm, as did several other prominent architects.

Besides colleges and schools, other cultural factors acted as educational forces in the arts. Many private galleries were opened, usually catering to the preference for European art, but nevertheless broadening a taste which at its highest level produced such important collections as those of J. P. Morgan, Benjamin Altman, and Henry Clay Frick in New York; of John G. Johnson in Philadelphia; and of Isabella Stewart Gardner in Boston.

The first really important museums in the country were founded in the first decade after the war, helping to supply a need only partially fulfilled before by the Boston Athenaeum, the Pennsylvania Academy, and the National Academy of Design. These were the Museum of Fine Arts in Boston, the Metropolitan Museum in New York, and the Corcoran Gallery in Washington, soon followed by the Art Institute in Chicago in 1879, the museums in Cincinnati and Detroit in 1881 and 1885, and the Brooklyn and Worcester museums and the Carnegie Institute in Pittsburgh in 1895.

Besides these permanent sources of inspiration and learning for artists, temporary expositions had considerable influence on the development of taste. The Centennial of 1876 in Philadelphia included in its myriad exhibits a summary of American and European accomplishments in art. More particularly, by showing the Barbizon and realist painters of France to a large public for the first time, it helped prepare both artists and public for what was to become an important influence in American painting. The Centennial was equally stimulating to architecture. The colonial revival was introduced at this time, as well as new trends in English domestic building and, for the first time, Japanese architecture. The more famous World's Fair, held in Chicago in 1893, was not as forward-looking as the Philadelphia Centennial except in the direction of the "city beautiful," in which architecture, painting, sculpture, and planning were all united in a common program.

Such educational stimulants, in addition to the increase in book and magazine publication and the improvement of reproductive printing processes, especially the invention of photogravure, caused the naïve isolated artist to become an anomaly. Thus, significant folk art died out, as did vernacular architecture. At the same time the general level of sophistication and accomplishment brought a kind of deadening academic competence and slickness to run-of-the-mill work, which was now unrelieved by the unconscious boldness of the folk artist. This was especially true in architecture at the end of the century: the correct Beaux Arts formulas made undistinguished buildings even more so, though they were more palatable to "good taste" than were their more naïve predecessors of the vulgar but vigorous period immediately after the Civil War.

Architecture

A thorough survey of the architecture of the post-Civil War period is impossible in a general history: there was far too much building during these decades to permit more than a study of the most noteworthy architecture as pointed out by scholars. Ignoring a host of other architects, we shall single out Henry Hobson Richardson, Louis Sullivan, and a few others, and shall attempt to find the most important trends of the period.

Though most architecture remained eclectic, the significant buildings of these years either straddled several styles or seemed to emerge entirely from revivalism. New techniques and new requirements finally led architecture away from the various manners into a style for our time; though briefly set back by the academic reaction of the 1890's, this style eventually became predominant in the twentieth century. Nevertheless, eclecticism remained the most conspicuous characteristic of the period; it can generally be divided into classical and romantic, using these terms in the broadest sense. The most widespread manifestation of the first, derived from the Paris of Napoleon III and generally called Second Empire, was a revival of seventeenth-century French classicism. The second stemmed from the Italian Gothic popularized by John Ruskin in England—though other medieval manners were employed as well, especially the Romanesque, handled in a very personal way by Richardson. More often than not, however (at least in America), various revival styles were combined apparently without rhyme or reason, as can be illustrated in Richard M. Upjohn's State Capitol at Hartford, Connecticut, 1878 (*AB 703), where classic forms are clad with Gothic details in a very bold and original, if hardly archaeologically rational way.

At the beginning of the period the archaeological aspect of eclecticism, especially in the medieval revivals, was handled with considerable freedom, though detail was inclined to be more correct, due to the greater knowledge of actual prototypes derived from published examples, especially as photogravure came into general use.

The revivalism of this period has a certain vigor. That of its first phase, in the late 1860's and the 1870's, was later considered vulgar, especially by genteel taste at the end of the century. Perhaps too aggressively picturesque, it had at least a plastic strength which the academicism of the 1890's did not. The lack of strong archaeological bias also gave greater scope for originality than might otherwise have been the case. Buildings like Harvard University's Memorial Hall (Illustration 5–6) and, later, those of Richardson are an unusual amalgam of revivalism and originality, giving the architecture of the period a vitality that is curiously attractive in spite of its often ungainly aspects.

Toward the end of the period, in the work of both original and conventional architects, a general stylistic trend became evident: the lessening of the picturesqueness of the mid-century and of the 1860's. Richardson's Trinity Church, Boston (Illustration 5–15), is more massive and more conspicuously unified than the medieval revival churches of the mid-century, and his Marshall Field Warehouse in Chicago (Illustration 5–19) has almost as simple a silhouette as the buildings of romantic classicism. In domestic architecture, the native shingle style shed its excrescences and became almost "streamlined"; the picturesque irregularities of the medieval styles gave way to the self-contained and symmetrical refinement of the colonial revival. Sullivan's protomodern skyscrapers and McKim, Mead & White's Renaissance palaces, though different from one another in other respects, are similar in their smooth precision and unaccented elegance.

New materials, tools, and processes implemented new forms. The large office building, the most conspicuous of the newer building types, was made possible by a number of factors: the wrought iron beam came into use in the 1850's; the later steel beam began to be mass-produced at low cost in the 1880's; Portland cement and plate glass became available, and the steam elevator was perfected in 1872. The exploitation of metal in the skyscraper, train shed, and exhibition hall introduced an entirely new dimension to architecture which was formerly dependent on wood and masonry, post and lintel, arch, vault, and dome—all essentially unchanged in principle since the time of the Romans. With the development of new techniques the cleavage between architect and engineer became greater. The older architects were at the same time masons, as witness the vaults of Latrobe and Mills. But such a structure as the Agriculture Building by McKim, Mead & White at the Chicago Fair of 1893 is an almost schizophrenic building, its interior a great span of steel and glass powerfully designed (and quite comparable to the more famous interior of the Salle des Machines of the Paris Exhibition of 1889), and its exterior an envelope of imperial Roman reminiscences.

Yet the new forms that resulted from the use of new materials and techniques are only the most obvious aspects of the building of the period; domestic architecture, not dependent upon these new factors, continued in the organic tradition that had begun in the 1840's and 1850's. The development of what Vincent Scully has called the stick and shingle styles brought the emphasis upon structure and open plan into a phase that can hardly be distinguished from modern architecture except by the persistence of a few eclectic details. Wood—light, strong, and easily workable and available—remained a popular material and was used to its fullest advantage in these houses. (Another aspect should not be overlooked, for it illustrates one more instance of the influence of the machine on building during this period: the torturing of wood into all sorts of shapes by the power saw, with ridiculous but exuberant results, as in the wooden vernacular known as "gingerbread.")

The training of architects now became more professional—the American Institute of Architects was founded in 1857, and the Massachusetts Institute of Technology opened its school of architecture the year before. But most students of architecture preferred to study abroad. Richard Morris Hunt was the first. He returned to the United States from Paris in 1855, having initiated a tradition of study at the École des Beaux Arts, a practice which reached its peak in the 1890's. The apprentice system, however, remained the best way of achieving professional competence. Working in a large firm, such as Richardson's, the burgeoning architect became acquainted with the functions of an increasingly complex profession.

Naturally the influence of source and design books persisted to a certain degree, especially among the carpenter-builders. These publications were legion, and in general were much inferior to their mid-century predecessors. *Examples of American Domestic Architecture* (1889) by John Calvin Stevens and Albert Winslow Cobb is, however, in a sense the culmination in book form of the organic tradition as developed before the time of Frank Lloyd Wright. This is not to say that books of a more general or theoretical nature were not influential. The eloquent prose of John Ruskin's *Stones of Venice* and *Seven Lamps of Architecture*, for instance, was almost solely responsible for the shift of architectural taste from English to Italian medieval prototypes. In his *Discourses*, Viollet-le-Duc, the French architectural theorist and restorer of Gothic cathedrals, introduced a kind of personal vocabulary of form and detail which had a greater influence in the United States than has been generally noted. Late in the period P.-M. Letarouilly's *Édifices de Rome Moderne*, published early in the century, had a belated but strong influence on the architecture of the academic reaction of the 1880's. On the whole, however, magazines gradually took the place of the pattern and design books. The most prominent was the *American Architect and Building News*, founded in 1876, which familiarized its readers with buildings important in the history of architecture and, more significantly, published both contemporary designs and executed buildings.

Eclecticism

The rampant eclecticism of the 1850's seems almost restrained in comparison with that which succeeded it during the boom years of the Grant

5–1. Illustration from *Houses of America*, M. J. Lamb (ed.) (New York: 1879).

Administration. The villa at Glendale-on-Hudson built in 1867 by Frederick Church, the landscape painter, outdid the earlier Longwood on the Mississippi in the variety of its architectural sources, incorporating forms which derived not only from relatively familiar prototypes from Switzerland and Italy but also from Greece, Syria, and Palestine, where Church had recently traveled. Even the aging Alexander Jackson Davis, as eclectic as any architect of the mid-century, could not quite stomach the excesses of the postwar period. In his diary he contemptuously classified the varieties of suburban dwellings and country houses as "American log cabin," "French suburban," "Oriental Moorish," and "Swiss Collegiate Gothic."

The whole period could be summed up by a view of a row of three respectable houses on a suburban terrace, appearing in *Houses of America* in 1879 (Illustration 5–1). (The text below announced that "countless styles from all climes have been made subservient to the convenience and taste of a mixed population.") The excesses of architecture were matched by those of interior decoration. Old photographs and a few actual furnished rooms preserved in museums bear out the advice of the writer on taste who stated that, provided there was space to move about in without knocking over the furniture, there was hardly likely to be too much in the room.

Overweening, ill-assembled, and repellent to modern taste, nevertheless the architecture of the Grant era, for all its lack of restraint, has vitality and imagination. Its frequently vulgar overstatement is at least more vigorous than the genteel restraint of the end of the century, as can be seen in comparing Ware and Van Brunt's Memorial Hall in Cambridge (Illustration 5–6) with the Boston Public Library by McKim, Mead & White (Illustration 5–27). Such buildings as Memorial Hall, and designs like Richardson's for Trinity Church (Illustration 5–15) and Furness' for the Provident Trust Company (Illustration 5–7) have a certain undeniable grandeur and power. The more vernacular buildings of the time, though often ridiculous, also have a kind of picturesque vitality and thus have enriched the American scene. Buildings like the No. 15 Fire House at San Francisco, 1885 (AB 679), and those comprising whole streets of false fronts in western mining towns, as at Black Hawk, Colorado (AB 324), possess a potentially humorous quality that has endeared them to artists like Saul Steinberg and the *New Yorker* cartoonists. Some of these structures, in spite of their absurdity, also have a surety of statement which gives them a certain dignity, as can be seen in Ansel Adams' superb photograph of a ghost town in California (Illustration 6–83).

Among the many styles of the post-Civil War period the three most prevalent were Second Empire, High Victorian Gothic, and Romanesque Revival.

The Second Empire style was developed under Napoleon III in emulation of the great seventeenth-century designers of the Louvre and Tuileries in Paris, and was exemplified best in the new additions to these buildings, which soon became international symbols of metropolitan elegance. Architecture inspired by the new Louvre, three-dimensionally varied in its projecting pavilions and steep-roofed towers, satisfied the continuing taste for the picturesque, and became the more or less classically derived opposite number for the steepled and pointed Gothic and Romanesque revivals. Sometimes the Second Empire style is simply called "mansard" after the curb roof shape originated by Jules Hardouin-Mansart in the seventeenth century, for the mansard (or "French") roof was an almost ubiquitous feature of the style (Illustration 5–2). The Second Empire provided modest suburban villas with a literally palatial character; even stables had mansard roofs.

The origin of the Second Empire style in the United States—whether directly from France or from earlier reflections of it in Britain—need not concern us. It was seen first in a group of New York houses by the Paris-trained architect Dietlef Lienau as early as 1849, and in the early work of Richard Morris Hunt. The style was found to be especially adaptable to official architecture because in it the classical orders continued to be used, though they were more ornate and combined with greater picturesqueness. A. B. Mullett's familiar old State, War, and Navy Department Building (now the Executive Office Building) in Washington, 1871–1875, is a typical example, but perhaps the masterpiece of the style is the Philadelphia City Hall, 1871–1881 (Illustration 5–2), by John McArthur, Jr. This grandiose but handsome structure, incorporating fourteen and a half acres of floor space, outdid the new Louvre (which it closely resembles) in scale, richness of form, and sculptural ornament, and called on more sources of inspiration, including Palladian. The five-hundred-forty-eight-foot tower is unique in its piling up of tier upon tier of florid archaeologisms, and is crowned by an elongated convex shape topped by a thirty-seven-foot statue of William Penn. The building took ten years to build and twenty more to decorate, and cost over twenty-four million dollars. In comparison to buildings by Mullett (whose New York Post Office, long since replaced, Davis likened to a diseased courtesan), the Philadelphia City Hall is relatively temperate in detail, perhaps because Thomas U. Walter, as an assistant to McArthur, was in charge of its construction. This magnificent

5–2. City Hall, Philadelphia, Pennsylvania, 1871–1881, by John McArthur, Jr.

prototype was emulated throughout the country, especially west of the Alleghenies where the bold silhouettes of the local city hall or county courthouse are the chief accents in prairie towns otherwise so often characterless.

Other important buildings—colleges, libraries, and civic institutions—were housed in the new cosmopolitan style. Among the more pleasing examples were the great resort hotels, their facades usually prefaced with long piazzas as were the famous Grand Union and United States hotels at Saratoga Springs. Unfortunately, these two hotels have been demolished, but the type is still represented (though less grandly) in many other places, notably at Cape May, New

Jersey, and Block Island, Rhode Island. The Eagle Inn at Orwell, Vermont (*AB 669), may be taken as typical of some of the less pretentious examples.

The Second Empire style was particularly popular in commercial building, conspicuously advertising the prosperity of the owner, and at the same time adding an air of elegant respectability. Its many details, derived from a variety of palatial buildings, were particularly useful in hiding the basic metal structure and in disguising height, a quality unwelcome in the early skyscraper since it drew attention to the fact that the proprietors were deriving the greatest possible return from their original real estate investment. A typical example is Hunt's Tribune Building, New York, 1873–1875 (AB 369), though here the Empire style is adulterated with further eclecticisms.

Textile and other mills used the Second Empire style perhaps as successfully as did any other type of building, since their scale and functional character resulted naturally in a simple monumentality that was admirably adapted to the largeness of conception of the baroque, if not to its penchant for ornamentation. One of the finest examples (though atypical in lacking the mansard roof) is the splendidly massive building of the Coventry Company Mills at Washington, Rhode Island, by Stone and Carpenter, 1870's (Illustration 5–3). The mill is distinguished for its scale, its colorful contrast of brick and stone, the projection of its window enframements, its conspicuous quoining, and the accent of its monumental tower. There are, of course, many other notable examples of mill architecture in the style, some of them reduced to quite functional forms. Especially interesting are some in Manchester, New Hampshire, and in Fall River, Massachusetts—impressive and picturesque enough to have served as subjects for the contemporary American painters Charles Sheeler and Edward Hopper.

The Second Empire style was particularly appropriate for the mansions of the very rich. Château sur Mer, the William S. Wetmore House in Newport, Rhode Island, 1872 (AB 405), an enlargement and remodeling by Richard Morris Hunt of an earlier "Italian villa," is a typical example. Towers, "French" roofs, and a play of projecting and receding areas make a bold composition of sculpturesque masses. The ponderous proportions of the exterior are continued into the interior, which is equally heavy and typically Victorian—dark, lofty, and laden with elaborate decoration (AB 366, *AB 367, AB 368). This ornament epitomizes the taste of the 1870's, since it incorporates the recommendations Sir Charles Eastlake set forth in his influential *Hints on Household Taste* (London: 1868; New York: 1872), which introduced a confusing variety of treatments for wood, torturing it into countless shapes and

5–3. Coventry Company Mills, Washington, Rhode Island, 1870's, by Stone and Carpenter.

textures in an elaboration of colonnades, brackets, lambrequins, and consoles derived from various classical and postclassical sources and some medieval ones. Hunt handled this detail with a kind of lavishness which almost excuses its overornate and unfunctional character.

The Second Empire style was employed in smaller houses as well, those in masonry and brick being usually quite dignified in spite of the Eastlake details, which were confined largely to eaves, brackets, and porch supports. Adaptation of the style to wood—with or without the mansard roof—was, of course, to be expected, and can be seen in the houses put up in rows by builders in many American cities (*AB 678), and in individual houses in smaller towns and throughout the countryside, as illustrated in the pretentious "French"-roofed cottage at Eastham, Cape Cod, Massachusetts, 1874 (AB 708), a successor to the typical "Cape Codder."

The medieval revivalism of the post-Civil War period is not as clear-cut as that of the mid-century when the Gothic, Romanesque, and other revivals could be more or less distinguished by the sources that inspired them, no matter how naïvely they were interpreted. The two most easily distinguishable medieval styles of the 1870's and early 1880's are the English Victorian Gothic and the "Queen Anne," though they were only the most conspicuous among

others, including Romanesque (especially in the hands of Henry Hobson Richardson) and the influence of Viollet-le-Duc's adaptation of Gothic.

Just as the Second Empire style was more picturesque than the Greek Revival, Victorian Gothic was more picturesque than the Gothic Revival of the 1840's. The variety of mass and silhouette and the equally various use of materials, textures, and polychromy derived from the Italian Gothic (so admired by the persuasive critic Ruskin) were the principal ingredients contributing to this effect, though they were often combined with the more conventional English Gothic to a greater or lesser degree. This variety permitted a freer and more individualistic handling by mid-century architects than had been the case with the generation inspired by Pugin.

The more Italian phase of the Gothic Revival is best represented by a building which had been begun before the Civil War, the Nott Memorial Library at Union College, Schenectady, New York, 1858–1876 (AB 380), by Edward Tuckerman Potter, inspired by the Romanesque baptistry at Pisa. Though its medieval character is inconsistent with the classicism of Ramée's surrounding buildings, constructed earlier, its circular form at least fitted better into the symmetry of the campus plan than some other medieval prototype would have. Most of the examples of the more strictly Italian aspects of Victorian Gothic among public buildings have been either demolished or superseded by later structures—as, for instance, the old Boston Museum of Fine Arts. More typical are a number of churches which combine elements from the Italian Gothic and from other medieval sources as well, put together with little logic as far as sequence of styles is concerned. The best of these, though somewhat ungainly, are characterized by the boldness and monumentality which are typical of the period. Among the most original examples is the South Congregational Church, Springfield, Massachusetts, 1872 (Illustration 5–4) by William A. Potter (the brother of Edward Tuckerman Potter), a building notable for an unusually rich variety of texture, color, and decorative motifs and for the

5–4. South Congregational Church, Springfield, Massachusetts, 1872, by William A. Potter.

5–5. Interior, Central Congregational Church, Worcester, Massachusetts, 1886, by Stephen C. Earle. (From *American Architect and Building News*, Vol. 19, No. 546, June 12, 1886.)

forcefulness of their composition. Many of these churches are also distinguished for the spaciousness of their interiors, which are roofed with complex wooden bracing deriving from the tradition that served Upjohn so well in the First Parish Church at Brunswick, Maine. They are, in fact, often even bolder in their large sweep, since the spaces are greater and the dimensions nearly square rather than longitudinal—a development which occurred in the less liturgically oriented Congregational churches. One of the most impressive examples is the interior of Central Congregational Church at Worcester, Massachusetts, by Stephen C. Earle, 1886 (Illustration 5–5).

None of these buildings sums up so typically and so well the Victorian Gothic as does Memorial Hall at Harvard University, Cambridge,

Massachusetts (AB 432, AB 432A, AB 434; Illustration 5–6), designed by Ware and Van Brunt in the late 1860's and erected from 1870–1878 as a memorial to the Harvard men who had died in the Civil War. This large cathedral-like building is one of the most impressive in the history of American architecture. Its spacious interiors are roofed by ceilings which bring to a culmination the tradition of wooden bracing, and its bulky exterior builds up through a boldly conceived complex of form, texture, and color to the climax of a tower which (until it was recently destroyed by fire) was capped by a multipinnacled roof. In recent decades, when a genteel classicism represented by a watered-down Adamesque revival was considered in good taste, Harvard was ashamed of this elephantine monument to the "vulgarity" of the post-Civil

War era, though it could hardly ignore it. Lately, however, the sheer bulk and the bold vigor of Memorial Hall have won it respect. Especially when seen at twilight, this vast building, isolated on a triangle between two busy lanes of traffic and surrounded by structures puny and characterless in comparison, shows itself to be an edifice conceived three-dimensionally and not a reproduction of a flat drawing-board design, like so many of its successors at Harvard and elsewhere.

Among the more distinguished edifices of the period is another academic building, Farnum Hall, Yale University, New Haven, Connecticut, by Russell Sturgis, 1868 (AB 640A), a structure generally admired for the restraint of its almost

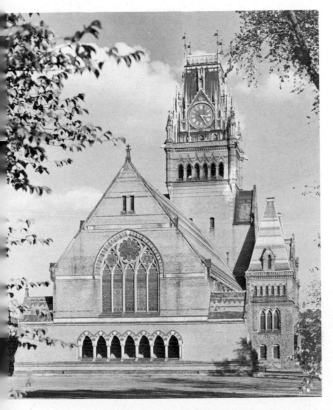

5–6. Memorial Hall, Harvard University, Cambridge, Massachusetts, 1870–1878, by Ware and Van Brunt.

planometric brick walls, which are interrupted by the accents of three projecting pavilions supported on heavy engaged columns, the only conspicuous ornament of the facade. This somewhat austere area is contrasted with the series of busily gabled dormer windows above, resulting in a composition in which the viewer is given an opportunity to grasp both simple massiveness and picturesque accents, each an outstanding characteristic of the eclecticism of the 1870's at its best.

The Connecticut State Capitol at Hartford, 1878 (*AB 703), by Richard M. Upjohn, the son of the elder Upjohn, is far more typical of the period in its confusion of stylistic sources and what seems to present-day taste its inconsistency of design. This edifice, begun in 1873, was one of the major public buildings of the era and is notable for its impressive exterior mass, contrasting with what must be a deliberate interior openness, and for its elaborate detail and richness of material. In it, the combination of medieval detail with classical proportion and symmetry (even to the choice of a dome instead of a tower) makes it difficult to classify it simply as Gothic Revival. In fact here the two principal aspects of the eclecticism of the period seem consciously to be combined.

The individualistic eclecticism of this period is more often mishandled than not, as in the Connecticut Capitol. But in the hands of great architects like Richardson, it is done with restraint and authority as in his Trinity Church, Boston (Illustration 5–15). Sometimes there is more authority than restraint, as in the work of Frank Furness whose extravagantly pictorial architecture epitomizes what used to be considered the worst aspects of the period. It is irresponsibly eclectic, heavy, ungainly, indeed almost ugly. Though a student of Hunt, Furness revolted against Beaux Arts correctness, and developed a strongly personal style. His eccentric detail and formal juxtapositions seem almost a travesty on the already ponderous masses and relentlessly emphatic ornament of the most obtrusive neo-Gothic of the time. But the powerful effect of his buildings cannot be denied. Their eccentricity is partly explained by the fact that the principal source of his ideas was not English, but derived from the Frenchman Viollet-le-Duc, whose designs are unusually idiosyncratic for an archaeologist, his gawky, bold forms seeming to arise from no specific origin. Something of the relative heaviness of form and detail that distinguishes American "General Grant" Gothic from English High Victorian Gothic could possibly be ascribed to this influence, for Furness was only the most conspicuous and original representative of a number of architects working in a similar way.

What seems to modern taste an almost surrealist crankiness in Furness was hardly considered so during his life, for he received in the 1870's and early 1880's some of the most important commissions in a city where there were twenty-six registered architects. To compare Memorial Hall at Harvard with Furness' Pennsylvania Academy of the Fine Arts in Philadelphia, 1871–1876 (AB 363), is to find it to be a model of restraint in contrast to Furness' building. The banking area of the old Provident Trust Company Building, 1879, later the Philadelphia National Bank (recently demolished) (AB 364; Illustration 5–7), is typical of Furness' several banks, only one of which still remains. Perhaps no uglier, yet at the same time no bolder, more masculine, or more dramatic a small building (shown at the far left of the photograph) could be found anywhere. Such monuments as Memorial Hall and the works of Furness are beginning to be appreciated again for their bold plasticity, variety, and originality, especially when they are compared with the aseptic academicism of the buildings of the next generation.

Victorian Gothic was not so well adapted to utilitarian and commercial architecture as was the style of the Second Empire, though a number of important buildings could be pointed out, typified at their best by Richardson's Marshall Field Warehouse (Illustration 5–19) or Sullivan's Auditorium (Illustration 5–21), both in Chicago.

In domestic architecture it is difficult to single out examples which are as specifically medieval

5–7. Provident Trust Company Building (destroyed), Philadelphia, Pennsylvania, 1879, by Frank Furness.

in their inspiration as were the castellated mansions and Gothic Revival cottages of the pre-Civil War period. The mansard style was more adapted to the grandiose taste of the time than was the medieval, with the consequence that when the Gothic did appear in the large houses it was often combined with elements of the Second Empire in such a way that it was not certain whether the building was a castle or a palace.

Some large houses, however, show little mansard or other classical detail. Typical in its medieval picturesqueness, and an unusually eloquent example of bold composition and rich juxtaposition of textures, colors, and materials is the Mark Twain House in Hartford, Connecticut (Illustration 5–8)—now a public memorial—which Edward Tuckerman Potter built for the humorist in 1874. Less typical are the complexity of its plan and the variety of its elements, among which are three towers, five balconies, an "ombra" (shaded deck), and a kind of three-sided veranda on the third floor which was intended to recall a pilot house. Gothic was frequently employed in smaller houses, though it was usually combined with the heavier forms of Viollet-le-Duc's eccentric medievalism, or, more often, with the "Queen Anne" and stick styles, both of which are also represented in the rich amalgam which is the Mark Twain House.

"Queen Anne" (best represented by the work of the English architect Norman Shaw) is strangely misnamed, for it is largely late Gothic in derivation (exploiting at the same time certain medievalisms which persisted in provincial seventeenth-century vernacular architecture in England) and is not at all like the Renaissance style used in the houses of Christopher Wren's

followers during the reign of Queen Anne. In it the country house tradition of open plan and structural integrity is combined with the usual eclecticism, deriving from many sources, but principally medieval. An emphasis on horizontal extensions and picturesque grouping is supplemented by the use of half-timber, hung tiles, and other details and materials evocative of "olde" England. The "Queen Anne" style enriched the functional and formal vocabulary of domestic architecture, and in America was an impressive addition to the long list of domestic types imported from England; though similar in feeling to the relaxed early Georgian dwelling, it was very different in plan and detail. "Queen Anne" became very popular in the United States, particularly after examples had been seen at the British exhibit at the Philadelphia Centennial. The more superficial elements of Norman Shaw were copied by his followers in England and especially in this country, but in the hands of more original architects only the significant elements were exploited: horizontality, open plan, and the use of rich material. Richardson's Watts Sherman House, Newport, Rhode Island, 1874 (AB 438, AB 439, AB 442, AB 443), is probably the outstanding American example. The open stairway, great hall, half-timber construction,

5–8. Elevation of the Mark Twain House, Hartford, Connecticut, 1874, by Edward Tuckerman Potter.

5–9.   The Cram-Sturtevant House, Middletown, Rhode Island, 1871–1872, by Dudley Newton.

and rich contrasts of textures are all very English and in the manner of Norman Shaw. Even the usual American piazza or porch has been omitted. The only indigenous element is Richardson's substitution of shingle for Shaw's hung tile. Yet the openness of the plan and the horizontal accents in the exterior design (seen in the emphasis on the floor divisions and in the continuous enframement of rows of windows) in the Watts Sherman House are at least analogous to native American developments.

In some ways the stick style is not any less eclectic than the "Queen Anne," for it utilizes details derived from many sources, including, sometimes, even Mohammedan. Yet it is the logical outgrowth of the mid-century cottage typified by Upjohn's Hoppin House (Illustration 4–38) and thus fits less into the history of revivalism than into the mainstream of the development of the indigenous country house from

the cottage of the pre-Civil War period to the prairie houses of Frank Lloyd Wright.

One of the best examples of the stick style is the Cram-Sturtevant House in Middletown, near Newport, Rhode Island, by Dudley Newton, 1871–1872 (Illustration 5–9). A more available example, though not quite so fine, is the present Newport Art Association, formerly the Griswold House, 1862–1863, by Richard Morris Hunt. Like the cottages built earlier in the century, houses like these are partly romantic in their recall of medieval and other picturesque forms. Such elements are to be expected in the tradition of eclecticism, but here these nostalgic details are considerably modified and subordinated to the emphasis on structural elements. More important than these essentially superficial details are the openness of plan and the flow of space seen in the interplay between interior and exterior, a relationship which is dramatized by a plethora of porches, stairways, bay windows, and French doors, further elaborated in the complex juxtaposition of eaves and dormers with the various planes of the roofs.

The stick style was one of the last to be popularized by the carpentry or pattern books. The best designs were published by George E. Woodward in the late 1860's and early 1870's. In *Woodward's Country Homes* (1865), as well as in books by other authors, both the open plan and the emphasis on structural framing in the design were stressed. The lightness of construction inherent in the balloon frame, and recommended by Woodward and others (AB 288, AB 309), was by the 1870's almost universally preferred over the older methods of framing and had much to do with the spread of a popularized stick style for smaller dwellings.

At its best the stick style, though short-lived (an interruption in building activity following the panic of 1873 brought it to a premature close), helped break through the heavy forms of the Second Empire and the Victorian Gothic, and prepared the way for the shingle style. But unfortunately the simplicity of such designs as those by Woodward was not the rule. Ill-digested eclecticism usually concealed structural honesty, and the stick and "Queen Anne" styles were combined with other stylistic ingredients, and even with a kind of vernacular Second Empire, in which ornament came to be increasingly elaborate and various. This emphasis on detail became more and more exuberant (or ostentatious, according to one's taste) after the invention of the power-run scroll saw which could turn out the most inventive variations on conventional decorative motifs in a matter of minutes. A somewhat extreme example is the Carson House (now a club) at Eureka, California, 1886 (AB 385); it would be difficult indeed to distinguish its various stylistic elements.

The Shingle Style

The elements that went into the making of the shingle style were the stick and "Queen Anne" styles, American colonial architecture of the seventeenth century, and even some Japanese influence inspired by buildings at the Philadel-

phia Centennial and by a house in the Japanese manner published by Viollet-le-Duc.

The best of the pre-Richardson examples is the elevation and plan for a house on Mount Desert Island, Maine, 1879 (Illustration 5–10), by William Ralph Emerson, an architect who worked very successfully in the style from its beginning to its end. The house is open and flexible in plan and there is considerable variety in the interpenetrations of space. Its pleasingly picturesque massing is not too busy or unreadable, and the "Queen Anne" detail is kept to a minimum. The coherence of its design is enhanced by the use of shingle throughout—the first such usage not combined with clapboard or masonry. (It is the employment of shingles as a unifying element—like a kind of skin spread over the frame—that chiefly distinguishes the shingle from the stick style, though one grew from the other.) Other architects besides Emerson were working in similar directions in designs for smaller houses as well as for cottages scattered along the length of the New England coast, and to a certain extent in New Jersey.

Richardson's contributions to the suburban and resort dwelling are the most successful manifestations of the shingle style; in his hands it became an almost contemporary manner, very nearly severed from eclecticism. The John Bryant House at Cohasset, Massachusetts, 1880; the Percy Brown House at Marion, Massachusetts, 1881–1882 (AB 452; Illustration 5–11); and the M. F. Stoughton House, Cambridge, Massachusetts, 1882–1883 (AB 454), all of shingle, are his best designs in the style. The first two are entirely lacking in eclectic detail, at least in the exteriors; this is not the case in the majority of Richardson's other work. Though the Stoughton House has Tudor chimney pots and a seventeenth-century overhang, and though the housing of the stair area recalls a Romanesque turret, these details are relatively inconspicuous. All three of the houses are irregular in plan and elevation and free-flowing in distribution of space, and they display considerable interpenetration between exterior and interior. The Bryant House is a little more "studied" or more obviously sophisticated than the latter two in

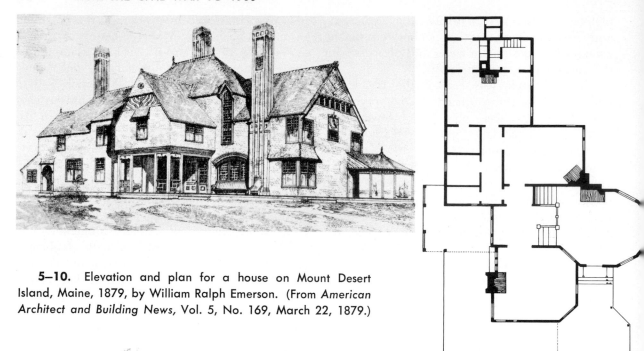

5–10. Elevation and plan for a house on Mount Desert Island, Maine, 1879, by William Ralph Emerson. (From *American Architect and Building News*, Vol. 5, No. 169, March 22, 1879.)

its Shavian manor house "hall" and stairway, and in the nicely proportioned asymmetry of its facade—though its plan is less open and flowing. The simpler Brown House is notable for the carefully studied interrelation between the two main rooms and the porch. More remarkable, however, are the almost continuous opening extending from the porch to the study and the literally continuous fenestration across living room, hall, and study, which seems thoroughly contemporary. The horizontality of the design and its relationship with the porch are further emphasized by the low roof line of the second floor, penetrated not by the usual acute-angled gables, but by a gambrel shape and by dormers with obtuse-angled pediments. The Stoughton House is not as satisfactorily simple as are the other two, but its plan, while more complex, is more flowing, and the three-dimensional composition of the house is the most successful.

In these three houses, and perhaps best in the Brown House, Richardson accomplished for the resort, suburb, and residential areas of the Northeast what Frank Lloyd Wright was later to achieve for the Midwest in his prairie houses.

Of the many architects besides Emerson and Richardson who built dwellings in the shingle style, among the more successful were Lamb and Rice in New York, Wilson Eyre in the fashionable Philadelphia suburbs on the Main Line and Chestnut Hill, Arthur Little in the Boston area, John Calvin Stevens in Maine, and Bruce Price in Tuxedo Park, New York. The last three are the most interesting. Little's work is a trifle too quaint; he was fond of incorporating exotic shapes such as those of lighthouses into his seaside houses on the north shore of Boston (a failing sometimes shared by William Ralph Emerson until he came under the chastening influence of Richardson). John Calvin Stevens took over the best aspects of Emerson's style as represented in his Mount Desert House, and epitomized it into a kind of classic expression of the shingle style, bringing to it a more conspicuous sense of order and coherence, in accordance with a theory of organic architecture

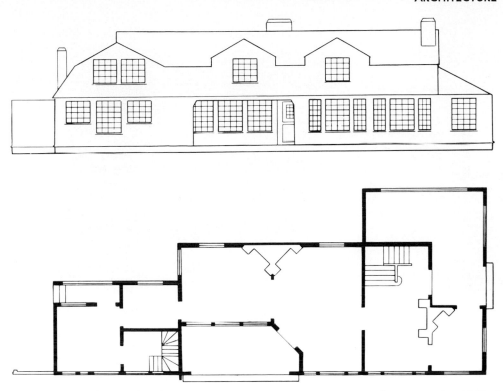

5–11. Elevation and plan for the Percy Brown House, Marion, Massachusetts, 1881–1882, by Henry Hobson Richardson. (Adapted from Richardson's drawings deposited in the Houghton Library, Harvard University, Cambridge, Massachusetts.)

developed in his book, *Examples of American Domestic Architecture* (1889), already mentioned. A typical Stevens house is the James Hopkins Smith House at Falmouth Foreside, Maine, 1885–1900, remodeled in 1945–1946 (*AB 529), in which an unusually open plan and a fine feeling for the site are combined with a clear-cut ordering of complex areas. The C. A. Brown House by Stevens, at Delano Park, Cape Elizabeth, Maine, 1885–1886 (AB 529A), one of the finest examples of the style (the more so since it has not been remodeled, and some of the original color is preserved in its interior), is notable for a greater refinement than is usual in the relating of stone to shingle, often rather insensitively handled by other builders of the time. A quite late example of the shingle style, but one which sums up the best of both the style and of Stevens' own work is the Fred

Gignoux House, also at Delano Park on Cape Elizabeth, 1905 (Illustration 5–12), remarkable for a feeling of symmetry where actually none exists.

The later work of many other architects in the shingle style, particularly that of Little, became not only symmetrical but was overwhelmed by a revival of eighteenth-century detail. (This influence from the colonial past succeeded that of the previous, still medieval, colonial style that had coincided with the Tudorisms of the "Queen Anne" style.) The houses by Bruce Price at Tuxedo Park exhibit these classicizing tendencies only in their rather strict symmetry; in other respects they are very original. Both their formality and their individuality may derive from Price's employer, the developer of Tuxedo Park, Pierre Lorillard, whose enthusiasm for Mayan architecture (im-

5–12. Fred Gignoux House, Delano Park, Cape Elizabeth, Maine, 1905, by John Calvin Stevens.

portant examples of which he had helped discover) may have influenced the monumental symmetry and heavy stone chimney of his own house by Price, and also the terrace of the William Kent House, 1885 (Illustration 5–13). The use of shingles and clapboard, the prominence of terrace and porch, and the exploitation of the view in the Kent House are in the best of the shingle style tradition, albeit interpreted in a very personal way.

Some of the early work of McKim, Mead & White in the shingle style before they entered their period of academic classicism is worthy of comparison with Richardson's. Indeed, it may have been very much influenced by the older man, since White had worked first in Richardson's office. White's native overrefinement, however, given fuller scope than was allowed in Richardson's office, was responsible for the somewhat less vigorous quality of the firm's work in comparison with that of Richardson. This refinement can be seen in the Newport Casino, 1880–1881 (*AB 544)—not a house, of course, but a complex of buildings domestic in feeling—and, at its most exquisite, in the dining room added by White to Upjohn's Kingscote in 1880 (AB 509), for which the inspiration was specifically

Japanese, and at the same time remarkably "modern" in its simplicity and lightness. Southside, the Robert W. Goelet House at Newport, 1882–1883 (AB 511), is interesting for its unusually open and flowing plan, but its great hall is so cluttered with eclectic detail and its facade so cut up that it lacks the coherence of a house by Richardson or even by Emerson. Yet it is more delicate in scale and elegant in feeling than the work of either, reflecting the personal style of White. The Isaac Bell House, also at Newport, 1882–1883 (AB 500, *AB 501), is perhaps the most successful of the firm's houses in the shingle style. Though less coherent than the Stoughton House, it is even freer in plan, making use of sliding doors, for instance, in emulation of the moving screens of Japanese dwellings. But again the detail is too refined and small-scaled and there is something mannered in the use of arches over the third-story windows and in the spindly Japanese imitation bamboo pillars of the porch—neither of which seems really part of an integrated design. The William Low House (now the Paul C. Nicholson, Jr., House) at Bristol, Rhode Island, 1887 (AB 510), the last of the firm's houses which can be said to be in the shingle style, is sym-

5-13. William Kent House, Tuxedo Park, New York, 1885, by Bruce Price.

metrical, like those of Bruce Price. In spite of this and the arbitrarily unifying pitched roof, its all-embracing sweep gives a certain grandeur to the long walls of shingle, to the bay windows and the wide porch. This assurance of design, coupled with a rejection of "Queen Anne" and other eclecticisms, makes the Low House one of the most impressive examples of the shingle style—and one in which the absence of White's usual detail compensates for a certain lack of freedom in plan. The symmetry seen in the Low House and in some of Price's houses influenced the early work of Frank Lloyd Wright leading to the development of his prairie houses. Wright's own house at Oak Park, built only two years later than the Low House, greatly resembles one or two of Price's houses at Tuxedo Park.

Perhaps the best general manifestation of the shingle style occurred in the estate or "development" house, as in the small dwellings at Tuxedo Park, and those of the Land Trust on Easton's Beach, Middletown, Rhode Island, near Newport, built in the 1880's (Illustration 5–14). There is a pleasing irregularity of plan and profile in the Land Trust Houses and a variation in shape and orientation. Porches, bay windows, and ample halls are elements of their open planning and integration of interior with exterior, while the use of shingles and of an occasional gambrel or overhang recalls the older indigenous architecture of the region. The several cottages are arranged with freedom and variety of placing and with attention to spaciousness and exposure, even in a relatively confined

5-14. Land Trust Houses, Easton's Beach, Middletown, Rhode Island, 1880's.

area. Excellent in design, sensitive in use of material and in a feeling for the site, this group of houses of anonymous authorship (it is known, however, that Olmsted laid out the site) is greatly superior to the average development housing of today.

The shingle style became almost ubiquitous on the eastern seacoast and in many suburban areas. At its most pretentious it became graceless and monstrous, characterized by too many badly integrated relationships of solids and voids, and by the use of too many materials. Unfortunately, all too often the worst aspects of the rampant eclecticism of the 1870's are combined with the shingle style; thus by association our judgment of the more restrained examples by Richardson and others is influenced negatively.

An interesting offshoot of the shingle style was its employment in the large seaside hotel, which became an elephantine shingled cottage surrounded with rings of stick-supported porches, and covered with great roofs cascading between protuberances of turrets and sharply pitched dormer windows. Fine examples at Jamestown, Rhode Island, and on Mount Desert Island, Maine, existed before the depredation of time, fire, and hurricanes; perhaps the best surviving example (though atypical in that it is not actually shingled and is therefore more accurately described as stick style) is on the west coast, the Hotel del Coronado, in Coronado, California, near San Diego, 1887–1888 (AB 671, *AB 672, *AB 673, AB 674), by James W. and Merritt Reid.

By 1890 the shingle style was nearly outmoded. By then the well-known firm of McKim, Mead & White had turned its back on this indigenous style and embraced the new classicism with enthusiasm and equal accomplishment— as seen in the first completely colonial revival house (actually Georgian–Adamesque), built for H. A. C. Taylor in Newport in 1886. By 1897 even Dudley Newton, the architect of the exuberantly original Cram-Sturtevant House in the stick style, built for himself in Newport an academic residence complete with pilaster strips, broken curved pediments, a fanlighted doorway,

and a classical portico—a house thoroughly conventional, symmetrical, and, of course, in "good taste." Meanwhile the very rich were building Roman *palazzi* and French *châteaux*. Thus the colonial revival and the Beaux Arts tradition overwhelmed the shingle style. Symmetry and grandiose spaciousness replaced subtle proportions and spatial sensibility. Henry James was undoubtedly describing a house in the stick or shingle style in *The International Episode* when he wrote of its "verandas of extraordinary width, with such an accessible hospitable air, such expansive thresholds and reassuring interiors"— the kind of house he so much preferred to those "white elephants," the neighboring marble palaces by Hunt. So ended for all intents and purposes one of the best periods in the history of the detached dwelling, though a kind of emasculated version continued in the East for about twenty years longer. In the Midwest, however, the spirit of the style was continued by the dogged Frank Lloyd Wright, and in the Far West it was combined with the indigenous California ranch tradition.

Henry Hobson Richardson

In the results of a poll conducted in 1885 by the *American Architect and Building News*, four of the ten most popular buildings in the entire United States were by Richardson. He was not only admired in his own time, but among all the architects of the nineteenth century he is the most accepted today—with the possible exception of Sullivan. He epitomized the typical architecture of his age and at the same time almost transcended it, prefiguring certain modern developments. But whatever Richardson's importance in the history of architecture, his work speaks to us with an assured and commanding eloquence as sheer building, irrespective of styles and theory. We look at his work and we must admire it, even if we may be a little overpowered by its sheer strength or too much reminded by it of the confused eclecticism of such contemporaries as the Potter brothers. Richardson was seldom led astray by ill-conceived stylistic juxtapositions, for, even though he sometimes combined French Romanesque, Byzantine, and Early Christian Syrian with Renaissance, he did so with a creative imagination which made their lack of logic believable. Richardson had the vigor and strength of the best of his period, and in him they became monumental and grand yet hardly ever pretentious. He shared the taste of his generation for rich and contrasting materials, colors, and textures, but never settled for shoddy imitations, for he personally supervised the choice or manufacture of his building materials. Richardson was an end product of the old masonry tradition; he loved stone and brick for their own sakes, and in general rejected the new metal construction—though when he used it, he did so honestly, as in his Fenway Bridge and the Harrison Avenue Ames Store (Illustration 5–20). Similarly, he accepted the fact of the railroad, designing his small stations not in imitation of English gardeners' cottages, but with an emphasis on horizontality expressive of the far-reaching tracks upon which the stations are an occasional accent.

His ability to express the identity of a building was one of Richardson's outstanding characteristics. It not only contributed toward making him greater than his contemporaries, but also made him more significant than as a mere link in the chain of the early development of modern architecture; for if expressiveness can be thought of as an architectural concept, Richardson is the architect who best illustrates it. His buildings clearly express their function not solely architecturally, but in the broadest or most poetic sense. The Allegheny Courthouse (Illustration 5–17) symbolizes the power of the State; the attached Jail, the inescapable strength of the imprisoning walls. The Marshall Field Warehouse (Illustration 5–19) conveys the power of wealth of a merchant prince; and Richardson's shingle style houses (*AB 452, AB 454; Illustration 5–11) suggest the relaxed freedom of the resort or suburb and the love of the open air. Both the powerful massiveness of Richardson and what may be called his symbolic expressiveness are becoming more appreciated now that architecture in the 1960's seems to be swinging more in these very direc-

tions and away from the open, light forms and obvious functionalism of the earlier decades of this century.

Henry Hobson Richardson, born into an aristocratic Louisiana family, was educated at Harvard and studied further at the École des Beaux Arts in Paris. This experience was supplemented by work in the offices of Théodore Labrouste, the brother of the better known Henri Labrouste. Richardson's work can be divided into two categories, but only for purposes of discussion, since each partakes of something of the other and both share their author's expressiveness. First, Richardson sums up the picturesque eclecticism of his era, beginning his career with the two most popular styles, the Second Empire and the High Victorian Gothic. These he replaced with his version of the Romanesque, making it more personal than any of the revivals had been in the hands of his contemporaries. Something of the forthright bulk and vigorous richness of the Romanesque suited Richardson's own expansive nature and even his physical person, for he was enormous, black-bearded, and vital—one of the "figures of earth" who inhabited the America of this era of expansion, energy, and ostentation. The second important facet of Richardson's work was his less eclectic production, for he took part in perfecting the shingle style and stopped just short of participating in the other important architectural development at the end of the century, the skyscraper.

Richardson produced only a few buildings in the style of the Second Empire, and these were very restrained and almost classical in comparison with those by other American architects. He soon turned to the Gothic, producing in the Unity Church, Springfield, Massachusetts, 1866–1869, a less chaotic amalgam of medievalisms than was usual among his contemporaries. In his Brattle Street Church, Boston, 1870–1872, Richardson showed his feeling for texture and color in the use of rough pudding-stone and varied polychromy; there is also a fine sense of composition in the campanile-inspired tower, beautifully proportioned and not strictly imitative of any Italian prototype.

Trinity Church, Copley Square, Boston, 1873–1877 (AB 435, AB 436, *AB 437; Illustration 5–15), is Richardson's masterpiece in what might be called his traditional as opposed to his forward-looking manner, though it is certainly not a merely eclectic building. Trinity is Richardson's first important essay in the Romanesque, but he did not employ northern European sources for inspiration as did Renwick in the earlier Romanesque Revival. Instead, he found his prototypes in more directly simple examples from southern France and from Spain, combining them in a design very cleverly adapted to the triangular site at Copley Square, which faces in one direction almost as much as another. This problem of orientation is solved in the interior by a central plan rather than the more conventional one on a longitudinal axis. The rich Byzantine-inspired decoration, applied under the direction of the painter John La Farge, was the first large-scale mural program in the United States, a far cry from the austere classical interiors of the Adamesque and Greek Revival meetinghouses. At the same time the decoration in Trinity is a great deal subtler and less brutally scaled than most neo-medieval ornament of the time. Trinity's chief virtue is its simplicity. Massive and commanding, the building holds its own among its neighbors: the New South Church by Cummings and Sears, 1874–1875, typically High Victorian Gothic, more aggressive but less sure; the elegant and self-consciously restrained Boston Public Library by McKim, Mead & White (Illustration 5–27); the more effete good taste of the Hilton-Plaza Hotel; and the tall white neutralities of the neighboring new insurance companies, flaunting their ideal of security in commonplace conservative design. Trinity Church was extremely influential, as were many of Richardson's other revivalist structures, especially the Hampden County Courthouse Building in Springfield, Massachusetts.

Nearly as eclectic as Trinity but more interesting from the point of view of their somewhat functional approach are a group of library buildings by Richardson. The first, the Winn Memorial Library, 1876, Woburn, Massachusetts, is

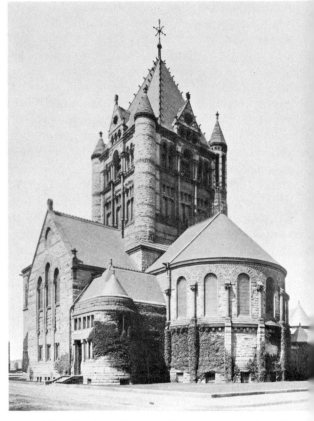

5–15. Trinity Church, Boston, Massachusetts, 1873–1877, by Henry Hobson Richardson. [From *Monographs of American Architecture, V* (Boston: 1888).]

more archaeologically picturesque on the whole than the others, though it introduces into the long stack area an almost continuous band of fenestration, and into the reading room an adaptation of the tall Gothic window in a form that amounts to a window-wall at the end. Thus Richardson demonstrated his appreciation of the importance of light in a library and expressed it in the design. He exploited these solutions of the lighting problem with greater clarity and effect at the Ames Free Library at North Easton, Massachusetts, 1877–1879 (*AB 444, AB 446), while also simplifying the building as a whole. Richardson employed here for the first time the huge entrance arch (associated from then on with his style) derived from Syrian examples which impressed his imagination with their powerful forms and cavernous darkness. At the Crane Memorial Library at Quincy, Massachusetts, 1880–1883 (AB 451), a further refinement of the problem of library illumination was attempted, for here the fenestration of the stack area becomes a continuous band. The plan is also functional despite the picturesque asymmetry of turret, gable, and arch. Very original are the curious "eyelid" windows of the roof which repeat in their arched shape the curve of the entrance, a repetition needed in a building otherwise fairly rectangular.

Less forward-looking, though not less formally inventive, is Sever Hall, Harvard University, Cambridge, Massachusetts, 1878–1880 (AB 475; Illustration 5–16), a building much admired for its adaptation to its architectural environment and for the refinement of its "Queen Anne"-derived detail. Here Richardson turned to red

5–16. Entrance, Sever Hall, Harvard University, Cambridge, Massachusetts, 1878–1880, by Henry Hobson Richardson.

brick, symmetry, and even a pediment to echo the earlier architectural traditions of the neighboring buildings in the Harvard Yard. He retained, however, the basic medievalisms of the turrets and the deep Syrian entrance arch, a feature which in no way improves the almost Stygian darkness of the halls. Richardson reverted to the prevailing esthetic of the primacy of appearance over function, and designed a building whose exterior is pleasing because of its proportions and its beautifully chosen brick, but which is gloomy and cramped within, as were so many public schools derived from it.

More successful is the Allegheny County Courthouse and Jail, Pittsburgh, Pennsylvania, 1884–1886 (AB 455, AB 456, *AB 487, *AB 487A; Illustration 5–17), the most assured and expansive of Richardson's primarily revivalist buildings. The Courthouse has the impact of a classic building in its emphatically symmetrical facade, encompassing three cave-like entrance arches, and crowned by a central tower. Though the Romanesque detail is almost pedantic in its correctness, and the masonry is somewhat monotonous in its lack of contrasting textures and of polychromy, these defects are compensated for by the repeated heavily voussoired arches, which serve to tie together the total design both in the formal facade and in the more functional courtyard. The assurance of this motif is echoed in the arches of the lower floor and in the vaults of the entrance lobby, reminiscent of those in Piranesi's prisons, but not so oppressive. The Jail, attached to the Courthouse, is perhaps the only building worthy to be compared with the products of the sinister imagination of the great Italian engraver. Though the building's structure recalls the fortified towns of southern France and Castile, and though the towers (necessary for ventilation) are also perhaps too picturesque, the eloquence of the sheer rough-hewn granite in almost Cyclopean proportions is overpowering. The voussoirs of the arches over the few openings in the great wall are eight feet in length, and comprise only a mere detail in the gigantic enclosure surrounding the prison complex—made more impressive because it meets at several

5–17.   Allegheny County Courthouse and Jail, Pittsburgh, Pennsylvania, 1884–1886, by Henry Hobson Richardson.   (From *Inland Architect and News Record*, Vol. 13, No. 5, May, 1889.)

obtuse angles, since the area which is confined is polygonal. Even the huge functional chimney, in its proportion and feeling for material, partakes of the formal quality of an exercise in abstract columnar form, a dramatic vertical cylinder among a complex of cubes and flat surfaces.

It is in domestic architecture that Richardson's highest achievement occurs, especially in the resort or suburban house, where we have already seen his progression from the masterly Watts Sherman House in the "Queen Anne" style to the finest examples of the shingle style. One other of his country or suburban houses, though too large to be strictly shingle, is the R. T. Paine House, Waltham, Massachusetts, 1884–

1886 (AB 457, AB 458). The wide living room (or hall) and the parlor with the subsidiary area which is contained in one of the towers are imaginative in their handling of space. Some details, however, such as the incongruous Palladian window on one of the facades, are sadly out of place and lead to the suspicion that they were additions by someone in Richardson's office rather than his own.

Closer to Richardson's smaller resort and suburban houses is the remarkable Ames Gate Lodge at North Easton, Massachusetts, 1880–1881 (AB 448, AB 450; Illustration 5–18), singled out here because of the expressive power of its gate and wing, combined in a simple mass punctuated by a turret which acts as a kind of anchor for the roof covering the gateway, a great arch of enormous proportions. The whole complex is constructed of boulders, relieved only by the simplest window enframements and by "eyelid" dormers in the roof. In the words of Richardson's biographer, Henry-Russell Hitchcock, it looks like a great "glacial moraine roofed and made habitable."[2]

Richardson's urban houses are not quite so interesting as his country ones, when judged from the viewpoint of the history of domestic architecture in the nineteenth century. Not that they were without distinction, as were the rectory for Trinity Church, and the attached John Hay and Henry Adams houses (now demolished) in Washington. The best and most original of Richardson's city houses is the J. J. Glessner House in Chicago, 1885–1887 (AB 460), which presents to the street a forbidding wall surface barely penetrated by the relatively small openings, while the other side of the house looks out on a courtyard. This contrast was not a mere whim of design but was motivated by the

proximity of the Michigan Central Railroad tracks. Thus the house is like some on the Mediterranean which are inhospitable from the street and concentrate on the amenities of the patio. This is not to say that the street facade of the Glessner House is not handsome, for Richardson solved the problem in the vigorous and frank way that would be expected of him.[3]

Richardson's place in the evolution of the commercial building is not unimportant. In the recently demolished Marshall Field Warehouse, 1885–1887 (Illustration 5–19), he achieved a masterpiece of the masonry tradition just as it reached its end with the invention of the new metal-supported skyscraper construction. Rejecting the picturesque variety of form and material typical of earlier commercial buildings, Richardson in this great cubical structure seems also to have almost entirely done away with archaeological reminiscence. Only the cornice recalls a medieval prototype. The beautifully integrated design is relieved from monotony by a lower story whose flaring curve expresses the weight-bearing function of the lower stages of the masonry, which carry the burden of the seven upper stories, and by a trabeated attic, between which are two sets of arcades; one, incorporating three stories, is twice as wide as the other which in turn encompasses the other two floors. Less noticeable is the remarkable subtlety shown in the variety of the masonry coursing, which grows smaller as the walls rise, though not in an absolutely consistent rhythm, which would have been monotonous.

Constructed mainly of self-supporting masonry walls, both the large size of the building and its extensive fenestration were facilitated by the use of interior metal supports. Thus technologically the Marshall Field Warehouse was not behind the times, though it was certainly not progressive, like the buildings of some of Richardson's Chicago contemporaries. But the grand simplicity of its design was of the most masterly authority, a logical conclusion and culmination of the masonry-constructed commercial building.

This important structure was torn down recently to make way for a parking lot.

5–18. Ames Gate Lodge, North Easton, Massachusetts, 1880–1881, by Henry Hobson Richardson. [From *Monographs of American Architecture, III* (Boston: 1886).]

5–19. Marshall Field Warehouse (destroyed), Chicago, Illinois, 1885–1887, by Henry Hobson Richardson.

One other commercial building by Richardson, however, the Harrison Avenue Ames Store in Boston, 1886–1887 (Illustration 5–20), shows intimations of an understanding of the new method of metal framing, a factor reflected also in its design, so unlike the first metal-framed skyscraper, the Home Life Insurance Company Building, Chicago, where the construction was *not* expressed. Though there are more medieval reminiscences in the Ames store than in the Marshall Field building, the main motif of windows grouped vertically under arches between piers, used by Richardson in all his commercial buildings, is here treated with iron I-beams between the floors, rather than with masonry. These beams are simply exposed as such and not hidden, an example of Richardson's always honest employment of materials. This usage is completely consistent with the long tradition in Boston commercial architecture of trabeated post and lintel, which Richardson used in the lower floor. Here, in a dramatic juxtaposition in downtown Boston, is a demonstration of the conscious continuity of a structural device from masonry to metal, a commentary on the basic sensitivity of an architect who, had he lived longer, would have made some contribution to design in the use of the new material and new methods (though the eventual development toward light, volumetric forms would not have been consistent with Richardson's taste for the massive). Richardson was quoted as having said that the things he wanted most to design were a grain elevator and the interior of a river steamboat.

The series of suburban stations for the Boston and Albany Railroad illustrate more effectively Richardson's adaptability to contemporary con-

5–20. Harrison Avenue Ames Store, Boston, Massachusetts, 1886–1887, by Henry Hobson Richardson.

ditions. One of the best is at Chestnut Hill, Massachusetts, 1881–1884 (AB 453), where the low pitched roof blends into the covering of the platform. This station and others, notably the one at Auburndale, Massachusetts, are expressive as structures within the larger complex of the railroad as a whole.

In sum, Richardson was a superb designer, comprehending in his work the best aspects of his era. Even if he was not in the vanguard of technological advance, he erected some buildings which are masterpieces of formal and expressive architecture, and in his domestic building in the shingle style he brought to a culminating formula a long indigenous tradition hardly to be excelled even in the twentieth century.

Richardson was so important and influential a figure that after his death picturesque eclecticism could almost have been called Richardsonian, so pervasive were his formal ideas.

Though some of the work of Richardson's followers, including that of his own firm, Shepley, Rotan, and Coolidge (continuing today as Shepley, Bulfinch, Richardson, and Abbott), was either respectable or innocuous enough, the majority of it seemed to reflect those aspects of his style which are least attractive to the taste of our own time. We should be careful, therefore, not to allow our opinion of Richardson's work to be influenced by that of his myriad lesser imitators, represented by the insensitive proportions of a hundred Trinity churches and Sever Halls, by gloomy and forbidding interiors unrelieved by the beauty or variety of materials, and by misguided medieval travesties shoddily constructed and painted in depressing colors, which can be seen in almost any American city or town.

The Development of the Skyscraper; Louis Sullivan

The skyscraper was the most important new architectural form of the nineteenth century and, like domestic building in the shingle style, looked ahead into the twentieth century. But unlike the house, in which old traditions and materials were adapted to new ways of living, the skyscraper was made possible by technological advances.

Yet the history of architecture is by no means the history of technological progress alone. Though many skyscrapers were built during the final two decades of the century, only Louis Sullivan and a few other architects contributed a clear architectural form to the new building type, giving it a kind of perfection which after a hiatus of several decades the twentieth century is only now approaching again.

The subject of the skyscraper is more involved than might at first be apparent, for the development of the tall building was not due exclusively to the introduction of new techniques. In fact, many of the early skyscrapers had self-supporting load-bearing walls, using metal (in the form of iron beams) only for supplementary interior support. The subject is further complicated because the principal dimension of buildings of metal construction need not, in theory, be vertical, since the structure is essentially a series of cages indefinitely extendable in a horizontal direction as well. Thus some of the most architecturally interesting skyscrapers are essentially tall masonry buildings, like Richardson's Marshall Field Warehouse; and the most significant example among the large commercial buildings, Sullivan's Schlesinger and Meyer Department Store (now Carson, Pirie, Scott & Company) (Illustration 5–25), a structure in which the design exploits metal construction more brilliantly than any other until our own time, is longer than it is high. Nevertheless, the *American Builder* was correct when it stated as early as 1874 that height was the outstanding architectural feature of the age.

Two factors were chiefly responsible for the development of the skyscraper: the invention and perfection of the elevator, and the increasing use of metal, at first only as supplementary support in the form of iron beams but later for the entire frame.

The earliest large commercial structures which could be called skyscrapers had the appearance of being constructed totally of masonry, though interior support of metal was employed and the masonry walls could have been lightened, to allow more illumination. Typical examples were two buildings in New York, George Post's Western Union Building (destroyed), and the Tribune Building, 1873–1875 (AB 369), by Richard Morris Hunt, which is nine stories high and crowned with a tower. The possibilities inherent in metal support as supplementary to load-bearing walls were not exploited in the Tribune Building, though some attempt at an integrated composition was made by the introduction of tiers of Second Empire detail sandwiched between a pretentious lower floor and a mansard roof. Richardson's later Cheney Building, Hartford, Connecticut, 1875–1876, was more successful (within the framework of eclecticism) in incorporating tiers of windows in a blind arcade, a device the architect perfected later in the Marshall Field Warehouse and the Harrison Avenue Ames Store. Louis Sullivan in the Troescher Building (now the *Daily Times* Building) in Chicago, 1884 (AB 569), actually

preceded Richardson in the use of the undisguised I-beam as a part of the facade support. Though the detail is typically eclectic and, unlike Richardson's, not at all distinguished as an architectural design, the building is important in that a large expanse of glass was made possible by a technical device which is frankly exposed. Thus Sullivan's Troescher Building and Richardson's Harrison Avenue Ames Store, built two years later, were the first buildings in which the technological factor of metal support was consciously expressed in the design.

But these examples were only abortive beginnings. Not until Sullivan's Wainwright Building in St. Louis, 1890–1891 (AB 590), was the new type esthetically formulated.

Meanwhile, two kinds of skyscrapers were being constructed: first, essentially masonry buildings with only minimal supplementary metal support; and second, those which were basically of metal construction, whether this fact was disguised or not. The majority of examples in both categories are buildings without particular distinction.

The first group is characterized by an unimaginative piling up of tiers of poorly integrated copy-book revivalisms; the second (using much the same procedure), by a failure to realize the design potentials of the metal frame. However, there were the following exceptions (all in Chicago) in both categories. Among the masonry structures were the Auditorium by Sullivan, 1887–1889 (*AB 570, AB 571; Illustration 5–21), and the Monadnock Building by Burnham and Root, 1889–1891 (AB 603, AB 604); and among those of metal frame construction were the Reliance Building, 1890–1895 (AB 605; Illustration 5–22), by John W. Root, and the Tacoma Building (destroyed), 1887–1889, by Holabird and Roche.

It is interesting that all these structures are in Chicago; the need for a completely new commercial section in the rapidly growing midwestern metropolis had been acute since the great fire in the 1870's. The *American Slang Dictionary* of 1891 defined the skyscraper as "a very tall building such as now are being erected in Chicago."

Sullivan's Auditorium consists of a group of structures comprising a hotel, an opera house, and an office building (all now preserved as Roosevelt University). This huge edifice of weight-bearing masonry would not have been possible without interior metal support—and without considerable engineering ingenuity as well (the contribution largely of Dankmar Adler, Sullivan's partner). The devices for weight-carrying in the form of elaborate spreading foundations sunk in the soggy lakeside soil (originated by Burnham and Root in the Montauk Building of 1882, an invention without which the skyscraper would not have developed in Chicago), and the excellent acoustics of the opera house were the contributions of Adler, whose work was essential for the success of this huge complex. But Louis Sullivan's design is the finally impressive element. The building is certainly Richardsonian in its scale and its feeling of mass. It also reflects the simplicity of Richardson's late commercial architecture, as exemplified in the Marshall Field Warehouse, which was indeed the principal inspiration for the Auditorium's final design. (It is interesting to compare the final building, so massive and simple, with the two preliminary rejected designs, which were cut up with bay windows and oriels, and spiked with turrets and gables.) The interiors also reflect the largeness of Richardson's concepts. But Sullivan surpassed the older master in the magnificent hotel dining room, which is roofed by a boldly soffited vault supported by five arches that spring from the floor itself. Lit by a skylight (the room is on the top floor), and with the areas between the exterior arches completely glazed, affording a sweeping panoramic view of Lake Michigan, the dining room is one of the finest spatial concepts of the period.

5–21. Interior, Auditorium, Chicago, Illinois, 1887–1889, by Louis Sullivan.

The decoration throughout the building is especially fine, deriving from sources other than the usual heavy, angular Victorian Gothic detail inspired by Viollet-le-Duc and Sir Charles Eastlake. It is more original and complex, stemming from "Queen Anne" motifs and the floriate designs of William Morris and the late pre-Raphaelite Sir Edward Burne-Jones, with some influence from the ancient Anglo-Irish manuscript illuminations, then only recently reproduced. Sullivan's decorative enthusiasm occasionally ran away with him, but at its best his ornament either accents structural areas or is used simply as an all-over pattern on flat areas. The interior of the Auditorium (Illustration 5–21) itself is a good example of Sullivan's skill, for in contrast to the representational murals which are out of keeping with the magnificent architectural sweep of the vast vaulted space, Sullivan's ornament picks up and enhances both the flat areas and the various structural elements. Even the electric light bulbs are part of the integrated decorative scheme; their unshaded pinpoints of light are not only functional but become essential decorative accents in the total effect.

Though the Monadnock Building (AB 603) is one of the tallest edifices of the era, it is constructed almost entirely of brick. Basically the structure is an undecorated slab penetrated with openings, relieved only by the projection of tiers of bay windows to afford more light, and flared slightly at the base (as was the case in the Marshall Field Warehouse) not only to afford more support, but to give the impression of a solid base for the many stories of brick. The only non-functional element in the design is a flaring out of the top of the building in an elegant curve which recapitulates the similar treatment at the base. The uncomplicated eloquence of great size, restrained fenestration, and sweeping proportion with no need for eclectic or other decoration creates an effect which has hardly been matched in the history of architecture. The Monadnock Building is a late monument in the long tradition of masonry (albeit supplemented by interior metal support) which was soon to

disappear entirely in the large commercial building—at least in the form of self-supporting masonry walls.

Before turning to the Reliance and Tacoma buildings (structures with some architectural distinction, if not quite equal to the Monadnock in design), the Home Life Insurance Building in Chicago, 1886, should be mentioned. The designer, William Le Baron Jenney, an army engineer turned architect, was the first to use an entirely metal skeleton—a fact which was made clear during the building's recent demolition when the external masonry cladding was found to be carried on metal beams bolted into the internal skeleton. But important as this innovation was, no intimation of its structural character was seen in the design, a fact which was typical for decades after, with the exception of the brilliant Chicago school of the next few years, in which Jenney also took part.

The Tacoma Building (destroyed), 1887–1889, and the Reliance Building, 1890–1895 (AB 605; Illustration 5–22), by John W. Root, were two of the first metal skyscrapers to express that fact in their design. In these very similar structures, little masonry was used as fill-in and there was only an apology to eclectic decorative motifs. The rows of windows were barely interrupted by the cladding of the metal frame, and the resulting airy and suspended effect was enhanced by the rhythmic projection of tiers of bay windows. (This device for capturing more light increased the impression of volume and weightlessness but, oddly enough, was not carried on much after this date.)

Contemporaneously, perhaps under the influence of his partner William B. Mundie, Jenney rejected the conventional architectural mannerisms of the Home Life Insurance Building, and in the second Leiter Building (now Sears, Roebuck and Company), Chicago, 1889–1890 (Illustration 5–23), produced a very handsome, simple design in which only the heavy corner piers and the alternating smaller ones between the tiers of windows deny the fact that each bay and each support of the frame differs in no way from its neighbor. Otherwise, the

5–22. Reliance Building, Chicago, Illinois, 1890–1895, by John W. Root.

of structure. But in its design, Sullivan had another purpose besides that of illustrating his later dictum that form follows function: he wanted to express height. Here is his famous credo for the skyscraper in his own words:

What is the chief characteristic of the tall office building? And at once we answer, it is lofty. This loftiness is to the artist-nature its thrilling aspect. It is the very open organ tone of its appeal. It must be in turn the dominant chord in his expression of it, the true excitant of his imagination. It must be tall. The force and power of altitude must be in it. It must be every inch a proud and soaring thing, rising in sheer exaltation that from bottom to top it is a unit without a single dissenting line. . . .[4]

It could be argued that before Sullivan's formulation of its design solution the tall building had already been accepted—economically, as a form of advertisement, and, to a certain extent, esthetically. But it is also true that many architects seemed to be apologizing in their designs for the fact that the real estate owner was deriving the greatest possible income from his footage, by diverting attention from the height of a building through an emphasis on horizontal detail, as in the Tribune and Home Life Insurance buildings.

5–23. (Second) Leiter Building (now Sears, Roebuck and Company), Chicago, Illinois, 1889–1890, by William Le Baron Jenney.

clean lines and nearly continuous fenestration have a style that is both fairly expressive of structure and elegantly simple in effect.

At about the same time, in 1890, the year in which Burnham and Root started the Reliance Building, Sullivan created the first deliberate or conscious design for a tall building—or at least the first that was justified by a specific esthetic —the Wainwright Building in St. Louis, 1890–1891 (AB 590). Actually it is no more advanced than some of its predecessors in the expression

5–24. Guaranty Building (now Prudential Building), Buffalo, New York, 1894–1895, by Louis Sullivan.

In such a context the eloquence of Sullivan's words is amply justified in the Wainwright Building, for the vertical accents between the windows are the principal element in its design. There is a strange inconsistency, however, in the replacement of the usual classic entablature with a kind of heavy slab, which seems like a lid pressing down on the aspiring height of the structure. The distinction of the building, which derives from its smooth edges, its beautiful proportions, and its delicate and original decoration in Sullivan's characteristic non-eclectic style, makes us forget that actually the cage or "honeycomb" frame of the building is not being consistently revealed: the corners are unnecessarily

heavy, and the vertical piers between the windows are equal in width, whether they cover a basic supporting member or not. Actually the Reliance Building is more expressive of the tensile strength and airy lightness of the steel frame, even if it is not so refined in design. Sullivan's Schiller Building (later the Garrick Theater and now considerably changed) in Chicago, 1891–1892, is a variation on the Wainwright Building, though far taller. The Guaranty (now Prudential) Building in Buffalo, 1894–1895 (AB 580, AB 581; Illustration 5–24), marks a stage of further refinement. This structure is notable for its delicate coved cornice, which mitigates the harsh right angle of Sullivan's more usual crowning slab. Also, its use of columns on the shop front of the lower floor shows more clearly than the upper structure how open the construction actually is, since at the very base the open space is interrupted only at key points by support (AB 579). Unfortunately the lower floors have been considerably remodeled.

Sullivan's masterpiece, and the finest skyscraper until the mid-twentieth century, is the Schlesinger and Meyer Department Store (now Carson, Pirie, Scott & Company, and considerably altered), in Chicago, 1899–1904 (AB 582, AB 583, AB 584; Illustration 5–25). The cantilevered corner is the first expression of this potential of metal construction, and the articulation of the upper stories expresses perfectly the basic metal framing and takes full advantage in its design of the openness which makes this framing possible. The resulting design, especially the elegant formulation of the "Chicago window" (the division of the otherwise monotonous window area into three main parts by mullions) is almost twentieth-century in its precise and simple elegance. The lower floors, however, are not at all contemporary, for they are covered with the most elaborate floriate design—of great originality and vitality, but to modern taste somewhat incongruous with the unadorned areas above, which depend for their effect upon beautiful proportion alone.

Sullivan's principal achievement was the creation of a new style for a new building type. He was therefore the first modern architect, since he

5—25. Schlesinger and Meyer Department Store (now Carson, Pirie, Scott & Company), Chicago, Illinois, 1899–1904, by Louis Sullivan.

expressed structural facts in his design a basic tenet of contemporary architecture. It is not surprising, therefore, that Sullivan should have a quite conscious philosophy of architecture. It was based on the theory of organic growth, derived from the philosopher Herbert Spencer and to a lesser degree the botanist Asa Gray, and was not unlike the organic theory of the transcendentalists who were undoubtedly read by Sullivan, since he grew up in Boston and attended the famous Latin School there. He felt, as did Horatio Greenough and a number of now forgotten theorists, that "form follows function." But this statement must not be interpreted in a purely mechanistic or utilitarian way. Form to Sullivan was not merely the reflection of structure. It was this, but it was also the use to which a building was to be put. To Sullivan, function was what a thing is, its native identity. He felt that the difference be-

tween a church and a library should be expressed, and he was particularly aware of the absurdity of using past solutions for present problems—a Greek temple for a bank, for instance—for he was convinced that every problem had its own solution. Architecture was not to be turned out by clichés; it was not "a prescription to be filled out in any architectural department store."

So far Sullivan's contribution to the development of skyscraper design in general has been emphasized. But the prominence of ornament in all of his buildings should also be pointed out; this has been touched on in connection with the Auditorium and the Schlesinger and Meyer store. In the former the decoration may be effusive to modern taste but it is not inappropriate, for the building belongs to a long tradition of which ornament was a part. But in such a contemporary-seeming building as the Schlesinger and Meyer store it is almost shocking, since modern architecture has for some decades been largely devoid of ornament. Yet in Sullivan's mind there was no inconsistency, for his organic theory encompassed both structure and ornament as being outgrowths of the same creative impulse that gave the building its basic form. Thus Sullivan illustrated the organic concept of form following function by relating his buildings to organic life. The use of ornament derived from organic life was therefore for Sullivan a kind of architectural metaphor, giving a poetic meaning to his theory. This is illustrated clearly in Sullivan's building in the Gage Group, 1898 (AB 607), otherwise free from ornament, where the two central piers suddenly blossom into elaborate floriate designs as they terminate at the top of the building, creating the illusion that the masonry cladding of the vertical metal supports are tree trunks.

To some modern taste, which feels that structure should be revealed and then expressed, Sullivan's ornament is obtrusive and inconsistent; but the recent trend toward a greater acceptance of ornament is more sympathetic to Sullivan's use of it and is inclined to praise it as highly as the more functional aspects of his style. It certainly cannot be denied that Sullivan's ornament is very distinguished and as original as other aspects of his architecture (though in this instance his accomplishment was parallel to and did not actually precede other practice). Sullivan's decoration is an early manifestation, and one of the most beautiful and mature examples, of the international movement called generally *art nouveau*. This movement is characterized by four principal aspects which are amply illustrated in Sullivan's work, beginning tentatively in the Auditorium: a flat linearism, continuous and dynamic; exotic origins (oriental or ancient Irish, for example, as opposed to conventional western styles); personal individuality and rejection of conventional eclecticism; and, finally, the combination of its own complexity with a contrasting simplicity of form.[5] This last quality is particularly well illustrated in the Schlesinger and Meyer store.

Some of Sullivan's most distinguished ornament appears in two extraordinary little buildings which are as much objects of abstract ornament in three-dimensional design as they are architecture: the Getty Tomb, Chicago, 1890 (AB 573, AB 574), and the Wainwright Tomb, St. Louis, 1892 (AB 578, *AB 593B). Sullivan's biographer, Hugh Morrison, goes so far as to say of the Wainwright Tomb that in its architectural form and its decorative richness it is "unmatched in quality by any other known tomb."[6] In both structures Sullivan employs somewhat oriental or exotic motifs combined with rich foliate forms, beautifully incised and complex, in juxtaposition with contrasting plane surfaces of beautiful proportion.

The decoration of all of Sullivan's skyscrapers is noteworthy, but at the Guaranty Building in Buffalo, both in the interior and exterior, it is particularly so: richly curvilinear in the repetition of the curved architectural elements, and contrastingly geometric in the areas that recapitulate the rectilinear forms prevailing in the structure as a whole. In this building Sullivan was assisted in his designs by George Elmslie, then a draughtsman in his office (and later a prominent architect in Minneapolis). Elmslie also was responsible for the final form of the decorative areas of two other later buildings, the

Gage Group and the Schlesinger and Meyer store—though Sullivan was of course responsible for the final conceptions.[7] The flat panels at the Guaranty Building, designed by Elmslie, and the more three-dimensional accents of botanical forms on the capitals and elsewhere, designed entirely by Sullivan, combine to create some of the most individual and pleasing ornament in the recent history of architecture.

Some of the finest decorative work connected with the name of Sullivan occurs in the small banks executed in the first decades of the twentieth century, during the architect's frustrated last years—buildings also notable for their abstract originality of form as a whole. Among these are the former Merchants' National Bank, at Grinnell, Iowa (now Poweshiek County Bank), 1914 (*AB 770); the People's Savings and Loan Association Bank at Sidney, Ohio, 1917–1918 (AB 771, *AB 772); and the Farmers and Merchants Union Bank at Columbus, Wisconsin, 1919 (AB 773). But these seem a little awkward and unintegrated when compared with the best of the small banks, the National Farmers' (now Security) Bank, Owatonna, Minnesota, 1907–1908 (AB 767, AB 768), which is not only bold and sure in design but decorated with magnificent ornament; the calligraphy of floriate forms is unbelievably lush, yet disciplined within an equally elaborate but relatively restrained geometry. Unfortunately for the reputation of Sullivan it is quite clear that Elmslie designed the Owatonna building before he left Sullivan's office, while the somewhat less distinguished banks that followed were by Sullivan alone. (The Owatonna bank—considerably changed in the 1930's—has recently been remodeled into its original state.)

Though Sullivan was undoubtedly the leader in skyscraper design, there were others who achieved distinction in the field (for the most part in Chicago), including the two firms already mentioned, Holabird and Roche, and Burnham and Root. The addition by Holabird and Roche to the Gage Group, 1898–1900 (AB 607), adjacent to Sullivan's section, is actually more sophisticated and surer in design than its neighbor, though the proportions of the "Chicago window" are not quite so refined as in Sullivan's later Schlesinger and Meyer store. The firm's McClurg (now Crown) Building, 1899–1900 (AB 764), is perhaps the most successful of the early skyscrapers in the expression of volume, since it is unaccompanied by the divertingly elaborate lower story of the Schlesinger and Meyer store which is in other respects the masterpiece of the genre. A later building by Holabird and Roche, the Champlain (now Powers) Building, 1903 (AB 765), is not so advanced, the supports being more emphasized in the design. Less sensitively proportioned than the Gage Group or the McClurg Building and vitiated by Gothic decorative motifs, Solon Spencer Beman's Studebaker (now Brunswick) Building in Chicago, 1895 (AB 601, AB 602), is perhaps the "openest" of all the Chicago buildings, the supports being as tenuous and narrow as possible, seemingly hardly more than mullions for a completely glass facade.

Outside of Chicago two skyscrapers should be mentioned as being especially interesting for their interiors—an area not generally exploited in this building type even though large open spaces were made possible as a result of metal construction. These are the Bradbury Building in Los Angeles, by George Wyman, 1893 (*AB 613, AB 613B, AB 613C, AB 614B), and the Northwestern Guaranty Loan Company (now Metropolitan Insurance) Building in Minneapolis, 1890 (*AB 609, *AB 610, *AB 611, *AB 612), by E. Townsend Mix. Each has a large, open courtyard running the full height of the building, covered by a glass roof, and exposing on all sides the undisguised metal supports of many stories. To these are added the varied forms of stairways and elevator shafts composed of open metal work, the whole complex forming a maze of structural elements that are almost breathtaking in their ordered complexity. (The Minneapolis building is further enhanced by glass floors.)

Chicago remained preeminent in the building of skyscrapers until the turn of the century. In fact the term "Chicago construction" became synonymous with technical skill and expressive design in the field. New York, well on the way to becoming the multitowered metropolis of today, in the 1890's began to outdistance Chicago in the number of its tall buildings, but even when they were of metal construction, the entire vocabulary of eclecticism was called upon to disguise rather than reveal this fact. The man who set the style for the skyscraper in New York was Bruce Price,[8] the architect who had developed Tuxedo Park. Not as famous as Sullivan is today, his influence was actually far greater, for the principle of the isolated tower, which makes New York's skyline so striking, and which is the ideal form behind Frank Lloyd Wright's and Le Corbusier's tall buildings, was first articulated by Price. It is undoubtedly his eclecticism (for he clad his buildings in classically detailed masonry) and his denial of everything but height in his designs which have made him less significant in later years than Sullivan. (Only one of Sullivan's structures, the Schiller Building, could be called a tower. The still free-standing Guaranty Building in Buffalo is enclosed on two sides—in the expectation of neighboring structures which never materialized.) Price felt that it was an esthetic mistake to design commercial buildings only in relation to the street, since their total aspect was more important.[9] The tower form which Price opposed to the slab was based on the classic prototype of the column: the base was the ground floor or floors, the shaft was analogous to the stretch of identical fenestration, and the top floors were adorned like a capital, often with a blind colonnade repeating the taller order of the ground floor. Even D. H. Burnham and Company (the successor to Burnham and Root), when they built the Flatiron Building in New York, where Fifth Avenue and Broadway cross, 1902 (AB 763), followed Price's precedent, at least in the two sides of the building from which its picturesque name derives.

The tradition of the skyscraper as a tower persisted until recently—one of the last examples being the Empire State Building—and not until after World War II was there a significant swing back to the slab and the kind of volumetric expression so brilliantly pioneered by Sullivan and some of his Chicago contemporaries, though

Frank Lloyd Wright's unexecuted designs for skyscrapers show that the tradition of Sullivan did not die in the interim.

The Chicago school [10] of the 1880's and 1890's reflected a still vital pioneer spirit in its technical advance, and a kind of frontier honesty in the acceptance of a form which was a true expression of the building. But the academic reaction, signalized by the World's Fair, when the Chicago architects bowed out to Richard Morris Hunt and the Beaux Arts-trained eastern architects, killed the local school. Sullivan, who designed the only large non-classical building at the Fair, the Transportation Building, was increasingly ignored because, unlike his colleagues, he did not shift to what he knew was a false revivalism, remaining true to his theory that "every building tells its own story, tells it plainly." Embittered, most of his energies were spent in expressing his ideas in an eloquent though somewhat turgid and poetic prose, much of which is incorporated in *Kindergarten Chats* (1901–1908), an exposition of the organic theory prefiguring the equally voluble Frank Lloyd Wright, and almost as important.

Sullivan did have time for the small banks already mentioned and for one or two other buildings. The Farmers and Merchants Union Bank at Columbus, Wisconsin, 1919 (AB 773), is remarkable not only for its beautiful exterior ornament but also for its largely unembellished interior, where the flat planes and simple masses are suggestive of Frank Lloyd Wright. Also remarkable is the forceful geometric shape of St. Paul's Methodist Church, Cedar Rapids, Iowa, 1910–1912 (AB 769), where a curvilinear auditorium is juxtaposed to a rectangular block incorporating the Sunday School, a configuration crowned by a great tower. This building is excellent in its functionalism and design but lacks the final touch of Sullivan's own ornament, since he resigned as architect before this was decided upon and executed. St. Paul's is certainly one of the boldest and most original structures in the early history of modern architecture. Had Sullivan possessed the stamina and doggedness of Wright and been able to swim more forcefully against the tide of genteel academicism, he

might have advanced into the theoretical position of the younger man and continued to produce buildings as important as his earlier ones and as those of Wright, who actually carried on his tradition.

Some Utilitarian Architecture

Aside from the skyscraper, there was little in the post-Civil War period to show an integration between engineering factors and architectural design. When metal was used imaginatively from the functional point of view, its esthetic expressiveness was disguised, as in such descendants of James Bogardus' cast iron structures as the Robins Paper Company (formerly the Cast Iron Building), Baltimore, c. 1870 (AB 306), or the curious Z. C. M. I. Department Store, Salt Lake City, Utah, 1868 (*AB 305), which has an extended facade consisting almost wholly of continuous fenestration made possible by the entirely metal construction—a fact, however, not exploited in the design, which is conventionally classical. Among textile and steel mills and other industrial buildings, as well as in arsenals and structures requiring the spanning of large areas with metal, very few examples of an integral relationship between structure and appearance occurred, the great spaces being disguised by facades, Second Empire embellishment, or medieval castellations. A few railroad stations, however, are more clearly successful as functional buildings, combining architecture and engineering in an integrated design. Certainly among the best of a nearly vanished group of important buildings was the Union Passenger Depot at Worcester, Massachusetts, 1875–1877 (Illustration 5–26), now demolished, by Ware and Van Brunt, one of the best examples of picturesque eclecticism in the period as well. Two sets of tracks entered the station at angles, not parallel, so that the plan of the depot posed a problem which in its successful solution resulted in an especially interesting composition. The rhythm of alternating arches and gables in the head house and subordinate areas, the repetition of the great curve of the train shed vaults in the plan of part of the station area, and above all the expres-

5–26.   Union Passenger Depot (destroyed), Worcester, Massachusetts, 1875–1877, by Ware and Van Brunt.

sion of the volumes of the interpenetrating sheds, foiled by the masses of masonry elsewhere and by the accent of the tower, comprised a forceful and consistent design.

No other station expressed so well in the interior design the important factor of the train shed. In a few, however, there is some relation between the shed and other parts of the building. An imposing concourse in Union Station, St. Louis, 1891, by Link and Cameron, repeats in its general shape and scale the adjacent shed, as does the rotunda at the Illinois Central Sta-

tion in Chicago, 1892–1893, where the architects very frankly used metal supports similar to those in the shed.

Something should be said about the sheds themselves, even though in nearly every instance they were merely attached to the building complex, and not actually incorporated into it. The largest was at the old Broad Street Station in Philadelphia, which was added by Wilson Brothers and Company to a building by Furness, and reached the spectacular span of nine hundred feet in width. The nearly contemporaneous

Reading Terminal shed, also in Philadelphia, though much smaller than Broad Street Station, still remains to give an impression of spaciousness filled with steam and smoke and the romance of train travel, which was more dramatic in the pre-diesel days before the competition of bus and plane. One of the most pleasing of these stations was that of the Baltimore and Ohio Railroad in Philadelphia, also by Furness, long abandoned and recently destroyed by fire. Though it did not reflect any better than most the span of the train shed in its all-over design, nevertheless Furness did emphasize the fact of metal structure by a concentration of decorative metal elements in supports and barriers which were handled in a delicate and light manner.

Though bridges may not be strictly architecture, the works of James B. Eads, especially the Eads Bridge at St. Louis, 1868–1874 (AB 294, *AB 295B), and of the Roeblings, John and Washington, are so beautifully designed that the achievements of these builders cannot be overlooked. Aside from the spectacular engineering involved in the great spans hung on cables, the relation of the curves of the bridge to the masonry supports is superbly handled. This is especially true in the Roeblings' Brooklyn Bridge, 1867–1873 (AB 296, *AB 297). Even the particular eclectic style chosen for the strictly architectural supports, the Gothic, is more appropriate than any other, the curved forms of its pointed arches repeating those of the span itself.

Late Eclecticism: The Academic Reaction

It has already been noted that Richardson's Marshall Field Warehouse was more self-contained and symmetrical than his earlier buildings, which were more consistent with picturesque eclecticism, and that Bruce Price in his houses at Tuxedo Park turned to more studied balance and restraint. This stylistic trend, seen even in Gothic Revival churches, which became less picturesque, was supplemented by the discipline and the classical bias of the École des Beaux Arts, where Americans increasingly studied, and also by an additional historicism whose greater correctness was due to a more accurate knowledge of famous buildings derived from photographs, which were now more easily reproduced. The authority of famous examples became the chief criterion of architectural merit. The consequence of these factors was the creation of a new academicism, grandiose as in the work of Richard Morris Hunt, or genteel as in that of McKim, Mead & White. In comparison with the more vigorous and original work of the 1870's and early 1880's, the academic reaction substituted a somewhat empty expansiveness for elasticity of space, and borrowed forms for inventiveness.

A perusal of the *Architectural Record and Building News* in the late 1880's reveals the shift from the picturesque to more restrained forms and styles, both medieval and classical, as seen, for instance, in the various competitive designs for Grant's Tomb and for the Cathedral of St. John the Divine in New York. At the same time a more correct and far-ranging eclecticism is evident. A conspicuous example is the large resort hotel, the Ponce de Leon, in St. Augustine, Florida, 1885–1888 (AB 492, *AB 494), by Carrère and Hastings, in which the presence of indigenous Spanish colonial building suggested the use of Hispanic forms, and initiated a revival in California and Florida.

The work of Richard Morris Hunt during the late 1880's and in the 1890's, typifying the more pretentious aspect of the eclecticism of the time, is illustrated in the residences in several styles which he built for the Vanderbilt family. The Vanderbilt Mansion (now demolished) on Fifth Avenue, in New York, and Biltmore, the family's great estate at Asheville, North Carolina, 1895 (AB 536), were modeled after French *châteaux* in the transitional style from Gothic to early Renaissance. The Newport palaces—Belcourt (the O. H. P. Belmont House), 1894, (AB 709), and The Breakers, 1892 (AB 496, AB 497, AB 498)—the grandest of the Vanderbilt residences, derive from more classical prototypes, Italian High Renaissance and French baroque. None of these buildings is a mere replica, for Hunt combined various sources with a certain skill and bravura, and he had a grandiose conception of scale. The enormous expanse of Biltmore and the size and elaboration of The Breakers make them at least quantitatively impressive if somewhat empty monuments to the sociological phenomenon of the American millionaire. In any case they are certainly a far cry from the typical Newport cottage admired by Henry James.

Aside from Richardsonian Romanesque, which became more classical in composition if not in detail, the revivalism of the end of the century eventually became thoroughly classical, culminating in the overwhelmingly popular success of the Chicago World's Fair, whose architecture derived almost exclusively from classical sources, ancient or Renaissance. By the end of the century the academic reaction had won out. Hunt's work began to seem too vigorous, and even his classical buildings had too much robust exuberance to be acceptable. Edith Wharton in her first book, *The Declaration of Houses*, wrote that the way to correct the bad taste of the time was "only by a close study of the best models"—those of the Italian High Renaissance. Even as early as 1878, a writer in the *American Architect and Building News* suggested that American architects should spend their holidays making notes on colonial architecture which, "in spite of its faults," was at least "superior in good building to what followed."

Joseph M. Wells, one of the members of the firm of McKim, Mead & White, the most representative architects of the era, summed up the new point of view very well when he stated that the classic ideal suggested not only "clearness, simplicity, grandeur, order and philosophical calm," but, significantly, "a fine and cultivated society." [11]   A comparison between McKim, Mead & White's Ross Winans House, Baltimore, Maryland, 1882 (*AB 521), and the Henry Villard Houses (now the Catholic Archdiocesan House), New York, 1883 (AB 518), dramatically summarizes the change in taste that occurred in that firm, which in turn represented a similar shift on the part of the general public. The Winans House is boldly three-dimensional, picturesque, asymmetrical, and inspired by medieval prototypes. The Villard Houses are relatively flat, symmetrical, and classical.

A lack of originality and personal flair was a concomitant of academic good taste. To quote Wells again, "In architecture individuality of style is at best a doubtful merit." [12]   The eccentricity of a Furness, or even the forceful statement of a Richardson, would have been unthinkable at this time.

McKim, Mead & White in their post-shingle style designs epitomized the academic reaction. Their undeniable distinction lies in the fact that they were undistinguished so well. The refinement of proportion and detail, the high standards in the use of materials, the restraint—in a word, the "good taste"—of this firm led the way in helping to transform the bold and ugly architectural scene of picturesque and original form into the dignified and genteel one of the classical norm. Adapted first to domestic architecture and later to the larger scale of commercial and public buildings, museums, clubs, and urban mansions, the production of the firm stands up as the best of its kind.

The Villard Houses (said to have been designed by Joseph M. Wells himself) marked a return to as strict a classicism as had been seen since the Greek Revival, though in this case Rome in the early 1500's was the inspiration—Rome as seen through the eyes of the French neo-classicist P.-M. Letarouilly, whose beautiful drawings influenced even the architect's renderings. The Boston Public Library, 1887 (AB 502, *AB 505, AB 506; Illustration 5–27), derives from the same sources, though its arcuated facade also resembles the mid-nineteenth-century Library of St. Genevieve in Paris by Henri Labrouste (but without its metal-supported reading room). The library's restrained refinement and simplified block-like form are especially notable, since it faces the bold picturesque mass of Trinity Church on Copley Square. The University Club in New York, 1900 (AB 522, AB 523; Illustration 5–28), may well be the masterpiece of the firm. Impressive in scale, magnificent in material, and thus a little less genteel than most of their work, it is a successful adaptation of the palace ideal of the Italian Renaissance (with even a trace of the Louvre), sensitively interpreted, to the larger scale of urban

5–27. Boston Public Library, Boston, Massachusetts, 1887, by McKim, Mead & White. [From *Monograph of the Work of McKim, Mead & White* (New York: 1915).]

New York. This edifice on the corner of Fifth Avenue and Fifty-fourth Street became a prototype for the many clubs, hotels, residences, and apartment houses whose rusticated lower floors, fine detail, and refined proportions recall the Florentine and Roman *palazzi* of the Renaissance; but it is still outstanding in comparison to its less vigorous imitators.

The distinction McKim, Mead & White lent to the new academicism had much to do with its success and with the turn of events that shaped the architectural character of the World's Fair of 1893. When the Chicago authorities turned from their own architects to Hunt, to McKim, Mead & White, and to younger architects who were trained in the Beaux Arts tradition, they created, under the leadership of McKim, a white plaster city on the slopes of Lake Michigan which staggered the susceptibilities of a generation, and moved an Edgar Guest

of the day to write a verse that began: "Oh, say not Greece is no more!" The vast project was an impressive example of cooperation among architects, landscape designers, painters, and sculptors. Laid out with sweep and regularity in an awe-inspiring scale, its combination of classical planning and building became the inspiration for the "city beautiful" movement, one of whose results was the refurbishing of L'Enfant's long neglected plan for the city of Washington. On the other hand, the classical ideal swept aside all possibilities of architectural advance by making the academic reaction so impressive in its scale, consistency, largeness of conception, and stylophilia that to follow it became almost compulsive. The antique grandeur of Charles B. Atwood's Columbian Exposition Art Building (now Rosenwald Museum of Science and Industry), 1893 (AB 738), can be taken as typical of the Fair: its porticos and

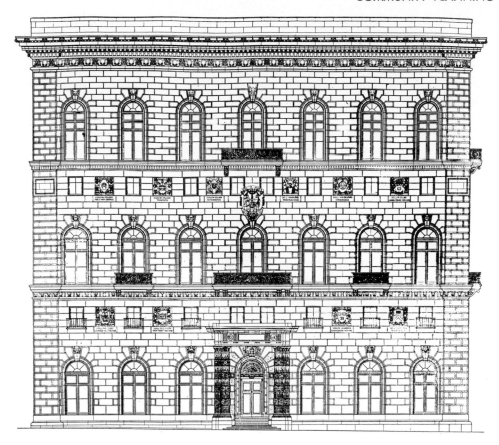

5-28. Elevation of University Club, New York, New York, 1900, by McKim, Mead & White. [From *Monograph of the Work of McKim, Mead & White* (New York: 1915).]

entablatures were intended to hide the great metal-vaulted exhibition spaces within—so unlike the Paris Exposition of 1889, dominated by Eiffel's tower and the great metal-framed interior of the Salle des Machines.

The Columbian Exposition gave the *coup de grâce* to the progressive and indigenous elements in American architecture. Only Sullivan in his brilliant Schlesinger and Meyer store of nine years later stemmed for a time the tide of classicism even in the skyscraper. Sullivan was right when he prophesied that the damage done to architecture by the World's Fair would last fifty years.

Community Planning

Community planning in the period following the Civil War was chiefly characterized by an accentuation of the worst and the best aspects of the preceding decades, by the growth of slums, and their amelioration in the park system and in the "city beautiful" movement.

The slums became worse as they expanded, with every penny of profit being extracted from the original investment—a procedure naturally supported by landowners and mortgage institutions. Tall brick tenements with increasingly smaller courtyards in New York, interminable lines of row houses in Philadelphia and Balti-more, wooden tenements of three or four stories with rows of identical porches in Boston and in the New England mill cities—these were only the most outstanding instances of poor planning. The slums of America, which in this period was becoming the richest country in the world and the mecca of repressed people everywhere, are among the most conspicuous examples of the public cost of private enterprise. Not until speculation and exploitation had been pushed to the point of diminishing returns was it possible for the efforts of reformers like Jacob Riis to make inroads on this national scandal.

The abuses of the slum were accompanied by lack of control in the siting of industry and by the spread of commercial and retail districts into residential areas. The consequence was the creation of an extensive urban blight which still plagues most American cities, many of which are involved in the enormous expense of urban renewal in order to survive.

Movement to the suburbs was the natural consequence of urban decay. The former residents of Euclid Avenue in Cleveland went to Shaker Heights; the recently occupied squares of South Boston were emptied for Brookline and Chestnut Hill; Philadelphians moved to the Main Line, and New Yorkers to Long Island, Greenwich, Connecticut, and other "dormitory" suburbs. One of the first of these suburban communities was Riverside, Illinois, 1869 (*CPB 61), designed by Frederick Law Olmsted, in which he introduced some of the traffic control devices he had developed in his parks. Other informal park-like communities followed, modeled after Riverside and the earlier Llewellyn Park. Outstanding examples among these were Tuxedo Park, New York, in which Bruce Price's shingle houses were built; Easton's Beach, Middletown, Rhode Island, near Newport, laid out by Olmsted, as already mentioned (see Illustration 5–14); and Delano Park, Cape Elizabeth, near Portland, Maine, a seaside community beautifully oriented toward the ocean, where John Calvin Stevens built two houses (see Illustration 5–12 and accompanying text). The principles of landscape gardening and town planning

incorporated in exclusive suburbs and garden cities of this kind were extended in general to the higher-income residential suburbs, making of them very pleasant places in which to live, and these communities drew away from the cities the very persons who were most capable of coping with the problems of urban decay. In any event, the best community planning of the period took place in the garden cities, suburbs, and resorts.

Social responsibility and civic foresight were exercised on a large scale, however, in the metropolitan park systems. Large parks in Buffalo and Detroit succeeded those which were developed before the Civil War, while Franklin Park in Boston, 1885, also designed by Olmsted, became the keystone in a system that was gradually extended to include the whole metropolitan area. Working with Charles W. Elliott, the landscape gardener, Olmsted devised for the Metropolitan Park Commission of Boston in 1893 a belt system of open spaces involving thirty-five communities in the greater Boston area, and incorporating a varied terrain of forest, meadow, river, and seashore—an ambitious project which has been of enormous benefit to an entire region. In Boston itself, Olmsted used Commonwealth Avenue, notable for its extensive planting and separated vehicular and pedestrian ways, as a precedent for the extension of a system of wide avenues radiating from larger open areas, actualizing what he had originally recommended for New York in connection with his plans for Central Park.

Admirable as such civic developments were, they were in the final analysis only a respectable facade for the substandard areas behind them, though they served as a partial incentive to the inception of the "city beautiful" movement. This ideal was further stimulated by the Chicago World's Fair, largely the creation of Olmsted, which was a magnificent example of a certain kind of community planning notable for its integration of the arts under a master plan, and for its consistency in architectural style, scale, and formal character. But the Fair's grandiose and formal classicism, although appropriate enough for a world exhibition, was too backward-looking, and hardly suitable for American cities on the threshold of the automobile age.

There was little besides the suburb, the park system, and the beginning of the "city beautiful" movement to mitigate the generally low level to which community planning fell in the post-Civil War period. Only a few company towns, for instance, carried on the sometimes still paternalistic community planning of pre-Civil War industrialism. The most outstanding example was Pullman, Illinois (now part of South Chicago), 1874–1884 (*CPB 66), by Solon Spencer Beman, architect, and Nathan F. Barnett, landscape architect. Though the style of its buildings is heavy and awkward, a remark-able variety of composition and orientation has been achieved, considering that eighteen hundred dwelling units are incorporated in it. In most cases, however, the consequences of rapid industrial growth and a relaxed social responsibility combined to permit living conditions of unimaginable squalor that had to be endured because of competition for jobs and the availability of cheap labor—circumstances which were exploited by owners and investors. Thus the jerry-built company towns proliferated in Pennsylvania and West Virginia, and slums increased in the larger cities like Pittsburgh, as the steel mills expanded with the application of the Bessemer process.

Painting

More than for any previous era, to understand American art of the post-Civil War period it is necessary to examine the simultaneous course of European painting, especially in France, which had become, and to a great extent still remains, the chief school of western painting.

During the mid-century decades, American art had been far less dependent on European art. The work of painters like Mount, Bingham, and the "luminist" landscapists possessed a definite native tang. But after the Civil War a large proportion of American art was indistinguishable from European; much of it (and some of the most important) was the work of actual expatriates like Whistler. Even such thoroughly American painters as Eakins and Homer either studied abroad or were strongly influenced by European painting, though each gave his borrowings a more original and even more national flavor than was customary or fashionable.

The principal change which had been occurring in Europe during the 1850's was the flowering of realism, three successive aspects of which it is convenient to isolate, if perhaps a little arbitrarily: *romantic realism; descriptive realism*, to distinguish it from the first, though it is generally referred to simply as realism; and *impressionism*, the outgrowth of descriptive realism.

Romantic realism was a reaction against the prevailing academicism of neo-classicism, and also against romanticism itself, which became nearly as stereotyped, though less officially accepted. Artists like Millet and Daumier dealt with themes concerning common people, while Corot and the landscapists of the Barbizon group painted simple and unpretentious scenes. This realism was qualified, however, by elements of romanticism persisting in their work: a tendency to intensify certain human characteristics for greater expressiveness, as in the idealized monumentality of Millet's peasants, and to sentimentalize landscape, as in the poetic nuances of Corot's forest glades, which sometimes are even peopled with nymphs.

The style and technique of romantic realism were also distinct from both neo-classicism and romanticism, differing from the precise outline and modeling of the former, and from the neo-baroque painterly handling of the latter. There was a closer approximation of total visual effect, rather than an arbitrary manner, either linear or coloristic. Lines and edges were blurred; forms remained strongly modeled but were realized in an ambiance of surrounding atmosphere. The colors themselves were not brilliant like those of the romantics or of the later impressionists. Corot's paint was not as thickly applied as that of some others, but an almost palpable atmosphere was created by his broad suggestive passages of varying tonality expressing space and air. (This new and more personal technique was used occasionally by the more academic painters as well, a fact which was especially significant in the career of Thomas Couture; his fame as a successful salon exhibitor and his prominence as a teacher caused his influence to be widespread.) The new technique, fairly pervasive among French painters by the 1850's, was brought back to the United States in 1855 by William Morris Hunt, an influential teacher and artistic propagandist; by the 1870's it was more or less endemic in America, receiving its final stamp of approval at the Philadelphia Centennial Exhibition in 1876 with the prominent showing of Corot, the Barbizon group, and others who painted in the same general manner.

Realism became less romantic in Gustave Courbet, whose forceful anti-idealism was summed up in his remark: "Show me an angel and I will paint one." Courbet's objectivity, however, was tempered by his sensibility; for, though he rejected the world of the imagination, he infused his best work with so much color, richness of paint, and grandeur of form that the real world took on a marvelousness which compensated for the loss of literary or ideal subject matter. The painterliness of romantic realism was heightened in the work of the realists by a more dashing and direct stroke, derived largely from the example of Spanish painting, especially that of Francisco de Zurbarán, whose broad areas of richly applied paint in the robes of monks, saints, and martyrs in the Louvre taught Courbet as much as did his teachers. The young Édouard Manet was impressed not only by Courbet, but by the realism of the Spaniards, especially Velázquez, and by the even more summary bravura portraits by the Dutch painter Frans Hals. The direct image captured as instantly as possible, as in some of Goya's work, also influenced Manet's style. Thus, in Manet, the important transitional ar-

tist between realism and impressionism, realism was heightened by a feeling of visual immediacy expressed by a spontaneous and lively handling. But Manet—unlike Goya, for instance—made no comment on the prostitutes or similar themes he occasionally used for subject matter. This detachment of observation led to a concentration on the way a picture was painted instead of on its subject.

The realism of Courbet and the more spontaneous proto-impressionism of Manet were brought to the United States at first indirectly by American students abroad, especially at Munich, where the bold brush work of the local school derived largely from Courbet and Manet. The Munich-trained artists most influential as exemplars and teachers in America were Frank Duveneck and William Merritt Chase, who performed a function in the late 1870's similar to that of William Morris Hunt a decade or so earlier: they gave a new character to American painting.

Impressionism grew naturally out of Manet's spontaneous realism, but with the important and distinguishing addition of a brilliant and more scientific palette (which in turn also influenced the late Manet, who became practically an impressionist) and an even more thoroughly detached and purely visual point of view. Claude Monet, the leader of the movement, once said that he wished he could have been born blind and later recovered his sight, since he could then simply paint without knowing what the objects were. The brilliant palettes of Monet and of other pure impressionists were characterized by unmixed hues applied side by side on the canvas, instead of being blended first on the palette; by an ignoration of local color (that is, taking into account the influence of surrounding hues); and by the introduction of color into shadows. The resulting brilliance was that of nature itself, an enormous advance in realism causing nearly all previous painting to look dull and dark in comparison. This new color was combined with the spontaneity of the instantaneous vision, realized in quick dabs or dots of the brush. The result was a vibrating, dynamic, variously textured play of paint on the flat canvas, causing a paradoxical and exciting tension between a kind of almost scientific realism reduced to pure sensation, and a richly formal abstract beauty.

The work of Claude Monet, and of Camille Pissarro and Alfred Sisley, his closest followers, coupled with the realist–impressionist work of Manet and the Munich school, comprised the greatest single influence on American painting from the 1880's well into the twentieth century. But another aspect of impressionism was also influential: the impressionism best represented by Degas, whose work (though spontaneous in technique and often brilliant in color) is characterized by a carefully worked out formal composition, which is combined with a desire to represent the casual moment, instantaneously caught. The chief impetus for this seemingly incongruous combination was the influence of the Japanese prints of the late eighteenth and early nineteenth centuries. These were known in Paris in the 1850's, were exhibited in large numbers in the Exposition of 1867, and became generally familiar in the 1870's. The representation of scenes from everyday and transient aspects of life, genre, or landscape and genre combined, coincided perfectly with the subject matter of realism and impressionism. Further, the tendency among Monet and the impressionists to catch the passing moment was reinforced by a similar purpose in the Japanese print.

All the complex and overlapping aspects of impressionism were brought to bear on American art to a lesser or greater degree. Even a painter considered as indigenously American as Winslow Homer was influenced, consciously or not, by all of them, while expatriates like Mary Cassatt were practically impressionists in the Degas and Renoir tradition. Among the important painters only Albert Pinkham Ryder was not very much influenced by the three French movements, though many others, less typical and of less importance, were also relatively uninfluenced.

There were, of course, other trends in the world of art that existed simultaneously with these main tendencies; most of them can be summarized under the somewhat vague terms, classicism and romantic idealism. These were usually joined to the persisting classicism of academic and official artistic circles, represented most conspicuously in the United States in mural painting.

William Morris Hunt and John La Farge

William Morris Hunt was the most important figure in painting at the beginning of this period, but chiefly as a catalyst. Like Allston a half-century before, Hunt was responsible for broadening the taste of a generation of artists by introducing to America the newest and most pervasive point of view in Europe at the time. As Allston had brought neo-classicism and a form of early romanticism to provincial Boston, so Hunt brought to the same city the new romantic realism, which was a reaction against both styles. Through his social position Hunt influenced public and private taste (Bostonians bought Corots and Millets almost before they were accepted in France) and as a teacher his influence was incalculable.

Hunt's early work executed in France vacillated between sentimental genre treated rather grandly in the manner of Millet (near whom he lived for two years) and a more ideal type, but both were executed in the then prevalent broad and suggestive manner. It was also in France that the first ideas for Hunt's famous and influential mural, the *Flight of Night*, were executed, under the direct inspiration of Delacroix, who was painting his decorations in the Louvre at the time. Hunt also painted landscapes strongly influenced by Corot.

Hunt's early work in the United States includes some Newport landscapes that look disconcertingly like the forest of Fontainebleau where Corot and the Barbizon landscapists worked, and some genre inspired by the Civil War.

In the late 1850's and early 1860's portraiture was still the most important branch of painting, and Hunt's best work is in this category. His portraits of *Lemuel Shaw*, Chief Justice of the Massachusetts Supreme Court, 1859 (PB 599; Illustration 5–29), and of *Charles Sumner* (The Metropolitan Museum of Art, New York) are among the most impressive of the era, and presage a series of distinguished portraits. Shaw's magnificent head is modeled in large,

5–29. William Morris Hunt, *Lemuel Shaw,* 1859. Oil on canvas. 79 x 50 inches. (Courtesy of the Essex County Bar Association.)

classicism is replaced by a more delicate charm which in the *Marguerite* would be almost sentimental if the picture were not so solidly painted. Hunt's portraits are not simply records. They are penetrating, thoughtful, and not unlike those of Eakins, a quarter of a century later, in their grasp of the fundamentals of form and space and in the respect shown for the dignity of the individual. It is no accident that both men acquired from Couture the broad handling of paint beginning to prevail at the time, as well as a sound academic background.

Hunt's later easel work, aside from portraiture, has a pervasive lyricism which gives it great charm, but it is not the work of a powerful artist. His evocative little landscapes painted in the 1870's are no longer vaguely reminiscent of Corot's pleasant vales, but at the same time are not much more specific in their reference to the coast north of Boston, except in their titles. In these pictures, Hunt is not concerned with recording nature or with transforming it to fit a romantic ideal. A vegetable garden or a casual ball game in a field served as well as the next subject to instigate a purely artistic response to the scene. The landscapes painted at Magnolia, Massachusetts, as exemplified in *Ball Players,* 1874 (Illustration 5–30), or in others such as

broadly handled areas, appropriate to the impressive character of the man so dramatically presented in the daguerreotype by Southworth and Hawes (Illustration 4–72). Both paintings portray men of solid worth, in compositions which are simple and direct. Hunt's *Self-Portrait,* 1866 (°PB 601), has a similar dignity and simplicity, and his portraits of women are equally fine. That of *Mrs. Richard Morris Hunt and Child,* c. 1865–1870 (PB 596), represents his sister-in-law, the wife of the architect, in a forceful pyramidal composition as she stands in a voluminous dress, holding her child in a Renaissance-like pose. In *Miss Ida Mason,* 1878 (PB 600), and *Marguerite,* 1870 (°PB 598), this

5–30. William Morris Hunt, *Ball Players,* 1874. Oil on canvas. 16 x 24 inches. (Courtesy of the Detroit Institute of Arts.)

5–31. William Morris Hunt, *Flight of Night,* c. 1878. Pastel. 62 x 99 inches. (The Pennsylvania Academy of the Fine Arts, Philadelphia.)

Gloucester Harbor, 1877 (PB 597), are extremely sketchy and suggestive; and, though misty and indeterminate, they have a formal subtlety of value transitions almost as refined as that found in some of Whistler's *Nocturnes.*

Hunt probably thought that his most important work was the mural he executed for the New York State Capitol at Albany, which he hoped would be the first of a series. The disappointment he suffered when the other paintings were vetoed by the legislature perhaps contributed to his decline in health and his relatively early death, possibly by suicide. Unfortunately, faulty construction of the Capitol damaged the painting, and eventually the area in which the mural was placed had to be covered in order to shore up the collapsing masonry. The subject, *The Flight of Night,* was derived from a Persian legend which had interested the artist from his early student days. The concept exists now only in the form of sketches, the best being a pastel at the Pennsylvania Academy, c. 1878 (PB 251; Illustration 5–31). Another done in oil at about the same time is in the Boston Museum (°PB 251A). *Flight of Night* is a lively composition,

dynamic and well-realized, and possesses much of Delacroix's neo-baroque vigor as well as his brilliant color. To judge from Hunt's sketches and from photographs of the work in progress on the Albany walls, the *Flight of Night* was more competent than any large paintings by Allston, and far superior to the murals by Trumbull, Vanderlyn, and others in the National Capitol.

The abortive *Flight of Night,* a few fine portraits, a group of charming but not memorable genre and landscape pieces—these are the contributions of Hunt which can be definitely assessed. He had talent in abundance, and perhaps a potential which was never quite realized. Yet his influence and example were important in leavening the provinciality of American art. He indicated the way to a richer handling of paint, and (in his later, more unpretentious work), to a more personal idiom of expression in which commonplace experience was given significance in itself, without the infusion of literary or other extraneous reference. As a prelude to the more overt realism of the Munich school and of the impressionists, Hunt's still romantic realism left a residue of lyrical feeling and humanism which mitigated his matter-of-fact point of view. At its worst this influence tended toward genteel sweetness or pretentious allegory; at its best it gave a form language for the more individual statements of Inness, Fuller, and Ryder.

In the work of Hunt, romanticism and realism are fairly well integrated. In Hunt's most important pupil, John La Farge, realism and romanticism—the latter might better be called romantic idealism in La Farge's case—set up a kind of dichotomy which caused a curious inconsistency in his work. (This struggle between reality and the ideal was the basis of the frustration of a generation of cultivated men like Henry Adams, who could not bear the vulgar realities of his own time and place, a position eloquently set forth in *The Education of Henry Adams* and in *Mont-Saint-Michel and Chartres*. La Farge was an intimate of Adams, and the circumstances of his wealth, social position, and European connections must also have made him more than usually sympathetic to Adams' point of view.)

La Farge's very early work could in general be called realistic, but, like that of Hunt, it was mitigated with the poetry of personal expression. However, the young La Farge possessed a surer and more vigorous talent than his master, as is amply demonstrated in his early *Portrait of the Artist, 1859* (PB 289; Illustration 5–32), in which La Farge portrays himself in a graceful pose, silhouetted boldly against a sun-bathed landscape. The figure is convincingly established in the surrounding atmosphere, and the landscape itself is a successful realization of the artist's stated purpose to represent the exact time of day and circumstance of light. La Farge's careful observation gives to this picture, and to his landscapes of this period, an impressive tonal consistency. He sometimes combined this accurate observation with a native decorative sense (note the treatment of the figure in the self-portrait), as can be seen in such a study as the *Magnolia Grandiflora*, 1870 (*PB 291).

La Farge was first diverted from the realism of his early work by the architect Henry Hobson Richardson, who put him in charge of the decorations of Trinity Church, Boston. The al-most Byzantine luxury of color and form in the interior of the building, complementing the forcefulness of the exterior, comprised the first ambitious instance of a unified program of decoration after the Civil War, and remains perhaps the best of a long progeny. La Farge himself executed the most important murals, which were essentially large easel pictures. Relatively realistic in comparison with their elaborate medieval enframement, but idealistic in recalling masters of the Renaissance, such subjects as *Christ and Nicodemus* (PB 612) reflect the assiduity of La Farge in rummaging through the past to meet the challenge of Richardson's assignment.

5–32. John La Farge, *Portrait of the Artist, 1859*. Oil on canvas. 16⅛ x 11½ inches. (The Metropolitan Museum of Art, New York. Samuel D. Lee Fund, 1934.)

5–33. John La Farge, *The Ascension*, 1887. Mural. Oil on canvas. (Church of the Ascension, New York, New York.)

The great treasury of world art was being opened at this time through the medium of photography, which made it possible for a cultivated painter such as La Farge to borrow from any source that appealed to his artistic curiosity —for better or for worse. Many of La Farge's pictures reflect the artist's knowledge of Renaissance and baroque art especially, though in general they are executed with his own rather personal variation of Hunt's lyrical and painterly technique, as, for example, in the *Halt of the Wise Men*, c. 1868 (*PB 610).

La Farge's learned eclecticism achieved its finest expression in his huge mural of *The Ascension*, 1887 (Illustration 5–33), at the Church of the Ascension in New York. The conception, derived largely from Raphael's treatment of the same subject, has Renaissance grandeur and amplitude. The composition is impeccably symmetrical and the figures have a classic stability. But at the same time this balanced presentation is dissolved by rich and various color, by subtle and nervous modeling, and by great realism in the details. There is even a glimpse of a landscape in the background whose inappropriate exoticism derived from La Farge's memory of Fujiyama, which he saw on a trip to Japan. *The Ascension* is painterly in the manner of Couture and Hunt, coloristic like Delacroix (whose decorative work La Farge, as the pupil of Hunt, must have admired), grandiose in the manner of the High Renaissance, but also meticulous in detail. But in spite of the combination of so many stylistic inconsistencies, the total impact of the composition, modeling, and color of *The Ascension* is a far richer sensuous experience than is the work of most of La Farge's contemporaries and successors, whose eclecticism is generally exclusively classical and executed with the pale, almost monochromatic flatness of Puvis de Chavannes, the most famous contemporaneous French muralist.

La Farge executed many other murals, notably at the Minnesota State Capitol and the Baltimore Courthouse. A mural at Bowdoin College, Brunswick, Maine, entitled *Athens*, 1898 (*PB 294), may be taken as typical of La Farge's developed style. Ample figures of the most ideal neo-classical type are arranged in a balanced composition. They are painted with a loaded brush in vivid colors, and are modeled with sculpturesque richness and realistic detail against a landscape of luxuriant tonality, mysterious depths, and atmospheric subtlety, which is nothing if not romantic. This combination of the three outstanding stylistic tendencies of nineteenth-century taste—neo-classicism, romanticism, and realism—is not quite fused, and therefore not quite satisfactory. The extremely cultivated, capable, and sensitive La Farge was perhaps too artistically educated, and as a consequence not sufficiently aware of the components and the extent of his personal talent to make a satisfactory fusion or choice among the many influences upon his art. As in the case of Stanford White and Augustus Saint-Gaudens, the "Renaissance complex," that learned facet of the genteel tradition, stood in La Farge's way to complete fulfillment.

La Farge did not return completely to his early realism until late in his life, during the relaxation of a trip to the South Seas in the company of Henry Adams, when he produced a series of pictures of Samoa and Tahiti which precede Gauguin's as records of a disappearing pagan culture. The savage and exotic in Polynesian life appealed to La Farge less than its idyllic simplicity, evocative of a classical Arcadia. The paintings, of which *Bridle Path, Tahiti*, c. 1890 (PB 611), is typical, were executed in watercolor. Their spontaneity of handling and transparency of color reflect a sensitive accuracy of observation. Though without quite the brilliance of execution which Winslow Homer and John Singer Sargent brought to the medium, La Farge's watercolors compensate with a more studied sense of decoration. Whether this quality may have come from the boldness of design in the native arts, a factor which influenced Gauguin's Tahitian paintings, is problematical. It is far more likely to have been the natural result of La Farge's long experience in decorating wall surfaces and stained glass windows. An oil from this period, *Maua—Our Boatman*, 1891 (*PB 614), has some of the freshness of observation seen in the watercolors.

La Farge typifies the cosmopolitanism of the post-Civil War period, but his educated sensitivity led him to emulate only the best. Together with Hunt, he served for the late nineteenth century a function similar to that of Allston at its beginning: his importance as an exemplar and teacher—insofar as he trained a generation of muralists—raised the general standards of artistic judgment and competence. Even if he and what he stands for seem indeterminate in comparison with more independent geniuses like Homer, Eakins, and Ryder, La Farge's realism and sense of color save him from the emptiness of many of his equally eclectic and overrefined contemporaries. Perhaps the passage of time will give more perspective to our present judgment of La Farge, and his inconsistencies may seem less glaring.[13]

Ideal Painting

In the post-Civil War period, ideal, literary, and history painting, though more difficult to distinguish from one another as clearly as before, persisted as aspects of late romanticism to the very end of the century, even in the face of growing realism.

A kind of history–literary genre deriving from the English painter Sir John Millais and the related pre-Raphaelite school was the most current form of ideal painting, though symbolic allegory based on the French academic tradition was almost equally prevalent. These influences were fortified by that of La Farge, whose literary subjects emulated the Italian Renaissance masters. The extensive mural painting at the end of the century developed from this school under the leadership of La Farge, and became eventually very close in spirit to the antique and Renaissance tradition prescribed at Paris by the École des Beaux Arts and the Salon. In contrast to this more public art, and to the literary, historical, and allegorical subjects of the more obvious ideal artists, there was also an ideal painting of a subtler and more introspective sort which culminated in the work of Ryder.

History and literary painting was largely in the hands of expatriates (living mostly in England) whose work is characterized by a learned nostalgia for the past, great technical competence, and an illustrative flair. Past eras were recalled with historical accuracy and with a pre-Raphaelite attention to detail in pictures dealing mostly with European subjects, but occasionally with incidents from American history. Among the latter are a number of paintings which, as visual stereotypes of our national past, have been reproduced on the walls of schoolrooms and in the pages of countless textbooks. The images are remembered but their creators are mostly forgotten. Among them are George H. Boughton, author of the *Pilgrims Going to Church* (New York Public Library), and Francis D. Millet. Incredibly deft, these *tableaux vivants* in paint are worthy of mention not only on account of their former popularity, but because of their meticulous accuracy, which gives them an insistency that cannot be ignored. Perhaps the best of these painters was Edwin Austin Abbey, better known as an illustrator, and remembered now largely because of his murals in the Boston Public Library. Abbey's sense of the past, particularly of medieval England, was projected with a literalness that was mitigated by a certain decorative sensibility influenced, probably inadvertently, by the art of the medieval world whose quaintness he so admired.

Of the symbolic or allegorical artists, some were easel painters exclusively, but others were often muralists as well. Abbott Thayer, who was both, is perhaps the most prominent of this group. His allegorical women were very impressive to his contemporaries. Samuel Isham, writing at the turn of the century, describes them as "a sort of revivifying of the figures of Phidias with modern spirituality." [14] Today these somewhat empty and ample figures, female in appearance yet sexless in feeling, are less attractive. The flesh and blood figure is there, but it is etherealized, like some of Saint-Gaudens' allegorical sculptures. Typical Thayer creatures are the *Stevenson Memorial Angel*, 1903 (PB 661), and the Florence in *Florence Protecting the Arts*, c. 1894 (PB 662).

Thayer is the best of the idealizers of women, because his somewhat banal conceptions are mitigated by painterliness, breadth of handling, and rich tonality similar to Hunt and La Farge. George de Forest Brush was almost as famous for his pictures of his wife and children, inspired by the madonnas of the Italian Renaissance. The critic Philip Hale, in reviewing an exhibition in which a typical Brush was shown, summed up the artist's work when he said: "The usual affair: Madonna della Mrs. Brusho con bambino brusho quite nudo." Brush's pictures, painted in Florence, are neither in the technique of the Renaissance or in the best contemporary manner—that of Hunt and La Farge; they are executed with a slick neo-classical realism that gives ideal conceptions an inconsistent specificity, as seen in his *In the Garden*, 1906 (PC 58).

The exalted notion of womanhood in the work of Thayer and others permeated much of American art in this period, not only that of the idealists. Even Winslow Homer's otherwise normal young women have something of this quality in their Junoesque figures and physiognomies; the most famous cartoonist of the day, Charles Dana Gibson, immortalized the type into the "Gibson girl"—still a phrase in common usage.

The mural painting of the period began with that of Hunt and La Farge who, though eclectic, were painters of ability and taste. Their borrowings were accompanied by a painterly and coloristic flair which derived ultimately from the great baroque decorative tradition through Delacroix, the admirer of Rubens. But the persisting neoclassical bias of official decoration in Europe, the appeal of antique mythology and allegory, and a revived interest in the classicistic murals of the great Renaissance masters exerted a constantly greater appeal and influenced the work of La Farge himself, and more especially that of his assistants and followers, of whom the best was Kenyon Cox.

This new neo-classicism was accompanied by a gradual rejection of the broadly handled coloristic romantic realism of Hunt and La Farge and its replacement by the hard and smoothly rendered detail of the academic neo-classic school, supplemented by the meticulousness of the pre-Raphaelites. The pale color and flat forms of the popular French muralist Puvis de Chavannes also exerted some influence, so that while mural painting became perhaps more appropriately decorative in its respect for the two-dimensional surface of the wall, the Hunt–La Farge tradition was diluted into an even greater restraint and refinement. The net result was conventional, bloodless, and unimaginative—though there were, of course, exceptions.

The most ambitious mural decoration before that of the Chicago World's Fair was at the Boston Public Library, commissioned in 1890 and executed over the next decade and a half. Though it was not typical of what was to follow, intrinsically it is important because it included the work of John Singer Sargent, whose biblical subjects in the stair hall are certainly the finest mural decorations of the century in America, though neglected by critics for decades. (Sargent's work at the library is so atypical that it does no harm to the discussion of mural painting to omit its consideration here and to include it in the treatment of the artist's work as a whole.)

The other work in the building was executed by Puvis de Chavannes and Edwin Austin Abbey. The decorations by the then aging Frenchman are not among his most successful, though it must be said in extenuation that he had never seen the building where they were to be placed. Those by the expatriate illustrator Abbey, depicting the story of the Holy Grail, seem to be blown-up miniatures, but the topical appeal of the artist's medievalizing detail and love of the picturesque gives a certain charm to their popular story-telling.

Mural painting was enormously stimulated by the challenge of acres of white walls at the World's Fair at Chicago in 1893, and the Roman bias of the architects led naturally to decorations of a classical nature. Though the actual work was intrinsically not very significant, it was an accomplishment from the point of view of cooperative effort on a large and showy scale, which reminded the participants of the great days of Medicean patronage in Florence. A tremendous surge of mural activity, stimulated by the Fair, accompanied the wave of the academic reaction in architecture. Among the most prominent commissions was that at Bowdoin College, where the work of La Farge and Thayer, already mentioned, competes, in an arrangement lacking in unity, with that executed by Kenyon Cox, the most typical of the three in his accomplished norm of classical decorousness. Other important work, on a much larger scale, was done at the Appellate Division Building of the New York Supreme Court, and at the Library of Congress in Washington. Typical of the former is Edwin Blashfield's *The Power of the Law*, 1899 (PB 515), in which the symmetrical composition and neo-classic figures, thrice removed from the Renaissance, are appropriate to the equally unoriginal classicism of the building. The decoration of the Library of

Congress was one of the largest unified mural programs since the days of the High Renaissance. Though the decorators felt themselves to be more nearly Florentines than Yankees, the results are disappointing on the whole. There is nothing of distinction to be pointed to except the achievement of a dead level of competent good taste. Similar work continued to be done in a succession of state capitols, banks, and foyers of office buildings until well into the 1920's, executed by Cox and Blashfield and by other competent artists such as Henry Oliver Walker, Edward E. Simmons, Henry Siddons Mowbray, Will H. Low, and John W. Alexander, and typified by such academically unimpeachable examples as Cox's *The Light of Learning*, 1910–1913 (PB 530).

Probably E. P. Richardson has said the last word on the whole sorry waste of time and space in this phase of American art, which is more "dated" than any other—though we may need more perspective to render a fairer judgment:

The men who produced these decorations were apparently convinced that the secret of mural painting was to represent a vaguely pretty woman in a long white robe. Standing with the Duomo and the Ponte Vecchio behind her, she represented Florence; seated or standing with appropriate emblems, she was Law, Fate, the Pursuit of Learning, the Telephone, or the Spirit of Ceramic Art; walking with Bible clasped in her hands, eyes upturned, the Pioneers crossing the Plains.[15]

Landscape: Inness and Pre-Impressionism

The large and meticulously painted landscapes of the late Hudson River school remained generally admired through the 1870's, but the more casual naturalism and broader handling in the work of Inness, and inspired ultimately by the Barbizon school, gradually gained ground, especially after the return of Hunt from France in 1855.

Inness is undoubtedly the outstanding landscapist of the last third of the century. Beginning with the somewhat classic compositions of the epic *Peace and Plenty* and the more lyrical and smaller landscapes of the mid-1860's—similar to his less pretentious early work, like

The Lackawanna Valley (Illustration 4–54)—he progressed through a more overtly classic phase in the 1880's, achieving finally a very personal style in the 1890's.

The inspiration of Claude and the effects of short trips abroad had already given Inness' work a certain classical serenity before he went to Italy in 1870 for a stay of four years. This visit resulted in the production of some of his finest work, of which *The Monk*, 1873 (PB 262), is among the best. This picture, depicting a white-clad monk in an expansive landscape dominated by the flat-topped pines of central Italy, has a grand simplicity of form bathed in a rich opalescent light, all treated with the artist's characteristic breadth of handling. An added sweep and clarity appear in the paintings executed after Inness' return to the United States. In the magnificent *Autumn Oaks*, 1875 (PB 602), the brilliant colors of the American autumn are combined with the voluminous forms of the trees receding in a stately rhythm into the sun-splotched distance. In this picture there also appears the beginning of a certain fuzziness of atmosphere, rendered with an even greater breadth than Inness had shown before.

Two pictures of the same title, *The Coming Storm*, the first painted in 1878 (Illustration 5–34) and the second in 1880 (PB 603), exploit this greater suggestiveness by a blending of solid forms with clouds and atmosphere in an effect which is most evocative of the mood of uneasy anticipation preceding a thunderstorm. The earlier painting especially, with its great banks of clouds rolling in over a lush and expectant countryside, has a power of suggestion that is almost contemporary in its emotional exploitation of shapes and colors.

Paintings of this sort are certainly successful illustrations of Inness' own remarks that a "work of art does not appeal to the intellect," that its "aim is not to instruct, not to edify, but to awaken an emotion." [16] Inness' works are as far as possible from the programmatic paintings of his predecessors of the mid-century and before. They appeal directly to the observer's senses and emotions, in a manner which it has since become more and more customary to think of as the

5–34. George Inness, *The Coming Storm*, 1878. Oil on canvas. 26 x 39 inches. (Albright-Knox Art Gallery, Buffalo, New York. The Albert Haller Tracy Fund.)

proper function of a good painting. Yet a considerable residue of realism is preserved in some of Inness' later work, derived from his feeling of respect for nature, proper in an artist who was an admirer of the theologian Swedenborg. The limpid forms of *June,* 1882 (*PB 261), for instance, have some of the specificity of his earlier work.

Though Inness had earlier remarked that Corot was "incomplete and slovenly," [17] his own work of his final years (1886–1894) might be described by an unkind critic in much the same terms. Inness' very personal and sometimes almost melancholy lyricism becomes more introspective in feeling and crepuscular in both mood and appearance. Thin veils of muted color textured with pure impasto passages reveal an image which becomes more and more elusive.

This late style can be traced back to *Grey Day, Goochland,* 1884 (*PB 263); it is less emphatically evident in *The Clouded Sun,* 1891 (PB 605); *The Home of the Heron,* 1893 (PB 264), represents it at its most extreme.

The relative formlessness of the late Inness relates him to the impressionist landscape painters, Monet, Sisley, and Pissarro, even more than did the breadth and sparkle of his earlier handling. Nevertheless, this must have been largely an independent development, since Inness is known not only to have disliked the impressionists but also to have held himself more and more aloof from all worldly contacts the older he grew.

Alexander H. Wyant's work, though of considerably less distinction, is not unlike that of Inness during his middle years. Early in his career Wyant rejected the teaching of both the Hudson River and Düsseldorf schools for the more naturalistic style of Inness, whom he had admired since he was a young man. In fact, Wyant's *The Mohawk Valley,* 1866 (PB 502), painted on his return from Düsseldorf, is not unlike Inness; it depicts a large, sweeping vista of fertile country basking tranquilly in the summer sun's warmth. But it is characterized by less artistic generalization than appears in Inness' pictures of the same time, and resembles in its surface treatment, if not in its composition, the more detailed work of the Hudson River school.

This somewhat precise handling was replaced by a more attractive summary treatment in Wyant's later work. After learning to paint with his left hand when his right became paralyzed, the artist produced smaller, more lyrical landscapes very much under the influence of the Barbizon painters and of Corot, but with some of the heavy impasto of men like Diaz de La Peña and Monticelli, painters associated with the Barbizon group who had an eccentric way of piling on the paint in rich proto-impressionist handling of brush and palette-knife. Characteristic of Wyant's later paintings is *An Old Clearing,* 1881 (PB 686).

The work of Henry Ranger was more precisely influenced by Monticelli and especially by Diaz de La Peña's representations of idealized forest glades with patches of speckled sunlight breaking through the verdant shade. Ranger's pictures of dark woods brightened by the autumnal foliage of North America become almost abstract in the heavy texture of the sensuously manipulated paint surface, and in the refinement of color organization. Such a painting as *Connecticut Wood* (National Collection of Fine Arts, Smithsonian Institution, Washington) is typical of the work of his best period. His almost Ryder-like use of vaguely evocative shapes is also characteristic. Ranger's later realist–impressionist work is much better known and more conventional, and these factors have militated against a greater appreciation of his earlier work.

Though their influence is less direct than in the paintings of Ranger, something of Monticelli and Diaz de La Peña can be seen also in the use of dots and slabs of color in the work of Ralph Blakelock. The facts of Blakelock's tragic life, marked by poverty, neglect, and madness (coinciding so well with the stereotype of the romantic artist), may have had something to do with his rediscovery in recent years. There is also more than a superficial resemblance to Ryder in his work—so much so that it remains a problem whether to discuss him as an "ideal" rather than a landscape painter. Most of Blakelock's pictures are landscapes, but they have very little reference to specific places. Usually visions of Indian encampments with great trees silhouetted against twilight, pale sunset, or moon glow, and with glimpses of misty distances, these pictures are essentially not landscapes, but ideal recreations of some boyhood nostalgia for the mysterious forests inhabited by the exotic indigene. *Indian Encampment* (PB 514) and *Moonlight,* c. 1885 (PB 512), use these props essentially as shapes and patterns which project the artist's dream-like vision, and are very reminiscent of Ryder's early landscapes. This ethereal quality is especially notable in such a picture as *The Vision of Life,* c. 1895 (PB 513), in which the figures are so amorphous as to be hardly distinguishable from the surroundings with which they are entangled.

Somewhat related to Blakelock is the little-known landscapist Joseph Meeker, whose *The Land of Evangeline,* 1874 (PB 624), has a haunting quality, though the dank, shaded bayou represented in the picture is treated in a less personal, more meticulous and conventional manner.

Homer D. Martin is an artist who, like Inness, was influenced at first by the Hudson River school but later developed a more personal lyricism. His early paintings *The Logging Camp* (PB 620) and *Lake Sanford in the Adirondacks,* 1870 (PB 303), are detailed and rhetorical, but their horizontal format (perhaps deriving ultimately from the panoramic tradition) and the misty or rain-obscured distances of their melancholy weather lift these pictures above the ordinary; they are landscapes of mood and contemplation. This generally reflective character persisted in Martin's work after his return from

France. He also derived from the Barbizon school a richer handling of paint, as in *Sand Dunes, Lake Ontario,* 1887 (PB 622). A later residence in France during the early 1880's introduced Martin to the brighter tonality and the even more spontaneous brush work of the impressionist landscapists, an influence reflected in his most famous painting, *The Harp of the Winds: View of the Seine,* 1895 (PB 619). But even this cheerful and extroverted scene, with its horizontal emphasis and the slow rhythm of its row of thin-trunked trees, has a kind of quietness which is faintly melancholy or at least elegiac.

The work of Dwight W. Tryon, another painter popular in his day, is not unlike that of the middle and later periods of Martin. It is characterized by a muted reflective quality which almost distinguishes American landscape, as influenced by the Barbizon school and the early impressionists, from the generally more extroverted naturalism of its French prototypes.

On the whole, with the possible exception of Inness', the great landscapes of the day were not painted by men who were nearly exclusively landscapists, as in the mid-century, but by artists of less limited range, men of the stature of Winslow Homer, Thomas Eakins, and Eastman Johnson.

Genre

The most typical painters of anecdote after the Civil War, Thomas Waterman Wood and Edward L. Henry, were less trained and less competent than those of the prewar years, and reflected the decline of genre painting as a distinct type. Only artists like Winslow Homer and Thomas Eakins, who transcended compartmentalization, produced genre pictures equal to or even surpassing in quality those of Mount and Bingham.

Such canvases as Wood's *The Village Post Office,* 1873 (PB 495), show little of the competence he might have been expected to acquire from his studies in Paris. Wood's sentimentalizing of American rural life in an industrial age is not heightened by the formal and emotional qualities found in the genre work of Winslow Homer. Henry is equally sentimental, reviving the American past in a series of historical genre scenes, and celebrating its rural present with hay rides and country schoolhouses. Like Wood, Henry studied in Paris with the most thoroughgoing of the mid-century academicians. But his drawing remained inadequate and his color harsh; in only a few pictures did he transcend his norm. One of them, painted before his trip to Paris, is *The 9:45 Accommodation, Stratford, Connecticut,* 1867 (PB 588), an early work with an enthusiastic and almost primitive naïveté. *The 9:45 Accommodation* is certainly an engaging picture. With much of the overt story-telling of the popular Currier and Ives prints, it appeals instantly to our curiosity, which is rewarded by a wealth of particulars. These details are held together by a skillful composition of diagonals leading around and beyond the "carpenter Gothic" station, where various rigs and buggies are unloading passengers for the brightly colored cars behind the pot-chimneyed engine with its shiny brass trim. The cheerful colors add to the general gaiety of the scene, and the activity has an almost rococo liveliness. Oddly enough, after study in Paris with one of the most exacting academicians of the time, Henry's work became less incisive, his drawing slovenly, and his color brash. At the same time, his sentimentalizing became more open in a series of historical genre scenes and rural episodes.

Immigrants from Great Britain added to the ranks of anecdotal painters, and brought with them a meticulous mid-century English realism. Perhaps the most interesting among them was John G. Brown whose best work reflects the almost scientific treatment of detail which is the mark of early pre-Raphaelitism. After coming to America he became extremely popular for his paintings of urchins, particularly newsboys, which were stereotyped in conception and compulsively accurate in detail—an unpleasant combination. Yet in some of Brown's less famous pictures he was a much better painter. His *Country Gallants,* 1876 (PB 93), depicting two swains assisting a couple of rustic young ladies over a rickety foot bridge, has something of

Winslow Homer's directness, and much of his almost impressionistic light; Brown was probably somewhat influenced by the greater artist. Brown is also the author of a remarkable picture, *The Longshoremen's Noon*, 1879 (Corcoran Gallery of Art, Washington), unusual for its close and discriminating observation of the various racial types portrayed and for the subject—workers listening to a labor leader. Other paintings, such as *The Music Lesson*, 1870 (The Metropolitan Museum of Art, New York), display such careful drawing and close, unsentimentalized observation that it is a pity the artist was diverted from realizing his true potentiality by the popularity of his street urchins.

Another painter of children, whose work was hardly ever as superficial as Brown's, is Charles Caleb Ward who, though a Canadian, was actually more closely connected professionally with New York than with his native New Brunswick. In what is certainly his best picture and one of the most charming genre paintings of the time, *The Circus Is Coming*, 1871 (Stephen Clark Collection, New York), he demonstrates a meticulous technique, linear and planometric composition, and close observation, and sums up the best of a tradition extending from Mount and the early Homer to Ben Shahn in the twentieth century (one of Shahn's favorite pictures is *The Circus Is Coming*). The bold arrangement of buildings and posters gives the painting a remarkable compositional strength, while the small scale, meticulous brush work, and precise observation lend it a jewel-like preciousness. The touchingly observed stances and clothing of the children contribute a poignant intensity rare in the anecdotal painting of the time.

An artist who should be better known is Conrad Wise Chapman, the son of the painter–illustrator John Gadsby Chapman. His series of small genre-filled landscapes concerned with the harbor defenses of Charleston are a kind of "sport" in art history, for they have a high-keyed tonality, heavy impasto, and even an eccentric composition, recalling the Japanese-influenced early Degas and Whistler. These characteristics of early impressionism can perhaps be explained through the possible influence of the Florentine

"Macchiorelli," [18] whose work Chapman may have seen in Italy where he was taken at the age of six by his father and remained until the outbreak of the Civil War, when he enlisted in the Confederate forces. His *Fort Sumter, December 8, 1863*, as well as *The Confederate Submarine Torpedo Boat H. L. Hunley*, both painted in 1863 (PB 105, *PB 106), demonstrate his quasi-impressionist characteristics. Both paintings are also very bold and sure compositions. After the defeat of the Confederacy, Chapman, rather than remain in the United States, went to Mexico, where he painted one of the last panoramas (and certainly the best of those which are still extant). *Panorama: the Valley of Mexico*, 1865 (PB 108), is a remarkable picture inspired by the Mexican landscapist Velasco, but lacks the immediacy of Chapman's paintings of the defenses of Charleston.

Another artist whose best work appeared early in his career was John F. Weir, the son of Robert Weir, the painter of literary genre and professor of art at West Point, and the brother of J. Alden Weir, the American impressionist. A few pictures dealing with industrialism, represented by *Forging the Shaft: a Welding Heat*, 1877 (PB 674), exploit the dramatic chiaroscuro caused by the glow of molten metal. It is strange that the emergence of the United States as a great industrial giant during the Civil War and after should have been celebrated so little in art. Most artists preferred to remain aloof in the world of dreams and allegory or in unspoiled nature. Only one other artist besides Weir (and Brown, in a similar theme) dealt with a subject at least somewhat related to industrialism: Thomas Anshutz, in his *Steel Workers' Noontime*, c. 1890 (PB 59). This vigorous study of figures relaxing outside a steel plant, their bodies strongly modeled in the noon sunlight, shows the influence of the sturdy realism and exacting knowledge of anatomy of Anshutz's great teacher Thomas Eakins. (One of the last genre painters of the old school, Anshutz is also important as the intermediary between Eakins and his own pupils at the Pennsylvania Academy, the next generation of genre painters: Robert Henri, George B. Luks, John Sloan, and William

J. Glackens, who remain as much realists as they are impressionists largely through inheriting the Eakins tradition.)

Among the vast number of genre painters of the period, only Eastman Johnson is of sufficient caliber to be compared with Homer and Eakins in that field, though his work in general is too uneven to be in quite the same category as theirs.

Old Kentucky Home, 1859 (PB 270), with its mid-century anecdotalism and slick Düsseldorf technique, hardly prepares us for the greater honesty and directness of some of Johnson's work during and after the war. In fact even his *Corn Husking,* painted only a year later (PB 607), though still meticulous in treatment, has something of Mount's strength of composition, and though the rustics are a little "quaint," they are not stereotypes. Johnson's work was always varied. Some of his paintings done before *Kentucky Home,* such as his Indian sketches, have the freedom and lack of pretension seen in some of his later work, like *In the Fields,* done in the 1870's (PB 272; Illustration 5–35). Many others, like the *Old Stage Coach* and the *Nantucket School of Philosophy,* done in the 1870's, are as anecdotal and carefully painted as the *Old Kentucky Home.* Certainly the most attractive of Johnson's works (besides the two group-portrait masterpieces to be discussed shortly) are those which the artist called "finished sketches" (to distinguish them from the larger, carefully worked out exhibition pieces). Such pictures as *In the Fields* or the brilliant little *Winnowing Grain* (Museum of Fine Arts, Boston; M. and M. Karolik Collection), and others done at Kennebunkport, Maine, in the late 1860's and on Nantucket during the following decade, are charming documents of rural life told with great economy of means and with a brilliant, almost impressionistic light quite suggestive of the early Winslow Homer.

Johnson's group portraits, *Family Group,* 1871 (PB 273), and *The Funding Bill,* 1881 (*PB 274; Illustration 5–36), are among the masterpieces of American painting in the second half of the century. Though the *Family Group* is almost overwhelming in its size and in the skillful projection of the heavily furnished and

5–35. Eastman Johnson, *In the Fields,* 1870's. Oil on canvas. 17¾ x 27½ inches. (Courtesy of the Detroit Institute of Arts.)

draped New York room of the early 1870's, it is a masterly realization of figures in space, brilliantly composed and utterly convincing. The meticulousness of Düsseldorf, where Johnson studied, is very nearly compensated for by the solid drawing and painterly technique derived from later study under Couture and from observation of the old masters, particularly Rembrandt. Perhaps it is only the color—which is not quite as subtle and unifying as it should be —that prevents the picture from fulfilling its potential success. In *The Funding Bill,* the influence of Rembrandt is even clearer. In the powerful modeling, Johnson almost achieves the grand solidity and formal realization of his great contemporary Thomas Eakins, who was equally influenced by Rembrandt.

The recent reappraisal of Johnson's less finished works, and the discovery of artists like Charles Caleb Ward are indications of current re-evaluations which are changing the view of late nineteenth-century genre. An example is the work of Edwin Romanzo Elmer, a small manufacturer and inventor in western Massachusetts, whose *Mourning Picture,* c. 1890 (Smith College Museum of Art, Northampton, Massachusetts; on loan from a relative of the painter), is a touching, if naïve, representation of the painter's deceased daughter standing with a pet lamb, her doll-baby in its carriage beside her, in a rather

5–36.   Eastman Johnson, *The Funding Bill,* 1881.   Oil on canvas.   60½ x 78¼ inches.   (The Metropolitan Museum of Art, New York. Gift of Robert Gordon, 1898.)

stark landscape graced with a new, conspicuously "bracketed" house before which her father sits with his wife as if for a formal portrait. The picture would be called a primitive if it were not for the careful observation, so meticulously rendered.   Even more impressive because it is less ambitious and more concentrated, is the portrait of the artist's wife at a loom contrived by the inventive Elmer to manufacture whiplashes. Entitled *A Lady of Baptist Corner, Ashfield, Massachusetts,* c. 1880 (private collection, Amherst, Massachusetts), this remarkable picture is composed with the greatest mathematical sensibility.   Its perspective is impeccable, its light closely studied, and its detail uncanny.

The mood of quiet work in the clearly defined and lighted space is emphasized by the view of the countryside seen through the window. (The painting is remarkably similar to contemporary examples of "magic" or "sharp focus" realism, especially the work of Andrew Wyeth.)

A word must be said about art concerned with the Civil War and with the West, which was so important a subject earlier in the century. With the exception of Winslow Homer, there were no outstanding artists among the many who were involved in the war as commentators, whether actually journalistic or not.   Among the most competent were William Waud and Edwin Forbes.   Waud's *Signaling by Torches from Gen-*

eral Butler's Headquarters, a wash drawing, 1863 (°GB 206), is quite dramatic, and among the best of a generally more mediocre production. Forbes's drawings, reproduced in his later etchings such as *Going unto Camp at Night,* 1876 (°GB 80), are far less satisfactory, both in formal organization and intensity of feeling, than the photographs of the war by Mathew Brady and Alexander Gardner.

A comparison between the work of most of the artists who represented the West and that of contemporaneous photographers again shows the latter to be esthetically more rewarding. Nevertheless, the paintings of the expanding frontier, where the life of the mining camp, the army post, and the range had been added to that of the Indian, pioneer, and trapper, became an invaluable source for the documentation which has kept the legendary "old West" alive in films and on television as part of American folklore. Most of the painting of this kind was done by countless illustrators whose work appeared in the magazines of the 1880's and 1890's, translated by means of wood engraving. Among them, only two painters of the period, Henry F. Farney and Frederick Remington, are in any way outstanding. The first was a competent realist who appealed to an audience that was sentimental about the passing of the red man. But the popular bias of his painting is too obvious and dated. Remington's work, on the other hand, though equally illustrative and popular, was based not on overdramatization or sentiment but on the truth and accuracy of his presentation, and reflected a deep knowledge gained first-hand from an intimate association with the range from the time of his youth, which he spent on a ranch in Kansas. Much of Remington's work is actually illustration

5–37. Frederick Remington, *Dismounted: The Fourth Troopers Moving,* 1890. Oil on canvas. 34 x 49 inches. (Courtesy of the Sterling and Francine Clark Art Institute, Williamstown, Massachusetts.)

(up to the time of his death in 1909 he was still doing effective covers for *Collier's*) and many of his paintings are variations on themes first intended as illustrations. Yet, because of his extraordinary powers of observation, his powerful technique as a draughtsman, and his impressive knowledge of both human and animal anatomy, Remington's work is not only invaluable as documentation but attractive as well. When his technical prowess was coupled with a sense of pattern or a dynamic composition, some of his paintings became important works of art. What prevents many of them from being more acceptable is a tendency to overfinish, and a somewhat brash and often unharmonious sense of color—though this is not inconsistent with the raw light of the plains and desert. Remington's cowboys, range hands, cavalrymen, Indians, and "bad men" can be seen in quantity at Ogdensburg, New York, in a museum devoted to his work. Two fine examples in more available collections are *Dismounted: The Fourth Troopers Moving*, 1890 (Illustration 5–37), a masterly presentation of cavalrymen leading a group of unmounted horses that seem to gallop right out of the canvas, and the *Flight of Geronimo* (Houston Museum, Houston, Texas), less pretentious in its show of skill, but no less dramatic, and more sketch-like and painterly than much of the artist's other work.

The Expatriates: Whistler, Cassatt, and Sargent

Many artists of American birth who worked in Europe are intrinsically as important as others who remained in the United States. Some have been mentioned—Edwin Austin Abbey and Francis D. Millet, for example—but in general they were so Europeanized that there is little incentive to include them in a history of American art. By the same token, James Abbott McNeill Whistler, Mary Cassatt, and John Singer Sargent could be omitted. But in view of their outstanding positions in world art and the fact of their American citizenship, they are always categorized as Americans. Perhaps only of Mary Cassatt can it be said that she belongs more to another school, the French, than she does to the

American. Much of Sargent's work was actually executed in the United States. Also, both Whistler and Sargent were true internationalists, limited to no school, painting and exhibiting in France, England, and America; on these grounds alone, irrespective of their citizenship, the United States therefore has as much claim to them as do the other countries.

All three artists reflect in their work the characteristics of late realism and impressionism. Sargent and Cassatt were distinguished followers of the great innovators Courbet, Manet, Degas, and other impressionists, and each contributed something personal. But in Whistler we are dealing with one of the leaders and innovators of his time. If it were not for the fact that early in his career Whistler left Paris for London and has therefore often been considered a member of the British school, it would have been more generally recognized how important a figure he was in the development of impressionism, especially in the direction of that formal refinement which Whistler represents almost as well as Degas—and contemporaneously, if not indeed earlier. Furthermore, Whistler's attitudes, as expressed in his famous *Ten O'Clock* lecture and dramatized in his libel suit with John Ruskin (who likened his technical performance in a painting of Old Battersea Bridge to "flinging a pot of paint in the public's face"), reflect an anti-Philistinism and art-for-art's-sake attitude which had a great deal to do with the preparation of the Anglo-Saxon world for the acceptance of impressionism and ultimately of modern art itself. If Whistler's pictures are not as arresting today as they were in his own era, it is largely because he himself has conditioned modern taste to accept what was once unacceptable, by his insistence on purely esthetic and intrinsically sensuous elements in a work of art, in contradistinction to story-telling or extrinsic qualities.

Born in Lowell, Massachusetts, James Abbott McNeill Whistler was taken at an early age by his father, an engineer, to St. Petersburg, Russia (where the son would have preferred to have been born, and on occasion said he was). His childhood was passed in European capitals. At the age of fifteen, Whistler returned to America to spend a few years at West Point (where he failed), and a few months at the Coast and Geodetic Survey, where he learned rudimentary drawing and etching. As soon as he was able, in 1855, Whistler departed for Paris where he became the pupil of Charles Gleyre, a follower of Ingres and one of the best of the academic teachers. But the young American soon fell in with the artistic revolutionaries Courbet, Manet, Monet, and Degas. Whistler's early landscapes, such as *Alone With the Tide: Coast of Brittany,* 1861 (PB 472), show the influence of Courbet, but demonstrate Whistler's more refined sensibility, already somewhat decorative in contrast. It was in his genre portraits, however, that Whistler came into his own. One of the first, *Music Room,* 1860 (PB 471; Illustration 5–38), is as advanced as those of Degas in refinement of composition, and was painted only one year later than the Frenchman's group portrait of the Bellelli family, generally considered a precedent-breaking picture. Whistler's *Music Room* is no less distinguished, though it must be admitted that it is much less rewarding on the whole than the Degas, since the French artist combined with his formal sophistication a psychological insight not attempted by Whistler. Nevertheless the *Music Room* is a thoroughly delightful picture. Subtly realistic in the casual, almost accidental posing of its figures, it is at the same time carefully thought out in its formal relationships. Here Whistler (as early as Degas) employed the compositional devices which were to become familiar in the following decades, and which are generally associated with the influence of the Japanese print: oblique perspective, the seemingly arbitrary cutting-off of important parts of figures and objects by the limits of the picture, and the prominent use of silhouette and of flat pattern—all combined in an essentially decorative way. Though the handling of paint recalls Courbet and Manet in its thick richness and is therefore not original, the treatment of the elements of composition is extremely advanced.

At about the same time, Whistler was producing the most satisfactory of his landscapes (or, more properly, city-scapes) in the sense that the decorative quality of these paintings is combined

5–38. James Abbott McNeill Whistler, *Music Room,* 1860. Oil on canvas. 37⅝ x 27⅞ inches. (Freer Gallery of Art, Washington. Gift from Colonel Frank J. Hecker, Detroit, June, 1917.)

with sufficient definiteness of statement to be readable, in contrast to the almost oversubtle suggestiveness of his later subjects. *The Last of Old Westminster,* 1862 (PB 475), and *Old Battersea Bridge, Symphony in Brown and Silver,* c. 1865 (PB 678), are typical, both showing the inspiration of the Japanese print. In another version of the subject, *Old Battersea Bridge, Nocturne in Blue and Gold,* c. 1865 (Illustration 5–39), the motifs of the tall bridge and the boatman in his barge are both derived from two specific works of Hiroshige.

Several full-length portraits of women done in the 1860's are more consciously oriental in inspiration than the *Music Room* and therefore a little mannered. *La Princesse du Pays de la Por-*

celaine (PB 679) and *Lady of the Lange Lijsen* (PB 677), both dated 1864, are typical in their use of actual oriental props such as fans, porcelain, and kimonos, and of such compositional devices as the casually cut off but decorative objects in the front plane which serve to lead the eye into the picture. Less self-conscious but as beautifully composed is the earlier *The White Girl*, 1861–1862 (°PB 474). Three masterly portraits of the next decade show the mature Whistler at his best: *Harmony in Grey and Green, Miss Cecily Alexander*, 1872 (Illustration 5–40); *Arrangement in Grey and Black No. I, the Artist's Mother*, 1872 (National Gallery, London); and *Arrangement in Grey and Black No. II, Thomas Carlyle*, 1872–1873 (Illustration 5–41). All three portraits show a change from the earlier bolder handling of pigment to a flatter and more decorative surface, inspired somewhat by Veláz-

5–40. James Abbott McNeill Whistler, *Harmony in Grey and Green, Miss Cecily Alexander*, 1872. Oil on canvas. 74¾ x 38½ inches. (Reproduced by courtesy of the Trustees of the Tate Gallery, London.)

5–39. James Abbott McNeill Whistler, *Old Battersea Bridge, Nocturne in Blue and Gold*, c. 1865. Oil on canvas. 26¼ x 19¾ inches. (Reproduced by courtesy of the Trustees of the Tate Gallery, London.)

quez' restrained and patterned handling in his late portraits of Philip IV of Spain. [These characteristics are seen even better in later portraits such as *Arrangement in Flesh Color and Black, Portrait of Theodore Duret*, 1883 (PB 484).] All three paintings are extremely clever in their organization. The studied silhouettes, the subtle harmonies and contrasts of color, the decorative

5—41. James Abbott McNeill Whistler, *Arrangement in Grey and Black No. II, Thomas Carlyle,* 1872—1873. Oil on canvas. 67⅜ x 56½ inches. (Glasgow Art Gallery and Museum, Glasgow, Scotland.)

elements of sprig and screen in *Miss Alexander* and of framed pictures and architectural elements in the other two, combine to make these among the most formally pleasing paintings of the century. This is not to say that Miss Alexander is not a very appealing little Victorian girl, or that the dour personality of the melancholy Scot and the strength of character of the artist's mother are not made evident by Whistler. But as portraits they do not possess the psychological insight of Degas or the profound physical realization of Thomas Eakins. The pictures remain finally decorations—even if very good ones.

The decorative character of Whistler's work became increasingly prominent during the 1880's. One of the artist's most important productions during these years was the wall decorations for the Peacock Room (now in the Freer Gallery in Washington) which he executed for a London house. But Whistler's easel pictures themselves began to become almost abstract decoration. Characteristic are the *Nocturnes* which Whistler was painting at this time. An outstanding one, *Nocturne in Black and Gold, The Falling Rocket,* c. 1874 (PB 481), representing a shower of fireworks in a night sky over the Thames, is as refined and abstract a piece of decorative painting as can be found until the advent of non-representational art in the twentieth century. In fact, many of Whistler's landscapes in this later phase, depicting twilight or night and therefore very subdued in color, are hardly different in final effect from certain paintings of contemporary abstract expressionism. Whistler's use of abstract terminology as titles for his pictures, especially from the vocabulary of music, is significant in showing a conscious bias in favor of abstraction, an attitude which is eloquently and cleverly presented in his *Ten O'Clock* lecture, delivered at London, Oxford, and Cambridge in 1885:

Nature contains the elements, in colour and form, of all pictures, as the keyboard contains the notes of all music.

But the artist is born to pick and choose, and group with science, these elements, that the result may be beautiful—as the musician gathers his notes, and forms his chords, until he brings forth from chaos glorious harmony.

To say to the painter that Nature is to be taken as she is, is to say to the player, that he may sit on the piano.

Whistler was the first critic or artist to express the point of view—supplemented and illustrated by his own productions—which has led to the present acceptance of abstract "harmonies" and "arrangements" as the proper content of figurative art, while its former province, representation, has been absorbed in partial abstraction, as in Whistler's own work, or has disappeared entirely.

In spite of the implications of modernity in Whistler's work, that of his last years is permeated by the *fin de siècle* overrefinement of his English contemporaries in the art-for-art's-sake movement, and therefore is characterized by a lack of vigor which a continued contact with the more central tradition of the French school might have prevented.[19]

Mary Cassatt was one of the best half-dozen or so American artists of this period, and certainly the best woman painter, the equal if not the superior of Berthe Morisot, her French counterpart among the impressionists. Because she studied and developed in Europe, lived in Paris, and exhibited with the impressionists, Mary Cassatt is only incidentally American. Yet her determination to succeed as a woman in what was then still a man's world and, as a gentlewoman, to astonish her friends by associating herself with a radical artistic group, indicate an originality and determination which could perhaps be said to be American traits, but are certainly not necessarily so. After a brief period of instruction at the Pennsylvania Academy, she went to Europe, never to revisit the United States for any length of time. A news item which appeared in the *Philadelphia Ledger* in 1899, long after Mary Cassatt had been accepted in Paris as one of the outstanding members of the impressionist group, suggests the reasons why the artist preferred Europe: "Mary Cassatt, sister of Mr. Cassatt, President of the Pennsylvania Railroad, returned from Europe yesterday. She has been studying painting in Paris and owns the smallest Pekingese dog in the world."

Though she studied in the Paris schools, Cassatt's true masters were Correggio, Rubens, and Hals, and among her contemporaries, Courbet, Manet, and the impressionists.

It is questionable whether she would have developed so brilliantly without her association with Manet, Renoir, and above all Degas. From Manet she acquired her fresh, lively brush stroke, augmented by her admiration for the similar handling of Hals; from Renoir her richer, more intense color and her feeling for the quality of flesh, again supplemented by her interest in the old masters, in this case Rubens and Correggio; and from Degas her sensitive drawing, compositional skill, casualness of treatment, and lack of pretense in subject matter, the latter qualities being reinforced from the same source that influenced Degas, the Japanese print. However, her work is still very much her own, and cannot be mistaken for that of any other artist.

The Bath, c. 1891 (°PB 99; Illustration 5–42), sums up these varied influences, while displaying Cassatt's own sure and direct touch. *The Bath* has a Degas-like pleasure in the shapes and patterns of the rug, pitcher, and striped bathrobe, the oblique perspective that Degas borrowed from the Japanese, the fine painterly quality of Manet, and the richly colored flesh of Renoir. Together with these characteristics, Cassatt's

5–43.   John Singer Sargent, *The Daughters of Edward Darley Boit*, 1882. Oil on canvas. 87 x 87 inches. (Courtesy, Museum of Fine Arts, Boston.)

work of Van Dyck, that epitome of the fashionable portraitist.

When we have looked at the Boit children and at portraits like that of *Madame X*, we have seen Sargent at his best, and are aware of the "slightly 'uncanny' spectacle," to quote his admirer Henry James, of a "talent which on the very threshold of its career has nothing more to learn." [21] Sargent's work did not decline until his late murals. Some of his fashionable portraits are hardly more than documents of Edwardian splendor, yet even these have a certain insight into the shallowness or triviality of their subjects. Furthermore, technically, Sargent was never really superficial. One head he painted sixteen times; and the face of Mrs. Stokes in the *Mr. and Mrs. Isaac Newton Phelps*

Stokes, 1897 (PB 649), which looks so summary and virtuoso-like, was actually repainted nine times to achieve its look of gay confidence.

At his best, Sargent is not only a superb craftsman, but a painter of considerable psychological profundity—that is, within the limits of the visual bias of the realist–impressionist tradition he represents, as opposed to the profounder realism of Eakins. In the *Stokes* portrait, one of Sargent's most characteristic and best (and largest), the paint is applied with an ease and virtuosity which are breathtaking; the pattern is bold to the point of being overwhelming; the space in which the figures exist is shockingly real; and the gay, debonair stance and smiling face of the vivacious and carefree Mrs. Stokes (just in from a tennis match) are most convincing. The picture has a breezy freshness which is completely appropriate to the subject, the place, and the time—the carefree world of the wealthy in the secure era before the First World War.

A very different portrait is that of *Robert Louis Stevenson,* c. 1885 (Illustration 5–44), a *tour de force* of the capacity of the impressionist method to represent the passing moment. Nevertheless, within the limit of this transient approach Sargent transcends mere deftness in his suggestion of the nervous creative energy in the frail and restless body of the dying poet passing before us in the shaded room.

Sargent was more than a portraitist; indeed, he grew to hate the tedious succession of commissions from important people—noblemen, bankers, and millionaires. In a fit of revulsion he once answered a peeress who was anxious for a portrait by the best international artist in

the field that he would paint anything else for her, "but not the human face." [22] Among Sargent's most attractive works were his watercolors. Casual notes made during his travels, and undoubtedly a welcome relief from his portraiture, they have the easy brilliance of his oils but are more intimate and personal, reflecting the relaxation such sketching obviously afforded him. Sargent's watercolors are not unlike Homer's, whose equally brilliant aquarelles undoubtedly influenced his own, since no one else had carried the medium so far into such economy of statement. To compare Sargent with Homer, however, is to find the former lacking in the convincing plasticity of the more realistic artist. But Sargent is Homer's equal in facility and in that spontaneity which is the essence of watercolor's quick suggestibility, as can be seen in a much later example, *Muddy Alligators,* 1917 (PB 411). Sargent perhaps even excels

5–44. John Singer Sargent, *Robert Louis Stevenson,* c. 1885. Oil on canvas.   20¼ x 24¼ inches. (Collection of Mr. and Mrs. Harry Payne Whitney.)

Homer in the subtlety of his tonal relations, which attain an almost photographic accuracy yet were achieved with all the cursory rapidity suitable to the medium.

Another aspect of Sargent's work, his murals, also afforded him relief from portraiture. This phase of Sargent's career is usually passed over, due to the falling-off in the quality of his work during the 1920's, seen in his conventional decorations in the dome at Boston Museum, 1916–1921 (PB 402), and at the Widener Library at Harvard. But those at the Boston Public Library, such as *Doctrine of the Trinity* (PB 400), begun in the mid-1890's and finished twenty years later, are certainly among the best in a category of painting which, in retrospect, is on the whole extremely unrewarding. The conception is elevated, the iconography is complex, the use of gilt and low relief adds decorative variety, and the imitation of medieval styles, especially Byzantine, is evocative of the grandeur and mystery of the subjects: the Christian faith, its Hebrew precedents, and False Doctrine. The decorations fill the rather constricted stair space, where they are placed grandly and effectively, and are rich and varied enough in form and content to interest the observer time and again—qualities which are necessary in an effec-

5–45. John Singer Sargent, detail from *The Prophets,* 1895–1916. Boston Public Library, Boston, Massachusetts. Mural. Oil on canvas. (Photo through the courtesy of the Trustees of the Boston Public Library.)

tive mural, as E. P. Richardson has pointed out.[23] The more abstract and decorative symbolic subjects, such as the *Doctrine of the Trinity,* are not unlike those at Trinity Church across the way, but they are more sophisticated in their author's knowledge of art history, being closer to actual medieval precedent than are La Farge's. Though the treatment is flat, and therefore consistent with the purist ideal of respect for the two-dimensionality of the wall, there is some modeling in the figures, a procedure inconsistent with the styles being emulated. Yet perhaps Sargent did this deliberately, for the frieze of *The Prophets* (Illustration 5–45), begun in 1895, is thoroughly three-dimensional as well as comparatively realistic in treatment. To quarrel with the inconsistency of this section in its juxtaposition with the more abstract areas is justified; but to object to the strongly modeled treatment of the prophets themselves is to deny the validity of most of the great Renaissance muralists from Giotto through Michelangelo and Raphael and those of the baroque period. (A more valid justification for caviling might be the employment of a somewhat broad Manet-like handling, derived in part from the Spanish masters, rather than the carefully contrived and more abstract three-dimensionality of the High Renaissance.) The realism of the hooded and robed figures, recalling the monks by the Spaniard Zurbarán, is supplemented by the individuation of the prophets' faces, reminiscent of the *Four Evangelists* by the great master of the northern Renaissance, Albrecht Dürer, a work which Sargent must have known well. Undoubtedly eclectic, nevertheless the frieze is impressive with its thoughtful and monumental figures arranged in a slow rhythm of gesturing attitudes.

These murals are an unusual production for a man who was otherwise almost exclusively a portraitist. Their existence points up the fact that mere visual reality was not everything for an artist of Sargent's generation. For in these works he was caught up, like La Farge and Saint-Gaudens, in the persisting idealism of the late nineteenth century. (Sargent's Hosea—the fourth figure from the left in the frieze—is very similar to Saint-Gaudens' brooding figure in the *Adams Memorial* (Illustration 5–74). Sargent's career thus represents one more instance of the conflict between real and ideal in the art of the West, and certainly in that of America.

Duveneck and Chase; Impressionism; Landscape

The romantic realism of Hunt and of the early La Farge was superseded in the late 1870's and the 1880's by a realism stemming from an entirely different source, the Munich school, followers of Courbet and Manet and of the Dutch seventeenth-century painters. Frank Duveneck, who himself ran a school in Munich for a number of years, and William Merritt Chase were the chief American protagonists of this realism, later to be called "the New School," which dominated the Society of American Artists, founded in 1877.

The paintings of the group are matter-of-fact in subject matter, impetuous and suggestive in technique, and especially notable for the quick slash of the brush and a feeling for the medium of paint. Duveneck in particular illustrates these qualities, which he combines with a dark palette recalling the rich "old master" tonality of the Dutch painters. When Duveneck first exhibited in the United States—at Boston in 1875—Hunt led an enthusiastic chorus of praise which was never to die down during the artist's influential lifetime. Duveneck's dashing manner is almost a *tour de force* in the *Whistling Boy,* 1872 (PB 542), but in *The Turkish Page,* 1876 (*PB 161), the bravado is richer in its suggestion of the complexities of space and texture. Portraits like that of the *Woman With Forget-me-Nots,* c. 1876 (PB 160), or the young *Mary Cabot Wheelwright,* 1882 (PB 543), have the assurance of the well-placed, deft stroke, together with a more traditional feeling for solid form, the more remarkable because so cursorily noted.

Many other Americans studied in Munich, among them J. Frank Currier, a kind of lesser Duveneck. But after Duveneck returned to the United States, most American artists abroad began to come under the influence of the brighter palette of the later Manet and the impressionists in Paris. Of this slightly later group, Chase (starting like Duveneck as a Munich painter and gradually becoming more impressionistic) is the most typical as well as the most prominent. Unlike some of his equally impressionistic but slightly more sentimental compatriots, Chase never lost his respect for the facts of appearance, and though he is hardly profound, his work is always enlivened by a fine sensuous feeling for the objects he paints and for the material of paint itself. Chase instructed hundreds of students from 1878 to 1896, and was during these years what Hunt had been twenty years before, the most influential innovator and teacher of his time.

Although the dark palette of Munich gave way to impressionistic luminosity, the slashing brush work of Hals and the broad areas of Velázquez remained in Chase's work. The influence of Whistler's composition added a strength of design to his pictures of the mid-1880's; later, the brilliant shorthand of Sargent's version of impressionism was given an even more slashing impetuosity by Chase. The artist's many still lifes done throughout his career represent his joy in things and in paint. His portraits, such as that of *Miss Dora Wheeler*, 1881–1883 (PB 521), have an admirable fluidity and, especially in this example, considerable subtlety of design quite reminiscent of Whistler, as has the simpler *Lady With the White Shawl*, 1893 (*PB 117). *In the Studio* (PB 114) shows Chase's ability to deal with a complex order of forms in space more brilliantly than Duveneck in his *Turkish Page*, and with a breathtaking dexterity. The late landscape, *Near the Beach, Shinnecock*, c. 1895 (PB 522), has an impressionistic freshness equal to that of any of his contemporaries, carrying further the already brilliant palette and the handling of his earlier genre scene, *The Open Air Breakfast*, c. 1888 (*PB 523). *A Friendly Call*, 1895 (PB 520), represents Chase at his best. Better composed and brighter in tonality than *In the Studio*, it recalls Whistler in surface design and Sargent in liveliness of handling.

On the whole, Chase was a brilliant imitator or follower of contemporary trends, never as bold or original as either Whistler or Sargent.

He typifies the non-idealist taste of the period from 1880 to 1900 better than any other artist, though in the 1890's the more strictly impressionist group was beginning to take over, even as Chase himself became more and more impressionist.

Among the leaders of this group were Theodore Robinson, Edmund C. Tarbell, and Thomas W. Dewing. Robinson found in the work of Monet a point of view and a technique which suited him perfectly, and he became like Mary Cassatt, an accomplished American painter in the impressionist school, as is demonstrated in his sensitive landscape, *The Vale of Arconville*, c. 1888 (PB 639), and in his fine figure study, realized in intense luminosity, *The Watering Pots*, 1890 (PB 640). But Robinson died too soon after his return to the United States to adjust his French palette to the American scene. Edmund C. Tarbell and Thomas W. Dewing, who turned their backs on Munich for the Paris of Manet and Monet, are more typical of a group of artists who domesticated the impressionist palette and technique to a kind of refined genre very typical of the time and place. Tarbell's women, as in *Girl Crocheting* (Library and Art Gallery, Canajoharie, New York) and *Josephine and Mercie*, 1844 (Corcoran Gallery of Art, Washington), seem to be relatives of those by Saint-Gaudens and Abbott Thayer and to have just stepped down from a pedestal into the pleasant interiors of shingle style cottages on the New England coast. Dewing retains a little more of a poetic quality derived ultimately from Hunt but made livelier by the color and brush work of the impressionists, as in *The Recitation*, 1891 (PB 146), or *The Spinet* (PB 536). In 1895, Dewing and Tarbell joined with eight other artists, some from New York, to form "the ten." Among the others were John Twachtman, Childe Hassam, and J. Alden Weir, in whose work the characteristics of French impressionism can be clearly observed.

Twachtman and Hassam were almost exclusively landscapists; toward the end of the century they initiated a landscape tradition which is even now lingering on in conservative circles. In the work of the American impressionists the last vestiges of romanticism died out. Land-

5–46. Childe Hassam, *Yachts, Gloucester Harbor*, 1899. Oil on canvas. 33 x 36 inches. (Collection, San Francisco Museum of Art, San Francisco, California.)

primarily an illustrator. Hassam came into his own at the end of the century, by which time his style had formed. The muted luminosity of Twachtman and Dewing is reflected to a certain degree in some of his Cape Cod and moonlit landscapes. But in general Hassam was obviously delighted with the clear brilliance of American light, which he interpreted with a vigorous impressionist stroke, as in *Southwest Wind*, 1905 (PB 213). Sometimes his treatment turned to a rawness of color if the subject warranted, as in his New York city-scapes. Less raucous is the brilliant but still somewhat brash color of *Yachts, Gloucester Harbor*, 1899 (Illustration 5–46), which represents the fully developed Hassam at his vigorous best. Yet the artist could be quite restrained both in color and composition, as in his charming glimpse of city life, painted later in his career, *Little Cobbler's Shop*, c. 1912 (PB 580). Of all the American artists who brought back the impressionist palette developed in the limpid, nacreous light of the Île-de-France, Hassam was the least tempted to transform the color which is native to New England, New York, and Long Island into that of the fields of France.[24]

J. Alden Weir sums up the impressionist influence in American landscape and genre at the turn of the century. His landscape has some of the subtle glow of Twachtman, but is more specific in its topography, usually the rural New England scene, which he manages to touch with sentimental nostalgia for a passing agrarianism, in spite of his objective technique of impressionistic luminosity. Typical is *Upland Pasture*, 1905 (National Collection of Fine Arts, Smithsonian Institution, Washington). *The Red Bridge*, c. 1905 (PB 673), is more objective. But even here a kind of sweetness fills the air, which, though not as full of nuance as Twachtman's, has none of the brashness (one is tempted to say the strength) of Hassam. This same gentleness is seen in Weir's genre scenes and in his portraits, in which the figures become almost insubstantial. Among the former, *Visiting Neighbors*, 1900–1909 (PB 671), has a certain strength of modeling which makes it somewhat more interesting than his usually softer forms, which become almost flaccid in their envelope of

scapes and figures became more important as shapes and colors seen in changing or shimmering light than as subjects for their own sakes. Yet the subtleties of Twachtman's visual records possess a convincing personal lyricism, especially in his seascapes, such as *Sailing in the Mist* (*PB 445), with its opalescent color, and in his winter scenes, such as *Snowbound*, 1885 (PB 446), or *Hemlock Pool*, 1902 (PB 666), in which the vapor of the melting snow and ice permeating the scene seems like the breath of coming spring. An impressionist's delight in the sensuous sweetness of light and air is seen in Twachtman's less moody paintings, among them *Holly House, Cos Cob, Connecticut* (PB 667), and *Summer* (PB 668).

Childe Hassam's early work, represented by *Rainy Day, Boston*, 1885 (PB 578), is realistic in the manner of Hunt and Chase, but already demonstrates the artist's eye for color and pattern. Hassam undoubtedly knew the work of Whistler, but the influence of Monet made itself increasingly felt in the somewhat descriptive views of cities done while Hassam was still

subtly graded strokes. There is little of the bold sureness of Mary Cassatt, for example, in Weir's pleasant impressionistic approach to the figure. His women even take on some of the disembodied "niceness" of that period, demonstrating a link at the end of the century between the older tradition of romantic idealization and the new visual realism of impressionism.

Winslow Homer

Even during the last years of his life, Winslow Homer was beginning to be called the greatest American artist. A recent comprehensive exhibition of his work not only has corroborated this judgment, but forces us to consider whether Homer may not be one of the most important artists of his era anywhere. The exhibition, which was sponsored by the National Gallery, far from transforming the artist into a monument in the history of the nation's culture, showed instead how fresh and alive the work of Homer remains. His pictures are among the least "dated" of those painted in his generation. Among Homer's American contemporaries only Ryder, Eakins, and the three great expatriates Whistler, Cassatt, and Sargent are comparable in quality.

To compare Homer with Ryder is pointless since these artists so perfectly represent the opposite poles of American art, the real and ideal. But Homer shares many of the characteristics of Whistler, Sargent, and Cassatt, being subject to the same influences, consciously or not. At any rate he belongs to the realist–impressionist tradition, and not to that of La Farge's cultivated eclecticism. In fact Henry James (who was fascinated by Homer, though he did not like him) stated well that ". . . the best definition of Mr. Homer to the initiated would be, that he is an elaborate contradiction of Mr. La Farge." [25] On the other hand, Eakins and Homer have much in common. Like Eakins, Homer was not concerned with idealization, but was dedicated to the recording of the physical world, less profoundly than Eakins but with much greater variety, and occasionally more poetry, or even charm. Both men belonged to their generation—Homer perhaps more so, since

he continued to develop even beyond impressionism. During much of his career Homer, like Eakins, was interested in ordinary scenes involving ordinary people, as were the realists and impressionists everywhere. Finally, both artists were preoccupied with American scenes and American people. Homer also sums up the general artistic trends of his period, developing from mid-century anecdote to a forceful personal expression within the framework of the realist–impressionist movement, and at the same time carrying on certain stylistic qualities indigenous to American art. There is in Homer's work, especially in its early phase, a very close similarity to the traditions in earlier American painting: design in flat planes, a pleasure in sharp edges, in detail, and in pattern, and a luminosity that is as American as it is impressionist. A comparison of such pictures as the *New England Country School* (Illustration 5–47) and *Dad's Coming* (Illustration 5–48) with the work of the luminists, for instance, makes this clear, though Homer's technique is much more painterly. Like Mount, Homer felt that he was always realistic, though it is perfectly evident from his work that he took considerable artistic license. But the assertion of his respect for facts was almost a fetish. When answering a question whether he took liberties in painting nature, he replied, "Never! never! When I have selected the thing carefully I paint it exactly as it appears." [26] He was equally emphatic about his not being influenced by other artists, least of all by Europeans. He once said, "If a man wants to be an artist he must never look at pictures"—in spite of the clear evidence in his work of inspiration from impressionism and Japanese prints.

The outer circumstances of Homer's life are simple. His energies were artistic; he never took on the responsibilities of marriage, becoming, during the latter half of his life, even misanthropic, living alone in a cottage at Prout's Neck on the coast of Maine. This lonely existence was varied only by seasonal trips to the north woods in the Adirondacks and Quebec, and to the Bahamas and the Caribbean in winter. Earlier, Homer had been more involved in an active life, having been an artist–correspondent for *Harper's Weekly* during the Civil War and for over a decade afterward. A trip to Paris in 1867 undoubtedly influenced his work, but only to further it in the direction it had already taken. After a stay in England in the early 1880's Homer turned from the recording of the "more smiling" [27] aspects of American life in genre painting to the more universal themes of the earth and sea and man's involvement with them. The cause for this sudden change in the artist's point of view has often been speculated on, but Homer himself left no hint. He simply told his biographer that "as the most interesting part of my life is of no concern to the public I must decline to give you any particulars in regard to it." [28] In any event the change from the carefree young gallant, interested in pretty girls playing croquet, to the crusty Yankee of the later years, was as profound as that which occurred in his work.

Homer was largely self-trained, beginning his professional career in Boston when hardly more than a boy as a designer of lithographed covers for sheet music. These and the woodcuts made from his early drawings have a kind of retardataire rococo quality not unlike Henry Inman's pretty genre conceits. But the reality of the Civil War and the necessity to record events rapidly and forcefully pruned off his decorative flourishes and brought out the young artist's latent strength. The directness of Homer's vision is seen in the rather well-known wood engraving, *Army of the Potomac—A Sharp Shooter*. This is factual reporting, but its bold design alone would impress itself on the memory. The *Bivouac Fire on the Potomac* from *Harper's Weekly*, 1861 (GB 520), is a less serious but equally effective example of lively reporting, depicting a Negro dancing before a group of soldiers, the whole scene dramatically lit by a fire. Many of the oils from the Civil War period are remarkable not only for their vivid reporting, but for their proto-impressionist quality of light and their painterliness. The latter two characteristics cannot be explained entirely by the probable influence of Hunt, and suggest the possibility of Homer's being familiar with George

Loring Brown's "Macchiorelli" technique, which that artist had brought back to Boston in the 1850's. [A painting done just after the war, *A Veteran in a New Field*, 1865 (Collection of Adelaide de Groote, New York), demonstrates very well the character of Homer's work at this time, that is, his ability to portray action brilliantly, his boldness of design, and especially the surety, verve, and breadth in the passages of paint which suggest rows of wheat tumbled by the scythe. Only the slight pun in the title dates it as surely pre-impressionist.]

A more important, larger, and better-known painting, *Prisoners From the Front*, 1866 (°PB 224), demonstrates better the stature of the young Homer at the end of the war. Painted from sketches made at the front, the picture represents a typical group of Confederate soldiers at the bitter end of the war; led by a cocky southern aristocrat, the men, including old men and mere boys, none of them in proper uniform, are lined up before a Union officer in a barren battlefield marked with the stumps of shattered trees. The figures are correct and well-realized, the air is charged with light, and the composition is impressive. No other American—with the possible exception of Eastman Johnson—could have executed such a picture at this time. Had Homer died then, he would still have been a figure to reckon with in the history of American art.

During the next decade Homer explored the carefree activities of the middle class at leisure and on vacation and recorded the life of farm and seacoast, particularly the world of children in school and out. Most of this work took the form of wood engravings for *Harper's Weekly*, but Homer also produced a number of paintings as well, inspired by the same subjects and often variations on the subjects of the wood engravings. The painting of *Long Branch, New Jersey*, 1869 (PB 225, °PB 225A, °PB 225B, °PB 225C), for example, is repeated in *On the Bluff at Long Branch, at the Bathing Hour*, which appeared in *Harper's Weekly* in 1870 (GB 517). The paintings are notable for their composition, showing a remarkable sensitivity for flat decorative pattern. This characteristic was perhaps indigenous enough in the American tradition, especially in folk art and among the more native professional artists like Mount, to account for Homer's awareness of it. All of these early pictures are also notable for their freshness, brilliant color, and lively brush work, qualities which have little connection to the sequence of their production from the mid-1860's to the late 1870's. If it were not for this fact, it would be very tempting indeed to assume that after Homer's trip to Paris in 1867 there was a marked increase in his proto-impressionism, both in technique and composition. But some of the most "French" of his pictures, such as the *Croquet Scene*, 1866 (PB 589), were executed before he went to Paris. In this painting the fresh color, the broad handling, and, above all, the bold pattern of the silhouetted women in their bustled dresses are very reminiscent indeed of Manet, Monet, and Degas, not to mention the Japanese prints.

The seemingly impressionist qualities in Homer's work may not have derived actually as much from impressionism itself as from a combination of various factors in the artist's own artistic environment and personality, which resulted in an effect analogous to impressionism. It has already been suggested that the "Macchiorelli" tradition brought back from Italy by Brown may have been a very strong ingredient of this result—indeed, the early Homers resemble strikingly the work of the Italian group. The combination of Hunt's painterliness with the tradition, if it can be called such, of the luminists may have produced by coincidence a similar effect. (It is interesting to note in this connection that Homer was a member of a hunting club in the Adirondacks to which David Johnson—who was almost a luminist—also belonged.)

It may well be that Homer saw some early impressionist work, or at least work by such proto-impressionists as Johan Jongkind and Eugene Boudin at the Boston Athenaeum in the 1850's and later in New York, and that he knew La Farge's collection of Japanese prints in Boston. But, as is so often the case when an attempt is made to explain genius, the historian when dealing with the origins of Homer's style is almost compelled to resort to an appeal to the *Zeitgeist*, that mysterious force which brings about contemporaneity of attitude and creation in various separate instances where there is apparently no cross fertilization. In any event, Homer's visit to Paris certainly stimulated him further in the direction he was already going, perhaps sharpening his eye for composition and for brighter color and subtler light.

Long Branch, New Jersey sums up as well as any other painting Homer's early work at its best, for it is typical both in subject matter and technique. (Though it could be argued that its qualities as a painting may have derived from impressionism, it is still similar enough to Homer's works executed before he went to Paris to be taken as characteristic of his entire work roughly within the decade 1865–1875.) The technique is certainly analogous to that of early impressionism: even the subject is similar to the beach scenes by the proto-impressionists and by the impressionists themselves. Long Branch, a resort made fashionable by President Grant, is depicted on a summer day, the ocean not too intense a blue, the paler sky speckled with small fleecy clouds. The fresh breeze from the sea is blowing the bright calico and muslin dresses of the girls as they walk on the bluff with colorful parasols to protect their complexions, while below a man hangs out bathing clothes outside a bathhouse. The combination of sea, sand, and grass with the small cubical bathhouse and the gaily dressed girls comprises an exciting composition. The colors are especially attractive: large masses of contrasting cool and warm colors, accented by spots of intenser hue, as in the red hat of the girl at the right, and the yellow shadow inside her parasol. The engaging scene belongs to a series devoted to the portrayal of attractive young ladies at various sports and at resorts ranging from the Jersey coast to the New Hampshire mountains. Simpler in composition, grander in conception, but with the same impressionistic handling of light and color is *The Bridle Path, White Mountains*, c. 1868 (PB 591A), another typical painting of the period.

During these years Homer was also interested in depicting activities involving the farm and the sea in pictures usually peopled by children or adolescents, seldom by adults. Executed mostly at the farm of some friends in central New York, and at the fishing port of Gloucester in Massachusetts, they are more appealing to us than they were to Henry James, who was appalled by Homer's "freckled, straight-haired Yankee urchins" and his "flat breasted maidens, suggestive of rural doughnuts and pie." [29] Yet here was the pictorial equivalent of the idyllic world of Huck Finn and Tom Sawyer, the innocent world of childhood and of the earlier America that existed before the time described in Mark Twain's disillusioned *The Man Who Corrupted Hadleyville*. These pictures by Homer seem almost elegies for the passing of the rural world, a theme overtly or unconsciously present in much of the art and literature of the nineteenth century, from the English lake poets and landscapists to the authors of local color and the painters of the local scene. This feeling had even been expressed in an indirect and grandiose way by the artists of the Hudson River School, but in Homer's work it takes on a peculiar poignancy, a quality which may be somewhat due to a contemporary regretful nostalgia for an earlier, less complex America; but not entirely, for when Homer described it, this world still had an actual existence, and was not yet artificially preserved in the stereotyped folksiness of Norman Rockwell. The honesty of Homer's approach is underscored when a typical work, *Snap the Whip*, 1872 (PB 590), is compared with a similar subject depicted by an artist of the previous generation, Henry Inman, entitled *School's Out*. Homer deals with real barefoot children in overalls in a scene dominated by a typical red schoolhouse and by a hillside sprinkled with maples turning red and yellow in the early autumn. There is something raw and brash about the picture, but it is fresh and real. The Inman painting is a confection; the children are like Boucher's cupids dressed in homespun in a landscape out of Gainsborough or Watteau, thrice removed through steel engravings.

Homer did dozens of such subjects as *Long Branch* and *Snap the Whip*, summarizing a whole facet of American life—some of it gone, some remaining as part of an American iconography, whether true or not, but at least too deeply felt to be stereotyped or ridden with clichés, even in such a picture as *Dad's Coming* (Illustration 5–48), in which artistic force succeeds in overcoming the Victorian sentiment of the appalling title.

Homer's pictures are frankly story-telling and therefore represent an aspect of art which is far from popular today, at least in critical and sophisticated circles. Yet in spite of the titles and a frank appeal to surface emotions, the subjects are not illustrations to literature, moral tales, or mere anecdote. Homer is too deeply involved in the sensuous aspects of experience to be in any way ideological or conceptual and consequently literary. His people are involved in nature: sailing, strolling, clam digging, and (toward the end of the period) hunting or fishing. Homer had an intimacy with his subject matter, and an understanding of it which was genuine enough to impress even Henry James, who had complained of Homer's "blankness of fancy." [30] For James realized that these unpretentious anecdotes were essentially pictorial, remarking with his usual perception, that Homer "saw everything as one with an envelope of light and air." [31]

New England Country School, both in the 1872 version shown here (Illustration 5–47) and an earlier one in the City Art Museum of St. Louis, 1871 (°PB 226), demonstrates this pictorial character very well. The story is obvious enough: the conventionally pretty young schoolteacher with children of all ages under her control in a one-room schoolhouse; it is sunny and warm outside and the children are restless, forced to stay indoors on such a day. One can almost hear the flies buzzing in the lazy heat of an Indian summer day. The technical and formal elements of the picture are very satisfactory. The interior light is cleverly indicated through panes and blinds; the air of the school room, stuffy and sleepy, is suggested by the

5–47. Winslow Homer, *New England Country School,* 1872. Oil on canvas. 21 x 38 inches. (Addison Gallery of American Art, Phillips Academy, Andover, Massachusetts.)

broad handling of the brush, the blending of edges, and the rich granular pigment which depicts the permeating glow of the afternoon sun in rich umbers and ochers. The almost geometric formality of the composition is equally remarkable in its play of rectangular forms, and in the way the observer is led into the picture by the bold placing of the school bench in the foreground. The unfortunately titled *Dad's Coming,* c. 1875 (Illustration 5–48), is an excellent example of how Homer could make a sentimental subject almost monumental. A mother and two children waiting for the return of a fisherman, the boy sitting on a dory drawn up on a beach, and the mother standing, holding the younger child in her arms, are the elements of a composition which is almost Renaissance in its static symmetry and its parallelism to the picture plane. The strength of Homer's composition is seen in the bold perspective of the dory

which nevertheless is finally a silhouette on the flat surface of the design as a whole, an odd shape cutting the horizon and contrasting with the parallel horizontality of the logs and with the isolated vertical of the mother and child. Yet together with this formal abstraction there is an intimacy of observation which is touching, not only in the attitude of the young boy perched on the dory waiting for the return of his father, but also in such a subtle detail as the seaweed which clings to the rope tied to the boat, caught there when the last tide ran out.

This painting is one of a number of seaside sketches which are among the most charming of Homer's early works. Many of them also appeared in wood engraved versions, and a word must be said here about Homer's wood engravings. The artist drew directly on the block and his conceptions for this medium exist therefore only as prints, contrary to the usual practice in this ordinarily purely reproductive medium, in which the drawing was copied on the block by the engraver. Homer's drawing, then, literally became the engraving. His wood engravings therefore have an autographic quality which makes them more personal and far closer to being original works of art than the customary copies. When a particularly sensitive engraver was employed to turn the drawing on the block into the series of raised and incised areas necessary for printing the image, the result was often very successful. Typical are the bold composition and sensitive texture in *A Winter Morning—Shoveling Out*, which appeared in *Every Saturday* in 1871 (*GB 518). In the best of Homer's wood engravings—or, more properly, wood engravings after Homer—there is a remarkable retention of the ambient light of his drawings. This is seen particularly in the seaside sketches, as in *The Raid on a Sand-Swallow Colony*, which appeared in *Harper's Weekly* in 1874 (GB 519), in the wood engraved version

of *Dad's Coming*, and in many others, among which *Waiting for a Bite*, also in *Harper's Weekly*, in 1874 (Illustration 5–49), is especially notable for the hazy atmosphere in a swamp where some boys are fishing from a great fallen stump, and for a composition of considerable power in the arrangement of its simple elements.

Homer in these early years also worked in watercolor as well as in oil. Though much less distinguished than his brilliant performances in this medium during his later years, some of these paintings have great charm. Their small format and somewhat meticulous rendering (in the old, conventional tradition of watercolor before it was revolutionized later in the century—largely by Homer himself) make them less satisfactory than the oils with their broader, richer handling. But in some instances the freshness and spontaneity of the later years begin to be seen, as in *Children on a Fence*, 1874 (*PB 222A), notable also for its composition.

5–48.   Winslow Homer, *Dad's Coming*, c. 1875. Oil on wood. 9⅜ x 13⅞ inches. (Collection of Paul Mellon.)

5–49. Winslow Homer, *Waiting for a Bite*. Wood engraving after Winslow Homer. (*Harper's Weekly*, August 22, 1874.)

In summary, some general remarks can be made about the early Winslow Homer: his rejection of the old-fashioned, tightly rendered studio light for the natural light of out-of-doors; his attention to the rendering of the particular place, time of day, season, and kind of weather —even his focus on the gay and pleasant, the innocent and sportive; his total lack of ideological pretension; and finally his subtle decorative or formal sense—all these qualities relate him to the impressionists, whether they are attributable to a direct influence, to a coincidental American development, to a combination of the two, or, for lack of anything more precise, simply to the *Zeitgeist*. At the same time, his tendency toward the planometric and toward parallelism to the picture plane, his feeling for rectangles and sharp edges, and his underlying geometry of the flat

surface coincides (whether influenced by it or not) with a visual tradition which may be called American, if we consider such pictures as Hicks's *Residence of David Twining* (Illustration 4–82), Mount's *Banjo Player* (Illustration 4–63), Bunting's *Darby, Pennsylvania, after the Burning of Lord's Mill* (Illustration 4–84), and Tirrell's *View of Sacramento* (Illustration 4–59), as well as work by David Johnson and Fitz Hugh Lane.

On a more obvious and less stylistic level, certainly Homer's work has an undeniably American flavor in its realization of the particularities of the American scene, not only in its stubbornly accurate depiction of places, people, and activities, but also in the precise selective rendering of certain times of day and season. Homer's sharp American light defines rocky pastures, blueberry fields, bright autumn foliage, leaf-flecked ponds, snowdrifts, and bare apple trees; beaches, piers, and chips from the shipwrights' awls, and plain Yankee mills and fishhouses, or, to quote the eloquent if unsympathetic Henry James, "his barren plank fences, his glaring bald blue skies, his big dreary vacant lots of meadows." [32]

Lyrical rather than epical in his rural scenes, descriptive rather than penetrating in his social commentary, the early Homer is more analogous to James Greenleaf Whittier and William Dean Howells than to Herman Melville or Walt Whitman. Yet Homer was honest, never rhetorical, and much less sentimental than most of his contemporaries. He was not profound, but he was brilliant, sensuous, and richly formal.

The later Homer is a very different artist from the one of the earlier years. The sharp, defining light and caressing detail of his early work are succeeded by a greater breadth and suggestiveness, and the charm of the particular is replaced by a more impersonal generality which is grander if less touching. Though much of Homer's work during the last decades of his life could be called genre it is much less topical, dealing with the elemental themes of man's relation to nature, or simply with the conflict of the elements themselves, as seen in his magnificent seascapes. The later Homer is not less concerned with the realization of physical experience than he was before. He is simply more universal and not so specific in his reference. Far broader in range than his contemporaries, the impressionists, it is not their visual world alone which he records, but a world in which tactile form and movement are still important, and in which even sound and smell are suggested. Though the word "sensuous" has connotations hardly compatible with the Yankee crispness of Homer's work, nevertheless his ability to express his response to the evidence of all the senses can hardly be described more accurately. In Homer's pictures there exist very real physical experiences: the surge and sweep of the sea, the excitement of running the rapids or riding to the chase, the stillness of moonlight, the barking of hounds in the distance, the hardly perceptible flutter of a bird's wings, the crack of a gun in the silent woods.

Some of the pictures which Homer painted in the five or more years before his stay in England, and the subsequent change in his style, already presage his later development. They are a little less decorative and charming, and display an interest in hunting, fishing, or similar activities, that is, in some relationship of men with their natural environment. Perhaps the best of these is *The Two Guides,* 1876 (PB 591), in which the theme and treatment are more general than in Homer's early paintings.

But it was in England that Homer's work really changed. Motivated by some reason we do not know, since Homer was so reticent about his personal life, he seems to have fled from the pleasant rural and resort life he had been describing for fifteen years, to the Yorkshire coast near Tynemouth where he depicted the harsh life of the fishing people on the shores of the North Sea. Here his themes become grand, his figures more solid, and the atmosphere of his pictures more embracing and less defining. The last factor can be explained by the influence of the English climate, and the broadening of technique which it inspired, possibly augmented by familiarity with the English landscape painters. Also, the massive and generalized figures of Homer's later work may have been influenced by English art of a kind not so accepted today but extremely popular in Homer's time—the work of the prominent painter–illustrators like Sir John Millais, whose usually banal work, so typical of British Victorian taste, should not blind us to their sometimes excellent pictures, notable especially for their grand figures and spacious compositions.

In any event, Homer's English experience and work, typified by *Inside the Bar, Tynemouth,* 1883 (*PB 592), left him with a very different feeling for the human figure—more three-dimensional and idealized; and a very different handling of light and paint—broader, more permeating and painterly.

After Homer's return from England he settled on the Maine coast, where the sea and man's struggle with it became the main themes of his work. A few pictures done during the early 1880's are, in a sense, transitional to his less

5–50. Winslow Homer, *Huntsman and Dogs,* 1891. Oil on canvas. 28¼ x 48 inches. (Philadelphia Museum of Art. William L. Elkins Collection.)

overtly dramatic later work, since they depend on story-telling content almost as much as did his earlier work. *Life Line,* 1884 (PB 231), and *Fog Warning,* 1885 (Museum of Fine Arts, Boston), are among the best known, but perhaps the most noteworthy is *Eight Bells,* 1886 (PB 233). In these pictures the paint is broader and more atmospheric, the figures are bigger and solider than in Homer's earlier work, and the ocean moves with a mighty and elemental force. The sea continued to be Homer's chief inspiration in the large oils which he produced until the end of his life, its eternal battle with the granite coast of Maine gradually becoming equated as subject matter with man's struggle against its awesome forces. Typical are *Northeaster,* 1895 (PB 240), and *West Point, Prout's Neck,* 1900 (PB 595). In representing the mountainous seas crashing against the rocks and casting spray and spume high against the turbulent sky, Homer simplifies the complex shapes and movements

into their basic forms, achieving an effect of elemental power very different from the meticulous imitation of surface effects which causes the seascapes of his imitators to appear frozen and static.

The forest and the life of the woodsman and hunter had for Homer a fascination almost equal to that of the sea. One of the finest canvases dealing with this subject is *Huntsman and Dogs,* 1891 (PB 235; Illustration 5–50), a composition almost Renaissance in its static balance, in which a young huntsman is represented pausing beside a thick tree stump on a hillside speckled with the subdued but rich colors of late autumn; the partly overcast sky is filled with fast-moving clouds.

In such a picture, and in the marines, the breadth of the brush work and the illusion of transparency in water and sky (even in the opaque medium of oil) reflect the influence of Homer's watercolor. This medium as a means of expression was carried farther by Homer than by any other artist until that time. He completely changed the point of view and technique of watercolor, sloughing off the residue of the topographical approach and of the meticulous treatment still displayed to a certain extent in his earlier watercolors. Homer realized the potential suggestiveness of the medium by developing a brilliant shorthand of free-flowing washes executed with a rapidity that retained the impact of the original experience. Yet the appearance of extraordinary ease of manipulation masks a surety which is never a mere *tour de force* or formula, but a grasping of the essential structure of appearance and movement. Watercolor became for Homer an ideal tool for recording the nuances of landscape, his immediate impressions of the activities of men in the northern woods and streams, and also his vivid experience of the contrasting world of the Bahamas and Caribbean with their intenser colors and darker people. Some of Homer's best papers are from this area,

as, for instance, the brilliant *The Turtle Pound*, 1898 (*PB 594), with its azure sea and the brazen glint of the sun on the wet skin of the Negro divers. *After the Hurricane, Bahamas*, 1899 (PB 242), showing a drowned sailor cast up with the remains of a dory on the beach, is perhaps a little overdramatic, but the subject afforded the artist a fine opportunity for the use of color, the reddish browns of the sailor's skin and of the seaweed and dune grass contrasting with the cold blues and greens of the tumultuous sea and sky. One of Homer's most famous oils, *The Gulf Stream*, 1899 (PB 243), is based upon such a watercolor, but is even more macabre, for it represents a colored sailor on a wrecked boat which is still afloat, being watched by waiting sharks; such overt story-telling was rare in Homer's later works.[33]

Of the northern watercolors, *The Adirondack Guide*, 1894 (*PB 238), and *Adirondacks*, 1892 (PB 236; Illustration 5–51), are characteristic.

5–51. Winslow Homer, *Adirondacks*, 1892. Watercolor. 13⅜ x 19½ inches. (The Fogg Art Museum, Harvard University, Cambridge, Massachusetts.)

Bold, but subtle in design, they are filled with the silence of the sun infiltrating the deep woods. The *Guide* is seen fishing, silhouetted against the grotesque shapes of dead trees; in *Adirondacks*, a young hunter pauses beside a decayed fallen tree in a forest of infinite verticals arranged in a complexity of planes suggested by the simplest means. In contrast to the static qualities of these two watercolors is the brilliant dynamism of the *Canoe in Rapids*, 1897 (PB 593), in which Homer represents the frail craft being maneuvered skillfully as it careens down the frothy boiling water between rocky shores, under a lowering sky. The transparent water, the rain-filled clouds, the rocky scrub-covered shores are dashed in with an impetuosity which suggests that Homer was actually in a canoe closely following the one depicted, and just put down the scene before him. The incredible immediacy, coupled with Homer's accuracy of vision and touch, make such a surmise not implausible.

Among Homer's greatest works—and in sequence of time, his culminating works—are a series of oils of great originality, in which the contemplation of nature and its forces is heightened by the presence of living creatures, sometimes man, or even by a story, now no longer sentimental but almost symbolic. Among these is *Fox Hunt*, 1893 (PB 237), in which the strange moonlit winter drama of starved crows chasing their unusual prey is told in a skillfully decorative composition. The silhouettes of animal and birds, the high horizon, the device of the little berries emerging from the snow drift are as refined in their placing as in a painting by Whistler, though the latter, of course, would have avoided such a subject. The subtle organization of the composition and the deft drawing of the figures would do justice to an oriental artist. Even more

5–52. Winslow Homer, *Right and Left*, 1909. Oil on canvas. 28¼ x 48⅜ inches. (National Gallery of Art, Washington. Gift of the Avalon Foundation, 1951.)

5–53. Winslow Homer, *Moonlight on the Water,* 1906. Oil on canvas. 15½ x 31¼ inches. (Los Angeles County Museum of Art, Los Angeles, California. Paul Rodman Mabury Collection.)

curious, and equally arresting in its composition, is *Right and Left,* 1909 (Illustration 5–52). A picture of great originality, it is also an excellent illustration of Homer's unrealistic point of view, for though the picture is logical in arrangement the question might be asked, where is Homer himself? Here, as in many of Homer's pictures, this question qualifies the matter-of-factness of his realism by adding an element of mystery. In *Right and Left,* Homer depicts two golden-eye ducks, one arising from a stormy sea, the other shot down and falling. Though very reminiscent of a Japanese print, both in the decorative placing of the shapes and the sensitive observation of the characteristics of the birds themselves, the composition derives not from an oriental source, but from an American one: Audubon's plate of *The American Golden Eye,* the only change being that the shot duck is reversed.

Self-trained, basically independent, but extremely sensitive to any change in the artistic climate, Homer's creative energy continued to the very end of his life. Had he retained his physical vitality it is likely that he would have continued in the forefront of his generation, if we may judge from one remarkable picture of his later years, *Moonlight on the Water,* 1906 (Illustration 5–53), which comes as close as is possible for art which is still representational to being an abstract pattern of shapes arranged in an emotionally expressive way, and is thus almost contemporary.

Throughout his career, Homer's work paralleled developments in European art, and at the same time epitomized certain indigenous traditions. The combination of these two factors with an unmistakable personal touch, as individualistic as his independent personality, makes of Homer a thoroughly American artist, but not a provincial one. The strength of his formal organization, and his remarkable sensitivity to the quality of his media—oil, wood engraving, and particularly watercolor—recommend him to the connoisseur. But of all American artists, Homer appeals most to simpler, less sophisticated tastes. His early work—charming, perhaps a little sentimental, and filled with nostalgia (at least to our generation)—has become increasingly appreciated not merely for its anecdotal qualities but for its pictorial ones, while the more general themes of his later work have an immediacy of elemental physical experience which must remain a valid form of artistic expression, even though their specificity may now be unfashionable.[34]

Thomas Eakins

With Winslow Homer, Thomas Eakins is a contender for first place in the roster of American painters. He is more limited than Homer because he is such a thoroughgoing realist, but for the same reason he is perhaps more profound.

The always prominent realistic strain in American art coincided in the late nineteenth century with the stylistic development of western art in general. Eakins' own artistic temperament was deeply realistic—he considered idealism a form of "untruth." Walt Whitman, one of Eakins' friends and admirers, said of him, "I never knew of but one artist and that's Tom Eakins who could resist the temptation to see what they thought ought to be rather than what is."[35] Eakins did not appeal to those whose taste for the grandiose or the sugar-coated had survived from the mid-century, nor to those who admired the cultivated eclecticism of La Farge and Saint-Gaudens. He was also ignored by those who preferred the more superficial realism of the impressionists, especially when, as in the case of Sargent, the glint of fashion was added. Eakins was never popular. He seldom received a portrait commission, for when he did, the sitter was frequently shocked at what the painter's stubborn honesty had revealed. Eakins felt the necessity to express the truth as he understood it. He was contemptuous of "esthetic" art, and for him imagination was suspect. Once when he was asked his opinion of a Whistler portrait of a girl, which he was observing, he replied that he thought it was a very cowardly way to paint.

When pressed further about whether the painting did not have "charm and beauty," he simply did not answer.

It was not Eakins' purpose to transcend reality; he wanted to realize it. And he knew he had to work for the reward of imminent beauty in his paintings. The tools he used for the comprehension and projection of the factual truth were chiefly scientific: mathematics, perspective, and, above all, anatomy. Eakins used geometry and perspective in various complicated ways to render the figure and objects in space as accurately as possible. In his drawings for *Max Schmitt in a Single Scull*, 1871 (PB 163, *PB 163A, *PB 163B), for instance, even the distortions of reflections in the rippling water are worked out logically. But it was anatomy that Eakins adored. He studied the subject at medical school during much of his career, and like the Renaissance masters, even required his students to dissect corpses. Eakins' knowledge of the human body was so professional that he once read a learned paper on physiology before a scientific body. His belief in the importance of anatomy even lost him his job at the Pennsylvania Academy, where his insistence that his female students understand the entire male anatomy was too much for current squeamishness. Photography was another one of Eakins' tools (as it would doubtless have been to the artists of the Renaissance), but he used it discreetly and only as a check.

To present-day taste, in which preference for the products of the "third eye of the imagination" has been bolstered by the free expression and association stimulated by the discovery of the unconscious, Eakins' point of view and performance seem ploddingly pedestrian. But taken within the limits of the factual truth in which he believed, Eakins' paintings are so profound that they have a kind of inevitable dignity which we must respect even if we may not like it or approve of it.

It could be argued that Eakins' scientific enthusiasm comes somewhat late in the history of art, since the first excitement over perspective and anatomy occurred five centuries before, when the Renaissance artists discovered these devices to express the new realism of the fifteenth century in reaction against the semiabstraction of medieval art. But, as an artist belonging to the tradition of late nineteenth-century realism, Eakins brings to it an honesty and profundity which are impressive. If this is too much praise, it can at least be said of Eakins that, like the factually oriented artists of the Renaissance, he was not merely a scientist, his realism cannot be condemned as mere verisimilitude. He never "sat down monkey-like and copied a coal scuttle," [36] as the artist himself described the seventeenth-century Dutch painters of still life.

Thomas Eakins was born in Philadelphia of solid Quaker stock. He subjected himself easily to a life-long discipline which began in the Paris studio of Jean Léon Gérôme, the most exacting mentor of academic thoroughness—a kind of Ingres without style. But though Eakins studied with a neo-classicist, he could not help absorbing some of the realism of the contemporary French school. Eakins admired Courbet later, but the main French influence during his early years was Couture, that is, the Couture of the unpretentious genre scenes, not the painter of the huge neo-classic–romantic Salon piece *The Decadence of the Romans*. (A visit to the Philadelphia Museum where Couture's *Little Gilles* is on display, not too far from a magnificent collection of Eakins, will show how similar are the techniques of the two artists.) But Eakins' most important masters were the great realists of the seventeenth century. A trip to Spain made him further acquainted with the Spanish school, especially Velázquez of whom he said, "so strong, so reasonable, so free from affectation." [37] His admiration for Velázquez was almost equaled by his liking for Hals. In these tastes Eakins is typical of his generation, but in his enthusiasm for Rembrandt he is less so; it was the great Dutch master who influenced Eakins most. He called him "the big artist," [38] admired the profundity of his grasp of truth, and realized the primary importance of the contrast of light and shade (he called it Rembrandt's tool) in the artist's work. As much as Eakins was impressed by Velázquez, the predominantly visual realism of that artist

was rejected for Rembrandt's more comprehensively constructed realization of form. Rembrandt's influence in the development of Eakins' style links his work to a more thoroughgoing and perhaps profounder tradition of realism than that of Manet and the impressionists, which is more superficial in the literal sense. Eakins' strong modeling in contrasts of light and dark, his generally rich dark tonality, and even the breadth and suggestiveness in the handling of pigment resemble Rembrandt's practice. Anyone familiar with such a painting as Rembrandt's *Bathsheba* is struck by certain similarities in Eakins' *William Rush Carving the Allegorical Figure of the Schuylkill*, the 1877 version (PB 173, *PB 173A; Illustration 5–54). The knowledgeable and sensitive treatment of the nude, the reality of interior space, and the handling of texture are all quite traceable to Rembrandt. It is not suggested here that the breadth, profundity, and insight of one of the world's greatest artists are matched by Eakins, but at least the American artist learned much from Rembrandt, and shared to a certain degree his ability to express the significance of reality.

When Eakins returned to the United States in 1871, the academic painters of overblown landscape and sentimental genre were still the most prominent artists, though Hunt's interpretation of French romantic realism—to be supplemented within five years by the showing of paintings by Corot, Millet, and the Barbizon group at the Philadelphia Centennial—was already gaining ground. Eakins' more descriptive realism never made much impact since, after a few years, the more visual realism of Munich impressionism (brought back by Duveneck and Chase in the late 1870's) was far more pervasive, although its influence was later succeeded by that of Manet and the impressionists. Eakins' lack of popularity can thus be partly explained by his position between two successive schools represented by Hunt in the earlier years, and by Chase and Sargent in the later. (Sargent, a man of cultivated sensibility, was far more ready to accept a painter quite different from himself than Eakins would have been, and was surprised to find on a visit

5–54. Thomas Eakins, *William Rush Carving the Allegorical Figure of the Schuylkill*, 1877. Oil on canvas. 20⅛ x 26½ inches. (Philadelphia Museum of Art.)

to Philadelphia that his hosts did not even know of the existence of Eakins, the one man Sargent wanted to meet there.) Eakins kept to his own path, changing hardly at all in the forty years of his productivity, but deepening always. There is no decline in quality noticeable in his later paintings, as there was in those of Ryder.

Eakins' early work, which can be conveniently grouped within the decade of the 1870's, is somewhat related to the genre tradition but less permeated than usual by sentiment or mere storytelling. Some of it involves his family and friends in interior scenes, as in *The Pathetic Song*, 1881 (PB 175), and *Chess Players*, 1881 (PB 172); or it depicts outdoor activities such as fishing or hunting, as in *Starting Out After Rail*, 1882 (PB 544). The best paintings are those concerned with the sport of rowing, as *Max Schmitt in a Single Scull*, mentioned earlier, *Turning Stake-Boat*, 1873 (PB 165), and *John Biglen in a Single Scull*, 1871 (Illustration 5–55). The interior genre scenes are notable for the intense absorption of the artist in the realization of the figures in the dark space they inhabit, and for the exaggerated chiaroscuro and the mood of sobriety it suggests, both reminiscent of Rembrandt. The outdoor scenes are observed with equal care and, in the case of some of the rowing pictures, with a meticulousness which might give an impression of almost mechanical rendition to the reader familiar only with reproductions.

It is true that the *Max Schmitt* is an experiment in a sharp focus technique not customary in Eakins' work. But the still figure resting on his oars in the pellucid light of the river atmosphere is wonderfully realized, and the spots of red color of his neckerchief and that of a distant rower upriver are such melodious notes in harmony with the pervading cool greens and blues, that meticulousness is transcended. In the *John Biglen* the careful studies of the figure and of its reflection in the rippling water are completely absorbed in a final product in which form, color, and paint become paramount. The design of the figure and the craft is impressive, aside from the competent presentation of anatomy and motion;

5–55. Thomas Eakins, *John Biglen in a Single Scull,* 1871. Oil study for larger watercolor, 24 x 16 inches, 1874. (Courtesy of Yale University Art Gallery, New Haven, Connecticut. Whitney Collection of Sporting Art.)

the color of the water, painted in thin washes of blue and green over an earth-colored ground, not only perfectly represents the movement of the muddy waters of the then already polluted Schuylkill, but creates an abstract web of interplaying cool and warm hues. The touch of red in the bandana around John Biglen's sweating forehead is not only pleasing and correct, but mandatory in the totality of the formal organization as a contrast to the prevailing blue. Finally, the rich combination of granular pigment and fatty oil is painted, glazed, dragged, and otherwise manipulated with a remarkable sensibility for all the possibilities inherent in the medium. Such a picture is more than mere representationalism. It is a comprehensive realization of the facts of three-dimensionality, space, and movement made into a sensuous totality of color, forms, and paint.

Such qualities, easily analyzed in a small picture such as the *John Biglen,* also exist in Eakins' larger pictures, such as *The Gross Clinic,* 1875 (PB 171, PB 171A, °PB 171B; Illustration 5–56), one of the great pictures of the era. Based on the "anatomies" of the seventeenth century—of which Rembrandt's *Dr. Tulp's Anatomy Lesson* is probably the best known—it was a logical subject to be commissioned by a medical institution where Eakins as a rigorous student of anatomy was an intimate of many of the staff. The impact of this huge picture when it is suddenly encountered on the stair landing of the college is overwhelming. The medical arena, crowded with hushed students intently watching the great surgeon as he makes a point concerning the incision on the patient's thigh, is depicted with a reality nearly as impressive as that of the quiet, shaded room in Madrid inhabited by Velázquez' maids in waiting. Its illusion is certainly more impressive than the more cleverly and not so painstakingly rendered room from which the daughters of Mr. Boit look out at us. People objected to the blood on the knife and hand of Dr. Gross, but Eakins was anything but squeamish, and it was part of the scene and therefore not "untruth." Its rich red is also a very necessary secondary accent that draws attention away from the powerful head of the surgeon, haloed in white hair, which

5–56. Thomas Eakins, *The Gross Clinic,* 1875. Oil on canvas. 96 x 78 inches. (Courtesy of Jefferson Medical College, Philadelphia.)

would otherwise be too attractive. In comparison with *The Gross Clinic* the other anatomy, *The Agnew Clinic*, 1889 (PB 178, PB 178A, °PB 178B), is almost matter-of-fact. The room with its silent observers is not so spacious. Dr. Agnew is not so dramatically isolated, and the white-clad figures in the operating area are less impressive than those in *The Gross Clinic*, who are still black-clad in the era before antisepsis was known. Perhaps the dogged and unimaginative objectivity of the later picture has its virtues, in contrast to such devices in *The Gross Clinic* as the light playing about the head of Dr. Gross, the blood on his hand and scalpel, the incised flesh, and the cringing watcher in the operating area (a relative of the patient, required by law to be present). Yet, leaving out of consideration the appeal to our emotions, *The Gross Clinic* remains the more impressive, if only for its more effective rendering of figures in space and more interesting composition in both form and color.

During the 1880's and 1890's Eakins did other pictures which could be broadly classified under the category of genre: some landscapes with figures depicting ordinary people fishing, mending nets, and otherwise relaxing in the country; in contrast to similar scenes by the impressionists they are quite matter of fact, even stolid, as might be expected from the brush of the sober Philadelphia realist. Among these are some involving the nude and near-nude. *The Swimming Hole*, 1883 (PB 545), is an impressive exercise in its rendition of the nude divers, and is almost Renaissance in feeling. The most interesting of Eakins' figure studies are boxing pictures. (Eakins, incidentally, was one of the first to make sports—with the exception of horse racing, which has a long history in painting—the subject of important works of art. Besides boxing, and rowing, he depicted wrestling and baseball as well.) The opportunity to treat the human figure almost in the nude, and at the same time to deal with large interior spaces filled with people, as in the clinics, appealed to Eakins. Consequently, such pictures as *Salutat*, 1898 (PB 550), and *Between Rounds*, 1899 (PB 551), are among his best.

During the last two decades of his life, Eakins turned more and more to portraiture, a branch of painting which had always been important to him, and which now became his almost exclusive concern until his death. He painted portraits of a few important people, among them *Walt Whitman*, 1887 (°PB 174), but commissions were rare. He therefore had to fall back upon his relatives and friends as subjects. His men all sit or stand impressively, from the early *Dr. John Brinton*, 1876 (Collection of Dr. Ward Brinton, Philadelphia), to *Professor Rowland*, 1891 (PB 548), and *The Thinker (Louis N. Kenton)*, 1900 (°PB 552). They frequently wear old rumpled clothes, shaped by their own characteristic attitudes and movements into a very personal covering, like another skin. They are often surrounded by objects indicating their occupations, and are shown in dark Philadelphia interiors filled with unpretentious furniture—old swivel chairs and roll-top desks. These portraits have a warm reality, are full of character, and possess a solid (perhaps even stolid) plasticity and, above all, Eakins' masterly realization of form in a completely comprehensible space. Most important, his sitters have an interior life as well.

Eakins' psychological insight is seen better in his portraits of women than of men. Even in what might be called his most stylish portrait, that of *Letitia Wilson Jordan Bacon*, 1888 (PB 177), for which he asked the subject to pose after he had seen her in the ball gown shown in the picture, there is a great deal more than the obviously becoming black dress with red, buff, and blue accents complementing its wearer's dark and somewhat sedate beauty. In his picture of *Miss Van Buren*, 1891 (PB 547), depicting a student of Eakins, the observer is impressed not only by the profound realization of form in space—perhaps as eloquent here as in any other of Eakins' paintings—but also by the fact that this perfectly understood body is inhabited by a real personality. To compare this picture with a typical Sargent portrait is to see the essential difference between Eakins' descriptive realism, built up from the evidence of many kinds of knowledge, and the realism of impressionism, based more upon visual evidence alone. Not that Sargent lacked insight; but when Eakins combined psychological penetration with such realization of form, the result is very moving indeed. Sometimes Eakins' objectivity is almost too intellectual, as in *The Concert Singer*, 1892 (°PB 549), in which the careful study of the singer's throat becomes almost an anatomical illustration. But usually, no matter how scientific the realism, it is relieved by variety of design and by effective color and handling of paint, as well as by an understanding of personality.

This is especially true of *A Lady With a Setter (Mrs. Eakins)*, 1885 (PB 546). Here the artist depicts his wife in a light blue dress, red stockings, and black slippers, sitting in a room in which the colors of the oriental rug and of the old secretary are rich and warm, and the hangings are a golden umber with accents of brighter warm colors against the foil of the pearl-gray walls. Yet for all this sensuous charm the final impact of the picture comes from the somewhat sad look in Mrs. Eakins' face, revealing a touching but at the same time almost frightening penetration into the very soul of the childless woman the artist knew best.

Among the finest of the late portraits are a group executed from about 1900 onward, usually only heads but including a few bust portraits. In these, Eakins concentrated in the face the energies he usually expended on the body and its surrounding space. The best known and most frequently reproduced is the handsome *Signora Gomez d'Arza,* 1902 (The Metropolitan Museum of Art, New York). Among the finest of the later, more intimate portraits are those of the pianist *Mrs. Edith Mahon,* 1904 (Smith College Museum of Art, Northampton, Massachusetts), *Clara,* 1900 (The Louvre, Paris), and *Addie,* 1909 (Philadelphia Museum of Art). But by any measure the most impressive is that of *Mrs. Thomas Eakins,* 1899 (Illustration 5–57), so penetrating that it transcends the familiar physical presence. It has been said of Eakins that under more favorable circumstances he would have had more scope, and that essentially his work is limited. In looking at this last picture in particular, and bearing in mind the entire serious

5–57. Thomas Eakins, *Mrs. Thomas Eakins,* 1899. Oil on canvas. 20 x 16 inches. (Collection of Joseph H. Hirshhorn.)

production of the artist, it must be realized how deeply he probed the human personality.

Eakins has finally come into his own in his native city and country. He represents the bedrock America beneath the glitter of the gilded age and the overrefinement of the genteel tradition. As in his paintings, he eschewed in his life all superficial grace and nicety. He was thought to be uncouth and boorish, resembling in this respect, as in others, his friend Walt Whitman, who, when asked if Eakins lacked the social graces answered no, but that, like himself, he put them in their proper place. It was not necessary for Eakins to seek, as did Whistler, Henry James's "denser, richer, warmer, European spectacle," and the genteel niceties that weakened stay-at-home contemporaries like Saint-Gaudens did not touch him.

Though Eakins has been accepted in the United States, he has not been in Europe—an interesting commentary on international taste. The American stereotype of materialism is always brought up in any discussion of Eakins abroad, unfortunately creating a prejudice where otherwise there might be appreciation. It is oversimplification to equate Eakins' scientific factualness with the materialism of the post-Civil War age. It would be far more just to compare him with the Renaissance artists, who were equally scientific but who have never been dubbed materialistic. And who are actually more materialistic in attitude than the universally beloved impressionists? Eakins' work is less appealing than that of either group, but at least its seriousness should recommend it to more appreciative consideration.

The Introspectives and Albert Pinkham Ryder

In contrast to the illustrators of history and legend, like Abbey, and the painters of allegories, like Thayer and the muralists, there was a group of introspective artists who were too individualistic to fit into either category, yet who shared a common anti-realism. Their work, no matter how diverse, has a common origin in a tradition, deriving from Allston's lyrical painting, which in the pre-Civil War period was scarcely manifested except in occasional isolated work by artists like William Page. All of those introspectives, except William Rimmer and Elihu Vedder, also shared to a certain extent the permeating influence of Hunt and La Farge, but that of Hunt predominated, for though La Farge executed a number of literary subjects, Hunt's rich and somewhat indeterminate and suggestive technique was particularly adaptable to the expression of vague poetic emotion—the stock-in-trade of these artists.

William Rimmer, whose earlier work in sculpture was discussed in Part Four, and Elihu Vedder, both painters of the mysterious and strange, retained the literary point of view of the mid-century and a still meticulous technique. Rimmer's sculpture was more important and far more original than that of his Italianate contemporaries. This might have been true also of his painting (most of which was done late in his life), had he had more time and training —that is, if we can judge from the few examples that have been preserved. All of them show (as do a few fascinating drawings also) Rimmer's grasp of anatomy and the powerful energy of his sculpture, though a Michelangelesque exaggeration reminiscent of William Blake's misunderstanding of the Italian master is more evident than in the sculpture. (Rimmer admired Blake; and casts of the *Day* and *Night* from Michelangelo's Medici tombs were at the Boston Athenaeum.) *Flight and Pursuit*, 1872 (PB 373), has an element of real terror in the powerfully drawn figure rushing through a maze of rooms, accompanied by a similar figure in a further chamber running also, in a nightmarish repetition of action.

Vedder was more technically competent as a painter than Rimmer. His meticulous rendering of imaginative subjects would place him among the run-of-the-mill artists of the period who were little more than illustrators if it were not for the quality of inner vision which occasionally breaks through his conventional treatment. While executing commercial art and illustration with a competent academic technique acquired in Paris, he painted a few pictures in the 1860's which are genuinely haunting in spite of the overly literary point of view reflected in their titles, such as *The Lost Mind*, 1864–1865 (°PB 461), and *Lair of the Sea Serpent*, 1864 (PB 460). The last is typical in possessing a power deriving from the nightmarish reality with which the fantastic subject is treated, for it is simply an eel enormously exaggerated in size, slithering across some Long Island or Cape Cod dune. After retiring to Europe more or less for good at the end of the decade, Vedder continued to paint similar pictures more restrained and classical in feeling, and on the whole less effective, such as the *Ideal Head*, 1872 (°PB 462). As a result of his admiration for classical art, he developed a conventional academic technique of considerable competence which stood him in good stead as a mural painter. *Rome*, 1894 (PB 465), one of the four decorations at Bowdoin College, is typical. In comparison with La Farge's mural, it is uninspired, though it competes well enough with the others. (It is interesting to note that Vedder did some charming landscape sketches in Italy, Egypt, and elsewhere, when he was foraging for material to be used in his more pretentious productions.)

Turning to the more introspective artists who reflected the influence of Hunt (or at least his technical method and personal expressiveness), it is appropriate to discuss Robert Loftin Newman, since he was the student of Couture and the associate of Millet at the same time as was Hunt. Newman shares little of the greater man's ability to realize a convincing object in space, in an ambiance of sensuous paint and with poetic expression. The mysterious quality of his figures is due as much to the artist's inadequacy as a constructor of convincing anatomy as it is to his deliberate creation of a mood. Though George Fuller and Albert Pinkham Ryder shared this same lack to a certain extent, they compensated for it by richer pictorial and evocative powers. Newman's *Landscape With Figures*, 1903 (PB 635), and *Madonna and Child* (PB 634) are typical of his work.

George Fuller, a farmer from Deerfield, Massachusetts, was largely self-taught, but his method of painting owes a great deal to the example of Hunt. After a trip to Europe to study the great artists of the past, particularly the Venetians, Fuller supplemented Hunt's painterliness with an "old master" technique achieved by a rich, low-toned palette and a surface haze like that of old varnish. His undefined figures brooding in a twilight obscurity are almost sentimental— for example, *Winifred Dysart*, 1881 (PB 570), the *Ideal Head* (*PB 192), or *Quadroon* (The Metropolitan Museum of Art, New York)— but they are saved by their very amorphousness, which gives them a strangely haunting quality. When landscape became his chief subject, Fuller was more convincing, since he was no longer primarily concerned with the construction of anatomy. In *The Tomato Patch* (*PB 193), the summer is very palpable, the land swells convincingly, the apple trees have struc-

ture, and the late summer humidity of the Connecticut valley finds a happy realization in Fuller's customary envelope of heavy atmosphere.

Except for Ryder, whose importance requires a separate discussion, and for Blakelock, who is more a landscapist than an ideal painter, the other idealists, mostly expatriates, dealt with literary and historical subjects or were eclectic followers of La Farge and the academic tradition.

Albert Pinkham Ryder is an artist whose work seems almost to transcend time and place. His pictures have an eloquence of form and color which is a far cry from the pervading naturalism of the nineteenth century; they are actually far closer to the abstract expressionism of today. It has often been said of Ryder that he represents in paint the introverted and mystical aspect of the nineteenth-century American imagination identified in literature with the work of Poe, Hawthorne, and Melville. But of all the figures in the history of American art, Ryder can least be considered from the point of view of tradition and environment; he was a most personal, if not an entirely autonomous artist. To place Ryder in the mainstream of American art, let alone that of western art in general, is therefore difficult. His work has more affinity to Allston's than to any one else's: both artists have a moonstruck quality in their landscapes, as a comparison of Ryder's *The Temple of the Mind*, c. 1885 (PB 381), and Allston's *Moonlit Landscape* (Illustration 3–43) demonstrates, and both depend for their effects upon the superrealistic evocation of shapes and their organization. It might be said that the lyrical mysticism in Allston seems to reach its culmination three quarters of a century later in Ryder. But the connecting links are hard to find, since Ryder was largely self-taught and paid little attention to the work of others. In fact, it is debatable that Ryder knew the work of Allston at all. Two more probable influences, however, can be mentioned as having had some effect on Ryder's development. Their significance seems to have been minimal, but no artist can be entirely with-

out roots. The first was the general painterliness and lyrical realism initiated by Hunt, and
practiced and carried further by artists like Newman, Blakelock, and Fuller. (There is such a
striking resemblance between some landscapes
by Fuller and by Ryder that the possibility of
a cross influence is suggested.) The second was
the Dutch painter Mattijs Maris, whom Ryder
met living as a recluse near London, and who
painted pre-Raphaelite subjects with vague and
amorphous forms almost as indeterminate as
those of Ryder. It is significant that Ryder
should have sought out Maris during a trip to
Europe (paid for by friends), and neglected the
museums and the better-known artists. After
this meeting, Ryder's subjects became less pastoral and more ideal or allegorical.

Ryder's early work, done in the 1870's, consists
mostly of landscapes and pastoral genre, such as
the *Pastoral Study* (PB 375), exhibiting the
broad handling of Hunt and resembling similar
subjects by Fuller, but more directly eloquent
than either in the use of a few large masses and
colors. Color and the texture of the paint itself
are as prominent as the objects represented,
which are made even more indeterminate by being "bathed in an atmosphere of golden luminosity," [39] to use Ryder's own words. Yet the
essential forms of hills and trees and of an occasional horse or human being are there, rescu-
ing these landscapes from a formlessness too
often seen in Newman and Fuller. Though
Ryder may never have drawn from nature, as he
himself asserted late in life, he must have observed the New England countryside around his
native New Bedford very closely.

Ryder began to develop as a painter of literary
and ideal subjects around 1880 and continued at
the height of his powers until about 1900. After
that the painter originated few subjects, preferring to "improve" his older ones, a procedure
which his failing powers made somewhat dubious, though some of his late pictures, like the
Grazing Horse, 1914 (PB 643A), indicate the
artist's earlier power. In these twenty years an
intense imagination was at work, creating a series
of haunting images which seem to link romanticism with twentieth-century expressionism. Ry-

der's romantic themes were drawn from Chaucer,
Shakespeare, and the Bible, as well as from the
romantic poets. At least one of his subjects was
taken from Wagner's operas, which greatly affected the artist. After hearing *Siegfried* he went
home at midnight and worked on the initial idea
for *Siegfried and the Rhine Maidens,* 1875–1891
(PB 384), for forty-eight hours without sleep or
nourishment. Ryder's interest in the fantastic,
the weird, and the remote in time and place are
thoroughly romantic. Like Ishmail in *Moby
Dick*, he was "tormented by an everlasting itch
for things remote," and like Melville himself he
was fascinated by the fathomless sea. Yet Ryder
was never merely literary or illustrative; his very
method prevented that. He made no sketches
from nature, but instead he blocked out the picture according to what he felt it needed, as he
told an interlocutor. The forms themselves,
simple and massive in shape, are expressive without representing any objects too specifically, as in
the recurring triad of swelling sea, scudding sailboats, and moonridden skies with shredded
clouds in *Moonlight Marine* (PB 643) and *Toil-
ers of the Sea,* 1884 (PB 641). Often Ryder's
forms are amorphous or ambiguous, as in *Macbeth and the Witches,* 1890–1908 (PB 383; Illustration 5–58), and *Jonah,* 1885 or later (PB 376;
Illustration 5–59), yet they are all the more evocative. The startled stance of the horse in the
Macbeth, the garments whipping around the ill-
fated man's body, and the stark towers of Glamis
Castle are intensified by the vaguely suggestive
forms of the witches and of the torn and tattered
sky. In the *Jonah* the boat is not shapeless simply
for the sake of shapelessness. It is not drawn
realistically, but its fragility is nevertheless conveyed in the midst of the turbulent water agitated by the raging storm and the great whale.
This kind of suggestive drawing, which Ryder
employed with such skill, his critics felt was not
drawing at all. The artist himself described his
method perfectly when he said, "Perhaps you
wouldn't say it had much drawing, but it has
what you might call an *air* of drawing." [40] The
simple shapes of boat and sky in *Constance,* 1896
(PB 642); the whipping branches of the trees in
Siegfried and the Rhine Maidens; the lush volu-

5–58. Albert Pinkham Ryder, *Macbeth and the Witches*, 1890–1908. Oil on canvas. 28⅛ x 35¾ inches. (The Phillips Collection, Washington.)

minous shapes in *The Forest of Arden,* 1897 (PB 644), redolent with midsummer's mood; the ominous silhouettes of the fence and rider in *The Race Track,* c. 1910 (PB 385); the mysterious forms and colors in *The Flying Dutchman,* before 1890 (°PB 645)—all are powerfully evocative. Ryder's use of color augments the impact of his forms. They seem to have the richness of precious stones, as though his pigments were composed of powdered azurite, ruby, and alabaster, manipulated and built up in an almost three-dimensional way on the surface of the canvas. The organization of form and the sensuous richness of handling and color combine to create an experience that eludes analysis. A passage in Melville's *Moby Dick,* written in 1855, describing a picture hanging over the bar of the Spouter Inn at New Bedford, seems to presuppose the quality of Ryder's work, especially his *Jonah:*

A boggy, soggy squitchy picture truly, enough to drive a nervous man distracted. Yet was there a sort of indefinite, half-attained, unimaginable sublimity about it that fairly froze you to it, till you involuntarily took an oath with yourself to find out what that marvellous painting meant. Ever and anon a bright, but, alas, deceptive idea would dart you through. —It's the Black Sea in a midnight gale. —It's the unnatural combat of the four primal elements. —It's a blasted heath. —It's a Hyperborean winter scene. —It's the breaking up of the ice-bound stream of Time. But at last all these fancies yielded to that one portentous something in the picture's midst. *That* once found out, and all the rest were plain. But stop; does it not bear a faint resemblance to a gigantic fish? even the great leviathan himself? [41]

Both Melville and Ryder were intrigued by the mystery and symbolism of the sea, and both were familiar with New Bedford; Ryder grew up there, and his youthful imagination was daily stimulated by the salty drama of the then greatest whaling port in the world.

His "squitchy" indefiniteness relates Ryder to the present, that is, to expressionism and even to abstract expressionism. Ryder's shapes in themselves set up a kind of reverberation in the viewer, irrespective of what they represent. Among all the painters before our own time, Ryder can be said to have somehow tapped the common residue of form perception in the unconscious of the race—if we can accept the implications of Jung's theory of the archetype. That is to say, Ryder at his best. Sometimes his work has an unrealized quality, and imagination is not enough to compensate for lack of actual experience, or for an intellectual and technical sloppiness which makes his meaning tentative, as in *The Temple of the Mind,* or even the physical

existence of his painting perilous. Some of Ryder's canvases are nearly ruined, and most of them are pale reflections of what must have been their former vibrant and jewel-like appearance. This is due to the artist's eccentric and bullheaded habits of applying paint, which (though building up a fine surface effect) put great strain on the adhesion of different layers of pigment and various media to each other and to the canvas. Ryder passed off his unscientific method by remarking, "When a thing has elements of beauty from the beginning, it cannot be destroyed." [42] Such an attitude is consistent with an extreme form of romanticism—the mystic's imagination untrammeled by the dimension of time. Ryder said of his *Jonah:* "I am in ectasies over my Jonah; such a lovely turmoil of boiling water and everything." [43] Just as this quotation, so expressive at its beginning, ends in an anti-climax, so in some

5–59. Albert Pinkham Ryder, *Jonah,* 1885 or later. Oil on canvas. 26½ x 33¾ inches. (Courtesy of the National Collection of Fine Arts, Smithsonian Institution, Washington.)

5–60. Albert Pinkham Ryder, *Dead Bird,* 1890–1900. Oil on wood. 4¼ x 9⅝ inches. (The Phillips Collection, Washington.)

of Ryder's paintings the final effort to make his statement effective is lacking.

But the best Ryders are saved by some residue of reality, transfigured in the night scenes from the experience of many moonlit walks; or used as a foil for more abstract forms, as in the *Macbeth;* or lying behind the seemingly amorphous forms of the early landscapes. Occasionally realism even takes precedence over the forms of the imagination, as in the intense and touching observations in the *Dead Bird,* 1890–1900 (PB 382; Illustration 5–60), in which the textures of feathers, bill, and claws express the very essence of soft, pathetic deadness. This saving grace of attachment to real experience preserves Ryder's best work of the 1880's and 1890's from the pretentious vagueness too often characteristic of romanticism and expressionism.

The critic who in 1883 dared Ryder to come out into the clear light and show whether his poetry was "strong enough, healthy enough to stand the wear and tear of life" [44] would be satisfied today. Ryder's work at its best can do just this, and matches that of any other imaginative artist of the century.

Still Life

Still life in this period occupies a very special place, for the best of it is so extraordinarily skillful that it forces itself upon our attention to an extent which this category would not otherwise deserve.

Only a few examples done between the time of Raphaelle Peale and the late nineteenth century are worthy of mention. Charles B. King's *The Vanity of an Artist's Dream,* c. 1830 (PB 285), is a curious juxtaposition of evocative objects in a fairly painterly style not as illusionistic as that of the Peales, though probably inspired by their pictures, since King lived for a while in Philadelphia. The Peale family itself continued to be the chief purveyors of still life, Rubens and Margarita Angelica carrying on the tradition into the 1860's. John F. Francis of Philadelphia was the best of the still life painters of the mid-century, mitigating the Peale tradition with a softer touch and a slightly less rigorous austerity of design.

Though a few painters imitated the baroque still lifes of seventeenth-century Holland, the continuing tradition was closely tied to the Peales. It is not surprising, then, that it was in Philadelphia that the illusionist still life school flourished toward the end of the century. William Harnett was undoubtedly the master of the group. From the beginning of his career, in the late 1870's, his work bore a close resemblance to that of Raphaelle Peale. His style was enriched and broadened but not essentially changed (except in the introduction of old world objects of quaint, curious, or associative character) by a stay of several years in Europe, principally at Munich, during the early 1880's. A drawing done in Munich, *Head of a Woman,* 1881 (*GB 85), demonstrates the extremely realistic competence Harnett acquired abroad, which he combined with his own precisionist sensitivity.

Harnett's most characteristic pictures after his return are those in which objects are represented hanging on or placed before a wooden door. In two examples musical instruments are included: *The Old Violin,* 1886 (PB 208), and *Old Models,* 1892 (PB 211). A similar painting is the relatively simple *The Faithful Colt,* 1890 (*PB 210), a kind of apotheosis of the famous pistol, here hung against a board wall with nothing but a scrap of paper to divert attention from it. *After*

the Hunt, 1885 (PB 206), is one of the most remarkable *trompe l'oeils* in existence. Harnett represents guns, game, and other instruments and symbols of hunting against an elaborately hinged door in a composition beautifully arranged in form and color. The objects are depicted with an uncanny consistency of modeling and texture, which is sustained throughout the large area (the picture comes within an inch and a half of being six feet tall). Harnett also did still lifes in depth, like the incredibly skillful *Emblems of Peace,* 1890 (PB 209); the observer has to restrain himself from snuffing out a small flame in the newspaper, which has been ignited by a hot ash dropped from a pipe laid upon it. *Just Dessert,* c. 1891 (Illustration 5–61), is a better example of Harnett's connection with the Peale tradition

5–61. William Harnett, *Just Dessert,* c. 1891. Oil on canvas. 25¼ x 26¾ inches. (Courtesy of the Art Institute of Chicago. Friends of American Art Collection.)

than are his more elaborate subjects, which have European connotations even though they demonstrate his incredible technique. In *Just Dessert* it is evident that he was able to cope with every nuance of form and texture, from the luminous marble tabletop and the equally white meat of the coconut to the moist bloom of the grapes. But, as usual with Harnett, this miracle of representation is accompanied by an organization of form in both two- and three-dimensionality which is as impressive as the artist's surface realism.

John F. Peto was inspired by Harnett and was nearly as fine an artist. He differed slightly in his choice of still life objects that were hardly ever pretentious (often they were pathetic discards), but his compositions were similar. In technique he differed a little more, for he was more painterly and therefore, in a way, more naturalistic than Harnett. Peto's pictures are easier to take in at a glance, and for that reason lack some of the intensity derived from Harnett's basically non-naturalistic all-over focus, the sharp detail of which cannot be comprehended at one glance. *After Night's Study* (*PB 364) is a good example of Peto's compositions in depth, and *Old Scraps* (probably) c. 1890 (Museum of Modern Art, New York), one of the finest of his numerous "rack" pictures (in which miscellaneous papers and related objects are held to the wall by tapes), is perhaps the finest of his more two-dimensional pictures, displaying an abstract organization on a flat plane that is as subtle as those of the best abstract artists of today. *The Poor Man's Store,* 1885 (PB 365), is a flat composition painted in depth, and with great subtlety of values as well as with the artist's usual compositional skill. The beautifully organized *Still Life With Lanterns*, c. 1890 (Illustration 5–62), is characteristic of the best of the still lifes of the period, typifying the compositions of both Harnett and Peto and of Harnett's other followers and imitators, and demonstrating the subtle difference between Peto's broader, more suggestive touch and Harnett's absolute precision as exemplified clearly in *Just Dessert.*

Among Harnett's several imitators, J. D. Chalfont and John Haberle must be mentioned. Chalfont's work was closest to his mentor's; he chose

5–62. John F. Peto, *Still Life With Lanterns,* c. 1890. Oil on canvas. 50 x 30 inches. (Courtesy of The Brooklyn Museum, Brooklyn, New York.)

similar subjects and treated them with a similar consistency. Haberle, though more famous and more original, was not the past master of representationalism that Harnett was. His *Time and Eternity*, c. 1890 (PB 199), is illusionistic enough, but *Grandma's Hearthstone*, 1890 (PB 200, *PB 200A), is very inconsistent in treatment, the believability of the upper part competing with a very unconvincing representation of depth in the burning logs in the fireplace. When such pictures as this, poor in composition and deficient in representationalism, are compared with the masterly work of Harnett, the accomplishment of that artist and of Peto is all the more remarkable.

Harnett and Peto sum up the haunting, almost surrealist quality of the "magic" realism of a group of painters who not only made a unique contribution, but who brought to an intense, if narrow, point of concentration tendencies traceable to the beginning of American art—the precisionists' point of view and a sense of flat pattern.

The Graphic Arts

At the beginning of the post-Civil War period, the chief function of the graphic arts remained the reproduction of paintings and drawings, a function retained to a certain extent until the end of the century when the efficiency of photography made the hand processes obsolete, at least for reproductive purposes. Meanwhile, however, the graphic media became increasingly expert means of interpretation, as can be seen in the illustrations for the spectacular *Picturesque America* published in 1872, in which the engravings are often far more excellent than the inferior examples of the Hudson River school which they reproduce. In the hands of the abler cutters of woodblocks, such as those who cut Winslow Homer's better illustrations, wood engraving could be equally sensitive. In fact, the medium reached a point of such technical brilliance toward the end of the century that for a while it successfully competed with photography. The most significant graphic work of the period, however, appeared not in the reproduction and interpretation of works of art produced initially in other media, but in original artistic expression, as in the etchings and lithographs of Whistler.

Before the impact made by Whistler's etchings of Venice, produced in 1884, etching had already made considerable progress as a means of original expression, largely stimulated in the United States, as well as in England, by the work of Sir Francis Seymour Haden and Philip Hamerton, the author of an influential book, *Etching and Etchers,* which was inspired chiefly by the example of Rembrandt's economy of line and his exploitation of the empty white areas of the paper.

At first this influence was combined in American etching with the grandiose and graphically complicated approach of the mid-century landscapists. Painters like Thomas Moran were happier in the medium of lithography [his *Solitude,* 1869 (GB 142), exemplifies his work], which was more adapted to the rendition of tonal values. The summary approach of the newer, more suggestive technique of etching, however, finally overcame the descriptive variety of the Hudson River school, and its dramatic romanticism was succeeded by less pretentious subject matter. Stephen Parrish and Charles Adams Platt are the outstanding print makers of this phase of American etching, being the first really notable etchers in American art before Whistler and Duveneck (the work of both of whom influenced their later production). Both artists exploited the eloquence of empty space (especially Parrish, in his snow pieces) and adopted a sketchy technique which forces the line to imply more than it states, a method derived from the influence of the later Rembrandt. These characteristics are well illustrated by Platt's *Buttermilk Channel,* 1889 (GB 173), and *Three Fishermen,* 1886 (GB 172).

The simultaneous etchings of Whistler and of Duveneck executed in Venice from 1879 to 1880 had an enormous impact on American printmaking. Together with the general influence of impressionism, these were the mainsprings of American graphic arts for the next fifty years. During his lifetime, Whistler was accepted more readily as an etcher than as a painter. Even when his critics disparaged his oils, there was always a market for his prints. During the last years of his life, and until recently, Whistler was considered as one of the great graphic artists of all time, though this judgment is not so generally accepted today.

Even though the monetary and intrinsic value of Whistler's prints may once have been somewhat inflated, their relative neglect today is unjustified, for Whistler was always an important creative figure. His prints, like his paintings, are charming, and their originality is prophetic of future artistic developments. This last aspect of his graphic work has hardly been touched on by critical analyses, though in some of his late lithographs especially, his originality is as prominent a factor as in his paintings.

Whistler's earliest graphic art, in the 1850's, possessed much of the bold directness of his Courbet-influenced paintings, and technically was reminiscent of the large and simple conceptions of Millet. The etchings comprising the Thames series of 1859–1860, well represented by *Black Lion Wharf*, 1859 (GB 216), continued to be executed in a realistic vein, as were the paintings done at the same time in the Wapping section of the London river front. But their objectivity was tempered by an interest in pattern and design which must have been somewhat inspired by the Japanese print, as was their effect of calculated casualness.

During these early years in London, when Whistler was executing such paintings as the *Music Room,* similar qualities appeared in his genre prints, of which several involving the members of the Seymour Haden family (Whistler's sister was Lady Haden) are very distinguished compositions. One of them especially, *The Music Room,* c. 1858, translates the realism, studied casualness, and sophistication of design which appear in Whistler's paintings of this period into a print of considerable power. A similar graphic competence appears in his etched portraits of this period and later, the etching often combined with drypoint [45] or executed in drypoint alone. Several of Whistler's drypoints realize very well the direct and incisive potentials of the medium, as seen in such portraits as those of his niece *Annie,* 1860 (GB 218), and of the engraver *Riault,* 1860 (GB 219).

5–63. James Abbott McNeill Whistler, *Speke Hall, No. 1* (Seventh State), c. 1865. Etching and dry point. 8⅞ x 5⅞ inches.

Some of the etched city-scapes of the 1860's, similar in conception to Whistler's paintings of Old Battersea Bridge, are as strong in design as the figure subjects but simpler in graphic means, showing a development in the direction of a more suggestive eloquence that is premonitory of the artist's more impressionistic work of the 1870's. Perhaps one of the finest and most representative prints by Whistler before this later development is the *Speke Hall, No. 1* (Seventh State), c. 1865 (Illustration 5–63), which sums up many of the characteristics of the early Whistler, so similar to those of Degas. The oblique perspective, the silhouetted figure, and the sense of pattern are all similar to the work of that artist and to Japanese prints. (The figure even recalls one of Degas' few prints, representing Mary Cassatt in the Louvre, done several years later, in 1872.) But a sense of place and weather, surviving from Whistler's early realism, and doubtless augmented by the pervading English romantic attitude toward nature, gives *Speke Hall* a very different character. The print is further distinguished by the artist's fine sensibility for the decorative effect of the black accents (many of them executed in drypoint), for the pattern of lines in general, and for their sparse eloquence.

The Venice etchings are in a way the culmination of Whistler's early and middle periods. In them he continued to record his sensitive observation and combined it with an even livelier sense of pattern. At the same time these prints marked a transition to the more abstract point of view of his later work. Evocative in subject matter, using the suggestive power of line at its most economical [as in *Nocturne* (GB 221)], and rich in design, they deserve the praise they have received. Perhaps an overdelicacy, which becomes attenuated into slightness, mars many of them, but this (as in Whistler's later paintings) is compensated for by a certain abstract quality to which modern eyes are particularly sympathetic.

The characteristics that began to appear in the Venice prints are seen to an even greater degree in Whistler's work after his return to London, especially in his lithographs and lithotints. In the lithograph of the *Tall Bridge*, 1878 (GB 225), he had already exploited the greater tonal subtlety of the medium. In the later lithotints, such as *Nocturne* and *Thames Embankment*, he further refined the value variations. This was made possible by the use of lithography as a wash, which, combined with the grain of the stone, produces an effect of subtle abstract delicacy analogous to the artist's effects in his *Nocturnes* and late seascapes. The understatement seen in all of Whistler's late work becomes almost a *tour de force* of economical line and tone

5–64. James Abbott McNeill Whistler, *Interior of the Louvre*, 1894. Lithograph. 8½ x 6 inches.

in such a lithograph as *St. Giles-in-the-Field*, 1896 (GB 227), and in a few of his last prints in that medium. In these, the artist's notations of appearance come as close to being abstract as art which is still representational can be. *Interior of the Louvre*, 1894 (Illustration 5–64), representing the Grande Gallerie spotted with little figures dwarfed by its spaciousness, is essentially a composition of small abstract objects distributed over a generalized space, not unlike a work by Mark Tobey today. More typical is *The Tea Party*, 1896, which is equally abstract in its manipulation of tones on a white background, but also retains something of Whistler's earlier sense of oriental decorative pattern and silhouette, and his Degas-like sensitivity to the gestures and attitudes of the human figure. Such prints demonstrate, as do his later paintings, Whistler's importance as a transitional artist between the realist–impressionist tradition and the abstract art of today.

The originality of Whistler's Venice etchings must have influenced Frank Duveneck's interpretations of that city, done while the greater artist was working there, for they lack the brash directness that might be expected of an artist whose paintings were so much more vigorous in handling than those of Whistler. Yet to compare Duveneck's *Riva Degli Schiavoni II*, 1880 (GB 75), with any of the prints in Whistler's series, is to find it much more realistic and less decorative. Not at all evanescent in effect, with rich strokes like the handling of paint in the Munich school, Duveneck's prints are far less "modern" than Whistler's, though strong and effective in design.

There were many print makers inspired indirectly by Whistler or more directly by the actual teaching of Duveneck, but on the whole there was little that was original or powerful about them. Similar work was done by artists more influenced by the French print makers than by the British or American followers of Whistler. The landscape painter Henry Ranger was among the best of these; his lithograph *View on the Seine*, 1896 (GB 174), reflects the impressionist landscapists and the popular topographical artist Louis Lepère.

The graphic art of Mary Cassatt is comparable in quality to that of Whistler, though it could not be said that her prints go beyond the formalistic realism–impressionism of Degas, as Whistler's do. Her early work was tentative, and imitative especially of Manet, but with none of the brilliance of touch or authority of that artist's etching and lithography. In the late 1880's, however, and into 1891, Cassatt did a few distinguished prints which, though somewhat reminiscent of Degas, are more original than her earlier work. Of these, several are lithographs, which have considerable charm and at the same time a certain directness; but the best are drypoints, of which the brilliantly suggestive genre scenes, *The Map*, 1890 (*GB 40), and *The Stock-*

5–65. Mary Cassatt, *The Letter*, 1891. Soft-ground etching and aquatint. 13⅝ x 9 inches.

ing, 1890 (GB 41), are among the best. There is not quite the boldness of abstract design in Cassatt's prints which one sees in Degas and which was to develop a little later in her own work, but there is a Degas-like casualness combined with her own charming genre quality in subjects dealing with children, as one would expect from her paintings. The drypoint quality, particularly in *The Stocking*, is beautifully exploited in all its tonal range with an easy spontaneity, sweep, and immediacy. In 1891 Cassatt produced her graphic masterpieces in a set devoted to genre subjects and executed in soft-ground etching and colored aquatint. The soft-ground afforded a broader line than the conventionally etched one, and the aquatint gave a tonality to portrayal of the color areas, printed from as many plates as there were hues. Inspired specifically by Japanese woodcuts, these prints are, however, very original in being executed in an entirely different medium—though the use of several plates for color was analogous to the employment of several woodblocks for the same purpose in Japanese prints. As color prints, Cassatt's set is hardly surpassed in western art. *The Fitting,* 1891 (GB 43), is typical, but *The Coiffure,* 1891 (GB 45), and especially *The Letter,* 1891 (Illustration 5–65), are among the best. Areas of flat color, sometimes with patterns superimposed, are the background for outlines of great descriptive sensitivity and decorative power. *The Letter* is the most oriental—the woman's features are even Nipponese. Yet this print has some of the solidity derived from the western tradition which Cassatt never lost in spite of her Japanese predilections.

Among the American impressionists who were print makers, J. Alden Weir and Childe Hassam are the most distinctive. Weir's *Christmas Greens,* c. 1888 (GB 209), an etching with dry-point, and *Woman Sewing,* c. 1890 (GB 208), a lithograph, are typical of his genre work. In these prints there is more of his persisting romantic realism than of the impressionism which is seen more prominently in his paintings. This is natural enough, since on the whole the vagueness of the impressionistic vision is not wholly suited to those graphic arts whose means of expression are linear. Childe Hassam is more successful in his impressionist etchings, but since they were all done in the twentieth century, they will be taken up in Part Six.

Photography

Floods of photographs inundated the country during this period: portraits in tintype, ambrotype, and *carte-de-visite* form; sentimental genre scenes and "art" photography. Most of them can be passed over as run-of-the-mill. The more significant photography of these years was largely documentary; that is, it authentically recorded facts or events, the most important examples being concerned with the Civil War and the exploration of the West. Toward the end of the period, the work of Jacob Riis and Alfred Stieglitz is outstanding. Riis was concerned with the social problems caused by the slums, Stieglitz with fundamental questions of the esthetic of photography. Interesting from the technical point of view was the development at the end of the century of a photography of action, by Eadweard Muybridge and the painter Thomas Eakins.

The Civil War was a great challenge to the photographer. The cameramen of Mathew Brady, including Alexander Gardner and Timothy O'Sullivan (both of whom later worked independently) in the North, and George S. Cook in the South, took photographs at great personal risk, narrowly escaping death because their awkward paraphernalia and their exposed positions (necessary for focusing) attracted enemy fire. Brady's buggy for wet-plate developing—the soldiers called it the "what-is-it wagon" —became a familiar sight on the battlefields.

These photographers recorded whatever aspects of the war and its aftermath were possible with their equipment; the necessary exposure time was too long to permit any action to be caught by the lens. Consequently there are no scenes of actual combat, no charges or engagements—only portraits of individuals or groups, and landscapes. Among the former are photos of Lincoln visiting McClellan's quarters on the battlefield, in which the president is standing, towering above the bearded officers of the general's staff; of the aristocratic Charles Francis Adams, Jr., captain of the First Massachusetts

Cavalry; of the dapper George A. Custer as a young officer. Timothy O'Sullivan's photograph *General U. S. Grant and Staff Officers; Massapomax Church, Virginia*, 1864 (F 48), is especially dramatic. There are also touching genre studies reminiscent of the work of the contemporary photographer Henri Cartier-Bresson, as, for instance, the anonymous photograph of *Hanover Junction*, c. 1864 (Illustration 5–66), showing a group of people waiting on the station platform at the important junction where the tracks for Gettysburg left the main line. Others were of soldiers: bored with an interminable siege, swimming in the James within sight and shot of the enemy, or wounded and resting in the sun. The landscapes are of all sorts; some show action: trains crossing the skeletal bridges across tall gorges, wagon trains arriving at Antietam. More

often they are landscapes of desolation: Fredericksburg utterly ruined; July wheat fields reduced to stubble at Gettysburg; Missionary Ridge stripped naked, with gaunt stumps where a forest had been a few days before; dead horses sprawled at Mary's Heights, their wagons cast over at grotesque angles; derailed trains at Manassas lying crazily on their sides. And there are the dead: rows and rows of them at Bull Run and Gettysburg, and pathetic individual casualties—a boy on the road to Fredericksburg, a soldier from Ewell's Corps propped against a picket fence, his gun and canteen useless beside him. *Gardner's Sketch Book*, a collection by Alexander Gardner and others, includes two especially memorable prints: O'Sullivan's stark *Harvest of Death*, a measure of the massive human toll of the war, and Gardner's own *Home of a*

5–66. Anonymous, *Hanover Junction*, c. 1864. Photograph. (National Archives, Library of Congress.)

Rebel Sharpshooter, Gettysburg, 1863 (F 33), showing the fallen marksman curled up between the rocks of his impromptu defenses, his gun now silent.

Even more eloquently recorded than the war itself in these necessarily static photographs is the war's aftermath: the skeletal men, like those of Buchenwald, at the notorious Andersonville prison; the grim symmetry of the utterly deserted courthouse and business district at Petersburg, Virginia, before the arrival of federal troops; proud Charleston equally deserted, its elegant buildings pitted with shell holes; Columbia, South Carolina, reduced to a row of battered Tuscan columns; and Richmond, with its blocks of silent and empty ruins (F 21). The towns and buildings seem to be posing for their melancholy portraits, guarded by an occasional soldier or watched by some eccentric derelict who stayed behind. Such pictures were particularly adapted to the static effects necessitated by the "view-box" requirements of the old wet-plate camera.

Who took these photographs? Most are attributed to Mathew Brady because he published them; whenever the actual photographer is not known, it has become conventional to give credit to Brady, the most famous of the Civil War photographers. Gardner took many of those that appeared in his *Sketch Book,* after he left Brady over a dispute about copyright; O'Sullivan, who is known to have done distinguished work later, left with Gardner. George N. Barnard stayed with Brady for a while, but his signed photographs of the western front and of the collapsing South taken later in the war are so fine that it is tempting to attribute to him rather than to Brady some of the best prints of similar quality. In fact, one is inclined to discount many of the attributions to Brady, especially since it is known that his eyesight failed him more and more, so that only his fame kept him in the business of photography after the war, when he was assisted by a younger relative. A comparison of his prewar portraits with his later ones shows a decline into mediocrity. The prints of the late 1860's are pedestrian in effect, the focus is not sharp enough, light and dark are not sufficiently contrasted, and the sleek softness of many of the faces portrayed cannot be attributed entirely to the slackness of the disillusionment and graft of the Grant era.

Barnard's photographs of Columbia and Nashville are so precisely focused, so beautifully composed, that he remains one of the greatest of architectural photographers. Gardner's studies of the dead are so poignant, his scenes so typical, that he is the tragic and epic poet of "the times which tried men's souls." Perhaps it was Barnard's eloquent camera that took some of the photographs of the ruins of Richmond (usually attributed to Brady) and of Charleston, and the long row of *Sutters' Houses* at Chattanooga, c. 1863 (Illustration 5–67), the ancestor of the many photographs of buildings that soon covered the booming West, with their prismatic facades and sharp edges, so fascinating now to photographers like Edward Weston, Ansel Adams, and Walker Evans. Certainly Brady's later portraits have nothing of the impact of Gardner's recording of the visages of the conspirators of Lincoln's assassination, all with the romantic and melancholy mien of plotters in a mid-century production of Shakespearean drama—the long locks and desperate eyes of Samuel Arnold, Michael O'Laughlin, and the anticlimactically named Dr. Samuel Mudd; and the mad, hunched form of little George Atzeroot, looking at us like a small and unpleasant animal at bay.

The best of these photographs, whether by Brady, Barnard, Gardner, O'Sullivan, or others, are invaluable as sincere and varied documents; but they also stand up as images of form and content quite as convincingly as "hand painted" works of art. Among the artists of the war only Winslow Homer can compare in quality with these artists of the camera. This cannot be accidental, for a comparison of their work with that of George S. Cook, the bold and courageous Confederate photographer, shows a man inferior as an artist. His work is never so beautifully composed formally; he was an almost casual recorder, requiring only that the object of the record be in the survey of his lens. His group and individual portraits are too posed, and not even conventionally arranged to give them some formal organization. In comparison, the sense of

5–67. George N. Barnard (?), *Sutters' Houses, Chattanooga, Tennessee,* c. 1863. Photograph. (National Archives, Library of Congress.)

immediacy achieved by the northern artists—as in the *Hanover Junction* group, when the pose took minutes, not a portion of a second, to catch —is all the more remarkable.

After the war, Gardner and O'Sullivan photographed the continuing opening of the West. Gardner recorded the slow progress of the Eastern Division of the Union Pacific Railroad across the plains of Kansas, advancing to meet the rails approaching from the Western Division, being photographed by Captain A. J. Russell. Gardner's are much better on the whole. But O'Sullivan was the real genius of the two, and was responsible for some of the best of the photographs in *Gardner's Sketch Book.* (Gardner's photos after his return to Washington are relatively lacking in distinction.)

O'Sullivan's photographs of various expeditions in the West are superb. By this time, the photographer had replaced the painter in the official expeditions to the West and O'Sullivan was the best of the lot. In 1867, 1868, and 1869,

working for the official geological exploration of the fortieth parallel, he photographed subjects ranging from the highest mountain peaks to the depths of mines, the latter lit by magnesium flares. In 1870, O'Sullivan went on an expedition to the jungles of Panama. After his return, he photographed the Pacific Coast, and joined yet another expedition, the first one *up* the Colorado. The last important photographs he took were on an expedition to Arizona and New Mexico. His recording of the desert, the old Spanish-American towns, the Indian pueblos, and the dramatic cliff dwellings are masterpieces of poetic observation—as the famous and much reproduced *Canyon de Chelly, Arizona,* 1873 (F 49), testifies. O'Sullivan's Celtic lyricism touched all his work, making even the aloof impersonal majesty of nature somehow intimate with glimpses of man or his artifacts. His careful realization of texture and tone and his fine compositions are remarkable, as in a print of a bay in Panama, as subtly atmospheric and carefully arranged as a

Chinese or Japanese landscape print. He had a consistent directness of vision, as seen in the *Gould and Curry Mill, Virginia City,* c. 1880 (Illustration 5–68).

William Henry Jackson was nearly as fine a photographer of the West as O'Sullivan, though he was not so poetic as the latter. There is a sweeping grandeur in Jackson's work, which comprises more than 2,000 negatives. He first photographed along the Oregon Trail, on the North Platte, and at Pike's Peak. In an expedition in 1871, the landscape painter Thomas Moran accompanied him to the Yellowstone. Moran's paintings of the site seem empty and rhetorical in comparison to Jackson's prints. The bombast of the paintings is shown up by the inevitable honesty of the direct image on the un-retouched plate. Jackson at his best was as beautifully composed and as sensitive to values and texture as was O'Sullivan.

Jackson later covered the whole eastern range of the Rockies in Colorado and the Tetons; then the cliff dwellings at Mesa Verde and the pueblos of New Mexico. His views of the more spectacular natural wonders of the West had much to do with stimulating the government toward the establishment of the national parks, and attracted visitors to them. In fact, Jackson's photographs and propaganda were important in making the West part of our national consciousness. Among his best work are his documents of the construction of the Union Pacific Railway, such as *Devil's Gate Bridge Over Weber River, Utah,* 1869 (Illustration 5–69).

5–68.   Timothy O'Sullivan, *Gould and Curry Mill, Virginia City,* c. 1880.   Photograph.   (George Eastman House, Rochester, New York.)

5–69. William Henry Jackson, *Devil's Gate Bridge Over Weber River, Utah*, 1869. Photograph. (George Eastman House, Rochester, New York.)

If one of the ways of judging a work of art is to take into consideration the artist's realization of the limitations of his medium and his ability to exploit its possibilities, then certainly a large part of the esthetic of the photograph consists in taking advantage of those qualities which photography has over all other media. These are the recording of detail, the rendition of values, and finally, a subtler and less technical but most elemental aspect: the acceptance of the visible world itself, which is the quintessence of photography. These early documentary photographers have given us images so penetrating, and often so beautifully composed, that they remain among the most arresting in the entire history of the medium. In their hands, the thing *found* was as expressive as the thing *made*, and as creative.

In the 1880's and 1890's, three developments in the technique of photography changed its course and its character: the invention of the dry plate, the development of the platinotype, and the process of photogravure. The invention of the dry plate (or gelatin plate, taken with the portable "detective" camera) was not as revolutionary as the others, but it made photography a great deal simpler, for it became possible to take a picture anywhere without the necessity of lugging along a portable dark room for the immediate development required by the wet-plate process. With it came the platinotype (or platinum print), a way of printing on paper, allowing great subtlety in range of values, and more atmospheric and textural variety within a small area. These prints were reproduced by photogravure, in which little of the quality of the original was lost. The platinum print tended to reduce harsh contrasts and allow for a greater naturalness, a "fuzziness" more visually realistic than the undifferentiated precision of the older methods, and resulted in an interesting coincidence with the blurred atmospheric effects of impressionism in painting. The misuse of the blurred image, however, fostered a tendency toward sentimentality that was much more difficult to indulge when the older methods were being used.

The English photographer Peter Henry Emerson, a prolific writer on photography in the 1800's, advocated a blurred focus on the edges of the picture for the sake of greater naturalism. But otherwise Emerson's theories on photography describe perfectly the method of the older photographers. Disgusted by the sentimental genre prints of the current "salons," so obviously imitative of the second-rate popular painting of the time, and repelled even more by the "combination prints" (wherein separate prints of figures and objects were pasted together), he formulated an esthetic which, though based erroneously on the premise that photography was better "art" than painting because it could be more naturalistic (except for color, which he hoped would soon be perfected), nevertheless does sum up the properties peculiar to photography as distinguished from painting and the graphic arts. These in essence were "truth to subject," composition without rules and formulas, and respect for the pure, untouched photographic image. With the exception of his notions about focus, Emerson's theories fit not only the work of men like Gardner and O'Sullivan, but also, by extension, that of their spiritual descendants, the "straight" photographers who still use the tripod, the sharp focus, and the long exposure of the mid-nineteenth-century masters —that is, the esthetic of "view-box classicism," still one of the strongest contemporary schools.

The great American photographer Alfred Stieglitz was the link between Emerson and the "straight" and documentary photographers of the 1930's and 1940's. Stieglitz, while studying in Berlin, had taken up photography, working at first in the manner of the sentimental genre painters of his time. But, undoubtedly impressed by Emerson's ideas, he took prize-winning photographs in northern Italy in 1887 and later in Berlin, which were immediately recognized by Peter Henry Emerson as the best of their kind. Subtle in both psychological insight and in the qualities of their texture, composition, and value, these prints are masterpieces of "straight" photography. The subjects are seemingly unposed, the compositions are arranged with great sensitivity, and the photographic technique is brilliant, as, for instance, in the *Venetian Gamin*, 1887 (F 74).

When Stieglitz returned to the United States in 1890, he exploited the portable "detective" camera (the "Kodak" was the most popular of this type). This combined with the dry plate made exposure a matter of parts of a second instead of minutes, and therefore made possible the catching of the split second of time as well as the subtlest variation of atmosphere. Furthermore, the portable camera was inconspicuous, permitting the photographer to snap a picture practically unobserved.

By exploiting speed Stieglitz added two other dimensions to the static grandeur of the old photography: the impact of the transitory moment in pinpointed movement, and the nuances of atmosphere and weather. But he continued to respect the principles of Emerson's naturalism, for he did not change the basic "classical" esthetic of photography, only expanded it by exploiting the added variety made possible by new technical developments. Stieglitz' best work of the 1890's deserves to be classed with the greatest in the century. He called his pictures of this time "exploration of the familiar." They have the evocative power and even the poignancy of the transitory found in certain phases of French impressionism, especially in Degas. A print by Stieglitz during this period could be compared with Sargent's *Robert Louis Stevenson* in that it catches the effect of the moment, while retaining the added virtue of the factualness of the clearly perceived object. For Stieglitz did not join with some of his contemporaries in following Emerson's "soft-focus" advice (carried to extremes in the "art" photography of the later 1890's), except in his remarkable photographs of

5–70. Alfred Stieglitz, *The Terminal,* 1893. Lantern slide. (George Eastman House, Rochester, New York.)

blizzards, in which speed was essential to catch a momentary effect, and the result is a blurred quality which is actually very appropriate to the representation of falling snow. Perhaps the masterpiece of this period is *The Terminal,* a lantern slide, 1893 (F 76; Illustration 5–70), in which even the steamy flanks and frosty breath of the horses drawing the street cars are recorded in a composition of the subtlest relationship of forms and of dark and light values.

The story of Stieglitz' activities of the last years of the century, his editorship of *Camera Notes* and the founding of *Photo Secession* and *Camera Work,* belongs with the new century,

when the conflict between naturalistic and "art" photography entered a new phase.

Before closing the discussion of nineteenth-century photography, a few words should be said about the journalist–photographer Jacob Riis, who would have wanted to be remembered first as a social crusader and not necessarily as a great photographer. (Actually he has been remembered as both; a housing development built on the site of the worst of the slums he had much to do with condemning has been named for him.) One of the first of the reforming newspaper reporters, Riis's articles and lectures, illustrated with lantern slides from his photographs, were very effective in arousing the conscience of New Yorkers. Such penetrating photographs as *House of an Italian Ragpicker*, 1888–1889 (F 54), and *Bandits' Roost*, 1888 (F 55), are documents of the reeking tenements, of child labor, and of vice and corruption. Gripping in their stark actuality, they are at the same time works of art made powerful by the force of their author's indignation. Riis had no worries about esthetics. He wanted to do a job; and because he wanted to do it effectively, his success was due to the technical or compositional devices he used. His work possesses formal and artistic qualities of which he was probably not aware. In the next years, Lewis Hine was to carry on in Riis's tradition, acting as a bridge between the social commentary of the reformer–journalist and the great documentary photographers of the depression years.

Toward the end of the century there occurred a development which was less important to photography as an art than it was a technical achievement significant in the early history of the motion picture: the action photography of Eadweard Muybridge and the painter Thomas Eakins. This technique was begun as a result of a bet by Leland Stanford concerning the way a horse ran. To explore the problem, Muybridge devised in 1878 a series of cameras in sequence, the shutters of which were set off by strings broken as the horse galloped by (F 44). With the invention of the dry plate, action photography became simpler and more effective as the result of quicker exposure. Eventually Muybridge came to the University of Pennsylvania to work on similar problems in a series of action photographs in sequence. His experiments were carried further by Eakins in a remarkable series of studies of the male and female nude in action, in 1884–1888 (F 24). These documents, together with other photography, Eakins used in the construction of his paintings. He also did other work in platinum prints for its own sake as photography, but some of it is unfortunately sentimental in feeling and "fuzzy" in focus. In some cases Eakins was able to realize the relation between the potentials and the limitations of the medium, as in his *Margaret*. This print has almost the impact of his painting, but it is essentially different, having none of his moody, crepuscular, Rembrandt-like light, but a clear and direct illumination.

Sculpture

The Civil War eased somewhat the stranglehold of neo-classicism on American sculpture. After the conflict, dying centaurs and brooding Medeas gave way to "Defenders of the Flag and personifications of the Republic," in the words of the art historian Lorado Taft. Martin Milmore's *Soldiers' and Sailors' Monument*, 1871–1877 (SB 75, SB 75A), in the Boston Common, is the most conspicuous, if not the very first, of a series of monuments of a type—apparently developed exclusively in America—consisting of a column crowned by some allegory, with figures on the base at each of the four corners. Milmore's work was also typical in combining a sort of naïve realism in the representation of contemporary figures with a surviving classicism in the allegorical ones. As a matter of fact, neo-classicism did not disappear as abruptly as Taft's statement implies, for the academic style died slowly. William Rinehart, William Wetmore Story, and Harriet Hosmer, for instance, worked well beyond the Civil War in their characteristic manner. Indeed, there was little real change evident in American sculpture until the Philadelphia Centennial dramatized the new combination of naturalism and the Renaissance revival currently flourishing in France. One important exception, however, was John Quincy Adams Ward, the pupil of Henry Kirke Brown, in whose work, along with that of Thomas Ball before the Civil War, there had been the first stirrings of revolt against neo-classicism. Ward's very considerable talent was influenced neither by neo-classicism nor the new French school.

He persisted in his own native well-observed realism until his death in 1910, not even touched by the elegance, subtlety, and sentiment of his contemporary, the greatest American sculptor of his day, Augustus Saint-Gaudens. In fact, when compared with the forthright Ward, Saint-Gaudens, for all his skill, seems refined to the point of prettiness, and ideal to the point of being vapid. Ward's neglect of both surface affectation and pictorial effect, so fashionable in late nineteenth-century sculpture, gives his work a kind of burly vigor and simplicity which are often more attractive to twentieth-century eyes than the comparatively overrefined productions of his contemporaries, more popular in their day.

In his very early *Indian Hunter,* 1868 (*SB 77), in Central Park, New York, Ward already showed his naturalistic skill in both the human figure and the dog. The group is remarkable for its springy agility, and for an excitement visible even in the quiveringly alert dog. Ward's study of actual Indians contributed to the naturalism of the work, but this alone would not have brought so much life to it. To compare Ward's Indian to those of Thomas Crawford and Horatio Greenough demonstrates how naturally Ward came by his art. His gift is all the more remarkable when it is realized that he had none of the advantages of the technical training at the École des Beaux Arts from which Saint-Gaudens and so many of his contemporaries benefited.

Ward's *Henry Ward Beecher,* 1891 (SB 76; Illustration 5–71), in Borough Hall Park, Brooklyn, shows the sculptor at his best, though the *Horace Greeley,* 1890 (SB 139), in Greeley Square, New York, is also impressive. The strong individuality of both men—Beecher, whose powerful voice moved millions; Greeley, whose equally powerful pen influenced two generations —is seen in the direct and simple treatment of feature and stance, not qualified by an over-elaboration of detail. This is true especially of the clothes; Beecher's greatcoat, for instance, becomes a kind of modern toga rather than a sculptured replica of Broadway dry goods. The sculptor's *Washington,* 1883 (*SB 138), on the

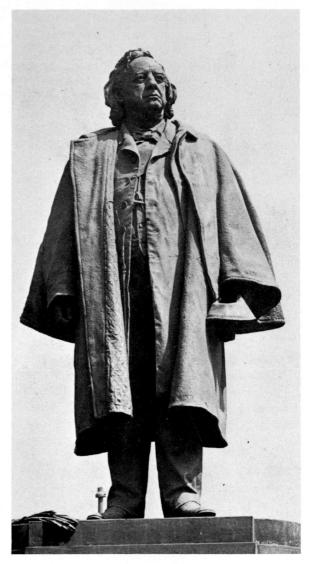

5–71.   John Quincy Adams Ward, *Henry Ward Beecher,* 1891. Borough Hall Park, Brooklyn, New York. Bronze. Height: c. 7 feet.

steps of Town and Davis' Subtreasury, is less realistic. Even Ward's customary directness faltered in the presence of this symbol, but the great sweep of the military cape gives the figure a more than ordinary effectiveness. Ward's statues can be seen in many public places: in the pediment of the Stock Exchange near the Subtreasury; in Central Park; and in Washington, notably the Garfield monument there.

Another sculptor, some of whose work preceded the Centennial Exposition, was Olin Levi Warner, who seems somewhat slight and over-idealized in contrast to the solid Ward. Warner was the first to represent the new trends: study in France, where great technical skill could be acquired; and the influence of the Italian Renaissance, so much richer, warmer, and more varied than neo-classicism. Warner is best known for the bronze doors of the Library of Congress, of which the *"Oral Tradition" Door*, 1896 (SB 142), is an example. Executed in the low relief which he and Saint-Gaudens introduced to the United States from Italian Renaissance precedent, the technically refined reliefs are the quintessence of genteel dignity, though a little more robust than some of Saint-Gaudens' work in the same vein. Perhaps more satisfactory are Warner's portrait figures in the round, of which the *William Lloyd Garrison*, 1885 (SB 140), on Commonwealth Avenue, Boston, is a good example. Here a greater naturalism than is usual in the artist and a knack for characterization save the work from the too great generality of over-idealization.

The sculpture of the last quarter of the nineteenth century is dominated by the figure of Augustus Saint-Gaudens. He was undoubtedly the most impressive American sculptor, at least until our own times, in spite of his frequent sentimentality and overrefined pictorialism—qualities which he managed to overcome in his best work, but which are all too evident in his less successful productions—especially when seen from the vantage point of the twentieth century. But Saint-Gaudens was never incompetent; on the contrary, his thorough training made him, if anything, too facile. He was first an apprentice to a gem cutter from whom he learned a subtlety of carving which lent refinement to all his work. He then became an apprentice to the Baltimore sculptor Rinehart in Rome, a mentor whose neo-classicism was less hard and mechanical than that of most. Finally, through the machinery of the École des Beaux Arts, he worked with two prominent Parisian sculptors as an apprentice, benefiting from the atelier system inherited from the Renaissance. From one, François Jouffroy,

he learned the discipline of the academy, where the nude in all its poses was so emphasized that it became as much a part of a sculptor's vocabulary as language itself. From the other, Jean Baptiste Guillaume, he learned a greater realism and an enthusiasm for the Italian Renaissance, classic and realistic at the same time, a style then being revived in France, especially by Paul Dubois, whose work Saint-Gaudens greatly admired.

When such a background is combined with a very high degree of native ability, it is not surprising to find that the first important work of the young sculptor was commendable. But the *Admiral David Glasgow Farragut*, 1881 (SB 134), in Madison Square, New York, is far more than that. It is the first mature work by one of the great artists of the century, perhaps equaled in Saint-Gaudens' subsequent work, but hardly surpassed. The influence of realism and of the Renaissance, especially that of Donatello, the most expressive as well as naturalistic of the Italians, is evident; but the subject is so different from those of the fifteenth century that eclecticism seems completely absorbed. The admiral's face is a forceful portrait in the best realistic tradition, while his body, in its vigorous though static pose, recalls Donatello's *St. George*, in which the figure is also standing still, expressing in its stance a similar reserve of potential energy. Farragut's pose suggests also the rolling of a deck, an impression increased by the lively edge of the cloak whipping in the sea wind, while the slight turn of the head and the piercing glance give the impression of the alert seaman. The base of the monument is not less interesting than the figure of the admiral, and is, besides, thoroughly original. Here the usual pedestal is extended into an exedra-like architectural form, in the design of which Saint-Gaudens was assisted by Stanford White—a solution to the problem of a base which became a prototype for subsequent monuments by Saint-Gaudens and by his imitators. But it is Saint-Gaudens' relief on the exedra which is the most interesting aspect of it. The very difficult problem of the combination of the representational and the decorative is nicely solved by fitting the allegorical figures and the lengthy inscription into a flowing linear rhythm depicting the waves of the sea, all executed in very low relief. At a short distance the gently sweeping watery motif appears almost as abstract as a pattern made by the natural striation of a prominently marked stone. The influence of Italian Renaissance low relief (*rilievo schiacciato*) and of the linearism of Botticelli's paintings, much admired by Saint-Gaudens, were probably the main sources of this unusual and finally original conception, though the analogous linear and decorative qualities seen in Japanese prints could also have played a part. (In connection with the originality which Saint-Gaudens displays in this design, it is interesting to note how similar it is to *art nouveau*, which was not yet quite formulated at this date, but the development of which was influenced by the same and analogous sources.)

Three other figures in the round compete with the *Farragut* in distinction: two Lincolns and *Deacon Samuel Chapin*. Saint-Gaudens' interpretations of the great president, both in Chicago—a seated figure in Grant Park, and a standing one in Lincoln Park, 1887 (SB 84)—have become a part of American patriotic iconography, yet are still not trite, in spite of subsequent imitation. Powerfully modeled, they are realistic evocations of a great human being, and at the same time eloquent national symbols in their dignified simplicity and effective silhouettes. This is especially true of the brooding figure in Lincoln Park standing before a heavy but decorative curule chair, a realistic but at the same time sculpturesque device. The *Puritan*, or more exactly, the *Memorial to Deacon Samuel Chapin*, 1887 (SB 135; Illustration 5–72), in Springfield, Massachusetts, is another symbolic work. The strength and energy of this figure, aggressively confident in his self-righteousness, is admirably suggested by the rigidly erect, striding form—the notion of a Puritan embodied in a very real man, of whom, of course, no actual representation existed. The bold rhythm of the cloak gives unity to the composition, and its energetic sweep, combined with the vigorous stride of the Deacon, results in an effect not only monumental but even exhilarating.

5–72. Augustus Saint-Gaudens, *Memorial to Deacon Samuel Chapin*, 1887. Springfield, Massachusetts. Bronze. Height: 8 feet, 5½ inches.

Comparable in quality to these figures in the round is the *Shaw Memorial*, 1884–1897 (SB 86; Illustration 5–73), the famous high relief on the edge of the Boston Common opposite the State House. In this Civil War monument, surely the finest among thousands, Colonel Robert Gould Shaw, on horseback, is accompanied by his marching Negro troops, led by a drummer. It is a sober work, not infused with the false enthusiasm usual in such monuments. The rhythmic repetition of the marching feet and the silhouetted guns (giving the sense of inevitable progress urged forward by the tattoo of the drum-

5–73. Augustus Saint-Gaudens, *Shaw Memorial,* 1884–1897. Beacon Street, Boston, Massachusetts. Bronze. Height: c. 10 feet.

sticks), and the interplay between high and low relief in an abstract and dynamic contrast of highlight and shadow, are strikingly effective devices to raise realism to a higher expressiveness. Unfortunately, the rather overgentle linearism of the figures of Death and Victory floating over the group mitigates the powerful effect of the whole.

A more satisfactory figure is the nude *Diana* in bronze, 1892 (SB 83), which formerly graced the cupola of Madison Square Garden. Now in the Philadelphia Museum, it dominates the entrance hall with a svelte, pagan grace, as befits the subject and its original airy perch. Here Saint-Gaudens' linear refinement is seen in a figure of huge size which demonstrates his great competence in the treatment of the human figure.

Saint-Gaudens' last productive years, from 1892 until 1903, were largely occupied with the *General William Tecumseh Sherman Memorial* (*SB 82), in the southeast corner of Central Park in New York, representing an equestrian General Sherman led by the figure of Victory—the most famous and conspicuous piece of sculpture in the United States, if not quite the most successful. The general himself embodies all of the best qualities of Saint-Gaudens' realism. The intense nervous face with its short stubby beard and sharp all-seeing eyes is vigorously modeled, and not too suavely, as is too often the case in much of Saint-Gaudens' later work. The figure as a whole is unified by the great sweeping cape; the horse is impeccable, but not remarkable, and a little too busy in silhouette; but the figure of Victory, arms spread out, wings and drapery fluttering, qualifies the sculptural effect of the whole with an overelaboration and delicacy of form and silhouette. The work fails principally because of the disturbing combination in one monument of the expressive realism of the general, his clothes modeled vigorously over a real frame, and the vacuity of the Victory, to which drapery clings indeterminately and from which wings sprout as though from some "spirit" substance unpleasantly closer to ectoplasm than to flesh and blood. The head of Sherman alone, in a study now in the Pennsylvania Academy, shows how Saint-Gaudens, even in his late work, was not always overcome by genteel refinement.

To see Saint-Gaudens' real stature, we must look at the *Farragut*, the *Puritan*, and the *Lincoln* and *Shaw* memorials, and at one other remarkable work, perhaps his masterpiece, the *Adams Memorial*, 1891 (SB 85; Illustration 5–74), in Rock Creek Cemetery, Washington, D. C., a monument to the wife, dead by suicide, of his friend Henry Adams. Here Saint-Gaudens succeeded in creating a personification which is not amorphous, in spite of its androgynous or sexless character. *Grief* (or the *Peace of God*, as Adams preferred to call it) is eloquently suggested by the massive bronze figure seated in the simplest architectural setting—basically two smooth stones at right angles—and swathed in great folds of drapery, one of which shadows the meditative head. The grave sobriety, largeness of conception and treatment, and above all the abstract plasticity of Saint-Gaudens are seen at their best in the *Adams Memorial*.

After Saint-Gaudens, Daniel Chester French is the most prominent American sculptor of the period, and comparison with his more distinguished contemporary is inevitable. French had far less training than Saint-Gaudens, though his study of anatomy with Rimmer in Boston gave him as great a mastery of the figure as could be obtained without going abroad. French's early work, like the bronze *The Minute Man*, 1874–

5–74. Augustus Saint-Gaudens, *Grief*, from *Adams Memorial*, 1891. Rock Creek Cemetery, Washington, D. C. Bronze. Height: 5 feet, 10 inches.

1875 (SB 89), at Concord, Massachusetts, and the *John Harvard*, in the Harvard Yard, have a kind of smooth generality never present in Saint-Gaudens, who is texturally interesting even in his least sculpturesque idealizations. After a trip to Paris in the 1880's, French brought to his work more realism and a little Gallic liveliness of surface, but except in his very best productions his underlying preference for heavy idealized types persists—dull in form, vacuous in expression, massive but not alive. A case in point is his seated *Lincoln* in the Lincoln Memorial at Washington, which, though undoubtedly competent and impressive, owed much to Saint-Gaudens, and when compared with the latter's seated figure in Grant Park is too relaxed and lacking in impact. Saint-Gaudens' figure is equally static, but imbued with an inner fire, expressed in the gesture of the hand and the intensity of the gaze. The figure of the angel in French's *The Angel of Death Staying the Hand of the Sculptor*, 1893 (SB 88), a memorial to Martin Milmore, in Forest Hills Cemetery, Boston, is without the convincing power of the analogous figure in the *Adams Memorial*. Flatulence is substituted for mass, though the design as a whole is impressive and the figure of the sculptor is convincing and graceful. When French is more realistic he is more satisfactory, though even his infrequent work of this type is marred by his tendency to generality. His somewhat heavy-handed idealization is best represented by the colossal bronze *Alma Mater*, 1902–1903 (SB 90), on the steps leading to McKim, Mead & White's Library at Columbia University, New York, a perfect adjunct to the dry academicism of the building. Similar in spirit to mid-century neo-classicism, although with more plastic richness and more competence, it is equally lacking in inner vitality. The torpid figure covered with its great slabs of drapery is the sculpturesque equivalent of countless similar figures in the murals of the time.

Henry Kitson was a spiritual follower of Saint-Gaudens and French; his *Roger Conant*, c. 1890, at Salem, Massachusetts, is derived closely from the *Puritan*, though his other figures, usually dealing with New England colonial history, are somewhat empty. They make French seem more vital in comparison, though Kitson's *The Minute Man*, 1900 (SB 953), at Lexington, Massachusetts, does demonstrate how the general level of competence had risen in the quarter-century since the young Daniel Chester French had done his version of the subject at nearby Concord.

It is a relief to turn from the unimaginative seriousness of the more pedestrian sculpture of the period to the movement and gaiety of Frederick MacMonnies, whose Gallic élan is almost rococo in its energetic and decorative charm. Influenced by eighteenth-century revivalism in France, typified by Jean Falguière; by the dynamism of the great romantic François Rude, the sculptor of the *Marseillaise* on the Arc de Triomphe in Paris; and by Jean Baptiste Carpeaux whose dancing and musical figures on the Paris Opera are almost as well known, MacMonnies is almost entirely French, in spite of much of his American subject matter. His *Bacchante* in the Boston Museum is typical of his vivacious and dynamic style, while the *Nathan Hale*, 1889 (SB 123), in City Hall Park in New York, though basically naturalistic, is treated in so crisp and lively a way as almost to require description in rococo stylistic terms. As might be imagined from the foregoing, MacMonnies' monumental work is perhaps too busy, as seen in the frenetic activity and decorative complexity of his work for the Soldiers' and Sailors' Memorial Arch in Brooklyn, and the *Washington, at the Battle of Princeton* at Princeton, New Jersey (SB 122).

Before closing the discussion of the period, a few sculptors should be mentioned who dealt with the Indian and other aspects of the frontier, often giving prominence to animals as well as to humans. The Indian was a favorite subject: picturesque, indigenous, and, of course, nearly nude and therefore a figure much more adapted to treatment in sculpture than one clad in a frock coat. Cyrus E. Dallin was perhaps the most famous of the Indian sculptors, though he executed some work dealing with other subjects. His equestrian figures, among them *The Medicine Man*, 1899 (SB 96), in Fairmount Park, Philadelphia, and the *Supreme Appeal*, 1909, in front of the Boston Museum, typify his work. Accurate, a little hard and graceless, these pieces of sculpture are nevertheless sincere, well-observed documents. The painter Frederick Remington, however, in a few rare works, was the best of all those who dealt with western themes in sculpture. His *Bronco Buster*, 1895 (SB 94A), possesses the accuracy and documentary value of his paintings, but like them is perhaps over-meticulous and therefore essentially unsculpturesque—though plastically interesting, varied, and certainly full of tremendous vitality.

velopment. The Winslow House in its symmetry and studied proportions, especially when compared with familiar examples of contemporaneous architecture, is far closer in feeling to McKim, Mead & White's colonial revival house than to any by Henry Richardson, William Emerson, or John Stevens. It will be remembered, however, that as the shingle style became less prominent, a sense of order and balance (parallel to the then developing colonial revival) began to assert itself, especially in the work of Bruce Price at Tuxedo Park. (Wright used one of Price's houses as the prototype for his own house at Oak Park, built in 1889.). This general tendency toward classicism was thus part of the environment of taste in which the young Wright developed; but his originality was such that the desire for harmonious order was satisfied by the emulation not of conventional classical prototypes, but of examples of exotic architecture similar in general effect to the classical style. The studied and balanced proportions of the Winslow House are certainly basically "classical," but so also were the Turkish and Japanese pavilions at the Chicago World's Fair. The wide, overhanging hipped roof and the high windows connected by a continuous band in the Winslow House were also seen in both pavilions; the prominent geometric ornamentation nearly duplicates that of the Turkish Pavilion in general effect, in scale, and in detail. The somewhat monumental character of the Winslow House may well reflect still another influence—the Mayan architecture reproduced in plaster at the Fair. In any case, Mayan architecture became increasingly more influential in Wright's work; the most obvious examples are the A. D. German Warehouse at Richland Center, Wisconsin, 1913 (AC 418), and the magnificent Charles Ennis House in Los Angeles, California, 1923 (AC 429). Another stylistic characteristic which appears in the Winslow House, and which Wright shares with Sullivan, should not be ignored: a feeling for the flat plane and the sharp edge, seen in such buildings as Sullivan's Walker Warehouse and Wainwright Building, and in a much reproduced house from Sullivan's office but designed by Wright, the Charnley House, built in 1891 in Chicago.[7]

In sum, the basic classicism and simple monumentality of the Winslow House depend as much on its harmony and refinement of proportion as upon actual emulation of exotic prototypes, though the latter certainly were inspiring to Wright. As would be expected in such a symmetrical building, the interior plan is closed (it opens out somewhat at the rear) and almost as arbitrary in its balance as is the exterior.

The River Forest Golf Club is one of the earliest and also one of the most interesting of Wright's structures in what might be called a continuation of the shingle style; at the same time it is an early example of what Wright was to term his "organic" architecture. Open and flowing in plan, with many instances of interplay between exterior and interior space, the Golf Club utilized wood, as did the shingle style. Wright's original contribution is the emphasis upon easy transition from one part of the building to another and upon the interrelation among the various areas, expressed in the long lines of the broadly projecting hipped roofs and in the continuous window bands. (Both elements were of exotic inspiration, domesticated to blend with the native tradition, though the continuous fenestration had been prefigured to a certain extent in Richardson's libraries.) In the Golf Club, Wright took the elements of the shingle style and ordered their complex forms into harmoniously intersecting volumes and masses, while still preserving an informal rural quality that is somewhat domestic but gives appropriate spaciousness and largeness of conception to this communal building.

The Golf Club is of further interest because of its cross plan (probably partly derived from Japanese example)—a plan that not only sustains convenience and movement, but is adaptable to the potentials of bold design. Only the symmetry of the River Forest Golf Club is atypical of the more "organic" examples of Wright's early work. More characteristic is the Bradley House at Kankakee, Illinois, 1900 (AC 370), a skillful design in which the intersection of planes is exploited even more dramatically than in the Golf Club.

The Arthur Heurtley House (now the Nick Forte House) at Oak Park, Illinois, 1902 (AC

371), represents an early attempt at a synthesis of Wright's two trends, the monumental or "classical" being more prominent in this case. Its proportions and massiveness are derived from employment of many of the characteristics of the Winslow House, though the continuous fenestration, again imitative of Japanese design, is more consistent with Wright's organic style, as is the interrelation of interior and exterior, emphasized by porches and terraces.

The Ward W. Willitts House, Highland Park, Illinois, 1902 (AC 373, AC 373A; Illustration 6–5), is the first mature example of the "prairie style," a generic term for a group of Wright's houses in the Chicago region. Wright's design related these houses organically to their immediate surroundings through an evident interplay between interior and exterior, and to their regional environment through an emphasis upon horizontality which reflected the spacious flatness of the plains.

In the Willitts House, the cruciform plan is developed with more sophistication than in the still somewhat arbitrarily symmetrical River Forest Golf Club; perfect balance is modified by the demands of convenience. The consequences of this irregularity are beautifully worked out in a series of interpenetrations that are less angular than in the Bradley House and more related to the horizontality of the hovering eaves, the string courses, and the generally extended design of the structure as a whole. The porches, terraces, and porte cochere extend almost weightlessly from the denser center of the house, seeming almost to reach out to encompass part of the surroundings. The concentration on the horizontal is balanced by the vertical accents of the living room area, which repeats the verticals of the surrounding trees. The division of this facade into panels, and the clustered fenestration immediately under the eaves, compromise a very distinguished design. It is questionable whether the strips that define the panels are a reflection of the studs' skeleton beneath the panels themselves or are a continuation of the Japanese influence evidenced in the projecting eaves and in the fenestration. The interior, especially the living room, is refined in proportion and possesses far more of the stripped-down, simple elegance

of Japanese architecture than the more literally imitative work of McKim, Mead & White, as in their remodeling in the Japanese manner of the dining room of Kingscote, Newport, Rhode Island, 1880 (AB 508, AB 509). (Though the living room of the Willitts House was originally stained dark and the furniture was designed by Wright, it must be confessed that the present owners' changes, involving the highlighting of the color scheme and the replacement of the heavy furniture—no matter how original, certainly cumbersome when compared with Japanese or contemporary furniture—by cushions and low tables, show the basic simplicity of the room to better advantage, though the purist may regret this disregard for Wright's original scheme.)

The Willitts House is one of the least "dated" of Wright's early buildings, prophesying more than any other until the spectacular Falling Water Wright's emphasis on flow or continuity radiating from a solid center—the opposite of the static, enclosed form of classical design. It is the first house to demonstrate with complete surety Wright's intention to "destroy the box."

While designing structures like the Willitts House, Wright was also executing buildings of an entirely different sort, for which the impressive "classicism" of his less organic manner was more appropriate. The most important of these were the Larkin Company Administration Building (destroyed), in Buffalo, New York, 1904 (Illustration 6–6), and the Universalist Church in Oak Park, Illinois, 1906 (AC 394, AC 395, AC 396). The Larkin Building was an office building remarkable for the structure and planning of its interior, and for the monolithic effect of its exterior. Essentially an open court with tiers of balconies illuminated by a skylight, the bright and cheerful interior was practically sealed off from the noisy manufacturing in the surrounding area by massive walls penetrated by few openings, and by four pylon-like unfenestrated brick masses on each corner, containing the stairways. Though at first glance the building may have seemed arbitrarily massive, Wright's organic principles were not denied, because the exterior form was actually functional: its almost solid walls shut out the noisy and ugly environment. The Univer-

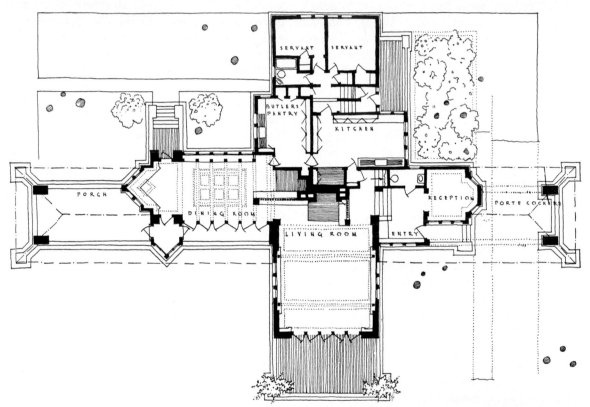

6–5.   The Ward W. Willitts House, Highland Park, Illinois, 1902, by Frank Lloyd Wright. (Floor plan from Henry-Russell Hitchcock, *In the Nature of Materials;* New York: 1942.)

salist Church is a more abstract design, wherein the large-scale forms of the Larkin Building are reduced in size and used frankly to create an effect of dignity and solemnity. Its poured concrete (Wright's first use of this material) was particularly adapted to the heavy forms, which in turn were conditioned by the thickness of the concrete slabs. The formal character of the edifice is somewhat relieved by the Mayan-like geometric design of the pier capitals. The interior, which reflects the rectangular outer mass, is designed as a series of interlocking

6–6. Larkin Company Administration Building (destroyed), Buffalo, New York, 1904, by Frank Lloyd Wright.

planes encompassing auditorium, galleries, clerestory, and a crossed ceiling grid, the decorative elements being logical extensions of the structural ones. The monumentality of this church (even though it is quite small in scale) and of the Larkin Building impressed Europeans who knew the buildings through photographs and drawings, and exerted considerable influence on the abstract, non-organic phase of early modern architecture in Europe.

The Avery Coonley House, Riverside, Illinois, 1908 (AC 398, AC 399, AC 400), represents a synthesis of Wright's organic style with the abstract formality of the Winslow and Heurtley houses (now supplemented in Wright's vocabulary of forms by the Larkin Building and the Universalist Church). Its spread-out plan, which incorporates extensive landscaping including gardens, a pergola, and a pool, thoroughly relates the Coonley House to its environment. It is also organic in the sense that structural elements have been expressed in the design. In the ceiling of the living room, for example, an asymmetrical complexity of various interlocking planes meets in a beautifully articulated series of beams and cross studs. Yet at the same

time the large plane surfaces and slab-like areas have a formality which makes the house essentially less intimate and rural (in spite of its site and extensive planting) than Wright's smaller houses. But this may be because the house is a large and elaborate one, more a mansion than a cottage. A small house for Isabel Roberts, in River Forest (°AC 401A), built in the same year as the Coonley House, shares many of its characteristics but is less formal or heavy.

The Frederick C. Robie House, in South Chicago, 1909 (AC 405, AC 406, °AC 406A, AC 407), is generally conceded to be the masterpiece of Wright's early domestic buildings. Illustrating all of Wright's points in his apologia for the organic style, the house is also a magnificently composed and authoritative design. It seems almost classical in spite of obvious openness of plan and lack of arbitrarily imposed canons of overt balance and symmetry, and thus seems to sum up the best facets of the seemingly antithetical trends in Wright's work. The heaviness of the masonry walls, partially supported by steel beams, is contrasted with the lightness of the balconies and roofs, which have an almost dynamic sweep when seen from a slight perspective. The interrelation between heavy and light and between mass and openness is probably the key to the compelling beauty of this house. Though the plan is not like any other of Wright's, it is a logical extension of the free-flowing openness of earlier ones in which a long wing with continuous fenestration incorporated both the living room and dining room.

The Robie and Willitts houses (the latter less "classical" and therefore more characteristically informal) illustrate Frank Lloyd Wright's principles of organic architecture as inherited from Sullivan and from the indigenous tradition of domestic architecture that culminated in the shingle style. In a group of statements in *In the Cause of Architecture, I* (1908), and *II* (1914), both published in the *Architectural Record*, and in the introduction to a publication in Berlin in 1910 of a monograph of his work, *Studies and Executed Buildings* (*Ausgeführte Bauten und Entwürfe*), Wright explained these principles, which are closely related to his concept of style. (The basic principles of Wright's theory were outlined in the 1908 article, and clarified in the statements of 1910 and 1914.) The most important of these, which Wright called the principle of simplicity and repose (words which sum up most accurately the feeling of the prairie houses), is achieved in two ways: first, by replacing a plan divided into many units and fixed by an imposed esthetic with one that is open and flowing; second, the replacement of arbitrarily applied ornament by the "natural" integration of structural elements, such as openings, into the formal design and the assimilation of appliances, fixtures, and furniture designed for the building itself. In the *Studies*, Wright states this point most succinctly: "Do not add enrichment for the sake of enrichment. If the structure is achieved organically, the ornamentation is conceived in the very ground plan, it is in the constitution of the structure." An incidental corollary to this principle is that each building designed with an appreciation for all the circumstantial and environmental factors involved, including the personality of the client as well as that of the architect, will be different from any other.

Other important principles emphasize the importance of harmonizing the building with its immediate and general environment, respect for the specific nature of the materials, and the use of colors closest to those of nature.

These fundamentals of an architecture which Wright called "organic" were further clarified by his idea of style, which he called in 1914 "the integrity of fashioning to purpose." He had said in 1910, "When we perceive a thing to be beautiful, it is because we instantly realize its rightness." Thus, by answering the recurrent question of nineteenth-century architecture—what style to have—with the concept of style as the natural result of a certain set of circumstances, Wright solved the problem of eclecticism. Even though his early buildings by no means consistently illustrate his principles (he either was not conscious of exotic eclecticism in his own work, or minimized its influence, and he was inclined to ignore contradictions of his organic theory in his buildings, as in the Winslow House), nevertheless it is remarkable that such

a clear statement of many of the principles of contemporary architecture should have been made more than a half-century ago. This fact, together with the publication of his buildings abroad as early as 1910, should underline Wright's seminal importance in the development of both modern architecture and theory.

The significance of Wright as a pioneer of the International Style—surely one of the most important developments in architectural history—poses an interesting question: Without discounting Wright's own synthesizing genius or the contribution of the western tradition as a whole, and especially the English, to American thought, was there anything in Wright's American cultural environment which acted as a catalyst to his creative originality? It need not be reiterated how Wright's principles were prefigured in the development of nineteenth-century domestic architecture in America, and in some of its spokesmen from Downing to Stevens; nor how much Wright's thought derived from Sullivan's architectural philosophy. Wright brought Sullivan's practice and theory to a fruition. Especially significant was his clarification of Sullivan's "form follows function" into "form *is* function." In this way Wright substituted the organic building itself for the organic ornament that Sullivan felt was necessary as an architectural metaphor.

It is interesting to notice the remarkable similarity of some of Wright's ideas to those of the literary and critical figures of the nineteenth century, especially to Emerson and his circle. Some of Emerson's remarks on sculpture and architecture, already mentioned, become more pregnant in the framework of Wright's principles. Emerson's delight in such functional buildings as the New England barn and the Eddystone light, was reflected in his remark that "the modern architecture is shipbuilding";[8] his statement, "Ask the fact for the form,"[9] even though deriving from Coleridge's theory of organic poetry and not referring specifically to architecture, sounds like Wright himself. It was largely the sculptor Horatio Greenough, whose esthetic was so different from his own artistic practice, who stimulated Emerson's thoughts in this direction. Greenough, who admired the trotting wagon and the yacht *America* and was "enamoured of the old, bold, neutral-toned Yankee farmhouse which seems to belong to the ground whereon it stands, as a caterpillar to the leaf that feeds him," [10] made statements which are remarkably close to those of Wright. "By beauty I mean the promise of function," [11] Greenough said; and, specifically referring to architecture, recommended, ". . . instead of forcing the functions of every sort of building into one general form, adopting an outward shape for the sake of the eye, or of association, without inner distribution, let us begin with the heart as a nucleus." [12] Wright's organic principles, his anti-eclecticism, and even his metaphor of the heart as a house are here prophesied to a remarkable degree. Greenough was only one (though perhaps the most articulate) of a whole group of men surrounding Emerson in the 1840's and early 1850's, who were developing similar functional or organic doctrines. It is unlikely that Wright read the remarks of Greenough, Emerson, or others, published in various issues of the *Dial* and *Atlantic Monthly* during the mid-century decades. Emerson's essays, however, were common educational material during Wright's youth. The thinking of both Sullivan and Wright is permeated by Emerson's concept of "fitness" as enunciated in his essay "On Nature."

Walden, by Emerson's friend Thoreau, brims with insights into the principles of organic architecture, and his statement that the only true architectural beauty is that which "has gradually grown from within outward, out of the necessities and character of the indweller" [13] could have been made by Wright, who asks us to "conceive now that an entire building might grow out of conditions as a plant grows up out of soil." [14] But Thoreau's comment on architecture had a more moral than esthetic orientation, and should not be distorted into having more significance than any other illustration of the Transcendentalists' concern with organic theory in general. Walt Whitman, on the other hand, though equally moralizing in his occasional remarks on architecture, addressed himself in his *Complete Writings* (1902) more specifically to the problem. His objections to current eclecticism and ostentation were based on his ideas of simplicity and economy, and he was concerned with the expression of structure, site, materials, and function, which he felt were the facts of architecture just as words are the raw stuff of poetry and should express organically the content of experience. Like Emerson, Whitman admired "the huge hull'd, clean shap'd New York Clipper." [15] Whitman's *Leaves of Grass,* Sullivan tells us in his *Autobiography of an Idea,* gave him "this most compelling suggestion of how art could grow organically from the forces of American life," [16] a remark which could be extended in its implication to include some of Frank Lloyd Wright's ideas on organic form and building for democracy.

It may well be that Wright's principles owe as much to the organic theories of Pugin, and to Ruskin and his followers, as they do to the Transcendentalists, but they differ on an essential point: they are not eclectic. The Englishman believed that a return to medieval architecture and craftsmanship was necessary to restore organic functional principles. Wright followed Emerson and Greenough in rejecting this eclecticism while recognizing the practical necessity for using the mass-produced product of the machine, provided it was well designed.

Wright's architecture was not limited by the principles of his organic theory. The classic authority of the Winslow House, the monumentality of the Universalist Church, and the richly sculpturesque qualities of all his work are as important as his more informal functionalism. Though not neo-classical in any sense, much of it possesses the ordered cubical massing and clear geometric volumes of the classic or Mediterranean formal tradition, supplemented by the analogous qualities of indigenous pre-Columbian architecture of the western hemisphere. All his statements to the contrary, Wright's eclecticism cannot be denied, though, as a late romantic, he was imbued with the conviction of his own unique individuality, and could not acknowledge his indebtedness. But Wright's eclecticism is so creative that it infused his cultural inheritance with a new ingredient.

In the decade following 1910, the overtly organic aspect in Wright's executed work tended to diminish. Only his own residence Taliesin I, at Spring Green, Wisconsin, 1911 (AC 411), was an exception. This house, beautifully incorporated into the rolling and fertile countryside, was one of the best examples of Wright's organic style until then, but it was destroyed by fire and replaced by subsequent buildings which represent a later phase. Not until Taliesin III, begun in 1925 (AC 434, AC 434A, AC 434B), and his famous houses of the 1930's, did Wright return to a more deliberate expression of his organic principles. Meanwhile such buildings as the Imperial Hotel at Tokyo, 1916–1922 (Illustration 6–9), and several houses in California seem to emphasize other aspects of Wright, especially his exoticism, a strong ingredient in his work.

In the closing years of this early period, the future direction of Wright's work was beginning to emerge. The extremely Mexican appearance of the A. D. German Warehouse at Richland Center has already been mentioned. The City National Bank Building, and the hotel at Mason City, Iowa, 1909 (AC 408), have an equally Mayan massiveness and a sophisticated use of heavy horizontal elements in the wide eaves, string courses, and moldings contrasted with a pattern of openings. Less derivative than these buildings was the charming Avery Coonley Playhouse, Riverside, Illinois, 1912 (AC 413), in which the block-like shapes, recalling the heavy horizontals of the Universalist Church, are combined with a lively interpenetration of interior and exterior space, enhanced by lattices and trellis-like overhangs which are frankly decorative. The increasing tendency toward applied decoration in Wright's work at this time was seen at its best in the Midway Gardens in Chicago, a "beer garden" and music hall in the popular German tradition, erected in 1914 but destroyed in 1923 after being made unprofitable by prohibition. A photograph (Illustration 6–7) of one of the street fronts gives no idea of the huge area of the building or of the rich complexity of its composition, but it does show the

originality and beauty of the abstract decorative forms. The prominence of this ornament would seem to deny one of Wright's foremost principles. But the decoration was not, in the strictest sense, inorganic, for here its function was to suggest (as much as was the case in his domestic architecture), the relation between exterior and interior, but in this instance symbolically or metaphorically. The variety and playfulness of surface, form, and texture were dynamic, creating an effect of gaiety. Furthermore, the forms themselves were not arbitrary, for they derived from Wright's own formal vocabulary, which had developed from circumstances of program and design in buildings whose function was more practical than was this architectural fantasy. Adapted here to a less utilitarian purpose, the forms which were evoked in the Midway Gardens closely resembled abstract sculpture.

In the sculpturesque architecture of the Midway Gardens, Wright achieved a form of abstraction which prophesied much of the later Dutch "de Stilj" movement in architecture, painting, and sculpture, as well as the more abstractly formal architecture elsewhere in Europe. In fact, European design seems to have been considerably influenced by the publication there of Wright's work in 1910, illustrating the designs and forms which he developed into abstract motifs in his later work.

None of the architects of the progressive school centered in Chicago possessed Frank Lloyd Wright's powerful imagination or his originality. The work of Charles H. Purcell and George Elmslie (who later formed a firm in Minneapolis) represents the continuation of the Chicago tradition better than any other; guided by Sullivan at first, they gradually assimilated the influence of Wright. Elmslie worked with Wright in the firm of Adler and Sullivan, and acquired increased importance after Wright left. In addition to contributing to the vocabulary of Sullivan's later skyscrapers, as the older man's health and spirits declined, Elmslie actually designed buildings which were at one time attributed to Sullivan. (The National Farmers' Bank in Owatonna, Minnesota, as we have

6–7. Midway Gardens (destroyed), Chicago, Illinois, 1914, by Frank Lloyd Wright.

noted, owes more to Elmslie than to Sullivan.) Elmslie's Merchants' National Bank at Winona, Minnesota, 1913 (AC 293), which he helped design as a member of the firm of Purcell, Frieck and Elmslie, is better in proportion and mass than the later and relatively much less effective banks designed by Sullivan after Elmslie left the former's office in 1909. Purcell and Elmslie's Stewart Memorial Church in Minneapolis, 1911 (AC 288, AC 289), is directly inspired by Wright's Universalist Church in general plan and exterior composition, yet the brick of the exterior and the wooden trim of the interior are too different in character to be treated effectively with the same proportion and scale that Wright achieved using concrete. The firm's Bradley House, or Seashore Bungalow at Woods Hole, Massachusetts, 1911 (AC 291), is their most original building. The architects felt they were designing in what they called an indigenous

organic American form. Though the house is constructed of frame and shingle and demonstrates interpenetration of interior and exterior space, its absolutely geometric symmetry (further emphasized by the juxtaposition of the forms of cube and circle) is actually quite inconsistent with the informality of the shingle style.

The work of Purcell and Elmslie is on the whole derivative and less distinguished than the work of Wright, but it demonstrates the continuing influence of the progressive Chicago tradition by at least two practitioners in the Midwest.

Only in California was there an impressive continuation of the progressive school represented by Sullivan and Wright. There were several reasons why a local school came into existence there and was able to persist so long in the face of prevailing eclecticism. The mild climate, the superb views, and the tradition of outdoor and informal living oriented building naturally in the direction of the open plan and encouraged the extensive use of porches, terraces, and patios. Also, the local Spanish-American tradition (carried on by the early Anglo-Saxon settlers) of the ranch or hacienda included a patio, as well as long porches with or without arcades. Of these ranches there were two kinds: those built in adobe and plaster, which had a somewhat cubical look, like the Castro House at San Juan Bautista, 1838 (*AA 165); and the sprawling hacienda of wood, with many porches and balconies, like the old Pantula Ranch at Vallejo. The last was the more popularly emulated, partly because of the availability of the beautiful and lasting redwood. Even the absurdly pretentious eclectic houses of the 1880's, like the Carson House at Eureka (AB 385, AB 386), were of wood and had an expansive openness of plan and largeness of conception, incorporating towers, cupolas, bays, and jigsaw decoration in an exuberant set of devices to relate interior and exterior space. Another important factor was the influence of the Orient, especially of Japan. There were Japanese shops and tea gardens in San Francisco and Pasadena, so that Japanese taste was familiar. Furthermore, there was the coincidence of a similar climate in San Francisco and Japan. Their interest in its culture made many Californians feel they were as close to Japan as to the eastern coast of the United States.

The architects who best incorporated all these factors in their work were the brothers Charles S. and Henry B. Greene—a combination of such compatibility that their buildings seem almost to have been designed by one man. Trained in architecture at the Massachusetts Institute of Technology, on arrival in California the brothers worked through the various prevailing styles— colonial revival, "Queen Anne," Old English, and Spanish mission—before they found their own original expression. The catalyst was the commission of a bungalow for Arturo Bandini in Pasadena in 1903, a U-shaped dwelling in the manner of the Spanish ancestors of the client. The building was constructed simply of redwood vertical board and batten, with an enfilade of rooms opening onto a continuous porch enclosing a patio-like area on three sides. Open, flowing, with none of the enclosed feeling of the adobe, it resembles the Vallejo hacienda, though it is of only one story and much smaller.

The influence of the Japanese was equal in importance to the local tradition in the work of Greene and Greene. This is seen in the flexibility of their plans, in broken roof lines, projecting eaves, and a complex variety of supports —as complicated sometimes as the most intricate of stick style structures. All their buildings display a love of craftsmanship, demonstrated particularly in the refined framing, joining, and finish, all of which were supervised by the architects from the milling onward. Though not so open in plan as Wright's and a little more complex in their spatial division, the Greenes' houses are more elaborate in their interrelation between interior and exterior, which is expressed in a greater number of porches, terraces, and lattice work. This complexity of openings and of structural members (such as railings, louvers, and brackets) was the basis for a personal style which is staccato, lively, and broken, and thus very different from the continuity and unity achieved by Wright. These differences can be seen in a comparison of the Willitts House with two by the Greenes: the Blacker-Hill House, 1907 (AC 120, AC 121, AC 121A), and the David B. Gamble House, 1909 (AC 122, *AC 122A, AC 122B, AC 123, AC 123D; Illustration 6–8), both in Pasadena. Another characteristic and important example, notable also for its superb craftsmanship, is the Thorson House, 1909 (AC 1025) (now the Sigma Phi House), in Berkeley. In the somewhat smaller Charles Pratt House near Ojai, 1909 (*AC 124), the architects achieved a remarkable effect of organized informality by means of broken roof lines and projecting eaves, a design as beautifully integrated into the landscape as any of its predecessors in the shingle style or by Wright.

The houses of Greene and Greene, built for wealthy clients who could afford the care the

6–8. David B. Gamble House, Pasadena, California, 1909, by Charles S. and Henry B. Greene.

architects lavished on the slightest detail, were so successfully adapted to the climate of California and to suburban and rural living that many of their plans and details, in a vulgarized form, contributed to the California bungalow type—the last descendant of the shingle style and the predecessor of the "ranch house"—which withstood the almost universal eclecticism of the second and third decades of the century, not only in California but throughout the country. This vulgarization, together with shoddy imitations of their work, the impracticality of the old handicraft tradition in an industrial civilization, and finally the success of the Spanish Revival all conspired against the Greene brothers, who ceased to practice in the early 1920's.

This was not the case, however, with Bernard Maybeck, another California "original," who was more varied in his creativity and production than the Greenes. Maybeck used the informal California tradition more casually, putting up redwood houses and schools like summer cottages of stud and boarding, permitting ordinary carpentry and redwood to speak for themselves, but utilizing interesting spatial arrangements involving clerestory and dormer lighting, split levels, and open screening of vertical studs.

His earlier houses resemble the "Swiss chalet" style of the 1850's (without the excrescences); the David Boyden (AC 1037) and Denzel and Vida Allen houses, 1900–1909 (AC 1035), both in Berkeley, are more typical. Their informal and open plan, and the stick and shingle traditions, reinforced by Japanese influence, are combined in a way which is almost contemporary. As a matter of fact, these houses, adapted to more popular use than the mansions of Greene and Greene, have exerted a strong influence on the so-called San Francisco Bay school of the present day. Maybeck's nondomestic work is also of unusual interest. Especially notable is the First Church of Christ Scientist at Berkeley, 1912 (AC 240, *AC 241), a potpourri of medieval and oriental architectural motifs and detail arranged with startling originality and imagination in a brilliant orchestration of heavy and light elements. The interior is especially impressive: a great space supported by two colossal diagonal beams contrasted against a screen of glass walls. The rich and plastic imagination of Maybeck is also seen in his Fine Arts Building, 1914 (AC 243, *AC 243A, AC 244), which, because of its popularity, was the only structure permitted to remain after the

Panama Pacific Exposition at San Francisco. Though it is a completely classical building in detail, its powerful shapes and volumes are evocative of a Piranesian antiquity and make all other traditional architecture of the period seem stodgy, uninspired, and merely academic. Even Maybeck's more eclectic houses, less interesting to us than his more unpretentious cottages, have a personal stamp, as do his later collegiate buildings in the prevailing Spanish Revival, as in the Hearst Memorial (Women's) Gymnasium at the University of California at Berkeley, 1925 (*AC 1039, *AC 1040).

Other California architects lacked the stature of the Greenes or Maybeck, although their work has a regional stamp. The most important is Irving Gill, whose work in masonry (or masonry and stucco) was inspired as much by the local

Spanish adobe as was that of the Greenes by the Spanish-American work in wood. The clear cubical forms of his early houses are accompanied by an open plan and an expressive use of wood framing and trim that is essentially less eclectic than the orientally inspired joinery of the Greene brothers. This is especially evident in his Melville Klauber House, San Diego, 1907–1910 (AC 104, AC 104C, AC 104D), which has something of the stripped-down eloquence of the contemporary style. Another architect, John Galen Howard, carried on the informal tradition in some of his work, as in the building for the School of Architecture at the University of California at Berkeley and in several houses (AC 160), though his most important work is in the Hispano-Italian manner with which he stamped the Berkeley campus (AC 1026).

Modern Architecture: Through World War II

With the exception of Frank Lloyd Wright and a few of his Californian contemporaries, very little happened in the progressive tradition of American architecture until the 1930's. Eclecticism remained practically unchallenged. But when traditional architecture was attacked in the 1930's, first by the propaganda of modernism and then by the arrival of actual European practitioners, it soon lost its hold. Cass Gilbert's Supreme Court Building in Washington, 1935 (*AC 102), seemed antedated before it was finished, and the new plantation houses in Atlanta, the Spanish baroque haciendas of Miami Beach, and the Tudor manors of Long Island have become as dated as the bizarre movie palaces of the 1920's.

Wright: The California Period

Even in California and in the work of Wright himself the thrust toward a contemporary style begun in the first decade of the century seems to have been deflected. Irving Gill, for instance, began to clothe his simplified version of the

California mission style with Spanish baroque detail (*AC 1021, *AC 1023). And, though Wright's work remained no less original or essentially organic than before, its outward appearance was influenced more than formerly by exotic eclecticism and by a further exploitation of abstract forms similar to those used at the Midway Gardens (Illustration 6–7). Both of these tendencies are illustrated in the Imperial Hotel in Tokyo, Japan (Illustration 6–9), which Wright began in 1915. Though the roof profiles are somewhat reminiscent of Japanese architecture, as are the interlocking forms and free-flowing plan, and though local brick and volcanic stone were used in the construction, the final effect, while exotic, is not oriental. The heavy forms are pre-Columbian, and the abstract ornament is not strictly Japanese but can be traced to the decorative vocabulary of the Midway Gardens, here almost grossly exaggerated in scale. Yet for all this, certain features of the hotel in its relationship to its environment represent the persistence of aspects of Wright's organic theory.

6–9.   Imperial Hotel, Tokyo, Japan, 1915–1922, by Frank Lloyd Wright.

The incorporation of gardens and courtyards into the total design and the use of specifically Japanese plantings illustrate Wright's interest in relating the building not only to its physical setting but to local tradition.

A more interesting aspect of Wright's concern with the environment is the fact that he took into account the prevalence of earthquakes in Japan. His design introduced a flexible system of interlocking cantilever construction, and provided garden pools that could be used as reservoirs to combat fires in case of earthquake. The Imperial Hotel was, in fact, one of the very few structures to survive the great cataclysm of 1922, and its pools were invaluable in quenching fires in its neighborhood.

In Wright's California houses of the early 1920's, the tension between the organic and the monumental continued. The heavy Amerindian forms, however, were more suited to the bold and harsh terrain of southern California than to the gentler landscape of Japan and were more compatible with Mexican forms, developed on the same continent and in a somewhat similar region. The first of these houses, Hollyhock House in Los Angeles, 1920 (AC 424), resembles certain Yucatán structures in mass and detail; at the same time, its total design, incorporating gardens, a pool, and pergolas, is actively interrelated with the surroundings. For his subsequent California houses, Wright developed his "textile block," a perforated hollow concrete block that permitted the passage of air but prevented the penetration of sunlight. Particularly suited to a hot and dry climate, the textile block, when combined with others filled with concrete for strength and united by steel rods for tension, was extremely adaptable and permitted consistent yet varied surfaces, monolithic forms supporting piers, and even spanning members. La Miniatura (the Millard House) in Pasadena, 1923; the John Storer House, 1923 (°AC 428B); the Charles Ennis House, 1923 (AC 429, °AC 429B); and the Samuel Freeman House, 1924 (AC 430A, AC 430B, AC 431, °AC 431A), all in Los Angeles, demonstrate various exploitations of the textile block in both structure and design. The Freeman House is like a graceful pavilion, in which the relationship between supports and openings is emphasized; the Storer and Ennis houses are massive and block-like, the latter crouching like a great Mayan monument astride a tall escarpment that affords a stunning view of Los Angeles far below and the sea beyond. Each of these houses is sensitively coordinated to its environment, especially La Miniatura, nestled in luxurious foliage, its textured patterns and the leaves of the surrounding trees mirrored in a pool. The decorative quality of the textile block is particularly attractive here, and suggests the later use of masonry screening by Edward Stone and Minoru Yamasaki.

The Richard Lloyd Jones House in Tulsa, Oklahoma, 1929 (AC 435), in which Wright also employed concrete blocks, illustrates in another way the play between abstract mass and enclosed volume, expressed here in the alternation of heavy vertical piers and fenestration, which results in a curious effect of penetrated massiveness. As in the California houses, protection against glare and the need for circulation of air are reflected in the design.

During the years in which Wright was building in Japan and California, he planned a great deal of work which was never executed, including skyscrapers and two large community programs. A small Wright skyscraper was finally built [the Price Tower at Bartlesville, Oklahoma, 1955 (AC 438)], but his designs for the Edward Doheny Ranch development in the Sierra Madre Mountains overlooking Los Angeles and for a large hotel for San Marcos in the Desert, near Chandler, Arizona, were never actualized. Both would have been notable for their unified concept and for the realization on a larger scale of the technological and formal developments in Wright's executed California houses. Furthermore, the Doheny Ranch project would have exploited the inherent grandeur of a range of hills now spoiled by chaotic development and subject to flash fires.

Not until the early 1930's did Wright come into his own again.

The Skyscraper

Meanwhile the influence of contemporary European architecture was beginning to make itself felt in the United States. Though a few other buildings, mostly domestic, were put up by the first of the European émigrés in the 1920's, it was in the skyscraper that modern architecture was first noticed publicly. After winning (with John Mead Howells) the contest for the Tribune Tower in Chicago in 1924, Raymond Hood, in his McGraw-Hill Building, 1929–1930 (AC 152), and in the Daily News Building (with Howells), 1930 (AC 153), both in New York, finally broke through the prevailing eclecticism to design two buildings which were the first direct and unadorned expression of the horizontal and vertical cage structure since the era of Sullivan.

The McGraw-Hill Building followed the tower tradition of the Wainwright and Schiller buildings and of Bruce Price's New York skyscrapers, but did not emphasize the vertical at the ex-

pense of the horizontal, for pier and spandrel were given equal importance in the design. The Daily News Building was a fairly early expression of the "slab" form of the skyscraper (the length is considerably greater than the width, a difference in dimension which is more noticeable the taller a building becomes). Both buildings were less pretentious than William Van Allen's Chrysler Building in New York, 1930 (AC 360), with its superficial "modernistic" decoration. Shreve, Lamb, and Harmon's Empire State Building, 1931 (AC 339), is a crisper, more clean-cut design than the Chrysler Building, and depends almost entirely for its effect on proportion and height, the latter emphasized by continuous vertical aluminum strips. Both structures are towers and, like the McGraw-Hill Building, symmetrical. The Daily News Building, however, is asymmetrical and the most studied in composition among the five, exploiting more imaginatively the possibilities of the setback required by the zoning laws.

In Rockefeller Center, a complex of buildings erected in New York between 1931 and 1939 (AC 154, AC 158) and designed by various architects (including Wallace Harrison), the tower form was rejected for the slab; its effective use in this group composition depends in large part on the fact that much of the area of the site was left free of buildings—the first prominent use of open space in skyscraper design. Since the zoning ordinance put no limitation on the height of a building if it occupied only one quarter of its site (as an alternative to the setback), the setback was not used as extensively at Rockefeller Center as elsewhere, thus enhancing the effect of its slab forms. Though the structures have little individual distinction, their composition as a group of simple flat shapes separated by various intervals of space is most effective. When viewed from a succession of various angles, their interrelationships provide an interesting visual and spatial experience.

Though the high-rise buildings of the early part of the twentieth century were generally larger and more technologically complex than those of the golden age of the Chicago skyscraper, few could compare with the best of the

6–10. Philadelphia Savings Fund Society (P.S.F.S.) Building, Philadelphia, Pennsylvania, 1932, by George Howe and William Lescaze.

latter in the formulation of the expression of structure in their design. One interesting exception is the former Hallidie Building (now Atkins Clothing Company) in San Francisco, by Willis Polk, 1915–1917 (AC 287). This structure, otherwise quite typical in its eclectic detail, is unique in possessing a curtain wall (the first of its kind), a glass facade cantilevered out from the supporting piers and beams so that only mullions interrupt the long, glazed facade.

The finest skyscraper of the twentieth century until after World War II, and the pacesetter for those that followed, was the Philadelphia Savings Fund Society (P.S.F.S.) Building in Philadelphia, by George Howe and William Lescaze, 1932 (AC 162, AC 163, AC 164; Illustration 6–10). Open in plan, asymmetrical, and relying on the beauty of proportion and material

rather than applied decoration, the P.S.F.S. Building was the first in which the stylistic characteristics of the International Style were conspicuously displayed in the United States, but in combination with a building type and a technology which were American. The massive, unfenestrated, tower-like section housing the equipment and services, the clearly expressed volume of the banking room (made possible by cantilevering), the flexible spaciousness of the cube containing the twenty-eight stories of offices, interrupted only by the vertical supports, and the curved shape of the five floors at the base of the tower comprise a composition both rich and subtle in its asymmetry and contrasts. The materials used are of the finest quality: on the exterior, highly polished black granite, glazed brick, and glass; in the interior, metal, glass, and marble combined in elegant juxtapositions, the marble being so highly polished that surfaces seem to interpenetrate as they reflect each other. Thus the open plan, the asymmetry, and the replacement of applied decoration by formal elements inherent in the materials and their arrangement illustrate three stylistic aspects of the International Style. The fourth—emphasis upon volume—is somewhat qualified by the bold composition of the three principal cubic areas and the massive solidity of one of them, and by an emphasis upon structure itself, that is, the prominence in the design of the relationship of pier and spandrel. This is particularly effective in the contrast between the projecting piers of the longitudinal facade of the office section with its interwoven spandrels, and in the windows and spandrels projecting beyond the piers in the narrower cantilevered facade. The somewhat cubic massiveness may be explained by the prevalence in the United States of the Beaux Arts tradition with its concentration on mass, solid construction, and defined areas. (Howe was trained in this tradition, and most American architects thought in it.) The emphasis upon the expression of structure is a recurring American practice which can be traced back to the simplified post and lintel construction of early nineteenth-century commercial buildings. Another aspect of the combination of the International Style at its most refined with certain traditions of American building in the P.S.F.S. Building is the integration between design and industry: the refinement of proportion and finish given to mass-produced materials, for instance, as illustrated in the striking effect created by the curved surface and huge dimensions of the window in the banking room, made possible by improvements in the manufacture of glass. The functional tradition in American building is also represented in the P.S.F.S. Building by the use of the large area needed to house the air conditioning machinery (this was the first large building to be so equipped) as the background for the huge illuminated letters "P.S.F.S." which stand out in the Philadelphia skyline both day and night as a bold and effective design—in addition to being excellent advertising.

The thoroughly modern design of the P.S.F.S. Building was urged upon his conservative clients by Howe, one of the first propagandists for contemporary non-eclectic architecture in the country, and was changed and refined over a long period, at first by Howe alone and later with Lescaze. The chief problem was the relation between vertical and horizontal accents, which was finally solved in the present elegant alternating structural rhythm. The result is a building which is a masterpiece of the International Style and which set a standard for what followed. The authority of its design and the use of materials so elegantly finished and juxtaposed that they rival the refinement of Mies van der Rohe's European work are qualities which alone would make the building outstanding; their combination in a dynamic design of intersecting surfaces is one of the most sophisticated exemplifications in architecture of the esthetic of the interpenetration of space and time, epitomized by cubism in the figurative arts. The integration of the plan of the P.S.F.S. Building with the industrial processes has hardly been equaled until the Seagram Building (Illustration 6–21); its emphasis on the expression of structure as well as mass and volume preceded the postwar Miesian esthetic by a dozen years; and its rhythmic articulation of horizontal and vertical elements is as fine as in such later examples as Pei's Mile-High Building, 1954, in Denver.

Architects of the International Style

The way had been partly prepared for the acceptance of the P.S.F.S. Building by the immigration to the United States a few years before of pioneers of the modern movement in Europe. After the success of Eliel Saarinen's design for the Tribune Tower (though it was not the winning design), which had opened American eyes to the possibilities of non-eclectic design in a way that was not too shocking, Saarinen himself came to the United States. His Cranbrook School, Bloomfield Hills, Michigan, 1928–1941 (AC 322), illustrates the Finnish architect's blend of craftsmanship and feeling for materials which, allied to a contemporary reinterpretation (as distinguished from imitation) of traditional forms, made his work popular in the years when modern architecture was gaining a foothold.

More essentially contemporary were two Europeans who came to Los Angeles in the mid-1920's, Rudolf Schindler and Richard Neutra. Schindler's work from the beginning was characterized by the clear-cut geometry and plane surfaces of the International Style (*AC 1057, *AC 1059A), qualities which continued on the whole unchanged in his later work, such as the Falk Apartments in Los Angeles, 1939 (AC 1056), its units interestingly juxtaposed on a steep incline, and the former Ralph Walker (now Alfonso Giella) House, also in Los Angeles, 1937 (AC 1060), which also takes advantage of a steep slope, with one side dramatically raised on concrete supports.

Richard Neutra was more influenced than Schindler by his new American environment. Arriving from Vienna in 1923, he made the ac-quaintance of the dying Sullivan in Chicago and met Frank Lloyd Wright, two experiences which imbued him with a greater respect for both the expression of structure and the relationship of a building to its site. His Lovell House in Los Angeles, 1929 (AC 266), is almost as classic an example of the integration of the International Style with certain American traditions in domestic architecture as is the P.S.F.S. in a larger building. The rectangular nicety of proportion and the clear sense of volume are European; the use of prefabricated parts, the machined precision of its detailing, and the emphasis on the structural members are American, as is the exploitation of the site, for the house opens out to a view of the canyon at whose apex it is situated. Another important building by Neutra was the Corona School, Bell, California, 1934–1935 (AC 269; Illustration 6–11), a beautiful and practical structure incorporating new ideas which became extremely influential.

6–11.   Corona School, Bell, California, 1934–1935, by Richard Neutra.

The classrooms are all on one floor; each has its own lavatory and closets, and each has light and ventilation from two sides and is equipped with a sliding glass door, one of the first uses of this device in the United States. Each classroom has a small yard (or transitional area between exterior and interior) which can be enclosed or left open by means of large canvas shades. On one facade each unit is clearly expressed in the design; on the other the unity of the whole is defined by means of a full-length cornice (with louvers for roof ventilation) and by recessed continuous fenestration above the entrances, which are further tied together by a canopy that stretches the length of the building. The light wood construction and the openness and flexibility of plan are given a deceptively monumental unity by the smooth transitions and the nicety of detail and proportion—characteristics of Neutra's work as a whole. The Corona School, together with several others in this period (to be noted later), marked the beginning of a development in a building type which after World War II comprised one of the most distinguished aspects of contemporary American architecture. [Only one other prominent school before Neutra's exemplifies the breaking away from the usual depressing box-like buildings several stories high, characteristic of secondary education architecture until then. This was the Polytechnic Elementary School at Pasadena, 1907 (AC 1027), built by Myron Hunt and Elmer Grey in the manner of Maybeck's dispersed, rambling California redwood houses—the result of an effort to find appropriate housing for the projects and programs of John Dewey's teaching theories, which required varying space needs.]

Another prominent European to arrive in America during the early 1930's was William Lescaze who, as we have seen, joined George Howe in the design of the P.S.F.S. Building. Later, working without Howe, Lescaze brought a European abstract refinement of proportion and elegance of surface to a number of commissions, most notably the handsome C.B.S. Building in Hollywood, California, 1937–1938 (AC 218), which he designed with Earl T. Heitschmidt. This crisp structure stands free in a vast parking space—one of the first designs to take into account the fact that Los Angeles was even then a completely "motorized" city.

After the coming to power of the Nazis in Germany and the eventual closing of the Bauhaus, its director, Walter Gropius, came to the United States in 1937, followed by Ludwig Mies van der Rohe in 1939. The prominence of these men, and the importance of their academic positions—Mies became director of the Illinois Institute of Technology, and Gropius head of the School of Design at Harvard—finally broke the back of eclecticism. Mies received a large and influential commission at the time of his appointment: the entire new campus of the Illinois Institute of Technology in Chicago, 1939–1956 (AC 248). This complex marks a change or development in Mies's style: the plan is axial and rigidly symmetrical, and the buildings, while retaining openness and clearly defined structural articulation, are almost classically formal in their balanced composition. (These deviations from the principles of the International Style, prefiguring the gradual breakdown of the style after World War II, occur in the work of one of its founders.) Among the buildings themselves, which have gradually made their appearance since 1939, are the Power House and the Metallurgical Research Center (AC 250), built just before the war. Even the former is notable for the care with which detail, proportion, and materials have been worked out in its design. In these buildings Mies reduced his vocabulary to an almost mannered simplicity, emphasizing the clear statement of exposed frame, painted black, with in-filling of glass and bricks. There is no concession (except to an efficient and flexible space within the framework) to any local circumstance or accident to mar the almost Mondrian-like purity of surface and proportion. Only the emphasis on the structural frame indicates any awareness on the part of Mies of the tradition of his American environment (that is, in the design; Mies took full advantage of mass-produced elements made possible by American industrialization).

Gropius was more amenable than Mies to local circumstances and traditions. Though more active as a teacher than a builder until he resigned from Harvard in 1953, he designed, with his former Bauhaus associate Marcel Breuer, a few unpretentious houses in the suburbs of Boston which are far from being doctrinaire examples of the International Style. His own house at Lincoln, Massachusetts, 1938 (*AC 33A, AC 34), and a weekend house for Mrs. Henry G. Chamberlain at nearby Wayland, 1940 (AC 43), are the most attractive of these. In both houses the architects used the traditional material of wood, and in the latter, particularly, they adapted themselves to the more informal plan of the American rural tradition. In the house at Lincoln something of the arbitrary rectilinearity of the International Style persists, though the angles and overhangs are adapted to the circumstances of orientation and shade. The Chamberlain House has an abstract beauty of silhouette with openings arranged in an elegant asymmetry which, combined with the informality of porches and the rustic free-standing stone fireplace, has considerable charm.

The work of Saarinen, Neutra, Mies, Gropius, and Breuer before the war was only the beginning of an important subsequent production. Meanwhile the influence of their ideas and the designs of others like Lescaze, together with the critical influences developing at the same time, created an atmosphere suitable for the cultivation of modern architecture by Americans.

Wright: The Middle Years

It is difficult to ignore the probable influence of the International Style on the later work of Frank Lloyd Wright, though he was the first to deny it. In a sense he was correct in doing so, for it could just as easily be said that the influence was the other way around, since the formulation of the International Style was partly inspired by Wright's early work published in Berlin in 1910. The greater elegance and simplicity, the more studied flow of space in Wright's work in the 1930's may just as well have been the result of the logical and natural development of a sensitive artist, refining what had already existed in his early work, as of the consequences of outside influence. In any event, Wright's

later work, from the formal point of view, became characterized by a greater crispness and a less dated abstraction, while retaining its organic aspects.

The building that prophesied the closing of the hiatus between Wright's organic prairie houses and those of the 1930's was Taliesin III, Spring Green, Wisconsin, 1925 (AC 434, AC 434A, AC 434B). More sophisticated in both plan and elevation than the Willitts or Robie houses, in it Wright adapted their open plan and formal subtleties to a site that is higher and more irregular than the flat areas of the Chicago suburbs. Taking advantage of view and contour, and using the local stone for building material, the house with its tall split-level living room and low-lying wings is as thoroughly adapted to its more complex environment as the prairie and California houses were to theirs. Taliesin III offered a foretaste of a further fulfillment of Wright's organic theories, combined with a greater formal refinement, which were to be demonstrated later both in houses for wealthy clients and in less pretentious variations on what Wright called his "Usonian" house. Both kinds of dwellings were explored in theory in Wright's designs for Broadacre City, where he was concerned with the problem of city and regional planning in general and with the skyscraper. Broadacre City was Wright's answer to Le Corbusier's City for Three Million People, to which (in spite of obvious differences) it can be compared. Both plans deal with the relation of living, working, and producing units to each other and to the total environment, and with the problem posed by automotive traffic. But whereas Le Corbusier's plan has much of the arbitrary formality of the Mediterranean tradition, Wright's is unschematic, loose, and varied. This is true not only of the site itself, which he would have kept as it was and not bulldozed into an area uncomplicated with contour lines, but also of the informal arrangement of its structures. In the models for individual buildings such as the large House on the Mesa and the Walter Davison Sheet Steel Farm Units, both shown at the epoch-making exhibition in 1932 at the Museum of Modern Art, it was clear

6–12. Falling Water (the Edgar J. Kaufmann House), Bear Run, Pennsylvania, 1936, by Frank Lloyd Wright.

that here was a new Wright whose work fitted nicely into the categories of the recently coined term, the International Style. His buildings were free-flowing, volumetric, and sparing of extraneous decoration, though they were at the same time less deliberate in their asymmetry and far more related to environmental factors.

The most prominent of the executed large houses of the 1930's, Falling Water (the Edgar J. Kaufmann House), a summer residence built over the stream called Bear Run in the western slopes of the Alleghenies near Connellsville, Pennsylvania, 1936 (AC 446, AC 446A, AC 447, AC 448, AC 448A; Illustration 6–12), epitomizes both the organic theories of Wright and the characteristics of the International Style in what is generally considered to be one of the architectural masterpieces of the century. The exploitation of the immediate environment is as

brilliant and imaginative as in the gardens of baroque Italy. The stream, especially, is exploited in every possible way: as a flooring seen through glass, as a swimming pool, and as a cooling waterfall, its splashing heard throughout the house and its spray cooling the air. The hillside is utilized as a foundation from which the cantilevered structure dramatically springs, and the forms of its horizontally striated rocks are repeated in the emphasized horizontals of the building; local stone, laid in roughly quarried horizontals, is employed for the central mass of the building. Orientation to the sun and to prevailing air currents are other aspects of the adaptation of the house to its environment and, together with the site and the planning of functions and facilities, control its plan and elevation. But the architectural forms resulting from these circumstances, and the structural device of cantilevering, which is so prominent, are then organized by Wright into a culmination of his "form is function" theory in a design as sophisticated, ordered, and refined as any by Mies, and with as much subtlety of spatial relationship. The combination of all these factors has resulted in a house which, in the organization of its rectilinear forms, its two-dimensional pattern, and its three-dimensional interpenetrations, not only sums up the esthetic of the twentieth century from cubism to constructionism, but adds an even greater dynamism in the relation between building and environment. (In contrast to Wright, Le Corbusier remained essentially static, sculpturesque, and Mediterranean, and Gropius confined his movement rather arbitrarily within his walls.)

The character of Falling Water is as different from that of the projected House on the Mesa as are all Wright's houses from each other. His buildings are as varied as the sites on which they were built. The Paul R. Hanna House (now owned by Stanford University) in Palo Alto, California, 1937 (AC 456, AC 456A, AC 457, *AC 457A, *AC 457C), for instance, demonstrates an adaptability to an environment entirely different from the other two, in this case a sparsely wooded hillock with twisted trees that appear almost oriental, in a countryside with some grass and a reddish earth. In this landscape (as clear and sun-struck as southern California, but greener), the red brick, redwood framing, and lattice work of its structure and the studied irregularity and openness of its plan combine to give the house a rural character. The irregularity, however, is deliberately deceptive, for the house is carefully organized in plan, depending on a hexagon as the basis of its design. This geometric form is very adaptable to Wright's desire for flexibility of orientation and for flow and interpenetration of plan; at the same time it prevents the design from becoming chaotic.

Each commission in domestic architecture evoked from Wright a particular solution. For example, the Boomer House, built about 1946 at Scottsdale, in the Arizona desert, seems like a great lens focused on the mountains, for the two-story living room opens out to the view like a rectangular cornucopia, while the remaining rooms trail out behind in a carefully integrated system of interpenetrating angles. In the George D. Sturges House, Brentwood Heights, California, 1939 (AC 467), Wright used the cantilever again, as at Falling Water, but here to extend the structure out over a canyon; the long horizontality of the house is emphasized by a roof terrace and by continuous lapped redwood siding surrounding the balcony upon which the main rooms open.

Like its larger counterpart, the House on the Mesa, the small dwelling was included in Wright's proposal for Broadacre City, and was eventually realized in several versions. The first was the Malcolm Willey House, Minneapolis, Minnesota, 1934 (AC 443, AC 444), in which the kitchen or "work space" as Wright called it, is partially incorporated with the living–dining room, another exemplification of Wright's adaptation to contemporary conditions, in this case the decline in domestic service. However, the slightly later Herbert Jacobs House, 1934, in Westmoreland near Madison, Wisconsin, represents a closer approach to Wright's "Usonian" ideal— that is, a house which a person with an average income can afford. Resting on a concrete slab that incorporates radiant heating, the core of the structure, housing the kitchen and bathroom, is raised above the rest of the house for ventilation. The remainder of the house, which could be attached in other versions to the central core according to the desired orientation and spatial relationships, is of wide board and batten, with all posts eliminated except the frames of the French doors opening out from the living room and from the bedroom wings. The Jacobs House, quite inexpensive and potentially viable as a model for mass production, was succeeded by a number of variations, the most sophisticated being the Goetsch-Winkler House, 1939 (Illustration 6–13), the only executed example of a number proposed for a site at Okemos, Michigan. Here the horizontal accent of the main mass is an improvement over the rather nervous repetitive uprights of the Jacobs House, and a clever use of clerestory fenestration adds the drama of light to that of

6–13.   Interior, Goetsch-Winkler House, Okemos, Michigan, 1939, by Frank Lloyd Wright.

volume and mass. In both plan and elevation the design of this house is not unlike Mies's Barcelona Pavilion, with its refinement of proportion and movement. The Lloyd Lewis House, Libertyville, Illinois, 1940 (AC 468, AC 468A, AC 469), a somewhat more ambitious variant of the Okemos house, is built on a terrain involving different levels.

Wright's experiments with the skyscraper began in his very early (1895) design for the Luxfer Prism Building, which preceded Sullivan's Schlesinger and Meyer Department Store by three years and was almost as expressive of the steel cage. But Wright did not return to the high-rise building until his project, almost thirty years later, for the National Life Insurance Company Building in Chicago, in which he preferred the principle of the cantilever to that of the cage. This structural system was more simply and beautifully expressed in the 1932 project for St. Mark's Tower (Illustration 6–14), which would have been the first building in New York by the country's greatest architect had it not been for the financial discouragement of the architect's backers during the depression. The design for the tower was polygonal in plan and consisted of interlocking duplex apartments at different levels with carefully worked-out exposures, clustered around a hollow core of concrete (from which the floors were cantilevered) containing elevators, entrance halls, and the services for each apartment.

The basic formula for St. Mark's Tower was increased in scope in projects for grouped apartment towers at Chicago and in the proposed Crystal Heights Hotel in Washington, but it was not actually realized (and then on a much smaller scale) until the Price Tower, Bartlesville, Oklahoma, 1955 (AC 438). This building represents one of the few actualizations in the United States of a principle in skyscraper design which is quite different from the usual cage; it is equally practical (and, if we can believe Wright, less costly), as well as susceptible to more varied and imaginative treatment.

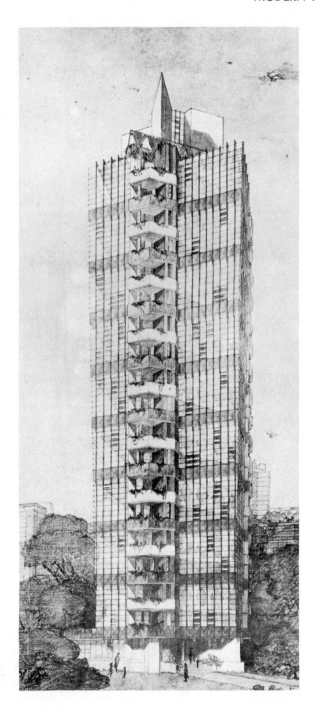

Two of the large-scale projects designed during the period between the two World Wars were executed, however: Taliesin West, 1938, Wright's school and residence in the desert at Scottsdale, Arizona; and Florida Southern College, Lakeland, Florida, 1940 (AC 471). Of Wright's many ambitious programs the latter is the most extensive to be realized, for it incorporates an entire college in the setting of a large orange grove sloping toward a lake. Planned around two axes, the Annie Pfeiffer Chapel (AC 472, AC 473) and the library, the ordered asymmetry of the campus is held together by diagonal axes and long colonnades and is separated from its immediate surroundings by an encircling pavement. The design has both monumentality and movement and takes into account the need for extensive parking areas. The architectural forms and their details show a reversion by Wright to Mayan or Aztec prototypes, though the colonnades and some of the geometric detail also recall the architecture of the Spanish missions. The chapel is the most distinguished single building in the complex, being especially notable for its tower, a source of light for the interior, and for the treatment of light itself, indirect and permeating.

Taliesin West, Scottsdale, Arizona, 1938 (AC 459, AC 460, *AC 460A, AC 460B, AC 460C, AC 461, AC 462, AC 463; Illustration 6–15), is as much of a unit though not as large in scale as Florida Southern College, and more original. Here Wright found the perfect expression of the settlement in the desert, the isolated "camp" for himself, his family, his students and followers. The basic forms of Taliesin West, constructed mostly of a richly textured agglomerate of reddish-purple desert rock and concrete (used also in the Boomer House), seem in shape, color, and texture to be a very part of the mountainous desert land upon which the buildings are situated. The solid architectural masses are combined, however, with the openness of the large drafting room (which is roofed with movable canvas louvers adjustable to light, air, and very occasional rain) and with the open loggias, which are covered with pergolas to

6–14. St. Mark's Tower (project), New York, New York, 1932, by Frank Lloyd Wright. (Drawing published in *Architectural Forum*, January, 1938.)

6–15. Detail of Taliesin West, Scottsdale, Arizona, 1938, by Frank Lloyd Wright.

create passageways not too brilliantly sunny and yet open to every breath of passing air. The whole complex is dynamically oriented toward the desert and the mountains, and incorporates the desert flora into its design—the spiny cactus planted in specific areas are nearly as important in the total effect as are the structures themselves.

In the last years before the war Wright experimented with formal devices beyond the hexagon, including the circle. The 1938 project for the Ralph Jester House was conceived entirely in terms of circles and curves, and was to be executed in masonry, concrete, or plywood (the last a relatively new material which Wright used with characteristic originality). Far less formal and arbitrary and more related to Wright's essential organicism were the curved forms developed at the Johnson's Wax Admin-

istration Building, Racine, Wisconsin, 1936–1939 (AC 451, *AC 452, AC 453, AC 453A; Illustration 6–16). Here function, equipment, and movement (that is, the pattern of activity) motivated the total design in plan, elevation, volume, and mass. The "nostrils" (Wright's term for the air conditioning) serve as the axes around which the outlines of the sections in the plan seem to be stretched like elastic bands. The resulting curved walls are composed of layers of horizontally alternating brick and glass which surround (but do not support) the great cave of the principal office room, whose roof areas, consisting of circular surfaces alternating with glass, are supported by hollow concrete piers tapering from a narrow base and spreading out to support the discs above. The relationship of the parts of the building to each other as one area seems literally to move

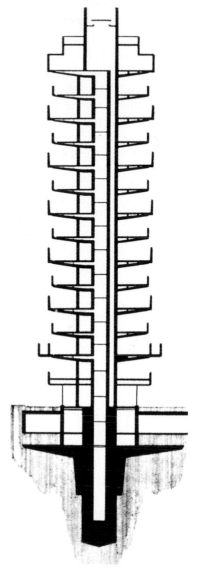

6–16. S. C. Johnson and Son Administration Building, Racine, Wisconsin, 1936–1939, by Frank Lloyd Wright.   Detail (*top*), view of building at night (*bottom*), cross-section drawing of Research Tower (*right*).

into contact with another displays itself in a dynamic plasticity reminiscent of constructivist sculpture and of the abstract work of artists like Pevsner and Gabo. Perhaps the beauty and formal refinement of this extraordinary building are seen best at twilight or at night, when the bands of glass become bands of illumination —the first, and still the most successful, use of artificial lighting as a deliberate part of the total design, a fact which again demonstrates Wright's receptivity to the possibilities of a given situation.

Domestic Architecture

The most prominent houses in the modern style in the 1920's and early 1930's were those by European émigrés or by architects influenced by them. By the mid-1930's, however, Wright's theories and executed buildings were the most influential factors in shaping the course of domestic architecture. Wright's organicism was paralleled and supplemented to a certain degree by the work of the elder Saarinen and later by the more contemporary Scandinavians (especially Alvar Aalto) and, after the 1939 World's Fair in New York, by the Brazilian architects Lucio Costa and Oscar Niemeyer. Besides being somewhat influenced by Le Corbusier, the Brazilians used native materials and curved and cellular forms (as did the American master), and built with a certain informality of plan. Their architecture represented in some respects a reaction against the coldness, austerity, and technological finish of the International Style, particularly as these qualities became more pronounced in the work of Mies van der Rohe after he came to America. At the same time, the California tradition of the Greenes and Maybeck was being revived by William W. Wurster and his associates at the University of California at Berkeley. The net results of all these factors in domestic architecture were freedom of plan and elevation, a fuller relationship to site and environment, and more variety of form. But few examples had the assurance and adaptability of Wright's work, with the possible exception of the Weston Havens House by Harwell Hamilton Harris. However, Wright's similar Sturges House preceded the Havens House by a year.

Of all the California architects, Harris is the closest link between the generation of Maybeck and the flourishing post-World War II school in that state. A house by him in Fellowship Park, Los Angeles, 1937 (*AC 134, *AC 134B, *AC 134C), is of wood, with conspicuous framing, wide eaves, and sliding panels opening to the surrounding wooded landscape. These elements are treated with a sensitivity to craftsmanship, detail, and site which is as Japanese

6–17. Weston Havens House, Berkeley, California, 1940, by Harwell Hamilton Harris. (Photo by Man Ray.)

in its refinement as the design itself. Less obviously inspired by Far Eastern sources is Harris' masterpiece, the Weston Havens House, Berkeley, California, 1940 (AC 136B, AC 136C, AC 136D, AC 137; Illustration 6–17), still one of the most admired examples of contemporary domestic architecture, a combination of modern technology with the organic tradition as it had developed in California. The house is situated at the very climax of the high ridge overlooking Berkeley, the bay, and San Francisco. By cantilevering the building from the steep hillside, Harris took full advantage of a most magnificent site. From the porch, soaring out over empty space, the vast prospect seems funneled into the living room by the slanting roof. In contrast, the other side of the house opens into an enclosed court, whose restriction is a welcome foil to the spaciousness of the western view. The use of redwood throughout lends informality to a quite large residence and at the same time links it both to the wooded hillside and to local tradition; the prominent framing, in its emphasis on construction, echoes the bold engineering of the cantilever. No one else in California until that time had exploited the native tradition and the landscape to such an extent as Harris did in this house.

The Marvin L. Heckendorf House, Modesto, California, 1939 (AC 97), by John Funk, offers agreeable solutions to the regional problem of hot weather, by orientation to the prevailing breeze, and to a local problem of traffic-filled streets: one side faces a shaded court and the other a covered porch bordered by a garden which is enclosed from the street. Such a house sets the pace for an architecture that is less consciously reminiscent of local tradition than is Harris' work. But the regional emphasis was to be revived later not only in California, but especially in the Northwest. John Yeon's A. R. Wetzek House, Portland, Oregon, 1937 (AC 501), is the first important example of this trend, which was to become more prominent after the war. Constructed on a height with a superb view that includes Mount Hood, the house takes full advantage of its location in its design, the environmental relationship being emphasized in a courtyard and portico. The plan has the informal, spread-out character of a large hunting lodge or mountain guest house. The material is wood, employed in such a way as to bring out the qualities of its framing and the angles of its pitched roofs.

Except for a few outstanding exceptions, modern domestic architecture in the East followed more closely the principles of the International Style than it did the native organic tradition. Even Neutra in the John Nicolas Brown House on Fisher's Island, off the Connecticut coast, reverts to an abstract elegance more related to Mies than to his own more organic California architecture, and Edward Stone's house for the collector A. Conger Goodyear, in Old Westbury, Long Island, employs an almost Miesian geometry and machine-precise nicety of detailing. The actual disciple of Mies, Philip Johnson, followed his master well in the charming small house he built for himself but later sold in Cambridge, Massachusetts, a beautifully proportioned and detailed box, one wall of which, all glass, looks out on a yard which in its proportions and in the height of the wall protecting it from the street is an extension of the building.

The most distinguished exception to these houses in the International Style is George Howe's Fortune Rock House, Somesville, Maine, 1939 (AC 166, AC 166A), situated dramatically at the very end of Somes Sound, on Mount Desert Island. Howe used cantilever to project the living room and its porch out over the water to encompass the splendid view down the length of the Sound to the distant Atlantic. At the same time he used the framed structure, pitched roof, and stone fireplace of the indigenous vernacular tradition in the remainder of the house, qualifying it only by the inclusion of larger areas of fenestration, made possible by the improvements in glass manufacture. In the use of modern techniques and materials, the exploitation of site, and the continuation of local structural and formal traditions, Wright himself could hardly have done better in this locale.

Aside from Fortune Rock House in the East, there is little to match the work of Wright or Harris, except Carl Koch's Snake Hill Houses, 1940, at Belmont, near Cambridge, Massachusetts. These are more organic even than Howe's house, being freer of arbitrary symmetries, and going as far as any dwellings—especially in the one Koch built for himself (now owned by A. G. Hill) (AC 204, AC 204A)—to exploit the view (a panorama of greater Boston) and actually to incorporate part of the rocky hillside and its vegetation into the house itself. The intimacy of relation to the exterior is further enhanced by the use of native rock for the fireplace.

Non-domestic Architecture

Aside from the skyscraper, the house, and the work of Wright in general, the most interesting modern architecture before the Second World War was educational or industrial (excepting community housing programs, to be discussed in a later section). In addition to Neutra's Corona School there were three other pacesetting schools (incorporating some features of Neutra's design: the Kensington (Maryland) Junior High School, 1938 (AC 52), by Rhees E. Burket; Acalanes Union High School, Lafayette, California, 1940–1941 (AC 214, AC 215, AC 215A), by Ernest J. Kump (then of Kump and Franklin); and the Crow Island Elementary School, Winnetka, Illinois, 1940 (AC 327), by Eero and Eliel Saarinen, and Perkins, Wheeler, and Will. The three buildings typify characteristics which were to become standard in the postwar period. They are attractive in form and color, exploiting a good site or improving a mediocre one; they are seldom too repetitive, no matter how large, and areas for various functions and age groups are differentiated in the design. Dispersion over a large site was first solved at Kensington, though the large rural school at Lafayette met the problem more deliberately two years later. The Kensington School is the most informal in appearance, making conspicuous use of wood; Kump's Acalanes School is of straightforward loft or factory-like metal and glass construction, efficient and sensible, if a little too technological in appearance. The Crow Island School is subtler in design and execution, implementing the Winnetka School Board's advanced educational ideas, which required not only practical efficiency but encouragement of the child's sense of freedom and security. Each classroom has its own workshop, lavatory, and court, and each age group has its separate area (features similar to Neutra's Corona School). The building, however, is characterized by a heavy massiveness that makes it less prophetic of the future than Kump's building in Lafayette.

A building somewhat related to these schools is the former United States Merchant Marine Cadet School (now San Mateo Junior College), San Mateo, California, 1942 (AC 1013), built by Gardner A. Dailey. An emergency building of simple and easily erected construction, the school has what the Museum of Modern Art called an unregimented order which is refreshing. The rooms, all on one floor, are arranged in a flexible and meandering plan that avoids monotony by the surprises of new perspectives and vistas as the building accommodates itself to the forested terrain.

The swing to contemporary design was slower in higher education than in primary and secondary schools. Mies's Illinois Institute of Technology and Wright's Florida Southern College were the most prominent exceptions in a field still overshadowed by the eclecticism displayed in the "medieval" Colleges at Yale and the Georgian Houses at Harvard. There were one or two exceptions, however. Anderson and Beckwith's swimming pool at the Massachusetts Institute of Technology, Cambridge, Massachusetts, 1940 (AC 8), is a handsome unadorned area illuminated by a huge window across its length. The simple elements of two pools, walls, fenestration, and a slanted spectator area are combined with interesting color in a composition of considerable distinction. The Recreation Building, at Great Lakes Naval Training Station, Illinois, 1942 (*AC 340, *AC 340A), an early work by Skidmore, Owings & Merrill, is distinguished for the display and variety of its wooden structural elements and for the informal character it retains in spite of its large size.

Public buildings and churches were even more ridden by conservatism than were colleges and universities. The First Christian Church (formerly Tabernacle Church of Christ) at Columbus, Indiana, 1940 (AC 324, AC 325), by Eliel and Eero Saarinen is among the first of the modern churches (excluding those by Frank Lloyd Wright and Purcell and Elmslie before World War I). Though the massing of the towers and the block-like forms generally date the building, the exploitation of light and space and the refined brick work give an impression of eloquent simplicity and restraint which is distinctive. Franklin, Kump and Associates' City Hall at Fresno, California, 1941 (AC 92), has a similar rectilinear heaviness— a concession to the need for monumentality in a public building, but resulting in an unfortunate qualification of its design, which otherwise reflects an efficient organization. The Museum of Modern Art, New York, 1939 (AC 119), by Philip Goodwin and Edward Stone, is perhaps the most distinguished public building of the period. Its exhibition areas are entirely flexible, being interrupted only by the supports, and separated from the business and service areas, which are concentrated in one section. The building also contains a fine auditorium with undulating walls and ceilings (for acoustical reasons), and a Members' penthouse with a balcony affording a view of the mid-Manhattan skyline.

Two hospitals are notable for their pioneering modern design: Ganster and Pereira's Lake County Tuberculosis Sanitarium, Waukegan, Illinois, 1940 (AC 98), and the Triboro Hospital, Jamaica, New York, 1941 (*AC 84). Open in plan and oriented for light and air, their efficiency is unhampered by the requirements of eclecticism or the tyranny of the cube.

In addition to Frank Lloyd Wright's Johnson's Wax Administration Building, in the field of industrial architecture only the buildings of Albert Kahn are outstanding—as much for their engineering as their architecture. During the second and third decades of the century, Kahn's factories were already the only structures comparable in their modernity to the work of Wright and his progressive contemporaries. The Third Ford Factory, Highland Park, Michigan, 1910–1917 (AC 187, AC 188), is notable for its direct and functional architectural approach, unqualified by eclectic reminiscence, and for a sense of spaciousness in its huge glass-covered courtyard. In the Ford Motor Company Administration Building, Dearborn, Michigan, 1928 (*AC 189A), Kahn eschewed all decoration and let the building speak for itself in the direct language of its shapes alone. As the century advanced, the logistics of large-scale planning and mass-produced units made of Kahn's office a kind of "plan factory" more typical of the architectural offices of the post-World War II period. Yet the very scale of his work gives it a sweep and expanse which are impressive and enhanced by what seems to be a somewhat conscious elegance of proportion, though this may simply be the natural consequence of efficient design. The Burroughs Adding Machine Company Building, Plymouth, Michigan, 1938 (AC 193), for instance, articulates a flexible plan for mass production into a quite formally satisfying structure.

For extent and for logic of arrangement, Kahn's factory for the Ford Motor Company at Willow Run, Michigan, 1942 (AC 196), is an impressive monument to the industrial age. His Dodge Half-Ton Truck Plant, Warren Township, Michigan, 1938 (AC 191, *AC 192), a quarter-mile long, with cantilevered areas of great expanse, is a masterpiece of functional architecture expressing in its design various structural and spatial organizations.

The fact that Albert Kahn employed rectilinear forms exclusively and had little use for the more expressive forms of concrete is simply a reflection of the circumstances of American mass production of steel and the greater labor expense involved in the use of concrete. In contrast, Ely Kahn's municipal asphalt plant in New York, 1944 (AC 197), constructed of reinforced concrete, is curvilinear; but both of these factors are the result of the efficient use of space to house the various functions of the edifice, and not the consequence of a deliberate design program. As impressive as the work of Albert Kahn and, like his, as much engineering as architecture, are the great dams and power houses of the Tennessee Valley Authority (T.V.A.). Two can be pointed out for their unusual esthetic merit, the Norris Dam in Norris, Tennessee, 1936 (AC 359), and the Watts Bar Steam Plant near Dayton, Tennessee, built in 1942 under the direction of Roland Warak.

Some of the great engineering structures built to meet the necessities of increased motor traffic should not be overlooked, though they may not be strictly architecture. The Pulaski Skyway, Hudson County, New Jersey, 1930 (*CPC 170), an elevated highway between Hoboken and Newark, is one of the most visually dramatic structures of the century. The suspension bridges —the George Washington, 1927–1931 (AC 101), and Bronx-Whitestone, 1939 (AC 7), both in New York; the Golden Gate, 1933–1937 (CPC 274D, CPC 274E), connecting San Francisco to Marin County; and the San Francisco-Oakland Bay, 1936 (CPC 274A, CPC 274B, CPC 274C)—are triumphs of engineering and worthy successors to the Brooklyn Bridge as beautiful and visually exciting landmarks.

From World War II to the Present

The years immediately after World War II were dominated by technological classicism in the form of a Miesian adaptation of the International Style to American technological conditions and stylistic traditions, ranging from large-scale programs to houses for individuals. Romantic naturalism was temporarily in eclipse but gained ground in the 1950's, and more recently these two basic aspects of modern architecture have tended to blend. Meanwhile, advances in technology found expression in an architecture of greatly enhanced spatial and structural richness. During the last few years the introduction of an abstract beauty which is not primarily the expression of structure and function has evidenced a widespread reaction against the principles of the International Style and of technological classicism, a trend supplemented by the use of forms derived from exotic or historical sources. At the same time there has occurred a restatement of the expressive relation of function and form in a new monumentality characterized by a rejection of the linear interpenetrations of the International Style, and deriving its unity not from fluidity but from the composition of separate and defined parts dramatically and even eccentrically composed.

The revival of building after the war benefited from the continuing revolution in technology, which had been accelerated by the war itself. The invention of new materials such as translucent plastic added new dimensions to the formal vocabulary as well as to the practical function of architecture, while the development of various kinds of molded forms—reinforced concrete, plastic, and laminated wood—destroyed the tyranny of the rectangle and afforded opportunities for new kinds of beauty and expressiveness. Less conspicuous than such innovations in material and structure, but often as far-reaching in their effect on architecture, were developments in what could be called services: heating and air conditioning, lighting, acoustics, and even the control of form, light, and color by the application of the principles of the psychology of perception, formerly left to "taste" or, more accurately, to chance. These factors, hidden or ignored by most architects, served others, such as Wright and Mies, as opportunities for formal treatment. Artificial illumination especially (particularly after the perfection of fluorescent lighting in 1938) presented a variety of possibilities ranging from ambient and fluctuating interior luminosity to exterior spotlighting and modeling.

New building types which are the consequence of the highly technological civilization of the present, for example, airport terminals, atomic reactor plants, parking garages, motels, and shopping centers, are so obvious that they are taken for granted. More specifically, the rapid increase in the use of the automobile has resulted in the growth of suburbia, the decay of the city center, and the expansion of the superhighway or throughway systems—developments which have been accompanied not only by new building types but also by other consequences to architecture. The need for parking space, for instance, has played as important a part in the new landscape as the superhighway and its approaches. Some buildings are designed to stand isolated in a large parking area, and whole complexes are planned with parking space as important as any other element in their program. Many buildings, singly or in groups, are now seen more frequently from a mobile than a static (or relatively static) point of view. Yet very few single buildings or even groups of buildings have been designed with this factor in mind, Neutra's Channel Heights, 1943 (Illustration 6–34), being an outstanding exception, since the architect deliberately laid out his plan according to this principle. Much of the brash liveliness of the American scene derives from the appearance of buildings catering to the motorist, yet few architects of distinction have been involved in

6–18. Crown Hall, Illinois Institute of Technology, Chicago, Illinois, 1952, by Ludwig Mies van der Rohe.

the design of any of them. Hardly a filling station, for instance, has benefited from their attention, and motels have fared only a little better.[17]

Technological Classicism

The first decade of the postwar period was dominated by the work and influence of Mies van der Rohe. The impact of his master plan for the Illinois Institute of Technology, executed before the war, was increased as the actual buildings appeared one by one. The design of the structures is appropriate both in relation to the technology taught within them and in the character of their execution. At the same time, they retain that elegance of material, detail, and proportion for which Mies was noted in Europe. Mies's guiding principles, summed up in his own phrase *"Wenig ist mehr"* ("less

is more"), have resulted in buildings whose functions are hardly distinguishable, since the means of their construction are so simple; each unit is essentially only a given amount of space enclosed by horizontals and verticals in a modular system. In fact, the Power Plant, the Alumni Memorial Hall, and even the chapel are variations on the basic structural theme of the Metallurgical Research Center, 1939 (AC 250), the first of Mies's buildings on the campus. The principles of Mies's construction are as elementary as the post and lintel system of Greek architecture, and he handles his steel, glass, and brick as carefully as the Greek masons did their stone. Crown Hall, the Architecture Building, 1952 (AC 256, AC 257, AC 257A; Illustration 6–18), is somewhat different from the other structures in being even simpler and thus in fact *"beinahe nichts"* ("almost nothing," another of Mies's favorite expressions). The edifice is essentially a glass-walled volume hung on four great girders, the only prominent additional element being the large entrance platform which seems to hover in front of the building, repeating the horizontals of its roof and floors. Subtle in proportion and scale, meticulous in detail, Crown Hall is a paradigm of Miesian architecture: functional, modular, and beautiful.

It might be thought that the Miesian simplicity would be too limited for adaptation to domestic architecture. Nevertheless, Mies's apartments, essentially identical volumes in a larger transparent one, are successful because of the mobility of their areas and the compatibility of their proportions. Mies's Promontory Apartments, 1950 (AC 260), and those at 860 Lake Shore Drive, 1951 (AC 262; Illustration 6–19), both in Chicago, and later ones which are part of urban complexes at Detroit and Newark, are similar to one another except for slight variations in the treatment of the supports and in their color. The two buildings which comprise the apartment houses at 860 Lake Shore Drive are the most effective, due to their relation to each other and to the surrounding area. The attenuated volumes are transparent when seen in certain lights and from certain angles; from other angles they reflect each other as well as the sky and nearby Lake Michigan. The even rhythm of their surfaces is further varied by the chance arrangement of the window draperies, which are all a uniform gray on the side facing the exterior, acting as a foil for the black framework of the structure itself. Tall, dark, and austere, these buildings have a brittle quality well-suited to their northern site. They are especially effective in winter, when they are silhouetted against the snow and the gray waters of the lake.

Mies's other structures are similarly simple in conception: the new wing of the Houston Museum of Fine Arts, 1958–1959, is a curved variation of Crown Hall, and the Seagram Building (done with Philip Johnson), in New York, is the culmination of his high-rise buildings.

Mies's elegant cages and suspended volumes have served as the ideal of an architecture which

6–19. Apartment house, 860 Lake Shore Drive, Chicago, Illinois, 1951, by Ludwig Mies van der Rohe.

can be easily designed and built and which offers within its limits both flexibility of plan and the potential of ultimate refinement. Steel and concrete frames; glass, plastic, or other envelopes; concrete or ferroconcrete slabs or shells used for floor or covering—these are the given elements which can be mass-produced in modular sections and areas, and which in various combinations have a natural tendency to develop in certain systems and forms. In the hands of its originator, the Miesian manner can be developed and refined in structures of exquisite articulation and precision. On the other hand, its logic can be turned into a vernacular adaptable to the mass production and technological organization required by much present-day construction. Such work, almost "bureaucratic" in its efficiency and practical appropriateness, lacks the personal statement of Mies's emphasis on the beauty of structure for its own sake. At its best it is impersonal and anonymous; at its worst it errs in the direction of added decorative effects and strident color in its attempt to avoid monotony and to achieve the appearance of originality.

The persisting popularity of this Mies-derived style in the United States can be explained by characteristics that appeal to certain aspects of the American temperament and taste: its almost scientific objectivity, its adaptability to technological processes; and, at the same time, its smooth, flat surfaces, its neatness and precision, and its rectilinearity (which coincides with the grid plan of most American cities).

Miesian bureaucratic architecture is particularly viable for large architectural firms and for the extensive programs commissioned by corporate clients. The research and preparation involved in such enterprises as the Air Force Academy or a large skyscraper, and the organization, scheduling, and dovetailing of various engineering procedures are facilitated by the adaptation of the Miesian formula. Such national firms as Skidmore, Owings & Merrill are large corporations equipped to handle any architectural problem no matter how massive, largely because they act within the framework of an esthetic which is as contemporary as their own technological problems.

Since the modular system of this style is equally adaptable to vertical or horizontal extension, not only the skyscraper but other large-scale designs have benefited from its application. Outstanding examples in three categories of building are the complexes at the General Motors Technical Center, Warren, Michigan, 1949–1956 (AC 309, AC 310, AC 311, AC 312, AC 313), by Saarinen, Saarinen and Associates; the Connecticut General Life Insurance Company Building, Bloomfield, Connecticut, 1957 (Illustration 6–20); and the Air Force Academy in Colorado, the latter two by Skidmore, Owings & Merrill. Of these the earliest and probably

6–20. Connecticut General Life Insurance Company Building, Bloomfield, Connecticut, 1957, by Skidmore, Owings & Merrill.

the most interesting is the General Motors Technical Center, in which a large sum was expended to create an environment intended to be conducive to creative thinking and research. The modular beauty of proportion and the ordered spaciousness of arrangement in this complex demonstrate that practical or functional architecture can be esthetically satisfying, a fact which is emphasized by the contrast of the Research Center with the tawdry, unplanned, and characterless landscape of the industrial suburbia surrounding it. The general plan of the Center is similar to that of the Illinois Institute of Technology in its rectilinear regularity (but not quite so well integrated) and is varied with picturesque or romantic forms such as domes and cylinders and with pools and fountains. The individual buildings, essentially steel cages faced with glass or brick, are adaptable to flexible adjustment for various uses and employ the newest technological processes. Here, for instance, an associate of Eero Saarinen adapted the principle of the automobile engine gasket for weatherproofing large areas of glass.

The General Motors structures are, however, only superficially Miesian, for their potentially eloquent structural statement is qualified by the employment of colorful glazed brick on the exteriors and by interior ornament that is sometimes elaborate in form and color; there are even several fountains. Though some of the decorative elements, such as the stairways, are effective in themselves, they are somewhat inconsistent with the basic austerity of the modular design. The Connecticut General Building is not so ambitious as the General Motors Technical Center but as much attention has been paid to amenity in its design. The four courtyards are beautifully arranged by the sculptor Isamu Naguchi, who also executed a large group of monoliths on the grounds. The landscaping is extensive and includes the use of water, and ample parking space is integrated into the total concept. Particular care has been taken in the selection and orientation of colors, furniture, and lighting fixtures, in the interests of an attractive psychological and physical environment.

Naturally the skyscraper, because of its indefinitely extendable verticality, is most adapt-able to the bureaucratic phase of the Miesian method and vocabulary. A building type which had languished during the depression and war years (no really distinguished example had been built since the P. S. F. S. Building), it became the most widespread form of architecture after World War II. Only a few examples which were either prototypical or interesting as variations on the norm will be singled out here. The earliest of them is Pietro Belluschi's Equitable Savings and Loan Association Building, Portland, Oregon, 1948 (AC 16), which introduced the curtain wall [18] (a covering which can be compared to a close-fitting skin or envelope, actually hung from the frame but giving the impression of being wrapped around it; it may be composed of glass, plastic, porcelain, or other material, and used to achieve transparency, opacity, or a combination of the two). In Belluschi's building the glass and plastic curtain wall clings closely to the frame, its sheer finish and its transparent and reflecting surfaces creating a visual precedent which has been emulated ever since. For example, in the huge United Nations Secretariat in New York, 1949 (AC 140, AC 141A, AC 141B, AC 142, AC 143), by Wallace Harrison and others, the wall is reduced to glass and thin strips of aluminum for spandrels and mullions, a pattern interrupted only by floors allotted to service areas. The prestige of this building, and the improvement of devices for fitting glass, sealing it against the weather, and treating it for glare and for heat resistance, resulted in the dispersal throughout the country of what have been disparagingly called glass boxes. Probably the handsomest and least elaborate example of the form is Lever House, also in New York, 1952 (AC 346), by Skidmore, Owings & Merrill, wherein the usual plan is varied by cantilevering one of the curtain walls. The glittering cubes or volumes of green glass comprising the various parts of the building are dramatized by being set off on two sides by a plaza, the first instance (since Rockefeller Center) in which open space is used to enhance the total visual effect and to make the building itself more livable, and the prototype of many to follow.

It was inevitable that the curtain wall would be varied after its novelty had been worn off by

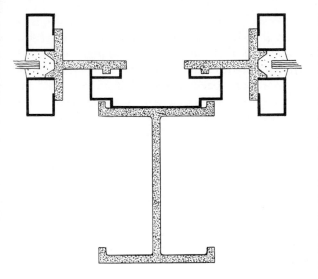

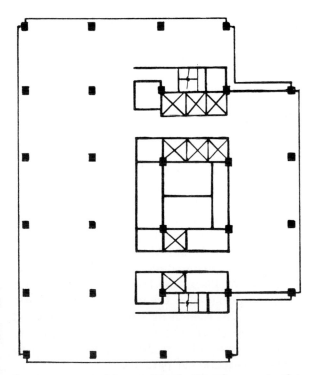

6–21. Section of bronze mullion (*above*), and plan of the tower (*below*), Seagram Building, New York, New York, 1957, by Philip Johnson and Ludwig Mies van der Rohe.

frequent repetition. (Saul Steinberg at this time summarized the situation in a drawing wherein he used a piece of graph paper to represent a skyscraper to which he added television antennas at the top and cars and people at the

bottom.) Several means were employed to achieve this variety. Harrison and Abramovitz, in the Aluminum Company of America Building, Pittsburgh, Pennsylvania, 1950 (AC 144, AC 144A), produced a bold pattern by alternating sheets of aluminum (pressed into three-dimensional forms) with small windows between the structural members. I. M. Pei at the Mile-High Office Complex, Denver, Colorado, 1954 (AC 1076, AC 1077), created an interesting pattern from the interplay between various functions frankly exposed rather than hidden behind the spandrels. By weaving together the structural members and the service ducts he achieved a realistic solution of the problem posed by the monotony of the large surface, a solution which exploited functional elements as the basis for the design. Other devices to achieve variety in the curtain wall have been more superficial: the use of projecting hoods and shields, for instance, and the addition of screens over the glass skin in egg-crate or corrugated forms, ostensibly as sun shades but sometimes frankly as decoration, as in Minoru Yamasaki's Michigan Consolidated Gas Building at Detroit, 1962.

Mies van der Rohe himself has used the subtlest and at the same time the simplest variations of the theme of the modular curtain-walled skyscraper, the building type largely initiated by his own theories. In the apartments at 860 Lake Shore Drive (Illustration 6–19), and in the Seagram Building, New York, 1957 (AC 264, AC 264A)—the latter done in collaboration with Philip Johnson—he qualified the sheer weightless quality of the volume by adding shadow-casting vertical projections to both supports and mullions (Illustration 6–21), achieving by this denser detailing an effect of mass which results in the illusion that the buildings are as much cubes as volumes, and thus approaching the effect of classical solidity. The scale, proportion, and detail of the Seagram Building are typical of Mies at all stages of his career. Yet the earlier, less austere architect of the Barcelona Pavilion is recalled in the richness of the materials—the exterior, for instance, uses bronze instead of stainless steel or aluminum. This richness, however, together with such subtleties as the rheostatic control of light (the interior illumination increases in proportion to the fading of daylight), may show the influence of Philip Johnson.

The Seagram Building is admired almost universally and with good reason, for it is a culminating example of the skyscraper as it has developed since the time of Sullivan and especially since World War II. It represents the perfecting of a building type made possible by modern technology and mass production, yet is constructed with such handsome materials, assembled with such precision, and conceived with such an elegant sense of proportion and detail that it is a masterpiece of the genre. A final judgment of this key building of the mid-century should not be made, however, without noting a certain anomaly. What seems to be an expression of the logic of modular structure is in the final analysis far more arbitrary than appears at first to be the case. An instance of this is the dismissal into a subsidiary space of service areas which would otherwise have interfered with the consistent and repetitive design of the main tower. Thus the Seagram Building does not entirely represent one of the basic principles of contemporary architecture, the expression in formal terms of structure and especially of function. In this sense it is in contrast to such structures as Wright's Johnson's Wax Administration Building, where the fortuitous shapes deriving from the functions of the building are exploited in the design, or to the buildings of Louis I. Kahn, each one of which is a unique expression of its particular requirements.

The Seagram Building, then, can be said to represent with distinction not only certain aspects of the International Style but also the reaction against it in the substitution of the primacy of formal beauty for the strict expression of function—a point of view to which Philip Johnson may be said partially to adhere, and which is popularly associated with the work of Yamasaki.

The Seagram Building also demonstrates how a building type which is easily susceptible to monotonous conformity can be refined by the careful design of all its aspects. In this respect it has served as a stimulus to a high standard of excellence in the field, which is represented at its best by the work of Skidmore, Owings & Merrill, whose skyscrapers are notable for the quality of their materials, detailing, and ancillary amenities (such as the incorporation of surrounding space in courts or plazas, and the inclusion of works of art), among which the Chase Manhattan Plaza in lower Manhattan, 1963, is outstanding. The firm's Inland Steel Building in Chicago, 1956–1958 (AC 347, AC 347A), initiated an interesting variation in the plan of the grid skyscraper: the floors are uninterrupted by communication and service areas, all of which are isolated in a tower separated from the main section, thus bringing to a logical conclusion a trend that began in the P. S. F. S. Building and was carried further in the main tower of the Seagram Building (Illustration 6–21).

Skidmore, Owings & Merrill are responsible also for an interesting variation in the framing and elevation of the grid skyscraper. In both the Alcoa Building in San Francisco, 1966, and their projected John Hancock Center in Chicago, diagonal bracing for greater structural strength is also exploited visually. This is particularly dramatic in the Chicago project whose ninety-eight stories will also be tapered from bottom to top—another innovation in grid skyscraper design.

The Marina City apartment house by Bertram Goldberg, also in Chicago, 1963, embodies a radical innovation in the grid skyscraper, since its reinforced steel columnar supports are arranged not rectangularly but in a circle, permitting balconied apartments radiating from a central core containing communication and services. Harrison and Abramovitz' Phoenix Life Insurance Company Building, 1964, in the new Constitution Plaza in Hartford, Connecticut, is the most original of the variations on the basic grid type, for, though its volume is emphasized in its almost complete transparency, the building is not a cube but is "boat-shaped"—or more precisely, a lenticular paraboloid.

There has been a tendency in recent years to qualify the volumetric emphasis in skyscraper design, a trend already signalized by Mies's use of shadow-casting projections to give an effect of greater solidity. One of Eero Saarinen's last works (completed after his death), the C. B. S. Building in New York, 1964, is a deliberate statement of a visual monumentality achieved by strongly modeled forms. Saarinen wanted his skyscraper to be a massive building and at the same time, like Sullivan's, "a proud and soaring thing." Its height is underlined by the emphatic granite-clad piers rising uninterruptedly throughout the building's entire thirty-seven stories, while its massiveness is brought out by their substantial and boldly triangular form, which casts deep shadows. Philip Johnson's Kline Science Center at Yale University, 1966, is another interesting attempt to vary the grid in the direction of a greater solidity. The supports (together with ducts for various services) are sheathed in brick so that the spandrels (themselves heavier than usual) seem to be supported on thin and elongated Romanesque towers.

The huge and brutally scale-destroying Pan American Building in New York, 1962–1964, in whose design Gropius and Belluschi played important roles, goes further in the direction of mass and solidity. A masonry aggregate is hung on the frame, giving an impression of heavy wall-bearing masonry, an effect which would almost ostentatiously flaunt the principle of the expression of structure in design if the massive tower were not paradoxically separated from the base of the building by a few floors which are obviously volumetric.

Even though such variations on the volumetric cube exist in high-rise buildings, there are few exceptions to the basic principle of the grid cage. The central stem with projecting cantilevered floors, for instance, has hardly been used in the United States except by Frank Lloyd Wright, though it has been popular elsewhere, especially in Latin America and in Italy. Wright's cantilevered Price Tower is unfortunately only a partial realization of the structural principles enunciated in his project for St. Mark's Tower and further elaborated in such seemingly impractical but basically feasible conceptions as the "mile-high" skyscraper that Wright proposed for Chicago.

The technological aspects of Miesian classicism are naturally more prominent in large building programs such as the skyscraper than in less spectacular architecture like housing, where the more "romantic" aspects of Mies's classicism are more prominent. Philip Johnson illustrates this aspect of the late Miesian phase of the International Style better in this dimension than does Mies himself who executed only one prominent house after his arrival in America. The earlier work of Philip Johnson was less personal than his recent buildings, and can be associated very closely with the International Style (Johnson was a co-author of the term). This was only natural on the part of a critic turned architect, a sometime Curator of Architecture at the Museum of Modern Art, and a biographer of Mies van der Rohe. Yet even at its very beginning Johnson's production differed somewhat from the style at its purest. That aspect of Mies which allows arbitrary beauty more scope than is consistent with a strictly functional theory was further emphasized by Johnson, but in a different way than in Mies's later work, for Johnson had little of the austerity of the older man's style. The houses that Johnson built from 1949 to 1956, beginning with his own in New Canaan, Connecticut, and continuing with the Richard Hodgson House, 1951 (AC 178), and the Wiley House, 1952–1953 (AC 179, AC 179A), also in New Canaan, and the Davis House, Wayzata, Minnesota, 1953 (AC 182A, AC 183), all emphasized Johnson's concern with beauty of proportion, material, and detail. His own house can be compared with Mies's Farnsworth House of about the same date. Neither structure is strictly functional as domestic architecture since there is little provision for privacy. Both houses are essentially glass-enclosed spaces sandwiched between floor and ceiling, the openness interrupted only by a cylinder in Johnson's house and a rectangle in Mies's which contain the bathrooms and utilities. Though the Johnson House is exquisite in proportion and in the detailing of the steel frame, it is essentially a dwelling designed to take the fullest advantage of its hilly and wooded site, which, in its careful landscaping, becomes an extension of the dwelling itself. Mies's house, on the other hand, seems an exercise in abstract form. Its three principal motifs—roof, floor, and stylobate-like terrace (essentially the three ingredients of Crown Hall without its girders)—appear to float slightly above the surface of the earth as though held at a precise elevation and in a perfect parallel relation to one another by a subtle magnetism, since the supports of both the floor and the terrace are too far under the building to be visible. Thus the Farnsworth House is like an object of constructivist sculpture, beautiful in itself regardless of its site, whereas Johnson's is more oriented toward a specific environment—a circumstance which is emphasized by its firm placement on the earth itself. Yet the geometry of the Johnson House is deliberately enhanced by the adjacent guest house, which is also a cube but almost solid brick—a witty contrast to its transparent neighbor. In the other three houses, Johnson continued to demonstrate his understanding of the International Style, especially of its rectilinearity, studied proportions, and sophisticated juxtaposition of materials, while at the same time consciously manipulating contrasts of enclosure and openness. In the Hodgson House an open area is countered by two closed ones; in the Wiley House, a formal, volumetric, glass-walled living room (AC 181, AC 181A) is placed above an informal stone-walled area half burrowed into a hill; the Davis House could be thought of as an inversion of Johnson's own, being essentially a solid mass built around a transparency. The rooms of the Davis House surround a large glass-walled patio-like area which houses a tropical garden—a dramatic contrast to the northern landscape seen from the windows in the exterior wall.

Mies and Johnson (in his work from 1945 to 1955; his style changed later) continued the International Style, but modified it in the direction of greater technological efficiency, greater formal refinement, or a combination of both.

Walter Gropius [working since the war with The Architects' Collaborative (T.A.C.)] adhered more closely to the original concepts of the International Style (with the glaring exception of the Pan American Building), continuing to integrate his esthetic with the technology of mass production. Though his idiom is flexible, there remains in his work a kind of anonymous quality in spite of the variety of his solutions. A case in point is the Graduate Center at Harvard University, Cambridge, Massachusetts, 1950 (AC 130, AC 131, AC 132, AC 132A), which is austere without being elegant. Efficient but lacking warmth, it seems less advanced than the Bauhaus of earlier in the century. The incorporation into the building of works of art by Josef Albers, Joan Miró, and Hans Arp does little to mitigate the building's bland impersonality. The arbitrary way in which the existing architectural surroundings of the building are completely ignored shows a certain callousness to the man-made environment. The brick pediment of an adjacent Georgian building, for instance, from certain angles appears to be actually surmounting one of the wings of the entirely different Graduate Center.

Unfortunately Gropius has had little opportunity to express his sense of social responsibility as architect and planner in large-scale housing or in urban renewal, except in the T. A. C.'s proposal for the University of Baghdad, Iraq, and, on a small scale, in a number of efficient schools. These, however, have some of the anonymity that seems to be the inevitable consequence of the combination of mass production and the collaboration of several architects. The T. A. C. is particularly strong, however, in the exploitation of the newest techniques—to which Mies seems indifferent—as seen in the use of folded concrete shells for one of the large structures at Baghdad and for a proposed auditorium at Tallahassee, Florida.

Among the followers of Mies working more or less in the tradition of technological classicism are Edward Stone, Peter Blake, and Ulrich Franzen, working in the New York area, and Bolton and Barnstone of Houston, Texas. Even on the West Coast, where the indigenous organic tradition is perhaps strongest, some of the most distinguished work in technological classicism is being done, at least in domestic architecture. This fact may be partly explained by the presence of Irving Gill's abstract protomodernism (in contradistinction to the more romantic work of the Greene brothers and Maybeck), reinforced by the urbane internationalism of Schindler and Neutra.

The combination of the features of two very different California houses built at the beginning of the period set the trend for subsequent development: the Charles Eames House, Santa Monica, 1949 (AC 82, AC 83), and the Lillian B. Ladd House, Pasadena, 1949 (AC 1029, AC 1030, AC 1031, AC 1032). The first, built by Eames for himself, is an ingenious structure composed of prefabricated materials—door and window units, steel framing, and plywood and plastic panels, some translucent and brightly colored. This cleverly composed structure demonstrates that mass-produced materials, when arranged with imagination and taste, can result in structures with individuality, the elements of which can be used in many different combinations. The Ladd House, on the other hand, epitomizes the custom-built house. Like Neutra's, it is finely proportioned and beautifully integrated with the landscape. Combining the formal and organic traditions, the suave distinction of its design is so great that it set a standard of almost Miesian elegance for the West Coast.

The use of mass-produced materials and formal beauty of composition are combined in the work of many Californians of whom Raphael Soriano, A. Quincy Jones (of Jones & Emmons), and Craig Ellwood (and, in an analogous development in the Northwest, Wendell Lovett) are especially important. Ellwood is the most interesting and productive of the group. Actually not an architect but a designer who came to architecture by way of contracting, his experience prepared him for the formulation of a partially prefabricated architecture which his formal sensibility has endowed with distinction. Due to the growing cost of labor and the increasing shortage of craftsmen, Ellwood feels that standardized frames, panels, and other structural units must be the basis for design. He also sets out, as Charles Eames did in his own house, to adapt these elements to each individual case in a different way. Ellwood has done just this in

a series of houses in the Los Angeles area which demonstrate a remarkable combination of practicality and formal sophistication. These qualities are well represented in the precise symmetry of the Frank Pierson House, 1955 (*AC 1019), and of the Victor Hunt House, 1957 (AC 1016, AC 1018), both in Malibu. The latter is composed of two units supported by thin steel trusses above the beach and has an expansive deck space funneling to the view. Recently Ellwood's talent has found expression in other than domestic architecture, for instance, in an all-aluminum office building and in two factory projects which do more than fulfill utilitarian requirements with the best possible expression of the structure and materials in the design, to paraphrase Ellwood's modest architectural credo.

One of the most successful manifestations of technological classicism has been in the area of school buildings. Among the most important and prototypical are Ernest J. Kump's Las Lomas High School, Walnut Creek, California, 1950 (AC 1053); Maynard Lyndon's Vista (now Santa Fe) Elementary School, Vista, California, 1950 (AC 220, AC 220B); John Lyon Reid's Hillsdale High School, San Mateo, California, 1955 (AC 1049, *AC 1050, AC 1052); and Donald Barthelme's Elementary School, West Columbia, Texas, 1952 (AC 13, AC 14). Kump's Las Lomas School is not unlike his earlier Acalanes Union High School in its rather formal character and its dispersed plan—the latter fairly ubiquitous in the even climate of California. But more advantage has been taken of the mass-produced unit, which Kump uses to tie together a large and sprawling but functional building. The school has a somewhat Miesian elegance. Lyndon's school at Vista is equally crisp and technological, but again designed with refinement of proportion. It is reminiscent also of Neutra's Corona School in the use of glass for one wall of the classrooms, here supplemented by louvered ceilings for back lighting.

Reid's Hillsdale High School in San Mateo is again a mass-produced building with loft-like areas of Miesian proportions, planned to be adaptable to fluctuating room sizes as the population and curriculum change. Barthelme's school in Texas is unusually sophisticated in design, as seen, for instance, in the way in which the steel truss frames are exposed for decorative effect. This school is also noteworthy for the prominent place given to an extensive undulating concrete canopy which announces the fact that the students are transported by bus from outlying districts, a far more appropriate symbol than the outworn clock tower. The growing tendency to create a consistent interior climate (as in a large office building) has aided the spread of technological classicism in school architecture throughout the country, even though the informality of the organic tradition seems more allied to modern education. This fact has contributed to the increase of the number of schools which are most conveniently adapted to modular coordination and prefabrication. In the hands of firms like Skidmore, Owings & Merrill and T. A. C., the results are commendable, but in most other cases the monotony of rote mass production has prevailed, with the exceptions of those noted above and others like them.

Modifications of Technological Classicism; Romantic Naturalism

Most architecture of the late 1940's and the 1950's either belongs within the category of technological classicism or is strongly influenced by it. This is true even on the self-consciously indigenous West Coast, where often the use of the open plan and native redwood amounts to only lip service to the local tradition. Yet, many buildings have such strong elements of romantic naturalism appearing side by side with those ordinarily thought of as belonging to the other school, that to categorize them as products of either school becomes arbitrary.

Among the architects who combined the two traditions during these years in a more than usually integrated way were two former representatives of the International Style, Neutra and Breuer. Neutra preserved in his work an abstract refinement combined with an application of Wright's organic theories. Occasionally his urbanity became a little "slick," as in the Northwestern Mutual Insurance Company Building, Los Angeles, California, 1950 (AC 278), which

is marred by excessive use of too many of the clichés of modern architecture such as louvers, smooth surfaces, and potted plants. Yet, in this structure, and even more clearly in the Amalgamated Clothing Workers' Building, also in Los Angeles, 1948 (AC 274), the emphasis on planes and rectilinearity is not merely modish but the result of the use of standardized parts. The abstract geometry of Neutra's style is particularly remarkable in houses in which standardization is not so essential and his formal sensibility is combined with the use of fine materials. When these qualities are united with a dramatic site the result is often very distinguished, as in the Warren Tremaine House, Santa Barbara, California, 1946 (AC 1044, AC 1045, AC 1046, *AC 1047), which is beautifully related to its garden and the surrounding landscape. The Kaufmann House (now the Lisk House), in Palm Springs, California, 1946 (Illustration 6–22), is even more successful in its integration with its environment; its swimming pool, terraces, and extended eaves seem to be a natural foil to the austere desert and the distant flat-topped mountains. These two houses are the prototypes of a series of large and small residences done by Neutra in southern California which are noteworthy for the variety and distinction of each individual solution of the relation of a structure to its surroundings, for Neutra is as emphatic as Wright in his recognition of the importance of the organic connection between architecture and its environment. One of Neutra's most successful achievements is the Holiday Motel at Malibu Beach, California, 1955, built on the dunes overlooking the sea. Here Neutra combines the various facets of his talents (including his ability to organize a number of structures into an efficient and agreeable whole, shown earlier in his housing projects) in one of the pleasantest examples of this fast-increasing building type. Neutra continues to maintain his position as one of the outstanding architects of the era.

In the postwar years Marcel Breuer continued to adapt himself to the indigenous domestic tradition as he had already done in the Mrs. Henry G. Chamberlain House, Wayland, Massachusetts,

6–22.   Kaufmann House (now the Lisk House), Palm Springs, California, 1946, by Richard Neutra.

which he designed with Gropius in 1940 (AC 43). He built a series of interesting houses during the first decades after the war: the Preston Robinson House, Williamstown, Massachusetts, 1947 (AC 47, AC 48, AC 48A); the Geller House, Lawrence, New York, 1952 (AC 41, AC 41A); and, on a smaller scale, the Harry A. Caesar House (now the property of Indian Mountain School), Lakeville, Connecticut, 1952 (AC 50). The last is a particularly successful small dwelling in which the solutions of the Chamberlain House are further refined. It is closely integrated with its rural environment; even a large tree is incorporated within the structure. Breuer's dor-

mitory at Vassar College, Poughkeepsie, New York, 1951 (AC 49), combines the best of the International Style with the American informal tradition, as can be seen in its pleasant proportions, its unpretentious use of brick and wood, and its interesting transitions in plan and elevation, as well as in the agreeable way in which it is situated on the campus. His auditorium for Sarah Lawrence College at Bronxville, New York, 1954, also possesses a pleasant unpretentiousness and an ingenious plan. (Breuer's later work is related to the new monumental functionalism of the 1960's and will be discussed later.)

Among the most interesting examples of the combination of the two main postwar trends during the 1950's are some early houses by Ralph S. Twitchell and Paul Rudolph (working separately and together), in which modern technology and the organic tradition are combined in an eloquent expression of structure in the design and in an adaptability to site and climate. Twitchell's Miller House (the Mario Lucci House), at Casey Key, Florida, 1947 (AC 303, AC 304, AC 304A), and the W. K. Healey House at Sarasota, Florida, 1950 (AC 306), by both architects, are representative. The latter is essentially a pavilion raised on concrete blocks above the sandy shores of a bayou, its principal feature being a roof of weather-tight plastic which can bend and stretch in the wind, and which is hung in a catenary curve from beams attached by tie rods to the projecting sill joists. This gracefully poised structure contains rooms that are open to the surrounding country on one side and controlled against the sun by wooden jalousies on the other. Rudolph's Umbrella House, Sarasota, Florida, 1953 (AC 301), also exploits tie-rod bracing to create an effect of such lightness that the main structure seems almost to float suspended over a part of the pool which is an important element in the total complex. The design is unified by a sense of continuous spaciousness achieved by means of a lattice work of sunshades covering the entire area of the pool, house, and subsidiary spaces. (Rudolph's quite different subsequent work will be discussed later.)

Among other architects who are somewhat more influenced by romantic naturalism than by technological classicism—at least in their domestic work (their other work is less easily categorized)—are Hugh Stubbins, whose office is in the Boston area, Eliot Noyes, John Johansen (in his work during the 1950's), Ladislau Rado, and Edward Larrabee Barnes, all practicing in the New York area. Of these perhaps the most interesting is Barnes, whose romantic naturalism is the most marked though he is not at all adverse to the simplifying convenience of the modular system, or the re-use of solutions already satisfactorily formulated. Barnes is a believer in what he calls continuity—continuity with the environment and with tradition. His dormitories at St. Paul's School, Concord, New Hampshire, 1962, accommodate themselves to the site relationship of the older buildings while preserving their shape and scale. His Haystack Mountain School, Deer Isle, Maine, 1962, demonstrates an eloquent use of native material and building tradition in a complex series of frame structures adapted in a most imaginative way to an unusual and magnificent site on a very steep incline overlooking Penobscot Bay.

A symptom of the eventual relaxation of technological classicism's hold on American architecture was the emergence during the mid-1950's of a reaction in favor of romantic naturalism in school building. One of the first to represent this trend was Perkins & Will's Heathcote School in Scarsdale, New York, 1954 (AC 286), comprised of a cluster of buildings (one for each of several age groups) constructed of natural materials in hexagonal shapes (which affords maximum natural light on all sides) and disposed informally over a pleasant terrain. This school was a prototype for many others, the most distinguished examples being in California, where the dispersed plan is most suited to the mild and even climate.

Frank Lloyd Wright is of course the most prominent exemplar of romantic naturalism after World War II, as well as the outstanding single figure of the period, with the possible exception of Mies van der Rohe. The years between the end of the war and Wright's death were not only among his most productive but were marked by the actualization of many projects that had been considered impracticable earlier. At the same time, Wright was by no means bypassed by the structural developments of recent years, as has already been noted in discussion of his buildings for the Johnson's Wax Company. During these years certain persisting trends in Wright's work continued to develop and new ones made their appearance. The most conspicuous among the former was the development of the curve, which became increasingly three-dimensional and dynamic and finally turned into the spiral. The

6–23. Interior, Solomon R. Guggenheim Museum, New York, New York, 1959, by Frank Lloyd Wright.

curvilinear forms introduced in the project for the Ralph Jester House, and realized in the curving enclosures of the Johnson's Wax Administration Building, are seen again in the second Jacobs House, Middleton, Wisconsin, 1948 (AC 479, AC 479A, AC 481). The curve became a spiral in the David Wright House, Scottsdale, Arizona, 1951 (AC 1068, AC 1069, AC 1070, AC 1071), and in the V. C. Morris Store, San Francisco, California, 1949 (AC 483, AC 484, AC 484A), culminating in the Solomon R. Guggenheim Museum in New York, 1959 (AC 475; Illustration 6–23). Regardless of whether he was influenced by the non-Greek Mediterranean architectural tradition, with its emphasis on rounded enclosure (as has been suggested by Vincent Scully), it is clear that in these buildings Wright exploited a new form but, as usual, not

without functional or organic application. The hemicycle of the second Jacobs House, for instance, encompasses a view of the plains, and the round tower-like form of the area housing the utilities repeats the drumlin shape of the hillock upon which the house is built and through which a tunnel leads to a garden—altogether a dramatic expression of the interrelation of the building with its environment.

In the David Wright House, the spiral is exposed; at the Morris Store it is enclosed in a contrasting rectangular box, its facade of impregnable brick penetrated only by an arch which is strongly suggestive of Richardson. The spiral ramp of the Morris Store is carried much further in the Guggenheim Museum, which can be thought of almost as a work of abstract sculpture. Here the dynamic flow and continuity of space are monumentalized as they never could have been before the twentieth century, when movement became part of the esthetic environment. Though the building has been criticized for functional difficulties in relation to the display of works of art and for awkwardness in the design of intersecting areas and of the central dome, nevertheless the great volumetric spiral is an exciting play of mass, space, tension, and their dynamic interrelationships, and is enhanced by the contrasting angular forms of the ancillary parts of the building. No structure sums up so well the differences between romantic naturalism and technological classicism. The Seagram Building, for instance, is static, formal, ordered, and rational—an expression of volumetric cubes in the most reduced terms of new materials and methods. The Guggenheim Museum, in contrast, is a sculpturesque volume, dynamic, irregular, organic, and intuitive—an eloquent expression not of mass production (though the modern technique of reinforced concrete is employed) but of romantic uniqueness. The Seagram Building seems to have been put together with laboratory instruments, the Guggenheim Museum to have been kneaded by hand like clay sculpture.

Rectangular forms appeared also in some of Wright's late buildings. They are used most effectively in the Unitarian Church at Madison, Wisconsin, 1947–1951 (AC 477, AC 478), whose basic triangular shape, as Wright described it, suggests hands in prayer. During the last years of Wright's life, two buildings carried on the themes of the angle and the curve: the Beth Sholon Synagogue, Elkins Park, Pennsylvania, 1957, and the Dallas Theater in the Round, 1958. The synagogue, which the rabbi wanted to be a "traveling Mount Sinai, a mountain of glass," is a translucent tent of corrugated plastic and glass, eighty-eight feet high. The Dallas Theater incorporates the ample bowl shape of the Guggenheim Museum, combining it with an area that houses a tantalizingly circuitous route from the entrance to the suddenly dramatic opening to the space of the interior.

In the Research Laboratory Tower for the Johnson's Wax Company, adjacent to the Ad-

ministration Building at Racine, Wisconsin, 1948–1950, and in the Price Tower, Wright's ideas for the skyscraper, epitomized in the St. Mark's project, were finally actualized, even if on a small scale. The Price Tower is closer to the project than the Johnson Tower, but is also somewhat backward-looking in its decorative detail and emphasis on angularity (a kind of recapitulation of much of Wright's earlier work in abstract design). The laboratory is more contemporary in feeling, since ornament has been entirely rejected. In it, Wright exploits the curvilinear shapes of the neighboring Administration Building in floors alternatingly circular and rectangular, with curved corners cantilevered from a central shaft (containing the functional elements of the building) sunk deeply in the ground.

Wright's imaginative concept of a mile-high office tower was that of a great showman carrying to a culmination the cantilevered principle embodied in the St. Mark's and Johnson's Wax towers—the gesture of an artist whose enormous creative powers had not been sufficiently challenged by a society which had not caught up with him. Other late projects were equally dramatic but more feasible. Many of them carried on Wright's preoccupation with the curve and spiral as, for instance, his plan for a Grand Opera and Civic Auditorium at Baghdad, 1947, and projects for civic centers at Madison, Wisconsin, Marin County, California, and the Golden Triangle at Pittsburgh. Such large-scale and dramatic conceptions were designed with the circumstances of vehicular and pedestrian movement in mind, and incorporated various devices of the modern highway. In these projects Wright exploited the possibilities of the spiral ramp, realized only on a small scale at the Guggenheim Museum but here enormously expanded for the accommodation of motor traffic.[19]

A small portion of the Marin County Center, the Administrative Center, 1962, has in fact been executed and embodies many of Wright's principles. The building seems to emerge from the landscape. Projecting from an auditorium area on one hill, it bridges a valley to another hill by means of a structure containing tiers of offices arranged around two parallel but separate corridor-like courts—all supported by huge arches —that are open to the sky. Though finished after Wright's death, the building is his own; the color and detailing, however, reflect the somewhat bizarre taste of the master's successors at Taliesin West.

Another imaginative project, never executed, was Wright's design for the Arizona State Capitol at Phoenix. Its angular forms would have suited the mountainous desert landscape of the region, and the largest interior space was to have been covered with a tepee-like structure as dramatically expressive or symbolic as a dome, by now a somewhat trite finial. The complex was to include shade trees and garden courts leading into one another, and was to be cooled by fountains and water courses. The buildings were to be joined together by canopies which would have filtered the sun like rows of trees, and this entire canopied area was to be enclosed by pierced screens to permit the circulation of air and to act as protection against the heat of the sun (a conception which obviously influenced Edward D. Stone's American Embassy in New Delhi, India, 1960).

These imaginative projects demonstrated not only the continuing creativity of Frank Lloyd Wright but also his awareness of new materials, methods, and needs, especially his recognition of the changes that had been brought about by the automobile. Furthermore, his projects seem practicable, unlike the somewhat Martian fantasies of his followers. The "nineteenth-century romantic," as Gropius called Wright, retained the humanism and individualism of that era, incorporating the organic theory of the Transcendentalists into his own theory of architecture. But in the process he adapted these principles to circumstances of mass population, communication, and production, except where a wealthy individual client permitted him to luxuriate in nineteenth-century individualism. Consequently Wright's work was not overwhelmed by monotonous conformity, no matter how viable or how refined the latter can be. His buildings are contemporary, but they are also traditional in the best sense, for they preserve the virtues of a humanistic naturalism adapted to a technological age. In fact, Wright exploited the benefits of the latter in a contemporary formulation of some of the universals which his "nineteenth-century" character represents. Thus, in the period of Miesian ascendancy the work of Frank Lloyd Wright cannot be relegated to a secondary position, even if its basically romantic individualism prevented it from being accepted as a vernacular for a technological style.

Though Wright's influence has been general, it is not surprising that the work of his own students should be the closest to his own. This can be seen in Alden Dow's domestic architecture, typified by his John Whitman House (now the John Van Stirum House), Midland, Michigan, 1935 (AC 81), and in Paul Schweikher's Louis C. Upton House, Paradise Valley, Arizona, 1950 (*AC 335), though the latter's Maryville College buildings, Maryville, Tennessee, 1953–1954 (AC 336, AC 337, *AC 337A), are more abstract and technological.[20]

Except for Frank Lloyd Wright, the strongest resistance to technological classicism has continued to be on the West Coast, where a number of architects in the San Francisco Bay area, the Los Angeles region, and the Northwest carried on (or at least partially incorporated in their work) the tradition of Maybeck and the Greene brothers, which had been revived before the war by such architects as Harwell Hamilton Harris and furthered by William Wilson Wurster at the School of Architecture of the University of California at Berkeley. Harris, in his Ralph Johnson House in Los Angeles, 1949 (AC 138, *AC 138B, AC 138C), developed his prewar style into an even more consciously regional expression under the increasing influence of Maybeck's framed houses. His later work in Berkeley and elsewhere is perhaps not as distinguished, but his Motel on the Mountain, 1956, on the New York Thruway near Suffern, New York, in its imaginative use of laminated timber and its fine exploitation of site, shows an adaptation of the principles of the California school to the East. The James Kelso House, Kentfield, California, 1953 (*AC 1074, *AC 1075), and the

Leonard Sperry House in Los Angeles, 1954 (*AC 489, *AC 489B, *AC 489C), by Wurster in partnership with Bernardi and Emmons, and Theodore Bernardi's own house at Sausalito, California, 1951 (AC 493B, AC 494), designed by Bernardi alone, are excellent and typical examples of California domestic architecture characterized by informal planning and adaptation to the environment. In the Center for Advanced Study in the Behavioral Sciences, c. 1954 (*AC 1072, AC 1073), in Palo Alto, California, Wurster, Bernardi and Emmons succeeded in giving to an institution a pleasant sense of informality and to its separate studies an air of domestic privacy.

Meanwhile the Northwest did not lag behind San Francisco and Los Angeles in the quality of its slightly different regionalism, which is adapted to a somewhat cooler and much rainier climate. John Yeon's Lawrence Shaw House, Portland, Oregon, 1951 (AC 502), is distinguished by the sensitive use of wood, both in framing and covering, continuing a tradition initiated by his Wetzek House, 1937 (AC 501).

Pietro Belluschi's domestic work in Portland is as successful as Yeon's. His churches, however, are better known. Two of them in Portland—Zion Lutheran Church, 1950 (AC 25, AC 26), and Central Lutheran Church, 1951 (AC 28, AC 29)—are especially effective in their use of huge laminated wood trusses, while the employment of open timbering (in the tower of the Central Lutheran Church) is reminiscent of the spirit of Gothic architecture, though not at all of its letter. In the Seattle area, the houses of Paul Hayden Kirk and of Robert B. Price in Seattle and Tacoma should be mentioned, since their work, though locally appreciated, has not yet gained national recognition though it is in its way as distinguished as that of some of the California school.

Among the California architects who represented romantic naturalism most prominently during the 1950's are Henry Hill, the firm of Campbell & Wong, Joseph Esherick, Charles Warren Callister, Mario Corbett, Vernon DeMars (who is also notable for his contribution to large-scale housing), Carl Warnecke and Ernest J.

Kump. Esherick's John Dern House, Redwood City, California, 1951 (AC 88, *AC 90), reflects the indigenous tradition in its timber construction, open plan, and organic relationship with the landscape—a contemporary adaptation of Maybeck's somewhat Japanese-inspired principles. Corbett's Moritz Thomsen House, Vina, California, 1952 (AC 68, AC 69), is an unusually attractive and original solution for a house situated in an insect-infested area of heavy rain and extreme heat, a solution arrived at by the incorporation of projecting areas covered with screening and further protected by sliding glass panels, though the total effect of the structure is symmetrical and crisp. Warren Callister's T. Carson O'Connell House at San Rafael, California, 1954 (*AC 1006, *AC 1007, *AC 1008), shows the influence of both the Japanese tradition and Frank Lloyd Wright's prairie houses. His Christian Science Church, Belvedere, California, 1951 (*AC 1009, AC 1010, *AC 1011, *AC 1012), one of the most pleasing structures of the postwar period, also reflects the theories of Wright and Maybeck in what is nevertheless an essentially original building. Callister's Corte Madera School at Portola Valley, California, 1960, is deliberately domestic, exploiting in the design both revealed framing and the presence of a grove of large oaks. Vernon DeMars' own house, in Berkeley, California, 1950 (AC 1015), like Callister's O'Connell House, is an up-to-date refinement of Maybeck's Japanese-inspired principles.

The work of Warnecke during the 1950's represents the best of the informal California tradition. Especially notable are his Mira Vista Elementary School at El Cerrito (near Richmond), California, and his del Monte Shopping Center in Monterey, California, designed in 1960 and still under construction. Both represent an organic and humanly scaled architecture perfectly suited to the environment and employing local materials when feasible. The Mira Vista School (a mature version of the Pasadena school built by Huntington and Grey in 1907 in Maybeck's informal manner), divided into several units, is scattered over one of the El Cerrito hills. Tiers of classrooms are covered by

6-24. Detail of Natural Life Sciences Building, Foothill College, Los Altos Hills, California, 1962, by Kump, Masten & Hurd, Architects Associated, A Joint Venture.

oblique and wide-eaved roofs, and are lit by skylights and by large areas of side light dramatically focused by the hovering roofs. Industrial materials are matched with the native redwood. The color is warm, the scale human, and the integration with the terrain conscious and successful. With the exception of his brilliant embassy at Bangkok and his almost as successful government buildings at Honolulu, Warnecke's domestically scaled work is more successful than his urban architecture, especially his huge Federal Building in San Francisco (in association with several other architects) and those at the University of California at Berkeley. This is also true of the work by Esherick and DeMars on the same campus, where the huge new Wurster Hall, 1963, housing the departments

of architecture, landscape architecture, and city planning, by Esherick, DeMars, and Donald Olsen, 1965, is inept in comparison with their less pretentious buildings which, no matter what their function, appears to be rural or domestic. Though Wurster Hall shares a certain rough directness of statement with other buildings of the mid-1960's, they are powerful while it seems merely awkward.

Among the great number of educational structures erected for the rapidly expanding state educational system in California, the best are those which remain small in scale (or appear to be so) and follow indigenous romantic naturalism. Of these it is generally conceded that Foothill College, Los Altos Hills, by Kump, Masten & Hurd, 1962 (Illustration 6–24), is the most outstanding. Set in an arresting landscape, the college is a masterpiece of the cluster or dispersed plan with which Kump had been experimenting since his Acalanes Union High School but here on a much larger scale, involving forty buildings on a 122-acre site. At Foothill, Kump rejected the more mechanical and mass-produced aspect of his former style, retaining only the modular system, and adapted himself to a regional romantic naturalism in the expression of informality, continuity, and openness, and in the use of local and natural material. The buildings are distinguished by their long-eaved shingle roofs and sensitive detailing, and the overall plan relates in a strikingly successful way the structures, courtyards, and paths (beautifully integrated in the landscape by Sasaki, Walker & Associates, landscape architects). In fact, this intimate (though ordered) and domestically scaled campus is almost an apotheosis of romantic naturalism, reflecting not only the local tradition but that of the shingle style and the organic work of Wright. Yet since it is a culminating example Foothill College is nostalgic, not prophetic.

The work of Charles W. Moore (who has recently succeeded Paul Rudolph as head of the School of Architecture at Yale) and his associated firm, Lyndon, Turnbull and Whitaker, is more timely. Moore's curious rural or suburban frame houses, as for instance, his own at Orinda,

California, 1962, built on an extremely steep slope, and another, the Cyril B. Jobson House at Palo Colorado Canyon, Monterey County, California, 1961, seem to do the impossible: to combine the informality, native material, and structural tradition of romantic naturalism with an eccentric, abruptly angular formality which is as deliberately dramatic as the monumental masonry or concrete structures of a Louis Kahn or a Paul Rudolph. West Plaza Condominium at Coronado (near San Diego), California, 1962, is a more suitable vehicle for the expression of such a formidable and ambiguous style, so consistent with one of the dominant trends of the 1960's. Powerful and heavy, the Condominium is not unlike Wurster Hall, although only superficially so, for it is not ungainly and immature but robust and sure—if perhaps a little overwhelming.

Developments in Structure and Materials

Recent developments in structure and materials have suggested new architectural possibilities wherein new dimensions of tension, compression, and their dynamics have been added to the traditional ones of space, volume, and mass. Particularly in the imaginative use of reinforced concrete, there is more opportunity for individual expression than in the mass-produced anonymity of the Miesian school at its most extreme. The United States has until recently lagged behind Latin America, Italy, and even Spain in this respect. This has been due to several causes, among them the persistence of antiquated building codes and the stylistic preference for rectilinearity, as well as the more obvious factors of abundant steel resources, mass-produced units, and highly paid labor. Technical improvements in the manufacture of concrete and ferroconcrete, however, together with a growth of rapport between architect and engineer, have tended to offset these disadvantages. The increased use of these new materials has stimulated the employment of folded, bent, warped, and twisted slabs, thick or paper-thin, in shell-like and other organic forms and in unaccustomed geometric shapes, comprising basically new structural conceptions

in no way reminiscent of the masonry vault and dome or of the post and lintel and its descendant, the metal grid system.

As in many other instances, Frank Lloyd Wright in his use of reinforced concrete was in the vanguard. The columns of the Johnson's Wax Administration Building were an early instance of the use of concrete over metal lath while the adjacent Research Laboratory Tower is the first executed example of a concept long in Wright's mind, the hollow concrete "mast" as the support for the cantilevered floor. His Guggenheim Museum in New York is one of the most original and expressive demonstrations of the use of ferroconcrete.

The airport Terminal Building in St. Louis, Missouri, 1954 (AC 499, *AC 499A, AC 500, AC 500B), by Helmuth, Yamasaki and Leinweber, was the first important building to express the use of reinforced concrete as an essential part of the design. The facts of enclosure and support are dramatized by three intersecting barrel vaults of great span and apparent weightlessness, separated at intervals by large areas of glass to give them a hovering effect. An equally bold use of reinforced concrete, in what is now a classic example, is seen in Eero Saarinen's Auditorium at the Massachusetts Institute of Technology, Cambridge, Massachusetts, 1954 (AC 317, AC 318, AC 318A, AC 319). In this structure a large auditorium and its ancillary functions and spaces are covered by a low dome-like shell, formed by a one-eighth section of a sphere, a roof load of fifteen hundred tons supported at three points which are only three and a half inches thick where they touch the ground. The total effect of the structure is one of great mathematical fastidiousness, an impression which is increased by the white paint covering the spherical section, the black color of the bolts which anchor it, and the smooth shimmer of the extensive glazed surfaces formed by the arched openings between the points. Other examples of less spectacular but more complex space-enclosing forms range from the rippling grace of the huge shell of the dining room which gives its name to the Concha Hotel at San Juan, Puerto Rico, by Toro and Ferrar

6–25. Ingalls Hockey Rink (model), Yale University, New Haven, Connecticut, 1956, by Eero Saarinen and Associates.

in association with Charles W. Warner, Jr., to the folded slabs (like folded paper projects come true) of José Luis Sert's American Embassy at Baghdad.

One of the most popular forms resulting from the introduction of new techniques and materials is the hyperbolic paraboloid formed of twisted or warped reinforced concrete or laminated wood (a material which, due to improvements in adhesives, is now almost as adaptable and strong as ferroconcrete). This shape has been utilized in the covering of all kinds of structures, some of them unfortunately more exhibitionist than practical. Yet, when its use is consistent with the functional needs of the building, interesting interior spaces as well as dramatic exteriors can be achieved. An example is the house built for himself by the architect Eduardo Catalano, at Raleigh, North Carolina, 1954 (AC 64), one of the first instances

of its use, or the large restaurant at Laguna Beach, California, 1957 (AC 1065, AC 1066, AC 1067), by Williamson and Johnson. (The possibilities of the hyperbolic paraboloid are more imaginatively demonstrated in I. M. Pei's design for a chapel at Tunghi in Taiwan, 1963, where four of them are joined together in a configuration which is not only technically brilliant but reminiscent of the curved roofs of Chinese architecture.)

Reinforced concrete has been combined with other uses of steel in many ways. One of the most interesting examples is another pacesetting structure by Eero Saarinen, the Ingalls Hockey Rink at Yale University, 1956 (Illustration 6–25), where the roof, covering an extensive playing area and spectator seating, is hung from steel cables stretched from a huge curved span of reinforced concrete. The somewhat ovoid shape of the building, together with the sweeping catenary curve of the hanging roof stretching from the spine high above to the top of the low walls below, make the interior more dynamic than would have been possible with masonry. Somewhat similar in its use of a combination of reinforced concrete and metal cables (and the first such building to be erected in the United States) is the State Fair Arena, Raleigh, North Carolina, 1953 (AC 281), by a Polish exile, Matthew Nowicki (in partnership with William Henley Dietrick). The cable-supported roof of the Arena is slung from two enormous overlapping arches slanting inward at oblique angles. (Hugh Stubbins' Congress Hall, built in Berlin in 1955, is more complex, combining two arches placed at an angle similar to those at Raleigh, with a tensile roof hung from a compression ring.)

The last decade has seen developments in structure more spectacular even than those of the previous one. One of the least dramatic of these, though impressive enough, is the improvement of prestressed concrete to make possible the spanning of larger areas by weight-bearing beams. This has especially affected skyscraper design, as in Yamasaki's recent projects, finally to be realized in his proposed Port of New York Authority Buildings, where the facades are uninterrupted by the intrusion of any supports beyond the corner ones. Prestressing will also facilitate the erection of structures which can take advantage of sites formerly unavailable for building, such as ravines, slopes, and valleys, exemplified in Luckman and Cadwalader's unexecuted project (1961) for a canyon-spanning restaurant at Oakland, California.

Some recent structural innovations perhaps belong more properly to the field of engineering than to architecture, but as the two have begun to meet again for the first time since their divorce at the beginning of the Industrial Revolution, the distinction becomes more difficult to make. Most of these innovations have taken place in the development of mass-produced materials for covering large areas and include domes suspended by steel cables or hung from compression rings, "space forms" of strutted networks of trussing, roofs suspended in catenary curves like the roadways of suspension bridges, geodetic domes, and other pneumatic structures.

Recent and continuing advances in structure and particularly in engineering are creating an increasingly important role for the engineer. In fact, if certain prophecies are right about the population explosion, the engineer, with his anonymous solution for mass housing, may supersede the architect entirely.

Among the most original of contemporary architect-engineers is Buckminster Fuller, who, though he has been developing his ideas for the last three decades, has been so far ahead of his time that his work can be discussed in the framework of the immediate present, if not indeed of the future. More deliberately than any other designer, Fuller thinks in terms of the total technological and social environment. From his Dymaxion House of 1927 through his Autonomous Living Package of 1959 he has been experimenting with improving what he calls "prototypes for world housing," and using various methods developed in industry, especially aircraft technology. Though ingenious, they have not been as practically feasible as have his experiments in the enclosure of great spaces. Largely theoretical until recently, some of these experiments have been realized on a vast scale as a result of recent advances in plastics, metallurgy, and alloy chemistry in commissions for such clients as the United States Armed Forces and the Ford Motor Company. The most successful are the space frames or "domes" based on a truss system involving the principles of the octahedron, as illustrated in the Ford Rotunda, Detroit, Michigan, 1953 (AC 94), and the accordion truss (geodesic dome). The latter combines the virtues of the sphere and tetrahedron, exploiting the compression and tension of these forms (the sphere encloses the greatest space in the least surface; the tetrahedron encloses the least space with the most surface) in what is referred to as a minimal dimensional energy system which has no inherent size limitation. This structural figure has been successfully adapted to multiple purposes, from its use by the Army in various circumstances and climates to its employment as a focal point of an extensive architectural complex in the Northland Center, 1954 (AC 95, AC 95A), a shopping area in Detroit.

Fuller, a descendant of New England transcendentalists, brings up-to-date a tradition of Yankee ingenuity, functional esthetics, and social responsibility which is as indigenous as the organic theories and democratic ideals of Frank Lloyd Wright but is more oriented to the future. Fuller's theories imply the nullification of individual creativity in architecture, because once a final solution is found, any variation on it would be redundant. The principles represented in Fuller's structures could conceivably create work areas and living spaces the size of cities in extremes of environment from ice cap to equator, not to mention under the sea and on other planets.

An aspect of the architectural use of new techniques and materials completely antithetical to that represented by socially oriented architect-engineers like Fuller is that which uses mass-produced materials and industrial technology for purposes of personal expression in formal terms which are nearly as sculpturesque as they are architectural. Buildings of this kind are the very antithesis of the almost anonymously objective products of the large architectural firms in which the esthetic of the International Style in its late Miesian phase has been reduced to its most practical formulation. Such a structure as Eero Saarinen's Trans-World Airlines Terminal at Kennedy International Airport, New York, 1956–1962 (Illustration 6–26), for instance, even incorporates a feeling of movement and the suggestion of biomorphic forms,

6–26. Interior, Trans-World Airlines Terminal, Kennedy International Airport, New York, New York, 1956–1962, by Eero Saarinen and Associates.

both characteristic of modern sculpture. The free-hand, ungeometric curves of a building like this are so structurally unconventional and mathematically complicated that models must be made before construction drawings can be prepared, as was actually done for the Trans-World Airlines Terminal. This controversial building suggests not only the dynamism of Flight (which would be impossible to project in a more conventional building), but also the flight of a bird, if not indeed its actual shape.[21] Even more dramatically sculpturesque are John Johansen's projected "airfoam" structures, to be constructed of concrete sprayed on steel-mesh forms supported by a steel armature. His models for houses in this medium are as shocking as the unconventional buildings by Antoni Gaudí in late nineteenth-century Barcelona, but suggest even more astonishing possibilities with the use of twentieth-century methods.

The work of Victor Lundy and Joseph Salerno, much of it in laminated wood, represented by the former's Unitarian Church at Westport, Connecticut, 1960, and the latter's House of Worship, Rowayton, Connecticut, 1962, show great ingenuity in the use of expressive free forms which almost transcend the limitations of conventional architectural practice and theory.

The formal possibilities inherent in the use of reinforced concrete and laminated wood, combined with the employment of new engineering techniques, are almost limitless. Such a building as the Trans-World Airlines Terminal challenges restraints imposed by outmoded structural and functional needs, as well as the esthetics of modern architecture, which emphasizes formal expression as the consequence of structural and functional circumstances. While the Terminal itself is an important personal statement, the potentials inherent in it are accompanied by the danger of unconventional architecture becoming mere showmanship or vulgar display. A prominent engineer who has worked with architects who have been among the most creative in the expression of new structural ideas, warns that to be truly architecture, structural forms should be "motivated by the mathematics of support and weight and not by poetic intui-

tion." Parts of Miami Beach are a nightmarish prophecy of what architecture could become in a riot of illogical convolutions.

The New Beauty; Exoticism and Historicism

Among the most arresting if not the most significant of recent architectural trends is a deliberate return to beauty for its own sake, considered aside from its relation to the honest expression of architectural facts. In most cases this does not involve a basic challenge to technological classicism, still the most viable of contemporary styles. The introduction of various decorative refinements to its basic rectilinear forms and mass-produced modular system ("gift-wrapping the Miesian box" as one critic happily phrased it) is of course exactly contrary to one of the premises of the International Style, from which technological classicism so closely derives. Occasionally it can be functional, however, as in Edward D. Stone's use of perforated screens as a device against heat in the American Embassy at New Delhi, but more frequently such screens simply become decorative motifs in themselves or are used to unify disparate sections of a loosely designed building complex.

The architect who uses decorative elements with the greatest skill is Minoru Yamasaki. His St. Louis Airport Terminal Building is fundamentally different from his later work. The delicate metal tracery surrounding his Reynolds Aluminum Building, 1959, and the precast concrete decorating the exterior of his Michigan Consolidated Gas Building, 1962, and that of his College of Education at Wayne University, 1961, all in Detroit, demonstrate Yamasaki's sense of scale and detail. The employment of water and foliage as part of the total complex at the Reynolds Building, and the introduction of narrow open spaces between the tenuous Miesian pavilions of the MacGregor Memorial Community Conference Center at Wayne University, 1957 (Illustration 6–27), are further illustrations of what Yamasaki calls quite frankly the "delight" in architecture. The change that has come over contemporary building in the half-century of its existence from Gropius to the present is nicely summed up in Yamasaki's

6–27. MacGregor Memorial Community Conference Center, Wayne University, Detroit, Michigan, 1957, by Yamasaki, Leinweber and Associates.

remark that the social function of the architect is first of all to create a work of art.

Much of the beauty of Yamasaki's work derives from his admiration of the architecture of other cultures, particularly Moslem and Japanese. The former has partially inspired his employment of screens and water as well as his repetitive detail and sometimes dramatic silhouettes, while the latter has suggested his prominent use of carefully designed landscape gardening and has enhanced his feeling for detail and variety of material. This exoticism, which has added variety and visual pleasure to the American architectural scene, makes of Yamasaki an ideal designer for the pleasure gardens of World's Fairs, such as his pavilion at the Seattle Exhibition in 1962. It also gives lightness and gaiety to such institutional structures as the Northwestern Life Insurance Building in Minneapolis, 1964, where the glass-clad offices are prefaced by a gracefully vaulted colonnade; or the Woodrow Wilson Center at Princeton University, 1965, where another exotic colonnade lends a classic dignity somewhat analogous to classical architecture.

The exoticism which is such a strong element in Yamasaki's work is perhaps best justified in the American government buildings abroad, particularly where the architects have adapted to modern technological terms appropriate stylistic elements which have developed in a particular country because of local climate and custom. Most successful in this respect is the American Embassy at Accra, Ghana, by Harry Weese and Associates, 1956–1957 (Illustration 6–28), where the concrete columns, set in the floor slab to withstand wind and earthquake, are shaped to resemble the finials and buttresses of West African mud architecture, while the wood members and slatted infillings recall the construction of local village huts and assembly places.[22] Among other distinguished buildings of this type are Carl Warnecke's American Embassy at Bangkok, Thailand, reminiscent of the Royal Sailing Pavilion there but not repeating it, and, on a less pretentious scale, Hugh Stubbins' American Legation (now the American Consulate) at Tangier, Morocco. Stone's Embassy at New Delhi is one of that architect's best buildings, for here his predilection for decorative screening, dramatic effect, and ingenious roofing coincides with native tradition and the need to compensate for the rigors of a hot climate.

Exoticism of this kind, which is very different from the revivalism repudiated by the pioneers of modern architecture, is matched by another kind of eclecticism which might better be called historicism, to distinguish it from its nineteenth-century counterpart. Historicism rejects the overt revivalism of picturesque eclecticism, seeking instead the great continuities of western architecture in general. Among the most successful of the architects whose work illustrates this new historicism is Eero Saarinen, whose buildings in this category comprise a considerable part of his protean production. His buildings for Concordia College, Fort Wayne, Indiana, 1953–1958, recall a northern European village, while Morse and Stiles Colleges at Yale University, New Haven, Connecticut, 1962, are quite successful in their integration with the architectural environment, since their irregular and unregimented plan, their picturesque massing and equally picturesque texture (a conglomerate of stone and mortar devised for these particular buildings) blend very well into the neo-Gothic of James Gamble Rogers' buildings of thirty years before. Saarinen's colleges display no eclectic detail nor do they recall any specific structures of the Middle Ages, but their impact is thoroughly medieval (a fact which some critics decry).

Buildings such as these demonstrate the usefulness of the new historicism as an appropriate solution for buildings which are adjacent to other structures of an earlier period, a particularly pressing problem for the campuses of the older colleges and universities.[23] It is not surprising, therefore, that college campuses are the site of a number of examples of overt or, more frequently, modified historicism. Saarinen's geometric chapel and auditorium, built in 1954, fit well into the literal classicism of the Massachusetts Institute of Technology (in a much less self-conscious way than his more recent pseudo-Gothic colleges at Yale). The complex delicacy of the pinnacles and screens of Paul Rudolph's Jewett Art Center, 1958, at Wellesley College,

6–28. Detail of United States Embassy, Accra, Ghana, 1956–1957, by Harry Weese and Associates.

suit the late Gothic revivalism of the adjacent buildings; and the recent Harvard Houses, by Shepley, Bulfinch, Richardson, and Abbott, 1961, though not as significant as Gropius' dormitories, at least recall in their material and proportions some of that University's traditional Georgian and neo-Georgian architecture. Another successful building which remains contemporary in structure and design while retaining the informal yet crisp character of the New England tradition of building with wood is the Library at Bennington College, 1960, in whose design Pietro Belluschi was a consultant. Marcel Breuer's informal dormitory at Vassar College, 1951, fits more successfully into the semirural campus than does Skidmore, Owings & Merrill's arbitrary though elegant dormitory at Smith College, 1961.

Of all the architects who have enlarged the architectural vocabulary of today with a sophisticated historicism, Philip Johnson in his recent work is the most significant, for he conceals the more superficial reminiscences of past styles in a genuine integration of their basic character with a thoroughly contemporary form language. Johnson's Kneses Tifereth Synagogue, Portchester, New York, 1954–1955 (AC 185, AC 186; Illustration 6–29), and his Boisannas House at New Canaan, Connecticut, 1954, can be considered as being transitional between his work in the International Style and his exploration of the formal language of other traditions. The crisp, smooth planes and the precisely delineated forms of the Synagogue are reminders of his earlier work, but the emphatic counterposition of the cube of the auditorium with the elliptical cylinder of the vestibule is new, as are the graceful butterfly vaults of the interior. The rigid rectilinearity of the Boisannas House and the contrast of its open areas with its thick walls and with the piers of its pergolas would not have been surprising during Johnson's earlier career, but the definition of the separateness of the

6–29. Interior, Kneses Tifereth Synagogue, Portchester, New York, 1954–1955, by Philip Johnson.

areas (which is emphasized by the repetition of the proportions of the open areas in the solid supports) is a flagrant denial of one of the main tenets of the International Style—open or free-flowing space. Such variations reflect Johnson's increasing interest in those aspects of past architecture which are stylistically analogous to contemporary taste, particularly the complex and ambiguous space of the Emperor Hadrian's villa near Rome, the restrained symmetry and monumentality of Palladio's classicism, and the abortive modernism of romantic classicism. The colonnades of the University of St. Thomas at Houston, Texas, 1957; the Brown University Computing Center, Providence, Rhode Island, 1959; the New York State Theater at Lincoln Center for the Performing Arts, New York, 1963; and the graceful vaults of the pavilion on Johnson's property in New Canaan, 1963, particularly evoke these sources. Other buildings show quite different inspiration, as evidenced in the Romanesque simplicity of the Benedictine Priory at Washington, D. C., the Mesopotamian monumentality of the atomic reactor plant at Rehovot, Israel, 1962, and the almost Adamesque delicacy which qualifies the scale of the shrine at New Harmony, Indiana, 1961, where a traditional American character is further suggested by a cedar covering reminiscent of the New England shingle style.

The Munson-Williams-Proctor Institute at Utica, New York, 1957–1960, sums up Johnson's combination of aspects of the International Style with a sophisticated historicism. He has created an original and beautiful building, if not an entirely novel one. Its urbanity, the laconic simplicity of its structure, even the use of heavy exterior girders, recall Mies's Crown Hall and his wing for the Houston Museum of Fine Arts, built about the same time. But the differences are as notable as the similarities. The emphasis on the separateness of each part, the isolation of the building itself as an abstract formal object unattached to its surroundings, and the grandiloquent statement of the two-storied central room, with its almost ceremonial stairway, give the Institute a monumentality in the tradition of the great architecture of the past.

Johnson's variety of solution, his exploitation of contemporary techniques, his sense of the appropriate, and as always, his refinement, are admirably represented in the New York State Pavilion, built initially for the 1964–1965 New York World's Fair, but retained as a permanent structure. Especially notable is the huge elliptical roof cantilevered from the columnar supports and suspended by cables from a compression ring.

To submit an architect's work to the kind of analysis which simplifies the process of its being categorized is always arbitrary. In the case of Philip Johnson it is especially unfair to limit his recent contribution to mere historicism. Furthermore, historicism has given sanction to much of the new monumentality of Kahn, Saarinen Associates, and others, though it has taken a very different course in the consistent elegance and spatial sensitivity of Johnson.

Emerging Trends

The various reactions against the established architectural tradition of the mid-century have diverted the public (and some critics) from realizing the importance of the renewal and re-interpretation of the mainstream of modern architecture. Though at its most obvious this trend sometimes becomes an overdramatization of the expression of function and structure ("muscle-flexing architecture," as Philip Johnson calls it), when it is subtler it is a genuine assertion of the essential character of a building and its use. What chiefly distinguishes this architecture from its immediate antecedents is a minimization of volume and of free-flowing continuity, and a return to an emphasis on definition of spatial areas and of mass. The last is achieved by a liberal admixture of steel, glass, and plastic with heavy materials such as stone and concrete. The result is often genuine monumentality or, where appropriate, even a formality that is unfamiliar in contemporary architecture as a whole (except in certain aspects of Wright's early work) and difficult to attain in terms of the open, informal International Style. Such a structure as the Larkin Company Administration Building (Illustration 6–6), representing the classical or formal aspects of Wright's functional organicism, serves as a link unifying a half-century of American architecture, for the impression made by Kahn's Richards Medical Research Building at the University of Pennsylvania (Illustration 6–33), and, to a lesser extent, Rudolph's new Art and Architecture Building at Yale (Illustration 6–32), is certainly similar to that which Wright's now destroyed building at Buffalo must have achieved. The new Boston City Hall by Kallmann, McKinnell and Knowles is an excellent exemplification of the characteristics of this trend in contemporary architecture at its most recent; the division between public, working, and ceremonial areas is clearly indicated, and a massive monumentality is expressed in the material, the structural elements, and the bold silhouette.

Since about 1958 the work of Marcel Breuer, Eero Saarinen Associates, and most of that of Paul Rudolph is representative of the general trend in architecture toward a more expressive and monumental functionalism, while that of Louis Kahn has been consistently so since 1950. Their buildings are not superficially alike, anymore than are Wright's, since in each case the structure takes the form which is given by the circumstances. Breuer's Lecture Hall wing, 1959, for the University Heights campus of New York University, in the Bronx, is one of the earliest examples of this contemporary trend. The important feature of this building is a large cubic area cantilevered out over a steeply sloping site, enclosing two lecture halls in an envelope of concrete and brick which perfectly expresses their shape. The building, picturesquely situated and strongly modeled, is a vigorous affirmation of function and form far more successful than the same architect's church for St. John's Benedictine Abbey at Collegeville, Minnesota (designed in 1953 and completed in 1961), where, though the dimensions are large, the forms are somewhat fragile and mechanical and the scale attenuated, thereby achieving size but not monumentality. The perhaps exaggeratedly robust character of the Lecture Hall and of the same architect's new building for the Whitney Museum of American Art in New

6–30. Dulles International Airport Terminal, Chantilly, Virginia, 1963, by Eero Saarinen and Associates.

large scale and daring simplicity of the great hammock-type roof slung on pylons that are equally grand in proportion. (Unfortunately, the scale of the interior elements is not well related to the magnificent covering.) But in spite of this, at least from the exterior the Dulles Airport Terminal is a structure which at first glance expresses visually what it is—an important monument and an example of functional engineering clearly defined in formal terms. Since the untimely death of Eero Saarinen in 1961, the firm's present designer, Kevin Roche, has been carrying on the tradition of the best work of the firm with an imagination and authority which are his own. Among the most impressive architectural conceptions of the mid-century are Roche's proposed building for the Ford Foundation to be built on Forty-second Street, New York, and the Fine Arts Center proposed for the University of Massachusetts at Amherst, 1964–1965 (Illustration 6–31). The former incorporates a section (to be extensively planted) enclosed in glass on two sides to resemble a huge greenhouse as high as the multistoried L-shaped building completing the enclosure; the two separated parts are joined at the top of the structure by balconies housing dining and other public rooms suspended above the enclosed plaza. The interrelationship of these areas, and the clear vista through the tall and grandly scaled entrance hall stretching from Forty-second Street to Forty-third Street continue the spatial continuities and organic functionalism of the mainstream of modern architecture, but add to it an emphasis on defined spaces and the monumentality given by generosity of scale and simplicity of form. The Fine Arts Center at Amherst is a larger and more complex structure involving the solution of the needs of the art, theater, and music departments of the University of Massachusetts as well as serving as an impressive architectural accent to define the entrance to the university's campus. Here the relation of structure, space, function, and environment is dramatically projected in a complex of buildings united by a continuity of actual passage from one to the other and by the sequence of repetitive and contrasting shapes magnificently scaled

York, 1966, is typical of the more brutal expressiveness of this kind of architecture, while Eero Saarinen's Dulles International Airport Terminal at Chantilly, Virginia, near Washington, 1963 (Illustration 6–30), is a more refined and complex example and at the same time is no less forceful. In what is perhaps his masterpiece, Eero Saarinen has created here a truly imposing building appropriate to a busy national capital. In this great structure, engineering is not subservient to the sculpturesque inclinations displayed in the same architect's Trans-World Airlines Terminal in New York, but has the very specific function of covering a large area. This fact is expressed eloquently in the

6–31. Model and detail (inset) of Fine Arts Center, University of Massachusetts, Amherst, Massachusetts, 1964–1965, by Eero Saarinen and Associates; Kevin Roche, designer.

and accented by large areas of light and shade.

In the work of Paul Rudolph visual effect is perhaps as much emphasized as is functional expressiveness, for Rudolph, like Yamasaki, is fond of beauty for its own sake though his means are more various and are seldom a mere decorative wrapping with no reference to the functioning of a building. Rudolph's early buildings (some done with Ralph S. Twitchell) were succeeded by a somewhat mannerist revolt against the International Style (as in his Jewett Art Center at Wellesley College, where the decorative role of the applied screens recalls the work of Yamasaki). Rudolph's addition to the Sarasota High School, Sarasota, Florida, 1961, is far bolder in its forms than is his earlier work,

for here Rudolph first forcefully demonstrated his belief that architecture should have a strong visual impact derived from emphatic modeling in light and shadow and not an effect of transparent insubstantiality. The boldly shaped rough concrete forms of the Sarasota High School and of his Florida houses built at the same time are powerful formal declarations that are difficult to ignore even when seen briefly from the highway. Rudolph's Yale Forestry School, 1958, and his Parking Garage, 1963, both in New Haven, Connecticut, are equally vigorous; the effect of the former derives largely from its boldly conceived rounded concrete supports, and that of the latter from its strongly modeled and dynamic concrete ramps. Rudolph's Art and Architecture Building at Yale, finished in 1963 (Illustration 6–32), is like the Larkin Building in its play of the three main elements against each other—open spaces, hollow piers, and rectangular massiveness. It is different, however, in the extent of its fenestration and in its asymmetry, factors which testify to its descent from the International Style as well as from Wright. An extremely complicated structure involving thirty-six levels, it is unified by what the architect calls a "pinwheel scheme" consisting basically of four overlapping platforms revolving around a large central space, tied down by paired hollow piers. In the manipulation of space, shape, and material (a striated concrete, as bold as Le Corbusier's, and even rougher), the building is plastically effective and spatially interesting, though perhaps a little busy in its complexity and the contradictions between open and closed, smooth and rough, and clarity and unclarity in plan—qualities which relate it to the work of some younger architects who employ

6–32. Art and Architecture Building, Yale University, New Haven, Connecticut, 1963, by Paul Rudolph.

these ambiguities even further. Rudolph's larger I. B. M. Laboratory at East Fishkill, New York, 1963 (in which the services are in closed towers), and the proposed Health, Education, and Welfare Center at Boston (a larger version of the pinwheel plan, related to open spaces and closed towers) are more unified and striking in the relative simplicity of their equally strong statement. Though structural and service elements are exploited in the design of these edifices, Rudolph does not make a fetish of the consistent integration of function and form, for he has stated that the satisfaction of functional requirements is not enough to produce good architecture. Consequently, some of the bold and forceful effects of Rudolph's later buildings are deliberate (or as some might say, arbitrary) and not necessarily the consequence of that process which results in the even more powerful forms of Kahn's buildings.

More than in the case of any of the architects just discussed, Louis I. Kahn's mature work is characterized by a clear restatement of the organic principle, by the use of mass and clearly defined spaces, by the individuality of each of his architectural solutions, and, finally, by an emphatic formal statement of these factors. In all of these respects there are affinities in Kahn's work to that of the early Wright, especially to the "classicism" of the Larkin Building and of the Universalist Church at Oak Park, Illinois. The clearly defined areas and volumes seen in Kahn's design for the First Unitarian Church at Rochester, New York, 1963, are very similar to Wright's church, and the tower-like service and communication areas of the Richards Medical Research Building (Illustration 6–33) recall the stair towers of the earlier Larkin Building.[24]

The most significant similarity between the two architects lies in their treatment of the relationship of form to function and structure. In fact, a clear restatement of the organic theory can be found in the somewhat hermetic language which Kahn uses to explain his philosophy of building. The most important task of the architect is, to Kahn, the discovery of that essential quality which makes a building what it is (its

6–33. General view (*above*) and detail (*below*) of Richards Medical Research Building, University of Pennsylvania, Philadelphia, Pennsylvania, 1958–1960, by Louis I. Kahn.

form, in Kahn's language), a quality to be expressed in terms of appropriate spaces, structure, and light, the choice of which follows from an understanding of "what the building *wants* to be"—the mechanics of design following naturally. Thus, the completed structure and its functions should be an unequivocal expression of the essential character of the particular building—which is another way of saying "form follows [or *is*] function" (though the meaning of form is different in Kahn's vocabulary). The relationship of "form" (in its conventional meaning, not Kahn's) to function and structure in Kahn's work is well illustrated by his concepts of "served" and "servant" spaces, and the clear characterization of each. At the Yale University Art Gallery, New Haven, Connecticut, 1951–1953 (AC 200, AC 200A), for instance, the heat, light, air conditioning, and other services are threaded into the concrete ceilings in a conspicuous tetrahedronal pattern which is as assertive as the gallery space itself, though it does not dominate it. The stairway is emphasized in an isolated vertical cylinder penetrating the horizontal panels in which are combined the floor, ceiling, and services.

At the Richards Medical Research Building at the University of Pennsylvania in Philadelphia, 1958–1960 (Illustration 6–33), Kahn's architectural philosophy was first consistently realized. Here, the "served" and "servant" areas are even more clearly defined. The laboratories themselves are open, appearing almost fragile between the lesser and greater towers which contain both vertical communication and the complex functions of a scientific building, including the housing of animals and disposal of waste gases. Though the contrast between open and closed space in this building has been criticized as being too great, the heavy masses of the service areas are compensated for by the powerfully eloquent structural elements (in the horizontal circulation areas and in the individual laboratories themselves), consisting of prestressed concrete members with interlocking joints laid up like dry masonry with severe clarity and, in most cases, standing dramatically free of the wall plane and straddling corners. In the recently completed laboratory building for the Salk Institute of Biological Studies at La Jolla, California, 1966, Kahn has carried further the separation of "served" and "servant" spaces than at the Medical Research Building or the newer, adjacent biology building at the University of Pennsylvania. At La Jolla the laboratory levels are totally separated from those devoted to service (which are, in fact, contained in separate floors tall enough for workmen to stand up in). The monotony of this arrangement (to which Kahn came after being convinced of the relative impracticality of an earlier, more visually pleasing solution) is compensated for by dramatically projecting stair towers which in the strong southern California light make an effective repetitive contrast of shapes.

The forms of Kahn's buildings are as expressive of function as those of Wright, and, as was the case with Wright, each of Kahn's buildings is a solution to an individual program. The appearance of the American Consulate in Portuguese Angola, for example, is largely the result of a solution to the problem of equatorial glare. Similarly, the pattern of an evenly alternating rhythm of closed and open spaces at the Jewish Community Center at Trenton, New Jersey, 1955, is the consequence of a program involving "served" and "servant" spaces in a recreation center where sports areas are juxtaposed with locker and bathing facilities. The Trenton building is also notable for illustrating very clearly Kahn's emphasis upon the definition of areas clearly isolated and non-continuous—the "thoughtful making of spaces," to use his own words.[25] (Kahn's rejection of continuity—though not necessarily of a dynamic sequence of differentiated space—is a relatively late development in his work. In his first notable building, the Yale Art Gallery, he left open space which could be freely changed to meet the demands of varying exhibition requirements—a solution which the architect later found unsatisfactory, for he would have preferred to have defined and accented the separate exhibition areas.) Kahn's project for the Museum School of Art at Philadelphia, remarkable for the boldness of its geometric ordering of space and masses and the strong play of light and shadow upon them, is the architect's strongest statement in terms of massive separateness and dramatic composition.

Kahn's strong sculpturesque shapes and his frequent use of rough concrete betray something of the influence of the later Le Corbusier and perhaps of what has been called brutalism [26] in contemporary English architecture. But this forceful plasticity is not employed for its own sake as sometimes seems to be the case with Rudolph and others. It stems rather from Kahn's search for the unique solution of what each building "wants to be" and from his emphasis on the inception of the building—the initial creative act of the architect—at the expense of later refinement. Consequently, the sometimes brash assertiveness of Kahn's buildings is a virtue to the architect, who has said that to make a building deliberately beautiful is a dastardly act—a remark which recalls the esthetic attitude of another Philadelphian, Thomas Eakins. Kahn's influence is perhaps as great as that of any living architect, though he has built relatively few buildings until recently. There are many young architects devoted to his principles, which are very similar in their organic bias to those of another great American architect and teacher, Frank Lloyd Wright.[27]

One aspect of Kahn's work, his dislike of the finished or perfected, is reflected in an interesting, somewhat eccentric aspect of the architecture of the mid-1960's (related to the principle of improvisation in the other arts): a sense of the provisional or the incomplete. This is well illustrated in John Johansen's recently constructed theater in Baltimore in which the large, almost clashing forms illustrate what he calls process rather than finality—a further development of principles enunciated in his Clewes Memorial Hall in Indianapolis, 1963, in which the architect permits interior free-form walls to compete with the still basically rectilinear shapes surrounding them. The element of ambiguity implied in such architecture, seen already in the contradictions and complexities of Rudolph's

Art and Architecture building at Yale, has become increasingly clear in recent years, appearing even in certain aspects of romantic naturalism in California where the work of Charles Moore especially seems consciously "crotchety" and complicated in the exaggeration of planes, shapes, and their relationships. In fact, Robert Venturi, one of the most interesting of the younger architects, has made virtues of complexity, contradiction, and ambiguity, feeling that a building should be readable and workable in several ways, insisting, contrary to Mies, that more is *not* less.

Whether the future of architecture lies in the direction of anonymous mass production according to a universally applicable formula, as suggested by the work and theories of Fuller; or whether there will still be a place for the individual solutions and the romanticism of a Frank Lloyd Wright, or even the subjective expression of a Saarinen, must of course remain unanswered. Meanwhile the present state of American architecture is as exciting as it is various. Confronted with such differing structures as the Guggenheim Museum, the Richards Medical Research Building, the blocks of shimmering glass skyscrapers, the Trans-World Airlines Terminal, and the ingeniously roofed great spaces by the architect-engineers, it could hardly be said that architecture has marked time since the breakdown of the International Style. As Paul Rudolph has asked: How can the golden age of modern architecture be over when so many unexplored or even undefined forms of society are crying for order?

Community Planning

Although it is difficult to prophesy which of the several trends in contemporary American architecture may eventually predominate, one direction is clear—its greater involvement within the larger context of community planning. At present, the architectural critic is faced with the realization that the history of individual buildings and their designers is becoming less significant than their relationship to their environment. Yet the problems in this field are so great, the still tentative solutions so recent, and the factors involved so complex that a survey can hardly do justice to a subject which is far more important than the treatment here suggests.

The Early Twentieth Century

At the beginning of the century, little concern was evidenced about such matters as public housing or the improvement of general living conditions, except in the creation of park areas. The energies of planners were devoted instead to the spread of the "city beautiful" ideal which had been largely inspired by the Chicago World's Fair. In fact, the controlling architect of the fair, D. H. Burnham, became the principal figure in the development of this concept, in which his European predilections were further confirmed. He was largely instrumental in imposing on American cities (by then already highly industrialized and soon to be inundated by the automobile and the dynamic concept of planning it would necessitate) an outdated, static, and grandiose esthetic suitable for the capitals of European royalty. Burnham's revival and revision, beginning in 1902, of L'Enfant's plan for Washington, in which he was assisted by Olmsted, McKim, and Saint-Gaudens, was the most appropriate expression of his ideas, because Washington, in the breadth and spaciousness of L'Enfant's essentially baroque plan and in the retrospective classicism of its buildings, is more European in feeling than any other American city—an impression Burnham and his committee increased. Elsewhere, notably in

Chicago, Cleveland, and San Francisco (and in many other cities, including Los Angeles and Detroit), Burnham's imposition of the concept of the "city beautiful" was not only inappropriate from a functional point of view, but was essentially a false front that concealed slums and industrial blight. "City beautiful" plans were usually accompanied by pretentious official buildings which reinforced the hold of the academic reaction in architecture on the expanding American city.

Yet, in spite of the negative aspects of the "city beautiful," its largeness of conception, seen in the tradition of open spaces, sweeping vistas, and the reservation of large areas for parks and parkways, has been of great benefit to many cities. For example, the Benjamin Franklin Parkway, connecting the central area with Fairmount Park, has been useful in the urban renewal of Philadelphia, and Burnham's most ambitious project, his plan for Chicago, has served that city well, especially his recommendation that the magnificent lake front be cleared of the encroachments of commerce, industry, and the railroad. Ultimately, however, the spatial conceptions of the "city beautiful" movement were as traditional as the buildings which accompanied them, for they were static, geometric, and oriented toward fixed axes of sculpture or architecture. They were thus ill-adapted, except occasionally by the accident of large scale, to the coming motor age.

Contemporaneous with the development of the "city beautiful" ideal was the movement to set aside large rural areas on the periphery of cities. These "green belts" have been a lasting contribution to community planning, especially when they have been preserved from the encroachment of parkways. (Related to this aspect of community planning is the much larger one of the national parks—and later, of the state parks —which grew out of the romantic nineteenth-century attitude toward nature and was supported by the conservationist movement to which President Theodore Roosevelt was devoted.)

One other positive contribution to community planning during these years was the replacement of the unsavory company towns of the late nineteenth century by a few which were more beneficently planned. Among these were Kohler, Wisconsin, for the Kohler Plumbing Company employees; the mining town at Ajo, Arizona, 1917 (*CPC 306); and the housing for workers at the Phelps-Dodge Copper Company, Clarkdale, Arizona, c. 1910 (*CPC 76).

In contrast to the enlightened policies of these few enterprises was the outrage of the slums, which men and women like Jacob Riis and Jane Addams were instrumental in mitigating. Though the worst aspects of the slums began to be controlled by legislation, slum clearance itself had to wait until somewhat later in the century. Accelerating an exodus begun in the post-Civil War period, an increasing number of people who could afford to do so moved to the suburbs. Prominent Philadelphians came to live in Chestnut Hill and on the Main Line rather than in the city, and Chicagoans moved to the suburbs where Frank Lloyd Wright would later build some of his prairie houses. Towns such as Radburn, New Jersey, in the more distant periphery of metropolitan areas and therefore more self-sufficient communities than suburbs, were modeled to a large extent on English garden cities,[28] incorporating curving streets, dead-end roads, and other devices to control traffic. There was variety in the architecture of these towns and, above all, they were adapted to the contour of the land and the character of the landscape. Excellent as such communities were intrinsically, especially from the point of view of health and well-being, they were nevertheless not the final solution to the problem of the interrelation of the city and country in what had become essentially an urban, industrialized society. They were no more twentieth-century in concept than was William Penn's desire for "a green country town" two and a half centuries before. As metropolises spread toward and even beyond these garden cities, they remained essentially apart. With the advent of the automobile, a closer relationship between the city and its surrounding communities, partaking of the advantages of each, could have been realized had the theory of their development been broad enough to implement a conception such as Frank Lloyd Wright's in his Broadacre City, a project embodying the proper distribution of function and amenity in a super-community that incorporated the best attributes of country, city, and suburb.

From the 1920's to the Present

The inadequacy, indeed the irrelevance, of the esthetic of both the "city beautiful" and the garden suburb became increasingly evident as the population and the number of automobiles increased. What might have been a mutual interchange of rural and urban values became instead a sharing of the disadvantages of each. With a few exceptions (such as the areas of Westchester County adjacent to New York City which took advantage of the new parkway system then beginning in the metropolitan region), a gradual erosion of many "exclusive" communities set in, as land speculators and real estate developers began to exploit the suburb as a status symbol for the white collar worker. Flimsy dwellings on bulldozed sites opened the way to relaxation of zoning laws and the encroachment of commerce and industry, creating a no-man's land which was neither rural nor urban, but chaotic, tawdry, and characterless. The situation was aggravated during the depression by the ease with which money for real estate could be acquired through government-guaranteed loans, one of the devices with which the New Deal sought to stimulate the economy. This factor, plus the continuing increase of automobiles and the reduction of the workweek to forty hours (permitting a longer weekend for the enjoyment of a house in the country), added to the exodus from the city, which was joined now by industry, eager to capitalize on a new market. The consequent creeping chaos of the countryside was matched by the urban blight caused by the depreciation of real estate values in the city. However, the economic crisis of the depression prepared the way for broad and long-range government planning of the community, from the Tennessee Valley Authority

(T. V. A.) to housing for migrant fruit pickers —programs which were supplemented by various public housing agencies, by the Slum Clearance Act of 1937, and by the cooperation of the American Federation of Labor and various civic groups.

The T. V. A., a program of flood control, power production, and soil improvement involving forty thousand square miles in seven southern states, was created primarily as an economic device to raise the living standard of a depressed area, but it also involved the social dimensions of physical and esthetic amenity. The success of the scheme has made the T. V. A. a paradigm for similar regional programs throughout the world, and has demonstrated that planning on such a large scale is possible in a free-enterprise society. The T. V. A. was a realization of the principles of community planning recommended by such theorists as Lewis Mumford, whose eloquent writing on the subject had much to do with forming the climate of opinion which made the program possible. The combination of the conservation and exploitation of natural resources with the relationship between an industrially efficient and at the same time physically and psychologically healthy social order was an impressive illustration of Mumford's "biotechnical" ideal. (It was also an exemplification on a much larger scale of Wright's Broadacre City, without the latter's architectural distinction, that is, with the exception of the dams and power plants mentioned earlier.) In the planning of the T. V. A. communities, the principles of ample and open space, variety of form, conformity with existing landscape, preservation of areas for recreational facilities, and separation of various kinds of traffic were all observed. With few exceptions this had not been the case before the depression, when most large-scale housing was handled by private developers, motivated less by social idealism than by the desire for quick profit.

With the advent of the Federal Housing Administration (F. H. A.) and other government programs, the best housing and community planning was done under the aegis of federal agencies, and, to a lesser extent, state and municipal authorities. During the later years of the depression, the government initiated new towns in country areas situated near centers of employment as an alternative to redevelopment of slum areas. Three were realized before the war: Green Hills near Cleveland, Ohio, Greendale near Milwaukee, Wisconsin, and Greenbelt, Maryland, near Washington, the last being the best known and most completely executed. In these towns—further exemplifications of Mumford's concept of the biotechnical community— the principles of good planning were again realized in complete and well-balanced garden cities protected from the infiltration of industry and commerce by a lateral wall of agricultural or park land; and characterized by a low density of building, numerous playgrounds, and various devices for the control and diversion of traffic. Though the design of individual buildings is not as satisfactory as the landscaping and planning in general, their basic functionalism is more adapted to a contemporary idiom than is the case in private "developments" which catered to the nostalgic taste for the colonial and other revivals.

There were, however, a few exceptions to the generally mediocre level of design in the government projects. Among the best were the communities for agricultural workers at Chandler, Arizona, by DeMars and Cairns, 1936–1937 (CPC 51B), and at Woodville, California, by DeMars and others, where there is an adaptation of plan and elevation to the character of the terrain. Some of the best government projects were done during World War II: a community at Center Lane, Michigan, by the elder Saarinen; the Baldwin Hills Development in Los Angeles, California, by Clarence Stein and Robert Alexander; Oscar Stonorov's Carver Court, Coatesville, Pennsylvania; and McLaughlin Heights at Vancouver, Washington, 1942 (AC 22), the first important work by Pietro Belluschi, which incorporates what amounts to the first shopping center. McLaughlin Heights is especially well suited to its environment. Open and spacious in layout, with a consciously emphasized core, it includes the best of the English "new town" principles and at the same time marks the emergence of a regional style which marked Belluschi's work and that of other architects on the northwest coast after World War II. Constructed of unpainted local wood, removed from through-traffic, designed with adequate and inconspicuous parking, and incorporating covered passages (necessary in this rainy region), the development in spite of its hugeness is intimate, informal, and not at all regimented. Neutra's Channel Heights, 1943 (Illustration 6–34), at San Pedro in the Los Angeles region, is one of the most successful of the government-sponsored communities. The units were mass-produced, yet are characterized

6–34. Channel Heights, San Pedro, California, 1943, by Richard Neutra.

by a consistent nicety of design which extends from structural details to furniture. Native redwood is used for frame and trim. Necessarily repetitive, the units are nevertheless varied in orientation and very much a part of the gullied terrain, and as many of the units as possible are situated to take advantage of the sweeping views to the sea. Neutra was concerned not only with the design of the houses individually and in groups as seen by the residents, but he took into account the effect of the project when viewed at a distance from moving cars, one of the first instances of the recognition of this new esthetic dimension. Neutra was also aware of other aspects of planning involving the automobile, for he has provided adequate space for parking and for separation of vehicular from pedestrian traffic.

Such communities as those just discussed are separate towns, similar to the company towns and the garden cities; there were also ambitious housing programs within the cities. Among the best of these are the Carl Mackley Houses in Philadelphia, by Barney, Kastner and Stonorov, c. 1935 (CPC 232), and the Williamsburg Houses in Brooklyn, New York, by Shreve, Bly, Del Gaudio, Holden and Lescaze, 1936 (CPC 176), both projects demonstrating an assimilation of the best of the International Style, though somewhat rigidly and mechanically. William Wilson Wurster's Valencia Gardens at San Francisco, California, 1943 (AC 490A) (begun as an F. H. A. low-rent project), is more distinguished. It is less regimented than the Mackley Houses, embodying the best of the vigorous regionalism of the Bay school, and its variety in both architecture and planting gives the project an air of relaxed and unmechanized leisure.

Unfortunately, after the period of international crisis not enough impetus was given by public or private capital to continue the support of these auspicious beginnings of public housing on a large scale. At the same time there was little response to community housing on the part of the typical American, who still preferred his handkerchief-sized plot with its tiny and inadequate detached house to any form of communal living, no matter how attractive.

Thus the problems of large-scale housing and the solution of urban decay were put off again, and most architects turned to work for individual clients. This is not to say that there was no public housing, or that some projects were not of superior quality. Two outstanding examples are Stonorov's Schuylkill Falls in Philadelphia, 1955, and Skidmore, Owings & Merrill's Lake Meadows in Chicago, begun in 1950, a realization of Le Corbusier's early town-planning ideas on a large scale.

However, much of the government-sponsored metropolitan housing programs and those financed by the large insurance companies are architecturally unimaginative and dreary, though they meet the basic demands of city planning. These buildings, characterized by monotonous repetition of geometric forms, texture, and color, are all the more undistinguished when contrasted with the liveliness and variety of public housing in other countries, especially in Latin America. Comparison of Stuyvesant Town in New York with Ciudad Juarez or Ciudad Alémán in Mexico City makes their differences all too apparent.

In the field of large-scale housing it must be confessed that private enterprise has been more successful than have publicly sponsored programs. Walter R. McCormack's Cedar Central Apartments in Cleveland, 1936 (CPC 78), is an outstanding example. Comprising three-story buildings covering only thirty-two per cent of the total area, incorporating several playgrounds, and exhibiting some variety of grouping, they rank with Valencia Gardens in their pleasant informality. Though perhaps not on a large enough scale to be considered in the same category as mass housing, Mies's Promontory Apartments, 1950 (AC 260), and the apartments at 860 Lake Shore Drive (Illustration 6–19), in Chicago, and the apartment building constructed in 1950 (AC 209) on Memorial Drive near the Massachusetts Institute of Technology in Cambridge (by a combination of distinguished architects including Carl Koch, Vernon DeMars, and members of the M. I. T. faculty), set a high standard which was upheld in the much larger projects by Mies in Lafayette Park in Detroit, and in Newark, New Jersey. These and the Zeckendorff housing projects designed by I. M. Pei, especially the units at Kips Bay in New York City, have the distinction to be expected of such architects, as well as the amenities of well-conceived town planning.

Some of the most satisfactory work of this type is being done in California, where the more informal and even rural character of the best of the California tradition has been applied to large-scale housing with excellent results. An interesting summary of the imaginative and original approach to this field on the West Coast is provided by the competition designs for the Golden Gateway Project for San Francisco, in which Wurster, DeMars, and Skidmore, Owings & Merrill (the San Francisco office) were among those competing. The winning design was by Warnecke and Beckett. One of the most satisfactory of the executed programs in California is Capital Towers Redevelopment Project, 1961, in Sacramento, by a combination of architects (Wurster, Bernardi and Emmons, Edward L. Barnes, and DeMars and Reay) some of whom are the most accomplished of the California school. Jointly planned by architects and developers—the kind of cooperation most needed in an era of large-scale building—this project is orderly, like those of Mies and Pei, yet it is also informal and more humanly scaled. Its blocks and closed courts are sufficiently urban to relate it to its immediate environment, and the parking garage is an important part of the design; yet the variation of alternating high and low-rise buildings, their staggered siting, and the prominent use of "breezeways" make Capital Towers one of the least monotonous of housing projects. The interesting plan, in which the upper apartments face one way and those on the lower floors face another, insures maximum privacy and gives the design heightened visual interest.

On the whole, the problem of large-scale housing has not been satisfactorily met. Unfortunately the most well-known examples are those typified by the Levitt towns, which are characterized by their combination of stylistic nostalgia and monotony, representing two prominent aspects of the American temperament—conservatism and conformity—as well as a curious

romanticism, for the split-level colonial ranch house is as self-contradictory as the concept of the hardtop convertible. Occasional rare exceptions, however, such as the Mill Valley Builders Development in California, 1956 (*CPC 305), and the new town of Reston, Virginia, are more encouraging.

One of the solutions to the housing problem, prefabrication, has always seemed feasible but has seldom worked out in practice. In the 1920's and 1930's, large firms such as the American Radiator Company and Johns Manville attempted the manufacture of prefabricated housing but found it unprofitable. Even Gropius and Mies worked on the problem, and one of the most original minds of the century, Buckminster Fuller, put his energies into it. Though mass production of standardized parts has been successful in supplying details in skyscrapers and other buildings, this system has been impossible to apply to entire buildings—a situation complicated by builders, plumbers, and unions, and by dealers in fixtures and other commodities. Carl Koch's "Techbuilt" House, as exemplified in the Stoddard House, 1953 (AC 207, AC 207A), has proved to be the most successful of a number of similar ventures, probably because it is largely of wood and because local contractors and suppliers are involved as cobuilders.

Housing is only one of the many problems facing the contemporary architect. He is forced to work increasingly with town planners in the larger dimensions of whole cities and regions, in programs which have been initiated to counter the decay of the older cities and to cope with the expansion of others, such as Los Angeles. Very little had been done before World War II on a large scale in this respect (with the outstanding exception of T. V. A.), but the effect of the automobile and related factors on the decay of the city center and the growth of urban sprawl inevitably resulted in the beginnings of closer cooperation among various civic and governmental groups. In its initial phases urban redevelopment was too diverse and overlapping in authority to be efficient, a situation which has gradually been rectified in more far-reaching and coordinated programs under more unified authority—generally referred to as urban renewal as opposed to urban redevelopment. Further cooperation among municipal, state, and federal agencies has accelerated and codified the process, and it has been implemented by the passage of legislation in the fields of zoning and financing. The first state to take advantage of such legislation was Pennsylvania; Pittsburgh became the first major city to embrace a plan of extensive urban renewal, and Philadelphia soon followed. A comprehensive exhibition in Philadelphia in 1947, designed to encourage citizen participation, initiated the most ambitious program in urban renewal which has occurred to date, setting a precedent for similar projects in many other American cities.

The rehabilitation of urban centers is one of the most significant architectural and sociological realities of the mid-1960's. The new downtown areas are generally characterized by improved circulation and parking facilities, an emphasis on shopping, entertainment, hotels, and cultural structures, and a minimization of warehousing, distribution, and manufacturing. In certain instances, motor traffic has been banned from these civic centers entirely, as in some streets in Philadelphia. Elsewhere small buses and trolleys have been proposed, following recommendations by Victor Gruen, an expert in town planning and design of shopping centers. In many instances these new city centers are partially bounded by and at the same time integrated with superhighway systems.

Constitution Plaza in Hartford, Connecticut, Charles Dubose, general designer and coordinator, 1960–1966 (Illustration 6–35), not only successfully exemplifies most of the best features of a civic center, but is also probably the most beautiful of the new urban renewal complexes. This is due not only to the incorporation in it of such a handsome structure as Harrison & Abramovitz' Phoenix Life Insurance Company Building, but also to the extra care lavished on such details as fountains and planting, the latter under the direction of Sasaki, Walker & Associates. (The excellence of Constitution Plaza is perhaps attributable to the in-

6–35. Constitution Plaza, Hartford, Connecticut, 1960–1966, Charles Dubose, general designer and coordinator.

volvement of private capital in its construction. No local civil agency was prepared to carry through such an ambitious plan, but business men in the area were sufficiently interested in stopping the decay of the inner city to risk greater expenditure in order to attract higher returns.)

Besides the urban renewal at Philadelphia and Hartford, other oustanding instances of successful downtown rehabilitation are Erie View Plaza at Cleveland, Weybosset Hill at Providence, and Charles Center at Baltimore. Rochester, New Haven, and San Francisco are also noteworthy for their programs, which are less concentrated in one area and distributed throughout the city. New Haven's renewal represents an outstanding instance of cooperation between government and citizens.

Boston is one of the most interesting and instructive examples of urban renewal. Two areas, the Back Bay Center Development and the Government Center, exemplify the complexity of the problem of privately versus publicly managed programs. The original proposal for the Back Bay Center Development, by a group of well-known architects who called themselves for this purpose the Boston Center Architects and who proposed to work closely with government agencies, was considered impractical, and was turned over to the Prudential Life Insurance Company, which was not equipped to accommodate the various problems of motor, bus, and railway traffic easements into the complex. The solution, by Charles Luckman and Associates, is dominated by the Prudential Tower and is not nearly as distinguished as Constitution Plaza where much more was at stake for the investors, who consequently spent more. The Government Center, however, comprising the Federal Office Building (begun too soon to be integrated from the beginning with the overall plan conceived later), the new City Hall, and the Boston Government Service Center, including the departments of Health, Welfare, and Employment Security, is a masterpiece of civic design involving a conception of urban spaciousness and monumentality unmatched in the twentieth century. The master plan is that of I. M. Pei, assisted by Walter Gropius, with Paul Rudolph as the consulting architect. Rudolph also designed the Service Center, incorporating a twenty-three story tower in a complex of variform structures. Rudolph's buildings and the City Hall by Kallmann, McKinnell, and Knowles give an imposing and spacious character to an architectural complex which surrounds a square larger than that of the Piazza di San Marco in Venice or St. Peter's Square in Rome, and which is kept intentionally urban since Boston is sufficiently graced with parks.

Such instances of a concentrated attack on urban evils are evidence that all American cities have not surrendered to the demands of the automobile, as has almost happened, for instance, in Los Angeles, where so much of the metropolitan area has been surrendered to parking places and to freeways and their approaches.

The large problems of community planning in our age of population and transportation expansion have challenged the best and most original architects of the century—Le Corbusier, Buckminster Fuller, Frank Lloyd Wright, and Louis Kahn. The latter's far-reaching recommendations, especially those of 1955–1956 for midtown Philadelphia, encompassing expressways, parking towers, subsidiary streets, culs-de-sac, and pedestrian ways, have influenced much that has occurred recently in Philadelphia (though somewhat indirectly) and elsewhere.

The fascination of starting fresh with a utopian situation has inspired others besides Wright, notably Paolo Solari, whose City on a Mesa, a proposed community for two million people, is a grandiose conception of a self-sufficient city on a plateau, its purpose being to demonstrate how a huge city of high density can be made workable and agreeable by exploiting automation and removing the "blight" of the automobile.

Such imaginative schemes, however stimulating and catalystic, are still in the realm of fantasy. Meanwhile the problem of the actual city remains, and in the process of its solution there is the danger that certain subtle human values may be lost by the imposition of arbitrary patterns of impersonal order and logic. (This danger is summed up by Philip Johnson's phrase "urban removal.") The personalities of individual cities, with their complex of associations, monuments, and that undefinable urbanity which still draws people to them in spite of their inconvenience and discomfort, should not be ignored by the doctrinaire city planner. The character of the older sections of Boston, for instance, has been greatly altered by a system of elevated highways which has imposed the dimensions of the twentieth century on the more intimate scale of the older areas in an unnecessarily intrusive way. A similar mistake was partially avoided by the citizens of San Francisco when they united to prevent continuing abuse of their city's personality, threatened by a further extension of the freeway system, the first link of which had ruined the character of the city's picturesque waterfront.[29] But even worse than the myopic logic of the highway engineers is the vandalism perpetrated in the name of culture, as in the case of the area surrounding Independence Hall in Philadelphia, where square miles of interesting and sometimes distinguished architecture have been razed because the structures were not in a particular period, the limits of which had been arbitrarily set. Not only has this section of the old city lost all its flavor, but notable structures such as Furness' Provident Trust Company Building have been unceremoniously removed.

Among the more interesting recent theories in community planning are those of Ludwig Hilbeersheimer (who has been assisting Mies in his large-scale housing programs), who recommends converting the grid pattern into superblocks, with every fifth block a green space. Victor Gruen's scheme of forbidding vehicular traffic in the city center (substituting slow vehicles to bring shoppers and visitors from parking areas situated on the periphery) is more interesting, for it would preserve the amenities of the city center and remove the disadvantages which have accrued to it as the consequence of the motor age. A most radical but at the same time attractive thesis has been expounded by Jane Jacobs in *Life and Death of American*

Cities (1961). She believes in the principle of controlled organic growth to preserve the diversity found in various urban neighborhoods, a diversity which is so often rudely shattered by mile-wide demolition in the name of logical planning. Consequently, she recommends not arbitrary simplicity but an ordered complexity to take into account intangible values which are as much a part of the total human environment as are physical ones.

But finally the problem of the individual town or city cannot be considered separately from its region. Among the more successful aspects of both the New Haven and Hartford redevelopments, for instance, is the incorporation of the Connecticut freeway system in their overall plans.

As a matter of fact, regional planners now consider the area stretching from Norfolk, Virginia, to Portland, Maine, as one huge urban district. The advantages to be gained from government and private cooperation in this megalopolis would permit an ideally balanced integration of residential, commercial, industrial, cultural, and recreational development. Residential overcrowding and proximity to industry would be relieved, and an increase in low-density housing as well as the retention of open space in a still varied and beautiful terrain would be encouraged.

Painting: Introduction

At the beginning of the discussion of the painting of the post-Civil War period, in Part Five, it was necessary to examine briefly the contemporaneous art of Europe to understand its influence on American art. Such a procedure is even more necessary in a discussion of art in the twentieth century, for European art, particularly in France during the late nineteenth century and throughout the Continent in the twentieth century, underwent a change as profound as the transition between the Middle Ages and the Renaissance—a change which was natu-

rally reflected in American art. Modern art, as the consequences of this change have generally been called, is as various as that of any period, ranging from the persistence of realism (in a form inevitably altered during the twentieth century) to the extremes of subjective abstraction. The main trend has been in the direction of antirealism, encompassing the most ordered and logical formality as well as the most undisciplined informality, but sharing one identifying characteristic: a reaction opposing the realistic or naturalistic bias of western art as it had prevailed since the Renaissance, reaching a climax in the completely visual and antiformal phenomenon of impressionism. The history of this movement in Europe from the 1880's to the 1960's can be summarized as follows. It began with the reactions against realism and impressionism in the generation of artists called the post-impressionists, who are generally agreed to be Seurat, Cézanne, Gauguin, and Van Gogh (though there is a growing tendency to include the Norwegian Edvard Munch among them). There followed the formulation of a new way of seeing, especially by Cézanne, and the expression of a more inner vision by Van Gogh and Munch. These two tendencies were reduced to the formalism of cubism and other intellectual abstraction on the one hand, and the emotional intensity of expressionism on the other. In the twentieth century, these two movements became to a certain degree—and at the risk of oversimplification—the continuing poles of classicism and romanticism, in the form-language of abstraction rather than of realism. Finally, an entirely new artistic dimension was added—surrealism, with its exploitation of the unconscious and of spontaneous improvisation.[30]

The complex interrelationship between Cézanne's flat and three-dimensional forms (or, reduced to simplest terms, planes and cubes), which led to cubism, produced variations on the theme of three-dimensionality represented two-dimensionally and the visual accidents accompanying this transformation. These were played upon by Picasso, Braque, Gris, and others, in some of the most formally sophisticated pictures ever painted. The transition from cubism to complete non-representation in painting and the graphic arts (and in sculpture) followed naturally but not immediately. The process can be traced from analytic cubism through synthetic cubism, in which the object became increasingly less important than the composition, to Orphism, in which dynamic color transformed the prismatic forms of cubism into curvilinear elements. The dynamic aspect of Orphism was paralleled in futurism, an Italian movement whose influence exceeded its intrinsic impor-

tance, and which emphasized motion as a significant part of contemporary life. Orphism was carried into pure color abstractions by Robert Delaunay, and back again into partial representation by Marcel Duchamp.

Purism in France, represented by Le Corbusier and Amédée Ozenfant, "purified" the object of much of its accidental aspect. Meanwhile, suprematism in Russia and the de Stijl movement in Holland produced abstract styles of mathematical clarity. The suprematist Casimir Malevich's *White on White,* 1918 (Museum of Modern Art, New York), represents a logical conclusion to this development, an almost hermetic subtlety which has had a significant revival in recent American abstract painting. Piet Mondrian's rectilinear and precise "neoplasticism" emerged as an artistic means for representing the universal order with the subtlest proportional relationships. The constructivism of Gabo and Pevsner, which succeeded suprematism, was characterized by its integration of artistic sensibility with principles of mathematics and concepts of space and time. Thus the constructs and sculpture of the constructivists are communications which are not strictly abstract but which incorporate universal experience. They are therefore somewhat less austere and restricted than the rectilinear paintings of Malevich and Mondrian, for in them there is implied a greater complexity of interpenetrations of time and space.

In abstract geometric art, the beauty of pure form, envisaged by Pythagoras and Plato, was at last actualized. Meanwhile the other pole of modern art—its emotional, romantic, and subjective aspect—was developing in France in the Fauve movement and in Germany in expressionism. The purpose of the Fauves was the expression (not the symbolizing) of feeling through color. Though Henri Matisse (a Fauve in his early work) in his classical French way sought for and achieved a pleasant and relaxed order, it was *feeling* that he wished to express, even if sometimes the results seemed merely decorative. The German expressionists [31] were in no way classical, for they wanted to express not order, harmony, and logic, but restlessness, fantasy, and the indeterminateness of the infinite and ineffable. Expressionism took two courses: the first, a continuation of the heightening and distillation of reality seen already in Van Gogh and to a certain extent in Munch; the second, a rejection of outward reality and an intensification of the connotative aspects of abstraction. The first group is represented by such artists as Emil Nolde, Ernst Kirchner, and Karl Schmidt-Rottluff (and, by association of place and time, Oscar Kokoschka, though he was never an expressionist in the strict sense), whose humanistically oriented art, like that of the Fauves and Matisse, was not overwhelmed by abstraction. The second is represented by the German Franz Marc and the Russian Wassily Kandinsky, whose combination of a subjective mysticism with the form language of cubism and futurism resulted in an increasingly abstract expression. Kandinsky felt that colors and forms alone, and not what they represented, would convey emotion directly in a way analogous to music, in which harmony, rhythm, and counterpoint are the materials of composition but are only rarely used for the reproduction of the sounds of nature.

Paul Klee, a Swiss who came under the same formative influences as did Kandinsky (and partly under the latter's direct inspiration), originated a more precise esthetic of modern art, formulated when he was teaching at Gropius' Bauhaus. Klee recognized the primary importance of subjective and intuitive processes as sources of creativity. But he insisted that the grammar and vocabulary of pictorial forms (line, shape, color, texture) must be thoroughly understood before the unveiling of the subjective could be entrusted to them. His own work, filled with fantasy and imagination, is projected with a delicate graphic and coloristic charm, and derives much of its inspiration not only from medieval and exotic sources but from the art of children and of primitive peoples. Klee created a various and lively formal vocabulary which has had as great an influence on twentieth-century art as have his theories.

Meanwhile the importance of intuition in the creative process was carried further by the sur-

realists in their acceptance of the unconscious as the only pure source of artistic creation; its activity was not to be interfered with by conventional logic. Surrealism was sired partly by Dada, a movement motivated by a desire to puncture all pretension, especially artistic, by employing the various devices of modern art for their shock value; and, more significantly, by the use of humor (especially the absurd) as an agent of ridicule, exemplified in the concept of Mona Lisa's mustache. Humor, depending for much of its effect on the pertinence of certain illogical relationships, is not unrelated to other aspects of the unconscious, the dream and automatic writing, both of which are the most important ingredients of surrealism itself. These, together with the exploitation of the accident (spilled ink, splattered paint) as a further stimulus for fantasy, contributed to the revolutionary character of surrealism. The meaning of surrealist forms lies in their reference to layers of experience entirely different from those of the conscious mind, that is, to experience projected and related through irrational and autistic logic, or "pure psychic automatism," as its cofounder André Breton described it in the *First Manifesto of Surrealism.*

Salvador Dali's showmanship, on the personal level and in his readily understood themes and technical dexterity, makes him the popular representative of surrealism, although his meticulous method of realizing his dreams is somewhat too conscious to be strictly surrealist. The strange images and metamorphosing forms of Hans Arp, André Masson, and, above all, Joan Miró are more consistent with surrealist theory, although the laws of chance in the work of these artists seem to coincide with the laws of beauty, which implies a process similar to that of Kandinsky's in his translation of his almost automatic *Improvisations* into his more studied and deliberate *Compositions.* Their work is not, therefore, pure surrealism, for their use of esthetic judgment (a function of the conscious mind) restricts the otherwise free play of the unconscious. What Sam Hunter has called the surrealist bestiary—the abstract shapes evolved from the disinterested processes of automatism and chance, refined and developed by such sensibilities as that of Miró—has served even Picasso well, and has been of inestimable value in the formation of the vocabulary of abstract expressionism.

No survey, however brief, can omit mention of the post-cubist Picasso. For, although he was not the innovator of movements subsequent to cubism, the integration into his own work of other aspects of contemporary art (together with his reinterpretation of ancient and medieval forms, especially Catalan) has created images and archetypes impossible to ignore. A whole artistic generation, for instance, has been influenced by his *Guernica,* whose powerfully expressive forms incorporate not only Picasso's many years of formal exploration, but also his familiarity with the methods and artistic products of surrealism as well as with aspects of expressionism.

The mainstream of modern art is made up of the three currents of abstraction, expressionism, and surrealism flowing together to a greater or lesser degree, combined or not with cross currents of representationalism—sometimes extensively, as in the case of Picasso. Abstract expressionism, the most central of the contemporary movements, is affected by representationalism hardly at all, and is perhaps more influenced by surrealism (especially in its exploitation of the automatic and the accidental) than by either of the two movements which compose its name—at best a misnomer, as recent criticism frequently points out.

Abstract expressionism flourished with particular vigor in the United States, if indeed it did not originate here. The story of the figurative arts of the 1960's in the United States can be summarized as a series of positive or negative reactions to it. These artistic trends range from an intensification of pure abstraction into a lyricism of form and color or into actual physiological optics (often referred to as "op art"), to a belligerent return to reality in terms of mass communication and even a kind of anonymity in "pop art."

Before the Armory Show

The situation in painting at the opening of the century was conservative, if not smug. Though men like Homer, Eakins, and Ryder were still at work, American painting as a whole was neither progressive nor very interesting. The revival of the academies, signalized in 1906 by the reamalgamation of the Society of American Artists with the National Academy, gave increased authority to the school of classicist mural painting (which found its most conspicuous expression in the decorations of the Library of Congress) and to a facile impressionism in landscape and figure painting. The work of "the ten," which seemed advanced in the 1890's, now appears pale in contrast to the vigor of the best painting that preceded and followed it. But just as the self-congratulatory optimism of established social and economic institutions was challenged by the reform movements of the early part of the century, so artistic conservatism was challenged and finally overthrown, first by a reinvigorated realism led by Robert Henri and his pupils, and later by the modern movement which was introduced into this country during the early years of the century.

In 1907 the conservative jury of the Academy of Design rejected the work of several young realist painters who had recently come into prominence. The following year, these men— George Luks, John Sloan, and William J. Glackens, together with their friend Everett Shinn, and their mentor Robert Henri—joined with Arthur B. Davies (an artist in the idealist tradition), Ernest Lawson (an impressionist landscapist), and Maurice Prendergast to form "the eight," and held an exhibition in 1909 at the Macbeth Galleries in New York. Lawson, Davies, and Prendergast were as different from each other as from the others taken as a group, for "the eight" were bound not by stylistic similarity but by a common attitude of revolt against the conventionalists of their time—the academic muralists, the suave portraitists, and the impressionist landscapists and figure painters, particularly those represented among "the ten," whose work had by this time become too genteel and overrefined.

Though the other painters, especially Prendergast, were far from negligible, the realists among "the eight" were the most significant. Led by the esthetic attitudes of Robert Henri, who believed life to be of greater importance than style, and having in common the reportorial experience of artist-journalists, theirs was a common point of view: the recording of the world around them. Their work is characterized by a return to the realistic aspects of early impressionism, and represents also a continuation of the post-Civil War genre tradition which was carried on best, though least topically, by such men as Thomas Eakins and Thomas Anschutz. From the perspective of the mid-twentieth century, this phenomenon of a revitalized genre in the style of early impressionism seems regressive, but its vitality—the consequence both of the teaching of Henri and of a genuine involvement and interest in the social scene—saves it from actually being so.

In addition to Velázquez and Hals, Henri admired Goya and Daumier for their humanity, though he little understood their style. The story-telling immediacy of the "ashcan" school (as it came to be called after the term was used in a derogatory review) is enhanced by a technical brilliance derived from training at the Pennsylvania Academy, undergone by most of the group, and from Henri's emphasis in his teaching on the quality of paint and its application. The topicality of the group's pictures is always expressed in a painterly and coloristic way and by lively drawing which is generally sound even in the most spontaneously executed canvases. They made the various and vigorous activity of New York come to life: the Bowery, Fifth Avenue, Central Park, the teeming slums, and the entertainment world of the theater, the music halls, and the early movie houses. Something of the exaggerated exuberance of vaude-

ville and ragtime spills over into the work of all these artists—almost raucously in Luks, more subtly and richly in Sloan, and literally in Shinn, whose subjects are often concerned with the spectacles of the stage.

The well-worn path blazed by the early impressionists and by Chase and Duveneck was followed closely in the portraits of Henri, which are very similar to those of Duveneck especially. The lively painting of a colored girl, *Eva Green,* 1907 (PC 212), and the broadly handled *Portrait of George Luks,* 1904 (PC 713), are notable for their brash directness and have little of the refinement and facility of Sargent's brand of impressionism. Henri's city-scapes, equally bold and spontaneous, are more interesting, such as *Fifty-seventh Street,* 1902 (PC 211). Henri replaced Chase's always pleasant subjects with the rawness of ordinary and even ugly scenes and figures which are depicted with bold chiaroscuro.

Henri's teaching was more vital and original than his paintings and had great influence on his pupils both in Philadelphia and later in New York. John Sloan was perhaps the best of them, as well as the outstanding member of the "ashcan" school. Delighted with the color, movement, and incidents of New York, he caught its every mood—the melancholy of the *Wake of the Ferry,* 1907 (*PC 920), the seriocomic drinking at *McSorley's Bar,* 1908 (Illustration 6–36), the humor of the *Hairdresser's Window,* 1907 (Wadsworth Athenaeum), the everyday poetry of cats and children playing in new fallen snow in *Backyards, Greenwich Village,* 1914 (PC 423). The metropolis was a source of continuous pleasure to Sloan (at least until his style changed late in his life). Even in the relatively late *Sixth Avenue Elevated at Third Street,* 1928 (PC 427), the artist celebrates a picturesque confusion of elevated trains, street cars, and motor traffic, the latter entangled in a gaggle of giggling and wind-blown girls. Like all great genre painters Sloan had a deep interest in the lives of the people he painted, from the inebriation of the habitués of McSorley's to the more Bohemian jollity of *Yeats*

6–36. John Sloan, *McSorley's Bar*, 1908. Oil on canvas. 26 x 32 inches. (Courtesy of the Detroit Institute of Arts.)

at Petitpas, 1910 (*PC 922). One of Sloan's most engaging subjects is *Three A.M.,* 1909 (PC 426), in which, during the preparation of a late cup of coffee, a half-naked girl in her nightdress is shown listening to her gaily dressed roommate tell of the evening's adventures. Sloan enjoyed other scenes, provided there were people in them, such as the *Picnic Grounds,* 1906–1907 (*PC 424), or the *South Beach Bathers,* 1908 (PC 425), with its sprawling, preening, playing humanity.

Sloan's broadly handled impressionistic brush work, the structure of his composition, and the solidity of his drawing give his lively and sympathetic comments on the metropolis a vigorous artistic foundation. The quality of his draughtsmanship is shown especially well in his etchings. *Turning Out the Light,* 1905 (GC 70), is boldly conceived in chiaroscuro and touching in its intimacy, while *Roofs, Summer Night,* 1906 (GC 69), is a strongly designed panorama of sleepers on rooftops escaping the heat of the tenements below.[32]

George Luks had Sloan's vigor but not his variety and love of people or his technical solidity. Luks preferred the more obvious and superficial, and made a fetish of the bold stroke, modeled after the surface brilliance of Hals but lacking the background of careful study which gave solidity to the Dutch painter's bravura. Luks enjoyed depicting brute force, as shown in his *Wrestlers,* 1905 (PC 289), a picture which comes close to caricature. Yet sometimes he could be quaint or even pretty in his portraits, as in the *Little Madonna,* 1907 (Addison Gallery of American Art, Phillips Academy, Andover, Massachusetts). His *Old Duchess,* 1905 (*PC 287), is more solid—like a Henri with more bombast and surface variety. Luks's emphasis on the quality of paint itself, at least in his earlier work (where it is still somewhat controlled), is rewarding, as in the *Spielers,* 1905 (PC 288), a picture which is also characterized by an attractive gaiety and movement. The artist's large composition *Armistice Night,* 1918 (PC 783), shows an explosive disorderliness which unfortunately became increasingly typical of his later paintings.

Everett Shinn's work is not so robust and heavy-handed as that of Luks, though perhaps his facile illustrator's touch is somewhat too mannered. He had a sensitive feeling for weather and time and place, as in his pastel of *Early Morning, Paris,* 1901 (*PC 419), and for the spectacle of the gay life in general, especially the theater and vaudeville, as in the *London Hippodrome,* 1902 (PC 420). In such pictures the influence of Degas and even of Toulouse-Lautrec is evident, though much diluted by the illustrator's point of view (with its emphasis on merely superficial commentary) and by too easy pictorial formulations.

William Glackens also loved the city and the entertainment world and his early work took on a vivacity similar to that of Sloan and Luks, as in his *Hammerstein's Roof Garden,* c. 1901 (PC 155). But Glackens' work is more studied and perfected than that of Luks and finally achieves an almost monumental quality, at least in his figure pieces. Reportorial like Sloan, Glackens is also somewhat more inclined toward the elegant and stylish, as seen in the bold yet quite subtly colored *Chez Mouquin,* 1905 (PC 156), which displays an organization of form and color

more refined than that employed by any others of the "ashcan" school. A trip to Paris in 1906 revealed the full glory of the impressionist movement to Glackens, and he was ravished by it. His themes became more Renoir-like, concentrating on landscapes, nudes, and still life, and more general in concept. His city-scapes of Paris and New York are a delight, revealing Glackens' joyous and uncomplicated point of view and his magnificent sense of color. His sensuous and formal sensibility is seen at its best in the *Nude With Apple,* 1910 (Illustration 6–37), in which his studies of the figure are brought to a culmination. The nude possesses all the solidity sought for during the 1930's by Sloan, who emulated the old masters also, but to much less effect than Glackens, who absorbed Renoir's color, sensuous surface, and three-dimensionality.

Though not members of "the eight," two other artists share sufficiently the point of view and subject matter of the "ashcan" school to be considered with them—Jerome Myers and Glenn O. Coleman. Myers' *End of the Street,* 1922 (*PC 340), and *Summer Night, East End Park,* 1919 (PC 339), are late examples of his broadly painted and colorful interpretations of popular life in New York. Never bitter or programmatic, Myers' paintings reflect instead genuine delight in the picturesqueness of the slums. Had Myers been more formally gifted, the gay patterns and shapes which appear in his paintings might have developed into more sophisticated designs, as did those of Prendergast, who was also fascinated by the pictorial possibilities of everyday life.

Coleman, who studied with Henri and Shinn, brought a quite different artistic personality to bear on the New York scene, for his *Downtown Street,* 1926 (PC 77), and his lithograph *Minetta Lane,* 1928 (GC 14), have a melancholy and even a mystery quite different from Myers and from his teachers. His dark palette, the strong, somewhat overwhelming shapes of his buildings, and the odd silhouetted figures which inhabit his twilit alleys give his pictures a romantic aura that is rare for the time and place. His *Fort Lee Ferry,* 1923 (PC 578), is less characteristic but

6–37. William Glackens, *Nude With Apple,* 1910. Oil on canvas. 40 x 57 inches. (Courtesy of the Brooklyn Museum, Brooklyn, New York.)

has a boldness of composition and drawing which combines the beginning of the influence of cubism with the tendency toward abstract form seen in the simplified rectilinearity of buildings in some of his other paintings. In fact, most of Coleman's works dated in the 1920's are actually reworkings of earlier pictures and sketches, all somewhat improved by the introduction of greater compositional strength derived from his contact with modern art. In the few years just before his death in 1932, Coleman's work became too consciously abstract for successful assimilation with the point of view of the genre painter of the early years of the century.

As we have noted, three artists, Ernest Lawson, Arthur B. Davies, and Maurice Prendergast, though members of "the eight," were not at all like the five others who comprised the remainder of the "ashcan" school, nor were they profoundly affected by the turmoil of modern art (except Prendergast to a certain degree).

Ernest Lawson was a somewhat more solid painter than John Twachtman and Childe Hassam, whose impressionistic style his own resembled. His brilliant and scintillating color is more forceful than that of Twachtman and more harmoniously rich than that of Hassam, as in *Early Summer, Vermont* (PC 275) and *Winter on the River,* 1907 (PC 764). In his later work, such as *Spring Night, Harlem River,* 1913 (*PC 274), Lawson almost succeeds in achieving some of the incisive solidity which Cézanne was bringing back to landscape painting, while at the same time he preserves some of the surface charm of impressionism.

A few other impressionist painters should be mentioned along with Lawson: in landscape, Daniel Garber of Pennsylvania; and in the figure, Gari Melchers and Cecilia Beaux, who carried the Sargent portrait manner into a more conventional realism.

The work of Arthur B. Davies, who was a prime mover of "the eight," the Armory Show, and many other artistic activities, was strangely uninfluenced by any of these programs, except toward the end of his career. A late romantic, he remained true to his own inner vision, painting a dream world of Cockaigne filled with castles, lush foliage, and idealized nudes. Davies resembles Ryder in subject matter but has little of that master's power. On the contrary, his work resembles that of the banal muralists of the turn of the century; yet he never quite sinks to their level of unimaginative clichés. *The Flood,* painted before 1909 (PC 618), and the *Dream,* painted in the same era (PC 96), are typical in their decorative quality as well as in a rather pleasant sweetness which barely avoids being cloying. The artist's later work became less attractive as he became more bound up in esthetic theory. His nudes began to float in a disconcerting lighter-than-air fashion (a consequence of the fact that Davies had embraced a theory of breath control). When this mannerism was combined with ill-digested cubist and futurist principles, as in the *Dancers* (PC 97), his pictures were almost grotesque, except for their fine color harmonies.

Among Davies' best works are his prints. Perhaps the somewhat more indirect character of print-making and the subtle tonal variations of the two mediums he employed most, aquatint and lithography, mitigated the oversentimentality which is less disguised by the medium in his paintings. In any event, such prints as *Doorway to Illusion,* 1922 (*GC 16), an etching and aquatint, *Uprising,* 1919 (GC 96), a colored aquatint, and the lithograph *The Spring,* 1895 (GC 95A), not only have graphic power in their exploitation of the potentials of the mediums used—to an extent hardly matched in aquatints

until the mid-century—but also achieve a vaguely poetic mood, an effect which in Davies' paintings is diluted by a greater specificity.

Before turning to Prendergast, Louis M. Eilshemius, another artist outside the main current of his artistic generation, should be mentioned. Like Davies, he was romantic and idealist in much of his work, though the best of his early paintings are based on a sound, if naïve, realism. Though mostly self-trained, Eilshemius, in some landscapes executed at the turn of the century, such as *Bridge for Fishing,* 1905 (PC 632), has a coloristic charm and serenity of composition that are as fresh as the impressionists, and he is almost as subtly suggestive in his brush work, while preserving a transparency reminiscent of the luminists. In *The Afternoon Wind,* 1899 (PC 127), floating female nudes are added to the landscape, but without giving the impression of illustrating some high-minded work of antique or medieval literature, as would have been the case with Davies.

Eilshemius' somewhat child-like quality gradually turned into eccentricity. About 1915, the artist, now a self-styled "genius," lost most of what discipline he had and compulsively painted stacks of canvases, only some of which are successful (as if by statistical chance in the midst of such volume), as, for instance, *Tragedy,* 1916 (PC 633). The majority of his late pictures are second- and third-rate hack work, though redeemed by a certain contagious enthusiasm.

Of all the artists of these early years of the twentieth century, none has quite the present-day reputation of Maurice Prendergast. Very nearly ignored in his lifetime, Prendergast's delectable watercolors and oils are now finding increasing favor. His sense of pattern is more appealing to modern taste than it was to his contemporaries of a half-century ago, who were shocked by his boldness in both composition and color. Also, Prendergast understood and absorbed something of Cézanne's analytic attitude toward space. Much of Prendergast's work is genre, as is the case with the "ashcan" school; and, like the artists of that group, he responded enthusiastically to the life around him. But he chose its gayer, more debonair aspects—beaches, parks, and picturesque foreign places—and he never made them banal, not even Venice. He infused these subjects with a kind of innocent freshness of vision, scattering his figures and foliage gaily about the surface of his pictures, as in the watercolor *Central Park*, 1901 (PC 326). There is also in Prendergast something of the French "intimists," especially of Pierre Bonnard, a follower of the impressionists who, like Prendergast, was fascinated with the color and pattern of contemporary life. Prendergast took the impressionist dots and made of them bolder elements than did Bonnard, using them like large pieces of mosaic and sometimes as substantial slabs of color, as in *Central Park*.

There is also in Prendergast's work, especially in his figures, something of *art nouveau* (which influenced the large curvilinear and outlined forms of Gauguin and Munch), a factor which adds to the effective, bold, and decorative quality of his pictures, as in the early *Ponte della Paglia*, 1899 (*PC 325). This characteristic persists in his later work, such as *Sunset and Sea Fog*, 1915 (*PC 370), which depicts a group of vacationers at evening by the sea.

Low Tide, Beachmont, 1897 (Illustration 6–38), sums up the best and most engaging qualities of Prendergast, and also shows, as does the *Central Park* and many others, his more than decorative use of pattern. For, what appears at

6–38. Maurice Prendergast, *Low Tide, Beachmont*, 1897. Oil on canvas. 19½ x 22⅛ inches. (Worcester Art Museum, Worcester, Massachusetts.)

6–39.   George Bellows, *Stag at Sharkey's*, 1909. Oil on canvas. 36¼ x 48¼ inches. (The Cleveland Museum of Art. Hinman B. Hurlburt Collection.)

first to be merely decoration is transformed by his use of color into Cézanne's property of form-definition. Prendergast's dots and slabs of color lead the observer into the painting much as do John Marin's and Lyonel Feininger's Cézanne-like planes.

The later Prendergast is not quite as attractive —or perhaps as subtle—as the earlier. In *Sunset and Sea Fog* there was already a tendency to transform areas of form and color into mere decoration and to omit the subtler spatial relationships of the earlier work. This change, though producing a luxurious and rich effect, caused his later paintings to resemble tapestries whose purpose is primarily decorative. *Autumn Festival*, 1917–1918 (PC 371), is an example of his later decorative style.

George Bellows was younger than the artists just discussed and was not a member of "the eight," yet his work is far closer to that of Sloan, Luks, and Glackens, both in point of view and in technique, than is that of Lawson, Davies, and Prendergast. Much of his best-known work postdates his early period, but he did his best painting before he was affected by the Armory Show. The early Bellows has the vigorous painterly touch of Luks, though his compositions—both in the action portrayed and in their organization—are far more dynamic than those of Luks, whose work in comparison seems relatively static in spite of the strenuous activity he often portrays. Bellows' early boxing scenes, *Both Members of this Club*, 1909 (PC 18), and *Stag at Sharkey's*, 1909 (Illustration 6–39), are pertinent examples. The action of the boxing ring is projected with extraordinary force in an impetuous, even violent style, utilizing the resources of that aspect of the impressionist manner which was derived ultimately from the slashing brush work of Hals and was carried further by Duveneck and Henri. Bellows' pictures are also quite large, which adds to their impact. This bigness, the masculine subject matter, the vigor of the brush attack, and the violence of the action portrayed make these sporting pictures extremely effective. Forty-two *Kids*, 1907 (PC 17), has the same largeness of scale and conception, and the same level of action, now distributed among many figures. The boys diving and swimming at a dock on the East River are painted with gusto and composed with considerable subtlety. A similar pleasure in life and movement is seen in another large canvas, *Cliff Dwellers*, 1913 (PC 20). Bellows could also compose well in black and white; his lithographs, such as *In the Park*, 1916 (*GC 7), effectively dramatize the picturesque.

Bellows was undoubtedly influenced by the Armory Show and by modern art in general, for between 1914 and 1920 his art changed radically. Part of this transformation was due to his adoption of the principles of dynamic symmetry, an esthetic doctrine promulgated by Jay Hambridge and based on the mathematical relation of a diagonal to the sides of a rectangle, and somehow paralleled to plant growth. Bellows' predilection for the big and impressive, combined with his self-confidence, now bolstered by his success, led him to attempt the expression of pretentious or "significant" content, as in some paintings and prints inspired by the First World War—often extremely chauvinistic—and in others deliberately competing with the old masters, with titles such as *Adam and Eve* and *Crucifixion*.

A comparison of *Dempsey and Firpo*, 1923 (Whitney Museum), with *Stag at Sharkey's* dramatizes the change that occurred in the work of this intuitive and unintellectual artist, possessed of great talent, technical bravado, and enormous *joie de vivre*, when he was stifled by the application of an arbitrary theory and by various modern surface manners which gave his figures a superficial, "slick" contemporary look. (This unfortunate change in Bellows typifies what happened to a number of the "ashcan" school—Sloan and Coleman in particular, though they were not further encumbered by dynamic symmetry as was Bellows—and what was to happen to a number of artists in the 1920's who never thoroughly absorbed the lessons of modern art.) The lithograph of *Dempsey and Firpo*, 1924 (GC 6), is more successful than the painting, the design in black and white being more powerful than in color. Most of Bellows' late portraits and figure compositions are deliberate and static; the bodies are affected and unconvincing, possessing a stock monumentality derived from the simplified abstracted forms of artists like the lapsed cubist André Derain. Some of Bellows' late portraits, however, have a certain conviction even if they are somewhat stiff and mannered, as in *Elinor, Jean and Anna*, 1920 (PC 19).

There are a few artists who can be associated with the "ashcan" school because of their basically realistic point of view, but who were more socially conscious. The most important of these was Eugene Higgins, whose best work was executed in France where he came under the influence of Daumier and his imitators of the early twentieth century. Higgins' figures have a massive simplicity, as do his compositions; these characteristics can be seen in his *Gamblers*, 1907 (PC 213). More typical than this picture, however, are a series of eighteen drawings reproduced in a French journal of social satire, *Assiette au Beurre*, in an issue devoted entirely to Higgins (January 9, 1908).

Working in America were artists like Higgins, who were associated with the leftist publication *Masses;* some of them were members of the "ashcan" school. Though hardly as committed to social criticism as painters in the 1930's, yet during the first decade of the century the mere fact that their subject matter dealt with the underprivileged gave them a radical tinge. Henri, Sloan, and Bellows were all involved in some way in radical activities and were identified with *Masses* until its suppression in 1916. Among the artist–contributors the best and most forceful was Boardman Robinson, who developed a strong lithographic crayon technique that more powerfully resembled Daumier than anything by Higgins, having more strength of composition and a more compelling articulation of the figures. This style stood Robinson in good stead in later paintings such as *Richard Bone,* c. 1942 (PC 879)—more so, in fact, than in his murals done in 1929 for Kaufman's Department Store in Pittsburgh, the style of which is derived from a crossing of cubism with the broad handling seen in his drawings. Other artists like Robert Minor, Maurice Becker, the young Stuart Davis, and Art Young joined Robinson in creating a forceful, socially oriented tradition which was to flourish later in the *New Masses* and elsewhere during the depression.

Pioneers of Modernism

The several modern movements in Europe during the first part of the twentieth century—expressionism, cubism, futurism, an early form of Dada—were all reflected in the art of the United States, but in nearly every case they took on a native character which distinguished the American work from its European influences: it was usually a little bolder, less complex or subtle, and certainly not as profound or as committed either theoretically or formally, and had a tendency to compromise with realism.

Those painters who initiated the two principal movements of abstraction and expressionism in America shared a courageous approach to the acceptance of the new forms and concepts. From the vantage point of the mid-century most of them have more stature than many who followed after modernism had become more generally accepted.

The first important American artists to come under modern influence were Max Weber, Alfred Maurer, Patrick Henry Bruce, Arthur G. Dove, and Arthur B. Carles—all of whom were in Matisse's painting class at Paris in 1908. John Marin and Marsden Hartley were also in Europe (in 1909 the latter had a show at Stieglitz' gallery) but their work, though showing contemporary influences, was to evolve in a more personal direction than that of the others.

Weber was the first to develop a forceful style. His early painting is so characteristic of the period of ferment both before and after the Armory Show in 1913, and so distinguished in its adaptation of both expressionism and abstraction, that he is perhaps the outstanding American artist in the first decade of modern art—though he continued to be an important figure until his death in 1961.

The Fauves, led by Matisse, were the most talked-about painters in Paris when Weber arrived there, and the great Cézanne exhibition in 1905 was the most exciting artistic event of the era. Before his return to the United States, Weber also absorbed cubism, and became aware of the primitive art which was currently inspiring Picasso. Like that artist, Weber also studied El Greco, who had partially inspired Picasso's blue period. *The Geranium,* 1911 (*PC 485), sums up Weber's earliest period: the figure is elongated like El Greco's, the forms are faceted and monumental as in early cubism, and the color is richly and blatantly Fauve. Parallels to Picasso continued in Weber's work. From 1914 to 1916 cubism played an important role, as can be seen in the *Chinese Restaurant,* 1915 (PC 486), though the richly painted surface is inconsistent with the austerity of early cubism. Weber's nudes of the middle and late 1920's are like those of Picasso's classic period in their weighty portentousness, as in *Tranquility,* 1929 (PC 487). In other pictures, such as *Rush Hour, New York,* 1915 (*PC 976), futurism (evident in *Chinese Restaurant* also) is the most conspicuous ingredient—though the hard edges of cubism are also evident. More personal, building on the "expressionism" of El Greco and the powerful images of primitive art, and inspired by Weber's deep interest in Jewish ritual and tra-

6–40. Max Weber, *Hasidic Dance*, 1940. Oil on canvas. 32 x 40 inches. (Collection of Mr. and Mrs. Milton Lowenthal, New York.)

dition, *Hasidic Dance*, 1940 (°PC 488; Illustration 6–40), typifies a far more individual style, but is less admired by the doctrinaires of abstraction than is his early work. The nervous and vigorous linearism and the evanescent spaces convey eloquently both the frenetic energy of the grotesque dance and the mystical possession of the dancers. *Winter Twilight*, 1938 (°PC 978), is equally expressive; its angular, gnarled tree is realized with a thick handling of impasto (a later technical development in Weber). In *Adoration of the Moon*, 1944 (PC 489), and *Three Literary Gentlemen*, 1945 (PC 980), the tenuous solidity of the *Hasidic Dance* has become more disembodied so that intellectual intensity is very successfully suggested by graphically dynamic forms oscillating in a polyvalent space. Shapes are still recognizable, but are very similar in effect to some of the far more abstract forms of Arshile Gorky at about this time. Weber never quite made the step implicit in *Three Literary Gentlemen* which would have brought him, like Gorky, closer to abstract expressionism.

Alfred Maurer was less sure of himself than Weber, less original and less productive. A frequenter of advanced circles in Paris from the early years of the century, under the influence of Matisse and the Fauves he soon dropped his early Sargent-like impressionism. His *Land-*

scape—in the Vineyard, c. 1912 (PC 809), is a rather vigorous demonstration of these influences. Maurer's somewhat unrobust temperament, however, found its real métier in still lifes derived from cubist principles, of which *Still Life With Doily*, c. 1930 (*PC 318), is a good example. A series of melancholy female heads—embodiments of the strange and disembodied women Maurer seems to be looking at with his haunted eyes in the distorted *Self-Portrait*, c. 1927–1928 (PC 317)—are the monotonously repeated human companions to these still lifes, and are finally made monstrous in a Siamese-twin juxtaposition in *Twin Heads*, c. 1930 (PC 319). Here the expressionistic violence of the concept is matched by the power of the shapes, creating an effect that transcends the shock of the deformed image.

The best known work of Arthur B. Carles consists of still lifes that are less powerful than those of Maurer though influenced by the same general sources of cubism, Fauvism, and futurism, but have a more interesting combination of movement, nuances of color, and spatial relationships. Typical is his *Arrangement*, before 1928 (*PC 576), and *Bouquet Abstraction*, 1930 (PC 73).

The work of Patrick Henry Bruce, Konrad Cramer, John R. Covert, and Arthur G. Dove, and of the synchromists Stanton MacDonald-Wright and Morgan Russell, represents a phenomenon unique in western art until this time: the appearance of a completely non-representational art (as distinguished, for instance, from cubism, which is more literally abstract). Only Kandinsky before them had taken this radical step, but his early *Improvisations* of 1910–1914 could hardly have been well known to these artists, even though his book *Concerning the Spiritual in Art* had been published in 1910. Bruce's painting is derived largely from cubism, but has more curvilinear elements and movement, implying some influence of Italian futurism or of its French near-equivalent, Orphism. *Composition II*, done before 1919 (PC 56), is a complex yet ordered arrangement of polygonal shapes disposed in a fascinating series of optical ambivalences. Bruce's later *Painting*, c. 1930

(PC 57), retains the artist's striking geometry, but loses much of the rich spatial orientation of his earlier work; its pictorial possibilities are hampered by being restricted to the representation of recognizable objects.

Konrad Cramer, a German-born artist who came to the United States in 1911, was as much influenced by futurism as by cubism. His pictures, less intellectual and mathematically controlled than Bruce's, owe a great deal to Kandinsky's *Improvisations*, with which he was familiar in Germany. His own *Improvisations*, however, are more limited and ordered than Kandinsky's, as can be seen in his *Improvisation No. 2*, 1913 (*PC 86).

MacDonald-Wright and Morgan Russell together founded a school of painting which they called synchromism, a combination of cubist elements with the dynamism of futurism and Orphism (though their imprecations against the latter—actually so close to their own work—would seem to deny this last influence). The backward and forward movement of color—the artists called it "color orchestration"—was the basic means by which they built their forms. Agreeable enough as a kind of non-representationalism, synchromism was by no means the final culmination of the development of painting, as its originators fondly thought, though their varied chromatic exercises embodied in pulsating shapes and oscillating directions have an appeal not unlike that of the work of the more articulated abstract expressionists of today. Typical paintings, showing also the variety still possible within the limits of the artists' restricting theory, are MacDonald-Wright's *"Conception" Synchromy*, 1915 (PC 290), and *"Oriental" Synchromy in Blue-Green*, 1918 (PC 291), and Russell's *Synchromy No. 3, Color Counterpoint*, 1913 (PC 391).

The work of John Covert is among the most original of this period. His *Temptation of St. Anthony*, 1916 (PC 84), a completely non-representational painting with little discernible reference to the subject, is rich in a sense of movement and planar relationships which are most compelling. Similar in form or stylistic configuration is his *Brass Band*, 1919 (PC 85).

But this picture and several others dealing with musical subjects achieve a remarkable visual equivalence of sound—perhaps the most successful manifestation in the figurative arts of something that is far more viable in modern poetry: the use of metaphor derived from more than one sense. A curious aspect of some of these pictures is their use of objects extraneous to paint, a procedure derived from the precedent of cubist collage. In the *Brass Band*, for instance, string is combined with oil to create three-dimensional ridges. Unlike the Dadaists, who used similar devices, the effects Covert created were not meant to be shocking or humorous, but were simply means to increase plastic richness and give greater spatial subtlety. In 1923 Covert gave up painting, at the same time destroying much of his work—circumstances especially unfortunate in the case of so original an artist.[33]

Arthur G. Dove is in many ways very similar to Covert. Like him, he is usually non-representational and he also employed extraneous objects in some of his works, which are in fact collages. Some of these are among the most amusing and poignant objects in the history of American art. *Goin' Fishin'*, 1925 (PC 188), is a pleasantly arranged assemblage of objects associated with that activity—pieces of a disassembled bamboo pole and a denim shirt, among other things. More evocative is *Grandmother*, 1925 (Museum of Modern Art), in which a piece of needlework, some weathered shingles, a title page clipped from a Concordance, and a pressed flower are pieced together with a certain prim warmth. But Dove's contribution in conventional oil painting is more significant than these playful *tours de force*. He is often compared to Kandinsky because of his non-representationalism, but he came to his

6–41. Arthur G. Dove, *High Noon*, 1944. Oil and wax emulsion. 18 x 27 inches. (Wichita Art Museum, Wichita, Kansas. Roland P. Murdock Collection.)

abstractions by another route. Kandinsky began with an inner vision which he projected; Dove was inspired by natural phenomena—though not necessarily visual. His *Fog Horns,* 1929 (PC 189), for instance, is as auditorily oriented as Covert's pictures dealing with musical themes, for it represents the blast of the horns blurred by the ambient softness of the fog. This picture also displays Dove's characteristic diffusions and interpenetrations, derived in part from the synchromists and in part from Kandinsky, though at first without the strong colors of either. Dove's tonality is soberer than Kandinsky's, for he preferred austere and earthy colors, though these are more frequently mixed with brighter ones in his later paintings, as in *Rain or Snow,* 1934–1944 (PC 191).

In Dove's earliest work, exhibited by Stieglitz in 1912, the abstract forces of nature have a rather amorphous and dynamic character similar in effect to synchromism. The pastel *Nature Symbolized, No. 2,* 1914 (PC 187), was derived from the same sources, which Dove discovered in Paris in 1907–1908. The landscape or animal motifs which he used then (and later) are not always completely non-representational but are derived from subjects and movements in nature. More often, however, he was inspired by a general feeling suggested by nature, both in his early work, such as *Nature Symbolized, No. 2,* and, decades later, in paintings such as *Green, Gold, and Brown,* 1941 (PC 190). In spite of a discouraging and even tragic life during the 1930's, Dove's painting continued to celebrate the beauty of nature and life. At his best he was a genuine poet of nature—abstract but not at all dry, emotionally convincing and formally satisfying. These qualities are summed up in the relatively late *High Noon,* 1944 (Illustration 6–41).

Joseph Stella and, to a lesser extent, Louis Lozowick, Abraham Walkowitz, Oscar Bluemner, and Samuel Halpert domesticated European abstract forms to the American scene. Stella is the most outstanding. His work at first is more futurist than cubist; in fact, it is filled with a rather furious dynamism which in *Battle of Light, Coney Island,* 1913 (PC 445), almost shreds the gay scene into ribbons of brilliant color. Stella's contact with Italian futurism is more telling in his work than in that of any of his American contemporaries, as can be seen in the quite different picture *Spring,* 1914 (PC 446), which is filled with a glancing scintillation of rustling foliage. In the finest of several versions of the *Brooklyn Bridge,* 1917–1918 (PC 447; Illustration 6–42), movement was controlled by a more static organization—still, however, filled with a dynamism of detail. Large in scale and rich and varied in color, its powerful composition carries great formal weight. Many excellent contemporaneous pictures in comparison seem like mere exercises in abstract sensibility. The *Brooklyn Bridge* has something of the stature of Hart Crane's poem of the same title, carrying with it adumbrations far beyond the splendid engineering presence. Something of the picture's powerful effect can be suggested by the intensity of the artist himself as he describes his painting: "Upon the swarming darkness of the night I rang all the bells of alarm with the blaze of electricity scattered in lightnings down the oblique cables, the dynamic pillars of my composition . . . of my metallic apparition." [34] The interweaving of line and tone, the iridescently glowing hues, the infinity of spatial and directional nuances are unified by a magisterial control of composition which comprises an order that is not actually symmetrical, producing a unity which is impressive in its dynamic balance.

Stella's love of New York whose "polyphony was ringing all around with the scintillating, highly colored lights," [35] and whose skyscrapers and bridges had been created by steel which had "leaped to hyperbolic altitudes and expanded to vast latitudes," [36] found expression in a summing-up of the city in a series of panels entitled *New York Interpreted,* 1920–1922 (Newark Museum), of which *The Bridge,* 1922 (PC 940), is another version of the familiar theme, now more contained and somewhat more literal, lacking the almost apocalyptic quality of the earlier picture.

6–42. Joseph Stella, *Brooklyn Bridge*, 1917–1918. Oil on canvas. 84 x 76 inches. (Courtesy of Yale University Art Gallery, New Haven, Connecticut. Collection Société Anonyme.)

The work of Morton L. Schamberg and Man Ray illustrates modern influences other than those affecting Stella. Schamberg turned from abstractions influenced by cubism, futurism, and synchromism to a concern with the machine, under the inspiration of Marcel Duchamp and Francis Picabia. These European abstractionists had derived from cubism their analytical method, which they had then turned to the incorporation of the machine with organic form. Meant primarily as a commentary on the mechanization of human life, their bitter wit discovered indirectly the formal patterns and the inherent beauty of the machine. Schamberg translated this beauty into charmingly decorative pictorial diagrams, with none of the metaphysical overtones of most of the Europeans, but rather in the spirit of the later and greater Frenchman Fernand Léger. *Machine* (PC 399) and *Telephone* (*PC 400), both painted in 1916,[37] are typical examples.

Man Ray, later famous as an expatriate photographer in Paris, also came under the influence of Marcel Duchamp when the latter came to this country in 1915. This event, added to the impact of the Armory Show, turned Man Ray's interest from architecture and engineering to art. *The Rope Dancer Accompanies Herself With Her Shadows*, 1916 (PC 379), totally non-representational, is strong and handsome in design, while at the same time showing some Dada influence in the humor of its title. Ray's *Admiration of the Orchestrelle for the Cinematograph*, 1919 (*PC 380), is closer to the spirit of Dada and surrealism than to cubism, and presages in its biomorphic forms and dilating atmosphere the qualities of his famous Rayographs—"photographs" without camera, in which sensitive paper is used to create images.

Other American artists who would later equal the stature of Weber, Dove, and Stella were beginning to paint in this period, but from among this oversupply of early work, only that of Marsden Hartley, who began his career at this time, deserves special mention. His early work is so different from that of his later years that it seems to be almost that of another artist. In 1912 Hartley went to Europe. At Paris he was made aware of cubism; moving on to Munich, which was more congenial to him, he fell under the influence of Franz Marc and Kandinsky. Out of these experiences came Hartley's first style, represented by the *Portrait of a German Officer*, 1914 (PC 203), and *Painting No. 5*, 1914–1915 (PC 704), depictions of symbols of German militarism in a bold personal style that combines the abstract patterns of cubism and of Kandinsky's *Improvisations* with the brilliant clashing color of Marc and other German expressionists. In retrospect, however, these vigorous paintings with their almost monumental brutality do not seem as genuinely felt as Hartley's later work executed in Maine during the 1940's—though many critics disagree.

From World War I to the Depression

In dealing with the artists who came into prominence during the years just before and after 1920 (many of whom are still painting significantly), we are struck with the heterogeneity of their styles. The work of individual artists is more important than that of any group during this period, but for purposes of convenience of discussion two fairly inclusive groups can be set up, not too arbitrarily, under the classifications of academic modernism and abstract realism. Painters in both groups were, of course, influenced to a greater or less degree by European abstract art; often the academic modernists were more superficially affected than the abstract realists who, in spite of their sometimes meticulous realism, are at the same time actually as abstract in composition as are, for instance, the cubists. Pure abstraction appeared during the 1920's to a less degree than before or since. This was also the case with expressionism, though an artist like Marin represents an almost indigenous form of the movement.

The abstract realists are more significant than the academic modernists, especially when their work is seen from the perspective of the mid-century.

Among the most advanced of the academic modernists was Maurice Sterne, who combined the influence of Gauguin's exotic subject matter and decorative treatment with the use of Cézanne's structural planes and color, as seen in the early and characteristic *Bali Bazaar*, 1913–1914 (PC 448). Bernard Karfiol was influenced not so much by Cézanne as by the elongated and melancholy figures of Picasso's blue and pink periods, as can be seen in the rather touching lean awkwardness of *Boy Bathers*, 1916 (PC 241). Later, Karfiol's work took on more of the physicality of Renoir, as in *Seated Nude*, c. 1930 (Museum of Modern Art), *Christina*, 1936 (*PC 243), and *Cuban Nude* (PC 734). Karfiol's work is permeated by a pleasant, slightly melancholy sweetness, partly due to its rich yet hazy color and tenuous drawing, suggesting the warmth of flesh, but not too intimately.

A master in portrayal of flesh was Jules Pascin, an expatriate in Paris, who was a great influence on painters like Karfiol and others who favored the nude. His *Reclining Model* (PC 352), and the drawing *Nude*, c. 1925 (GC 155), show the basis of his appeal. Pascin's work is sensuous, even a little perversely so, with something of the morbid commentary of Toulouse-Lautrec and the intimacy of Degas' late bathers. Pascin combined his own sensitive and evanescent line with Degas' suggestive pastel treatment and Cézanne's modeling in patches of color to create poetic erotic symbols out of his little street-girl models.

Leon Kroll, Eugene E. Speicher, Walt Kuhn, and Alexander Brook were of a caste somewhat different from Karfiol and Pascin. They are more three-dimensional and static, influenced by Cézanne and Renoir, but more in the direction of the former's plasticity than his subtlety of spatial relations. Kroll's mature work, such as *In the Country*, 1916 (PC 258), has some of the same overrounded modeling and ordered composition that appear in the later Bellows. This basically intellectual attitude made Kroll's work more academic than that of Karfiol, and even though spiced with Cézanne's monumentality and some of Renoir's lushness, he has little of the life and sparkle of the late Glackens. Speicher's *Katherine Cornell as Candida*, 1925–1926 (PC 434), has a similar somewhat academic solidity, seasoned with more Renoir-like painterliness. Kuhn was fascinated with the circus, which has inspired most of his pictures, but he rejected its gaiety and glitter for the somewhat lugubrious solemnity of posed figures which combine a Daumier-like three-dimensionality and painterly surface with the simplified modeling and broad handling of the earlier, less "classical" Cézanne. The total effect is one of impressive solidity, typified in the *Blue Clown*, 1931 (PC 261), and undergoing little change in *A Girl in White and Silver*, 1943 (PC 758), and *Clown in His Dressing Room*, 1943 (*PC 263). The rather oppressive simplicity of these figures contrasts considerably with the much earlier *Dressing Room*, 1926 (PC 260), a somewhat decorative and more various picture, or with the charming lithograph *Trapeze Performer*, c. 1927 (GC 112).

Alexander Brook gave a more poetic and personal character to what had become essentially, though not officially, an academic tradition. Somewhat influenced by Pascin in his nudes and seminudes, he is more solid in drawing, and his paint has more body, qualities which can be observed especially in his still lifes. *The Sentinels*, 1934 (PC 49), for example, is an impressive structure of richly luminous color and fine paint texture. Brook's figures have mood and insight, and are not mere studio poses, as illustrated in the wistful portrait of Peggy Bacon and her cat, *Peggy Bacon and Metaphysics*, 1935 (PC 50).

Abstract Realism

Abstraction as such largely died out in the 1920's; even Dove's work tended toward a greater naturalism than before. Yet, in being combined with native realism, abstraction found a metamorphosis. However, the geometric aspect of abstraction—not the Fauve or expressionist variety—was the principal abstract ingredient, finding fertile ground in what may be thought of as an unconscious revival of certain stylistic characteristics of American mid-nineteenth-century painting, seen most clearly in luminism (as defined in Part Five: a style distinguished by certain formal characteristics as well as by a certain treatment of light). For, the art of Charles Sheeler and others—sometimes called "the Immaculates" or, more lately, precisionists (when their work was first shown in Latin America in the 1930's they were dubbed the "Frigidaire school")—gives the same attention to the precisely rectilinear and planometric, shares the same concern with detail, and possesses a very similar static mood. Though the light of "the Immaculates" is not quite the same, it has something of the still transparency of the luminists. The influence of cubism is also very evident in the work of the two most important figures of this group, Charles Sheeler and Charles Demuth, who domesticated European abstraction in the United States. In fact, Sheeler once said that "pictures realistically conceived might have an underlying abstract structure."[38]

Charles Sheeler is more consistent and less varied than Demuth and is certainly the most outstanding among "the Immaculates." In his early work he painted in a geometrically abstract vein, but in 1917 he worked with the photographer Paul Strand in sharp-focus photography, which concentrated on an unrelieved and precise realism. The combination of these two approaches resulted in the formation of Sheeler's personal style, characterized by precise detail and an ordered geometry of edge, surface, and texture. This is summarized well in *Upper Deck*, 1929 (PC 415), a picture of almost machine-like austerity. Somewhat warmer in color and modeling are his numerous industrial landscapes, many of them painted at the Ford plants at Willow Run and River Rouge, such as the *Classic Landscape*, 1931 (*PC 416), and *City Interior,* 1936 (PC 417). The title of the first is particularly apt, for in pictures of this kind Sheeler brings to the seeming chaos of the industrial scene an order reminiscent of the classic landscapes of the seventeenth century.

6–43. Charles Sheeler, *Of Domestic Utility,* 1933. Conté crayon drawing. 21¾ x 15⅞ inches. (Collection, The Museum of Modern Art, New York. Gift of Abby Aldrich Rockefeller Fund.)

The elements with which Sheeler is concerned in these pictures are those which appear in most of his other work—functional architecture and its expression in clean and almost mechanically precise forms. He has also painted the functional integrity of the older vernacular architecture of Bucks County farmhouses, Colonial Williamsburg, and Shaker buildings with as much care as he lavished on his factories. Yet it is not so much the American scene which is important in Sheeler's work, but Sheeler's way of seeing it, which in its detail and precision is in fact a twentieth-century manifestation of an older way of seeing that can be traced from Hicks's *Residence of David Twining* through the early Winslow Homer.

The poet William Carlos Williams, an admirer of Sheeler, says that Sheeler turned from abstraction to particularization because he sought to realize the uniqueness of things as ends in themselves. This concentration may explain why Sheeler's photographs have the same intensity of vision found in his painting. Even early examples like the *Stair Well*, 1914 (F 60), and the *White Barn*, 1916 (F 61), center on the expression of particularity, a quality which becomes less consciously stylized in the direct and absolute precision of the photographs of his later years, such as the *Ford Plant*, 1927 (*F 62).

Sheeler's drawings are most effective in evoking the essence of things by means of a concentration on detail which, as Williams says, "is in itself the thing." [39] These were executed in conté crayon, a medium which in Sheeler's hands is capable of expressing every nuance of tone and texture. The relatively early lithograph *Yachts*, 1924 (GC 129), is still concerned chiefly with surface pattern, but such drawings as *Of Domestic Utility*, 1933 (Illustration 6–43), are miracles of verisimilitude which at the same time are comparable in composition to the finest abstract or cubist paintings.

In recent years, Sheeler has diluted the effectiveness of this statement by a reversion to a somewhat arbitrary abstract manner, as seen in *Architectural Cadences*, 1954 (PC 48), in which superpositions of industrial buildings comprise a more easily achieved abstract construct than that afforded by the scene itself.

A generation has passed since the death of Charles Demuth in 1935, and he is considered now one of the finest artists America has produced, if not perhaps the most powerful. His work is too complex to be categorized as easily as is Sheeler's, for his figure pieces and especially his illustrations can hardly be said to be dominated either by realism or abstract geometry. In fact, there are almost three Demuths. The best known is the artist of the 1920's, who perfected his personal version of "Immaculatism." Fully as important, more original, and at least equally interesting is the artist of the period from 1911 to 1915 who illustrated books (not

6–44. Charles Demuth, "Flora and the Governess," illustration for Henry James's *The Turn of the Screw*, 1918. Watercolor. 8 x 10⅜ inches. (Collection of Mrs. Frank C. Osburn, Manchester, Vermont; courtesy of Philadelphia Museum of Art.)

for publication, but for his own satisfaction) and recorded the world of circus, vaudeville, night club, and bar. The last phase, when Demuth devoted himself almost exclusively to still life, is perhaps a little too limited and cold, but still infused with the artist's delicate formal and sensuous sensibility.

Demuth's illustrations for Zola's *Nana* and for Henry James's stories are especially remarkable not only for their very personal stylistic refinement, but for the way in which the artist has grasped the essentials of the authors' intent. Examples are "At a House in Harley Street," from James's *The Beast in the Jungle*, 1918 (PC 111), and "Flora and the Governess" from James's enigmatic *Turn of the Screw*, 1918 (Illustration 6–44); both are watercolors. From what sources Demuth achieved these evanescent evocations of literary mood is hard to say, but they are a remarkably distilled blend. In his treatment of subject there is a little of the decadence of Aubrey Beardsley, the English illustrator of the 1890's (whose delicate virtuosity with the pen and *art nouveau* sinuosities Demuth admired), as well as something of the more robust viciousness of Toulouse-Lautrec, especially in the *Nana* illustrations. Demuth's style is as exquisite as Beardsley's but quite different, making use of overlappings and transparencies to lend an air of psychological ambiguity and to remove his objects and figures from the matter-of-fact, infusing them with a somewhat dream-like quality.

In Demuth's genre work there persists much of the delicate and subtle character of his illustrations and even a slightly ironic perversity of viewpoint, as in some of his bar scenes. His circus and vaudeville subjects develop more assertion in design and are at the same time more rhythmic, suggesting the forms of Arthur G. Dove. Though successful renditions of complicated and graceful action, they retain the refinement and the irony of Demuth's earlier work, as can be seen in the watercolors *Circus,* 1917 (PC 110), and *Acrobats,* 1919 (°PC 602).

In 1917, Demuth was beginning to explore the structure of those architectural and natural forms which were to become the subject matter of his "Immaculate" phase. *Trees and Barns, Bermuda,* a watercolor done in 1917 (PC 110A), is a good example of his manipulation of forms in space according to cubist principles, showing at the same time his exquisite and decorative linear and tonal suggestiveness. Some Province-town subjects, such as *After Sir Christopher Wren, Houses and Trees,* 1920 (Illustration 6–45), show an adaptation of the cubist vocabulary of planes to more ambitious pictorial constructions, aided by the "ray line" used by the futurists for directional purpose. In Demuth's better known industrial subjects, such as *My Egypt,* 1927 (PC 113), these devices are perfected, but their somewhat arbitrary and logically inconsistent character seems merely decorative in comparison with the more significant spatial explorations of the cubists. Yet such pictures, and the earlier *Paquebot Paris,* 1921 (°PC 112), have a pristine clarity, a love of clean mechanical shapes (reminiscent of Sheeler and Schamberg), and a sensitivity to prismatic geometric form which give them enough individuality to remove them from the necessity of competing on their own terms with cubist masterpieces.

6–45. Charles Demuth, *After Sir Christopher Wren, Houses and Trees,* 1920. Tempera on fiberboard. 27⅞ x 20 inches. (Worcester Art Museum, Worcester, Massachusetts. The Dial Collection.)

Perhaps too dry, too literal, too impoverished both in subject and medium to have wide appeal, Demuth's art of the 1920's, in its self-contained and conscious manipulation of limited elements, is most distinctive and at the same time a thoroughly native manifestation of American art. His refined precision and detail, accompanied by an abstract pattern frequently seen in American art, are particularly successful in the curious and important *I Saw the Figure 5 in Gold,* 1928 (PC 606), illustrating a poem by his friend William Carlos Williams, in which auditory associations are prominent (a clanging fire-engine is being represented).

Demuth's exquisite color, always decorative and evocative, becomes more structural in the remarkable still lifes of his last decade. The typical *Poppies,* 1929 (°PC 114), a watercolor, draws somewhat on Cézanne's paintings in the same medium and brings to a climax Demuth's own precisionist technique. In such papers as these can be seen the final expression of a talent which is reserved, precise, and sometimes perhaps too coldly clear, but always elegant and intense.

Demuth is too complex and various an artist to be placed arbitrarily among Sheeler's group of "Immaculates." Closer to Sheeler in subject matter and, to a degree, in style, but less distinguished, are Niles Spencer and Preston Dickinson; similar in style, though not in subject matter, is Georgia O'Keeffe.

Niles Spencer, like Sheeler, loved New York and the countryside of the Northeast, dividing his time between them and painting pictures which revealed his fascination for their crisp, prismatic architecture. His earliest characteristic work is well represented by *City Walls*, 1921 (*PC 436), which is rectilinear with cubist penetrations, thinly painted, and rather cold and austere, but with a delicacy more like Demuth than Sheeler. This last quality is exhibited even better in his prints of the same period, as in the striking yet subtle lithograph *White Factories*, 1928 (GC 131). In his work of the 1920's and 1930's, Spencer's paint becomes richer and his pictures in general show greater naturalism, as in the *Green Table*, 1930 (PC 437), though there is still the rigid control reminiscent of the geometric aspects of cubism. Spencer's later work, represented by *In Fairmont*, 1951 (PC 439), reverts to the greater abstraction of his earlier painting, combining it with the somewhat richer and denser paint quality of the *Green Table*. It is far bolder and more effective in design, however, and more nearly abstract than any of his earlier work.

Preston Dickinson's subject matter parallels that of Spencer, but his is a richer and more complex approach. Intent on the same smooth surfaces and angles, he is subtler and at the same time more realistic (because he eliminates less) than Spencer. His *Industry*, painted before 1924 (PC 118), is typical. In comparing Dickinson's *Still Life With Yellow-Green Chair*, 1928 (PC 119), with Spencer's *Green Table*, similar char-

acteristics emerge, though Dickinson's work retains a sensibility closer to Demuth's elegant refinement than to Spencer's more direct austerity. Dickinson is consistently tasteful if not always very impressive—qualities well illustrated in the *Still Life*. Had he lived beyond 1930, his sense of design, refreshed by the renewal of abstract art in the 1940's, might have carried him, like Spencer, to a more definite statement.

Georgia O'Keeffe is not simply an "Immaculate" nor is she interested solely in the architectural aspects of the American scene. She is more concerned with subjects drawn from organic life than she is with the man-made world, and she brings to them a feminine sensibility. Non-representational abstraction characterized her early work, such as *Blue and Green Music*, 1919 (PC 343), and certainly taught her the formal discipline which characterizes her later representational work as well. Though her painting has the precision and "edginess" typical of the translation of cubism by "the Immaculates," it has also some of the dynamic surge of Dove's abstractions, which are more organic than crystalline. While complete non-objectivity continued to appear in her work into the late 1920's, as in *Black Abstraction*, 1927 (The Metropolitan Museum of Art, New York), she eventually found such disembodiment less satisfactory than the specificity of a very particularized vision, which she began to perfect in her flower pieces during the mid-1920's. Such pictures as *Black Iris*, 1926 (PC 344), in their penetrating organic character reflect her admiration for Dove's work, and illustrate the general stylistic characteristics of "the Immaculates." O'Keeffe's paintings of flowers have inspired much enthusiasm, largely instigated by the female symbolism in them, which is almost clinically intimate. Such reaction, however, loses sight of the essential stylistic restraint, even the coldness, of the artist's clean surfaces, exquisitely subdued colors, and controlled design.

O'Keeffe's famous still lifes from the southwestern desert, which incorporate bovine skulls and other nostalgic regional mementos, as in *Cow's Skull, Red, White, and Blue*, 1931 (PC 345), are characterized by her consistently careful design and technique, but they are in the end too sentimental and overt in their symbolism. The overtones of literary suggestion too easily achieved by the startling juxtapositions in these pictures (some of her skulls are garnished with red roses) are omitted from the much more direct landscapes, also inspired by the Southwest, such as *The White Place in Shadow,* 1940 (*PC 346). In these her precise vision and flow of design, suggesting the rhythm of nature through its own existence rather than through slightly spurious metaphor, are allowed more play.

Other painters who illustrate somewhat the same stylistic character as Sheeler, Demuth, and O'Keeffe, but are more strictly recorders of the American scene and on the whole not so personal, include Stefan Hirsch, George C. Ault, and Ernest Fiene. The latter's *Hudson Navigation Boat,* 1927 (PC 148), represents a middle ground of pleasant realistic observation which is given some structure and stylistic precision by the introduction of cubistic abstract formulas, as do his numerous canvases dealing with various architectural subjects in New York.

Andrew M. Dasburg and Henry L. McFee were among the first American painters to have been influenced by cubism and by Cézanne. Both artists are best represented by still lifes, the subject matter most easily adapted to semi-abstract treatment. Dasburg's *Apples,* 1929 (PC 94), is a domesticated descendant of Cézanne's still lifes, and his *Autumn Fruit,* 1934 (PC 93), is only slightly bolder.

Although Lyonel Feininger is almost entirely outside the stream of American art (he matured in Germany, going there from the United States as a young man and remaining until 1936), his work is usually considered American, and it bears some resemblance to that of Demuth and "the Immaculates," or at any rate to that phase of their work which is closest to cubism. At first Feininger's painting depended on the obvious devices of cubism, as in the *Side Wheeler,* 1913 (PC 140), in which planes and prisms manage to move the ship through heavy seas. A little later, contact with expressionism influenced a change toward a more emotional con-

tent, though Feininger's means remained almost mathematical. He continued to use cubism's analysis of form in space to create a vocabulary of directional planes within which to compose his architecture and his ships—the former in a tectonic play of areas, the latter in movement suggested by spreading areas of space. Though the means seem mechanical and sometimes arbitrarily decorative, the purpose and effect are quite different, for the prismatic forms project a mood of eerie wonder, infusing the subjects with an air of northern mystery. This can be seen, for instance, in the *Church of the Minorities, II,* 1926 (PC 141), with its Gothic bays soaring above the eaves and gables of the tall houses, all tied together by a twilit play of connecting relationships. *The Glorious Victory of the Sloop Maria,* 1926 (PC 142), is very different, representing the dynamic sweep of the sails as they literally cut through the areas of space. The much later watercolor *Yacht,* 1952 (PC 144), has something of the same spatial quality, though here the vessel is careening over a great swell in a burst of sunlight. The artist's evocative but less disciplined New York city-scapes, such as *City at Night,* 1941 (PC 143), seem not to represent an advance, though their effects are achieved with very simple, even seemingly accidental, means.

Among all the artists who came into prominence in the 1920's and are still painting, Edward Hopper is the most respected by a generation of artists and critics oriented almost entirely toward the non-representational. His canvases, though thoroughly realistic, are distinguished by subtlety and strength of composition (characteristics which he shares with "the Immaculates"), and by his feeling for the medium of paint. Even Hopper's early work, such as *Corner Saloon,* 1913 (*PC 720), has the static and impressive simplicity of his later pictures, as well as their fine painterly quality and their curious lack of emotional involvement. The austerity of such a painting stands out in the midst of the lively genre of the "ashcan" school from which, as a pupil of Henri, Hopper actually emerged.

There is no question that Hopper's formal sensibility has been sharpened by living in the twentieth century; probably more than any other quality, his formal assurance has given him his position as a kind of "old master" of a surviving realist tradition which (largely through his own accomplishment) preserves a kind of respectability. Even a cursory glance at reproductions of his works indicates how they are informed with a sure sense of design; they are static, monumental, and final. *Early Sunday Morning*, 1930 (PC 226), is almost as carefully composed as a Mondrian. The contemporaneity of Hopper's formal sense, however, is more intuitive than it is deliberate, and by no means is it a manner assumed merely for the sake of fashion.

Hopper thinks of himself first as a realist, and has said that his aim in painting "has always been the most exact transcription possible of my intimate impressions of nature." [40] Yet he has also said, "Angularity was just natural to me. I liked those angles." [41] The first of these remarks is one which Winslow Homer might have made. Indeed, Hopper is close to Homer not only in his objectivity but in his sensitivity to the medium as a direct and simple statement. Hopper's oil paint is never meager or timid; it has the rich, fatty simplicity of Corot's Roman period and, as the artist Charles Burchfield, a friend of Hopper, has pointed out, it is adapted to the simple monumentality, strong modeling, and bright illumination of so many of his subjects. Typical is his *House by the Railroad*, 1925 (PC 233), representing a relic of Grant era grandeur standing bleakly in a treeless landscape against an empty sky; the railroad track, the cause of its isolation and desertion, is the only other element in a composition of classic simplicity. When more evanescent and atmospheric effects are required, as in *White River at Sharon*, 1937 (*PC 723), Hopper uses watercolor with appropriate fluidity (though he also employs watercolor for the static architectural compositions so characteristic of him; the fresh clarity of the medium lends itself to the depiction of objects in bright light). Composition and technique, however, are only the means for the expression of content in Hopper's work; they are not ends in themselves. Hopper believes that the "great painters . . . have attempted to force this un-willing medium of paint and canvas into a record of their emotions." He adds, "I find any digression from this large aim bores me." [42]

Hopper is a realist, but certainly not a romantic one. As Burchfield has said, he has "no sentiment, propaganda or theatrics." [43] His work is consistent in its lack of obvious emotion, its restraint, and its impersonality, for it is as basically classical in feeling as his ordered composition is in form. Hopper is never merely picturesque, nor is he ever merely descriptive. Yet his work is permeated by an intangible quality which is finally emotional—for all its restraint. Perhaps the key to this quality is his use of light. As would be expected of so consciously objective an artist, Hopper's light is very well observed; it models and illuminates with impressive tonal accuracy and consistency—never focusing more here or there, but representing generally what the eye sees. Yet this light is also adapted to the circumstances or mood of the particular situation. At its most obvious and most natural, as in *House on Pamet River*, 1934 (PC 224A), it describes the hard, bright, isolating atmosphere of North America, so different from the diffused radiance of Europe and England. It can also describe the harsh brillance of artificial illumination, as in *Nighthawks*, 1942 (PC 227; Illustration 6–46), or the nacreous seaside quality of the twilight in *Gas*, 1940 (*PC 722), in which the lights of the filling station seem diffused by sea damp. Hopper can also use light to isolate his figures psychologically either from the environment or from each other.

Hopper's *Nighthawks* can be taken as an epitomization of his work. The composition is masterly. The structure of horizontals and verticals, varied slightly with oblique diagonals, is foiled by the repetitive rhythm of the ovals of the seats in front of the counter. Even the small square of glass in the brightly lit kitchen door is an obbligato to the much larger rectangles of the composition. The counterpoint of the four primary colors is as carefully worked out as the shapes: intense in the important areas, they gradually diminish in intensity elsewhere. The static, even restful, composition of large areas and uncomplicated colors sets a mood, just as

6–46. Edward Hopper, *Nighthawks,* 1942. Oil on canvas. 33¼ x 60⅛ inches. (Courtesy of the Art Institute of Chicago. Friends of American Art Collection.)

the even more emphatic arrangement of forms in *Early Sunday Morning* gives the emotional tone for the projection of the precise kind of emptiness peculiar to Sunday morning. For, though the brilliantly lit island of the *Nighthawks* should be cheerful and gay in the surrounding sea of darkness, it is sad and, above all, lonely. The place is not deserted, but the people who inhabit it briefly are isolated—one mechanically performs his duties as waiter, and the others are connected only by proximity.

The casual observer may well ask what is the significance of Hopper, with his banal subjects, his matter-of-factness, his obsession with the ordinary. His figures seem to be uninvolved mannequins, his forms are rigid and without emotional context, his scenes are lackluster. There is no transfigured experience, no meaningful commentary, no beauty (in the conventional sense) in a gasoline station where an attendant waits for a passing car which may never come.

There is only the poetry of the commonplace, of light, of the moment reduced to its lowest common denominator. Hopper is almost unique in his ability to raise almost nothing to something very arresting, by pure force of formal statement. The emptiness of *Early Sunday Morning* is filled with a haunting sense of desertion, almost as though man, but not his artifacts, had been destroyed.

This emptiness is all the more poignant when peopled. The gasoline attendant in *Gas;* the single figure in the deserted street in *Night Shadows,* an etching done in 1921 (*GC 33); the girl alone in bed on a hot night in the city, turning her naked body to the sudden breeze in another etching, *The Evening Wind,* 1921 (GC 32)—all express the essence of loneliness. The situation is more moving when there is more than one person, especially a man and woman, as in the vaguely disturbing tension between the pair in *Nighthawks,* and the implied boredom of the couple in *Cape Cod Evening*, 1939 (Illustration 6–47). The melancholy of loneliness—either solitude or that greater loneliness between people who should be emotionally close—gives the work of Hopper a significance which he has probably never consciously intended but which he has intuitively caught.

For various reasons Charles Burchfield is often considered together with Hopper. They have both painted the American scene, probably with more force and distinction than anyone else, and with less chauvinism. Both artists admire one another, each ingenuously imputing to the other some of his own artistic characteristics. Yet they are basically different. Hopper is clas-

sical, static, and non-committal. Burchfield is romantic, his composition is often dynamic, and he has a message. The differences and similarities of both artists can be pointed out in a comparison of Hopper's *House on Pamet River* and Burchfield's *House of Mystery*, tempera and oil glaze, 1924 (PC 567). Both pictures have in common the use of architecture as expressive or evocative form. In the Hopper it is rigid and geometric, and seen in a hard clear light; in the Burchfield the architectural elements, though well composed, are less clear and the light is ambivalent. The deserted emptiness of the *House on Pamet River* is unexpressive when compared with the *House of Mystery*, where

6–47. Edward Hopper, *Cape Cod Evening*, 1939. Oil on canvas. 30 x 40 inches. (Collection of Mr. and Mrs. John Hay Whitney.)

6—48.   Charles Burchfield, *Insects at Twilight*, 1917. Watercolor. 17¾ x 21¾ inches. (Frank Rehn Gallery, New York.)

even the dull red glow of a piece of stained glass contributes to the effect of a house where, in Burchfield's words, "anything might happen or has happened." [44]

The work of Burchfield has not the impact or the monolithic consistency of Hopper's. The romantic attitude is far less restricting than the classical, and in Burchfield's case its lures have led in many directions, from the almost out-and-out expressionism of his youthful work, through the social commentary of his middle years, to the frank nature worship of his latest paintings.

From 1916 to 1918, between his graduation from the Cleveland Art School and his induction into the army, Burchfield produced a series of watercolors derived largely from childhood memories, fantasies filled with fear of the dark, the sound of wind, and even the songs of insects. These extraordinary pictures (so similar to early Expressionism) are the more remarkable since their author knew nothing about this artistic movement, only feeling a kinship with a mysterious "Northland" he had never seen, but which always haunted him (a country actually inhabited by the Norwegian Edvard Munch, whose work is coincidentally close to his own in feeling). Full of powerful rhythms and extremely decorative, the principal impact of these watercolors lies, however, in their uncanny subject matter. Probably no other artist has used visual metaphors for auditory sensation so successfully as Burchfield in the waves of sound in *Church Bells Ringing, Rainy Winter Night*, 1917 (PC 59), or in a watercolor *Insects at Twilight*, 1917 (*PC 565; Illustration 6–48).

After Burchfield returned from the army he turned to the recording of the passing of the small town, in pictures which are basically realistic and are similar in mood and effect to the writings of Sherwood Anderson, whom the artist admired. Though in these paintings Burchfield, like Hopper, was also celebrating the commonplace, he did so with overtones of commentary on the defeat and frustration in the backwater towns left behind when an earlier America was sidetracked by the industrial giant it now is.

Less overtly topical, but still matter-of-fact, Burchfield's paintings in the 1930's gain in structural organization, as in the watercolor *Six O'Clock*, 1936 (Illustration 6–49). This picture has an almost Hopper-like angularity of composition and, at first glance, something of Hopper's loneliness of mood. But on further acquaintance the scene begins to seem warmer, even cozy, as the housewife is seen going about her pleasant task of preparing the evening meal in the kitchen of a house which, as one of a row of identical dwellings, is not more anonymous, but, on the contrary, all the more friendly.

Black Iron, 1935 (PC 61), is an excellent instance of Burchfield's growing concern with form. The great metal mass of the awkward weight which controls the functioning of the drawbridge is powerfully silhouetted as the principal

6–49. Charles Burchfield, *Six O'Clock*, 1936. Watercolor. 24 x 30 inches. (From the permanent collection of the Everson Museum of Art, Syracuse, New York.)

accent in the shape of the bridge as a whole. Though most of Burchfield's pictures are topical —and perhaps even self-consciously ugly or in many instances simply dull—even the less distinguished examples possess powerful composition and scale, all the more remarkable for being executed in watercolor. The observer is often surprised when he comes upon an original Burchfield in a gallery or museum, for it has an impact which reproductions do not prepare him for, an impact which goes far beyond the everyday and sometimes sentimental subject matter.

About 1943 Burchfield turned again to a more imaginative and less realistic manner, partly in reaction against the increasing popularity of pictures of the "American scene" (largely inspired by his own work, but becoming banal through repetition), and partly because he had been made to realize through favorable criticism the virtue of his early work, which he had heretofore tended to disparage.

Sun and Rocks, 1918–1950 (PC 63), is an instance of the actual reuse of a watercolor from these early "expressionistic" years. The large rhythms, the symbolism, and even the anthropomorphic suggestions are controlled within a more or less logical framework, but the forms themselves take on the adumbrations of the earlier years. The best of the later watercolors combine this revival of expressionism with the clear statement and bold scale of the middle years. One of the most outstanding in this respect is *An April Mood*, 1946–1955 (*PC 569); the spiked trees and lowering sky are simplified into an impressive graphic vitality and tonal drama in a watercolor which is astonishing, as are so many of Burchfield's, in suggesting the substantial effect of oil.

If Burchfield is a romantic, or even an expressionist at times (if that term can be used in its broadest sense), so is John Marin, though there are elements of organization in his work which could be called classical as well.

To Europeans—critics, students, and connoisseurs, even those who have been in the United States long enough to have acquired a sympathetic feeling for American art in general—Marin still remains baffling for what seems to them his impromptu and unstructured casualness. Yet in a survey sponsored not too long ago by a popular magazine, among responsible museum directors Marin rated higher than did any other contemporary American artist. At the same time Marin is respected by the artistic *avant-garde* because of the importance the medium has always had for him. In fact, his late work is quite consciously oriented toward a greater emphasis on means than on subject, for he himself stated in 1947 that he was representing paint first of all and the motif secondarily. Thus, in Marin, more perhaps than in the work of any other American artist, his development, method, purpose, and achievement must be studied somewhat closely in order to avoid his being too easily dismissed as flimsy or insubstantial.

Marin was first occupied unsuccessfully as an architect and engineer; but his acquaintance with those skills did not actually have the effect on his work that some have supposed, since he turned his back on practical matters at the age of twenty-eight. After studying briefly at the Pennsylvania Academy, he went to Europe, where a somewhat innocuous Whistlerian style gave him some fame. Not until his introduction to Stieglitz' circle in New York did Marin become acquainted with modern art. It is evident that what he learned about the Fauves, the cubists, and Cézanne (especially his late watercolors) at "291" influenced his work, because from then on Marin changed. But to have his eyes opened was a very different experience from taking over the actual methods of other artists. By a kind of visual osmosis, Marin intuitively absorbed the general tendencies of abstraction and expressionism, becoming himself an actual innovator within the modern movement. Marin is quite just in denying any specific influences in his work, especially when his total accomplishment is compared with that, say, of Stella, or even of Demuth and Sheeler, who show a more specific cubist influence. This independence is part of Marin's appeal as a personality—a Yankee "character" who is so completely himself that he cannot be copied or imitated.

Marin's individuality, indeed his eccentricity, is first seen in the etchings and watercolors of New York done in 1912 and 1913. The disintegrated shapes and nervous, broken lines of the etchings, and the darting brush work and strident hues of the watercolors are the artist's response to the excitement of the force and vitality of New York, whose building boom was then turning the Victorian city into the towering canyoned one of today.

The formal devices of the cubists were not necessary for Marin, since, as he himself said, it was *movement* and not structure that concerned him. In New York, where he found "buildings, people alive," he felt "great forces at work, great movements . . . . The warring of the great and small. . . ." [45] To Marin this movement was not like that of the futurists, who employed large unifying rhythms, but was unordered and fragmented. Marin became, in fact, a kind of home-grown expressionist, reeling under the impact of New York and dizzy with what he called the reciprocal movement between its parts. Pictures such as *Movement, Fifth Avenue,* 1912 (PC 303), a watercolor, and etchings such as *Woolworth Building, New York,* 1913 (GC 50), and *Brooklyn Bridge,* 1913 (*GC 48), express eloquently the unplanned vitality of New York and give an impression of the same ugly vigor which Stuart Davis finds in the city, though Davis treats its frenzy more deliberately.

The next step in Marin's development was to bring some order into chaos, for it would have been impossible to have maintained excitement at such a high pitch. To compare a version of the *Woolworth Building* done in 1913 to one executed two years later is to find that the spontaneity has been ordered into a more deliberate pattern, even into arbitrary forms which are as much symbols as representations.

At this point in his career Marin discovered the coast of Maine, where he spent much of each year for the rest of his life. The calmer excitement of nature was added to the frenetic movement of New York as a continuing part of Marin's subject matter. Little patterns, free play on motifs suggested by natural forms and movements (as of water and clouds), were deliberately used as a kind of foil to the larger forms. It is hard to tell sometimes whether these are meant to reinforce the pictorial structure or are simply decorative grace notes adding a quality of gaiety or whimsy. In any case these elements became shorthand signs of certain natural events, and made it possible for Marin to paint more rapidly and spontaneously, capitalizing through them on experience already pictorialized, and therefore enabling him to get at the immediate problem of expressing, with as little mechanical interference as possible, his always intense contact with his subject. These signs tended increasingly to turn into indications of planes in space, not unlike the method used in cubism. But in such pictures as *Pine Tree, Small Point, Maine,* 1926 (*PC 307A), the observer is not simply made party to a formal analysis of static relationships in the manner of Cézanne or Braque (though the effect is not dissimilar); instead he is made aware of the tree's dynamic relationship to the surrounding space.

During the decade 1915 to 1925, Marin increasingly used abstraction, as seen in such pictures as *Sunset,* 1922 (PC 304), which is composed almost entirely of symbols of nature boldly arranged over the paper in a nearly abstract design, but one tingling with the excitement of experience nevertheless. *Lower Manhattan,* done in the same year (PC 305), is even more abstract, actually a pastiche of symbols or motifs arranged with no logic of naturalistic placement, but according to one of form and expression.

Marin's work during this time was by no means exclusively or even predominantly abstract, for the artist chose his method of approach according to the requirements of his subject (much as Picasso has alternated between realism and abstraction). *Maine Islands,* 1922 (PC 795), for instance, is typical of the more naturalistic watercolors of this period. But it is not entirely realistic, because its abstract lines and areas define planes and movement. In other pictures these devices become almost frames which enclose certain areas and sometimes the whole scene, as if to keep the inner explosive force of the picture under control. Marin says he "nailed the stuff down in these frames,"

It may be asked why, in a watercolor—such as *Maine Islands,* which needs no "nailing down"—there is such a dependence on lines and planes. Yet this subject, a breathtaking panorama of island-dotted Penobscot Bay, would surely be less exciting, even dull, without these lines and areas. Such a device must thrust the viewer into the adventure of exploring with his imagination these sheets of water scattered with islands, some in brightness and some in the shade of passing clouds. One unkind critic has remarked that windshield wipers would do as much as these lines in clearing the vision in the center. But Alfred Barr is fairer and more to the point when he says that this cubist angularization is used not only for organizational effect but to

sharpen the central impression of the subject, "as a diamond is cut to lead light to the heart of the stone."

The remarkable and much reproduced *Lower Manhattan* (the 1920 version, in Philip Goodwin's Collection) illustrates the validity of Marin's abstract and seemingly arbitrary lines and planes better than does *Maine Islands.* In *Lower Manhattan* (depicting in a rush of line and color an elevated railway as a dark diagonal, the Woolworth Building leaping to penetrate the sky, and the struggle and thrust of other buildings) these abstract, structural, or organizing devices are not as arbitrary as in some other cases but are more integrated with the scene represented. A further clarification of the artist's "frames" and

6–50. John Marin, *Two-Master Becalmed,* 1923. Watercolor. 16½ x 19⅞ inches. (The Metropolitan Museum of Art, New York. The Alfred Stieglitz Collection, 1949.)

6–51. John Marin, *Pertaining to Stonington Harbor, Maine, No. 4,* 1926. Watercolor. 15⅝ x 21¾ inches. (The Metropolitan Museum of Art, New York. The Alfred Stieglitz Collection, 1949.)

facets may be at least felt, if not explained, in comparing *Storm Over Taos*, 1930 (PC 797), with the New York and Maine subjects. The spaciousness and sweep of the New Mexico landscape are entirely different, its grandeur and big forms being encompassed by larger, broader planes.

Certainly Marin uses these enframing shapes most successfully in the depiction of movement, as a comparison between two watercolors, *Two-Master Becalmed*, 1923 (Illustration 6–50), and *Pertaining to Stonington Harbor, Maine, No. 4,* 1926 (PC 306; Illustration 6–51), dramatically demonstrates. The two-master is almost literally blocked by veritable walls of heavy windless air, whereas the schooner in Stonington Harbor appears to be actually pushed on its way by the diagonals of the windy space.

Some of Marin's watercolors or prints of the late 1920's or early 1930's, such as the *St.*

Paul's, New York, 1930 (GC 49), are almost conventional in their handling of spatial relationships and their avoidance of experience-heightening devices, while others of about the same time are so full of them as to appear willful—especially in the use of a heavy bar of color at the top of the picture. But usually even this is essential for the design, for it holds the picture down. Sometimes these bars or boxes in the sky seem annoyingly and inconsistently heavy, like great beams supported by or suspended from nothing. (This writer once asked Marin why he used them in this way, and was rewarded with the only answer appropriate for such a question, "Why not?")

It is not the scene itself which is important to Marin but his reaction to it, his excitement, and his desire to record the essence, not the mere appearance. Yet, though the forms may be abstract to the observer, they were not meant

6–52. John Marin, *Movement, Sea and Pertaining thereto, Deer Isle, Maine,* 1927. Watercolor. 16⅝ x 22⅜ inches. (The Metropolitan Museum of Art, New York. The Alfred Stieglitz Collection, 1949.)

to be, at least in the accepted sense. Marin himself disliked the word "abstract," as he disliked all current artistic "-isms": "The sea that I paint may not be *the* sea, but it is *a* sea and not an abstraction." [46] He grasps the bare bones, the essentials, but these are in nature itself. Marin feels that the "true artist must perforce go from time to time to elemental big forms—Sky, Sea, Mountain, Plain,—and those things pertaining thereto, to sort of re-true himself up, to recharge the battery. For these big forms have everything." And he adds, "But to express these you have to love these, to be part of these in sympathy." [47]

Only those persons who are unfamiliar with the locales of Marin's subjects—not only the sites, but the shift of mood which every hourly change of the weather brings—can assert that

his forms are abstract. As Marin moved his residence on the coast of Maine always further "down East," from Casco Bay and Small Point to Stonington on Deer Isle and finally to Cape Split, his paintings changed accordingly. The character of each place is clearly reflected and nearly always preserved in spite of the temptations to whimsy, eccentricity, or mere decorativeness which creep into his less successful pictures. This love for the *genus loci* is particularly evident in the Deer Isle watercolors, such as *Pertaining to Stonington Harbor, Maine, No. 4* (Illustration 6–51) and *Movement, Sea and Pertaining thereto, Deer Isle, Maine,* 1927 (Illustration 6–52). In these pictures Stonington is represented as it usually is, in a brilliant, scintillating light which defines its irregular shoreline, its crazy precipices covered with spikey pine and hemlock and a hodgepodge of angular vernacular buildings, and its choppy harbor filled with bobbing masts and sails. Or, the town is seen in the half-and-half brightness of a day when the sunlight comes bursting out of the fast scudding clouds, glancing off a white cap, a whirling gull, or a sail. The abstract elements will usually be found to be the necessary skeleton supporting the almost immaterial flesh of the color washes which define or suggest objects and, more important, movement in space.

In the mid-1930's Marin became so skillful in realizing his purpose that he began to depend somewhat less on his semiabstract devices. In giving up his planes and enframing lines he seems to accomplish as much with a more vigorous massing of objects, a tauter, more controlled wash, and an indication of the nuances of distance and depth by the use of a subtle progression of intensity. With only a few telling accents to indicate shifts of spatial relationships and movement of current, wind, or cloud, the scaffolding of lines can be omitted, for the building is so perfect. Sometimes this change can be seen more clearly in his oils than in his watercolors, as in *Movement—Sea and Sky,* 1946 (PC 799).

Though much has been made of Marin's oils —on the whole a fairly late development in his work—they are in general not as successful as his watercolors, even if less given to the use of arbitrary spatial devices. In watercolor Marin is decisive and incisive, no matter how free. But oil seems less appropriate to this freedom. Had he used oil transparently (as in the oil—or more correctly, varnish—glazes of the old masters and, more recently, of Turner), he might have been happier in this medium. But he used it opaquely in the current *alla prima* technique which employs viscous, non-transparent oil. Though Marin obviously enjoyed the manipulation of the medium, in contrast to his watercolors his oils are sometimes muddled in color and even indeterminate in spatial relationships, as in *Movement—Sea and Sky* and *Tunk Mountains, Autumn, Maine,* 1945 (PC 307). The surface of the canvases becomes a battlefield for background, middle distance, and foreground,

and sometimes there is no victory, not even a draw. Comparison of Marin with Cézanne in their use of the medium of oil is not inappropriate, for, unlike the great French master, Marin's areas of space do not incorporate themselves into a consistent relationship, either with themselves or with the surface of the canvas. His mountains, for instance, seem to come forward without Cézanne's compensating backward-directed planes. The artist's usual "blessed equilibrium" is simply not there.

This is not to say that Marin's oils are not significant. Among other things, they illustrate very well the concern, even the struggle, with the material itself, in which so many contemporary artists are engaged. Yet his oils (and probably his relatively few figural compositions also) will take a less important place in Marin's total work than his watercolors; in the latter, with great verve and originality, he carried to a culmination an indigenous tradition, making the medium more expressive than anyone else has before or since.

Aside from the successful projection of feeling and emotion in a pictorial language of extraordinary immediacy, Marin's watercolors also have considerable significance from a purely formal point of view. The excitement and satisfaction to be derived from the best and most characteristic of them depend chiefly on the tension between solid form and movement. Marin's use of the medium has often been compared to Cézanne's. Each artist pared the medium down to its essentials, but whereas in the work of Cézanne (in his oils as well) the polarity is between form and *space,* in Marin it is between form and *movement,* for Cézanne remains basically classic, Mediterranean, and static, while Marin is full of the vigorous dynamism of the northern temperament. Both artists are impressive because of the equilibrium of their polar equations, but in each the second term is different.

Marin sums up as well as any American artist the various influences from European modernism which permeate the art of the first half of the twentieth century, giving it at the same time a most native expression.

The Prewar Decade

The 1930's, or more precisely the years from the depression in 1929 to the entrance of the United States into World War II at the end of 1941, is a period characterized by increasing interest in the American scene, and by what may be called the art of social consciousness, either as commentary or as protest, coinciding with the depression and the economic and social problems which exploded in World War II. This was also the decade in which some artists, perhaps in negative reaction against the pressure of events, turned with nostalgia toward other eras and other places, or developed a more personal or subjective language within the various vocabularies of modern art.

Before turning to the individual artists and movements which are most characteristic of the decade, something should be said of two groups of artists who can be thought of as being more or less transitional from the 1920's. The first group emerged from the studio tradition of Kroll, Speicher, and Kuhn, and included a number of artists like Raphael Soyer and his brother Moses, who painted social commentaries which were dramatized or made more poignant by the economic stress of the time, or Reginald Marsh, who put more "bite" into the "ashcan" tradition. The second group, including such painters as William Gropper, Joseph Hirsch, and the satirists Adolf Dehn and Peggy Bacon, turned to more overt social criticism and irony; they were joined in 1932 by the German refugee, the great caricaturist George Grosz.

Of the artists in the studio tradition, Henry Varnum Poor is among the most impressive in convincing form and in the achievement of a poetic mood. Kenneth Hayes Miller, however, exerted more influence on the newer generation of studio painters. In the 1930's his quite conservative academic manner changed to one in which the simplification of the human figure was carried almost into abstraction, that is, as far as a continuing realistic tradition would permit, as seen in the *Box Party*, 1936 (PC 328).

Miller gave his students and followers a sound academic background in the realization of the human figure, as seen in the work of his pupil, Isabel Bishop. The three Soyer brothers, Isaac, Moses, and Raphael, have a broader scope and more penetration of subject than do Miller and Bishop, qualities which in Raphael become quite moving. His *Office Girls*, 1936 (PC 430), has the solidity of Miller, but far more subtlety as well as a mood of wistful charm. The latter quality can be seen more emphatically in a comparison of his *The Brown Sweater*, 1952 (PC 432), and Moses Soyer's *Girl in Orange Sweater*, 1953 (PC 429), which is less poetic and more socially conscious. Raphael Soyer's *Waiting Room* (PC 431) is more ambitious and shows a grasp of interior space, in which real and sensitively observed persons are situated. Isaac Soyer's *Employment Agency*, 1937 (PC 428), is equally well organized and painterly, but slightly more exaggerated in drawing and more poignant.

Isaac Soyer is nearer than his brothers to Reginald Marsh, whose bitter, boisterous, and sometimes probing genre scenes are generally more profound than the work of others in this decade. Marsh, like the artists of the "ashcan" school, whose paintings his own resemble in spirit and subject, was deeply involved in the multifarious life of New York, more often than not in its seamier side. Also, like several artists of the "ashcan" school, Marsh was at first chiefly a draughtsman. His treatment of the figure, not only in his vigorous prints, as in the etching *Tattoo, Haircut, and Shave*, 1932 (GC 118), but in his paintings, with their solidity and almost ostentatiously correct and exaggerated musculature, recalls the masters of the sixteenth and seventeenth centuries whose work he loved and emulated. (Marsh even adapted the technique of the Renaissance, egg tempera, so as to achieve the firmness and precision of the old masters.)

Marsh was fascinated with the human figure, especially nude or seminude, and even when

6–53.   Reginald Marsh, *Why Not Use the "L"?*, 1930. Egg tempera on canvas. 36 x 48 inches. (Collection of the Whitney Museum of American Art, New York.)

not overly attractive, as in his many depictions of Coney Island, crawling with flesh, or in his somewhat squalid burlesque and strip-tease subjects. The competence of Marsh's drawing is also revealed in his clothed figures, even in the decayed and battered denizens of Skid Row and the Bowery, as in *Tattoo and Haircut*, 1932 (PC 308). Marsh is usually fairly direct and uncomplicated, as in the jolly disorder of *The Bowl*, 1933 (PC 309), which depicts a Coney Island amusement device mauling a group of laughing girls. But occasionally a more serious and poetic mood appears, as in *Why Not Use the "L,"* egg tempera, 1930 (Illustration 6–53), in which the dull fag end of the day's activity plays itself out in the stale air of a subway car.

Marsh's understanding of the human figure was well adapted to mural painting, which he handled with considerable skill, especially in *Discharge of Cargo at Pier*, 1937 (PC 1005), executed for the New York Customs House. On the whole, however, his style was not monumental, and therefore was more appropriate to the scale and detail of the genre tradition.

Of the more militant socially oriented artists of the 1930's William Gropper is perhaps the most prominent. As an illustrator and caricaturist during the 1920's in the *Liberator* (which succeeded the *Masses* in 1918) and later in the *New Masses*, founded in 1928, his work utilized the more linear technique of German artistic journalism, as opposed to the still persisting tradition of the older generation, represented at its best by Boardman Robinson, whose broad handling was more in the manner of French social caricature deriving ultimately from Daumier. Gropper's later works in the 1930's, typified by *The Senate*, 1935 (PC 180), and the lithograph *For The Record*, 1936 (GC 106), show a broadening of treatment but also a continuing dependence on linear expression and exaggerated angularity to underline their satire. *Homeless*, 1938 (°PC 181), is more pictorial, not related to caricature, and therefore not so "dated."

Adolf Dehn and Peggy Bacon were satirists in the same tradition of line as Gropper, and both worked for the same magazines; but they were not as politically oriented, directing their wit instead against sham of all sorts. They drew, painted, and made prints in a biting yet lively and decorative manner that was realistic in its telling detail.

The most effective of the world's political cartoonists and social commentators of the 1920's, George Grosz, came to America in 1932, a refugee from the Nazis, whose regime he would have pilloried as unmercifully as he had the last days of the German Empire and the early years of the Weimar Republic. In America he at first retained his eye for the precisely telling detail, cruelly exposed and brilliantly isolated, as in the desiccated old and very rich pair who are epitomizations of selfish wealth in the *Couple*, a watercolor done in 1934 (PC 182). But relief from immediate concern with Europe's troubles turned Grosz toward other facets of the world of artistic expression. The peaceful spaciousness of Cape Cod and the sensual charm of women seduced him to their celebration in pictures of considerable merit, characterized by baroque exuberance, fulsome form, and dynamic composition. Premonitions of war, the war itself, and its aftermath brought Grosz back to social commentary. In several searing pictures, he painted the horrors of the conflict itself, as in the watercolor *Waving the Flag*, 1947–1948 (PC 186), a bitter commentary on last-ditch patriotism, and the nauseating misery

of a bombed-out world in the horrible *Pit*, 1946 (PC 185). These pictures are less tellingly economical in means than his German work or than his early paintings in America, but they have a greater sensuous appeal, due to the added richness of form and texture derived from his plastic explorations of the late 1930's.

During this decade the most conspicuous and publicized form of realism was an American variety which came to be known as regionalism, with which the names of Thomas Hart Benton, John Steuart Curry, and Grant Wood are associated, and which was popularized by the prolific critic Frank Craven. The reputations of all three artists have been in eclipse since World War II, partly because of the association of regionalism with Fascism, and partly because what once appeared to be interesting formal devices in the work of Benton and Wood now appear to be mere formulas. Yet these factors are compensated for by the vitality, enthusiasm, and topical interest of Benton, and by Wood's creation of several strongly designed pictures which have become almost part of the stereotyped image of America.

No matter how much Benton may protest that he has rejected modernism, his mature work indicates a considerable debt to it, as can be seen in his exaggerated dynamism and somewhat arbitrary color—derived from futurism and synchromism—and in his distortion, which is so pronounced that it is tempting to put Benton under the category of expressionism. Some of his early work, consisting of semiabstract nudes in swelling overlapping billows of light, owes a great deal to MacDonald-Wright, and his later work reflects not only expressionism but the distortions of late sixteenth-century mannerism. As a matter of fact, as an aid to composition and modeling Benton has even used little clay models, a device employed by Tintoretto, the great mannerist artist. The results of this method are especially clear in the artist's later work, as can be seen in the somewhat too conscious modeling of the figures and other objects in *July Hay*, 1943 (PC 24). This rather indiscriminate three-dimensionality does not interfere to the same degree with the dynamic composition and lively figure drawing of the earlier work, where an overall movement gives unity to pictures almost too packed with incident, as in *Boom Town,* 1928 (PC 22), and in many others depicting the South, Midwest, and Southwest. Sometimes Benton's prints present a clearer and more powerful statement than his paintings, where a too cacophonous color often confuses the already busy compositions. The lithograph *Going West,* 1929 (GC 86), representing a speeding train, in spite of its remarkable suggestion of rapid movement, is too close to caricature.

The sweep and vigor of Benton at his best are seen in his murals in the New School for Social Research (1928), and those done for the Whitney Museum in 1932 [now in the New Britain (Conn.) Museum of American Art] and the Indiana State Building at the New York World's Fair of 1939 (now at the University of Indiana at Bloomington). They represent a cross section of American life—social, industrial, and intellectual—in all its racy vitality and variety, interpreted not through the broad generalities of the idealism of the older mural school, but with an eye for significant and typical detail presented in a carefully worked-out dynamic design. In spite of their sometimes too stereotyped interpretation of a South which is too backward and a West which is too wild, and a debunking not only of obvious pretense but of honest liberalism and reforming, the murals remain a vivacious record of an America seen perhaps naïvely but with enthusiasm, as a typical section from the Whitney mural, *Arts of the West,* 1932 (PC 527), attests. The most interesting aspect of the murals is their formal organization, for Benton has managed to connect a series of often unrelated events in ways that are neither illogical nor visually jarring. Sometimes the problem of continuity or sequence is solved simply by change effected by the interjection of arbitrarily broken enframements. But usually the solution is more effectively achieved by a clever sequence not unlike that used in the motion picture, whose inherent dynamism, like that of music, is sympathetic to Benton's artistic temperament.

Benton's murals gave the final *coup de grâce* to the dying idealist school that flourished at the turn of the century, and set a precedent for an entirely new point of view in this field. Benton's belligerent celebration of the American scene and the example of his murals had a great influence on the art of the 1930's, especially in the government-supported art programs.

Grant Wood was an artist of considerably less scope than Benton, but much of his early work is impressive within its limits. Unlike Benton and many of his contemporaries, Wood was less influenced by modernism than by the past, which in his case was represented by the German and French masters of the Gothic and early Renaissance, whose meticulous realism he felt was appropriate to the delineation of the life of his native Iowa. Yet at the same time the simplified forms and flat patterns of the modern movement had a great effect on Wood. In fact, the irresolution in his combination of these two influences qualifies even his best work. *American Gothic,* 1930 (PC 491), undoubtedly Wood's masterpiece, shows the two influences at their most compatible. Here the meticulous recording of detail is enhanced by a concern with repetitive pattern and shape, as in the pitchfork and the seams in the man's overalls, while the angular austerity of the figures and the house is emphasized by an attention to the basic geometry of form.

In the much reproduced *Daughters of the Revolution* (private collection), representing three sour-mouthed and complacent figures silhouetted against a print of Leutze's *Washington Crossing the Delaware,* emphasis on the subject is mitigated not only by a loving attention to detail for its own sake, but by the introduction of obvious surface pattern, as in the dresses and collars of two of the ladies. The reduction of objects to their basic geometry, as well as a self-conscious simplification derived from folk art, partially destroy the impressive realism which still remains in Wood's somewhat pretentious comments on American history, such as *Parson Weem's Fable,* 1939 (private collection), and the *Midnight Ride of Paul Revere,* 1931 (PC 986), in which the neat, affectedly toy-like buildings are a travesty on the style of "the Immaculates." Wood achieved only a compromise, not an integration, between realism and abstraction.

John Steuart Curry was essentially an academic painter with a flair for the local scene, which he painted with energy and vivacity at a time when a reaction against abstraction and formalism was at its height. He expressed his feeling toward his native Kansas not so much by distorting or abstracting it as by dramatizing it. Adopting a painterly technique derived ultimately from Rubens, but without either the sound draughtsmanship or the mastery of color of the great tradition, Curry painted landscapes and genre subjects that are large in scale, grandiose in conception, and frequently violent in action. Typical are his *Hogs Killing Rattlesnake*, 1930 (PC 89), and *Tornado over Kansas*, 1929 (PC 90), the titles of which reflect their content and indicate the chief reason for their former popularity. Curry's work is on the whole sincere, if a little overstated, and his technical competence within the realist painterly tradition in the twentieth century is respectable enough.

A number of painters in the 1930's were influenced by this trio of regionalists, and also by Reginald Marsh, whom Craven included with the other three and praised as an indigenous artist. Perhaps the most famous, if not the most distinguished, instances of their influence were the murals commissioned by the government or painted under the auspices of the W. P. A. Art Project during the depression years. Boardman Robinson's somewhat mannered murals at Kaufman's Department Store in Pittsburgh, and those by Benton, were the only American examples from which to form a style which would supersede the classicizing manner inherited from the Chicago World's Fair, until then almost ubiquitous. There was also the example of the leftist humanitarianism and the modern forms of the famous Mexican muralists David Alfaro Siqueiros, Diego Rivera, and José Clemente Orozco, painted in the United States. The most influential examples of their work were Orozco's at Dartmouth and Rivera's at Rockefeller Center in New York (the last mentioned were destroyed

before they were finished, because of pro-communist references). Unfortunately, however, the opportunity for mural painting was not properly exploited. The old school was too moribund and its style no longer appropriate, and the new school was not yet sufficiently formed.

Doubtless the best murals were done by artists who were already distinguished: Curry, Poor, Gropper, and Ben Shahn. Though most of the projects, including the many Post Office decorations, were examples of misapplied combinations of realism with various types of inadequately understood modernism, not all of them were incompetent boondoggling. Some were even moderately distinguished. Usually concerned with local history or incident, they reflected the best of regionalism. Mitchell Siporin's Post Office decorations in St. Louis and Anton Refregier's at the Rincon Annex Post Office at San Francisco are among the best of these.

There were many other artists in the 1930's whose work reflected an absorption in the American scene, usually with a regional emphasis. Jon Corbino's *Flood Refugee*, 1938 (PC 82), is typical of his work; characterized by well-modeled figures, spirited composition, and rich painterly color, its style leans heavily on Rubens and is well adapted to active scenes and to pictures in which horses are the chief subject. Joe Jones' *American Farm*, 1936 (PC 1002), dramatizes the erosion of the dust bowl area, as does Alexandre Hogue's powerfully designed and realistic *Drought Stricken Area*, 1934 (PC 220). Fletcher Martin's *Trouble in Frisco*, 1938 (PC 313), deals with a longshoremen's strike, focusing on a fistfight seen dramatically through a porthole. All of these artists paint in a basically realistic way, but their work is tempered by the somewhat expressionistic distortions of both landscape and figure popularized by Benton.

Arnold Blanch is less influenced by the style of Benton, but his concern with certain areas of the deep South has a genuinely regional flavor, as in his *Swamp Folk*, 1939–1940 (PC 31), restrained in its melancholy mood, and delicate in its subtlety of drawing and tonality.

These qualities give his prewar work a distinctive flavor which is lost in his later, more abstract work, represented by the painting *Four Ships,* 1951 (*PC 32).

The artists who painted the American scene may well have done so even without being encouraged by the success of the prominent regionalists. The work of most of them seems simply a continuation of the "ashcan" school or some other phase of impressionistic realism more or less influenced by modern art. Typical of these artists is Louis Bouché, whose *Ten Cents a Ride,* 1942 (PC 549), treats the subject of the long, corridored waiting room on a ferry boat with a feeling for both design and paint that is not unlike Hopper's but has less impersonality and compositional restraint. The rather casual charm of his genre subjects and city-scapes, and the rich and pleasant handling of paint and color distinguish him among the realists, particularly since these qualities are usually combined with an impressive composition reminiscent of "the Immaculates." Another painter of place, Walter Stuempfig, is also notable for his handling of paint, as well as for a realism which is almost romantic in mood. Changes of weather and the anatomy of resort architecture at Cape May, New Jersey, have inspired some of his most evocative subjects, as in *Thunderstorm II,* 1948 (PC 456). He has also transformed the tiered and textured configurations of the mills on the Schuylkill River at Philadelphia and Manayunk into almost Poussin-like classical compositions, drawing attention to the colors and surfaces of neglected city streets.

Aaron Bohrod has done in the Chicago area very much what Stuempfig has done in the Philadelphia region. But he is more searching and sometimes acid in his commentary. His work is brash in color, vigorous in drawing and composition, and precisely realistic, carrying much further the tendency of the "ashcan" school to depict the ugly. His *Landscape near Chicago,* 1934 (PC 45), pinpoints the visual squalor of the suburbs of industrialism, while his genre scenes are particularly effective in underlining the sordid vastness of the huge and impersonal modern city.

Romanticism

Another category of realistic painting, little influenced by the rigors of geometric abstraction or the distortions of expressionism, is more romantic than naturalistic. Few of the artists in this group take great liberties with appearance beyond the suggestive use of the medium or the deliberate neglect of precise rendering. Among them are Eugene Berman, Julian E. Levi, and the painter who calls himself Leonid, three artists quite similar to each other in their feeling for the medium and their nostalgic melancholy. The world of Berman's twilit Mediterranean cities, Venetian lagoons, and denuded plains, dotted with decaying baroque splendors and inhabited by strange waifs and strays, is summed up in his typical *The Gates of the City, Nightfall,* 1937 (PC 26). Sometimes figures are more prominent than landscape and building, as in *The Muse of the Western World,* 1942 (PC 27), portraying actually no real figure at all but a configuration of cast-off objects hung on a chair and grouped around it. Less pretentious and with a tenderer melancholy are the seascapes and genre scenes of Leonid in which those whose livelihood is the sea are represented performing their quiet tasks in classically composed landscapes, usually under hazy summer skies on the coasts of France or the Adriatic. The sweeping view of *Entretat, Le Cabeston Capstan,* 1931 (PC 773A), is typical, as is *Malamocco,* 1948 (PC 773), evocative of the still, mirror-like water and nacreous light of the Venetian lagoon. Julian E. Levi, in *Last of the Lighthouse,* 1941 (PC 280), and other seaside pictures, creates a similar atmosphere, but the forms and colors peculiar to maritime architecture are sometimes more emphasized than the landscape itself, with results that are often more decorative than descriptive. A tendency toward greater abstraction and away from emotional overtones can be seen increasingly in Levi's more recent work.

The romantic point of view is too personal, and at the same time too limited to concentrated facets of experience, to permit easy categorizing into groups. Sometimes the narrowing of experience is so intense that lack of scope must be compensated for by depth.

Among the most distinguished artists who remain still primarily romantic without much admixture of expressionist and surrealist overtones are Yasuo Kuniyoshi, one of the most engaging artists of the period, Loren MacIver, whose feminine sensitivity makes her an outstanding American woman artist, second only to Georgia O'Keeffe, and Morris Graves, whose originality is fostered not so much by modern European expressionism as by analogous tendencies from the Orient.

Kuniyoshi was (until his fairly recent death) an important artist for thirty years. But unlike Marin, Sheeler, or Hopper, who in the 1920's arrived at a personal style which remained more or less constant, Kuniyoshi's work ranged from primitivist fantasy in his early years, through naturalism in his middle period, to a return to fantasy, but of a more sophisticated sort, in his last years. This lack of consistency makes him less impressive in the long view than the "old masters" of contemporary American painting, though he remains one of the more important twentieth-century artists.

The primitivism (or lack of western realistic tradition) in the artist's early work may be thought to be the consequence of his Japanese birth (he came to this country when he was sixteen). But the lack of perspective and of realistic anatomy is equally attributable to his interest in modern expressionist artists, who drew on folk art for inspiration. Kuniyoshi's exquisite draughtsmanship, however, surely has an affinity with that of the Orient. *Little Joe With Cow,* 1923 (PC 264), and *Strong Woman and Child,* 1925 (PC 763A), have a witty quality which is far from the naïveté of an untutored Nipponese. In these decorative pictures, with their charming color and draughtsman-like passages of the brush, the distortions and unreal spaces are part of a sophisticated total design which is consistent with the folk-story mood of their somewhat humorous fantasies.

Trips to Paris in 1925 and 1928 increased Kuniyoshi's sensitivity to the sensuous quality of paint, but also directed his interest to a more realistic point of view, rather than reinforcing his abstract tendencies. This came about largely through the influence of Jules Pascin, the American émigré, whose sensual subject matter and diaphanous technique exerted considerable influence on Kuniyoshi. Henceforth the exploitation of the material of paint, the effects of various technical processes of glazing, impasto, and texture, as well as the translation of his linear sensibility into brilliant and at the same time refined brush strokes, became the chief interests of the artist. He utilized these technical subtleties in the presentation of limited but deeply felt subject matter: charming still lifes representing objects in often humorous juxtapositions, as in the lithograph *Interior with Dress Form,* 1928 (GC 39), and sensuous and moody women, as in *I'm Tired,* 1938 (PC 265). But a growing tendency toward the enigmatic and fantastic is seen in *Headless Horse Who Wants to Jump,* 1945 (PC 266), and his voluptuous and indolent females begin to be troubled by overtones of mystery, as in *Look, It Flies* (*PC 762). A private symbolism becomes almost surrealist in the disturbing images in the paintings of Kuniyoshi's last years, such as *Revelation,* 1949 (PC 267), and *The Amazing Juggler,* 1952 (*PC 268). The ambiguous strangeness of these pictures reflects the artist's awareness of a world which has changed to such an extent that his languorous sensualities and witty incongruities no longer satisfied him. Unfortunately, disquieting as these pictures are, and though brilliantly painted and designed, they do not quite ring with the truth of Kuniyoshi's less pretentious and less concerned work. They also borrow a little too directly from the formal vocabulary of the postwar Ben Shahn, for they are flatter and more patterned, and have a general angularity which succeeds the sensuous surfaces and curvilinear passages of Kuniyoshi's middle period.

Loren MacIver is a subjective romantic whose visionary quality is tempered and strengthened by references to reality. She is also more or less in the tradition of Ryder, though his large forms are replaced in her work with ones of a more feminine delicacy. Her *Hopscotch,* 1940 (PC 294), is as abstract and suggestive as the work of non-representational artists such as William Baziotes or Theodoros Stamos; yet when examined it is seen to be a very careful rendering of the surface texture of a hot asphalt street with the underpaving showing through and with part of its surface covered with the lines and numbers of a child's game. MacIver catches in her tenuous forms and colors almost accidental glances of small segments of the passing world; as comments on the commonplace they become almost as eloquent as Hopper's, though his banality may be said to be epic in contrast to her more lyric expression. *Venice*, 1949 (PC 296), illustrates another aspect of her work, being less specific in reference but with as sensitive a grasp of the intrinsic quality of the thing seen, in this case the facades of the dream-like city hovering over the lagoons in a flickering evening light, described in rich but muted color. MacIver brings the same sensitive observation, lyrical yet specific, to her comments on the make-believe world of circus clowns. Her interpretations of Jimmy Savo and *Emmett Kelley*, 1947 (PC 295), differ as much as the subjects do themselves.

The work of Morris Graves has a very special place in the history of American art. Thoroughly contemporary, it nevertheless represents a continuation of aspects of nineteenth-century romanticism which found expression pre-eminently in America. Some of Graves's birds recall the compassion of Ryder's *Dead Bird;* others are infused with a magic not unlike that of Audubon, who put into his naturalist drawings something of the grandeur and excitement of the unexplored continent. This sense of nature's vastness, of its isolated and lonely places inhabited only by birds and beasts, seen in certain aspects of the Hudson River school and among the painters of the frontier, is also a very important ingredient in the work of Graves. His attachment to the northwestern coast, where he lived almost a hermit's existence for many years on an island in Puget Sound, is reflected in his absorption in the phenomena of nature which he so closely experienced there. Graves's almost pantheistic mysticism has been strongly reinforced by the affinity of the West Coast for the art of the Far East, and the presence of many distinguished oriental works of art at the Seattle Museum and elsewhere in the area. Graves is familiar with the Far East first hand, for he made several trips there as a sailor, with long stays in Japan in 1939 and again in 1954. He has also been strongly influenced by aspects of oriental philosophy, especially by Vedanta and by Zen Buddhism, which have amplified his western pantheism with an urge to even greater absorption of his identity with all creation.

Graves's romanticism is almost expressionistic. The sensibility of his line, the delicacy of his washes, and their abstract and semiautomatic quality recall the work of Paul Klee. But Graves's contemporaneity is not so directly influenced by western European art as it is reinforced by it. The tenuous white lines, for instance, which surround the *Bird Singing in the Moonlight,* 1938–1939 (PC 172), with a cocoon of moonlit sound, derive not from Klee but from the "white writing" he learned from Mark Tobey, who had brought the technique back after study with a famous artist-calligrapher in China. This happened in 1938, and it was then that Graves developed the style employed in the remarkable series of pictures painted between 1938 and 1942 (and more or less consistently since): watercolor or gouache (as *Bird Singing*), often on Chinese rice paper, executed with delicate sweeps and mere touches of the brush on backgrounds of wash, frequently supplemented by "white writing," and drawn with an exquisite linear sensitivity and tonal subtlety strongly relying on Far Eastern precedent. *Bird Singing in the Moonlight* is a characteristic early example; later ones include *Bird Maddened by the Long Winter*, tempera, 1945 (PC 175), and *The Flight of Plover*, 1955 (PC 174).

Graves's subjects in general are conceived not as specific instances, but, in the words of the artist, "essences with which to verify the inner eye," as indicated in such titles as the *Owl of the Inner Eye*, 1941, and *Little-known Bird of the Inner Eye*, 1941 (both in the Museum of Modern Art), and in such paintings as *Joyous Young Pine*, 1944 (Museum of Modern Art), in which the upper branches of the tree seem to embrace the moon. These pictures embody such large conceptions as the force of growth and the unity of all organic things in the cosmos. Yet for all the generality required for the expression of the essential, Graves also retains the poignant power of the very specific. His creatures are utterly right. The gesture of walk or flight, the turn of a claw, the ruffle of feathers are as accurate as in Audubon or the Far Eastern artists, touchingly specific as well as universal. The haunting and compassionate image of the *Blind Bird*, gouache, 1940 (Illustration 6–54), is effective largely because of this quality, depending as much on the convincingness of its hunched form as on the soft and clinging web of "white writing" which serves to chain the dark bird down with its white gossamer. In such pictures as these the artist is at his best, combining the sensitiveness of both his inner and his outer eye; he has not only meditated on the forces of the universe, but also "can tell us the exact weight of a plover's wing." [48]

There are other artists in whom romanticism is less intense, but whose eccentric and limited vision has nevertheless produced expressions of considerable artistic interest, even if somewhat restricted in scope. Darrel Austin's fairy-tale depictions of Beauty and the Beast, eerie landscapes, or pictures of feline creatures inhabiting twilit phosphorescent forests and swamps, as in *Catamount*, 1940 (PC 510), are not as convincing as are Graves's intensely felt creatures, but they are evocative enough.

John Carroll's sultry and fragile models, fashionably lovely and in negligee as in *White Lace*, 1935 (PC 74), his actresses drooping with suppressed temperament, and his spent and anguished adolescents are neurotic and somewhat dematerialized descendants of the models painted by the studio painters of the 1920's. Clarence Carter is obsessed with the folklore of the South and the "poor whites," in pictures such as *Jane Reed and Dora Hunt*, 1941 (*PC 557). The landscapes and seascapes of Henry E. Mattson, such as *Moonlit Landscape*, 1934 (PC 315), and *Wings of the Morning*, 1937 (PC 316), are compositions which recall the shapes of Ryder, but are more angular without the lat-

6–54. Morris Graves, *Blind Bird*, 1940. Gouache. 30⅛ x 27 inches. (Collection, The Museum of Modern Art, New York. Purchase.)

ter's sensuousness. Raymond Breinin brings something of the fantasy of exoticism from his native eastern Europe to his allegorical *The Night*, gouache, 1941 (PC 550). A more compelling figure is Edwin Dickinson, the mystery of whose buildings, still lifes, and foreshortened nudes enmeshed in an ambiance of ambiguous forms and tones, always remains enigmatic. The quality of his work can be seen at its most typical in *Composition With Still Life*, 1933–1937 (Museum of Modern Art). *The Woodland Scene*, 1933–1935 (PC 115), becomes almost nightmarish. Its well-realized forms, convincing modeling, and figures beautifully drawn in difficult perspective are as carefully and intensely observed as they are irrationally assembled, for its parts consist of a prostrate nude turning into a forest, an androgynous elderly figure in a great coat, and a reclining, fully clothed, but sensuous woman.

A very different artist is Ivan Le Lorraine Albright, the almost microscopic detail of whose technique might at first seem to justify his being placed among the realists. His detail is so closely observed, however, that it becomes an almost unreadable maze in its particularity, and it is so single-mindedly directed to the adumbration of sentiment that his paintings belong to a special brand of romanticism all his own. In such pictures as *Into the World There Came a Soul Called Ida*, 1927–1930 (PC 4), flaccid bodies and puffy faces are surrounded with the intimate appurtenances of squalor revealed in a harsh, raking, theatrical light. Albright's still lifes, *That Which I Should Have Done I Did Not Do*, 1931–1941 (PC 6), representing a funeral wreath on a battered and pockmarked door, and *Poor Room—There Is No Time, No End, No Today, No Yesterday, No Tomorrow, Only the Forever and Forever and Forever and Forever Without End*, 1942, unfinished (Art Institute, Chicago), describing an incredible assortment of objects tumbling from a packed room through a partially burned and broken window of a decaying house, are modeled to the finest degree, so that the cumulative effect is one of an indiscriminate piling up of the flotsam and jetsam of life. From a short distance these paintings have the effect of abraded soil—and something of its monotony—until the eye begins to pick out their appalling detail.

Surrealism and Its Influence

Romanticism is the common parent of expressionism and surrealism—expressionism carrying on its emotional projection, and surrealism drawing on the unconscious and the dream world.

Among the works of some of the romantics just discussed there were occasional suggestions of surrealism, especially in the mysterious incongruities of Eugene Berman and Edwin Dickinson. But "official" surrealism made very little impact in America—that is, the surrealism of dreams and of the unconscious, with its esoteric and sophisticated grotesqueries and its predilection for the erotic and obscene. Yet in a diluted or transformed way it influenced a number of painters and added to their concep-

tual vocabulary, and in one case, that of Peter Blume, had much to do with the formation of a major artist.

One of the most important European surrealists, Yves Tanguy, came to the United States in 1939, and remained the rest of his life. Though perhaps his best pictures were painted in America, his point of view is so thoroughly European that it seems almost arbitrary to include him in a history of American art. Almost the same could be said of Kurt Seligmann, nearly as famous, or of Jimmy Ernst, who, though he has spent the major part of his life in the United States is greatly influenced by his father, the prominent Dada-surrealist. Tanguy's landscapes, stretching to infinity and filled with ambivalent forms; Seligmann's bizarre and indeterminate creatures; Jimmy Ernst's protoplasms moving in an intangible geometry—all seem alien to any American tradition, as do also Kay Sage's beautifully built but illogical edifices and impressively complex but meaningless constructs, empty of inhabitants of this or any other world. These frightening landscapes of the unconscious have had little influence on American painters, except the abstract expressionists of the post-World War II period. Instead, the irrationality of the dream and of the humor inherent in the philosophy of surrealism has had a greater influence in the startling effects of illogical juxtapositions and the symbolic suggestibility of seemingly unrelated objects. At its most obvious, this aspect of surrealism contributed a great deal to the work of humorists such as James Thurber, Saul Steinberg, and other artists associated with the *New Yorker*. In a more serious guise it has added levels of meaning to the dream-like images of artists who are often otherwise realists in the tradition of "the Immaculates." The outstanding artist among these is Louis Guglielmi whose *Terror in Brooklyn*, 1941 (PC 192), does not belie its title and whose *The River*, 1942 (PC 193), has something of the pregnant silence and emptiness of the hallucinated city-scapes of the Italian proto-surrealist Giorgio di Chirico. Among similar artists can be counted Federico Castellon, whose forbidding *The Dark Figure*, 1938 (PC 75), is reminiscent of the work of Dali in its detail and dream-like clarity.

Walter Quirt is one of the few native American surrealists in the 1930's whose work is abstract. His swirling forms are meant to suggest (according to his own description) the psychoanalysis of public neurosis through free association, as in *Mutation,* 1940 (PC 375). Alton Pickens is sometimes a realist of great power but he often heightens his convincing presentation with elements of the bizarre which are surrealistic in spirit and create a kind of terror that is all the more graphic for being combined with the three-dimensionality, spatial understanding, and anatomical articulation of the great masters, particularly Goya and Daumier. *The Tightrope Walker,* 1947 (private collection), with his head bound in a rag and a false one at his crotch, and *The Carnival,* 1949 (Museum of Modern Art, New York), with its blue-featured ape, birds emerging from a woman's open mouth, and other arcane symbolism, are unforgettable images but hardly as disturbing as the horrid, grotesquely adult little girls mutilating their dolls in *The Blue Doll,* 1942 (PC 360).

Peter Blume is a difficult artist to categorize, for his is a strange world, depicted with the most exacting realism and with elements of incongruity that are closely related to surrealism. His precise description is like that of "the Immaculates," as seen most clearly in his early *White Factory,* 1928 (*PC 44A), but to his meticulous treatment of mechanical and natural objects Blume soon added overtones of subject matter that were symbolic or simply subjective, employing illogical juxtapositions similar to those of some of the surrealists—Dali in particular—which give to his pictures a nightmarish, dream-like character. In *Parade,* 1930 (PC 41), a suit of armor carried on a pole by a workman has a natural but unlikely affinity with the metallic forms of the modern factories past which it is being paraded. Pictures such as *South of Scranton,* 1931 (The Metropolitan Museum of Art, New York), a somewhat arbitrary assemblage of the artist's experiences on a trip from Scran-

ton, Pennsylvania, to Charleston, South Carolina, prepare the way for the huge picture *The Eternal City,* 1934–1937 (PC 42). Here Blume's representation of poverty, graft, and violence juxtaposed with the remains of the pagan world and with instances of superstition and degenerate Catholicism are overshadowed by a huge green *papier-mâché* head of Il Duce which has just emerged as a jack-in-the-box. Enormous effort has been expended by the artist on a picture which is a visual commentary on the times rather than primarily a work of art for its own sake. Though Blume's ambitious program in *The Eternal City* perhaps overshadowed its purely artistic qualities, the picture remains an important example of an artistic point of view in which the artist is involved with his society, an attitude represented at its most impressive in Picasso's *Guernica.*

Blume's energies for the next decade were largely devoted to the preparation and realization of *The Rock,* 1948 (PC 44; Illustration 6–55), an allegory of man's relation to the earth. Perhaps in reaction after the intense discipline of *The Eternal City,* Blume painted in 1940–1941 at Key West, Florida, a number of little pictures representing small objects—mostly the jetsam of the sea—whose organic forms fascinated him and whose surrealist overtones he emphasized. In these, however, he retained his meticulous treatment, which became a little less metallic and hard, indicating a greater affection for natural texture and organic form. These studies, together with an exploration of the possibilities of the automatic "doodle" and essays in the expressive drawing of the human figure (which he studied carefully in preparation for a painting commissioned by the U. S. Army Medical Department), prepared him for the accomplishment of *The Rock,* which evolved eventually from a series of studies and preliminary paintings. In the final version, rigid and jagged shapes are confronted with rounded organic ones in a composition more integrated than in *The Eternal City.* Between the still-smoking ruins of a partially burned mid-nineteenth-century house, and a partly built contemporary one (Frank Lloyd Wright's Falling

6–55. Peter Blume, *The Rock,* 1948. Oil on canvas. 58 x 74 inches. (Courtesy of the Art Institute of Chicago. Gift of Edgar Kaufmann, jr.)

Water), is seen a strange semiorganic, half-naturalistic object—the rock—placed on a mesa-like pedestal which supports also a skeleton and a great stump uprooted by the excavating activities going on under the pedestal. The figures involved are distorted and exaggerated (not at all dissimilar to those of Thomas Hart Benton, who, unlike Blume, is presently so much out of favor). In a more recent ambitious picture, *Passage to Etna,* 1954–1956 (*PC 996), Blume has put together similarly an accumulation of visual and psychological impressions, stimulated by a trip to the Mediterranean and the Orient.

Blume is a commanding figure in contem-porary art, not only because of his accomplish-ment but because his remarkable achievement is so completely at variance with the tendency of his time toward the non-conceptual in con-tent and the non-specific in style.

Expressionism

Of the two principal movements in contem-porary art—formal abstraction and expression-ism—the latter became increasingly influential from the mid-1930's onward. Max Weber, the grand old man of American expressionism, and John Marin, with his own peculiar version of it, remained the leaders; but many others were either quite close to the prototypical Germans or more remotely influenced.

Benjamin Kopman, in *Portrait—Bear,* 1928 (PC 256), recalls both the conception and the method of the German Franz Marc, who attempted to portray in intense and arbitrary color the way animals themselves might feel; Ben-Zion, in *Moses,* 1955 (*PC 22A), resembles the German expressionist Max Beckmann in his large, abrupt, angular forms packed with meaning; and David Burliuk, in *Harlem River Bridge,* 1926 (*PC 66), and *The White Cow,* 1936 (PC 67), adds a folk art quality—derived from Marc Chagall and Heinrich Campendonk—to the violence of his form and color, giving his pictures a somewhat terrible gaiety.

The work of the Philadelphia painter Franklin C. Watkins does not derive as closely from the expressionist movement, but is certainly violent in form and color. Some of his early paintings, such as the *Fire Eater,* 1933–1934 (PC 482), and *Suicide in Costume,* 1931 (Philadelphia Museum), dealing with the garish and tawdry life of the circus and sideshow, are dynamic, colorful, and somewhat melodramatic in the angular intensity of their distortion. Watkins' early portraits have a similar power, as in the jutting chin and angular shoulders of the man portrayed in *Soliloquy,* 1932 (*PC 484A). His later work is less fiery and more abstract, as in the allegorical paintings he executed in the late 1940's for the Philadelphia collector Henry P. McIlhenny, in which the influence of El Greco is quite evident. Perhaps Watkins' most impressive works (now that his early painting, so exciting thirty years ago, is seen with a longer perspective) are the solid portraits he has executed from the late 1940's until the present, wherein his distortions, somewhat abated but by no means eliminated, help to delineate the character and personalities of his often well-known sitters, as in the portraits of *Justice Owen J. Roberts,* 1947 (PC 483), and of *Prof. Henry Murray,* 1956 (Harvard University).

Abraham Rattner is another American expressionist (though he is almost as influenced by geometric abstraction) who combines somewhat cubistic forms with a richness of jewel-like color that recalls that of the great Frenchman Rouault but is even more brilliant and varied. His *The Emperor,* 1944 (PC 377), is even similar to the French master's subject matter, while *Figure and Mask,* c. 1948 (*PC 378), is more distorted and violent. Yet Rattner can be gay and lively, if rather forcefully so, as in *April Showers,* 1939 (PC 376); rhythm of form and color, however, is perhaps a little too geometricized in this early work.

Expressionism, in the broadest sense of the word, has permeated American art so generally that it is difficult to isolate in its various degrees of combination with abstraction, realism, social realism, and even surrealism. The strongest artists are those who emphasize one or more of these combinations in the most personal way. Among them surely must be counted Marsden Hartley, an early expressionist in a somewhat abstract way; Karl Knaths, even more abstract; and the two Boston painters influenced more by Chaim Soutine than by strict expressionism—Jack Levine and Hyman Bloom. Levine is as much a social commentator as an expressionist, as are the two painters associated with the depiction of Negro life—Robert Gwathmey and Jacob Lawrence—and the somewhat poetic and symbolic Philip Evergood, and Ben Shahn. Labels of any kind are too restricting for most of these artists, especially for Shahn whose very personal and original style utilizes his own combination of realism and abstraction as much as it does expressionism.

The later Marsden Hartley is reminiscent of Marin in the depth of his emotional response to Maine. But he is a very different artist. Hartley did not really find himself until the mid-1930's. A pioneer American in the modern movement, Hartley continued to experiment, reinterpreting Cézanne in a somewhat bold and rather obviously decorative way in the 1920's, producing some forceful representations of Alpine scenery at Garmisch-Partenkirchen which, however, by no means possess the formal subtlety of Cézanne's Mont Ste. Victoire. But upon Hartley's return to the United States, the strong simplifications of his reading of Cézanne were utilized to transcribe elements of the American scene in dramatic fashion, beginning with the "Dogtown" landscapes painted in a deserted area behind Gloucester, Massachusetts, remarkable for its strange rock formations. Shortly thereafter the artist discovered the coast of his native Maine, and during the last decade of his life he immersed himself in a subject matter which moved him greatly, bringing to bear on it a lifetime of preparation in abstract and expressionist art, plus one other essential factor, the influence of Albert Pinkham Ryder. The decorative shapes of abstract art and the rather raw

color and forceful handling of some German expressionism were now subjugated to the projection of shapes and forms to evoke the essence of the subject. In writing about Ryder, Hartley speaks of the essential importance for the artist of "the eye of the imagination, that mystical third eye in the mind that transposes all that is legitimate to expression." Hartley manages in some of his work to achieve that transposition—though never to the degree of effectiveness of the great protoexpressionist Ryder. In some of Hartley's work a deliberate primitiveness is coupled with a somewhat too consciously arranged design, as in the *Fisherman's Last Supper*, 1940–1941 (PC

6–56. Marsden Hartley, *Fox Island, Georgetown, Maine*, 1937–1938. Oil on canvas. 22 x 28 inches. (Addison Gallery of American Art, Phillips Academy, Andover, Massachusetts.)

206). But in others in which Hartley deals with landscape and the forces of nature, he is surer and less mannered, as in his treatment of birds (again reminiscent of Ryder). Among his large landscapes the views of Mt. Katahdin are among the most impressive, of which *Mt. Katahdin, Autumn, No. 1*, 1939–1940 (PC 205), is a good example. The dramatic bulk of the mountain is seen in a clear October day, with the jewel-like autumnal foliage contrasting with the intense green of the pines and the choppy dark-blue water of the lake. The shapes of trees, cloud, and mountain and the clangorous colors are as evocative of fall in inland Maine as Marin's more complex and subtle forms are reminiscent of the coast. Hartley's shapes lack the rightness and power of Ryder's, and for this reason are not as universal, for to receive the full impact of the scene (which Hartley obviously wants us to do) almost requires our past acquaintance with it. His seascapes are perhaps more readily comprehended, especially those of the surf at Schoodic Point, such as the *Wave*, 1940 (PC 207), which recalls the thundering immediacy of some of Winslow Homer's seascapes but is more abrupt and more overtly emotional; though Hartley gains in abstract simplification, he loses the older master's dynamism. These and many other Maine subjects, however, such as *Fox Island, Georgetown, Maine*, 1937–1938 (Illustration 6–56), effectively project a genuine if overdramatic feeling for a *genus loci*, which Hartley also expressed in distinguished verse.

The feeling for place is also very strong in Karl Knaths. During all his important painting years he has lived in Provincetown, Massachusetts, and though his work reflects Cézanne and the cubists, he has never been abroad. At the Armory Show, Cézanne was a kind of revelation to Knaths. He recognized that the Provençal master had a much more profound grasp of real color than did the impressionists, for Cézanne's color had volume (as Knaths said later) while theirs was merely visually naturalistic. Cézanne's structural use of planes and color became Knaths's principal tool, for he thinks of a canvas as "a density that can be pushed into."

Knaths uses Cézanne's approach, further distilled through the analytical methods of the cubists, for the expression of feeling, that is, the projection of sensations or ideas. In this respect his painting is analogous to the late work of Braque, for both artists use angles and planes, lyrically as well as structurally, as the collector Duncan Phillips has pointed out. In Knaths's case this feeling consists largely of his response to the land, sea, and town-scape of Provincetown and its environs on the tip of Cape Cod. This is often summed up in still lifes, which in their colors, textures, and shapes become quintessential commentaries on the things of Knaths's intimate world of experience, as in *Autumn Leaves*, 1948 (PC 254), and in *Duck Flight*, 1948 (PC 253), where the flight is the background of a picture in which a decoy is more prominent. The earlier *Cock and Glove*, 1927–1928 (PC 252), is brasher and less subtle, but exemplifies the artist's incisive use of line and plane to project the attitudes and movements of living things. This quality becomes more abstract but at the same time more convincing in the shorthand drawing of figures in his later work, such as *Overhauling the Trawl*, 1955 (Phillips Collection), characteristic also for its interesting spatial relationships and for the distillation of the seaside colors of salt-greyed shingles, the sunburned arms of fishermen, and the blue of their sun-bleached overalls.

Abstraction has always been present in Knaths's work; in the early 1930's it became at times almost non-representational. In such landscapes as *Number Zero—Adam*, 1948 (Albright-Knox Art Gallery, Buffalo), and especially *The Sun*, 1950 (Illustration 6–57), Knaths is seen at his most eloquent, employing the language of semiabstraction for the expression of deep feeling in color which is vivid and exciting and in drawing which is strong and very personal. He knows the language of formal analysis so well that it does not stultify his spontaneous response.

Everett Spruce, in such pictures as *The Hawk*, 1939 (PC 440), and Lamarr Dodd, in *Monhegan Theme*, 1949 (PC 123), are somewhat similar to Knaths and to each other in their sensitivity to the grandeur of landscape expressed in the ex-

6–57. Karl Knaths, *The Sun,* 1950. Oil on canvas. 36 x 42 inches. (The Phillips Collection, Washington.)

aggerated forms and colors exploited by German expressionism, and exemplified in the United States perhaps best by Hartley.

Jack Levine and Hyman Bloom are usually discussed together because of the similarity of their background and style. Bloom was born in Baltic Russia and Levine's parents were from there. Both were brought up in the slums of Boston, and both had the experience of being taught in a settlement house by an artist who introduced them, through the facilities of the Fogg Museum at Harvard University, to the world of art history and to the historical techniques of painting. As a consequence, both artists have a more than usual sensitivity toward the handling of paint. They also share an expressionistic style, considerably reinforced by realism and largely inspired by the painter Chaim Soutine, who was also of Baltic Russian origin.

Jack Levine is involved with man and his problems and tragedies, and admires most those artists who were similarly concerned: Rembrandt in the past and Rouault and Soutine more recently. Levine himself, however, deals more directly with the specific injustice and dishonesty deriving from economic inequalities, satirizing them with trenchant directness or sardonic humor. Yet he does so always with the subtlest technical means, in imitation of the old masters who used the Flemish and Venetian techniques of underpainting and glazing, and thus softens

6–58.   Jack Levine, *Street Scene No. 1*, 1938. Oil on canvas. 30 x 40 inches. (Courtesy, Museum of Fine Arts, Boston.)

his most uncompromising pictures. Typical of his early work is *Street Scene No. 1*, 1938 (Illustration 6–58), an impressive picture from the technical point of view, and an expression of the artist's absorption in the paradoxical beauty of urban squalor as well as his revulsion against the injustices of poverty.

In Levine's work during the 1940's, the increasing influence of Rembrandt tended to refine his light, and within its subtle chiaroscuro his sordid or bitter dramas play themselves out. Among the wittiest of these, as well as one of the most brilliantly painted, is *Welcome Home*, 1946 (PC 282), in which Levine's recent career as an army private is somewhat salved by this wry and telling caricature of army "brass" at a formal

dinner. In this picture there can also be detected an increase of the influence of Tintoretto and El Greco, in an added refinement of glazing and in the mannerist distortion of the figures. *Gangster Funeral*, 1952–1953 (PC 284), and *The Trial*, 1953–1954 (PC 777), become slightly more reportorial, and the handling of glazes, even more transparent and diaphanous than in earlier works, has an effect considerably less strong though possibly not less telling.

The persistence of Levine's concern with humanity and justice, taken together with his strong realistic bias, places his work of the 1950's out of the mainstream of the decade. Yet there is something admirable in his anachronism.

As Levine has become a more convinced realist, Bloom has approached nearer to abstraction. Even in his relatively early work, such as the *Synagogue,* c. 1940 (PC 34), the appeal of color for its own sake seems more important than the subject. In similar representations of Orthodox Jewish ritual, the depiction of oriental pageantry and mystery is blended with a feeling for paint and color and with an expressionistic distortion of the objective world. These pictures, and others such as the jewel-like trove in the *Treasure Map,* 1945 (PC 35), represent outstanding examples of the influence of both Rouault and Soutine in the United States.

Bloom's consuming interest in the sensuous beauty of color and the material of paint has led him even to the extreme of exploring the phosphorescence of organic decay, as seen in such studies of severed limbs and human corpses as *Corpse of Elderly Female,* 1945 (°PC 36). More recently the slightly less morbid but equally physical inspiration of surgery and butchery has produced some of the most magnificent symphonies of powerful color and form in contemporary art—quite equal to many of those of abstract expressionism but based on factual visual experience, as in *The Anatomist,* 1953 (PC 541). Perhaps the overtones of physical violence, death, and decay in the lacerated, bleeding, or putrifying flesh reflect not so much a morbid preoccupation as a frank and unsqueamish facing of some of the disagreeable facts of our time.

Levine and Bloom are products of the genteel but sensitively appreciative culture of Boston and Cambridge. The tradition of the Boston Museum School, where both artists studied, was later reinforced by the appointment of Karl Zerbe to the faculty in 1938. A modified German expressionist painter who had worked in France and Mexico, Zerbe's work as artist and teacher is important for the expressive correspondence between idea and rich painterly texture, the latter supplemented and reinforced by the introduction of the ancient wax medium of encaustic, which he modernized by the employment of synthetic materials. Both his qualified (or even somewhat academic) expressionism and his rich technical means are seen in *The Harlequin,* 1944 (PC 498).

David Aronson, a pupil of Zerbe and, like Levine and Bloom, from a Baltic Russian background, is a third member of what could be called a Boston school. His religious interests (he studied theology at one time) finally have led him to religious subjects, as in *Coronation of the Virgin,* 1945, encaustic (PC 8), in which the expressionistic distortion and richness of color characteristic of Levine, Bloom, and Zerbe are diluted by a certain technical smoothness and a satiric note which is more fey than profound.

Out of the tradition of social protest of the 1930's have come two artists whose principal concern has been the condition of the American Negro: Jacob Lawrence, a Negro himself, and Robert Gwathmey. Possessed of a less realistic bias than Levine, their work is more abstract in form and sometimes more symbolic or suggestive in content.

Like Levine and Bloom, Lawrence received his artistic start in a settlement house, was supported by the W. P. A. Art Project, and was further encouraged, from 1940 to 1942, by scholarships. His boyhood work in poster colors and cutouts predisposed him toward a decorative, flat, and patterned style which he has used with great eloquence, combining it with expressionistic exaggeration and a searching eye for the telling stance or gesture. The almost flat *Tombstones,* 1942 (PC 270), is remarkable for these characteristics, combined here (as in his early work) with a simplification of shape which is expressive of emotion. Later this simplicity became more formally sophisticated, though without much loss of expressive power, in a series dealing with the themes of the Negro and of war, of which *War Series: Another Patrol,* 1946 (PC 767), is an outstanding example.

Robert Gwathmey, a Virginian by birth and background, brings to his treatment of the Negro something of the guilt of the sensitive white southerner, as shown in his contemptuous treatment of mere palliatives against misery and discrimination in *Bread and Circuses,* 1945 (PC 196); his sympathy and feeling of fellowship are seen in the gayer, more carefree, but still moving *Vacationist,* 1946 (PC 197), representing a Negro crabbing. Gwathmey's work has not the eloquence of Lawrence's powerful simplifications, which make the latter's overtly literary or dramatic themes, through their formal statement, more art than propaganda. Yet Gwathmey shows considerable artistic sophistication in his employment of various aspects of abstraction and surrealism. His subtler methods make him a more pleasing and decorative painter than Lawrence, and his sincerity is obvious, though his personal involvement could never carry the force of Lawrence's inevitably deeper one.

Another artist concerned with the human condition is Philip Evergood. His paintings of the 1930's fit into the then current pattern of social protest but not so programmatically as, for instance, those of Gropper or Grosz. The overtones of social injustice in *Lily and the Sparrows,* 1939 (PC 136), are tempered by the artist's delight in the pleasure of the slum child blissfully unaware that she is underprivileged. The figures in Evergood's genre subjects have too much bumptious vitality to be solemn symbols of class struggle, and when the artist is deeply concerned, as in the *New Lazarus,* begun in 1927 and finished in 1954 (PC 139), his figures are never stock players but convincing and differentiated. Even if Evergood is occasionally sentimental, as in the incongruously cheery one-legged *Boy from Stalingrad,* 1943 (private collection), he is too sincere to be stereotyped. In fact his work is so unstereotyped that it seems almost inconsistent. Each subject—landscape, genre, or figure—and each mood—bitter, heroic, or gay—is treated differently, as though every new situation required a new solution. Sometimes the artist is bold, sometimes delicate; sometimes predominantly tonal, sometimes linear. Evergood usually makes a direct statement, but sometimes he is symbolic, frequently he ventures into fantasy, and often an individual painting can be interpreted on various levels or in different ways, as in *Lily and the Sparrows.* This formal and conceptual variety is the source of much of Evergood's appeal, but it also tempts some critics to dismiss him too quickly as an artist who has not really found a consistent personal style. But there is an underlying consistency in Ever-

good's work, and that is its deliberate naïveté. He seems consciously to choose to see things with the uncomplicated immediacy of the folk artist in order to preserve their freshness. Many of the devices of popular painting are used by Evergood, as is evident in nearly all of his pictures, not the least of which is the gay and charming *Dream Catch,* 1946 (PC 137), which has the brilliance of a Haitian primitive. But this well-educated artist has at his command other devices borrowed from more sophisticated artists, such as the attenuated figures and luminous visages of El Greco, and the angular and exacerbated drawing of the expressionists—especially, in his later work, of Max Beckmann. All of these influences, together with those of folk or primitive art, can be seen in the *New Lazarus.* Yet Evergood's basic humanism keeps him from being merely eclectic in this picture as in others, for formal considerations never gain the upper hand over his concern with people, his admiration for their courage, and his pleasure in their passing joys.

Ben Shahn is similar to Evergood in his subject matter, in his borrowing from popular art, and in his variety. But Shahn is more powerful and more consistent, and has developed one of the most personal and influential styles among contemporary American artists. For his treatment of subject matter, which is similar to those artists associated with the American scene and more especially to those sharing a leftist or reformist bias, Shahn can be described as a typical artist of the 1930's. But he is nevertheless atypical in having a far greater range of subject and a profounder sense of form and style. Shahn could be called a realist, yet he is not one in the conventional sense. His work is incisively real, acutely observed, and precisely expressed, but it combines traditional and logical consistency of appearance with the more conceptual realism of exaggeration, suppression, and, above all, simplification—almost to the point of using signs, as in the representation of the features of a face. Yet these abstracting devices, though often very prominent, are never used for the sake of mere formality or decoration. Thus Shahn is neither a conventional realist nor an abstractionist. In reacting against the outward realism of appearance and against formal abstraction employed only for its own sake, Shahn as an artist is as deeply involved in the formal as he is in the conceptual problems of his time, and is perhaps its most eloquent artistic spokesman.

Shahn's work throughout his career of thirty years has been concerned mostly with two themes that are fairly easy to differentiate: the social condition of mankind, and the more personal or lonely identity of man as an individual. The first played a more important role during the early 1930's; the second became more prominent in the late 1930's and early 1940's, and remained so even during the widespread holocaust of World War II. After the war both themes became more subjective, and the abstract element increased in tune with the general artistic tendency of the 1950's, a decade during which Shahn was perhaps not quite so much at home.

The sources of the elements which make up Shahn's style can be analyzed to a certain extent, but their synthesis is thoroughly his own. Though at times his eclecticism is evident, on the whole it has been absorbed in a personal expression which is individual enough to have left a stamp on much of the art of our time, from the magic realism of Bernard Perlin to the linear witticisms of Saul Steinberg. The influence of modern art in general is seen in Shahn's concern with abstract design, but, in his case, more attention is paid to flat pattern and line than to the problems of form in space. One is reminded in Shahn's work more of the graphic and decorative sensibility of Paul Klee than of the three-dimensional formalism of Cézanne or the cubists. Klee's influence has been supplemented by elements from popular and children's art (strong ingredients in Klee's work also), especially the use of conceptual rather than visual realism, the employment of symbols and signs, and an emphasis on bold and easily readable design, as is the case with the "comics."

The influence of photography, his own and that of others, is also important in Shahn's work. The exhibition of photographs by Cartier-Bresson, held in 1933 at New York, in which visual reality was transfixed in an almost surrealist unreality, especially when recording the trance-like, self-absorbed play of children, had a strong effect on Shahn, as his own sensitive treatment of children suggests. These photographs and those of his friend Walker Evans, which were concerned on the one hand with the poignancy and tragedy of the human predicament and on the other with a love of the abstract forms of architecture and advertising lettering, showed Shahn that the popular art of photography could have as much evocative force and as much formal subtlety as the older forms of popular art. This was undoubtedly one of the main factors in his shift from the somewhat self-conscious linearism and simplification of his earliest important work (which dealt with the Sacco and Vanzetti case) to a more inclusive vocabulary of form. Shahn's own photography, into which he was urged by Evans, helped sharpen his eye and gave him a backlog of pertinent visual facts and motifs to which to refer in his paintings.

Another important factor in the development of Shahn's style came a little later: the influence of mural painting. His work as an assistant to Diego Rivera, when the Mexican painter was working on the ill-fated murals at Rockefeller Center, gave Shahn a sense of large design and of three-dimensional form. These were supplemented by a study of the great Italian frescoists of the Renaissance, especially Piero della Francesca, the specific influence of whose dignified and simple treatment of the figure can be seen in such pictures as *Welders*, 1943 (*PC 411). To an artist who has always been attracted by linear refinement and who is happiest in a small format, this broadening of approach was very important, for without it Shahn might have remained an artist known principally for his graphic sensibility, and the murals, posters, and paintings of his later years would not have been so effective.

Still another ingredient in Shahn's style is subtler and less consistently permeating but nonetheless significant: the influence of certain aspects of the American environment, and even of certain American artists who emphasized them. The rigid rectilinear architecture of streets and buildings, the prominence of advertising lettering, and the precision of machines and their products are the most conspicuous elements of the environment which have appealed to Shahn in themselves and have influenced his own vision and design. The use of planes, lines, and edges, very much an American tradition, is a stylistic characteristic which Shahn incorporates in his work and adumbrates by the whimsical addition of such quaint absurdities as Victorian architectural detail. (It has already been noted that one of Shahn's favorite pictures is Charles Caleb Ward's *The Circus is Coming.*)

Shahn's earliest characteristic works consisted of a series of small paintings dealing with the Sacco-Vanzetti case (expressing the indignation among liberals inspired by what they considered to be a miscarriage of justice in which two naïve and innocent men were sent to their execution) and another concerned with the trial of Tom Mooney in California. Clear, bold, touching in their specificity, and painted with the flat, poster-like quality of popular advertising and the eloquent power of children's drawings, these pictures were meant to have a mass appeal, but ironically were admired only by the sophisticated and bought by the very wealthy. *The Passion of Sacco and Vanzetti,* 1931–1932 (PC 409), is typical.

The influence of photography and mural painting caused Shahn to develop a richer, less deliberately flat or meager style, as can be seen in the forceful modeling and perspective in *Scotts Run, West Virginia,* 1937 (Whitney Museum of

6–59. Ben Shahn, *Handball,* 1939. Tempera on paper over composition board. 22¾ x 31¼ inches. (Collection, The Museum of Modern Art, New York. Mrs. John D. Rockefeller, Jr., Fund.)

6–60.   Ben Shahn, *Willis Avenue Bridge*, 1940.   Tempera on paper over composition board.   23 x 31⅜ inches.   (Collection, The Museum of Modern Art, New York.   Gift of Lincoln Kirstein.)

American Art, New York), but not at the expense of incisive drawing, which in this picture is most successful in the characterization of the unemployed miners.   At this time Shahn was beginning to work on his own murals, at the Community Center of Roosevelt, New Jersey, in 1938–1939, and at the Bronx Post Office a little later.   These and subsequent ones done in 1940–1942 at the Social Security Building at Washington are certainly the outstanding wall decorations done under the aegis of the Roosevelt administration.   But they are not the outstanding work of Shahn; even the best of them incorporate motifs reworked from the artist's paintings of the late 1930's and early 1940's, which are in fact much more successful, perhaps because of their smaller format, and mark the high point of

Shahn's work.   Among the best are *Handball*, 1939 (Illustration 6–59); *Vacant Lot*, 1939 (PC 410); *Willis Avenue Bridge*, 1940 (Illustration 6–60); and *Girl Jumping Rope*, 1943 (Illustration 6–61).   All four are distinguished by Shahn's magnificently apt and telling drawing: the attitudes of the boys playing ball in the first two pictures; the gangling girl, and the boy in a paroxysm of awkwardness in *Jumping Rope*; the arthritic hands and ankles of the crippled colored woman resting on a bench on the Willis Avenue Bridge; and even the cut of the chain-store leather jackets worn by the handball players.   Emotional intensity is relieved and enhanced by abstract compositional elements of great effectiveness: the large blank area of the handball board enframed in the geometry of sign-covered and

6–61. Ben Shahn, *Girl Jumping Rope*, 1943. Oil on canvas. 19¾ x 27½ inches. (Stephen and Sybil Stone Foundation; courtesy of the Downtown Gallery, New York.)

window-filled masonry; the interminable brick wall against which the solitary boy is batting a ball in *Vacant Lot* (the small-patterned monotony of the wall makes his loneliness the more affecting); the ruined house with its exposed, gaily flowered wallpaper, which is the background for the psychologically separated boy and girl in *Jumping Rope;* and the belligerently gay orange-painted beams of the Willis Avenue Bridge criss-crossing behind the green park bench on which the sober and dignified colored ladies are sitting.

The war and its aftermath affected Shahn profoundly. Involved in active poster-making, he created a few unforgettable examples, such as the representation of the hollow-eyed and supplicating youth in *We Want Peace—Register, Vote,* which he did for the C. I. O. in 1946 (V 134), to which the painting *Hunger,* 1946

(The State Department) is related. The powerful oil painting *Welders* is one of the most impressive of Shahn's wartime pictures. Two paintings similar to one another and both done in 1945, *Pacific Landscape* (Museum of Modern Art, New York), and *Death on the Beach* (Collection of Mr. and Mrs. Sidney Berkowitz, New York)—particularly the latter, with its representation of a dead soldier's curly red head, his clenched hands, and his blood running out over a pebbly beach—bring to a climax Shahn's characteristic coupling of intense feeling and incisive observation. The impact of these tragic and grisly subjects is enhanced by his handling of form, line, color, and (especially in this case) texture, which make up the abstract design.

The desolation at the end of the war is summed up in *The Red Stairway,* 1944 (PC 904), depicting a crippled man in a ruined city-scape, mounting a red metal stairway that leads no-where. But the hope of the future is suggested in the poignant activity of half-starved children in *Reconstruction*, 1945 (°PC 905), in which Shahn's intimate understanding of children is especially notable.

With the return to a less frenetic life after the war, Shahn's best work is represented by his re-version to the eloquence of the particular [as in the touching *Spring*, 1947 (Albright-Knox Art Gallery, Buffalo, New York), in which two lovers are shown lying together on a little triangle of glass which is almost crushed between buildings] rather than to socially conscious subject matter, represented by *Death of a Miner*, 1948 (The Metropolitan Museum of Art, New York), which seems too pat and mannered.

On the other hand, Shahn's graphic work of these later years is as remarkable as any of his earlier pieces; its focus is on the essential, but now with more freedom and incisiveness than formerly. These qualities are seen especially well in his drawings around the theme of baseball (which are as typically American as Picasso's drawings of bull fighting are Spanish) and of jazz. The best of the latter are Shahn's illustra-tions for the life of Louis Armstrong, commis-sioned by Edward R. Murrow in connection with his film, *Ambassador Satchmo*, 1956. Even such merely decorative drawings as that used for an advertisement for C. B. S., *The Empty Studio*, 1940 (°V 135), indicate how far Shahn has ad-vanced beyond his own early work and the work of those who imitate him. Even the brilliant Saul Steinberg often seems merely witty in com-parison.

About 1948 Shahn's work became more subjec-tive (already hinted at in some of the pictures of the war years), expressed chiefly in an iconog-raphy which is more private or autobiographi-cal than formerly, incorporating a fusion of vari-ous experiences and memories which become symbolic. In *Everyman*, 1954 (PC 412A), for instance, the accurate drawing of the figures, the linear pattern, and the sense of all-over design are familiar, but the effect is new. Such a pic-ture, not precise in its references, is all the more disquieting, though its subjective and even her-metic imagery somewhat defeats the purpose of a theme of general reference and appeal. This tendency toward polyvalent meaning (some of its vocabulary is derived from the mystical writ-ings of William Blake, whom Shahn had come to admire) is seen even in his drawings and prints of the time, as in the serigraph, with watercolor added, *Phoenix*, 1952 (GC 65). Among the most successful of the artist's works of this kind are his variations on the theme of Hebrew letters. His concern with the decorative and stylistic as-pects of lettering, which was always strong and sure [as seen in such charming examples as the Christmas card published by the Museum of Modern Art in 1952, *Two Turtle Doves* (V 139)], was now supplemented by emotional content, as in the serigraph, *Where there is a Sword there is no Book*, 1950 (°GC 66).

When the later Shahn deals with a subject of general reference through the metaphor of the specific, it remains effective and is perhaps more subtly powerful because of the addition of sym-bolism. In the *Blind Botanist*, 1955 (PC 409A), for instance, the concentration shown in the face and the expressive quality of the hands explor-ing the spikey identity of a plant intensify the allegory of man's groping attempts to compre-hend the kind of world in which he finds himself today. Shahn's present preoccupation is in fact just this, as indicated by his pictures dealing with the fate of the crew of a Japanese fishing boat poisoned by the explosion of an atomic bomb. Eloquent and gripping, these paintings are not quite successful. But not even Shahn can be expected to find satisfactory expression for mankind's present dilemma.

Perhaps Shahn is more important as an elo-quent summarizer of a half-century of art in America than he is as a contributor to the present and future. His work has esthetic charm and the power to move. Yet when a collection of his paintings is seen together at one time, as at the Venice Biennale of 1954, both his formal and conceptual references seem a trifle too expected. Though Shahn has moments of high seriousness and poignant poetry, his too-various style, for all its sensitivity and expressiveness, has little of the consistent impressiveness of a Hopper, or of the image-making faculty of the abstract expres-sionists.

Abstract art as such did not flourish between its flowering after the Armory Show and its revival in the post-World War II period. This is especially true of the geometric constructivists, as opposed to the expressionists. Only one painter of great significance, Stuart Davis, became at the end of the period almost an abstract artist, one who nevertheless always kept his feet on the ground of the real world.

There are basically two kinds of abstract art: that which projects images from the imagination itself—what José Ortega y Gasset calls "intrasubjectivism," represented by the abstract expressionists—and that which derives from the actuality of the world surrounding the artist, reinterpreted or distilled into abstract forms. It is to this last group that Stuart Davis belongs, and he is probably its most distinguished representative in the United States.

Since Davis became a prominent artist in the 1920's, he should perhaps have been discussed before, but his subsequent work, beginning about 1938, is no longer concerned merely with a reinterpretation of the subject matter of "the Immaculates" in terms of more specific European modernism. Instead, it is a distillation of real experience—and an intensely American one; consequently, his work during and since the 1930's is far more important than that of the 1920's. Perhaps more than any other artist, except one of two of the abstract expressionists at this time, Davis speaks with the greatest authority as a thoroughly American painter.

Davis was from the beginning concerned with the American scene. As the son of the art director of the *Philadelphia Press* who employed Luks, Sloan, and Henri, Davis knew these men and shared their enthusiasm for the life they reported. A further affirmation of their point of view was gained by the young artist through studying with Henri himself. But a vague dissatisfaction with what he felt was a too great concern with subject matter on the part of the "ashcan" group was confirmed by the Armory Show, where Van Gogh, Gauguin, and Matisse especially impressed him. He realized that the beauty of the music played by Negro pianists in the bars he had been exploring could have a

counterpart in art, and he was thereby incited toward the exploration of new artistic dimensions. Initially this took the direction of Fauvist landscapes, where he first used color arbitrarily—a persisting characteristic. Then in 1920 he embarked on a course of serious self-discipline in the exploration of cubist and other formal abstraction. His *Lucky Strike*, 1921 (*PC 98), inspired by cubist *papiers collés*, shows his skill in the manipulation of form, texture, and color into a lively, amusing, and decorative pattern. Later in the 1920's Davis began a series of paintings confined to the exploration of the formal possibilities of an arrangement made up of an eggbeater, an electric fan, and a pair of rubber gloves—not the studio props of cubism, but, as in the case of *Lucky Strike*, objects chosen from his own American environment; *Eggbeater No. 1*, 1927 (PC 99), was one of the results.

After a trip to Paris in 1928 and his return to the United States (there was no question of his returning—he felt he belonged in America, even if Paris was the center of the artistic world), Davis continued this series and began another which dealt with a salt shaker, as exemplified in a version done in 1931 (Museum of Modern Art, New York), which is often illustrated. These later still lifes are more decorative and not quite so serious, an element of gaiety having been added in the form of brighter colors and a somewhat lively linearism, perhaps derived from Klee—a supposition reinforced by the presence in some of them of little directional arrows, one of Klee's devices.

This linearism, which was to become increasingly characteristic of the artist, was first seen conspicuously in the exuberant and arbitrary calligraphy of the clouds which appear in an otherwise rectilinear and disciplined canvas (the best known from his Paris experience), *Place Pasdeloup*, 1928 (PC 100). This picture is also notable for its frank acceptance of the decorative and patterned elements of the typical Paris scene, reformed into a delightfully bold and semiabstract design showing the influence of Matisse and Dufy. Davis' sensitivity to the character or essence of place is nicely demonstrated by the contrast between the relatively elegant and re-

6–62. Stuart Davis, *New York Under Gaslight,* 1941. Oil on canvas. 32 x 45 inches. (The Bezalel Jewish National Museum, Jerusalem, Israel. Gift of Mrs. Rebecca Shulman in honor of Herman Shulman.)

strained form and color of this picture with his harshly colored, hard, and decisively rectilinear American city-scapes, in which he achieves a synthesis of the method of later cubism and the depiction of the American scene which is boldly decorative in its arrangement of forms and hues. In his delightful prints of the early 1930's, such as the lithograph entitled *Barber Shop Chord,* 1931 (°GC 17), where there appears for the first time a whimsical play on words in the title, and in equally engaging pictures such as the *Windshield Mirror,* 1932, a gouache and ink drawing (GC 150), and the very lively oil *New York Under Gaslight,* 1941 (Illustration 6–62), Davis projects an image of America with the forms and colors of the local scene arranged in a brash, insouciant, and even witty way, which has a genuine native tang. Engaging as such work is, however, it is not profound, being essentially a reinterpretation of subject matter already made familiar by "the Immaculates," in the framework of a more sophisticated or fashionable abstraction and with a livelier tempo. Such pictures would be wonderfully appropriate as inspirations for stage sets for an American ballet or musical comedy.

In 1938 Davis began to make a more penetrating statement about the American scene, in which form and content are more integrated. The dynamics of jazz and of what Davis called its "numerical precision," which he had heard in the playing of the Negro pianists during his youth, now at last received a visual equivalent in his painting. (Davis' designs for record covers of jazz music are especially successful.)

The tempo and gratuitous linearism increase in such pictures as *Report from Rockport,* 1940 (PC 101), in which these elements take on almost a life of their own. Davis combines the quaintly picturesque elements of the little fishing port and artists' colony with those ubiquitous elements of the American scene which relate to the automobile and its services. In what amounts to a culmination of his development to this point,

in this picture Davis' loud hues, angularity, calligraphic line (now broadened into larger areas),
and references to actuality are incorporated into
a swarming maelstrom of raucous gaiety. In such
a painting Davis is now completely himself.

In his work of the 1940's, visual motifs taken
from the actual world around the artist become
less obvious, though the forms eventually always
refer back to nature. In a word, there is more
presentation than representation. As Davis becomes more abstract his references also become
more than merely visual. He is free to develop,
for instance, witticisms suggested by the title
Owh! in San Pao, 1951 (PC 999), in which the
play on the nasal sound of the Portuguese pro-
nunciation of the Brazilian city of São Paulo is
important to the final effect of the picture. In
such paintings, or in the impressive *Something
on the Eight Ball,* 1953–1954 (PC 102; Illustration 6–63), the characteristics of the later Davis
are evident, that is, a greater monumentality and
simplicity and the employment of fewer elements than formerly, superbly placed. These
compositions, dissonant (but at the same time
balanced by the reappearance of similar elements
throughout the canvas) and startling in their
unconventional juxtapositions, possess the element of surprise which is also characteristic
of jazz. In fact, many of them are actually inspired by "jam sessions," as the title of *Rapt at
Rappaport's* (Collection of Mr. and Mrs. Stanley
Wolf, Great Neck, New York) suggests. Incidentally, it is interesting to note that these pictures precede Matisse's jazz themes by a few
years.

In Davis' work, especially of the last two decades, the lessons of cubism, Léger, and futurism
have been absorbed into an American idiom in
pictures which, though they hint at their foreign
ancestry, could not have been produced anywhere else but in the United States. Like the
cubists and, indeed, every abstract and partly
abstract artist since Cézanne, Davis respects the
two-dimensional surface of his canvas, allowing
three-dimensionality to be largely the function of
color (in the sense that red projects and green
recedes). He employs color, to use his own
terminology, as an "interval" in space, and refers
to the dynamics of color–space relation. With

6–63. Stuart Davis, *Something on the Eight
Ball,* 1953–1954. Oil on canvas. 56 x 45 inches.
(Philadelphia Museum of Art.)

color, then, as the chief organizer of space, Davis
can ignore consistent vanishing points and horizon lines, and wander around the surface of the
canvas like the cubists—and also like Klee, whose
actual method his own gaiety resembles more
than it does the more solemnly analytical method
of the cubists. His composition, freed from the
illusionism of three-dimensionality, depends
largely on cubical and rectilinear forms for its
unifying elements—squares playing against
cubes, and often within frame-like limits—and
depends also upon a very careful asymmetry or
accurate balance in which color is very significant, its relative importance controlled by intensity more than by the size of its area. But color
in itself, aside from its space-relating compositional function, is also used in a wonderfully gay
and expressive way, exploiting contrasts but always controlled by greater or less intensity so
that, though cacophonous and brash, there is
unity in its organization.

Davis' late style is admirably suited for wall decoration. His *Mural*, 1955 (*PC 615), is superb and smashing, appropriately flat as wall decoration, yet more than usually effective because of the painter's exploitation of the color–space relationship.

A work such as *Mural* is almost pure abstraction, which seems to be the present direction of the artist, a trend that is illustrated also in the colored lithograph *Detail Study for Cliché*, 1957 (GC 97).

Davis has been a superlative recorder of America, at first in pictures clearly abstracted from the visual world, and later in those less related to it, but adumbrated by words. letters, titles, and humorous tongue-in-cheek attitude; and, above all, by the rhythm and beat of jazz —staccato and frenetic. The dynamism and rude ugliness of the American scene, reflecting the vitality of certain chaotic, uncontrolled, and unplanned aspects of our culture, have no more eloquent spokesman than Stuart Davis.

After 1945

This section deals principally with artists and movements that have flourished in the years after the war, although it includes some painters who, while well-known before the war, achieved greater prominence afterward, like Andrew Wyeth and Mark Tobey.

The fragmentation of modern art became more exaggerated as it became more contemporary; at the same time each fragment seemed more specifically itself. Realism became a culmination of precision; geometric abstraction became more doctrinaire; and, when combined with elements of expressionism and surrealism, modern art was apotheosized in abstract expressionism, still probably the most significant artistic manifestation of the present. That a painting by the precisionist Andrew Wyeth and one by the abstract expressionist Jackson Pollock can be considered equally important, indeed that they can be painted in the same era, symbolizes dramatically the heterogeneity of contemporary art.

"Magic" or "Sharp-Focus" Realism; Andrew Wyeth

Out of the American tradition of the precisionists or "the Immaculates" of the first third of the century has come a group of painters who, though ideologically quite separate, have in common a realism which has been called "magic" or "sharp-focus": [49] "magic" because the point of view is so precise that it gives to the ordinary world a sharpened intensity that sometimes makes it mysterious or even frightening, especially when it is accompanied with overtones of the illogical, unreal, or strange. The most straightforward of these artists are those who simply deal with still life. Kenneth Davies, for instance, in his *trompe l'oeil* carries on the precisionist tradition of William Harnett; Carlyle Brown gives a more cubist elegance (not unlike that of Demuth) to his complicated arrangements, as in the *Red Cabinet*, 1954 (PC 55). Honoré D. Sharrer, in a series of small-scaled paintings so incredibly precise as to suggest the technique of the fifteenth-century Flemish masters, made comments on the present-day world, some of them biting in their candid observation of lower middle class foibles and values; others, such as *Workers and Paintings*, 1943 (PC 908), are a little whimsical. Equally precise, frequently employing the medium of tempera, which is adapted to detail, and socially oriented almost to the point of brutality are Paul Cadmus' forceful commentaries on post-Freudian mores. These often embody a conflict between the artist's disapproval of his subject and his fascination with it, as in *The Bar Italia*, 1952–1955 (PC 70), and in the less ambitious and somewhat more objective *Playground*, 1948 (PC 69), in which a mastery of figure drawing, perspective, and design shows the artist's indebtedness to the Renaissance. Cadmus' technical skill, facility, and nostalgia for the ordered, logical, classical way of seeing are shared by Jared French, who adds to them more than a hint of the static and dignified quality of archaic Greek sculpture, both in composition and in the concept of the figure, as in the *Rope,* tempera, 1954 (PC 151). Bernard Perlin's work, also executed in a medium similar to that of the fifteenth century (casein tempera), is even more meticulous, reaching a kind of *tour de force* in the detail of the encompassing forest in *The Farewell,* 1952 (PC 357).

The enigma of the meaning of French's *Rope* and the aura of strangeness in the compulsive complexities of Perlin become more deliberate in the work of Henry Koerner, Robert Vickrey, George Tooker, and John Wilde, in which there are also elements of surrealist irrationality. In this respect, and in their meticulousness, Koerner's paintings are not unlike those of Peter Blume. Such a picture as *Vanity Fair,* 1946 (PC 255), with its references to many levels of experience in time and space (all the more effective because of the convincing reality of each separate but illogically juxtaposed segment), is an ambitious statement about mankind, in which autobiographical fragments are combined with episodes from the history of the race. Less ambitious and more lyrical, but also stranger and even terrifying, are Tooker's human automatons, wandering in mysterious Kafka-like passages and offices, as in the tempera *Government Bureau,* 1956 (PC 475), and Robert Vickrey's lost creatures, often children and nuns, caught inextricably in mazes or fleeing over ominous open spaces, as in *Fear,* egg tempera, 1954 (PC 479).

The use of pattern and other formal devices derived from abstract art in these paintings, as well as certain reminiscences of Ben Shahn (as in Vickrey's employment of lettering as a prominent feature of his composition, and Perlin's emphasis on gesture), are indicative of a certain degree of eclecticism. In the equally precise and detailed work of Andrew Wyeth, however, whatever influences there were have been integrated in a completely personal style. The objects and figures in Wyeth's temperas and drawings (and his watercolors, although in a more suggestive way) are made to speak for themselves, to be isolated in the significance of their uniqueness as in the work of the great photographers, and to

a certain extent in the drawings of Sheeler. Other artists among the sharp-focus realists feel called upon to give literary, psychological, or other clues extrinsic to the picture itself for the interpretation of their paintings; Wyeth's concentration upon a very carefully chosen segment of the physical world is so intense that it engenders its own meanings in each viewer. This is not to say that subject matter as such is not important to the artist. His watercolor and drybrush landscapes are redolent of place, either of Chadd's Ford, Pennsylvania, or the coast of Maine, and his figure pieces, mostly temperas, are filled with psychological drama. The dignity of the crippled girl in *Christina's World,* 1948 (PC 496), who crawls to visit the graves of her parents, is deeply pathetic, as is the look in the eyes of the old colored man in *A Crow Flew By,* 1950 (Illustration 6–64), as he interprets the bird as the coming of death.

Though detail is the main source of the power of Wyeth's naturalism, other time-proven devices of realism rejected by Cézanne and the abstract artists who followed him have been revived by Wyeth with the enthusiasm of rediscovery: first, geometric perspective, seen in the surge of the long hill in *Christina's World* and the sweeping landscape under the outspreading wings of the great bird in *Soaring,* 1950 (PC 990); second, the logically consistent use of light, both for purposes of modeling and for a subtler realization of the ambiance of atmosphere, which discloses the exact moment of the hour and season of the year, especially in the artist's watercolors; and third, the knowledge of anatomy and its articulation. All three are employed by Wyeth with the skill of the great realists of the past, as his superb drawings attest perhaps more directly than his paintings.

No picture could successfully project itself entirely on the basis of realism, no matter how expert and varied its instruments. Wyeth's feeling for the character of his medium and his compositional skill are two of the qualities with which he supplements his realism. In tempera nothing seems impossible to him, from the shimmering iridescence of water reflected on the gray-shadowed side of a dory, to the Van Eyck-

6–64. Andrew Wyeth, *A Crow Flew By*, 1950. Tempera on wood. 17½ x 27 inches. (The Metropolitan Museum of Art, New York. Arthur H. Hearn Fund, 1950.)

like stubble of a man's shaven beard; in watercolor the chaos of foliage or the complexity of life and color in a tidal pool reflecting the sky is projected with what seems sleight of hand, but is never mere showmanship. Wyeth's compositions are as carefully worked out as those of abstract artists, and with more elements to arrange, from those pictures with an emphasis on curves and undulations, such as *Soaring*, to those whose main accent is angular.

Wyeth's precision and sharply focused detail, seen with incisive clarity, relate the artist to one aspect of the American tradition, while his concern with every aspect of reality, not merely its surface appearance but its projected three-dimensionality, is reminiscent of Eakins (whom Wyeth admires), even though the method is not as broad and painterly in handling as Eakins' usually is.

The work of Wyeth seems to defy the common opinion that in our time the artist of quality is separated from the general public by an unabridgeable gap. The extent of Wyeth's popularity, not only with museum directors and sophisticated collectors but with the general public, must indicate that his work is vital even in a time which, we are told by many critics, is an age of abstract art and in which representational art is moribund, if not, in fact, dead.

Expressionist Realism

A number of artists are still tied somewhat to realism yet have transformed it through the various devices of contemporary art—abstraction, expressionism, or surrealism—to a much larger extent than have those just discussed. The strongest tradition among these painters is the continuing one of American expressionism, which could be described as a combination of Marin's more delicate sensitivity with some of the force and vigor of Hartley and Knaths, expressed with varying degrees of heightened realism and abstraction.

William Congdon's pictures, mostly of European subjects, such as *St. Germain,* 1954 (PC 80), raise reality to a higher power, much as Van Gogh and Kokoschka have done in their landscapes. The sweeping vigor of Congdon's style is seen in the equally angular though more fragmented manner of Herbert Katzman, as in *Two Nudes Before Japanese Screen,* 1952 (PC 238).

More disciplined by a cubism similar to that employed deliberately by Feininger and more intuitively by Marin are a group of artists including John Heliker, William Palmer, Arthur Osver, James Boynton, and William Kienbusch. The most distinguished is probably Kienbusch, who expresses eloquently the moods, movement, and energy of nature in highly emotional pictures which are made more effective by being restrained by a clear structural framework.

The work of Milton Avery and Lee Gatch is less obviously structural, though equally dependent on aspects of abstract art to heighten reality. Avery's *Gaspé Landscape,* 1943 (PC 9), is typical of the artist's landscapes, which are essentially decorative and formal shorthand notations, like Marin's, but in which there is a tendency for larger or flatter areas to be covered in bolder, more essentially decorative colors. In Avery's figure compositions, represented by *Two Figures at Desk,* 1944 (PC 10), there is a further simplification, the decorative areas being bounded by expressively distorted outline. Gatch is more complex than Avery, evolving from a semiabstract style of angular ordering in planes (not unlike the later Heliker and Kienbusch), represented by *Pennsylvania Farm,* c. 1936 (PC 153), toward a more dynamic kind of abstraction that encompasses the suggestion of movement and growth, as in *Greenhouse,* 1950 (PC 152).

The ordering of visual experience through the use of the form language of cubism (especially of Picasso's later more decorative or synthetic cubism) is seen in the work of Zygmunt Menkes and, in a more complicated form, in that of Vaclav Vytlacil and Carl R. Holty.

Perhaps the most prominent artist in the more realistic aspect of the expressionist tradition (excepting Leonard Baskin, who, however, is not a painter, but a print-maker and sculptor) is Rico Le Brun, who is deeply concerned with human society, especially the drama of man's inhumanity to man, heightened by being played out in the eschatological present. The various influences of cubism, Picasso, and the Mexican muralists have almost overwhelmed, rather than enhanced, Le Brun's native realism which nevertheless remains very powerful in pictures ranging from commentaries on Buchenwald to various reinterpretations of the Crucifixion in the light of recent history, as in *Wood of the Holy Cross,* 1948 (PC 277).

Expressionism, as well as surrealism, has been largely absorbed by abstract expressionism. There are a few artists, however, who could be said to have somewhat surrealist overtones, though they combine them with aspects of realism and abstraction. Among them are Attilio Salemme and Joseph Glasco (who is also a sculptor). Salemme's geometric totems, as in his *Caught in the Equinox,* 1953 (PC 398), and *Inquisition,* 1952 (PC 397), inhabit a clearly defined yet dream-like environment, and have the unfamiliar yet somehow convincing actuality of creatures from another planet and from a different kind of space. Glasco's nearly abstract compositions, such as his *Portrait of a Poet,* 1951 (PC 161), have a graphic charm, similar to Klee's detail, which becomes more deliberately childlike or primitive in his more representational work (in this quality also he is not unlike Klee). His *Salome,* 1955 (PC 163), is all the more arresting in her nudity because of this simulated naïveté.

Formal Abstraction

The tradition of formal abstraction was never strong in the United States and, before Mondrian's arrival in New York during the war, was usually combined with realism (as in the case of "the Immaculates") or with emotional expression (as in Arthur G. Dove and the early Georgia O'Keeffe) or was related to music (as in Covert and synchromism). In the 1930's Albert Gallatin and George L. K. Morris kept alive a tradition of exploration into various phases of purism, constructivism, and cubism, summarized in such a work as Morris' *Nautical Composition,* 1937–

1942 (PC 332). Morris was also a mainstay of the American Abstract Artists Group, which was founded in 1937 and held several exhibitions subsequently. Abstract artists such as John Graham extended Picasso's cubism, and Charles Howard added certain forms derived from Miró to his basically formal compositions, as in *Prescience,* 1942 (PC 229).

The formal effect of Ralston Crawford's work is similar to that of the abstract artists just discussed, though his purpose is different, for his abstraction does not derive from projections of an inner vision but from the distillation of the visual experience of the actual world, as is clearly demonstrated in his relatively early *Whitestone Bridge,* 1939 (PC 87). His later work is more abstract. Especially in his lithographs (among the most carefully executed and printed in the history of the medium), he achieves a formal beauty which is perhaps richer for having some elements of the recognizable environment reduced to essential shapes, patterns, textures, and their relationships. These Crawford arranges with a powerful subtlety, as in *Nets, Croix de Vie,* 1955 (*GC 15), and in many subsequent examples.

The great impetus toward purely formal abstraction came from the actual presence in the United States of Mondrian himself and of Josef Albers, the Bauhaus' most dedicated pure abstractionist.

Mondrian has a dedicated follower in the Swiss émigré (sometimes still considered a Swiss artist) Fritz Glarner, whose *Relational Painting,* 1949–1951 (PC 159), and *Tondo, No. 15,* 1950 (*PC 160), are variations on themes analogous to those of his master, though somewhat smaller scaled in their motifs. Burgoyne Diller is nearly as devoted a follower, while Ilya Bolotowsky varies Mondrian's rectangles with slight diagonals, as in *Blue Rectangles,* 1953 (PC 47). Irene Rice-Pereira has developed the inherently limited expressiveness of pure abstraction to a greater capacity. The most obvious distinguishing characteristic of her art is the addition of the third dimension to Mondrian's two by the introduction of transparent and overlapping space, both simulated on the flat surface of the canvas and actually built up in three-dimensional surfaces that are transparent or opaque. Some of these are composed of undulating transparent glass so that the slightest movement of the observer before the pictures effects a subtle change in the myriad interrelationships of the artist's forms.

Albers remains the high priest of abstraction. The subtlety and precision of his arrangements of form in black and white, as seen in such clever configurations as *Aquarium,* a woodcut, 1934 (GC 81), and *Ascension,* a lithograph, 1942 (GC 1), are increased in his handling of color relations, which have become almost the content of his paintings. Pictures such as *The Gate,* 1936 (PC 501), for instance, are so nicely balanced that any reproduction jars their exquisite rightness. Light, color, and form reduced to a minimum of restricted design are used by Albers like the most sensitive instruments, so that the sequences of color adjustments seen in such series as *Homage to the Square,* 1953, of which "Ascending" (PC 3) is especially notable, are in themselves an intense esthetic experience.

The influence of Albers has spread during the 1960's into new developments in geometric and optical experiments using the juxtaposition and repetition of certain shapes and colors to produce such visual effects as dazzle and afterimage, as in the work of Richard Anuskiewicz and Gene Davis, and reaching a purist distillation in the art of Frank Stella. This aspect of what has been dubbed "op art" is a refinement of European postcubist abstraction which approaches dangerously close to didactic exercises in the physiological effects of color and form, and is to be distinguished from the work of artists like Morris Louis and Kenneth Noland (to be discussed later) which, though equally abstract, derives from American abstract expressionism and is intuitional and emotional rather than scientific and detached.

Gorky and Tobey

Before turning to abstract expressionism, the most important phase of contemporary art, two artists who were instrumental in the formation of that style should be discussed: Arshile Gorky and Mark Tobey. They are by no means significant merely as forerunners. Gorky has assumed a place of importance second to none of the abstract expressionists except possibly Jackson Pollock, and Tobey is one of the most lionized of American artists abroad, being the first American to win first prize at the Venice Biennale (in 1960) since Whistler, and the subject of important European exhibitions since.

Gorky took many years to find himself, re-exploring in his early work the territory already discovered by the pioneers of modern art, especially Picasso. *The Enigmatic Combat,* c. 1936 (PC 164), is a late example of this period of apprenticeship, already showing some of the intensity of his later works, though still hidden under Picasso-like forms. The example of Matta, Miró, and the surrealists stimulated Gorky into a more personal vocabulary and freed his artistic imagination from the stabler and more massive forms of abstract art which he began to replace with fragile, insubstantial, and pulsating configurations more appropriate for the expression of his themes of desire, conflict, and fertility. Surrealism gave Gorky some of the method by which these shapes were arrived at and composed. Though he rejected the strict automatism and the deliberately induced accident of pure surrealism, he employed a semiautomatic procedure whereby he induced the invisible world of the unconscious to take shape in forms which he combined with his sensitive observation of organic life. As a consequence of this process, he achieved a synthesis of two levels of meaning which took effect through analogy, "the hybrid form in which all human emotion is precipitated," as the founder of surrealism, André Breton, wrote in the introduction of the catalog of Gorky's first one-man show in 1945 at the Julien Levy Gallery in New York. The drawings of this period, such as *Crayon Drawing,* 1943 (*GC 166), show these hybrid forms at their purest, and reveal the excitement of the artist's discovery of the potentials of expression in the interpenetrations and changes of the forms of the visible and invisible world.

The drawings of 1944 are perhaps clearer in their analogies between nature and the symbolic images of the memory and dream world, translated into new visual symbols. In these Gorky expresses his fascination with the diversity of nature's forms in the springtime awakening, playing on the theme of fecundity and turning grass to bone and bone to phallus. The addition of the bold and direct forms of dream symbolism—such as the boot shape (the fetishist symbol for woman) and extensive organic reference (the liver, viscera, and the genitals)—to the mutating forms of the drawings resulted in such a painting as *The Liver Is the Cock's Comb,* 1944 (PC 166). This typical and culminating example of Gorky's first phase, in which he is completely himself, has the spontaneity yet at the same time the delicate refinement of the drawings, combined with the bolder and more direct forms of the Freudian chamber of horrors in guises which at first mystify, but later reveal meanings in various levels of communication: natural, symbolic, and analogic. These forms are eloquent in themselves as shape and color and are arranged with a spatial and decorative sensibility of the utmost refinement.

In 1946 another series of drawings acted again as a partial catalyst for a series of paintings, Gorky's last ones. They were inspired by a familiar room which contained a fireplace, rocking chairs, palettes, boots, and figures, and by objects from the world outside the room—fields, flowers, thorns, the beaks of birds, and bones. These the artist interwove into metaphors of love and death. An additional formal element began to assume more importance in Gorky's work at this time: the shapes which occurred in the work of artists he enjoyed, seen not in their original meaning, but, in a sense, negatively instead of positively. The familiar forms of Ucello's *Battle of San Romano,* for instance, appear again in an entirely different context in his *Betrothal II,* 1947 (PC 167).

The paintings of Gorky's tragic last year and a half before his suicide combine a more complex but better integrated number of layers of meaning. These are made up of the stimuli of the visible world, the symbolism of psychoanalysis and of the dream, the automatism of the unconscious, memories of his Armenian childhood in the Caucasus, and various works of art. This

6–65. Arshile Gorky, *The Diary of a Seducer*, 1945. Oil on canvas. 50 x 62 inches. (Collection of Mr. and Mrs. William A. M. Burden, New York.)

personal cosmos of multiple meanings is made to express the most basic and agonizing of human biological and emotional activities: wooing, rejection, and drawing together in *Betrothal II;* the sexual cycle in the *Plow and the Song* (one version of which is at Oberlin College); passionate sensuality and psychic sadism in *Agony,* 1947 (PC 168); and poignant frustration and immolation in *The Diary of a Seducer,* 1945 (Illustration 6–65). This picture, one of Gorky's last, is a commentary on one of his besetting themes, the wooing of women. The title is taken from a chapter in a book by the nineteenth-century Danish existentialist, Sören Kierkegaard, and refers to a man who is by no means a libertine, but

who faces the universal problem of wanting a woman to give herself to him freely—a problem that cannot be solved because of the inherent paradox that any free act cannot be urged.

In pictures such as these (painted in his last months, when he was suffering from cancer and from a form of psychosexual frustration not necessarily connected with the disease), Gorky spoke out on the conflicts between love and rejection, life and death, hope and destiny, in a language whose vocabulary was derived from his personal and artistic experience, and he projected these in his paintings with an intensity stimulated by the activity of the unconscious.

Tobey, like Gorky, spent many years searching for a personal style, the first phase of which he arrived at in the mid-1930's. Until then he had vacillated between realism and various phases of abstraction, in the early 1930's coming under the influence of Picasso, like Gorky and so many of his generation. But he absorbed an important aspect of surrealism much earlier in his career than did Gorky, for he had been interested in automatic writing since the 1920's.

Realism and abstraction have been the continuing polarities of Tobey's art (except for a recent period when a form of oriental abstraction absorbed most of his attention), a fact which is often overlooked by those who, fascinated by his abstract form, ignore the reality which stimulated it and to which he remains attached.

In the early 1920's Tobey painted lumberjacks, sailors, and the denizens of Skid Row in a realistic genre style. A few years later he not only discovered the generally abstract and expressionistic formulations of modern art but became interested in some of the pictorial effects of the great Venetian masters of the mannerist and rococo periods, an interest which molded his contemporary sensibility more than did the classical and monumental aspects of twentieth-century painting. He found in Tintoretto's contrived perspectives and rippling highlights a new kind of space unified by the play of light, and discovered in Guardi's and Tiepolo's sparkling waves and scintillating air a similarly unifying web of brilliance. Tobey combined these visual revelations with a free form of drawing stimulated by automatic writing, achieving a tenuous linearism that began to envelop his figures and shapes in a gossamer of light, reducing their mass and drawing them together in a greater unity. In 1934, Tobey studied the calligraphy of the Far East with a Chinese master who was visiting in America, and in 1935 continued his studies in China itself. While in the Orient, he visited Japan, and lived for a while in a Zen Buddhist monastery, supplementing both his technique and his philosophy with an oriental analogy to the automatic gesture of surrealism and its release of the subconscious.

On Tobey's return to the United States, his varied experiences became integrated in a style typified by paintings done in the late 1930's and early 1940's, such as *E Pluribus Unum* (Seattle Art Museum) and *Broadway,* tempera, 1936 (PC 465), in which his humans become part of the conglomeration of cities, and his cities themselves become poems of glittering light and energy. In these paintings the figures and the urban configurations are unified by a dynamic pattern of white lines—the "white writing" which is commonly thought to be Tobey's reinterpretation of oriental calligraphy, but is actually a combination of this with his more usual elements of line and light. In fact, Tobey's excited line is utterly lacking in oriental serenity; instead, it has the frenetic and nervous dynamism of the twentieth-century Western world. Furthermore, its abstraction is only visual, for it represents energy.

This first, individualistic phase of Tobey's art was succeeded by one in which his interest in the occult and spiritual, which had drawn him to Zen and Bahai, led him to the forms and imagery in the art of the Indians of the Northwest coast, prominently displayed in the museums of Seattle where he had come to live. Totem poles and magic signs inspired such pictures as *Drums, Indians, and the Word of God,* 1944 (private collection), in which images are isolated in a ghostly ambiance of their own by the intricacies of white writing.

The next and best-known period in Tobey's career is that represented by *Universal Field,* tempera and pastel, 1949 (PC 467), in which solidity is now nearly destroyed by the proliferating glitter of "white writing," but still not dissolved (as was later to be the case in Pollock's pictures), for the space being acted upon is not emptiness but the Void, which in oriental thought is filled with mystical significance. Yet in spite of the abstract appearance of such a picture, its very title should carry with it a warning that something quite specific is being represented. Reality is easier to discover in such pictures as *Written Over the Plains,* 1950 (San Francisco Museum of Art), in which Tobey's interest in airplane views, contour maps, and other aspects of less familiar visual reality supplements the gratuitous gestures and whimsical flourishes of his semiautomatic calligraphy. *Above the Earth,*

6–66. Mark Tobey, *Above the Earth,* 1953. Gouache. 39¼ x 29¾ inches. (Courtesy of the Art Institute of Chicago. Gift of Mr. and Mrs. Sigmund Kunstadter.)

gouache, 1953 (Illustration 6–66), is a similar but more complex picture, typical of this period in his work. The *Fountains of Europe,* tempera, 1955 (*PC 466), is a slightly later example, and, though it is less typical than his pictures inspired by the multitudinous shapes of Seattle (its Pike

Street Market, its exposed electric and telephone wires, the lights of night traffic, and reflections in Lake Washington and in wet streets), the gay, nocturnal, flood-lit splashing of the European subject has been reduced to a lively and decorative maze of movement and brilliance.

In the mid-1950's Tobey was overwhelmed by the abstract near-automatism of oriental "sumi" writing, with its freedom and play of signs which need not be meaningful. More recently he has combined this renewal of the automatic and symbolic with continuing immediate contact with reality in the form of air views, electric light poles, rolled-up chicken wire, and autumn leaves to form a richer amalgam of reality and abstraction. Those who see glittering in his pictures "the reflection of the sidereal serenity which shines in the F Major Toccata of Bach," as one critic has commented, or those who see instead a summary of energy and vitality derived from the quintessence of things in themselves, can be equally happy in the rich formal satisfactions in Tobey's play of energetic line, delicate and oscillating color, and authority of gesture.

Both Gorky and Tobey have been called abstract expressionists. Gorky died too soon to deny the label, but Tobey has always rightly insisted that he is not one. Gorky's free and unspecific forms resemble the psychic automatizations of the abstract expressionists, but they do so only superficially, since they are deliberately formulated communications. The meandering gestures and insubstantiality of Tobey are not fortuitous, since they reflect the dynamism of actual, not merely psychic energy, the scintillating unity of actual objects and energies in the ambiance of light.

Abstract Expressionism

Although in recent years there have been various signs of reactions against it, abstract expressionism [50] has become so prominent during the last two decades that most other contemporary painting seems lackluster in comparison. In this movement American art has come of age, even in

the viewpoint of Europeans. Exhibited everywhere, taught in most art schools, bought by responsible museums and collectors—even the most conservative criticism can no longer disregard it.

Combining the vocabularies of abstraction and expressionism, and to a certain degree that of surrealism as well, it is a form of art which is generally non-representational,[51] ranging from the use of imagery derived primarily from the unconscious ("psychic improvisation," as one critic has called it [52]) to imagery with a more deliberate purpose but still abstract, as in Robert B. Motherwell's pictures dealing with the Spanish Civil War. The abstract expressionist seeks to express directly emotions such as fear, gaiety, anger, or anxiety, without the intervention of the formal structure and visual experience of the actual world which have been in the past the plastic equivalents of art in its relation to life. Realism (or naturalism), in its simplest terms, is the recording of visual experience; expressionism is the heightening of it; and abstract geometric art is either a distillation of experience into its essence or an uncovering of the universals beneath accidental forms of experience. Abstract expressionism is none of these, though paradoxically it is closest to realism. Like realism, it can be an unadumbrated record without implication or recollection—without ordering, heightening, or distillation—but it is a recording of the inner world, not the outer. What the abstract expressionist has to say is real; only his language is abstract. And what he creates is not an image of a thing, but the thing itself, no less real because it is a new thing created by him alone. Unlike realism, which is a statement with a subject and an object, it could be said of abstract expressionism that there is no subject or object, only the verb. The artist is alone with himself, with his own existence. As Harold Rosenberg has said, "The artist accepts as real only that which he is in the process of creating." [53] The abstract expressionist says, "I paint, therefore I am," to use Alfred Barr's happy rephrasing of Descartes.

Abstract expressionism seldom communicates in a conventionally logical way. The visual vocabulary of each artist is so personal to him that it is isolated from the common language of shared symbols or familiar images of experience or of order, artistic or otherwise. Yet the force of the abstract expressionist statement is such that the observer is overwhelmed by it, however annoyed or angered he may be at the same time.

The power of these configurations of shapes and color, often arrived at with as little interference as possible from the conscious will, is mysterious —not because of some magic or some cabalistic symbolism, but because their reality is not one of the recognizable world, but of another dimension of experience. Sometimes energy or movement is the principal content of the paintings; at other times shapes or images are being created which refer to no conscious experience but instead arouse reverberations in less conscious levels, images which are objective correlatives of feelings or emotions which are indefinable because ineffable. In general, the abstract expressionist artist has used two principal means to project his concepts and images—the medium itself, and the automatic act (both in its relation to the medium and as an analog to ritualistic and mystical experience).

The importance of the medium in much abstract expressionism is such that it can be thought of as the actual subject matter. In the process of wiping clean the slate of the past, the abstract expressionists had no choice but to re-explore the raw material of paint itself, the *sine qua non* of their art. (Similarly, the composers of *musique concrète* and other forms of contemporary music have tossed out the whole complex framework of harmony, counterpoint, and rhythm and started all over again with raw sound or noise.) Much of early abstract expressionism was involved with the exploration of the medium and its potentials—something which had to be done before anything else could be resolved. Even later, the effort to realize the potentials of the medium has sometimes been so significant a part of an artist's creative act that the marks of the struggle between the artist and his paint are among the most interesting aspects of certain abstract expressionist paintings.

Closely related to the importance of the medium is automatism, another method exploited in abstract expressionism in general, for the accidents which occur in the manipulation of paint and other materials serve as excellent devices for the release or projection of subconscious or unconscious expression—a device inherited from surrealism. One of the hero-figures of abstract expressionism, Jackson Pollock, has stated that the ultimate source of his painting was the unconscious, and asserted that when he was painting he was not much aware of what was taking place. Motherwell, in a lecture at Harvard, said almost the same thing when he remarked that "the painting knows more than I do." What emerges is a spontaneous invention which is very individual to each artist: Motherwell's forms, for instance, are rather aggressively heavy in pigment and application whereas Pollock's are a gossamer of delicate linear proliferations. Such methods of painting are analogous to non-directed or non-verbally oriented thinking—fantasy, daydreaming, or stream of consciousness—and, like them, are not consciously controlled. Yet out of this process certain fragments are undoubtedly isolated and developed by the artist, as though he were standing aside as a second being, consciously watching and partially directing the unfolding of his fantasy (a process such as that recommended by Paul Klee).

In the exploitation of automation and of the accidents inherent in the medium, abstract expressionism demonstrates as much resistance as does surrealism to the interference of the conscious mind, which might tend to change the image or *thing* brought forth by the artist, an interference which would be tantamount to wounding or killing something which literally has a life of its own. In fact, the respect which the abstract expressionist has for the unconscious is profoundly serious, and altogether a different thing from the "fun and games" of Dada and early surrealism. William Baziotes, for instance, speaks of emanations from the unconscious with the greatest awe, and many of the abstract expressionists give the impression of being somehow exalted beings in tune with the infinite, "dwelling in that secret place where primeval power nurtures all evolution," [54] to use the words of Paul Klee. Such an attitude is very close to mysticism, and had already been expressed in Kandinsky's *Concerning the Spiritual in Art*. It is no coincidence that oriental mysticism, as represented by Vedanta and especially Zen Buddhism, has played an important part in the life of many abstract expressionists.

Motherwell feels that modern painting is a great new human experience, with the intensity of mysticism though secular in background; many other artists speak as though they were trying to express (if not actually communicate) something ineffable. Mark Rothko has said, "To be inspired, that is the thing, to be possessed, to be bewitched, to be obsessed, that is the thing, to be inspired"—the very repetitiveness of the description of such seizure is ritualistic. Indeed, the paintings of Rothko executed at the time of the statement (1945) are filled with vague adumbrations and references to signs and symbols of primitive and archaic art, as were the works of Baziotes, Clyfford Still, and Adolph Gottlieb, illustrated in the latter's *Evil Omen*, 1946 (PC 169). The resemblance of these paintings (and of others, like those of Stamos, with their strange, mysterious, and compelling images) to exotic and primitive art has been remarked. Malraux, in the *Voices of Silence* says that the demons of Babylon, the early church, and Freudianism show us the same visage.

The formal characteristics of abstract expressionism cannot be as simply isolated as the methods used by the artists in producing them. Most examples are extremely large in scale—both in their total dimension and in the relative size of the motifs used—whether the surface is woven into a complex constellation of lines, slashed with a few enormous calligraphic gestures, or covered with huge, simple areas of color. But there are other paintings in the school which are not large, so that size in itself cannot be taken as a general characteristic.

Another very conspicuous aspect of much abstract expressionism is a strong sense of movement, seen especially in the work of Pollock (where the infinity of dynamic interweavings seems to be the residual record of a series of events which have comprised the action of painting itself) but also in that of other painters, where many of the formal elements depend on the swing of the artist's arm (de Kooning, for instance, has given that reason for the broad sweeps that define the exaggerated busts of his terrifying women). But dynamism is by no means a general characteristic, for there are other paintings, such as those of Rothko, which have an almost monolithic calm.

One characteristic which could be said to be more pervasive is a tendency to the vague or amorphous in area, shape, and image. For this reason the movement has sometimes been called "informal" painting by certain English critics, or "free-form." Physical, biological, and psychological boundaries are blurred in a rich and suggestive interpenetration of pulsating, polyvalent, and polymorphous forms, sometimes exquisitely erotic, sometimes with the obscene and anonymous indeterminateness of mutating flesh. Often these proliferating forms are either in a precarious balance, or are in a state of actual transience, which in a sense could be thought of as another aspect of potential or, in some cases, actual movement.

Another pervasive quality in abstract expressionism is what could be called polarity, though its appearance in other levels that are not exclusively formal makes it more difficult to isolate. Certainly a dichotomy or polarity in a state of tension often comprises the chief impact of an abstract expressionist picture. The clashing forms of Hans Hofmann, the precarious relationship of shapes and colors in de Kooning (and the almost painful clash between representation and non-representation in his *Women* series), and the conflict in Motherwell between automatism and the conscious desire to express specific meaning all exemplify this principle. Indeed, the character of the whole movement from the point of view of art history is its union of opposites, implied in its very name (in the purest sense of the two words), and its combination of these with surrealism. The attempt on the part of the abstract expressionist artists to cause opposites to exist simultaneously is the source of much of the excitement of their paintings, and, when resolved, of their success. Even when not resolved, which is more often the case, the record of the struggle has its pictorial rewards.

Abstract expressionism is not simply a new manner or a novel subdivision of painting as we have known it. Most of the critical apparatus used in judging western art, whether past or recent, is not applicable to it. This is especially true when those artistic characteristics which can be weighed quantitatively are considered, such as balance, harmony, sequence, or repetition. Some critics, however, insist that the most successful forms of abstract expressionism have met such esthetic criteria. Though this is indeed often the case, it is the result less of deliberate choice than of accident, for these classically accepted standards would seem to be almost a fortuitous byproduct in the work of certain artists, part of whose method has been the deliberate restraint of logic to make it possible for deeper levels of consciousness to emerge. The abstract expressionist, as emphatically as the surrealist, is inclined to reject standards of judgment and beauty as being irrelevant. Furthermore, in extreme forms of psychic improvisation it is impossible to judge by extrinsic standards a kind of non-objectivity which is not imitative of anything else, or even an abstraction or symbol of it, but is simply its own intrinsic self. De Kooning, for instance, makes it almost impossible for us to judge his finished painting since he says it cannot be judged in any way apart from the effort, struggles, and hesitations of its creator.

A critical vocabulary as new as the objects it criticizes must be forged before fair judgment can be attempted. Meanwhile, subjective criticism must suffice, inaccurate as this always is. (After an exhibition of Rothko's huge canvases, one critic compared them to stained sheets, another to "unspeakable vibrations evoking the experience of doom," and a third as possessing the "fatalistic quality of Greek drama.")

Anything which is the product of a process so close to the mystical experience as is abstract expressionism should perhaps not be judged rationally, for, as William James says, the mystic stands on unassailable ground. The almost religious intensity of abstract expressionism seems to demand a non-intellectual approach. In fact, the Spanish critic Mercedes Molleda, in a review in 1958 of the exhibition of abstract expressionism which circulated through Europe under the auspices of the Museum of Modern Art and was then in Barcelona, came as near as anyone can to the problem of understanding and judging when she simply stated that these pictures could not be comprehended by intelligence, but only by Grace.

Perhaps we cannot judge or should not; it may be inappropriate to raise such common-sense questions as the problem of communication, the demands for which Clyfford Still feels are both "irrelevant and presumptuous," considering the struggle the artist must go through to achieve "depth of insight" and the courage he has expended in "realizing his own vision." [55]

If questions concerning the validity of judgment and even of communication are raised in connection with abstract expressionism, it may well be asked why the movement has had such extraordinary success in a society which is still functioning in almost all other respects according to logical and rational processes. Abstract expressionism must reflect at least some aspects of contemporary western culture. It may be useful, therefore, from the point of view of the social history of art, briefly to point out certain coincidences between the movement and contemporary science, psychology, and social attitudes, whether there is any actual relationship between them or not.

Though there are some contemporary artists who are as excited by modern physics as Kandinsky was when he heard in 1913 about the disintegration of the atom, most of them have turned their backs on the complexities of space-age science, immersing themselves in their own psyches or returning to archaic or primitive forms of thought or expression. Nevertheless there is an interesting affinity between at least the outward appearance of abstract expressionist works of art and aspects of contemporary physics. Fluid, multidimensional, dynamic, with amorphous structures filling infinite space, abstract expressionism reflects the world of twentieth-century science as clearly as the solid forms and optical verisimilitude of realism and impressionism reflected that of the nineteenth century. Perhaps it is not merely chance that a painting by Pollock resembles a photograph of the interior of a "cloud cabinet," where the pattern of the collision of subatomic particles with clusters of electrons follows much the same path as the artist's markings.

It has been suggested that polarity and tension are important aspects of the formal character of abstract expressionism. This is surely analogous to that anxiety which Rollo May and other psychologists have stated to be the principal manifestation of present-day psychic maladjustment. Perhaps another aspect of contemporary neurosis, anger as the consequence of frustration on many levels, is also reflected in the slashing violent strokes of abstract expressionism and, in some instances, in the near-destruction of the image.

The non-conformity and lack of social involvement popularly associated with the "beat" generation could hardly be illustrated better than by the abstract expressionists. In them the commitment of the politically engaged artist of the 1930's has been succeeded by a monumental disengagement. Motherwell says that he and his fellow artists form a kind of spiritual underground, completely rejecting the values of the bourgeois world. The abstract expressionists have thrown away the whole imagery, both visual and conceptual, of a society which they consider pointless, decadent, and, above all, false. This antisocial attitude is felt to be related to the problem of individual freedom. By the assertion of his complete autonomy the abstract expressionist artist feels that, while rejecting society, he is at the same time making a significant contribution to it. Whether this is so or not, such an attitude must at least salve his conscience, and permit him to exert his whole effort stubbornly to the discovery of new reality.

A general survey is not the place to go into the tedious argument of whether abstract expressionism is actually an American development. Suffice it to say that it reached self-consciousness in the United States, for all its initiation by European sources. Many of its ingredients existed already in Kandinsky, in non-figurative surrealism, and in more recent European artists, such as the German Franz Hartung (now of the school of Paris). But the self-confident boldness of the movement and the creation of its most powerful images occurred in the United States.

The general artistic ancestry of abstract expressionism is implied in its name and needs no explanation. Its more immediate forebears were Kandinsky, Klee, Picasso, Miró, and Arp. Its surrealist ingredient was of the non-figurative sort, typified especially by the work of Max Ernst, André Masson, Yves Tanguy, and André Breton (the original propagandist of the surrealist doctrine), all of whom came to New York at the beginning of the war. There they were joined by the veteran French painter, most lately a surrealist, Marcel Duchamp, who has been a continuous influence on American abstract painting since the Armory Show.

Except for Gorky and, to a much lesser extent, Ryder, Dove, and perhaps Marin, the influence of the American artistic background was far less important than the European on the development of abstract expressionism, though certain aspects of the physical and psychological environment may well have been instrumental in the formation of the school. The large scale and dynamism of much of abstract expressionism could be related to the boundlessness of America (reflected earlier in the large landscapes of the Hudson River school) and to the strong element of energy and mobility seen in American economic, social, and cultural history, from the Great Migration to Sunday motoring. It may be no accident that the tortuous meanderings of a Pollock and the stabbing violence of a Kline are among the most direct translations of movement and energy into the pictorial arts.

The exaggeration of size and color, as well as of other formal elements, is characteristic of American romanticism in general. There is a tradition of hyperbole in American literature of the nineteenth century, especially in humorists like Mark Twain and in the expansiveness of Walt Whitman. Whitman's work is characterized by formlessness as well, a kind of improvised amorphousness which is also a characteristic of much of the man-made American scene—sprawling, chaotic, and unformed. Again, it is perhaps not accidental that the amorphousness prefigured in surrealism and in Miró became monumentalized

in abstract expressionism, supplemented, perhaps, by some influence from Ryder's vague but evocative shapes. In any event, American abstract expressionism projects such a degree of subjective emotionalism that it carries the American romanticism of the nineteenth century to its ultimate conclusion. Certain other more specific historical and environmental factors influenced the development of abstract expressionism. Among them was the W. P. A. Art Project, which served as a catalyst to bring groups of younger artists together to discuss and experiment. Another was the international crisis culminating in the war and America's role in world rehabilitation, factors which turned American artists away from their provincial self-satisfaction in regionalism and the American scene.

An important initial incentive in the formation and development of the school was the part played by a group of like-minded gallery owners and critics. From 1942 to 1947 Peggy Guggenheim's Art of This Century Gallery played a role similar to that of Stieglitz' 291 of an earlier generation, bringing young American painters together with European artists who had recently arrived in the United States, and supporting the early development of artists like Pollock who were later to become famous. The dealers Betty Parsons, Charles Egan, Sidney Janis, and Sam Kootz followed in the steps of Art of This Century, propagandizing for the new school. They were aided and abetted by critics like Clement Greenberg in the *Nation* and *Partisan Review*, and later by Thomas Hess in *Art News* and Harold Rosenberg, whose *The Tradition of the New* is among the best-known contributions to the criticism of abstract expressionism. The teaching of the semiabstract, semiexpressionistic Hans Hofmann (who immigrated to America from Germany before the war) was also influential, since many of the best-known artists in the group studied with him; Hofmann himself, in the process of teaching, gradually developed into a full-fledged abstract expressionist. Clyfford Still taught for several years at San Francisco, starting what amounted to a West Coast school. Motherwell, Sam Hunter, and many other abstract expressionists have since become prominent teachers, some of them at important colleges and universities, thus fostering what amounts to a contemporary academicism.

The first phase of the movement, more properly a sort of proto-abstract expressionism, lasted from about 1943 to 1948. This was the period when Gorky achieved his synthesis of formal abstraction, personal romanticism, and surrealism, which was in effect almost abstract expressionism, and when artists like Bradley Walker Tomlin, Jackson Pollock, Willem de Kooning, Franz Kline, Bernard Newman, James Brooks, and Philip Guston were turning from various degrees of representationalism to abstraction. The case of Guston is particularly dramatic. The quite successful style of his W. P. A. murals, with their fine formal organization and expressive drawing—represented in the easel picture *Martial Memory*, 1941 (*PC 194)—was suddenly succeeded by a style with no trace whatsoever of representationalism, and one which he has persistently followed since; *The Street*, 1956 (PC 195) is typical. At the same time other artists, including Hofmann, Motherwell, Still, and Pollock, were, like Gorky, rediscovering and transforming surrealism and combining it with elements of formal and expressionistic abstraction; Baziotes, Gottlieb, and Rothko (and to a certain extent Pollock, too) were reviving the myth and primitivism. All of these artists were exhibited extensively during these years, and some had one-man shows.

The second, mature phase of abstract expressionism was from 1948 to 1951, when de Kooning, Kline, Tomlin, Guston, and Rothko came into greater prominence, accompanied by newer men, including James Brooks and Jack Tworkov. The years since then have seen the death of Pollock and the coming into prominence of Kenzo Okada, Gabor Peterdi, John Ferren, and Joan Mitchell.

But chronology, artistic ancestry, and all the similar paraphernalia of art history may be just as much beside the point in connection with abstract expressionism as is an attempt at judgment. In fact one French critic, Michel Tapié, feels that such concerns are simply "codified ir-

relevancies" in the case of such art, while Clyfford Still disdains museums and all they stand for—although he can be induced to exhibit in them.

Not only would it be appropriate, in Tapié's or Still's frame of reference, to ignore an historical approach to abstract expressionism, but it would be very convenient to do so, since in a general history a discussion of such recent artists is a somewhat perilous task at best.

For purposes of discussion abstract expressionism is divided into three categories. The first is psychic improvisation, or free-form abstraction,[56] wherein artists like Pollock, Guston, Rothko, and Still project the image from the inner eye rather than transform the material of the outer world into other visual forms. The second is as abstract and non-representational as the first, but refers to conscious experience, as in some of Motherwell's and Kline's work. In the third category, semiabstraction,[57] the influence of the observation of the outer world is more evident, as in the early paintings of Pollock, Rothko, and Gottlieb, and continuing in the work of Stamos, Baziotes, and others.

Stylistically a quite definite division can be made within the first category of free-form or psychic improvisation, that is, between those artists who are stylistically dynamic, like Pollock and Kline, and those who are relatively static, like Newman and the later Rothko.

Pollock, de Kooning, and Motherwell are discussed first and at greater length than some other equally important artists, chiefly because they typify both the development and fruition of certain significant aspects of abstract expressionism.

A glance at any typical painting by Pollock, such as *No. 1 1948* (PC 366), *Autumn Rhythm*, 1950 (PC 367A), *Convergence*, 1952 (PC 1011), or *Blue Poles*, 1953 (Illustration 6–67), will immediately reveal the artist's originality. All four are typical. *Convergence* is a trifle later than the high point of what may be called Pollock's "classical" style, coming after his black and white paintings such as *Ocean Greyness*, 1953 (Guggenheim Museum), and reverting to the heavily

6–67.   Jackson Pollock, *Blue Poles,* 1953. (As installed at Sidney Janis Gallery.) Oil on canvas. 6 feet, 11 inches x 16 feet, 1 inch. (Collection of Mr. and Mrs. Ben Heller, New York.)

painted violence of his early work. *Blue Poles* is perhaps his most inclusive single work, for it sums up the artist's "classic" phase and incorporates the vertical accents of the earlier "totem" period to give the picture a certain satisfying stability. Pollock's work does not photograph well in black and white, and in color, especially in a reproduction, the complex gossamer-like refinement of his lines appears incorrectly like an unvaried all-over texture. When confronted with the pictures themselves, the observer is overwhelmed first by their size (scale is not even hinted at in most reproductions) and then by the multiplicity of their linear configurations, the residue of many passages of the artist's arm swinging a brush from which the paint has

dripped. What seems merely decorative in a reproduction turns out to be an almost endless proliferation of spatial comings and goings in an infinity of various colors.

These examples are hitherto unfamiliar statements in paint, and are the final distillation of a personal style or "handwriting" which was prophesied in the swinging dynamic pattern of the heavier forms and broader passages in the artist's early representational work. As a student of Thomas Hart Benton, Pollock was undoubtedly influenced by the older man's diluted expressionism, characterized by sweep, movement, and the use of large bold images. This influence was supplemented by that of Ryder whose simple lyrical forms carried with them a powerful impact over and beyond what they represented. The example of the Mexican muralists (especially Orozco), with their exaggerated and forceful large-scale statements, was another factor in Pollock's development. But it was the unreal creatures of the surrealist imagination—the brutal pseudo-flesh of Picasso, and Miró's biomorphic forms—and the exploitation of the automatic which finally stimulated Pollock into his thoroughly individual statement. Out of these influences there emerged in the paintings of 1943 savage-looking shapes seemingly expelled by the artist in a Dionysiac frenzy, their subjects concerned most often with primitive ritual and with sex, as in *Totem II* (Collection of Mrs. Lee Krasner Pollock). In these pictures, as in others, the surfaces were enlivened and unified by a kind of linear energy, the personal calligraphy of which began to take over the canvases entirely—at first brutally and with a heavily weighted brush, and later in the refined web of interweaving calligraphic gestures, examples of a radical new technique wherein Duco and aluminum paint were dripped from a brush or stick onto a canvas spread out horizontally. *No. 1, 1948* perhaps typifies this new manner at its best, while *Autumn Rhythm* is a variation in November hues of the earlier, more exuberant, and perhaps subtler picture, though a third again as huge (it measures 8 feet, 7 inches by 17 feet, 3 inches).

The paintings of Pollock's last years were, on the whole, recapitulations of his earlier achievement. The impression remains that Pollock could only repeat that initial vision of a kind of painting the possibilities of which were profoundly shocking, and which he somehow could not finally realize—a situation made all the more embarrassing in the light of an increasing fame which was becoming almost notoriety.

Willem de Kooning vacillates between the semirealistic, as represented in *Woman I*, 1950–1952 (PC 108), and the completely abstract *Asheville*, 1949 (PC 107), though the bulk of his work is in the later category.

As is the case with most of the older abstract expressionists, de Kooning began as a more or less representational artist, but in the late 1920's and early 1930's he developed a kind of fashionable surface cubism which he combined with experiments in somewhat amorphous forms. In the 1940's the curvilinear and ovoid shapes of Picasso's classicism were enhanced and supplemented with the biomorphic ones of Arp, Miró, and the later Picasso, but with the addition of de Kooning's own very personal color, culminating in such a picture as *Pink Angels*, 1947 (Collection of Jeanne Reynal), which incorporates conglomerations of protoplasmic pink fleshiness. This monumentalization of the biomorphic showed for the first time de Kooning's originality as an image maker. In 1946, black and white forms began to appear in his work; in their greater austerity of design and boldness of contrast they are even more powerful than his earlier paintings. Similar forms, but with rich color added, are seen in *Asheville*, and a combination of this later style with the earlier one of *Pink Angels* is represented in *Excavation*, 1950 (Illustration 6–68). In 1953 de Kooning began a series with *Woman I* (Museum of Modern Art); one of the latest is *Woman VI* (Carnegie Institute). These grinning travesties on the busty, toothy, ideal girl of American advertising are not only effectively satiric in their onslaught on bourgeois stereotypes, but are magnificent semi-abstract exercises in the handling of paint and color, embodying the formal experiments and technical freedom which the artist had developed in the preceding years (including a series of women done in the style of Picasso and Ingres, which he was executing simultaneously with the perfecting of his non-representational style).

About 1955 de Kooning began to evolve a style which is characterized by a superficially more chaotic color and the introduction of large-scaled passages of paint that are best described as enormous enlargements of the space-defining brush strokes of Cézanne's last works—perhaps instigated by the huge size of Franz Kline's motifs. This style is well represented in *Easter Monday*, 1956 (The Metropolitan Museum of Art, New York).

From 1945 until the present, the work of de Kooning, for all its variety, is characterized by

6–68. Willem de Kooning, *Excavation*, 1950. Oil on canvas, 6 feet, 8⅛ inches x 8 feet, 4⅛ inches. (Courtesy of the Art Institute of Chicago. Mr. and Mrs. Frank G. Logan purchase prize, gift of Mr. Edgar Kaufmann, jr., and Mr. and Mrs. Noah Goldowsky.)

recurring forms of pictorial ideas—especially the ovoid and the vertical stripe, as clearly defined as the latter has since become in Bernard Newman, for whom it is an obsessive theme. These are supplemented by other motifs recurring less frequently and deriving from accidental visual experiences such as the configurations of drapery, a row of paper matches which have been bent backward, old newspapers, and the use of a blue peculiar to drugstore cotton wrappings. But perhaps even more important as chance pictorial motifs are the fortuitous shapes which result from corrections, additions, subtractions, and especially those accidental "negative" shapes which occur, for instance, between an arm and a torso, and which are used "positively" in another place and in another context. These forms or shapes become both the vocabulary and the themes of the paintings. They are to de Kooning's personal style what the proliferating line is to Pollock's, and out of their polyvalent relationships his pictures are formed. When his work is totally nonrepresentational, de Kooning achieves a completely unique and personal world (symbolizing nothing outside the pictures themselves) wherein the obsessive shapes, subjective motifs, and negative–positive ambiguities are joined in a struggle, the outcome of which is a painting which seems to be teetering on the very knife-edge of disintegration.

De Kooning's semiabstract work is enriched by the expressive power of his shapes, brush strokes, and colors, while his non-figurative work is typical of psychic improvisation at its purest, illustrating especially well, among the formal characteristics of abstract expressionism, the factor of polarity or tension.

Robert B. Motherwell's painting usually has some extraneous reference (as indicated in his titles and recurring themes), but its formal characteristics, exploitation of the medium, and use of automatism are similar to those employed in purer forms of psychic improvisation.

By the early 1940's Motherwell had developed his own style out of cubist–constructionist studies, experimentation with Dada collages, and the influence of surrealism. It was marked by a fine sensibility for form, and by psychosexual symbolism which was not too esoteric, as in a series of western and Mexican subjects. Toward the

6–69.   Robert B. Motherwell, *Elegy to the Spanish Republic, LIV*, 1957–1961. Oil on canvas. 5 feet, 10 inches x 7 feet, 6¼ inches. (Collection, The Museum of Modern Art, New York.)

end of the 1940's, the artist had settled into two fairly disparate manners: huge mural-size statements in an epic mood, composed with classic equilibrium or massive poised tension, as in the Spanish Civil War and dance series, powerfully epitomized in *Voyage*, 1949 (PC 1013A); and smaller lyrical commentaries, more impulsive and dynamic (often employing collage), and built around such themes as *je t'aime*, which is sometimes written out on the picture itself. (The two styles are not always confined to the larger or smaller format, and occur sometimes irrespective of size.) Perhaps Motherwell has been more successful than any other contemporary artist in communicating his deep earnestness and moral concern on the one hand, and his joy in life and love on the other, through significant plastic equivalents of experience and emotion.

In a series of paintings on the same subject, titled usually *Elegy to the Spanish Republic*, especially number *XXXIV*, 1953–1954 (*PC 1013), and number *LIV*, 1957–1961 (Illustration 6–69), Motherwell has created particularly effective pictographs symbolizing the tragedy of the Spanish Civil War, which opened our era of mass destruction. These enormous black and white paintings of large and sometimes dripping ovoids pressed between thick vertical oblongs, together with earlier versions of the subject entitled variously *Granada* and *5 O'clock in the Afternoon* (referring specifically to the poet Garcia Lorca who was killed by the Nationalists), have always been powerful and arresting shapes from the time of the artist's first exploration of the subject twenty years ago. Perhaps the repetition of these obsessive ovals and oblongs, which have drilled themselves into at least a segment of the public's mind, accounts for a sense of real communication in these pictures; or it may actually be that the obvious sincerity of the artist's feelings have indeed created a viable language of communication through plastic equivalents of emotion that are no longer dependent on reference to the visible world.

In this somewhat arbitrary grouping, used only for convenience of discussion, two general subdivisions can be made, at least on stylistic grounds: dynamic and static.

Guston is perhaps the most prominent of the psychic improvisors who are still somewhat dynamic in style, though James Brooks and Jack Tworkov are nearly as noteworthy, and the late Franz Kline developed a personal style of enormous energy and calligraphic sweep. Guston's characteristic compositions, dating from the time of his shift from representationalism in the 1940's until lately, have been variations on the theme of linear brush markings, sometimes combined with more dot-like passages and piled up into an area somewhere near the center of the canvas. Though not nearly as dynamic as Pollock, de Kooning, or Kline, these works have a forceful energy directed toward an apex, and therefore none of the static calm of Newman or Rothko. A constant search for the expression of self led to a continuously greater subtilization of variations upon this single theme (or activity) of piling up pigment gradually in one area, as in the paintings done between 1950 and 1955. In 1956 Guston's forms began to become harsher and more aggressive as in *The Street*, though still preserving the basic focal arrangement (which is as personal to Guston as Pollock's calligraphy is to him). At about the same time a more dramatic quality entered the artist's work, which, as Dore Ashton has pointed out, became the arena for a conflict of dynamic and static forms, as in *Fable 1*, 1956–1957 (Illustration 6–70), in which black is contrasted with areas of intense green and orange.

A whole school of younger psychic improvisors are also dedicated to probing for the personal image, revealing something never seen or felt before. Among them are Ernest Briggs, James Brooks, and Jack Tworkov. All three artists paint big pictures filled with large and impulsive forms. Briggs arranges his in a coalescence of striated movement. Brooks, as in his *Ainlee*, 1957 (PC 53A), is far bolder, evolving shapes almost as impressive as de Kooning's and Kline's, but curvilinear ones, which the artist prefers to rectangular since they seem to him to reflect human gestures rather than mechanical things. Tworkov can be described as more impetuous, for he uses violent brush strokes similar to Kline's, but with more variation and subtlety.

6–70. Philip Guston, *Fable I,* 1956–1957. Oil on canvas. 6 feet, 3 inches x 5 feet, 5 inches. (Collection of Washington University, St. Louis, Missouri.)

The most forceful of the painters of the second wave of abstract expressionists is the late Franz Kline. He was not always strictly a psychic improvisor, for many of his pictures have titles which refer to a specific event or place about which, like Motherwell, he wanted to comment. His paintings seem to be even more spontaneous and impulsive, however, and thus in appearance are closer to pure improvisation than Motherwell's. Yet the impact of Kline's energetic and kinetic proclamations and images is so effective that conscious ordering must have played some part in their production, as in the powerful *Painting No. 7,* 1952 (PC 251), or *Shenandoah Wall,* 1961 (Illustration 6–71).

The effect of a Franz Kline painting is unequivocal as John I. H. Baur says, like a blow from a sledgehammer.[58] The observer–victim cannot help reacting, even if negatively.

There are other powerful image makers, less dynamic than Kline but, like him, creators of presences of a kind somewhere between psychic improvisation and Motherwell's more conscious and deliberate projections. Richard Pousette-Dart, Adolph Gottlieb, and William Baziotes are among them. In such pictures as Pousette-Dart's

6–71.   Franz Kline, *Shenandoah Wall,* 1961.   Oil on canvas.   6 feet, 8¾ inches x 14 feet, 3 inches. (Courtesy of the Egan Gallery, New York.)

The Magnificent, 1950–1951 (PC 323), and in the early work of Gottlieb and Baziotes, primitive art is invoked and its magical powers are suggested, as in Gottlieb's *Evil Omen* and Baziotes' *Dwarf,* 1947 (PC 12). In this last picture there is far more, however, than a recollection of primitivism, for the ambivalent forms evoke a very real presence as convincing as any Renaissance portrait or figure by Eakins, a veritable likeness of something never before seen, felt, or heard. Forms such as the monstrous tentacled shape and the pictograph sun seen vaguely through a semitransparency like that of an X-ray photograph in Baziotes' *Pompeii,* 1956 (PC 15), evolve from suggestions emerging from the accidents attending the manipulation of the raw material of forms and colors placed intuitively, out of which the artist says "a phantom must be caught and made real."

Gottlieb's more scattered motifs, arranged in an arbitrary but convincing order, as in *Hot Horizon,* 1956 (PC 171), seem to have definite meaning in terms of feeling, if not as visual fact or as symbols of verbal conceptualization. The

artist seems to corroborate this interpretation in the quite obvious connection of title and image in *The Frozen Sounds No. 1,* 1951 (PC 170). Though the subjective quality of Gottlieb's images is evident, their order is conscious and objective, as in *Transfiguration No. 2,* 1958 (PC 678A), and therefore perhaps resembles the production of those abstract expressionists who are static and meditative rather than dynamic.

Among these painters perhaps the most outstanding are Bernard Newman, Mark Rothko, Ad Reinhardt, and Clyfford Still. All except Reinhardt began as admirers and imitators of primitive art, illustrated eloquently in Rothko's watercolor *Vessels of Magic,* c. 1947 (*PC 388). The work of all four still retains a feeling of mystery, but now this is induced by an almost oriental calm, which in Newman is reduced to two basic motifs—lines or thin rectangles dividing other rectangular areas, like a ribbon dividing two fields of color—and which in Rothko is extended to larger areas less rigidly contained.

Gradually purging himself of magic symbols and biomorphic shapes, Rothko finally achieved (about 1950) a serene simplicity in the creation of large, irregular zones of color in pictures made up of ample rectangles, as in *No. 10, 1950* (PC 389), and which he has been refining ever since, as in *Painting*, 1953–1954 (PC 390). Both these pictures are typical of Rothko in the treatment of color, either vibrating in contrast or pulsating in harmony. The artist's latest work is so subtle in its color relationships and transitions that an exciting tension is created by the unresolved struggle between the throbbing hues and the rectangular enframements from which they seem to want to escape. (Because of their subtle color relationships Rothko's pictures reproduce particularly badly.)

Like Mondrian, Rothko is searching for universals and in the process destroys all extraneous associations. But unlike Mondrian, he is more concerned with the expression of emotion and mood than with abstract structure. The paintings which are the results of his struggle to arrive at this expression in a form which eliminates the accidental might at first seem trivial to the superficial observer were it not for their enormous scale. The slow and tortuous development of an artist sincerely dedicated to what he has called the elimination of all obstacles between the painter and his idea, should predispose the observer toward a tolerant attitude and help him to participate in these attempted visualizations of transcendent reality.

Ad Reinhardt is obviously aiming for the same ineffable effect as Rothko. He rejected an earlier curvilinear, spontaneous style for structured rectangles which are considerably less diffused than Rothko in their transitions, and more numerous, as seen in *No. 24, 1954* (PC 875).

Clyfford Still is even more literally ineffable than Rothko, to such a degree that he feels communication is irrelevant. He paints only because he feels committed to what he calls the "unqualified act." The results are brutally direct, from his early paintings of the late 1930's (which are still somewhat eclectic in their combination of the influence of Picasso's surrealist images with that of savage artifacts) to his later canvases, which have completely sloughed off all tradition and in no way illustrate what the artist calls our "outworn myths and contemporary alibis." [59] Instead, they stand huge, aggressively alone, and autonomous. Generally speaking they are of two kinds: some are almost totally covered with a certain color (or more frequently, black) relieved with one or more areas looking like jagged tears or scars; others have one or more images which are the gaping and ragged holes still evident after another color has been slapped unevenly over the underpaint. Both styles are represented in *Painting*, 1951 (PC 453). The second style in a more developed phase is illustrated in the powerful *1957–D, No. 1*, 1957 (Illustration 6–72).

These compelling objects are apparently the consequences of a dedication to the search for self and self-sufficiency, pictures painted by the artist for himself alone—if we are to believe his words and those who have talked with him. Still is the ultimate romantic, the artist containing within himself the universe and communicating with it alone, oblivious to accidents of ephemeral particularization, such as other people. In theory at least Still is the truly solipsist artist.

Sam Francis, in the simplicity of his motifs, in the huge size of his canvases, and in the impression of ineffability which his paintings give, is very similar to Rothko and Still, and is, in fact, the latter's pupil. Francis usually covers the tremendous areas of his paintings with one predominant color, over which he adds another layer with varying thoroughness but sometimes to the point of saturation. This second layer often consists of wriggling ovoid and amoebic shapes of a contrasting color or colors running across the canvas in a tremendous cascade. The combination of huge scale with a plethora of repeated forms accomplishes exactly what the artist wants to do, which is "to make something that fills utterly the sight"—a somewhat more modest purpose than that of his master, and as effective and personal a statement.

Except for those artists who are consciously influenced by nature itself (though their results are abstract) and who comprise a somewhat definable group, most of the second and third

6–72. Clyfford Still, *1957–D, No. I*, 1957. Oil on canvas. 9 feet, 5 inches x 13 feet, 3 inches. (Albright-Knox Art Gallery, Buffalo, New York. Gift of Seymour H. Knox.)

waves of abstract expressionists divide themselves between pure psychic improvisation and the expression of concepts in abstract terms similar to Motherwell's. At the same time they also combine elements of the dynamic "action" style with the static and meditative, though usually leaning toward one or the other. Among them are Edward Corbett, Kenzo Okada, Adja Yunkers, Corrado Marca-Relli, and Jack Youngerman. Corbett studied and worked in San Francisco when Clyfford Still was there and has as personal a style, but more varied, ranging from blazing jewel-like forms emerging from a cot-

tony atmosphere, as in *Number 15*, 1951 (PC 81), in which the use of chalk with casein promotes the evanescent character of the image, to more recent equally dark but more forebodingly rectilinear pictures.

Okada, a relative newcomer to abstract expressionism, brought from Japan a certain delicacy and refinement of touch and an elegant sense of placing which adapts itself well to free-form improvisation, as in *Tanabata*, 1956 (PC 341A). His recent paintings continue to be sensitive, but have gained in power. Yunkers is a more forceful image maker, as can be seen in the heavy, strong, and at the same time dynamic *Tarrasa XIII*, 1958 (Whitney Museum of American Art, New York). Marca-Relli's collages, made up of pieces of painted canvas, as in his *Sleeping Figure*, 1953–1954 (PC 300), are filled with shapes as strong and individual as those in de Kooning's pictures of the late 1940's, and were perhaps influenced by them. Enrico Donati, in such a picture as *Self-Born*, 1955 (Illustration 6–73), dilates upon an idea, like Motherwell. He expresses it in archetypal form, in *Self-Born* and in his other pictures, with a kind of richly textured series of rectangular blocks, often as

impulsive in technique as de Kooning, but as strongly architectonic in form as Rothko or Still. Youngerman's large forms are like blown-up sections of Still's torn or gaping areas, and as powerful. But he also suggests definite places such as Aquitaine and Coenties Slip, and creatures, such as rams, in pictures bearing indicative titles (all painted in 1959), using a more elaborate configuration of broken and torn forms; thus he is related to the more conscious improvisors. The former expressionist Paul Burlin and two women painters, Helen Frankenthaler and Rosemarie Beck [especially in her *No. 3, 1954* (PC

6–73. Enrico Donati, *Self-Born*, 1955. Oil on canvas. 5 feet x 5 feet. (Collection of Mr. and Mrs. Fred Olson, Guilford, Connecticut.)

520)] are more dynamic and nervous, while Milton Resnick, though equally dynamic, is more sensitive in the interweaving complexities of his delicate and shimmering brush work.

In contrast to the artists just discussed, Hans Hofmann and Bradley Walker Tomlin, though very different otherwise, share a somewhat more deliberate approach to their work than is common to most abstract expressionism, as well as a tendency to be motivated as much by outer appearance as by inner vision. Hofmann's *Magenta and Blue,* 1950 (PC 218), a still life with figures, summarizes much of his background and accomplishment. The structure of cubism, the color of Fauvism, and the strong pattern of Matisse reflect three of the principal influences of his European past, though combined and re-projected with the extraordinary boldness, sure-ness, and exciting cacophony of color which are typical of Hofmann. This picture also illustrates his theories (which were very influential) of modeling in space with planes and colors, there-by preserving surface integrity. It does not, however, demonstrate the more spontaneous as-pect of his work, or its image-making capacity, which developed simultaneously with the first wave of abstract expressionism. In fact, in one picture, *Red Trickle,* 1939 (private collection), as its title suggests, Hofmann actually preceded Pollock in many of the latter's dripping and linear devices. The assimilation of lessons de-rived from Kandinsky's *Improvisations* and from Miró, combined with his own exuberance, cre-ated images nearly as impressive as those of Motherwell and de Kooning, but always with some residue of conscious control in their for-mulation, as in *Embrace,* 1945 (Lane Founda-tion, Leominster, Massachusetts). The most typical of Hofmann's late pictures are those in which there is some reference to the shapes and colors of reality, which continue to reappear in the sequence of his varied work. All his pictures are exuberant [as indicated by some of their titles: *Ecstasy,* 1947 (Collection of the artist), and *Burst into Life,* 1952 (Collection of Mrs. Pauline Donnelley, Chicago), and one called *Exuberance,* 1955 (Illustration 6–74)], but not

6–74. Hans Hofmann, *Exuberance,* 1955. Oil on canvas. 50 x 40 inches. (Albright-Knox Art Gal-lery, Buffalo, New York. Gift through Seymour H. Knox Special Fund, 1955.)

really violent; John Baur calls them a "controlled explosion." [60] It is this formal control of passion and impulse which gives an underlying consist-ency to a body of work which is varied in in-spiration (he used the images of the real and of the subjective world) and in form, for he is both static (in form or pattern, never in color) and dynamic. Eclectic, and without the monolithic consistency of Kline, Rothko, or Guston, Hof-mann is perhaps not as impressive. How much of an originator of abstract expressionism in many of its phases he is, or how much only a catalyst, is difficult to assess. Certainly his teach-ing, with its background of European abstraction and expressionism, and his own native boldness and enthusiasm contributed immeasurably to the inception and growth of abstract expressionism.

The last few years of the work of Bradley Walker Tomlin sum up much of the character of several stylistic trends in abstract expressionism, but Tomlin had a more conscious desire to be well-ordered and even beautiful than is consistent with the theory of abstract expressionism in general. He was always an accomplished artist, from the time of his rather mild and decorative cubism, as illustrated by *Still Life,* 1939 (PC 470), to his *Number 20,* 1949 (PC 473), with its ordered array of interpenetrating abstract shapes, still largely rectilinear but with a freer play of movement within a limiting framework. Up to this time and a little later, formal order was the prevailing element in his pictures. But in the 1950's the vigorous spontaneity of the action painters affected his style more extensively, so that his final production illustrates a struggle between structure and energy, epitomized in some very effective paintings. *Number 13, 1952–1953* (PC 472), is still somewhat architectonic, but *Number 15,* 1953 (Collection of Mr. and Mrs. Ben Heller, New York) is full of movement and enlivened by the use of a kind of "white writing" probably derived from Tobey.

Some of the artists already discussed may have been somewhat influenced by natural appearance, but in general their purpose has been to lay bare an inner vision rather than to project nature transformed. If questioned about their relation to nature they would probably agree with Gottlieb who has stated that he never used nature as a starting point, or they would answer with Clyfford Still that they never paint nature, only themselves.

Yet at least two groups of abstract expressionists are influenced by nature, though still sharing with the psychic improvisors their stylistic or formal characteristics. The first group includes such artists as Theodoros Stamos, and they are inspired by the forces and processes of nature, using them, in a sense, as pictorial metaphors. The second group, represented by Joan Mitchell, among others, includes the representation of the actual visual object in some way in their pictures —either disguised, absorbed, or still somewhat recognizable.

Theodoros Stamos has a strong and conscious relationship with nature, unlike Rosemarie Beck who said, when she was still an abstract expressionist, that she only approached nature by analogy. Stamos' relationship, however, is not with the appearance of nature, but with its qualities, especially its vital change and growth, and reflects the artist's attempt to identify with the elemental rhythms and forces of the natural world. *Sounds in the Rock,* 1946 (*PC 442), is an early attempt to create an image of sound and feeling, a mood of nature; the shape is not unlike those of Baziotes, but in Baziotes' case, as we have seen, the image is engendered spontaneously and only afterward made more recognizable or communicable. In Stamos' *High Snow— Low Sun,* 1957 (Illustration 6–75), or *Greek Orison,* 1952 (PC 144), the forms are less forceful images, more dynamic and evanescent. The former belongs to a series devoted to the winter solstice, wherein movement, energy, and growth are more important than shape, thus reflecting the newer scientific concepts.

There are other artists (Baziotes to a certain extent is one of them as much as he is a psychic improvisor) who arrive at a natural image almost by accident, by what John Baur calls an oblique approach: Carl Morris, whose paintings certainly suggest though in no way actually describe or define the outer world, explains his relation to nature by saying that it entered by his back door; Helen Frankenthaler, within whose maelstrom of form and color there is sometimes a hint of something recognizable, says she will accept a natural image if it occurs spontaneously and by coincidence.

There is little question that John Ferren, in the gay shapes and brilliant color of *The Garden,* 1954 (PC 147), was not unaware of an inspiration from an actual garden; or that the elongated multicolored crystals magnetized into certain foci in Gabor Peterdi's *The Misty Ocean,* 1954 (PC 359), are meant to recall certain aspects of wetness on shipboard or seashore, an impression which is borne out by the title. In any event, Peterdi, like Stamos, is involved in nature, if not in its appearance; to clarify his point of view he has quoted an eleventh-century Chinaman: "If

6–75. Theodoros Stamos, *High Snow—Low Sun,* 1957. Oil on canvas. 4 feet, 5½ inches x 8 feet, 1½ inches. (Collection of the Whitney Museum of American Art, New York. Gift of the Friends of the Whitney Museum of American Art.)

you want to paint a bamboo, you have to become a bamboo yourself."

The West Coast artist Emerson Woeffler, in *Birds and Orange Sky,* 1956 (PC 1010), is also interested in interpreting nature, if not reproducing it, as is James Jervaise in his Hudson River series, though Jervaise's forms are as abstract as Marca-Relli's, which they strongly resemble. Carl Morris' pictures of the northwestern coast, such as *Autumn No. 3,* gouache and Chinese ink, 1954 (*PC 817), are redolent of a specific place in color, shape, and mood, as are such pictures as Boris Margo's *Winter Evening,* lacquer on aluminum, 1955 (PC 302).

Charles Schucker, Joan Mitchell, Jon Schueler, Ethel Schwabacker, Hyde Solomon, and Angelo Ipollito represent to a greater or lesser degree the intrusion of the image into abstract expressionism. Mitchell paints her emotions about nature or objects, rather than the objects themselves, but references to them sometimes intrude into her work. In *Hemlock,* 1956 (Whitney Museum of American Art, New York), there is some residue of the angular structure of that species of tree. Schucker in his *Bridge,* 1954 (PC 402), combines natural appearance, as he does in other pictures, with a feeling for great spaciousness suggested with sweeping areas of amorphous color very similar to that of non-naturalistic abstract expressionists. Schueler's *Snow Cloud and Blue Sky,* 1958 (Whitney Museum), approaches in color and handling the late impressionism of Monet; in fact, Schueler, Schwabacker, Solomon, and even Ipollito, who seems more abstract, have been singled out with a few others (and for less obvious reasons) as abstract impressionists.

By making artists and the public aware of the sensuality of paint and, as Sam Hunter says, teaching a younger generation of artists how to think in paint, abstract expressionism has been an enormous stimulant to American art as a whole. In another dimension, it has done much more by probing deeply into new levels of human experience to produce images of compelling power. The struggle and slow development of some artists is like a man with no motor coordination trying to learn to dance, and though some abstract expressionist paintings may seem paltry and ridiculous at first glance, they are the result of a sincere, if painful, search for a transcendent reality. It seems therefore almost ungracious to point out a few of the pitfalls implicit in abstract expressionism.

The problem of communication is unavoidable. In spite of the high-handed remarks of Still, most abstract expressionists are under the impression that they are communicating. Carl Morris says that he *assumes* he is tapping a common reservoir of human experience. In the case of the convincing and dedicated abstract expressionist this is undoubtedly true, but in the case of the imitators and hangers-on—or even of the less profound members of the school—the egocentricity typical of many artistic personalities may prevent them from sufficiently projecting into the perceptual processes of other persons to realize that they may not share the impulses and associations which motivate their own form-making.

The problem of extreme individuality is somewhat connected with communication. Paradoxically, out of complete freedom of expression has come a very monotonous production, not only in the works of a single artist but in those of groups of artists, which are sometimes hardly distin-

guishable. Thus a kind of pervasive consistency which is anonymous rather than individual began to occur in abstract expressionism during the 1950's.

This observation leads to a third point, the danger of academicism. The expressionistic ingredient in the movement can never be faked. Impetuosity and intensity cannot turn into habit. Some genuine experience, some real inner vision of the kind which produced Pollock's and Kline's personal autographic styles must be present; to repeat their discoveries without their involvement is to eviscerate the style completely. One critic writing on the students of Hofmann stated the situation nicely in the following way: "Without passionate commitment you get a *Dies Irae* arranged by George Melachrino." [61]

As with all academicism, there is the danger of pomposity, to which abstract expressionism is particularly susceptible, since from the beginning its esthetic has been riddled with mysticism. The movement is so earnest that it cannot conceive of being in any way ridiculous. One of the most attractive qualities of Dada and surrealism is the humor which accompanies their assault on pretension, and it is largely humor which keeps Picasso constantly renewing himself. It is refreshing after two decades of *ex cathedra* pronouncements emanating from the abstract expressionists and from their critics and dealers to learn that the painter Robert Rauschenberg has partially erased a drawing by de Kooning, framed it, and given it the title *The Erased De Kooning*.

Post-abstract Expressionism

During the last decade and a half it has been inevitable that an artistic movement as important as abstract expressionism would have both a positive and a negative influence. The pictorial effects of abstract expressionism, if not its purposes and actual methods, have been reflected in a number of painters who are to a greater or lesser degree either still representational or

bound to another abstract esthetic. William Kienbusch in his later work, for instance, replaces his nature-qualifying geometry with the gesture of "action" painting; and Balcomb Green, formerly a complete abstractionist, turns not only to overt content, but to a kind of surface design and texture more related (in spite of the artist's statements to the contrary) to abstract expressionism than to any other style. His nudes and landscapes, such as *Composition, the Storm,* 1953–1954 (PC 177), are propelled by semiabstract overlappings of form and the sweep and excitement of his surfaces; but it is still the subject matter of the exterior world (as he states categorically), not the promptings of the inner world, which direct him.

In George Mueller's *The Study,* 1955 (PC 336), the image of a table is reminiscent also of a certain phase of abstract expressionism, in which the overpowering abstract image is paramount. For, though this piece of furniture is recognizable, even with its unconventional perspective, its huge presence overpowers the canvas.

Hans Moller's *Forsythias,* 1956 (Hirshhorn Collection, New York), recalls free-form abstraction. In fact, the painter says that the title was suggested by the process of painting itself, during the early stages of which he applied a large amount of yellow to the canvas. Moller's *Crown of Thorns,* 1955 (PC 1014), is bolder and less abstract, which is the direction his present work is increasingly taking.

Robert Goodenough is still abstract in his initial motivation and, like Klee and many of the abstract expressionists, he experiments with form until suddenly an image appears which cannot be suppressed. It is then exploited, as in *Centaur,* 1959 (Collection of the artist, New York). Though Goodenough's canvases at first glance have the style and impact of abstract expressionism, his basic motivation seems very different indeed, as far removed as Balcomb Green's, for example. The latter says that nature has become "a tool to make the projecting and capturing of feeling possible," a statement which could only have been made by a young artist who had grown up since abstract expressionism became the prevailing mode.

Larry Rivers is another prominent painter who, though his point of view differs completely from that of abstract expressionism, has been greatly influenced by its scale, its amorphousness of form and space, and its exploitation of the accidents of the medium. These factors give a mystery and poetic mood to his figural compositions which make them a new kind of image, as in his quite realistic *Double Portrait of Birdie,* 1955 (PC 386), and in the more amorphous paintings involving the themes of Washington crossing the Delaware and the Civil War.

Rivers' later work has been influenced by developments which are also prominent in what has come to be called "pop art"; though impressive in its physical size and complexity (using three-dimensional forms at times) and in its themes—such as Africa, or the Russian revolution—it is perhaps not as personal and original a statement as that of a few years ago.

Several painters who were formerly abstract expressionists have turned to the natural world, but have retained the spontaneity and largeness of conception of the movement. Among the most interesting are three California painters: Elmer Bischoff, Richard Diebenkorn, and the late David Park. The broad handling, brilliant color, and emotionalism of their recent work is related in mood and actual technique as much to figurative German expressionism as to abstract expressionism.

Rosemarie Beck has also turned to realism, but brings to it the palette, texture, and even the forms of her earlier abstract expressionism, which greatly enrich it. This is true to an even greater extent of Grace Hartigan. Her early study of Matisse (which gave her a feeling for both boldness and refinement of color and pattern), the powerful slashing brush work, intense color, and great scale of her abstract expressionism, combined later with realism, produced some of the more interesting pictures of the 1950's, as can be seen in the vigorous *Grand Street Brides,* 1954 (PC 703), and even more effectively in the *Creeks,* 1957 (Collection of Philip Johnson).

The most conspicuous reactions against abstract expressionism in recent years, especially against its formless generality, involve a concentration upon the specific. This is expressed either in the simulation of objects by means of conventional painting techniques, as in the earlier work of Jasper Johns, or in the actual physical incorporation of objects into the works of art themselves, as in the "combine paintings" of Robert

Rauschenberg. Johns's subjects, which include numbers and letters, maps, shooting targets, coat hangers, and the American flag—either singly or in combination—are so ordinary and banal that they are almost non-subjects, thus permitting the viewer to enjoy their juxtapositions and repetitions as though the paintings were actually abstract. But the fact that they are not, and do indeed represent very familiar objects, puts them into a frame of reference entirely different from the contrasting generalities of both geometric (or post-cubist) abstraction and abstract expressionism. By drawing our attention to ready-made objects Johns's work is related (though not consciously so) to a similar phenomenon in literature, represented by the French novelist Robe-Grillet whose "naming" of things is analogous to Johns's pointing them out in paint. The final implication of Johns's work raises a new and profound problem in criticism, that of identity. This is illustrated more dramatically in Johns's sculpture than in his painting: his two cans of Ballantine ale, for instance, the result of much labor and skill, can be distinguished from actual cans of Ballantine ale only after the most careful examination.

Rauschenberg's work is not so revolutionary in its implications, being a bridge between the art of the immediate past and that of Johns and other contemporaries who have initiated new problems of meaning. Rauschenberg is richly formal, painterly to an extreme, and replete with connotation. At the same time the importance of the actual fragments of physical reality which he uses so conspicuously in his work (and which make them sometimes difficult to distinguish from sculpture) results in an ambiguity of identity which is as perplexing as in Johns's carefully simulated objects. Rauschenberg's *Canyon*, 1959, composed of conventional oil on canvas supplemented by wood, printed matter, a stuffed eagle, and a pillow, or his *Monogram*, 1961 (Illustration 6–76), a stuffed angora goat with a tire around its middle, standing majestic and melancholy in a welter of commonplace but incongruously combined objects, are works of art which surprisingly enough transcend the seeming absurdity of their materials to create a new

esthetic experience. This experience has its own peculiar validity, which is difficult to analyze yet nonetheless real. Perhaps this is so partly because Rauschenberg's vision is thoroughly contemporary, nourished on the actual experience of the paradoxically ugly beauty of the mid-century, the product of mass production and of the mass media. At any rate, in the organization of what he sees and chooses to isolate, he demonstrates not merely a dependence on chance juxtapositions but a conscious pleasure in the discovery of new configurations which are esthetically and emotionally convincing. This is especially true in Rauschenberg's illustrations for Dante's *Inferno* (1959–1962) wherein the combinations of the commonplace and familiar images of cheap illustration and advertisement, transferred to paper and manipulated with washes and other technical devices, have produced out of the painfully banal an eloquent and poignant commentary on a universal theme.

Frivolous or neo-Dada as such work may at first appear, even the most unsympathetic critic could not deny that it marks a return to the objective world from a solipsist subjectivity. Furthermore, its neo-Dadaism bears only a surface resemblance to the original movement, for Dada was iconoclastic, whereas the new art of "assemblage," as the Museum of Modern Art has called work such as Rauschenberg's and of his predecessors and contemporaries (like the "sculptor" Joseph Cornell), is an affirmation of the actual world, in either its matter-of-fact or its symbolic aspects. This world is expressed through the most effective and shocking visual means but with great formal sophistication. (The plastic and textural richness of such paintings makes them sometimes difficult to differentiate from sculpture. Furthermore, many sculptors also make use of the detritus of mass production and industrialism.)

Out of the background best represented by Johns and Rauschenberg, and strongly influenced by them, has come one of the most recent schools of contemporary art, at first called the "new realism" (1962) but more recently simply "pop art," in which both content and technique are influenced by the mass communication media

6–76. Robert Rauschenberg, *Monogram*, 1961. Construction. 4 feet x 6 feet x 6 feet. (Collection of the artist, New York.)

and the products of mass production and industrialization. Andy Warhol monumentalizes soup cans and food stamps, and drums into our eyes the vacuous public smile of Marilyn Monroe many times over in one canvas, compounding the confusion raised by Johns's ambiguity of identity by reduplicating his motifs through photographic and screen processes. Roy Lichtenstein fashions sinister and satiric comments in a monumentalized comic strip style, even copying with brush strokes the mechanical stippling of the cheap reproductive process. James Rosenquist who, like Lichtenstein, was formerly a sign

painter, uses the large scale and vapid smoothness of display art for his incisive pillories of a mechanized society, as in his *I Love You With My Ford*, 1961 (Moderna Museet, Stockholm), in which the car's bumper is juxtaposed with the ecstatic face of a woman. Robert Indiana has developed an elegant personal style analogous to geometric abstraction through the use of words and letters inspired by the sign board tradition and sometimes produced by stencils. Other artists associated with the "pop" movement, like Marisol and Tom Wesselmann, use the actual products of mass technology to supplement their work, such as the old sneakers and plaster members enlivening the former's poignant figures, and the bath towels, toilet seats, and "live" TV sets accompanying the latter's painted nudes.

Though from some points of view "pop art" may seem to be merely the most recent manifestation of an art form kept alive only by the impetus of sensationalism, at its best it has a sincerity and forcefulness of statement which may permit it to survive in spite of the tendency of the art market to treat art as any other commodity, subject to the same principles of planned obsolescence as the other products of our industrialized society.

"Pop art," in its rejection of the emotional subjectivity and loose painterliness of abstract expressionism, shares with contemporary American abstraction a cool detachment of attitude (even a similar anonymity) and a neatness or hard-edged precision of style, seen most clearly in the work of Richard Anuskiewicz and Gene Davis. But another phase of current abstraction, superficially similar, is more significant. Not so directly derived from European artists like Mondrian and Albers, it is a little closer to certain aspects of abstract expressionism as represented by Rothko, Newman, and Reinhardt. The use of vibrating color by Carl Morris and Kenneth Noland, for instance, is similar to that of these artists. At the same time the hard-edged shapes of Ellsworth Kelley are petrified or frozen translations of Jack Youngerman's informal and pulsating forms. These artists, and others like Larry Poons, whose motifs consist of dots rather than the stripes of Noland and others, are even more adventurous than their more conventionally abstract contemporaries in their exploration of relationships between forms, as in positive versus negative shapes and in sharply differentiated color; the results are dynamic equilibriums which are more exciting than restful. In some cases suspense or anxiety is suggested, as in the paintings of Leon Smith and Ellsworth Kelley; and in general, visual effects are emotional and connotative rather than detached and scientific.

The present importance of these artists in the current art world is another facet of the reaction against abstract expression. Yet, from the vantage point of the mid-1960's, abstract expressionism still seems to remain the most significant movement in American painting of the last decades.

The Graphic Arts

Print-making in the twentieth century has followed substantially the same course as painting: the last phases of nineteenth-century realism and impressionism; the genre realism of the "ashcan" school; the introduction of abstraction and expressionism in various degrees of integration; social realism and the American scene; and, since the war, an outburst of original creativity which has completely revolutionized the graphic arts.

The most prominent group of print makers at the turn of the century were those who carried on the tradition exemplified by Seymour Haden, Duveneck, and Whistler, and who imposed their artistic point of view on print-making in the United States almost until World War II. Among the most prominent was Joseph Pennell, a follower, intimate, and biographer of Whistler. In the 1880's and 1890's Pennell did quantities of etchings and a few lithographs which were competent notations of the pleased reactions of an American tourist in Europe, chiefly in London, Italy, and Spain. At first Pennell was influenced by Haden's romantic realism, which he interpreted with an etched line reflecting the facile pen and wash technique of an illustrator, as in *San Gimignano*, 1883 (GC 123A), but he turned gradually to a more Whistlerian statement—at least in its suggestiveness, if not in its subtlety. Pennell's etchings are somewhat marred by a too overt exploitation of old world quaintness, and are therefore quite different from the dispassionate approach of the impressionists. They do con-

6–77. Childe Hassam, *Easthampton*, 1917. Etching. 7½ x 11½ inches.

vey, however, a certain lyricism, though in a more popular, less exquisite, and certainly less modern way than those of his mentor. Pennell's work in the twentieth century becomes broader in handling, especially in his lithographs, many of which deal with industrial and urban subjects in direct and dramatic compositions, as in *The Gates of Pedro Miguel Lock,* 1912 (GC 124).

The more impressionist realism of late nineteenth-century British and American print-making was carried on by such artists as Frank W. Benson, whose etchings and drypoints of hunting and of wild life were enormously popular. But far superior to the others of this group is the painter Childe Hassam, whose prints were executed in the early twentieth century, later than most of his paintings. The impressionist vision is not wholly suited to those graphic arts whose means of expression is linear, but Hassam is an extraordinarily successful adaptor of the essentially atmospheric and painterly method of im-

pressionism to the line technique of etching. The pull between objects and their surrounding atmosphere is difficult to adjust to line, and Hassam is more consistently impressionist even than Whistler in this respect. He developed a very personal style consisting of areas of crosshatching of greater or lesser darkness to weave a surface that is not unlike that of the texture of paint in his own paintings and those of other impressionists. Objects and perspective (form and space) are sufficiently described to be readable, but are unified in an envelope of alternating sun and shade-filled air. Among the most successful and typical are *House on Main St., Easthampton,* 1922 (GC 31), and *Easthampton,* 1917 (Illustration 6–77). In such etchings Hassam actually achieved a style more original and more charming than the sometimes rather forced boldness of his later painting; they remain closer in feeling to his earlier canvases, which have greater atmospheric subtleties.

The more realistic aspect of the Haden–Whistler–Pennell tradition was continued by a group of artists whose work was characterized by an almost compulsive realism of detail. In the etchings of John Taylor Arms, such as *Gothic Spirit,* 1922 (GC 3), this realism is combined with great archaeological accuracy, feeling for texture, and some decorative charm. Another prominent member of what may be called a topographical and architectural school of etchers is Samuel Chamberlain, whose *Dentelles Gothiques, Clamecy,* 1930 (*GC 90), is typical in its sensitive but somewhat too accurate detail.

The illustrative tendencies of members of the "ashcan" school and their associates, such as Bellows, were naturally suited to the graphic media, as were those of other artists concerned with the American scene. None of the latter, however, possessed the vitality of Reginald Marsh or the muted eloquence of Edward Hopper, especially in his *Night Shadows,* 1921 (*GC 33). One or two almost captured the quality of the city as well as did Hopper, but without his laconic simplicity and formal power. The best of these is Martin Lewis, whose *Night, Greenwich Village,* 1930 (GC 115), and *The Glow of the City,* 1930 (*GC 45), are strongly designed and lyrical commentaries on the metropolis.

Other realistic artists produced woodcuts which brought a more stylized approach to the American scene, partly because the nature of their medium lent itself to more abstract or, at least, more decorative treatment than did etching and drypoint. The dean of these artists is Rudolph Ruzicka, whose *Louisburg Square, Boston,* 1914 (GC 127), a color woodcut, is typical of his meticulous but always formally distinguished work. The woodcuts of J. J. Lankes and the wood engravings of Thomas W. Nason, such as *Leaning Silo,* 1932 (GC 122), in the poignancy of their evocation of "North of Boston," could almost be illustrations for Robert Frost's early poems.

Another artist, Stow Wengenroth, a lithographer, is even more successful in distilling the essence of the same region in prints whose remarkable exactitude recalls that of the "magic" or "sharp-focus" realists, as seen in *Serenity,* 1951 (GC 78), but whose compositional power and remarkable feeling for the rich and varied tonal character of lithography make him an artist to be respected even in a period when verisimilitude is often to an artist's disadvantage.

Other print makers in the late 1930's and early 1940's were bringing a more powerful graphic approach to the older realistic tradition, a development facilitated by the relaxation of the hold of certain collectors (largely wiped out by the 1929 stock market crash and the subsequent depression) whose conventional taste had perpetuated a conventional product. Among these artists were Lawrence Kupferman and Harry Wickey. Kupferman's *Victorian Mansion,* 1939 (*GC 40), brings the boldness of drypoint used with the impressive precision of engraving to an urban aspect of the American scene. Wickey's *Sultry August Afternoon,* 1936 (GC 143), a lithograph, demonstrates a vigorous and exuberant approach to the rural scene, in a spirit similar to that of the regionalists, who themselves were not inactive as print makers (as we have seen in the case of Benton). John Steuart Curry's dramatic lithograph *Line Storm,* 1935 (GC 95), and Grant Wood's lithograph *Honorary Degree,* 1937 (*GC 79), are among the best of their graphic works. Of course there were other artists—mostly painters—who brought some degree of expressionism or abstract ordering into their graphic art during this period when new ways of seeing and organizing were being absorbed into American art as a whole. Max Weber's distinguished color woodcuts, such as the *Feast of the Passover,* 1918 (GC 76), and *Primitive Man,* 1918 (*GC 77), have the expressive power of his paintings, and are closer in technique to the work of Gauguin and Munch in the same medium than are those of any other American artist. By contrast, Franklin C. Watkins' woodcuts are cruder and less organized but still forceful in their exploitation of the medium, in the slashing knife strokes used, and in their bold contrasts. The lithographs and lithotints of Marsden Hartley, produced in the 1920's and early 1930's, have a boldness and graphic surety which put them well ahead of their time, and justify at least their mention.

Among similar artists who were more exclusively print makers were Earle Horter and Howard Cook, both of whom brought the disciplining distortions of cubism to bear on the conventional city-scape. Wanda Gag, in prints such as *Elevated Station*, 1925 (GC 27), lent a somewhat mannered expressionist distortion (not unlike that of the early Burchfield, but more deliberate) to the metropolitan scene and to natural objects. A later artist, but one who is still essentially realistic and not overly influenced by more recent technical and formal innovations, is Harold Sternberg, whose powerful factuality is aided by a sure sense of design, as in the lithograph *Steel*, 1941 (GC 133).

On the whole, except for the work of painters such as Weber, and that of others representing all shades of artistic opinion—Walt Kuhn, Raphael Soyer, Yasuo Kuniyoshi, William Gropper, Stuart Davis, Robert Gwathmey, and Federico Castellon—there was little that was distinguished, outside of the realist tradition in one form or another and the few exceptions mentioned above. The late 1930's and early 1940's seemed to be a period of exploration in the graphic arts, before the tremendous outburst of print-making in the late 1940's. Graphic artists began to investigate various aspects of abstraction in relation to the medium itself, rather than using the medium primarily to express in prints what could also be accomplished not very differently in painting or drawing. Paul Landacre, for example, in *The Press*, 1935 (GC 113), took advantage of the decorative ordering of planes and facets as interpreted by the patterned textural subtleties inherent in wood engraving. Other artists experimented with new combinations of old media and inventions of new ones. In the late 1930's, the serigraph (silk screen stencil print) was developed, a medium adapted to both the representational and the abstract points of view, though more readily to the latter. Leonard Pytlak's *Night Skaters*, 1941 (GC 125), an example of the former, handles the medium with a tonal subtlety equal to that of lithography; whereas Anthony Velonis shows in his work, such as *Decoration Empire*, 1939 (GC 135), the

more formal possibilities inherent in the medium, which is naturally adapted to the superpositions and interrelationships of forms characteristic of cubism and its descendants.

Another aspect of this transitional period in the graphic arts was the breaking down of the old prejudice in favor of the cabinet or portfolio-sized print (meant to be looked at close at hand), and its replacement by prints of greatly increased size, which eventually became comparable in dimension to medium-sized paintings. This innovation was prophesied in a few very large prints done before the war, such as Max Kahn's *Lithographer Contemplating a Roller*, 1939 (GC 110), a colored lithograph, the grand simplicity of which is enhanced by its size (25¼ x 18¾ inches).

The print departments of certain museums and institutions, such as the Philadelphia Print Club, contributed to the search for new ways of print-making to replace the outmoded ones favored by the older generation of collectors. But the most important agency was the W. P. A. Art Project, whose graphic workshops, especially in New York, brought together many artists with backgrounds in various print techniques and pooled their common experience. The serigraph was invented in the New York Project, and the first of the large-sized prints evolved there as well. It was here also that Louis Schanker developed the relief processes of woodcut and wood engraving into what amounted to a new graphic art by virtue of great size and the release of technical potentials never exploited before. At the same time he realized in his abstract subject matter the potentials of the colored wood block for bold expressiveness and decorative power, as in *Carnival*, 1945 (GC 62), and for subtler linear and tonal effects, as in *Arrangement of Forms*, 1949 (*GC 61).

An even more important factor in the achievement of a new point of view in the graphic arts was Atelier 17, a print workshop which Stanley W. Hayter, an English artist of the school of Paris, brought from France to New York in 1940. Hayter's methods performed for the intaglio processes (etching, engraving, drypoint, etc.) what Schanker's had accomplished for relief prints: they were released from the constrictions of the small scale of the conventional print of the past and from the kind of precise handling traditionally reserved for the specific print medium. This was especially so in the case of engraving, which Hayter freed from being minuscule and precise, using it instead for the expression of large and forceful linear motifs.

Hayter also combined the linear and tonal media, even experimenting with the introduction of extraneous objects for textural variation, so that the large-scaled prints of his group and those influenced by it are often of mixed intaglio media, sometimes even crossed with serigraph. Hayter's own work combines a mastery of technique with the surrealist methods of free association and automatism, a procedure which he urged on his pupils. Among American-born print makers, Karl Schrag's work is nearest to Hayter's, though generally, as in *Falling Night*, 1949 (*GC 63), he is not as controlled or sophisticated in design.

The influence of Hayter varied from the inspiration of his technical innovations alone, in work which is still basically realistic, to an emulation of his formal and expressive point of view as well. Armin Landeck, for instance, is still tied to the recognizable motif but, in such prints as the etching and engraving *Stairhall*, 1951 (GC 114), transforms the architectural print from a sentimental and decorative record into a vehicle for a richer expression of space and mood. Sue Fuller, in *Hen*, 1945 (GC 26), combines the media of engraving and soft-ground etching (that is, a precise and a blurred type of intaglio, respectively) in a unique way in order to realize the rich textural character of the feathers of the peahen. More frequently, Hayter's abstract linearism is applied to the expressionistic distortion of reality in dynamic compositions like those of Walter R. Rogalski and André Racz, and in purely abstract forms such as those of Raymond Jordan. The prints of Gabor Peterdi, who was associated with Atelier 17 from its Paris days, reflect the influence of Hayter's purely linear and tonal manner. Peterdi's gruesome *Price of Glory*, 1947 (*GC 54), an engraving, demonstrates a most expressive use of the sweeping line, derived

from automatism but applied to the representation of destruction and mayhem, and of drear landscapes inhabited by jackal-like creatures. A print such as this is typical of a recurring manner and theme in his work in which, to paraphrase his own words, he attempts to create an oppressive image haunted by the fearful images of destruction. In the 1950's Peterdi's work takes a calmer course, oriented more toward life than death, in which the theme of the triumph of life alternates with that of the fight for survival. Of the former group *Germination*, 1952 (GC 53), a colored aquatint, etching, and engraving, is a good example of richness and variety of texture; its shapes and colors are unified by a somewhat formal and static composition, very different in effect from *Price of Glory*. The vacillation between manners illustrated by this comparison occurs throughout Peterdi's work, indicating a fascination with techniques and manner but not a consistent artistic statement.

The influence of Hayter's book *New Ways of Gravure* (1949) and the prominence of his follower Peterdi and his pupil Mauricio Lasansky carried the principles of Atelier 17 far. Both artists taught at various schools and universities. Lasansky, who had been changed from a romantic realist to a powerful expressionist by contact with Hayter [as is testified by his *Self-Portrait*, 1947 (GC 42), a colored etching, aquatint, and engraving], influenced a whole generation of print makers through his position at the University of Iowa. Among his own pupils several have carried the Atelier 17 point of view to other universities, notably Lee Chesney, whose prints are as bold and expressive as the title of his *Pierced and Beset*, 1952 (*GC 12), a colored etching, engraving, and aquatint, would suggest. John Paul Jones' *Self-Portrait*, 1950 (*GC 34), a soft- and hard-ground etching, engraving, and aquatint, is typical of that artist's more realistic approach, which is ordered by a refined formal sensibility and enhanced by the powerful grasp of line and tone characteristic of the Hayter–Lasanski circle.

Other print makers associated with Atelier 17 and influenced by its principles are Fred Becker, Norma Morgan, Ezio Martinelli, and, among

Lasansky's pupils, besides Chesney and Jones, Glen Alps.

By the mid-1940's the influence of Schanker and his associates at the former Art Project and that of Atelier 17 had stimulated other artists into further technical explorations. Boris Margo invented the cellocut (dissolved celluloid, which, when reformed, can be printed in intaglio or relief), a medium admirably suited to the linear and spatial complexities of his own style, which is somewhat influenced by surrealist psychic automatism, as seen in his *Sea,* 1949 (*GC 47). In 1947 Margo joined with Schanker and others in a group called the Graphic Circle, which acted as a further catalyst for the spread of new ways of print-making. By the 1950's even more graphic methods had been made available: engraving on lucite, invented by Harold Persico Paris; the use of movable blocks and cardboard cutout and paper relief, resulting in prints which are literally monotypes, for each print can be the result of a different juxtaposition of these elements, as in James Forsberg's *The Family,* 1953 (GC 23); and even electron prints, as in the work of Caroline Durieux.

The basic graphic medium of lithography was not as easily subjected to radical change as were the relief and intaglio processes. But the greater use of color and the increase in scale have sufficiently altered the traditional lithograph so that it too is equal in impact to the other print media. The work of Benton Spruance typifies this change to a certain extent. His is a vigorous realism tempered or enhanced by aspects of abstract design aided by subtle and expressive color, as in *Anabasis,* 1957 (GC 132), and in many other prints dealing with a variety of subjects. Aubrey Schwartz' *Predatory Bird,* 1957 (GC 128), exhibits a more contemporary feeling for the expressive power of the large image on a large surface.

The influence of Atelier 17, the Graphic Circle, Lasansky and his pupils, Schanker and his pupils, and the propagation of the new approach by exhibitions (particularly the Brooklyn Museum Annuals) and publications, all combined to bring about a tremendous upsurge of creative energy in the graphic arts. The work of Seong Moy is a good example of the cross fertilization resulting from these influences, for his color woodcuts, inspired by Schanker, are not primarily angular, as are the latter's own or the woodcuts inspired by him, but display a curvilinear character which Moy acquired working in intaglio at Atelier 17. His gay carnival-like work is lively, boldly decorative, and unpretentious, qualities seen in an early print such as *Chinese Actor,* color woodcut, 1948 (GC 52), and later in such prints as the *Royal Maids of Waiting,* color woodcut, 1955 (Illustration 6–78), which is more subtly calligraphic.

Artists representing both abstract and realist points of view have reflected equally in their work the large scale and imaginative use of technique typical of the new ways of print-making. Milton Goldstein's semiabstract *Sun,* 1956 (GC 105), an etching and aquatint, for instance, is not only large in scale, but grandiose in concept and design. Rudy Pozzatti's more representational but still expressionistically distorted architectural subjects are greatly enhanced by large scale and bold engraving, as in his *Duomo,* 1952 (GC 56).

Gabor Peterdi says in *Printmaking Methods, Old and New* (1959) that the last thirty-five years have seen more technical innovation than the past five hundred in the procedures of the graphic arts. Prints are not only more pervasive than paintings, since they are multiplied and not unique, but they now almost rival paintings in size, and are certainly as expressive a vehicle, except in the case of the more extreme forms of automatism in painting. There are about three thousand serious graphic artists in the United States, and in a recent year there were thirty different exhibitions between June and April. Various organizations have come into existence to promote the exhibition and sale of prints, the most important being the Print Council of America, which has organized two international exhibitions.

There is no question that all this activity is a reflection of great artistic vitality stimulated largely by technical discoveries. But just as important, and indeed perhaps the reason for these

effects, that the final worth of the prints may be somewhat inflated.

There are a number of print makers who utilize the technical innovations of the revolution in print-making with a more evident purpose as means than as ends. Of these there are some in whose work the fascination with the medium is still so strongly stimulating that a consistent individual style has not emerged; Peterdi and Lasansky are among the most prominent in this category. But there are others whose personal statement is more consistent, or who have achieved an integration of all the technical devices, stylistic influences, and artistic points of view which have formed their artistic personali-

6–78. Seong Moy, *Royal Maids of Waiting*, 1955. Color woodcut. 18 x 11⅝ inches.

innovations, has been the general change of artistic tempo in the United States, a change which has found its most prominent manifestation in abstract expressionism. The works of Schanker and Margo, of Hayter and many others connected with Atelier 17 were abstract or partially so. Thus recent print-making, like painting and sculpture, is marked by technical innovation and a new artistic point of view; but since the technical aspect of print-making is more intrusive than in the other figurative arts, there is a tendency to be so impressed by the excitement of the new methods and the novelty of their decorative

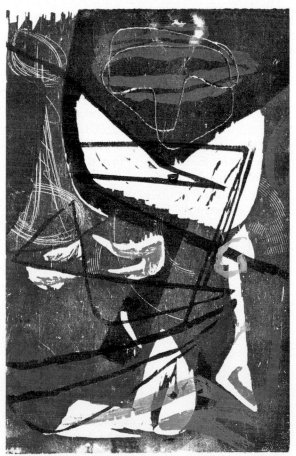

6–79. Adja Yunkers, *Composition*, 1955. Color woodcut. 21 x 13⅝ inches.

ties. Among these artists Misch Kohn and Antonio Frasconi may have less scope than some of their more adventurous and far-ranging contemporaries, but within their limits they possess perhaps more clarity and effectiveness of statement. The sure decorative effect, force of design, and clarity of statement seen in Kohn's early *Tiger*, 1949 (GC 37), have continued in a series of huge wood engravings, "sugar lift" aquatints (and more lately aquatint and etching), filled with pageantry and occasionally something of the grotesque. Though perhaps concerned with larger moral ideas like good and evil, as in his bullfight series, for instance, Kohn's prints are still primarily artistic rather than moral statements, demonstrating an esthetic detachment which some of his contemporaries lack in their almost hysterical treatments of eschatological subjects, as if they were depending on the importance of their subject matter to come to their rescue esthetically. Frasconi is even less concerned with man's fate, concentrating instead on the attractiveness of the visual world—human, animal, and architectural—in its varied forms and activities, in his decorative woodcuts, such as the *Fulton Fish Market*, 1952 (GC 24). At the same time he is not lacking in seriousness, as his simple and effective *Self-Portrait*, 1951 (*GC 25), indicates.

Adja Yunkers' prints have the controlled ease of the accomplished artist. Already a mature painter on his arrival in the United States in 1947, he brought to his prints a confidence of statement and surety of abstract language which make the dynamic forms of *Magnificat*, 1953 (*GC 146), surging and interpenetrating in space, and the static and classic calm of *Ostia Antiqua VI*, 1955 (GC 147)—both color woodcuts—equally effective. Typical of his powerfully designed work is *Composition*, color woodcut, 1955 (Illustration 6–79), whose evocative forms demonstrate the artist's relationship to abstract expressionism.

Among the most highly esteemed print makers today is Leonard Baskin (who is also an important sculptor). He is no less earnest in his commentary on man's moral situation than many of his contemporaries, but he is far clearer. This is true not only because he remains largely repre-

sentational and derives his artistic inspiration from such deeply committed humanists as Goya, Käthe Kollwitz (the German expressionist), and Georges Rouault (formerly one of the Fauves), but also because he is a superb draughtsman. He understands the character of his media (both relief and intaglio), and uses them with the expressive linear power of the great German woodcutters of the fifteenth and early sixteenth centuries. Baskin's images and symbols are more specific than are those of most of his contemporaries; at the same time they do not derive from Picasso's iconography of destruction developed in the *Guernica*, so popular among other artists whose work is still representational. Baskin's references are sometimes extremely concrete, as in the *Poet Laureate* woodcut, 1954–1955, whose flaccid and bloated face is a mordant commentary on the artist who sells or wastes his talent, and *Mantegna at Eremitani*, wood engraving, 1952 (GC 83), in which the dedicated creativity of the great Italian master is suggested

6–80. Leonard Baskin, *Tobias and the Angel,* 1960. Wood engraving. 14¾ x 15 inches.

in the strongly veined temples and jagged profile. Yet when Baskin's themes are more general, they are still projected in terms that have specific reference, as seen in his reinterpretation of such a traditional subject as *Tobias and the Angel*, wood engraving, 1960 (Illustration 6–80). Woodcuts like *Everyman*, 1960, and the earlier *Man of Peace*, 1952 (*GC 83A), though even more universal in context, nevertheless remain pointed in their poignant actualization. These pathetic, dogged, and gentle figures evoke the basic human dignity lying beneath the surface of what Baskin has called the "spoiled and debauched" condition of man today.

Though dealing with subject matter of scope and importance, Baskin (unlike many of his contemporaries similarly concerned) is neither pretentious nor vague, for his technical competence is never mere showmanship, and his formal sensibility is sure. The ideas and images he projects are first thoroughly explored and then realized with precision.

Photography

The history of twentieth-century photography should begin in the 1890's with Stieglitz' editorship of *Camera Notes*, and the beginnings of *Photo Secession* and *Camera Work*. *Camera Notes*, originating as a Camera Club journal, became a quarterly with an international reputation. One of its purposes was the insistence that photography was a fine art, a point of view then still considered somewhat outlandish, but almost universally accepted today, as is evidenced by the existence of a department of photography at the Museum of Modern Art, by the inclusion of photographic prints among the collections of graphic arts in several museums, and by the awarding to photographers of a number of Guggenheim Grants in the creative arts. After some disagreement with the Camera Club, Stieglitz founded *Photo Secession* and another quarterly magazine *Camera Work* (in which the illustrations were printed in the most carefully supervised photogravure), both of which stood for the use of the camera for the production of works of art. The success of the magazine and of the *Photo Secession* artists was international; Stieglitz had won his point that photography was art. But the question should be asked: Was it photography, or was it photography imitating art? For, the photographs of the early twentieth century, even the best in *Camera Work* and elsewhere were as imitative of late nineteenth-century genre painting as were those of the art photographers against whom Peter Henry Emerson had inveighed a generation before. But ironically Emerson's recommendations of blurred focus, together with the tonal refinement made possible by the platinum plate, combined to produce prints which had all the diaphanous effects of American impressionism as well as the somewhat sentimental subject matter of the impressionist genre painters; examples are Gertrude Kasebier's *Nativity* and "*Blessed art Thou Among Women*," c. 1900 (*F 38), and Edward Steichen's less sentimental but hardly less painterly portraits from *Camera Work*, especially those of *J. Pierpont Morgan*, 1903 (F 71), and *Rodin— The Thinker*, 1902 (F 70). Even Clarence White, Sr., who was among the most straightforward photographers of the time, was affected by the esthetic of painting, for his otherwise consistently focused and detailed platinum print *In the Orchard, Newark, Ohio*, 1902 (*F 99), is slightly hazy with more than autumn mist. Only Stieglitz himself, in such magnificently clear and precise (but for all that, atmospheric) prints as *The Steerage*, 1907 (F 77), continued to use photography as he had done in his earliest work: not as quasi- or pseudo-painting, but as photography exploiting those qualities of detail and precision which only the lens can achieve.

In a lecture given in London in 1923,[62] a young American photographer, Paul Strand, included this principle of precision among several

6–81. Paul Strand, *White Fence,* 1917. Photogravure. From *Camera Work,* No. 49–50, 1917, published by Alfred Stieglitz. (George Eastman House, Rochester, New York.)

others, in the first clear-cut statement of a photographic esthetic. Strand's standards for photographic criticism were remarkably like those of Peter Henry Emerson a generation before, except for this one principle of precise detail, which was at variance with Emerson's recommendation of the blurred focus. In effect, Strand's esthetic was held unconsciously or as a matter of course by the first photographers whose works are in a sense the "classics" of the art: Southworth and Hawes, O'Sullivan, and the early Stieglitz, in whose prints the reality of the given world and the recording of its detail are all-important.

Stieglitz was quick to recognize the significance of Strand's photographs as perfect exemplifications of their maker's theories, and devoted the last two issues of *Camera Work* to Strand's prints of places and of people, the latter taken without their subjects' knowledge by the simple device of pointing a large false lens elsewhere to attract their attention from the smaller one actually focused on them. Thus an instantaneous moment of passing expression was caught in such pictures as *Portrait, New York,* 1915 (F 82). Among the prints of places is the unforgettable *White Fence,* 1917 (F 83; Illustration 6–81), which can be taken as the *locus classicus* for the subsequent development of the main tradition of American photography into our own time: sharply focused, precise in detail, rich in contrast of texture and value, beautifully patterned in its abstract design, and still evocative of a point of view, an attitude, or a state of mind—in other words, having significant content as well as form.

In the example of Strand, Stieglitz found renewed strength for his own point of view, initiating a phase of his work which is even more precise and sensitive to every nuance of texture and atmosphere than before, as in his photographs of clouds, which he called "Equivalents." Among these reflections of his own various moods and feelings are *Equivalent No. 149-A*, 1931 (F 80), and portraits of his wife, Georgia O'Keeffe, such as *Portrait of Georgia O'Keeffe*, 1922 (F 79), and *Hands of Georgia O'Keeffe*, 1918 (F 78). Some of the most interesting of Stieglitz' photographs are the detailed architectural studies of his house at Lake George, and the city-scapes of New York taken from his hotel window or his gallery, An American Place, as seen in *New York: R.C.A. Building*, 1935 (?) (F 81).

Strand's point of view was also that of Charles Sheeler, whose talent seemed equally at home in photography or in painting, as we have seen. Even Edward Steichen, under the influence of Strand's esthetic and that of his former associate Stieglitz, changed his style completely after World War I, producing a series of portraits for *Vogue* and *Vanity Fair* which were as dramatic as before but now had the most precise focus and feeling for detail, with none of the more painterly effects of his earlier work. The technical expertness of these photographs is sometimes so underlined that they barely avoid the slickness of some of his fashion photographs (which are nevertheless masterpieces within the limitations of their subject).

Edward Weston, a little-known photographer in the *Photo Secession* tradition, may also have been inspired by Strand's example and theory to reject his soft focus lens and concentrate on the utmost precision, refining even further the Strand esthetic. This he achieved through a technique involving the use of an 8 x 10-inch "view-box" camera; the picture to be made was perfectly reproduced in the ground glass and thus capable of being composed there. The 8 x 10-inch negative was then printed on glossy paper of the same size, thus avoiding the loss of any detail through the additional focusing required by an enlargement. Weston's was a very deliberate technique, even requiring a certain length of time for exposure, since the greatest detail was achieved by the smallest possible aperture of the lens, a setting known as f/64

(Weston's work and that of some of his followers is sometimes spoken of as the "f/64 school"); this need for a longer exposure to light precluded action and movement, with a consequent tendency to emphasize the static. The photographs of Weston, since they required a completely immobile subject, are thus very similar to those produced by the daguerreotype and the wet plate processes, and it is no coincidence that some of Weston's architectural photographs, like his *Belle Grove, Louisiana*, 1941 (*F 96), should have the frozen timelessness of the work of George N. Barnard and Tim O'Sullivan. It is clear that Weston's development was away from the representation of action, which had appeared in the portrait of *Guadalupe de Rivera, Mexico, D.F.*, 1924 (F 90), and toward the non-dynamic, as in the sunlit geometry of *White Door*, 1940 (*F 95), and the *White Dune, Oceano*, 1936 (F 94). The formal potentials of the human figure as a whole, as seen in *Nude*, 1936 (F 93), or of its parts; of other natural or vegetable forms, as seen in *Shell*, 1927 (F 91), or *Artichoke Halved*, 1930 (F 92), and of the stones and trees of his beloved Point Lobos, near Monterey, California, have been the unmoving models for his formally sophisticated studies. He has infused the natural world with the formal principles of the abstract art of the twentieth century, while at the same time retaining the basic realistic esthetic of the camera.

Strand himself, in spite of the perhaps greater technical perfectionism of Weston, remains the chief exponent of his own principles, producing photographs of consistent quality through the years, though rejecting the immediacy of his early portraits. His portraits as a whole, however, have gained in profundity, if not in immediacy, as in *Young Boy, Charente*, 1951 (*F 88); and his architectural subjects have become more effective both formally and evocatively. *New England Town Hall*, 1946 (F 87), one of a group of photographs which he used in a book entitled *Time in New England* (accompanying texts were chosen by Nancy Newhall), is an unusually eloquent evocation of the *genus loci*. In addition, *Early Morning*, 1927 (F 84), and *Latch*, 1944 (*F 86), have an intensity of vision which is like that of Sheeler's drawings in their ability to state the quintessential.

The kind of photography represented by Strand and Weston comprises a distinctive genre in which strict adherence to the exploitation of the medium within its limitations remains the most clearly defensible esthetic of contemporary photography, as it was also in the earliest years of the medium. But the purpose of the early photographers was to document, and not necessarily or subconsciously to create a work of art. Jacob Riis used photography even more purposefully for extra-artistic reasons, as a means to an end: social reform. Yet Southworth and Hawes, Tim O'Sullivan, and Jacob Riis were effective documentators by virtue of the honesty and directness of their use of the medium. This fact, together with a natural gift for formal organization and an eye for a telling theme or detail made their work often as esthetically satisfying as that of the more deliberately artistic work of Weston or Strand. This is also true of the documentary photography of the twentieth century from Lewis W. Hine, through the recorders of the depression years, to the best of the *Life* photographers of today, whose work, besides exhibiting compositional sensitivity, has the added dimension of a greater involvement with persons or events, a factor which, when combined with artistic skill, creates images as moving as that of Alexander Gardner's *Home of a Rebel Sharpshooter*. Hine in the early twentieth century carried on the tradition of Jacob Riis, documenting the unpleasant facts of child labor and other social abuses in photographs even more formally satisfying (and more deliberately so) than those of the older man. Typical of his work is the eloquent *Carolina Cotton Mill*, 1908 (*F 36), in which a little girl at the spindles is shown overwhelmed by a long machine-filled loft which is photographed from an angle that gives the perspective an additional effect of loneliness. In such prints as *Italian Family, Ellis Island*, 1905 (F 35), Hine also documented the arrival of immigrants at Ellis Island and their first days in the new country; these photographs, a little more consciously studied and less crusading than some of his others, are still direct in their immediacy

and lack of pretension, if sometimes a little sentimental, as indicated in the title of one, *The Madonna of Ellis Island*. In his later years Hine devoted himself to the recording of the activities of labor. A series dealing with the erection of the Empire State Building was especially successful.

As the photographs of the Civil War so effectively demonstrated, the camera is particularly adapted to the registering of significant or evocative facts in a way which is poignant but not sentimental. This was again proven in the national crisis of the great depression following the stock market crash of 1929. The work of the photographers who concerned themselves with the social and economic problems of that era may well stand up as less "dated" and more satisfactory esthetically than will the equally documentary paintings of the regionalists and the socially conscious painters of the time, who represented strikers, migrant workers, the dust bowl, and the "Oakies." The best of these prints were done by photographers sent out by the various government agencies, especially the Farm Security Administration, under whose aegis Dorothea Lange, Arthur Rothstein, and Walker Evans did some of their finest work.

Dorothea Lange's *Bread Line*, 1933 (F 39), is a moving commentary on an era which most younger Americans find it hard to believe ever existed, and older ones find it preferable to forget. Such work prepared her for the production of her extraordinarily eloquent records of southern poverty, its causes and effects, in each case pinpointed in a human being (or even in a part of one), as in *Hoe Culture, Alabama*, 1937 (*F 41), or in a group of people, as *In A Camp of Migratory Pea Pickers*, 1936 (F 40), in which the expressions and gestures caught are those which most precisely make their point. These photographs are compelling in the power of their composition and in the quality of their detail, texture, and contrast of light and dark. Arthur Rothstein's statements are often more general and epic than Lange's, as in the panoramic *Father and Son Walking in Face of Dust Storm*, 1936 (F 56), but he, too, is the author of photographs with the telling efficacy of the very specific.

Among the socially oriented photographers who came to prominence in the depression years, Walker Evans is most closely related to the pure photographic esthetic of Weston and Strand, and is at the same time more influenced by the incisiveness and insight of the French genre photographer Cartier-Bresson, whose example was followed to a greater or less degree by the whole group. Evans' early work (and his latest) tends to emphasize formal values, though often with a slightly wry point of view in his choice of somewhat ridiculous architectural subjects, as in *Connecticut Frame House,* 1933 (F 27), *Maine Pump,* 1933 (F 26), an affectionate exploration of the wing of the Wedding Cake House in Kennebunkport, Maine, and *Country Store and Gas Station, Alabama,* 1936 (F 29). Evans can be as earnest as his colleagues in his interest in the human misery which his government assignments covered, and as effective in their presentation. At the same time his pleasure in purely compositional elements and in the often absurd character of his architectural subjects gives his work a personal quality. Consequently, many of his prints transcend the somewhat dated earnestness of others who seem less important now than formerly, largely because their pictures were less carefully composed as works of art. Evans' *View of Easton, Pennsylvania,* 1936 (Illustration 6–82), is as subtly composed in its tension between decorative flat surface and the illusion of depth as a painting by Cézanne or a cubist. Berenice Abbott, essentially a documentary photographer, was less actively concerned with the social problems of her time, but was intensely interested in the pictorial or graphic possibilities of the world of the commonplace, a point of view influenced by her admiration of the French photographer of the turn of the century, Eugène Atget. Abbott has explored New York and other cities in much the same way that Atget scrutinized the everyday scene of Paris, and with nearly as much understated poignancy and concentration on the formal delights of the accidental (see Illustration 4–13). Margaret Bourke-White approaches the documentation of an object with as much clarity and precision as Strand or Weston, in her industrial photographs, such as the *Construction of Fort Peck Dam,* 1936 (F 16), and in her remarkable records of the surface of America as seen from a low-flying aircraft, as in *Contour Plowing; Walsh, Colorado,* 1954 (F 18). At the same time she can become involved in a personal response to human situations, as in her fine study of *Mahatma Gandhi,* 1946 (F 17), and in the various "photo essays" she has done for *Life* magazine. Yet for all her technical brilliance, sympathy with the human condition, and formal sensibility, there is not the consistency of approach which marks the work of artists like Strand, Evans, or Abbott, a fact which derives partly from the nature of journalistic photography itself.

The photographers of the twentieth century discussed so far have followed the esthetic of "straight" photography, to a greater or lesser extent, even though few of them have wanted or have been permitted (due to the exigencies of their assignments) to follow Weston into the cultivation of ultimate refinement, with the loss of more immediate or topical interest. Each year technical devices have been perfected to make this photographic point of view more effective in presentation and more adaptable to the personal artistic projection of the individual artist. The improvements developed in the 1930's, such as more highly sensitive film, higher powered lenses, and the use of the flashbulb and electronic flash, have made possible scientific photographs of split-second events and of the enormously magnified geography of the microscopic world, which can be as fascinating esthetically as any other kind of photography. Technical advances have also brought about improvement in the presentation of the momentary in more conventional photography, as in Barbara Morgan's dance subjects, represented by her *Martha Graham in "Letter to the World,"* 1941 (*F 43).

As a matter of fact, the increase in speed, which permitted such a great degree of spontaneity in catching the unposed subject, amounted to a new and valid dimension in the art of photography. What action photographs may lack in perfection of value contrast, texture, and sometimes even compositional care (arrived at so deliberately by the Weston school), is compensated for by a sense of immediacy, a virtue

6–82. Walker Evans, *View of Easton, Pennsylvania,* 1936. Photograph. (Library of Congress.)

which is essentially photographic, since with the perfection of means to attain it, photography can exploit this aspect of reality also. The work of Alfred Eisenstadt is outstanding in this field, which is well adapted to journalistic photography, for the instantaneous and the unposed is particularly newsworthy. *Life, Look,* and other pictorial magazines have made use of this technique as well as of the more traditional ones (represented by Bourke-White) in picture essays, in which a series of photographs, with words, adds up to a single impact.

Ansel Adams, a younger photographer whose work Stieglitz exhibited in 1936 and who subsequently won a Guggenheim Grant for creative

photography, exemplifies the exploitation of the new techniques within the purest esthetic of the medium, an attitude based on Adams' admiration for Strand. Adams' employment of the most advanced technical equipment and his carefully calculated technique have added to his "straight" photography certain subtle atmospheric effects and the representation of movement in water, cloud, or leaf. Otherwise, Adams is a little less deliberately conscious of formal values, never permitting content to be instigated by form (as is often the case with Weston), but at the same time never presenting subject matter without great formal sensibility, as in the nostalgic and melancholy *Old Building, Bodie, California,*

(Illustration 6–83). The play between rectangle and curve, sunshine and shadow; the variety of texture; and the head-on composition that permits no perspective all give this photograph a purely formal richness comparable to that of an abstract painting. Yet these are only part of a totality that includes the important dimension of associative connotation. Adams' photographs, some of the finest in the history of the medium, have richness and variety (partly due to a greater technical range than that of Weston) yet retain the utmost precision and exactitude (equal to that of Weston himself). These qualities are further enhanced by Adams' attitude toward his subject, which he neither exploits solely for its formal possibilities nor uses

as an expression of his personal emotion, but presents with respect for its own integrity. His photographs range from the "view-box classicism" of the *Courthouse, Bridgeport, California,* 1938 (F 10), and a Strand-like sensibility to texture and value, as in *Grass and Burned Tree,* 1934 (F 7), to more personal records of aspects of nature, done in the late 1930's and the 1940's.

At the time when Weston was perfecting the photographic attitude which has been called "view-box classicism," an antithetical point of view was being developed in Paris by the expatriate American artist Man Ray, which he christened the Rayograph. (Similar work was also being done by Lázló Moholy-Nagy at the Bauhaus and in America after his prewar emi-

6–83. Ansel Adams, *Old Building, Bodie, California.* Photograph. (Wesleyan University, Middletown, Connecticut.)

gration.) To make such a print, objects are arranged on sensitized paper in the dim light of a photographic dark room, and then exposed to strong light, with the result that the space covered by the objects becomes a white or gray silhouette (depending on the extent of contact with the paper), as seen in *Rayograph*, 1923 (F 31). The Rayograph technique was essentially non-photographic since it dispensed with the camera and lens entirely; thus, it would be more appropriate to call it a new technique in the graphic arts than in photography. Ray also distorted the camera image itself by such devices as exposing certain areas of the negative to white light during development, thereby creating black areas in the print which he used as outlines; and by not exposing certain areas at all, which emerged in the print as white patches. Such graphic devices make interesting works of art, as in *Solarization*, 1929 (F 52); yet, though the lens was at least used in their production, they violate the basic esthetic of the medium—which Ray did very deliberately, since by this means he expressed his personal artistic conviction. [Ray can produce as fine a "straight" photograph as many a master of that medium, as in his *Portrait of Pablo Picasso*, 1933 (F 53), and his photograph of the Weston Havens House (Illustration 6–17).]

The realistic esthetic of Strand, either used as "view-box classicism" or adapted to the instantaneous approach or the casualness of the candid camera, is suitable for a variety of personal styles. Among a new generation of photographers who possess sensitivity, originality, and flair are W. Eugene Smith, Harry Callahan, and two outstanding students of Weston, his son Brett, and Minor White. Brett Weston's *Brooklyn Bridge*, 1946 (F 97), has a larger scope and a quite different approach from the work of the elder Weston. Minor White's *Point Lobos*, c. 1947 (*F 100), is equally different from Edward Weston's variations on the themes of that peninsula. White's *Side of Barn With Windows*, 1957 (*F 101), resembles a richer and at the same time a more austere Strand or Adams.

In contrast to work in the classic tradition, to the pseudo-photography of Man Ray, or to the specialized photography exploiting new technical devices, all of which are *sui generis*, there is at present a growing tendency on the part of photographers to fall into the old trap of imitating the figurative arts. Pollock's drippings and Motherwell's large forms are sought for in fortuitous drippings on walls or in the configurations of rocks, as in the photographs of Aaron Siskind. The coalescing blurred rectangles of Rothko and the dynamic effects of Kline and de Kooning are imitated in images made by the dipping or swerving of the camera, by its long exposure at night, and by other devices as inappropriate to the esthetic of the camera as the "combination" salon prints of the 1870's or the fuzzy halos of light in the New England mangers of Gertrude Kasebier at the turn of the century.

Sculpture

The situation in twentieth-century sculpture is quite analogous to that of the graphic arts. At the beginning of the century, and in certain cases almost as late as World War II, sculpture for the most part languished in the tradition of the nineteenth century, undergoing a revolutionary change in the 1930's, and becoming by the mid-1940's completely transformed from a lingering nineteenth-century realism, still strongly seasoned with traces of idealism, into a medium as adventurous in its exploitation of new materials and techniques as is print-making, and as expressive of basically new artistic points of view as is painting.

As in the discussion of painting, a few introductory remarks about the European background of modern sculpture will be helpful. Though painters were the principal initiators and promulgators of modern art in general, sculptors also played an important role, especially Constantin

Brancusi whose abstract formulations of objects and conception of movement brought to sculpture much of the elegant formality of the best of abstract art. The sculptured work of Arp is not dissimilar to Brancusi's, except for its surrealist overtones. Sculptors such as Alexander Archipenko (who moved to the United States in the 1920's) preserved a closer relationship with the analytical approach of cubism. Expressionism (that aspect of it which heightens reality) had several powerful representatives in sculpture, most notably Ernest Barlach who was influenced by the same northern medieval sources that inspired much of the painting of his fellow expressionists. A combination of formal abstraction with the abstract aspects of expressionism and surrealism marks the work of another sculptor who has had great influence on American sculpture of recent years, the Spaniard Julio Gonzalez. This is especially true in his approach to metal, which he uses not so much as solid mass, but more as a material to be treated almost graphically by means of techniques of cutting and welding.

Late Realism

Until the full impact of modern art had made itself felt in the 1920's, with a few exceptions sculpture continued more or less on the path laid out by Augustus Saint-Gaudens and Daniel Chester French, with the injection of a greater naturalism stemming from the influence of the great Frenchman, Auguste Rodin.

Paul Wayland Bartlett brought the competent naturalism and decorativeness of late nineteenth-century French academic sculpture to his work in the pediment of the House of Representatives at the Capitol, *Democracy Protecting the Arts of Peace*, 1909–1916 (SC 181). Dynamically composed, decorative and lively in its contrasts of light and dark, it is one of the most successful of numerous competent Beaux-Arts pedimental sculptures adorning banks and official buildings across the nation. One of the most skilled of the French-influenced group was Charles Grafly, whose allegorical nudes were not as vapid as their sisters painted in the murals of the time, since they retained something of the strength and

surety of the French tradition, plus a certain forthrightness derived from study of anatomy with Eakins at the Pennsylvania Academy. Grafly's *General Meade Memorial* in Washington, 1915–1925 (SC 183), is therefore less cloying in its allegorical treatment than is usual in such cases, and Meade himself is well realized. An even greater naturalism comes through in Grafly's portrait busts, which are strikingly realistic, as in his bronze portrait of *Frank Duveneck*, 1915 (SC 182).

The greatest American sculptor of the early twentieth century—one of the last important representatives of a dying tradition—was George Grey Barnard, a master of the expressive nude. Years of study in Paris, and the influence of Rodin's naturalism and Michelangelo's expressiveness formed his early style, represented in the vigorous and powerful *Struggle of Two Natures*, 1905 (The Metropolitan Museum, New York). In the sculpture for the State Capitol at Harrisburg, Pennsylvania, he achieved not only the perennial (but usually unfulfilled) wish of all sculptors, the opportunity to execute a really monumental commission, but also brought to a culmination, for our time certainly, the use of the nude as an expressive vehicle for human emotion. It is of course still the academic and representational nude, though with the exaggerated naturalism of Rodin. Barnard rejected, however, the picturesque surface modeling characteristic of Rodin's somewhat impressionistic realism, retaining a solider glyptic sense.

Another exponent of Rodin's naturalism who was possessed of enough personal force to exploit that master's handling of large rhythms and masses in a personal way was Gutzon Borglum. Among the most interesting commemorative statues in the history of American sculpture is his seated portrait, in the Sculpture Hall of the Capitol, of *Alexander Hamilton Stephens*, 1906 (Illustration 6–84), Vice-President of the Confederacy, and governor and post-Civil War senator from Georgia. Comparison with the mass of ill-assorted figures surrounding it shows this statue to be far superior to all of them in sculpturesque and expressive power. But even without this advantage, the *Stephens* is a remarkable portrait,

6–84. Gutzon Borglum, *Alexander Hamilton Stephens,* 1906. Statuary Hall, The Capitol, Washington, D. C. Marble.

capturing the nervous energy and physical weakness of this lame little "human steam engine," as Stephens was called, with his pock-marked face, agitated eyes, determined mouth, and his intense hands grasping the chair arms. The work is basically realistic but the physical and spiritual characteristics of the sitter are so underlined that it is almost expressionistic.

Unfortunately, the megalomania which seems endemic to many great sculptors afflicted Borglum in the form of a desire to express himself in a grandiose scale. This is first seen in the head of Lincoln in the Rotunda of the Capitol; it is so huge that it dwarfs every other representation of humanity in the building. The tremendous energy and ambition of Borglum led him eventually to do what no man before him had ever done, to

carve an entire mountain into the semblance of men, the *Presidents* on Mount Rushmore in the Black Hills of South Dakota.

Before turning to the more modern sculpture of Paul Manship and his imitators, mention should be made of two rather unusual but not prolific sculptors, Mahonri M. Young, also a painter and graphic artist, and Henry Shrady, who is known for only one monument, the Grant Memorial in Washington, after the completion of which he died. Young's figures of laborers and men represented in all kinds of activity, including boxers, are not only influenced by Rodin but are even reminiscent of the small bronzes of certain masters of the early Renaissance who were also devoted to the expression of energy. The bronze *Man With Pick,* 1915 (SC 119), is typical.

Shrady's bronze *Grant Memorial,* completed in 1922 (Illustration 6–85), is not only an impressive work of art because of its intrinsic merit, its great size, and its prominent position on the Mall at Washington, but it is also a kind of summation of the history of American sculpture from before the Civil War to the time of its execution. It embodies the idealism of Saint-Gaudens, the decorative liveliness of MacMonnies, and the naturalism and expressiveness of Barnard and Borglum. The large figure of Grant sits silent, brooding, and canny on his horse in the midst of such violent military action that it is no wonder the work took seventeen years to plan and execute. The subsidiary sculptural groups have been criticized because of their excessive realism and lack of sculpturesque character, but this realism is so embedded in an all-over dynamism of design and simulated action that the result is almost comparable to the baroque conceptions of the seventeenth century which are equally "unsculpturesque." Representationalism reaches a height of competence and expression in this work, which is a formidable performance even from the vantage point of today, when such accomplishment is denigrated or even ignored.

Two other sculptors later on in the century who belonged essentially to the realistic tradition are Malvina Hoffman and Jo Davidson. Hoffman's industry and perspicacious accuracy are

6–85. Henry Shrady, *Grant Memorial* (detail), 1922. The Mall, Washington, D. C. Bronze.

seen in her portraits, such as the bronze *Paderew-ski, the Artist: Head,* 1923 (*SC 59), and in the impressive collection of ethnic types executed in bronze for the Field Museum at Chicago, begun in 1930. Davidson crossed his realism with the expressionistic exaggeration of such artists as the American-born English sculptor Jacob Epstein, and the formal simplifications of modern art in general. These characteristics are well demonstrated in the almost hieratic bronze figure of *Gertrude Stein,* 1920 (SC 26), and in many other incisive and impressive portraits. The influence of Epstein's strongly modeled style, derived somewhat from Rodin but raised to a higher power of plasticity and psychic penetration, has continued to be an active ingredient in American sculpture, as seen in the work of Minna R. Harkavy and Anna Glenny.

The Beginnings of Modernism

It is, however, the formal rather than the expressionistic aspect of modern art which made the first strong impact on American sculpture, though at first quite superficially. The appeal of the archaic, primitive, and exotic, which had motivated the protomodernism of Gauguin and stimulated the early work of Matisse, the Fauves, and the German expressionists, acted as a catalyst to turn American sculpture from its realistic course. The glyptic sense and elegant linearism of archaic Greek sculpture, and the equally graceful and rhythmic character of the art of India exerted a strong influence on Paul Manship who in the 1920's still seemed to be the most contemporary of American sculptors. His bronze *Dancer and Gazelles,* 1916 (SC 82), sums up the graceful charm of his work, which is extremely competent in its casting and engaging in its content, but finally simply decorative—a judgment which would not have been made so easily at the time the statue was executed, for it must have appeared very advanced when compared with contemporaneous realism. Meanwhile, Manship seems to have become increasingly academic, with the result that his work, though remaining attractively and effectively decorative, as demonstrated in the popular *Prometheus* at the Lower Plaza of Rockefeller Center, New York, 1933 (SC 83), has come to represent a kind of official sculpture which holds the ,fort of traditionalism against the onslaughts of more original and experimental work. A similar formalism, perhaps a little more deliberate, informs the work of Alfeo Faggi, whose monument to St. Francis in San Francisco [a smaller bronze version, 1915 (SC 39), is at the Albright-Knox Gallery in Buffalo] is a simplified draped human form made more visually effective by its studied planes and relationships of surfaces. The sometime painter Maurice Stern is equally sophisticated in his planar simplifications in the bronze head entitled *The Bomb Thrower*, 1910–1914 (SC 171), and in the composition of figures in one of the few monuments to be erected between the wars, *Monument to the Early Settlers*, bronze and stone, 1927–1929 (SC 172), at Elm Park, Worcester, Massachusetts. Actually more related to European formalism than any of these artists was Elie Nadelman, a Pole who, having worked in Paris from 1903–1914 (years which were so important in the development of modern art), came to this country in 1915. Though his bronze *Wounded Bull*, 1915 (*SC 86), shows some of the devices of the interpenetrating planes and tensions of cubist sculpture, it is primarily decorative. His other figures are more pneumatic than volumetric, as in the *Man in the Open Air*, c. 1915 (SC 85), which in spite of its bronze medium looks more like rounded wood. Such figures as these, however, have a kind of prim coyness which must reflect the sculptor's interest in American folk sculpture, particularly the wooden dolls of the nineteenth century. Nadelman's *Sur la Plage*, c. 1917 (SC 154), of bronze

and marble, is even more mannered than Manship's work in its sinuous charm, and is eclectic in its reminiscence of various periods in the history of art.

Another émigré, Gaston Lachaise, supplemented his training at the École des Beaux Arts in Paris by working later as an assistant to Manship. He developed, however, into an artist of independent stature, bringing an increasingly contemporary accent to his work. To the Beaux Arts tradition of the human figure, he added an exaggerated voluptuousness which seems mannered to some critics and monumental to others. It is expressed in rotund, slim-waisted bodies poised grandly on tiny feet and slender ankles, as in the life-sized *Standing Woman*, bronze, 1912–1927 (SC 68), a svelte and civilized version of the ancient fertility figures. A sense of rhythm, together with a decorative refinement and a technical brilliance derived from association with Manship, characterizes Lachaise's bronze *Dolphin Fountain*, 1924 (SC 141), and the glittering, curved, and elegant bronze and nickel-plated *Head*, 1928 (SC 142). Two other pieces show a more impressive originality: the bronze *Floating Figure*, 1927, cast in 1935 (SC 66), and *Torso*, 1930 (SC 143). In the first a heavy-thighed, ponderously breasted creature is miraculously poised on a small surface, only barely touching it; she can almost be thought of as being not weighty but inflated. *Torso* is a frank abstraction of Lachaise's ideal female, with the meaty rotundities of the thighs, buttocks, and breasts held together by the thinnest of waists. Lachaise shows an unexpected realist–expressionist strain in the spontaneously executed bronze head of the painter *John Marin*, 1928 (SC 67), in which the subject's Yankee eccentricity is penetratingly portrayed.

The influence of Manship is more clearly noticed in such artists as W. Hunt Diederich, whose bronze *Jockey*, 1924 (SC 33), has a mannered grace and finished elegance that are more superficial than the work of Lachaise. In the 1920's, a reaction against the smooth finish and modeling of the current treatment of bronze found expression in the return to the direct carving of stone, a reaction led by the powerful artistic personality of William Zorach, who turned from painting to sculpture (in which he was self-taught) in 1924. Under the double stimulus of the formal discoveries of abstract art and a return to the appreciation of the character of the medium and its tools (also inherent in the contemporary point of view), he embarked on a career as a sculptor, and his productivity is hardly matched in the history of the art in America. Finding analogies to his own taste in the stone carvings of the Egyptians and the Romanesque sculptors, and supplementing these inspirations with the discipline of abstract formalism, he created images which are by no means merely formal or decorative, but have considerable expressive power. The effectiveness of their emotional communication is aided by the eloquence of the medium itself, which is employed in such a way that its particular qualities are enhanced in its treatment. The almost classical order and sense of containment seen in Zorach's group sculptures, especially *Mother and Child,* 1927–1930 (SC 122), in Spanish marble, or *The Future Generation,* 1942–1947 (SC 175), in Botticini marble, are due as much to his strong grasp of abstract design as to emulation of the carvers of antiquity. The basic similarity between these two groups, executed more than a decade apart, points also to the continuity of Zorach's style. However, the female figure in *Torso,* 1932 (SC 176), in Labrador granite, is very different both in form and texture from *Victory,* 1945 (SC 123), in French marble. The first is graceful, tapering, and almost abstract; the other is more svelte and linear, recalling just sufficiently the Nikes or Victories of antiquity. The early *Floating Figure,* 1922 (SC 121), in African mahogany, is as poised and wonderfully balanced as Lachaise's figure of the same title. Zorach's stonework is glyptic, as is borne out by the brash stoniness of the much later *Head of Moses,* granite, 1953 (SC 177).

A number of sculptors who came into prominence in the 1920's and early 1930's shared Zorach's enthusiasm for the direct approach to the medium. Among them are Reuben Nakian, Heinz Warneke, and Aaron Ben-Schmuel. Robert Laurent also followed Zorach's lead, not only in his treatment of the medium, as seen in

6–86.   John B. Flannagan, *Dragon Motif,* 1932. Bluestone. Length: 12½ inches. (Collection of Miss Eleanor Wolff, New York.)

the alabaster *The Wave,* 1926 (SC 72), but in his personal style, for his much later bronze *Kneeling Figure,* 1935 (SC 144), recalls similar figures by Zorach.

John B. Flannagan, another direct carver who worked mostly in stone, was also influenced by Zorach's style in his early work. Flannagan soon found a more personal and romantic style, however, which makes him one of the more significant figures in American sculpture before World War II. Flannagan's feeling for the medium of stone becomes almost the content of his work. He himself said that his aim was "to produce [sculpture] with such ease, freedom and simplicity that it hardly seems carved but rather to have endured always." [63] Flannagan's shapes, which have a kind of primordial simplicity and inevitability, are enhanced by his habit of choosing stones so formed that they are ready to express the artist's idea with very little additional shaping. His figures seem to emerge from the rock as the creature emerges from the granite egg in the *Triumph of the Egg, I,* 1937 (SC 42), or the dragon from the stone in *Dragon Motif,* 1932 (Illustration 6–86); or they are incorporated in it as is the flat bluestone whale in *Jonah and the Whale: Rebirth Motif,* 1937 (SC 40A), which needed little changing to be the vehicle for the Jonah incised in its belly. The themes of birth and of emergence and return are as primitive as the treatment of the stone, and combine with it to produce a statement which is often quite poignant in the specificity of its observation. Flannagan's later work done in Ireland, where he sought some atavistic comfort before his death, is more conscious in its effect and not quite as convincing, though still powerful in its imagery.

The work of Jose de Creeft is also remarkable for the expression of the character of the medium, again mostly stone, as in *Maya,* 1937 (?) (SC 127, *SC 127A), of black Belgian granite, and *Cloud,* 1937 (SC 29), of green stone. They are two very different conceptions, the former being as dense and hard as a stylized Amerindian figure, the other almost light and transparent. In *Saturnia,* 1939 (SC 28), a relief in hammered lead, the muted sheen of the material is effectively exploited in the heavy figures. On the whole, in comparison with Zorach and especially with Flannagan, de Creeft is too obvious in the sources of his inspiration from primitive art. This could not be said of Chaim Gross, whose bulbous and convoluted forms are *sui generis,* and are also somewhat related to the given character of the material, as in the bumptiously lively *Handlebar Riders,* 1935 (SC 52), carved in lignum vitae, and in the more refined but still protuberant *Reflection,* 1954 (SC 135), in pink alabaster. Among other sculptors who found a personal style during the 1930's through the exploitation of the medium are Bernard Reder, noted for his splendidly massive female *Torso,* limestone, 1938 (SC 96), Hugo Robus, and Emma Lu Davis. The last two evidence the influence of Brancusi (who reduced his forms to basic shapes and rhythms, while refining his surface to the utmost), who had been in New York in 1926.

On the whole it is remarkable how little abstract or semiabstract sculpture was produced in America until the great outburst of creative activity after the Second World War. This is probably due to the fact that experimental and original sculpture was relatively neglected by those in a position to give commissions; they were almost invariably dealt out to the artists of the National Sculpture Society, the followers of Manship's eclectic quasi-modernism, most of whose work, though executed so recently, is forgotten now. Originality languished, though there was enough interest to support fine sculptors like Lachaise and Zorach.

There was one artist, however, whose creative originality made up for all the rest—Alexander Calder. In fact, Calder's conception of lightness (as opposed to weight) and movement as being proper concerns of sculpture is as revolutionary as any in the history of art, and has had an enormous progeny, the most distinguished of which still remains Calder's own. His work is a felicitous combination of European influence with a thoroughly American temperament. Calder began as an original but not very profound artist with a nice sense of whimsy and a talent for gadgetry, as illustrated in the amusing *Horse,* 1928 (SC 15), in walnut, composed of folk art shapes and put together like a Tinker Toy, and the witty *Hostess* of the same year (SC 16), a kind of line drawing in twisted wire. The discovery of the abstract compositions of Mondrian, which Calder soon peopled with the biomorphic forms of Miró and Arp and made three-dimensional, opened up undreamed-of possibilities for his enthusiastic inventiveness, which was now no longer constricted by the requirements of representationalism. The free forms and automatic improvisations of surrealism, and the carefully constructed framework of abstract art were used by Calder as a springboard for an ingenious and ingenuous inventiveness in which a Yankee mechanical "know-how" was joined with a witty fancy to produce some of the most engaging objects of our time, objects which have now become part of our environment, fitting in perfectly with the dynamism of the age. For Calder's sculpture moves. At first he made it move mechanically by means of little motors, but later he refined his balance and interrelationships so precisely that his mobiles (as he called them) of wire-supported disks and other shapes undulate like foliage in every breath of air. Sometimes they are representational to a certain degree, as is *Lobster Trap and Fish Tail,* 1939 (Illustration 6–87), which has delighted nearly a generation

new wa
is stron
realism
charact
that of

Study
admirat
early w
(SC 90
its slab:
the mec
the sim]
the con
ism, bec
uration
1949 (S
but bot
niscent
sionism,
variatio
Miró. I
lithic st
the grou
surance
More re
Kasama
for Japa
tall decc
realist o

David
and is p
sculptur
native, f
of Euroj
and eve:
time, Sn
bolic cor
appeal t
spatial a
for spec
personal
may be
techniqu
which a
brazed.
can be t
ground i
ism simi
must als

6–87. Alexander Calder, *Lobster Trap and Fish Tail,* 1939. Mobile. Steel wire and sheet aluminum. Height: c. 8½ feet; diameter, c. 9½ feet. (Collection, The Museum of Modern Art, New York. Gift of the Advisory Committee.)

ot visitors to the Museum of Modern Art in New York, where it hangs conspicuously in the main staircase. Sometimes they are completely abstract, as in *Red Gongs,* executed before 1955 (SC 19). Usually some reference to organic or natural life is hinted at, but even when this is not the case, his mobiles are not merely mechanical; they are always playful. These artistic playthings are a delightful comment on the mechanization of our times, for here are machines executed with as much ingenuity as the better mouse traps and clocks produced by earlier Connecticut Yankees, though Calder's are ostentatiously and completely useless. To accuse Calder of lack of seriousness, as is often done, is to deny the sig-

nificance of play. Calder, therefore, makes the third of a trio consisting of Klee, Miró, and himself, who are to a large degree concerned with the free play of fancy, wit, and humor, so closely related to the basic spiritual energy and vitality emanating from the unconscious.

Calder's work is not limited to mobiles. His "stabiles" are nearly as interesting, if not quite so original. The formal inventiveness and variety of the sheared, bent, and welded shapes, and the excitement of their juxtapositions combine to create images which are not always funny, though fanciful. Sometimes Calder creates veritable presences out of his "stabiles," as in *Spiny,* in sheet aluminum, 1942 (SC 17).

Calder's ingenuity and inventiveness continue. Color has come to play an increasingly important role, his work has become even gayer, and recently he has added sound to his mobiles.

For sculpture, the period after the war (and the years just before it) was one of preparation for the future, as it was in the case of painting and the graphic arts. The W. P. A. Art Project and the arrival in America of European artists [64] acted as catalysts for the stirrings of the sculptural Renaissance, just as they had done in the other figurative arts. Chaim Gross and other important sculptors of the 1930's had been connected with the Art Project, as had Raoul Hague and others who were to become prominent after the war.

The Europeans

Among the European sculptors who came to the United States and were influential in the postwar development of American sculpture were Naum Gabo and Jacques Lipschitz. Gabo arrived in America at the end of the war, in 1946. His *Construction,* 1951–1952 (SC 45), of plastic and wire; *Construction in Space,* 1953 (SC 46), of plastic; and *Construction,* 1956 (SC 47), of lucite, plastic, and metals, are late examples of a style which found its final development in the United States. Both before the war, previous to Gabo's emigration, and afterward, his work and his constructivist theories (which he had promulgated with his brother, Pevsner) have been important factors in the development

given work space in the industrial village of Voltri. The incorporation of abandoned tools into these sculptures enriched Smith's formal vocabulary, lending piquancy to his geometric calligraphy, which, just before his recent death, was at its most powerfully expressive.

Seymour Lipton is another pioneering figure in the use of metal in original ways. In this respect he is not as revolutionary as Smith, however, though the total impact of his work is perhaps more powerful, being more single-minded. Drawn by a need as strong as that of Smith to express his feelings, his content is direct and simple, realized in forms "that have a catalystic force growing from an ambiguous but strongly felt fountainhead of Nature," but forms which also have the "sense of the dark inside, the evil of things, the hidden areas of struggle." [66] In Lipton's work this struggle propels itself in a convoluted energy which seems to force its way through the somber massiveness of the steel in brutally shaped contours. Lipton's metal is not as open and pierced as Smith's, or as that of the other sculptural "draftsmen," but it is used with as much inventiveness in its spiraling and shredded forms. *Menorah*, in nickel-silver on steel, 1954 (SC 77), at Temple Israel, Tulsa, Oklahoma, sums up Lipton's formal qualities and his personal style, but is more restrained and generalized than usual. *The Prophet*, 1956 (SC 78), nickel-silver on monel metal, is infused with the violence and passion of his earlier work, but made more telling perhaps because of its more specific reference.

Ibram Lassaw began to devise delicate metal cages at about the same time that Smith and Lipton were forging their personal idioms. Titles like *Clouds of Magellan*, 1953 (in Philip Johnson's Guest House, at Canaan, Connecticut), and *Galaxie of Andromeda* (Collection of Nelson A. Rockefeller) suggest in words the fragile space nets of which Lassaw's work is composed, which seem to be three-dimensional explorations of Tobey's "white written" two-dimensional world. The *Kwannon*, 1952 (SC 70), contrived of welded bronze and silver, is an ineffable oriental presence, a tenuously balanced construct or maze of interpenetrating rectangles; *Procession*,

6–89. David Smith, *Voltron XVIII*, 1961. Steel and iron. Height: 110⅞ inches. (Marlborough-Gerson Gallery, New York.)

1955–1956 (*SC 71A), wire, copper, bronze, and silver, is a scintillating enfilade of attenuated figures. Lassaw's *Pillar of Fire*, 1952–1953, at Temple Beth El, Springfield, Massachusetts, is more effective as monumental sculpture, because of its scale and its use of larger, more sweepingly inclusive motifs. Lassaw's decoration in Philip Johnson's Kneses Tifereth Synagogue, Portchester, New York, is less successful, for it seems inappropriately small in scale, overly busy, and too casual in its rectilinearity to be placed in the midst of such serene and perfect geometry.

These three very individual talents in the nontraditional use of metal, Smith, Lipton, and Lassaw, were the immediate precursors of a group of artists with similar sculptural intent. The most prominent of these are Herbert Ferber, Theodore Roszak, David Hare, and Richard Lippold. Arriving at a personal expression about 1949, Ferber integrated the symbols of his private world with forms of the outer one in artistic metaphors which are not dissimilar to those achieved by Gorky in his painting. Emotionally stimulating, his shapes and their arrangement in space are always fresh in their fanciful variety. His compositions are arrived at by proceeding from cursory sketches through a working model, from which he approaches the final sculpture with a battery of instruments for cutting, perforating, bending, hammering, and welding. Ferber works in this way not so much in a spirit of reproducing a preconceived idea (though this may have been his starting point), as with a mind open to the suggestions of the tools and materials themselves as they are being manipulated. This combination of psychic image with the exploitation of the accidents of process relates Ferber's work to that of the abstract expressionists in its strong surrealist ingredients. The personal imagery of his spikey and claw-like forms—delicate or heavy, tenuous or bulging, sometimes enmeshed in spiral cages, as in *Sun Wheel*, 1956 (SC 129), in brass, copper, and silver solder; or flickering around a pivot as in *The Flame*, 1959 (SC 43), in brass, lead, and soft solder—places Ferber among the most original and expressive American artists of today. Ferber's manner is particularly adapted to the statement of religious themes. Like Lassaw, Ferber has done work for synagogues, for which his style seems quite appropriate. Certainly the intensity of feeling expressed in his jagged, writhing forms are most successfully utilized in the semiabstract plant and flame motifs in *"and the bush was not consumed"* for the facade of Congregation B'Nai Israel, Millburn, New Jersey, 1951 (SC 44). Lately Ferber's work has become more tenuous and light: thin wafers and ribbons in which he has evolved new solutions in a characteristically spontaneous and personal way.

Like Picasso, Lipschitz, and many other artists, the pressure of world events drove Theodore Roszak from serene rectilinear reliefs executed in an abstract style, represented by *Vertical Construction*, painted wood and plastic, 1943 (SC 165A), to a semirepresentational style made up of forms which he intended to be "blunt reminders of those brute forces that not only produced life but in turn threaten to destroy it." [67] *Spectre of Kitty Hawk*, 1946–1947 (SC 99; Illustration 6–90), with its brutal and horned shapes welded and hammered from steel and glistening threateningly with brazed bronze and brass, is a frighteningly effective commentary on the misuse of the Wright brothers' invention to destroy humanity by bombardment. Later works, barbed and forbidding, are like modern totemic figures not too specific in reference, but filled with meaning for our own time, as in *Sea Sentinel*, 1956 (SC 166), of steel with brazed bronze. The technical skill represented in Roszak's now fluid, now an-

6–90. Theodore Roszak, *Spectre of Kitty Hawk,* 1946–1947. Welded and hammered steel brazed with bronze and brass. Height: 40¼ inches. (Collection, The Museum of Modern Art, New York. Purchase.)

Stonecutters, which is one of the most amusing as well as scholarly works on American art.

36 Gardner, note 35 *supra,* p. 22.

37 Quoted in Gardner, note 35 *supra,* p. 22.

38 Quoted in Oliver W. Larkin, *Art and Life in America* (New York: 1960), p. 181.

39 Quoted in Gardner, note 35 *supra,* p. 47.

40 Quoted in Gardner, note 35 *supra,* p. 71, from D. M. Armstrong, *Day before Yesterday* (1920).

41 Lorado Taft, *The History of American Sculpture* (New York: 1925), p. 54.

42 Quoted in Gardner, note 35 *supra,* p. 25, from C. Sumner, "Crawford's Orpheus," *United States Magazine and Democratic Review* (May, 1843).

43 A sonnet, of which these lines are a part:
"Appeal Fair Stone and strike and shame the strong By thunder of white silence overthrown."

44 Quoted in Gardner, note 35 *supra,* p. 35, from James, note 45 *infra.*

45 Henry James, *William Wetmore Story and His Friends,* 2 vols. (Boston: 1903).

46 Nathaniel Hawthorne, *The Marble Faun* (Boston: 1860), p. 182 in 1871 ed.

47 Gardner, note 35 *supra,* p. 35.

48 Nina Fletcher Little, "Mathew M. Prior, Travelling Artist," *Antiques,* LIV, 1 (1948), 44–48.

49 Musée du Jeu de Paume, *Trois Siècles d'Art aux États-Unis* (Paris: 1938), p. 23.

50 Alice Ford, *Edward Hicks, Painter of the Peaceable Kingdom* (Philadelphia: 1952), p. 29.

51 One other form of folk or popular carving should be mentioned, though most surviving examples postdate the Civil War: that is, circus and carousel carving. The early work of Samuel Robb (an erstwhile carver of trade signs and steamboat ornaments) for P. T. Barnum's circus wagons in the 1870's, has a kind of lissome charm in the elongated, rhythmic figures of his nymphs and other allegorical female figures. This restrained elegance was soon to be followed, however, by a gayer, more lavish mood of showmanship, as seen in the magnificently garish and vulgar wagon now preserved at the circus' headquarters at Sarasota, Florida. In contrast to the circus wagon figures, which are flat and primarily used in decorative panels, the carousel figures are three-dimensional. At their best, these figures, usually animals, have a lively gait or stance, and their realism is combined with a decorative rhythm of body, head, and tail. Some are almost baroque in their lavish ornament and dynamic, wheeling forms. The *Goat,* 1870, preserved at the Shelburne Museum, Shelburne, Vermont, is a typical example. These carved animals are among the last manifestations of the old craft tradition, already turning to more naturalistic forms. Trade signs, hitching posts, weather vanes, and carved ornamental figures were soon replaced by mass-produced iron castings. Only wooden decoys, still preferably hand-made, persist to represent today an important art form overwhelmed, like other folk art, by the consequences of the Industrial Revolution.

52 Some authorities date this figure about 1900. The assistant curator of the Taylor Museum has informed the author that José Lopez of Loredo, New Mexico, who died in 1938 at a little past 60 years of age, stated that the figure was made by his grandfather in about 1850.

Part Five: From the Civil War to 1900

For Part Five the author has depended chiefly on the following: for architecture, Charles Condit's *The Rise of the Skyscraper,* Henry-Russell Hitchcock's *Henry Hobson Richardson,* Hugh Morrison's *Louis Sullivan,* and Vincent Scully's *The Shingle Style;* for painting, Lloyd Goodrich's *Thomas Eakins* and *Winslow Homer,* and Albert Ten Eyck Gardner's *Winslow Homer.*

1 Vernon Louis Parrington, *Main Currents in American Thought,* Book IV (New York: 1950), p. 13.

2 Henry-Russell Hitchcock, *The Architecture of H. H. Richardson and His Times* (New York: 1936), p. 202.

3 Charles Price, "Henry Hobson Richardson, Some Unpublished Drawings," *Perspecta 9/10: The Yale Architectural Journal* (New Haven: 1965), pp. 204–208.

4 "The Tall Office Building Artistically Considered," *Lippincott's Magazine,* LVII (March, 1896), p. 403.

5 The characteristics of *art nouveau* have been abbreviated from a thorough analysis in Stephan Tschudi Madsen's *Sources of Art Nouveau* (New York: 1955).

6 Hugh Morrison, *Louis Sullivan* (New York: 1935), pp. 125–126.

7 David Gebhard, "Louis Sullivan and George Grant Elmslie," *Journal of the Society of Architectural Historians,* XIX, 2 (1960), pp. 62–68.

8 The author is indebted to Samuel Huiet Greybill's unpublished Ph.D. dissertation (Yale University, 1957), *Bruce Price, American Architect,* for much of the information on Price.

9 L. S. Buffington's design for a skyscraper in Minneapolis is, in point of fact, a very clear statement of the tower principle before Price, as is also the much less tall (only ten stories) Tower Building, 1888–1889, in New York.

10 The use of the term "Chicago school," popularized by Carl Condit, has been called into question by more than one critic who feels that it is too exclusive. For a general survey, however, the term is still useful.

11 Charles C. Baldwin, *Stanford White* (New York: 1931), p. 362.

12 *Ibid.,* p. 363.

13 A word should be said about La Farge's work as the

author of stained glass windows, an interest to which the artist's involvement in the decoration of churches led him. Dissatisfaction with current practice caused him not only to design but to execute his own windows, one of the results of which was the development of a kind of opalescent glass of his own invention. La Farge's rich color sense and decorative talent found a natural affirmation in stained glass and his work was in demand not only for churches but for private homes as well. La Farge's windows were much admired during the artist's lifetime and recently there has been a revived interest in them—one of them, *Welcome*, is now conspicuously displayed in The Metropolitan Museum of Art, New York. But in this medium, even more than in his paintings, La Farge's inconsistencies can be seen, as, for instance, in the jarring contrast between flat areas of color, similar to those of medieval windows, and areas of extreme realism, modeled three-dimensionally with all the subtlety of tonal oil painting. Such a contrast of styles is difficult to understand in a man of the sensitivity of La Farge, who surely knew and admired the great thirteenth-century French windows at Chartres.

14   Samuel Isham, *The History of American Painting* (New York: 1905), p. 472.

15   Edgar P. Richardson, *Painting in America* (New York: 1956), pp. 357–358.

16   Elizabeth McCausland, *George Inness* (New York: 1946), p. 65.

17   *Ibid.,* p. 472.

18   The work of this school, almost unknown outside Italy, has a proto-impressionist freshness, brilliance of color, and spontaneity of brush work, together with a persistence of the denser texture and heavier pigment of early realism.

19   Whistler's prints are discussed with the graphic arts.

20   Mary Cassatt's prints are discussed with the graphic arts.

21   Quoted in Oliver W. Larkin, *Art and Life in America* (New York: 1949), p. 302.

22   Frederick A. Sweet, *Sargent, Whistler and Mary Cassatt* (Chicago: 1954), p. 65.

23   Richardson, note 15 *supra*, p. 356.

24   Hassam's etchings are among the most successful by the impressionists anywhere, since he kept the evanescent quality of light, yet retained linear structure. (Since his etchings were done in the twentieth century they are discussed in Part Six.)

25   Quoted in Henry James, *The Painter's Eye,* etc. Selected and edited with an introduction by John L. Sweeney (Cambridge, Mass.: 1956), p. 97, from Henry James, "On Some Pictures Lately Exhibited," *The Galaxy* (July, 1875).

26   William Howe Downes, *The Life and Works of Winslow Homer* (Boston and New York: 1911), p. 11.

27   Quoted in Larkin, note 21 *supra*, p. 301, from William Dean Howells' *Criticism and Fiction* (1891), chap. XXI.

28   Downes, note 26 *supra*, p. 15.

29   James, note 25 *supra*, p. 97.

30   *Ibid.*

31   *Ibid.*

32   *Ibid.*

33   Mention should be made of Winslow Homer's few etchings, which, though essentially reproductive (since all but one of the published ones are copied from his oil-painted marines), are worthy of passing note as the work of an important artist. Large in size, they have the characteristic power of the master, reproducing in many lines—almost with the precision of an engraving—the large volumes and spatial nuances of his painting, as can be seen in the *Life Line*, 1884 (°GB 516). Though quite outside the contemporaneous trend in etching toward terse statement in a few lines, these prints by Homer have, on the other hand, none of the perfunctory facility almost inevitable in most reproductive etching.

34   In this connection it is interesting to know how Homer himself felt about the relative importance of subject matter. Referring to his *Gulf Stream* he writes in a typically crusty letter dated February 1, 1901, to his dealer in New York, M. Knoedler & Co. [quoted in *Art in America*, LIII, 4 (August–September, 1965), p. 56] as follows:

> "I regret very much that I have painted a picture that requires any description. The subject of the picture is comprised in its title and I will refer these inquisitive schoolmarms to Lt. Maury.

> "I have crossed the Gulf Stream *ten* times and I should know something about it. The boat and sharks are outside matters of very little consequence. *They have been blown out to sea by a hurricane.* You can tell these ladies that the unfortunate Negro who now is so dazed and parboiled will be rescued and returned to his friends and home, and ever after live happily."

35   Lloyd Goodrich, *Thomas Eakins* (New York: 1933), p. 123.

36   *Ibid.,* p. 17.

37   *Ibid.,* p. 28.

38   *Ibid.,* p. 18. Though not referring specifically to Rembrandt, the context is clear.

39   Lloyd Goodrich, *Albert Pinkham Ryder* (New York: 1959), p. 15.

40   *Ibid.,* p. 22.

41   Herman Melville, *Moby Dick* (London edition, Oxford University Press: 1958), p. 6.

42   Goodrich, note 39 *supra*, p. 23.

43   From a letter from Ryder written to Thomas B. Clarke, a major collector of American art, in April, 1855 [quoted in *Art in America*, LIII, 4 (August–September, 1965), p. 62].

44   Goodrich, note 39 *supra*, p. 16.

45   See Glossary.

sentational but quite strange, depicting mannequin-like dolls in odd poses and situations.

34 From an autobiographical manuscript in the possession of the Whitney Museum of American Art, New York.

35 *Ibid.*

36 *Ibid.*

37 The little-known work of a contemporary of Schamburg and a friend of F. Scott Fitzgerald, Gerald Murphy, though not picturing the machine, is not unlike that of Schamburg and Léger in its diagrammatic aspects. Both in their large size and their celebration of mass-produced objects, Murphy's paintings are premonitory of the "pop" art of the 1960's.

38 Museum of Modern Art, New York, *Charles Sheeler* (New York: 1939), p. 8.

39 *Ibid.*

40 Museum of Modern Art, New York, *Edward Hopper Retrospective Exhibition* (New York: 1933), p. 17.

41 *Ibid.*

42 *Ibid.*

43 *Ibid.*, p. 16.

44 John I. H. Baur, *Charles Burchfield* (New York: 1956). (Caption by Burchfield for Illustration 21.)

45 Museum of Modern Art, New York, *John Marin* (New York: 1936), p. 28.

46 *John Marin: A Retrospective Exhibition, 1947* (Boston: Institute of Modern Art, 1947), p. 27.

47 E. M. Benson, *John Marin, The Man and his Work* (Washington: 1935), p. 107. (Quotation from "John Marin by Himself" written originally for the magazine *Creative Art.*)

48 Museum of Modern Art, New York, *Americans 1942* (New York: 1942), p. 51.

49 Both terms were familiarized by Alfred Barr of the Museum of Modern Art.

50 Although generally accepted, the term "abstract expressionism" is not altogether satisfactory, for it covers a number of disparate artistic styles. Yet it is broader than "action painting" (which is an inappropriate description of the static meditative work of some of the group) or "School of New York," which is geographically too limiting.

51 Occasionally there occur references to appearance or compromises with it, as in de Kooning's series of women [represented by *Woman I*, 1950–1952 (PC 108)].

52 Werner Haftmann, *Painting in the Twentieth Century* (New York: 1960).

53 Harold Rosenberg, *The Tradition of the New* (New York: 1959), p. 32.

54 Paul Klee, *On Modern Art* (London: 1945), p. 69.

55 *Albright Art Gallery Bulletin,* Buffalo, N. Y. (November, 1959).

56 This term is that of John I. H. Baur, used in Lloyd Goodrich and John I. H. Baur, *American Art of Our Century* (New York: 1961).

57 Also a term used by Baur; *ibid.*

58 Goodrich and Baur, note 56 *supra.*

59 *Albright Art Gallery Bulletin,* note 55 *supra.*

60 Goodrich and Baur, note 56 *supra,* p. 220.

61 Leo Steinberg, "Hofmannism," *The Arts* (April, 1958).

62 Paul Strand, in a lecture, republished as "The Art Motive in Photography," *British Journal of Photography,* LXX (October 5, 1923), p. 612.

63 Museum of Modern Art, New York, *John Flannagan* (New York: 1942), p. 9.

64 Carl Milles, the great Swedish sculptor (SC 152, *SC 152A, SC 152B) and the Yugoslav Ivan Mestrovic (SC 151), one of the pioneers of modern art, both came to the United States before World War II to assume teaching positions, as well as to continue their own creative work. But their still semitraditional approach was not as influential as that of the more advanced practitioners of the art such as Brancusi, Arp, and Gonzales.

65 Sam Hunter, in *Modern American Painting and Sculpture* (1959), very appropriately entitles his chapter on recent sculpture "Sculpture for an Iron Age."

66 Seymour Lipton, in Museum of Modern Art, *12 Americans,* Dorothy C. Miller (ed.) (1956), p. 72.

67 *Daedalus* (Winter, 1960), p. 107.

68 Museum of Modern Art, *15 Americans,* Dorothy C. Miller (ed.) (1952), p. 28.

GLOSSARY

(Terms in *italics* are defined elsewhere in the Glossary.)

abacus. The slab or table at the top of a *capital* supporting the *entablature*.

abutment. The part of a structure that directly receives *thrust* or pressure (as of an *arch, vault, beam,* or *strut*).

academic. Art which conforms to traditional conventions. The term derives from the teaching of academics and is generally used today in a pejorative sense.

adobe. Sun-dried bricks. A building material used frequently in the Southwest of the United States.

aerial perspective. In painting and the graphic arts the achievement of the effect of distance or depth by the diminution of detail and precision in drawing and of *value* and *intensity* in color.

aisle. The area surrounding the *nave* of a church, and sometimes its *transepts* and *apse*.

antae (plural of *anta*). A square or rectangular pier formed by the thickening of a wall at its extremity, thus three-sided. Commonly has a *capital* and base conforming to the *order* used elsewhere in the building.

apse. The recess, usually semicircular, at the end of a church.

aquatint. A method of print-making in which tones (as opposed to lines, as in *etching*) are bitten into the surface of a polished metal plate (usually copper) by means of acid penetrating between particles of acid-resistant resin made to adhere to the plate by heating it. The resulting small holes create a tone when inked and printed. In a **sugar-lift aquatint** (sometimes called lift-ground etching), unlike a conventional aquatint, where an area is defined by coating its boundaries with an acid-resistant ("stopping out") varnish, a drawing is made on the plate with a brush and viscous liquid (often containing sugar). When partially dry, liquid acid-resistant varnish (etching ground) is laid over the plate and the plate is submerged in water. The areas covered by the drawing are removed by the water, exposing the bare metal where the drawing has been made. An aquatint ground is then laid and bitten as in conventional aquatint.

arcade. A series of *arches* with their supports. (**blind arcade:** An arcade applied decoratively to the surface of a wall.)

arch. A curved structural member spanning an opening and serving as a support.

archaeology. The scientific study of past cultures.

architrave. The lowest division of the *entablature*.

arcuated. Provided with or characterized by *arches* or arch-like curves. See also *trabeated*.

art nouveau. A stylistic term referring to the use of sinuous curvilinear forms, sometimes derived from organic life, both in the figurative arts and as decoration in architecture and its ancillary arts. The style flourished during the last decade of the nineteenth century and the first years of the twentieth.

ashlar. Hewn or squared stone; also, masonry of such stone.

astylar. Having no *columns* or *pilasters*.

atelier. An artist's or designer's studio or workroom.

atrium. The open court in front of a church.

attic. 1. A low story or wall above the main part of a structure. 2. A room partly or completely within the roof space of a building.

baluster. A turned or rectangular upright supporting a stair rail. See also *banister*.

balustrade. A continuous row of *balusters* surmounted by a hand rail.

banister. A corruption of *baluster*.

barge board. A board, usually ornamented, that conceals roof timbers projecting over *gables*. (Sometimes called verge board.)

baroque. A style of artistic expression prevalent in the seventeenth century (and, in provincial areas, into the first half of the eighteenth century), characterized in both architecture and the figurative arts by elaborate, exuberant, and dynamic forms and by a complex manipulation of space. Generally antithetical to the restraint and relative stasis of the *classical* and *Renaissance* styles. In the figurative arts, the style is often accompanied by intense emotional expression, and in painting and the graphic arts it is usually projected by means of a suggestive, *painterly*, or otherwise imprecise manner.

barrel vault. A semicircular *vault;* sometimes called tunnel vault, a more accurately descriptive term.

bastide. A small fortified town with grid plan.

batten. A strip of thin and narrow wood (usually vertical) used over the joints between two boards in the siding of framed buildings.

bay. A principal compartment of the walls, roof, or other part of a building.

bay window. A window which projects in the form of a segment of a circle or rectangle.

beam. A long (usually squared) timber used horizontally in building construction.

beam anchor. A bar of wrought iron fastened to the end of a *beam* and built into a masonry wall or carried through it and secured by a cross iron of various shapes, usually an **S.**

belt course. A course of masonry, usually projecting, to indicate the interior floor line on the exterior wall.

biomorphic. Shapes or forms used in abstract art, resembling those of living organisms.

board and batten. Construction utilizing battened boards. See also *batten*.

bolection molding. A heavy, wide, conspicuously projecting *molding*.

bond. The manner in which bricks (or stones) are laid to form a wall of masonry. (**English bond:** bricks laid in alternate courses of *headers* and *stretchers*. **Flemish bond:** bricks laid alternately in each course.)

bracket. A support projecting from a vertical surface. In *classical* architecture, if upright it is a console; if horizontal, a *modillion*. In medieval architecture, it is often called a corbel.

bulto. A statue of a saint, in the Spanish-American Southwest. A *santo* may be either sculpture, painting, or a print; a *bulto* refers only to a statue.

bungalow. A one-story, lightly built dwelling.

buttress. A projecting structure for supporting or increasing the stability of a wall, usually when the wall is supporting the *thrust* of an *arch* or *vault*.

calligraphic. Relating to calligraphy: elegant handwriting.

cantilever. A projecting *beam* or member supported at only one end; now usually steel.

capital. The uppermost member of a *column*.

casement (window). A window that opens on hinges at the sides.

catenary curve. The shape assumed by a wire, cord, or similar flexible material in equilibrium under given forces.

chalet. A Swiss dwelling with unconcealed structural members and wide overhanging *eaves*.

champfer. An angle cut diagonally.

chancel. The part of a church lying east of the *nave*.

chasing. The tooling of metal.

chiaroscuro. The use of strong contrasts of light and shade (from the Italian *chiaro:* light, and *oscuro:* dark).

chimneypiece. A *mantelpiece*.

clapboard. A narrow board, usually thicker at one end, used as a lapped siding.

classic. To be distinguished from *classical*. Refers to quality rather than to period style.

classical. The art of Greece and Rome from approximately 530 B.C. to 330 A.D.; also later art, especially the *Renaissance*, influenced by Greece and Rome. As a formal style it is characterized by order, symmetry, and refinement of proportion. In the figurative arts it is further characterized by idealized naturalism, by an emphasis on monumental three-dimensionality, and by restraint in the expression of feeling.

classicism. Art and architecture based on the study and emulation of *classical* art, especially that of Greece and Rome.

classicistic. Following *classical* standards.

clerestory. The uppermost wall of a building carried above an adjoining roof and pierced with windows.

coffer. A recessed panel in a ceiling, *vault, dome,* or *soffit*.

collage. The technique of applying paper or other material to the surface of a painting.

colonial. In the specific sense used in this book, the term refers to the period from the first settlement by Europeans of what is now the United States of America until the independence of the United States from Great Britain.

colonnade. A series of *columns* supporting other structural members spaced at regular intervals.

column. A cylindrical structural support (or occasionally free-standing as a monument) consisting of *shaft* and *capital,* and sometimes a base.

composite order. The fifth *order* of architecture introduced by the Romans, combining the *volutes* of the *Ionic order* with the acanthus leaf of the *Corinthian order*.

compression ring. A member designed to receive and balance loads exerted upon it by other structural members that normally would meet at a point.

console. See *bracket*.

coping. A material or a member used to form a capping or finish at the top of a wall, pier, or the like, to protect it by throwing off water on one or both sides.

corbel. See *bracket*.

corbel table. A projecting course of masonry resting on corbels; often connected by blind *arches*.

Corinthian order. The third *order* of *classical* architecture, characterized principally by its elaborate *capital,* whose motifs are derived from the foliage of the acanthus plant.

cornice. The crowning member of a wall or part of a wall; in *classical* architecture, the uppermost of its three principal members, the others being *architrave* and *frieze*. (In the *Doric order,* the frieze is replaced by horizontal alternation of *metopes* and *triglyphs*.)

cove. A surface of concave, more or less cylindrical, form.

coved ceiling. The upper side of a room which is so designed that *coves* join the vertical wall with the flat part of the ceiling.

crocket. A curved ornament consisting of a coiled or open leaf placed at intervals on sloping structural members.

cruciform. In the form of a cross. Usually referring to a church plan with *nave, apse* (or *chancel*), and two *transepts*.

cruck. Support formed from the trunk of a tree bent inward, used in two opposite rows at regular intervals, the bent ends touching to form the crown of a *gable*.

cupola. A *dome* or the rounded top of a dome.

daguerreotype. An early type of unique photograph on a silver or silver-covered copper plate.

dentil. One of a series of small projecting rectangular blocks, especially under a *cornice*.

diapered. A pattern consisting of the repetition of one, two, or more simple figures which connect with one another more or less closely.

dome. A hemispherical roof or ceiling.

Doric order. The first *order* of *classical* architecture. Its *capital* consists of a curved member (*echinus*) surmounted by a block (*abacus*); without a base. The *frieze* of the Doric *entablature* is divided into *triglyphs* and *metopes*.

dormer window. An upright window in a sloping roof. (**shed dormer:** A flat-roofed dormer, i.e., without a *gable*.)

droplet. A decorative element dependent from an *overhang*.

drum. Cylindrical wall between the structural supports at the base of a *dome* and the dome itself.

drypoint. *Engraving* in which the needle or burin is dragged as in drawing, creating either a very delicate line or a very dark one, the latter caused by the furrow raised by the passage of the needle through the metal, called burr. Subtler and more spontaneous effects can be obtained in engraving; and richer, more forceful darks than in *etching*.

eave. The *overhang* of the slope of a roof.

echinus. The curved member between the *shaft* and *abacus* of the Doric *capital*.

eclectic. Composed of elements selected from what appears to be best in various artistic doctrines, methods, or styles.

elevation. A geometric projection on a vertical plane. See also *plan*.

ell. A one-story, lean-to wing added to the main body of a house.

engaged column. A *column* partly built into, or attached to, a wall.

engraving (line engraving). A method of print-making in which lines are incised into a polished metal plate (usually copper) by pushing a sharp-pointed instrument called a graver or burin. The plate is then inked, and wiped, the ink remaining in the lines whence it is forced by the pressure of a press onto a piece of paper, making a print. Engraving, because of the need for a deeply incised line in order to print effectively, is not a spontaneous medium since it requires disciplined force in the process of execution. On the other hand, for this reason it can produce effects of refined precision and detail in contrast to the more "sketchy" effects of *etching* and *drypoint*, the two other most important intaglio (from the Italian, meaning "to cut into") media.

entablature. The upper part of any classical *order* consisting of three horizontal sections: *architrave, frieze,* and *cornice*.

entasis. The tapering bulge of the *shaft* of a *column*.

etching. A method of print-making in which lines are bitten into the surface of a polished metal plate (usually copper) by means of acid rather than incised by means of the pressure of the hand, as in *engraving* and *drypoint*. The plate must first be covered with a thin acid-resistant substance through which the lines are drawn with a needle handled like a pencil or pen, and not pushed as in engraving. Consequently, more freedom and spontaneity are possible in this medium than in engraving. See also *soft-ground etching*.

facade. The front of a building.

fanlight. A semicircular window with radiating bars, usually placed over a doorway, but sometimes used separately.

fan vault. Ribs spread out like a fan over a *vault* surface; used in English late Gothic architecture.

fenestration. The arrangement of the windows of a building.

ferroconcrete (reinforced concrete). Concrete reinforced by metal (usually steel) embedded in it.

figurative. Art characterized by the depiction of the human and animal figure. Used here to distinguish sculpture, painting, and the other graphic arts from architecture.

finial. An ornamental crowning feature of a *gable, pediment,* pinnacle, etc.

flamboyant. The last phase of French Gothic architecture, characterized by tracery with flame-like forms.

fluting. The use of shallow vertical grooves on the *shafts* of *columns* and *pilasters*.

flying buttress. A *buttress* separated from the principal mass of the building, but attached to it by one or more *arches*. In this way the *thrust* of *ribs* and *vaults* is carried off by a form of buttress which does not darken the windows by its shadow, as would be the case if the buttress were not flying.

fresco. See *mural painting*.

fret. Ornament consisting of interlocking angular motifs.

frieze. 1. The middle part of the *entablature* of the classical *orders*. 2. A horizontal band sculptured in relief or otherwise ornamented.

gable. The triangular wall at the end of a ridged roof, sometimes varied by stepped or curved *coping*.

gambrel roof. A roof with a lower steeper slope and an upper flatter one.

genre. Unidealized treatment of subjects taken from ordinary daily life.

geodesic dome. A term invented by Buckminster Fuller to define one of his structural forms: essentially a network of spherical triangles formed by intercrossing great circles, creating a *dome*-like structure.

Georgian. Used here to indicate the period which began with the reign of George I of England (1714) until American independence under George III (1776); but in English architecture until the end of the reign of George IV (1830).

giant order. A *classical* order which is more than one story high. (Sometimes referred to as colossal order.)

girder. A horizontal main structural member which supports vertical loads.

girt. A beam on the outer (and narrower) wall of a building to receive the ends of the floor *joists*.

glaze (glazing). Thin film of translucent (rather than the usual opaque) color.

glazier. One who sets glass.

golden section or **mean.** A system of proportional relationship obtained by dividing a line in such a way that the shorter part is to the longer part as the longer part is to the whole.

Gothic. A style of artistic expression which flourished during the late Middle Ages (after the *Romanesque*), from about 1200 to 1400 in Italy, until 1500 in the north, and later in provincial or isolated areas such as the English colonies.

gouache. *Watercolor* painting made opaque by the addition of white.

graphic arts. Drawings and, more especially, prints: i.e., *engravings, etchings, drypoints, lithographs, woodcuts, wood engravings,* etc.

grill. An ornamental or plain grating used to fill an opening.

groined vault. A *vault* formed by the intersection of two *barrel vaults* of equal span, either semicircular (as in *classical* or *Romanesque* architecture) or pointed (as in *Gothic*), the diagonal lines of the intersecting under-surfaces being the groins.

hacienda. A large estate (similar to a plantation) in Spanish or Spanish-speaking countries. See also *rancho*.

half-timber. Construction in which the structural framing is left exposed, and in which spaces formed by the framing are filled with brick, clay, or other material.

hammer beam. A late medieval form of roof construction in which short timber *brackets* (hammer beams) supported by *struts* take the place of *tie beams*.

header. The shortest dimension of a brick. See also *stretcher*.

hipped roof. A roof with inclined sides and ends, the diagonal lines formed by the intersecting planes being known as hips.

housewright. A carpenter skilled in house construction.

hyperbolic paraboloid. An overshooting surface generated by the rotation about its axis of a conic section (the intersection of a cone with a plane parallel to its side).

iconography. The imagery selected to convey the meaning of a work of art.

impasto. A thick paste-like application of paint to the surface of a painting.

in antis. *Columns* (usually two) set between two *antae*.

intaglio. The meaning used here is to distinguish among the graphic arts those printed from lines incised or etched in a metal plate (as in *engraving* or *etching*) as differentiated from those printed from lines in relief (as in *woodcut*).

intensity. Degree of hue in a color, i.e., amount of redness. See also *value*.

Ionic order. The second *order* of *classical* architecture. The *capital* is characterized by a double *volute* in the place of the Doric *echinus*. The *shaft* rests on a base. The *frieze* is continuous. The proportions are more elongated than those of the *Doric order*.

joinery. The craft of gluing together pieces of wood.

joist. Any one of the small timbers (or metal *beams*) ranged parallel from wall to wall in a building to support the floor or ceiling.

keystone. The central *voussoir* block of an *arch*.

knee. A *bracket*, generally rectangular, made out of a naturally bent limb of a tree.

laminated. To make by uniting superimposed layers of material.

lath. A strip of wood generally thin and narrow, a number of which are secured to *studs* for the support of finishing materials, usually plaster.

lattice. A framework or structure of crossed wooden or metal strips.

lean-to. A structure having only one slope or pitch.

limner. (Archaic.) One who draws or paints.

linear (or **geometric**) **perspective.** A scientific means, by the use of geometry, of determining the planes of recession in a picture. See also *aerial perspective*.

lintel. A horizontal architectural member spanning and usually carrying a load above an opening.

lithography. A graphic art in which an oily crayon is used to draw on stone or metal and which is printed through the chemical principle of the mutual incompatibility of oil and water. (The stone is dampened, then inked. The water adheres only to those sections of the stone which have not been drawn upon and the ink only to those sections which have been drawn upon. Therefore, only the drawn-upon areas print.) Lithography is the only print medium which appears in its execution as it will when printed (except, like all prints, the image is reversed). Great freedom of execution and richness of effect can be obtained.

lithotint. Like a lithograph, except it is executed not with a crayon but with a brush dipped in an oily ink.

loggia. A roofed open gallery within the side of a building.

louver. An opening provided with one or more slanted fixed or movable fins.

Mannerism. An artistic style which prevailed in Europe from c. 1525 to c. 1600, more conspicuously in the figurative arts than in architecture, but in both as a reaction against the standards of the *Renaissance*.

Expression was in terms of exaggerated and unnatural proportions, colors, and lighting, and in the breaking-down of *classical* order and mass or monumentality. There was also an increase in the expression of emotion, either in the direction of secular sophistication or religious and spiritual intensity (as in the work of El Greco).

mantelpiece. The frame which surrounds a fireplace, and often also the paneled and/or otherwise decorated area which surmounts it.

medallion. A circular plaque decorated in relief.

metope. In the Doric *entablature*, that part which is interposed in a horizontal sequence between two *triglyphs* in the area which is interposed between *architrave* and *cornice*.

mezzotint. A form of *engraving* in which tone rather than line is desired. This is achieved by scraping the halftones and highlights from a metal plate, usually copper, which has been roughened (and would therefore print black if not scraped away to a greater or lesser extent, as in the actual execution of a mezzotint).

miniature. A picture, most often a portrait "in little," executed in *watercolor* on parchment or ivory.

mobile. Movable sculpture, consisting of forms linked by wires or rods, which can be moved—sometimes even by currents of air.

modillion. A horizontal support projecting from a vertical surface; similar to a console or *bracket*, except not used singularly, but in a series.

module, modular. The use of a common denomination in measurement, especially in architecture.

molding. A continuous narrow surface projecting or receding (or a combination of both) from a wall or panel; plain or decorated.

monolith. A single stone.

mortise. A rectangular sinkage in a *beam* to receive a *tenon*.

mullion. A vertical bar which divides a window into separate "lights" or glazed sections.

mural painting. Painting executed directly on a wall surface into wet plaster (fresco) or on canvas applied later to it.

mutule. A flat member slightly projecting from a Doric *cornice* placed alternately over a *metope* and a *triglyph*.

nave. The central area of a church, in front of the *apse* or *chancel;* separated from side aisles, if any, by *arcades* or *colonnades.*

neo-classicism. The revival or adaptation of *classical* taste and style; usually referring to the revival during the late eighteenth and early nineteenth centuries, as opposed to that of the Renaissance.

newell (post). The end *post* to which the hand rail of a stairway is attached.

niche. A recess in a wall, frequently *arched* and usually intended to hold a statue.

obelisk. A tall, tapering monument terminating in a pyramid. Originally an Egyptian form.

octahedron. A solid or volume formed by eight sides.

oil painting. Painting with colors ground up and mixed with oil. Until the nineteenth century generally this oil could be opaque or transparent (glaze). Now generally opaque.

order. Designation of the five categories of *classical* architecture: *Doric, Ionic, Corinthian, composite,* and *Tuscan,* each consisting of a *column* and *entablature* and varying in proportion and detail.

oriel. A *bay window,* usually polygonal, especially in an upper story or stories.

overhang. The projection of one story over the one below.

painterly. Having the characteristics of a painting, as opposed to a drawing or a print medium which employs line. Much painting could be described as colored drawing; painterly refers to the technique used in those paintings where details and edges are not defined by lines but are blended into the surrounding areas. The painterly technique gives the illusion that all objects are surrounded by palpable atmosphere or immediate space.

Palladian. In general, architectural style derived from the practice and theory of Andrea Palladio (1518–1580); in particular an adjective referring to the Palladian motif, an *arched* opening flanked by two rectangular ones. (Sometimes called Venetian.)

panel. In woodwork, a board planed to a nearly triangular end. Each of its four sides are set into a frame or into a *molding.* The panel may be plain, or with various *moldings.*

parapet. Usually, a low wall to protect the edge of a platform roof.

patina. A surface appearance of something grown beautiful, especially with age and use.

patio. Courtyard; a roofless inner court.

pavilion. Here, used principally to describe a part of a building projecting from the rest, usually at the center.

pediment. 1. A triangular space forming the *gable* of a pitched roof. 2. A similar form used decoratively, but varied from the triangular shape by being broken or broken and curved.

pendentive. One of the three-sided spherical sections of vaulting that spring from the corners of a rectangular ground plan and serve to allow the area to be covered by a *cupola* or *dome.*

pent roof. The short end-section of a gable roof at its *eave* end, used as a projecting covering for a section of the first story of a two-story (or higher) house. Used almost exclusively in Pennsylvania. (Sometimes called skirt roof.)

pergola. A structure usually consisting of parallel *colonnades* supporting an open roof of *girders* and cross *rafters.*

peripteral. Surrounded by a single range of *columns.* See also *peristyle.*

peristyle. A *colonnade* surrounding a building (or court). See also *peripteral.*

perspective. See *linear perspective* and *aerial perspective.*

photogravure. A process for making prints from a metal plate prepared by photographic methods.

picture plane. The plane of the picture surface itself; the point where the space which the artist has depicted begins.

pilaster. A vertical architectural member analogous to the engaged *column* but rectangular.

plan. A geometric projection on a horizontal plane. See also *elevation*.

plastic. 1. (adj.) Capable of being molded or modeled, and indicating pronounced three-dimensionality. 2. (noun) Any of numerous materials (usually synthetic) which can be formed into shapes.

plate. A horizontal timber for carrying the *trusses* or the *rafters* of a roof.

porte cochere. A roofed structure extending from the entrance of a building over an adjacent driveway and sheltering those getting in and out of vehicles.

portico. A *colonnade* attached to the *facade* or to any elevation of a building. Also, a smaller structure, usually supported by two *columns,* before an entrance.

post. A piece of timber (or metal) in an upright position as a support.

program. A plan of procedure. As used in architectural practice, the term signifies the architect's solution of problems arising from all the circumstances connected with a building: site, purpose, materials, needs of the client, etc.

provenance. Place of origin.

pylon. 1. An ancient Egyptian gateway structure in the form of a truncated pyramid. 2. A monumental mass flanking an entrance to a bridge.

quoin. A block which is part of a series of blocks forming the angle of a building.

rafter. One of the sloping timbers of a roof.

rancho. Small ranch, or one devoted to specialized raising of a certain animal.

Renaissance. In general, the revival of culture and learning which took place in the fourteenth, fifteenth, and sixteenth centuries under the influence of *classical* literature and art. In the history of art, the term refers more particularly to a style of artistic expression influenced by classical artistic prototypes, characterized by monumentality of form (and, in the figurative arts, by idealized naturalism and emotional restraint), expressed in rational, harmonious, and balanced terms. It can be contrasted to the *baroque,* which is undisciplined and overemotional.

representational. Describes *figurative* art in which figures and objects are represented or depicted in the way they seem to appear or are known to be, in contrast to abstract and non-representational art.

rib. A narrow *arch* in *Romanesque* and *Gothic* vaulting which helps supplement the supporting function of the *vault.*

rococo. A style of artistic expression prevalent in the eighteenth century (especially c. 1735–1760). It could be thought of as a coda or extension of the *baroque* whose formal characteristics it shares, except that the elaboration, dynamism, and complex manipulation of space, as well as the suggestive painterliness of the earlier style are all increased or exaggerated, and made more decorative where this is possible. But the rococo differs more definitely from the baroque in other respects. Its forms have a more fragile attenuated character in contrast to the more massive and solid ones of the baroque. The rococo also possesses a certain gaiety and lightness, and often lacks a profound or serious treatment of subject matter.

Romanesque. A style of artistic expression which prevailed in Europe from c. 1000 to 1200 and which preceded the *Gothic.*

romantic. Impractical to summarize as a stylistic term except as the antithesis of *classical*. As a term defining a period, it parallels and follows *neo-classicism* (c. 1825–1865).

rosette. An architectural ornament resembling a rose; usually in the form of a disk in relief.

rotunda. A round building, especially one covered by a *dome*.

rustication. Masonry which is left rough or unfinished.

santo. The painted image of a saint, in the Spanish-American Southwest. See also *bulto.*

scallop. One of a continuous series of circle segments or angular projections forming a border.

segmental. Referring to a segment of a circle or arch; not a semicircle.

setback. The withdrawal of the surface of a section of the wall of a building some distance from the building line or from the wall below.

shaft. The central cylindrical part of a *column*.

sheathing. A covering of boards on the exterior of a timber house. Used either vertically or horizontally, but not overlapping, as in *clapboarding*.

shed dormer. See *dormer*.

shouldered post. A *post* with a projection at the top, usually flared as it rises.

sidelight. Window openings flanking a door.

sill. The heavy horizontal timber at the base of a framed house.

skirt roof. See *pent roof*.

soffit. The underside of an architectural member, such as an *arch, lintel, cornice,* etc.

soft-ground etching. A print-making process in which a greasy, tacky substance or ground is applied to a copper plate. Moist paper is then laid on the plate and drawn upon. The pressure of the pencil or stylus when drawn on the paper makes the ground adhere to the paper and thus it can be lifted from the surface of the plate, leaving an uneven or crumbly line, very different from the more precise line of conventional *etching*. Beyond this point the procedure is similar to etching.

spandrel. The triangular space between the curves of two *arches*.

spindle. A turned, decorative piece of wood, vertically placed.

spire. The staged and pointed portion of a steeple, above the tower.

stretcher. The long dimension of a brick. See also *header*.

string course. A horizontal band (as of bricks) in a building.

strut. A structural member, placed diagonally, designed to resist pressure in the direction of length.

stucco. A material made of cement, sand, and lime, and applied in a plastic state to interior or exterior walls; finished more roughly than plaster.

stud. An upright stick which fills spaces between *sill, posts, girts,* and *plates.*

stylobate. The continuous flat pavement upon which a row of *columns* is supported.

sugar-lift aquatint. See *aquatint.*

summer beam. The *beam* which crosses the ceiling of a room from *girt* to girt and carries the *joists* of the floor above. May be lengthwise or thwartwise.

swag. Something hanging from two points; often a suspended cluster of fruit and/or foliage.

tempera. A process of painting in which egg yolk or similar synthetic substance and water are employed instead of oil. Has more of a matte effect than oil.

tenon. A short projection from the end of a *beam.* It is pinned into a *mortise.*

tetrahedron. A solid or volume formed by four sides.

thatch. Coarse grass used as roofing.

thrust. The lateral pressure exerted by one part of a structure against another part, as of an *arch* or *vault* against an *abutment;* usually compensated for by a *buttress.*

tie beam. A *beam* connecting the lowest part of the principal *rafters* of a gable roof to prevent them from spreading.

tongue and groove. A joint made by a tongue (a rib on one edge of a board) fitting into a corresponding groove on the edge of another board.

trabeated. Constructed with horizontal *beams* or *lintels.* See also *arcuated, post,* and *lintel.*

transept. Any large division of a building lying across or in a direction contrary to the main axis.

triglyph. The area placed alternately with the *metope* in the *frieze* of the *entablature* of the *Doric order.* It consists of a flat surface in which three parallel vertical grooves are cut.

truss. An assemblage of structural members (as *beams*) forming a rigid framework.

Tuscan order. A Roman order similar to the *Doric,* but without fluting in the *shaft* or ornament in the *entablature,* and narrower and more attenuated in proportion.

value. The amount of light or dark added to hues to change their *intensity.* A component (with hue and intensity) of color.

vanishing point. The arbitrary point placed on the horizon used in *linear* (or *geometric*) *perspective* to which all parallel planes or lines recede from the picture plane and appear to converge there.

vault. An *arched* structure of masonry forming a ceiling or roof. See also *barrel vault* and *groined vault.*

verge board. See *barge board.*

volute. A spiral scroll-shaped ornament forming the chief feature of the Ionic *capital.* Also used as an isolated form in other architectural contexts.

voussoir. Wedge-shaped blocks of stone used in constructing an *arch.*

wainscot. The lower three or four feet of an interior wall when finished differently from the rest of the wall.

watercolor. A process of painting in which water is used as the medium; therefore transparent.

water table. A slope, plain or molded, at the top of the underpinning or at the first floor level or offset.

woodcut, wood engraving. Relief prints, as opposed to intaglio (line *engraving, etching, drypoint, mezzotint*) and planographic (*lithography*). Could be likened to pictorial type (type is also raised). In the woodcut the design is allowed to remain while the white areas (those not meant to print) are removed by knives and gouges. In the wood engraving the principle is the same, but the execution can be thought of as the reverse of the woodcut. The lines which are drawn (or more properly, incised) are those which will appear as white in the print (hence wood engraving is sometimes called white-line engraving), while the untouched part prints black. The tool used is similar to the burin or graver in line engraving, and the effects can be as refined—in contrast to the bolder woodcut.

SUGGESTED READING

Note: Extensive and well-selected bibliographies may be found in the following books, to supplement the sources listed here. For architecture in general: Wayne Andrews, *Architecture, Ambition and Americans* (1955). For architecture c. 1800–1850: Talbot Hamlin, *Greek Revival Architecture in America* (1944). For painting in general: Virgil Barker, *American Painting: History and Interpretation* (1950); E. P. Richardson, *A Short History of Painting in America* (1963) (paperback). For painting and sculpture in the twentieth century: Sam Hunter, *Modern American Painting and Sculpture* (1959) (paperback); Elizabeth McCausland, "Selected Bibliography on American Painting and Sculpture from Colonial Times to the Present," *Magazine of Art,* XXXIX (November, 1946), pp. 329–349. (More specialized.)

GENERAL SOURCES

Books covering one or more of the arts during the entire history of American art or an extensive portion of it:

Larkin, Oliver W., *Art and Life in America* (1960).

Pierson, William H., Jr., and Davidson, Martha, *Arts of the United States; A Pictorial Survey* (1960).

Cahill, Holgar, and Barr, Alfred H., Jr. (eds.), *Art in America, A Complete Survey* (1935).

Kouwenhoven, John A., *Made in America: The Arts in Modern Civilization* (1948).

Lynes, Russell, *The Tastemakers* (1954).

Architecture

Andrews, Wayne, *Architecture, Ambition and Americans* (1955).

Burchard, John, and Bush-Brown, Albert, *The Architecture of America, A Social and Cultural History* (1961).

Fitch, James M., *American Building: the Forces that Shape It* (1948).

Hitchcock, Henry-Russell, *Architecture: Nineteenth and Twentieth Centuries* (1958). (The sections on American architecture.)

Less recent but useful surveys, though "dated":

Hamlin, Talbot, *The American Spirit in Architecture* (1926). (Vol. 13 of "The Pageant of America" series.)

Tallmadge, Thomas E., *The Story of Architecture in America* (1936).

Community Planning

Tunnard, Christopher, and Reed, Henry Hope, *American Skyline: The Growth and Form of Our Cities and Towns* (1955).

Churchill, Henry S., *The City Is the People* (1945).

Painting

Barker, Virgil, *American Painting, History and Interpretation* (1950).

Feld, Stuart P., and Gardner, Albert Ten Eyck, *American Painting, A Catalogue of The Metropolitan Museum of Art,* vol. I (1965).

Richardson, Edgar P., *Painting in America* (1956).

McCoubrey, John W., *American Tradition in Painting* (1963).

———— (ed.), *American Art 1700–1900—Sources and Documents* (1965).

Less recent and "dated":

The American Spirit in Art, Frank J. Mather, Jr., Rufus Morey, and William J. Henderson (eds.) (1927). (Vol. 12 of "The Pageant of America" series.) (Includes some sculpture.)

Important earlier sources:

Dunlap, William, *A History of the Rise and Development of the Arts of Design in the United States*, 2 vols. (1834). (Revised 3-vol. edition, 1918.)

Jarves, James J., *The Art-Idea* (1864); 1961 ed., Benjamin Rowland (ed.).

Tuckerman, Henry T., *Book of the Artists* (1867). (Includes sculpture.)

Hartman, Sadakichi, *A History of American Art*, 2 vols. (1902).

Isham, Samuel, *The History of American Painting* (1905). (New edition with supplementary material by Royal Cortissoz.)

Sculpture

There is no recent survey.

Taft, Lorado, *The History of American Sculpture* (1903).

Post, Chandler R., *A History of European and American Sculpture*, 2 vols. (1921). (The sections on American sculpture.)

Gardner, Albert Ten Eyck, *American Sculpture, a Catalogue of the Collection of the Metropolitan Museum of Art* (1965).

The Graphic Arts

Again, there is no recent survey.

Weitenkampf, *American Graphic Art* (1912).

An excellent book on a special aspect of graphic art is:

Murrell, William, *History of American Graphic Humor*, 2 vols. (1933, 1938).

Photography

Newhall, Beaumont, *The History of Photography from 1839 to the Present Day* (1964).

————, and Newhall, Nancy (eds.), *Masters of Photography* (1958).

Folk Art

Christensen, Erwin O., *The Index of American Design* (1950).

Lipman, Jean, *American Folk Art in Wood, Metal and Stone* (1948).

————, and Winchester, Alice, *Primitive Painters in America, 1750–1950* (1950).

PART ONE: THE SEVENTEENTH CENTURY

Architecture

Briggs, Martin S., *The Homes of the Pilgrim Fathers in England and America* (1932).

Downing, Antoinette F., *Early Homes of Rhode Island* (1937).

Forman, Henry C., *The Architecture of the Old South* (1948).

Garvan, Anthony N. B., *Architecture and Town Planning in Colonial Connecticut* (1951).

Isham, Norman M., and Brown, Albert F., *Early Connecticut Houses* (1900).

Kelly, J. Frederick, *The Early Domestic Architecture of Connecticut* (1924).

————, *Early Connecticut Meeting Houses*, 2 vols. (1948).

Kimball, Fiske, *Domestic Architecture of the American Colonies and of the Early Republic* (1922).

Morrison, Hugh, *Early American Architecture* (1952).

Painting

Baker, C. H. Collins, and Constable, W. G., *English Painting of the Sixteenth and Seventeenth Centuries* (1930).

Burroughs, Alan, *Limners and Likenesses, Three Centuries of American Painting* (1936).

Dresser, Louisa, *Seventeenth-Century Painting in New England* (1935).

Flexner, James T., *First Flowers in Our Wilderness* (1947).

Hagen, Oskar, *The Birth of the American Tradition in Art* (1940).

Sculpture

Forbes, Harriette, *Gravestones of Early New England* (1927).

Ludwig, Allan, *Graven Images* (1966).

PART TWO: THE EIGHTEENTH CENTURY

Architecture in the English Colonies

Beirne, Rosamond R., and Scarff, John F., *William Buckland 1734–1774, Architect of Virginia and Maryland* (1958).

Bridenbaugh, Carl, *Peter Harrison, First American Architect* (1949).

Downing, Antoinette, *Early Homes of Rhode Island* (1937).

————, and Scully, Vincent, *The Architectural Heritage of Newport, Rhode Island* (1952).

Hitchcock, Henry-Russell, *Rhode Island Architecture* (1939).

Howells, John M., *Lost Examples of Colonial Architecture* (1931).
Kimball, Fiske, *Domestic Architecture of the American Colonies and of the Early Republic* (1922).
Morrison, Hugh, *Early American Architecture* (1952).
Shurtleff, Harold R., *The Log Cabin Myth* (1939).
Waterman, Thomas T., *The Dwellings of Colonial America* (1950).
———, *The Mansions of Virginia* (1946).
———, and Barrows, John A., *Domestic Colonial Architecture of Tidewater Virginia* (1932).
———, and Johnson, Frances B., *The Early Architecture of North Carolina* (1941).
Wertenbacher, Thomas J., *The Foundations of American Civilization: The Middle Colonies* (1938).
Whiffen, Marcus, *The Eighteenth Century Houses of Williamsburg* (1960).
———, *The Public Buildings of Williamsburg* (1958).

Non-English Architecture

Eberlein, Harold D., *The Manors and Historic Homes of the Hudson Valley* (1924).
Kubler, George, *The Religious Architecture of New Mexico* (1940).
Newcomb, Rexford G., *The Old Mission Churches and Historic Houses of California* (1925).
———, *Spanish Colonial Architecture in the United States* (1937).
Reynolds, Helen W., *Dutch Houses of the Hudson Valley before 1776* (1929).
Wertenbacher, Thomas J., *The Foundations of American Civilization: The Middle Colonies* (1938).

Community Planning

Garvan, Anthony N. B., *Architecture and Town Planning in Colonial Connecticut* (1951).

Painting

Burroughs, Alan, *Limners and Likenesses, Three Centuries of American Painting* (1936).
Chicago Art Institute, *From Colony to Nation* (Sweet, Frederick A., and Huth, Hans, eds.) (1949).
Flexner, James T., *First Flowers in Our Wilderness* (1947).
———, *John Singleton Copley* (1948).
Hagen, Oskar, *The Birth of the American Tradition in Art* (1940).
Little, Nina Fletcher, *American Decorative Wall Painting 1700–1850* (1952).
Parker, Barbara Neville, and Wheeler, Anne Bolling, *John Singleton Copley, American Portraits in Oil, Pastel and Miniature* (1938).
Rhode Island School of Design, Museum of Art, *Old and New England: An Exhibition of American Painting of Colonial and Early Republican Days, Together with English Painting of the Same Time* (1945).

Sculpture

Forbes, Harriette, *Gravestones of Early New England* (1927).
Ludwig, Allan, *Graven Images* (1966).

PART THREE: THE EARLY REPUBLIC

Architecture

Downing, Antoinette, and Scully, Vincent, *The Architectural Heritage of Newport, Rhode Island* (1952).
Frary, Ihna T., *Thomas Jefferson, Architect and Builder* (1931).
Hamlin, Talbot, *Benjamin Henry Latrobe* (1955).
Hitchcock, Henry-Russell, *Rhode Island Architecture* (1939).
Howells, John M., *Lost Examples of Colonial Architecture* (1931).
Kelley, S. Frederick, *Early Connecticut Meeting Houses*, 2 vols. (1948).
Kimball, Fiske, *Domestic Architecture of the American Colonies and of the Early Republic* (1922).
———, *Thomas Jefferson, Architect and Builder* (1916).
———, *M. Samuel McIntire, Carver, The Architect of Salem* (1940).
Morrison, Hugh, *Early American Architecture* (1952).
Place, Charles A., *Charles Bulfinch, Architect and Citizen* (1925).

Community Planning

Coolidge, John P., *Mill and Mansion* (1942).
Hitchcock, Henry-Russell, *Rhode Island Architecture* (1939).

Painting

Baur, John I. H., *American Painting in the Nineteenth Century; Main Trends and Movements* (1953).
Born, Wolfgang, *American Landscape Painting, An Interpretation* (1948).
———, *Still Life Painting in America* (1947).
Chicago Art Institute, *From Colony to Nation* (Sweet, Frederick, and Huth, Hans, eds.) (1949).
Flexner, James T., *The Light of Distant Skies, 1760–1835* (1954).
M. & M. Karolik Collection of American Painting, 1815–1865 (Introduction by John I. H. Baur) (1949).
M. & M. Karolik Collection of Water Colors and Drawings (Introduction by Henry P. Rossiter) (1962).
Little, Nina Fletcher, *American Decorative Wall Painting, 1700–1850* (1952).

Rhode Island School of Design, Museum of Art, *Old and New England: An Exhibition of American painting of Colonial and Early Republican Days, together with English painting of the same time* (1945).

Richardson, E. P., *The Way of Western Art, 1776–1914* (1939). (Chapters i and ii.)

———. *Washington Allston, A Study of the Romantic Artist in America* (1948).

Sculpture

Forbes, Harriette, *Gravestones of Early New England* (1927).

Gardner, Albert Ten Eyck, *Yankee Stonecutters* (1945).

Ludwig, Allan, *Graven Images* (1966).

Pinckney, Pauline A., *American Figureheads and Their Carvers* (1940).

PART FOUR: FROM JACKSON TO THE CIVIL WAR

Architecture

Downing, Antoinette, and Scully, Vincent, *The Architectural Heritage of Newport, Rhode Island* (1952).

Gallagher, H. M. P., *Robert Mills* (1935).

Gilchrist, Agnes A., *William Strickland, Architect and Engineer* (1950).

Hamlin, Talbot, *Greek Revival Architecture in America* (1944).

Hitchcock, Henry-Russell, *Rhode Island Architecture* (1939).

Kilham, Walter H., *Boston After Bulfinch* (1946).

Smith, J. Frazer, *White Pillars* (1941).

Upjohn, Everard M., *Richard Upjohn, Architect and Churchman* (1939).

Painting

Baur, John I. H., *American Painting in the Nineteenth Century; Main Trends and Movements* (1953).

———, "American Luminism," *Perspectives, U.S.A.*, no. 9 (August, 1954).

Born, Wolfgang, *American Landscape Painting, An Interpretation* (1948).

———, *Still Life Painting in America* (1947).

Cowdrey, Bartlett, and Williams, Hermann Warner, Jr., *William Sidney Mount, 1807–1868, An American Painter* (1944).

Flexner, James T., *That Wilder Image* (1962).

Larkin, Oliver W., *Samuel F. B. Morse and American Democratic Art* (1954).

McCausland, Elizabeth, *George Inness, An American Landscape Painter, 1825–1894* (1946).

McDermott, John Francis, *George Caleb Bingham, River Portraitist* (1959).

Richardson, E. P., *The Way of Western Art, 1776–1914* (1939). (Chapter iii.)

St. Louis, City Art Museum of, *Westward the Way*, by Perry T. Rathbone, *et al.* (1954).

Sears, Clara E., *Highlights Among the Hudson River Artists* (1947).

Sculpture

Gardner, Albert Ten Eyck, *Yankee Stonecutters* (1945).

Folk Art

Boyd, E., *Saints and Saint Makers of New Mexico* (1946).

Christensen, Erwin O., *The Index of American Design* (1950).

Ford, Alice, *Edward Hicks, Painter of the Peaceable Kingdom* (1952).

M. & M. Karolik Collection of American Painting, 1815–1865 (Introduction by John I. H. Baur) (1949).

Lichten, F., *Folk Art of Rural Pennsylvania* (1946).

Pinckney, Pauline A., *American Figureheads and their Carvers* (1940).

Wilder, Mitchel A., and Breitenbach, Edgar, *Santos: The Religious Folk Art of New Mexico* (1943).

PART FIVE: FROM THE CIVIL WAR TO 1900

Architecture

Condit, Carl W., *The Chicago School* (1964).

———, *The Rise of the Skyscraper* (1952).

Downing, Antoinette, and Scully, Vincent, *The Architectural Heritage of Newport, Rhode Island* (1952).

Hitchcock, Henry-Russell, *The Architecture of H. H. Richardson and His Times* (1936).

———, *Rhode Island Architecture* (1939).

Kilham, Walter H., *Boston After Bulfinch* (1946).

Morrison, Hugh S., *Louis Sullivan* (1935).

Mumford, Lewis, *The Brown Decades* (1935).

Schuyler, Montgomery, *American Architecture* (1892).

Scully, Vincent J., *The Shingle Style: Architectural Theory and Design from Richardson to the Origins of Wright* (1955).

Sullivan, Louis, *The Autobiography of an Idea* (1949).

———, *Kindergarten Chats* (1947).

Tallmadge, Thomas E., *Architecture in Old Chicago* (1941).

Van Rensselaer, Marianna G., *Henry Hobson Richardson and His Works* (1888).

Community Planning

Olmsted, Frederick L., Jr., and Kimball, Theodora, *Frederick Law Olmsted, Landscape Architect*, 2 vols. (1928).

Tunnard, Christopher, *The City of Man* (1953).

Painting

Born, Wolfgang, *American Landscape Painting, An Interpretation* (1948).
———, *Still Life Painting in America* (1947).
Chicago Art Institute, *Sargent, Whistler, and Mary Cassatt* (Frederick A. Sweet) (1954).
Frankenstein, Alfred, *After the Hunt: William Harnett and Other American Still Life Painters 1870–1900* (1953).
Gardner, Albert Ten Eyck, *Winslow Homer, American Artist: His World and His Work* (1962).

Goodrich, Lloyd, *Thomas Eakins, His Life and Work* (1933).
———, *Winslow Homer* (1944).
National Gallery of Art, *The American Vision* (film), written and directed by J. Carter Brown (1966 release).
Porter, Fairfield, *Thomas Eakins* (1959).
Richardson, E. P., *The Way of Western Art, 1776–1914* (1939). (Chapters iv and v.)
Smith College Museum of Art, *Winslow Homer, Illustrator, 1860–75* (Bartlett Cowdrey) (1951).
Whitney Museum of American Art, *Albert P. Ryder Centenary Exhibition* (Lloyd Goodrich) (1947).

PART SIX: THE TWENTIETH CENTURY

Architecture

Blake, Peter, *The Masterbuilders* (1961).
Coles, William A., and Reed, H. H. (eds.), *Architecture in America: A Battle of Styles* (1961).
Drexler, Arthur, *The Drawings of Frank Lloyd Wright* (1962).
———, *Ludwig Mies van der Rohe* (1960).
Giedien, Siegfried, *Space, Time and Architecture* (1949).
Hitchcock, Henry-Russell, *In the Nature of Materials* (1942).
———, *Modern Architecture* (1929).
———, with Arthur Drexler, *Built in U.S.A.: Post-War Architecture* (1952).
———, and Philip Johnson, *The International Style: Architecture since 1922* (1932).
Hudnut, Richard, *Architecture and the Spirit of Man* (1949).
McCallum, Ian, *Architecture U. S. A.* (1959).
Michaels, Leonard, *Contemporary Structure in Architecture* (1950).
Mock, Elizabeth B., *Built in U. S. A. 1932–1944* (1944).
———, *If You Want to Build a House* (1946).
Mumford, Lewis, *Roots of Contemporary American Architecture* (1952).
———, *From the Ground Up* (1956).
Neutra, Richard, *On Building: Mysteries and Realities of the Site* (1951).
Peter, John, *Masters of Modern Architecture* (1958). (A concise introduction; excellent photographs and surveys.)
Pevsner, Nikolaus, *Pioneers of Modern Design from William Morris to Walter Gropius* (1949).
Scully, Vincent, *Frank Lloyd Wright* (1960).
———, *Modern Architecture* (1961).
Tempko, Allan, *Eero Saarinen* (1960).
Wright, Frank Lloyd, *An Autobiography* (1932).
———, *On Architecture*, Frederick A. Gutheim (ed.) (1941).

Community Planning

Architectural Forum, Editors of, *The Exploding Metropolis* (1958).
Blake, Peter, *God's Own Junk Yard* (1964).
Jacobs, Jane, *The Life and Death of Great American Cities* (1961).

Journal of the American Institute of Planners, XXVI, 3 (August, 1960). (Issue devoted to Philadelphia.)
Mumford, Lewis, *The City in History* (1961).
Progressive Architecture (July, 1959), "The Emerging Urban Pattern."
Tunnard, Christopher, and Pushkarev, Boris, *Man-Made America—Chaos or Control?* (1964).
Weaver, Robert C., *The Urban Complex, Human Values in Urban Life* (1964).

Painting

Albright-Knox Art Gallery, Buffalo, *Andrew Wyeth* (1962).
Ashton, Dore, *The Unknown Shore: A View of Contemporary Art* (1962).
Baur, John I. H., *Revolution and Tradition in Modern American Art* (1951).
——— (ed.), *New Art in America* (1957).
———, *Nature in Abstraction* (1958).
Blesh, Rudi, *Modern Art U. S. A.* (1956).
Brown, Milton W., *American Painting from the Armory Show to the Depression* (1955). (Also valuable for thorough bibliography.)
Fogg Art Museum, Cambridge, and Morgan Library, New York, *Andrew Wyeth, Dry Brush and Pencil Drawings* (Agnes Mongan) (1962).
Friedman, B. H. (ed.), *School of New York, Some Younger Painters* (1959).
Goodrich, Lloyd, and Baur, John I. H., *American Art of Our Century* (1961).
Greenberg, Clement, *Art and Culture* (1961).
Haftmann, Werner, *Painting in the Twentieth Century*, 2 vols. (1960). (Especially pp. 347–373.)
Hess, Thomas B., *Abstract Painting: Background and American Phase* (1951).
———, *Willem de Kooning* (1959).
Hunter, Sam, *Modern American Painting and Sculpture* (1959).
Museum of Fine Arts, Boston, *John Marin Memorial Exhibition* (1955).
Museum of Modern Art, New York:
Abstract Painting and Sculpture in America (A. C. Ritchie) (1951).
American Realists and Magic Realists (A. H. Barr, et al.) (1943).

Americans 1942, Dorothy Miller (ed.) (1942).
Americans 1963 (1963).
Stuart Davis (James J. Sweeney) (1945).
Charles Demuth (Andrew C. Ritchie) (1950).
Lionel Feininger and Marsden Hartley (1944).
15 Americans, Dorothy Miller (ed.) (1952).
14 Americans, Dorothy Miller (ed.) (1946).
John Marin, Water Colors, Oils and Etchings (1936).
The New American Painting As Shown to Eight European Countries (1959).
Jackson Pollock (Sam Hunter) (1956).
New Images of Man (Peter Selz) (1959).
Ben Shahn (James Thrall Soby) (1947).
Charles Sheeler, Paintings, Drawings, Photographs (Introduction by William Carlos Williams) (1939).
Mark Tobey (William C. Seitz) (1962).
Twelve Americans, Dorothy Miller (ed.) (1956).
O'Hara, Frank, *Jackson Pollock* (1959).
Ortega y Gasset, José, "A Point of View in the Arts," *Partisan Review* (August, 1949).
Rosenberg, Harold, *The Tradition of the New* (1959).
———, *The Anxious Object* (1964).
Soby, James Thrall, *Contemporary Painters* (1948).
University of California, Berkeley, *The Morris Graves Retrospective Exhibition* (Frederick S. Wight) (1956).
University of California, Los Angeles, *Charles Sheeler, A Retrospective Exhibition*, Frederick S. Wight (ed.) (1956).
Walker Art Gallery, Minneapolis, *The Precisionist View of American Art* (1960).

Whitney Museum of American Art, New York:
   Edward Hopper Retrospective Exhibition (1950).
   The New Decade, 35 American Painters (John I. H. Baur) (1955).
   Young America 1957. Thirty American Painters and Sculptors under 35 (1957).

The Graphic Arts

Frost, Rosamund, "Lasansky and the Hayter Circle," *Perspective*, I, 5 (1947).
Hayter, Stanley, *New Ways of Gravure* (1949).
Johnson, Una, *Ten Years of American Prints, 1947–56* (1956).
Sachs, P. J., *Modern Prints and Drawings* (1954).
Sweeney, James Johnson, "New Directions in Gravure," *Museum of Modern Art Bulletin*, VII, 1 (1944).

Sculpture

Giedion-Welcker, Carola, *Contemporary Sculpture*, 3rd ed. (1960).
Museum of Modern Art, New York:
   Abstract Painting and Sculpture in America (A. C. Ritchie) (1951).
   Recent Sculpture U. S. A. (1959).
Ritchie, A. C., *Sculpture of the Twentieth Century* (1952).
Seymour, Charles, Jr., *Traditions and Experiment in Modern Sculpture* (1949).

ADDITIONAL PHOTO CREDITS

The author wishes to thank the following individuals, institutions, business firms, and museums who generously supplied the photographs listed below. Numbers indicate illustrations in text.

INDEX